Connecting with Computer Science

Greg Anderson
David Ferro
Robert Hilton
Weber State University

THOMSON
COURSE TECHNOLOGY™

Australia • Canada • Mexico • Singapore • Spain • United Kingdom • United States

Connecting with Computer Science by
Greg Anderson, David Ferro, Robert Hilton

Senior Product Manager: *Alyssa Pratt*
Senior Acquisitions Editor: *Amy Yarnevich*
Development Editor: *Deb Kaufmann*
Associate Production Manager: *Aimee Poirier*
Senior Marketing Manager: *Karen Seitz*

Associate Product Manager: *Mirella Misiaszek*
Editorial Assistant: *Jennifer Smith*
Cover Designer: *Steve Deschesne*
Interior Designer: *Resa Blatman*
Compositor: *Pre-Press Company, Inc.*

Printed in the United States of America

2 3 4 5 6 7 8 9 QWT 08 07 06 05

For more information, contact Thomson Course Technology,
25 Thomson Place, Boston, Massachusetts, 02210.
Or find us on the World Wide Web at: www.course.com

ISBN 0-619-21290-X

brief contents

table of contents

preface

Connecting with Computer Science is a fresh approach to the essentials of computer science. It evolved out of the desire of three colleagues, computer science professors, who wanted the students in their Introduction to Computer Science (CS0) courses to (1) actually read the assigned textbook and (2) learn the foundational material necessary to handle the rigor of a computer science program. They felt what was needed was an easy-to-read yet comprehensive introductory text for computer science majors that would also appeal to non-majors who wanted a broad-based introduction to the field. They wanted a text that students could connect to. They felt that the core knowledge outlined in the ACM/IEEE Joint Task Force on Computing Curricula 2001 (CC2001 for short) could be presented in a context suitable for beginning students, without "dumbing down" the material or patronizing the students. They had not been able to find such a text, so they decided to write it themselves. To meet their objectives, they opted for a more conversational style of writing, a more open design, and an optimal balance of text, figures, tables, and marginal features.

Connecting with Computer Science is written in a relatively informal manner, incorporating humor and numerous practical examples. Because students will read and enjoy the text, they will be better able to learn and retain the necessary material. *Connecting with Computer Science* is appropriate for students with varying levels of knowledge and expertise, and will help ensure that students move on to the CS1 course with a consistent level of knowledge.

approach

Our approach in this text is to present the breadth of the computer science discipline in a way that is accessible, understandable, and enjoyable. Specific elements of this approach are outlined in the next sections.

draw students in at the beginning of each chapter

Each chapter begins with a humorous vignette, "the lighter side of the lab," by CS student and journalist Spencer Hilton. These vignettes capture the students' attention and provide a bridge to the chapter material. Many studies have demonstrated that humor is an effective catalyst to learning. These vignettes were written in a way and with language that students can relate to.

explain why the material in the chapter is important

Students are more likely to read and study the material in a chapter if they understand why it will be important to them in their studies. A short section near the beginning of each chapter explains to students why they need to learn the material contained in the chapter and how they will benefit from it.

keep the pages informative and visually interesting

The chapters are filled with margin boxes and definitions that break up the text and add interest. Photos and conceptual figures are also used throughout to illustrate and provide examples. We took care to not clutter the text with excessive non-textual material, maintaining a good balance between text and supporting material. Additionally, appropriate humorous material is interspersed throughout the chapter to further encourage students to keep reading.

give key term definitions in the margins

Key terms for the chapter are defined in the margin at the point they are first used. The student doesn't have to turn to the back of the chapter or book to understand the definition of these key words. At the end of each chapter is a list of key terms with page references. At the end of the book, all of the key terms and their definitions are compiled in a Glossary for easy reference.

include ample end-of-chapter review materials

At the end of each chapter are many types of review materials to solidify students' grasp of the material presented, including the following:

- **test yourself questions:** At the end of the chapter there are ten to twenty questions that students can use to test their knowledge of the subject matter in the chapter. Answers to these questions are contained in an appendix at the end of the book.
- **practice exercises:** At the end of each chapter there are also ten to twenty multiple-choice practice exercises. The answers for these questions are not given in the text, but are available with the Instructor's materials. They would also work well as questions for weekly quizzes on the material to further encourage students to read and study the chapter.
- **digging deeper questions:** Five questions at the end of each chapter are designed to lead the student (and instructor) deeper into the chapter subject matter. These questions can be assigned as topics for research papers, oral

presentations, or to maintain interest for more advanced students. This section encourages students to emphasize critical thinking and reasoning skills as opposed to rote memorization.

- **discussion topics:** Each chapter includes five thought-provoking discussion questions. These are designed to be used in class, and will encourage student participation and engagement with topics related to the chapter. Many of these questions address ethical and societal issues while others lead students into a "which is better?" discussion. The questions in this section allow students to apply the chapter's material and their current understanding of computer science to society in general.
- **Internet research:** An effective method of enhancing learning on a topic is to perform research related to the material. This end-of-chapter section consists of five questions that direct the student to Internet research on topics related to the chapter. The authors have pre-researched the questions to ensure that Web materials are available for each one. This section helps students develop essential research skills and demonstrates the power of finding out information for themselves—as well as the danger of accepting everything they find on the Internet at face value.

include a companion CD chock full of exciting extras and support materials

To augment the text, and to help students effectively learn CS concepts and related computer skills, a free companion CD is included in the back of every copy of this book that includes extra resources and exciting features and links, such as:

- PowerPoint lectures
- Learning tools related to chapter content
- Tutorials on chapter topics
- Labs on selected topics
- Self test games
- Source code

organization

Connecting with Computer Science is organized into 14 chapters, as follows. The chapters are modular, that is, they can be covered in any order that the instructor chooses.

chapter 1, "a brief history of computing," is a short tour through the essentials of the history of computers and computing. Key figures are introduced along with their contributions to the computer science field. This chapter is presented first as a less technical topic to ease students into the curriculum.

chapter 2, "software tools for techies," introduces students to software tools that will be vital to them as they work on future courses. This chapter is also less technical and helps students ramp up.

chapter 3, "computer architecture," covers the basics of computer architecture focusing on the Von Neumann machine, including memory, CPU, I/O, and buses. Treatment is also given to digital logic circuits, and how they are used to build the CPU and other computer devices.

chapter 4, "numbering systems and data representation," is a key chapter designed to give the student a strong foundation in numbering systems and conversion between bases, with emphasis on binary, hex, and decimal conversions. Students are also introduced to forms of data representation including signed and unsigned integers, floating point, character, sound, and video.

chapter 5, "operating systems," provides students with an understanding of the fundamentals of operating systems. Additionally, the chapter contains a reference table comparing tasks in UNIX, DOS, and Windows that will help students prepare for using operating systems in later courses.

chapter 6, "networks," familiarizes students with the ISO/OSI network model and the operation of LANs, WANs and WLANs. Protocols and standards involved with networking are explained, giving students a basis for further networking courses.

chapter 7, "the Internet," expands on the knowledge gained in the networking chapter by explaining TCP/IP and higher-level protocols such as DHCP, HTTP, and FTP. Concepts such as NAT, DNS, and Web page addressing are also covered. Examples of HTML coding are given along with a basic explanation of how Web pages are created. Finally, students are given an introduction to using the Internet and search engines as a tool for research.

chapter 8, "database fundamentals," begins with an introduction to database theory and proceeds into database design, including normalization, and then into the basics of SQL. The history of other database models is also discussed.

chapter 9, "data structures," provides an understanding of the importance of data structures in computer science. Stacks, queues, linked lists, binary trees, and other structures are explained through theory and visual examples. Students are taught the basics of sorting and the use of pointers.

chapter 10, "file structures," gives insight into methods of storing information on mass storage devices. Specific information is given on FAT and NTFS. Students are introduced to the differences between sequential and random record storage and the use of hashing and indexing to retrieve stored records.

chapter 11, "programming," is an introduction to the concepts and practices involved in computer programming. Students learn about algorithm development and pseudocode, then are introduced to high-level programming. The basics of programming in Java are explained using object-oriented examples.

chapter 12, "software engineering," shows how software engineering is used to create computer applications. The main software engineering process models are discussed and students are introduced to design documents and UML. Team programming is also addressed.

chapter 13, "computing security and ethics," provides a grasp of the issues involved with computer and network security and the ethical use of computers. Hacking, social engineering, privacy and other issues are discussed to help students establish positions and policies on security and ethical issues.

chapter 14, "emerging technologies," looks at the current limitations of computers and how they might be solved in the future. Leading edge technologies are introduced in the areas of memory, I/O, and the CPU. The chapter concludes with an explanation of the basics of artificial intelligence.

In addition, there are three appendixes (appendix A, "answers to test yourself exercises," appendix B, "ASCII chart," appendix C, "Java reserved words"), a glossary of all key terms with definitions, and a comprehensive index.

instructor's materials

Connecting with Computer Science includes the following teaching tools to support instructors in the classroom:

Electronic Instructor's Manual. The Instructor's Manual that accompanies this textbook includes additional material to assist instructors in class preparation, including suggestions for lecture topics.

Solutions. Solutions to end of chapter practice exercises are included. (Solutions to the test yourself exercises are included in Appendix A of this book.)

ExamView®. This textbook is accompanied by ExamView, a powerful testing software package that allows instructors to create and administer printed, computer (LAN-based), and Internet exams. ExamView includes hundreds of questions that correspond to the topics covered in this text, enabling students to generate detailed study guides that include page references for further review. These computer-based and Internet testing components allow students to take exams at their computers, and save the instructor time because each exam is graded automatically.

PowerPoint Presentations. This book comes with Microsoft PowerPoint slides for each chapter. These are included as a teaching aid for classroom presentations, either to make available to students on the network for chapter review, or to be printed for classroom distribution. Instructors can add their own slides for additional topics that they introduce to the class.

Distance Learning Content. Course Technology is proud to present online courses in WebCT and Blackboard to provide the most complete and dynamic learning experience possible. When you add online content to one of your courses, you're adding a lot: Topic Reviews, Practice Tests, Review Questions, Assignments, PowerPoint presentations, and, most of all, a gateway to the 21st century's most important information resource. We hope you will make the most of your course, both online and offline. For more information on how to bring distance learning to your course, contact your local Course Technology sales representative.

acknowledgments

This book is a joint effort of three authors and many other talented people. All three authors would like to thank the following people:

Jennifer Muroff was instrumental in getting the project started. Her initial support enabled the project to go forward. We appreciate her belief in what we wanted to accomplish in this text.

We would still be just thinking about Chapter 1 without the organizational skills of Alyssa Pratt, our very competent project manager. Now that the project is complete, Alyssa's constant and firm deadline pressure is greatly appreciated.

Deb Kaufmann was absolutely amazing as a development editor, cheerleader, and counselor. We greatly appreciate her thoroughness and her overall editing expertise. Most of all we want to express thanks to her for her talent (and patience) in working with three different personalities and styles to create a consistent text.

Aimee Poirier, the production editor, did a great job of shepherding the chapters through production and keeping us informed about the process. Mark Goodin, the copyeditor, polished our prose and made sure the overall style of the book was consistent.

Spencer Hilton added a dimension to the book that kept us enthused with the topics. Thanks to Spencer, we got a chance to laugh at least once during the writing of each chapter. (It's too bad that the readers of this text didn't get an opportunity to laugh at all of the "lighter side of the lab" forwards that were rejected because they were too funny!)

We would also like to thank our reviewers for their candid and constructive feedback:

Mark Hutchenreuther, *California Polytechnic State University*

Eric Kisling, *Indiana University*

Steve Leach, *Florida State University*

Johnette Moody, *Arkansas Tech University*

Amy Woszczynski, *Kennesaw State University*

Because this book is a collaboration of three authors who each had support of associates, family, and friends, each of us would also like to separately acknowledge some special people.

Greg Anderson: First and foremost, I would like to thank my wife Gina for being patient and providing me with encouragement to write another book even though she swore that it would never happen again. Can't wait until the next one, right, dear? Thanks also to my great children Kelsi, Kaytlen, Marissa, and Miles. I now have time to play! A special thanks to Rob, Dave, and Spencer. Even though there were stressful times, there was always time for a good laugh.

David Ferro: I want to thank my students for their suggestions and help during the writing of this book. Many became instrumental in its creation—proving that undergraduates, research, and interesting and useful projects can co-exist fruitfully. Three students who went above and beyond are Matt Werney, John Linford, and Adam Christensen. I also want to thank my co-authors. The working relationship we established could not have been stronger or more enjoyable. Even on the darkest days, with deadlines looming, one or all of us could bring some sense of humor to the proceedings. Finally, I want to thank two very special people, my wife and daughter, Marjukka Ollilainen and Stella Ferro. This book frequently took me away from my family. Marjukka gave constant support despite the needs of her own academic career. Stella brought joy to my life in a way she cannot comprehend at this early age. She will realize later what her mother knows already: how much their love means to me.

Robert Hilton: I'm grateful to both Greg and Dave for their encouragement and patience throughout the process and especially to Greg for "making it happen." I came into this project with only a vague idea as to the amount of time that would be required. Many thanks to my wife, Renae, and my sons, Brent, Spencer, Joel, and Michael for allowing me to hibernate while I was writing. I hope they will still remember me as we become reacquainted now that the project is complete. Special thanks to my daughter, Jenn, for her encouragement, help in editing, and willingness to be a sounding board for thoughts and ideas.

Connecting with Computer Science

1

chapter

a brief history of computing

in this chapter you will:

- Learn why today almost everyone is a computer operator
- Learn about the predecessors of modern computer hardware and software
- Trace the development of computer hardware and software through several generations
- Learn that sometimes good ideas flop and bad ones survive
- Meet some interesting figures—some famous, some infamous, some wealthy, and some obscure
- See some issues facing modern computing

the lighter side of the lab

by spencer

My first memory of computers dates back to 1984. I was six years old, wandering through my house, looking for my dad to ask him how to spell the word "sword" so I could kill the ogre in Zork.

Most students won't remember Zork, but it was the hottest computer game around at the time. This was back in the days of no mouse, no joystick, no sound, and no graphics; just a blinking green line on a solid black screen. A green message would come up on the screen: "You are in a room with a door." The player would type "open door." The computer then printed on the screen "The door is open." The player would then type, "go north." Screen message: "You are now in a room with a big, scary ogre." This is where the user *should* type, "kill ogre with sword." Which is why I was wandering around my house searching for my dad. There I was, trapped in a room with an ogre, and the idiot(s) who invented English decided to put a silent "w" in "sword."

This brings me to my point—that we've come a long way since then. Not only do we have computers, but we have "super" computers. Within a year or two, we'll probably have "super-duper" computers. For example, a Pentium 4 is capable of completing about 500,000,000 tasks per second (approximately the same number of tasks my professors are capable of assigning per second).

We're all aware where this technology is headed because we've seen movies like *The Matrix* and *Terminator*—computers are eventually going to become smarter than humans and take over the world. (We could stop it from happening by destroying all the computers right now while we're still stronger, but then we would have to start paying for music again.)

In the meantime, we know we're still okay because of people like Vladimir Kramnik of Russia, world champion chess player. In October 2002, Kramnik took on Deep Fritz, the world's most powerful chess computer. Kramnik opened with the aggressive Scotch Opening (not the same thing that you bar-hounds may be envisioning), and by the second game, Kramnik was up 2–0. However, Fritz came back and the contest ended in a draw at 4–4. Kramnik was awarded $600,000, and Fritz was awarded a new surge protector. "We've learned a lot from this, and there is much we can do to increase Fritz's playing strength," said Frans Morsch, creator of Fritz.

I smell trouble. My next foreword will be hand-written, because I'll promptly be destroying my computer, right after a game of Zork.

why you need to know about...
the history of computing

Today, the computer has become so much more than its origins promised. With the advent of the Internet, the computer has become a communication device. With a video screen and a mouse, it has become a tool for artists, architects, and designers. With growing storage capacity and the growth of information in a digital format, the computer has become a device for archiving information of all kinds. By connecting the computer to sound and video at both the production and receiving ends, it becomes an entertainment device—potentially replacing your CD player, DVD player, television, stereo, and radio. Put four wheels on it and add a steering wheel and the computer turns into your Honda Civic. Add some wings and a couple of jet engines and it's a Boeing 777. You can find computers in everything from the coffee maker that starts brewing at 6 a.m. on your kitchen counter to a North Face jacket that monitors your body temperature.

Computers are everywhere, and unless you are living in a cave, you and everyone else is a computer operator. So what? Maybe you didn't grow up using an abacas and a slide rule, but how did you get to this stage of life where computers are found even in pet electronic dogs? How did the interface between the user and the computer go from thousands of switches and cables to a gas pedal or a play button? What does it mean for society, you the consumer, or you the potential software designer? What does it mean for the future?

ancient history

The most logical place to start when talking about the origins of computer science is ancient Assyria. Don't worry, we won't stay in Assyria forever.

At its core, the computer is basically doing math. Applied mathematics—numbers and their manipulation—allows you to play that MP3 file of the Ketchup song, display that F22 Raptor screen saver, and calculate last year's taxes. That brings us back to the Assyrians. The Assyrians invented tablets with the solutions to square roots, multiplication, and trigonometry right there on the tablet—easily accessible. With the proper training you could solve your mathematical problems easily using these tablets.

Why did the Assyrians need to solve mathematical problems? Because math was—and still is—a handy tool for solving personal and societal problems.

someone had to invent the zero?

It isn't that the ancients couldn't grasp the idea of "nothing." The use of the zero has to do with a number's position giving it value. Prior to this, numbering systems didn't work with place to the same extent that is used today. For example, in the Roman numbering system CXII is 112, because C is 100, X is 10, and II is 2. Around AD 600, the Hindus created a numbering system using the numbers 1 through 9, their value increasing by a power of ten for each place to the left. Evidence suggests the Arabs borrowed this concept and transferred it to Europe as early as the 10th century AD. The Hindus and the Persians also used the concept of zero as a placeholder. With the zero placeholder, the Roman number CI, for example, would translate correctly as 101. The new numbering system made complex math possible.

abacus – A counting device used from ancient times to the present that uses sliding beads, principally useful for addition and subtraction

slide rule – A device that can perform complicated math by using sliding guides on a rulerlike device; popular with engineers until the advent of the cheap electronic calculator

With the advent of civilization, humanity began to discard its nomadic ways and invent the concepts that you now take for granted. Ideas like property and ownership spurred the need for measuring that property—whether it was land or food supplies. When people settled and no longer ranged laterally, they built vertically. The Egyptian pyramids and the Greek Parthenon demanded more complex math than did the construction of tents and teepees. Later, navigation across both land and water also began to demand more complex mathematics. It also demanded more control over time.

You can thank the Greeks for some of the ideas of logic that you use in computer science. You can thank the Persians for refining or inventing algorithms, algebra, and the zero. These civilizations borrowed and improved many of the ideas of previous ones. Other civilizations (in China and Central and South America) either borrowed these mathematical concepts or, in many cases, invented them independently.

Pascal and Leibniz start the wheel rolling

For a long time, paper, wood, stone, papyrus tables, and increasingly complex ***abacuses*** were the "computers" through which mathematical solutions emerged. In Western society, where most of the rest of this story continues, you can probably credit the 1622 invention of the ***slide rule*** as the beginning of the solution of complex mathematical problems by mechanical devices with moving parts. In 1642, a man named Blaise Pascal designed a mechanical calculator with gears and levers that performed addition and subtraction. Gottfried Leibniz built on Pascal's work in 1694 by creating the Leibniz Wheel that added multiplication and division to the mechanical calculator's capabilities. The number and size of tables to solve the numerous problems society required had become unmanageable. Devices like Pascal's and Leibniz's allowed a user to "key in" the parameters of a problem and receive a solution. Unfortunately, cost and complexity kept use of these devices from becoming widespread.

Joseph Jacquard

In 1801, a major invention allowed for not only keying in the parameters of a problem but also allowed for the parameters themselves to be stored and used whenever needed. This freed the user from having to enter the parameters of a problem more than once. Interestingly, this invention addressed a problem that had nothing to do with solving issues in land speculation or navigation, and is seldom noted in the history of mathematical development. The invention, in fact, made fabric.

The invention has been called the Jacquard loom (Figure 1-1). The Frenchman Joseph Jacquard (1752–1834) invented a device attached to a loom where a series of pins would select what threads would get woven into a fabric. If a pin

Figure 1-1, The Jacquard loom; note the string of punched cards that feed into the machine

Courtesy of IBM Archive

was down, that thread would be selected, if the pin was up, the thread would not be used. Different patterns could be produced by changing the orientation of the sets of pins. The orientation of the pins was determined by a set of reusable cards. This worked similarly to a player piano (also an invention of the 19th century) where a paper roll with a series of holes and air blowing through those holes determined which notes would play. Both the Jacquard loom and the player piano thus had a "stored program" and could be "programmed" using the interface, a series of holes in either wooden cards or paper rolls. To this style of programming, as you shall see, IBM owes its great success.

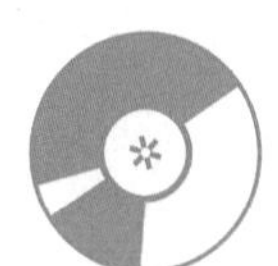

Already getting a bit lost with the names and dates? Check out the dynamic timeline on the student CD under Chapter 1, learning tools. See comparisons of hardware and software over the last century as well.

Charles Babbage

But the story is getting ahead of itself. First, you need to visit England's Charles Babbage. Babbage continued the work of Pascal and Leibniz by creating a prototype Difference Engine in 1823, a mechanical device that did addition, subtraction, multiplication, and division of 6-digit numbers. To the dismay of the British government, which had subsidized his work, Babbage abandoned his quest to improve it. Instead, he focused on an Analytical Engine that had many characteristics of modern computers. Unfortunately, he was never able to build it for lack of funds. Babbage died fairly poor and obscure, but by the middle of the 20th century, he was recognized as the father of the modern computer, and the British government even issued a commemorative postage stamp with his likeness.

Despite his failures, Babbage managed to design a machine that captured the key working elements of the modern electronic computer (an invention that was still more than a century away). First, he envisioned that more than human hand power would drive the machine, although steam, not electricity, would power the thousands of gears, wheels, shafts, and levers of his device. More importantly, his machine had the four critical components of a modern computer:

- An input device (borrowing the idea of punch cards)
- Memory (a place where numbers would be stored while they were worked on)
- A central processing device (that decides what calculations to do)
- An output device (dials that showed the output values, in this case)

program loop – The ability of a computer to "loop back" and repeat commands

This programmable device—despite never having been built—also introduced another critical figure in computing: Ada Lovelace Byron. Ada was a patron of Babbage and daughter of the poet Lord Byron. She also was a mathematician. Through a series of letters with Babbage, she described many instructions for the Analytical Engine. The concept of the ***program loop*** has been attributed to her, and she has been called the first programmer. In the early 1980s the U.S. Depart-ment of Defense named their Ada programming language after her. While research in the late 1990s showed that many of the concepts came from Babbage himself, her contributions to programming are still broadly recognized.

In 1991, the Science Museum of London actually constructed a working, historically accurate Difference Engine from Babbage's designs, attempting to use only materials and techniques that would have been available at the time. It was widely thought that Babbage failed to a large extent because of the difficulty in manufacturing the multiple complex and precise parts, but the success of the Science Museum team indicates that the main cause of Babbage's failure was that he simply could not secure adequate funding—not the last time you will hear that story.

Herman Hollerith

One character who *did* find adequate funding to develop a "computing" machine was American Herman Hollerith, although he never originally intended to create a mechanical adding machine.

The Constitution of the United States indicates that an accounting of its people shall occur every ten years. Hollerith was working for the U.S. Census Bureau during the 1890 census when he realized that with the counting methods of the day, they wouldn't even finish before the next census ten years away. Hollerith solved this problem by introducing electromechanical counting equipment using punch cards as input (Figure 1-2). Hollerith created a company around this technology and that company eventually became the International Business Machines (IBM) Corporation.

Strangely enough, IBM didn't build the first electronic computer. Hollerith, and later IBM, sold single-purpose machines that solved routine tabulation problems. This was a huge industry in the United States and included companies like Burroughs, Remington Rand, and NCR (National Cash Register). The machines these companies sold were not modeled on the multipurpose engine of Babbage.

IBM finally did invest in the development of a multipurpose machine in 1937: the Mark I. Howard Aiken led the Mark I project at Harvard. Only after starting did he become aware of the work of Charles Babbage from whom he later claimed inspiration. The machine was complete in 1944. It was a single 50-foot-long drive shaft powered by a 5-horsepower electric motor mechanically synchronizing hundreds of electromechanical relays. It was said to sound like a

Figure 1-2, The Hollerith census counting machine

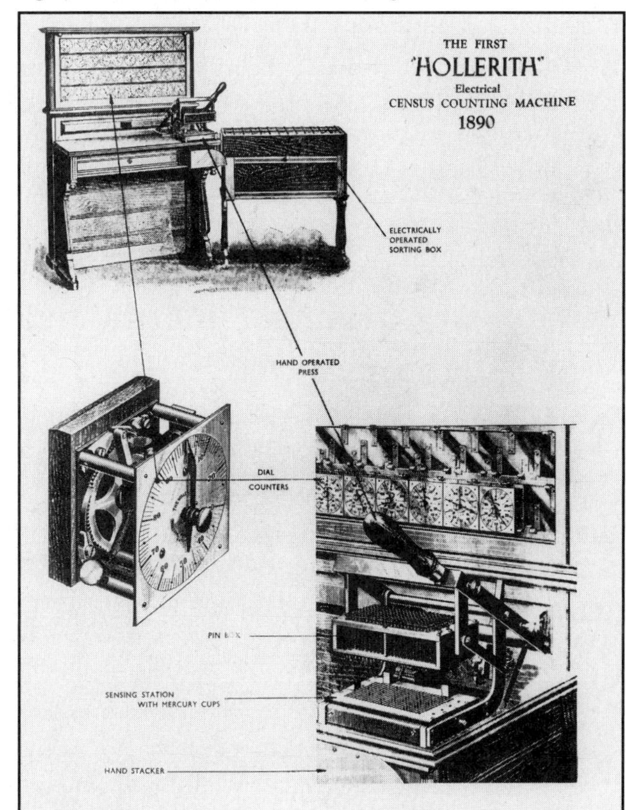

Courtesy of IBM Archive

very large room full of people knitting. Despite the massive press coverage it received, by the time of its introduction, a critical technological invention had already made it obsolete. The technology that really made electronic computing possible was one familiar to most Americans, sitting in their living room radios: the vacuum tube.

progression of computer electronics

Boolean algebra or Boolean logic – A logical system developed by George Boole that uses truth tables to indicate true/false output based on all possible true/false inputs; the computer owes a lot to this concept, because at its most basic level the computer is manipulating ones and zeros—in other words, true or false.

Developments in computing, though ongoing since the middle of the 19th century, were mostly the product of weak or poorly funded efforts. By the 1880s, American Charles Sanders Peirce, extending the work of Charles Boole, realized that electric switches could emulate the true/false conditions of ***Boolean algebra***, also known as ***Boolean logic***. A complex arrangement of switches could model a complex Boolean expression with on as "true" and off as "false." Benjamin Burack built a small logic machine that used this concept in 1936 (it was even portable) with electric relay switches. The series of electric switches was the approach adopted by the Mark I team as well.

vacuum tube – A signal amplifier that preceded the transistor. Like a transistor, it can be integrated into a circuit, but it takes more power, is larger, and burns out more quickly

John Atanasoff of Iowa State College realized that the switches could be replaced with electronics and be both much faster and less power hungry. He, along with Clifford Berry, designed and built a small limited-function prototype of the ABC (Atanasoff-Berry Computer) using ***vacuum tubes*** in the late 1930s. While proving the usefulness of vacuum tubes for computers, with only $7000 in grant money, Atanasoff and Berry couldn't realize the potential of their full design. Nor did they get much credit for their innovation until years later.

A momentous occasion spurred the development of the first modern electronic computer: the entry of the United States into World War II.

wartime research drives technological innovation

During WWII, the U.S. military had a huge problem: the pace of weapons development was so fast that often the men in the field were the first to truly test and learn to use the weapons. This was particularly problematic with gun trajectory tables, where field-testing often led to missed targets and, worse, friendly fire incidents. The U.S. Navy Board of Ordnance became involved in the Mark I project at Harvard in order to attempt to correct this deficiency. In 1943, the U.S. Army sponsored a different group at the Moore School of Engineering at the University of Pennsylvania. This team was lead by John Mauchly and J. Presper Eckert. They created the ENIAC (the Electronic Numerical Integrator and Computer)—a machine that could run 1000 times as fast as the Mark I. As it turns out, both machines were completed too late in the war to really help with the military's funded purpose of creating trajectory tables.

ENIAC and EDVAC

Although it was a landmark, by no stretch of the imagination could you argue that the ENIAC was portable. It was loud, even without thousands of clattering switches. It was a 30-ton collection of machines with banks of switches and switchboard-operator style connections that filled a huge basement room (Figure 1-3). A group of technicians ran around replacing the more than 18,000 vacuum tubes that continually burned out. Another team of women programmers meticulously flipped the more than 6000 switches that entered the many machine instructions needed to perform a simple arithmetic operation.

However, ENIAC was a functioning and useful computer that could perform both arithmetic and logical operations. It could use symbols for variables and operations and was therefore not limited to being used for one single purpose.

Von Neumann machine – A computer architecture developed by John Von Neumann and others in the 1940s that allows for input, output, processing, and memory; it also includes the stored program concept

The architecture of the ENIAC was a model for all subsequent machines except for one critical problem: it could not modify the contents of the program itself. In fact, its memory could only hold twenty 10-digit numbers at one time and had to be programmed externally. In 1944, a number of engineers and scientists including Mauchly and Eckert created the EDVAC (Electronic Discrete Variable Automatic Computer). This machine, which truly is the model for current computers, became recognized as the ***Von Neumann machine***, named after John Von Neumann, a mathematician who was critical to its success. Its

Figure 1-3, The ENIAC and some of its programmers

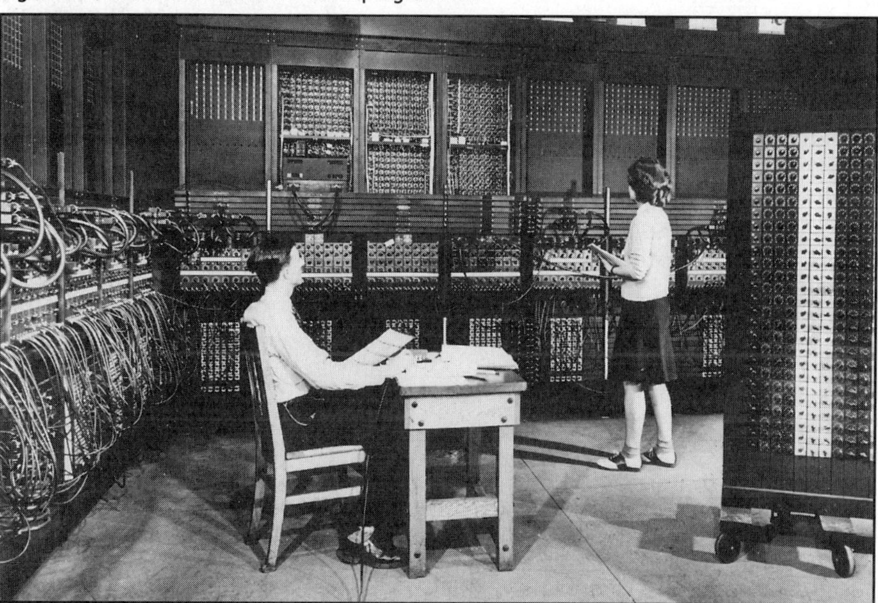

Courtesy of IBM Archive

stored program concept – *The idea that a computer can be operated by a program that is loaded into the machine's memory; also implies that programs can be stored somewhere and repeatedly loaded into memory, and that the program itself, just like other data, can be modified*

operation was governed by a program loaded into memory. The program could even modify itself during operation. It could be programmed to perform many different functions. Programs were entered just as data were. In fact, the programs, whether calculating logarithms or bell curves, were just more data. And, programs could be stored for repeated use. This became known as the ***stored program concept***.

World War II also spawned a few other secret computing machines. More than twenty years after the war's end it was publicly revealed that the British had also built a computer, ten of them in fact, named, collectively, Colossus. Its designers and builders returned to their prewar jobs, sworn to secrecy. All but two of those British machines were destroyed after the war with the remaining two being destroyed sometime during the 1960s.

The Colossus played a critical role in winning the war for the Allies by helping to crack the German U-boat Enigma code. (Figure 1-4 shows the German Enigma encoding machine.) It turns out the Germans had been developing a computer as well—the Z1 developed by Conrad Zuse. And so, the time was right. Technology and need came together to spur the development of the electronic computer.

John Von Neumann

During WWII, von Neumann, a professor at Princeton, worked with J. Robert Oppenheimer on the atomic bomb and it was there, faced with the complexities of nuclear fission, that he became interested in computing machines. In 1944 he joined the team working on the ENIAC. With his influence, the team was supported in working on the EDVAC. The origin of the key feature of this machine—the stored program—has been disputed ever since. There is evidence that Eckert had written about the concept months before Von Neumann knew of the ENIAC, although Von Neumann got most of the credit after the EDVAC was completed in 1952. Von Neumann also owes a debt to Britain's Alan Turing who created the Turing machine—a logical model that emulated the techniques of computing later put into practice through the hardware of the ENIAC and EDVAC. Regardless of this dispute, Von Neumann is recognized for his many contributions, and modern computers are still sometimes called Von Neumann machines.

Figure 1-4, The Enigma machine was used to encode German military intelligence in World War II

Courtesy of NSA

the computer era begins: the first generation

hardware – The physical device upon which software runs

software – The instructions that operate the hardware

The 1950s are generally considered the first-generation years for the development of both computer ***hardware*** and ***software***. Vacuum tubes worked as memory for the machine. Data was written to a magnetic drum and, typically, paper tape and data cards handled input. As the decade wore on, the computer industry borrowed magnetic tape from the recording industry to use as a cost-effective storage medium. The first line printer also made its appearance, and for the next 30 years and more, programmers read their output on wide, perforated green-barred printouts.

binary code – The numeric language of the computer based on the binary number system of ones and zeros; also called machine code

The '50s was also the decade when hardware and software personnel parted ways and software development became more specialized. Computer machine instructions were, and still are, written in what's called ***binary code*** or ***machine code***—something that uses only zeros and ones to mimic the on/off logic of the computer. An instruction for a machine to add a one to another number might be written like this: 1100000000110000001000000001. Now imagine thousands of lines of this to do anything useful!

assembly language – A human readable language to represent numeric computer instructions (binary code)

Writing programs in binary is a long, tedious, and error-prone process. To remedy this, a programming language was developed called ***assembly language***. An assembly instruction version of the above binary code might look something like this: "add x, y". It might still be somewhat cryptic, but easier to manage than the straight binary. It also meant you had engineers and programmers who worked in binary and others who worked in assembly to create applications. Programmers soon split into "system engineers" (those who programmed the system) and "application engineers" (those who programmed applications—accounting programs for example—that ran on the system).

You'll learn more about assembly language and other programming languages in Chapter 11, "Programming."

During the 1950s a major shift began in almost all disciplines of science, engineering, and business. Prior to this time, making scaled-down mechanical models of the intended devices or systems—be they dams, airplanes, cars, electrical grids, or whatever—was the most widely used method of creating new technology. In the 1950s and 1960s, this analog model of development began to be replaced with digital electronic mathematical models. Before this, using mathematical calculations to model systems, while possible, was often far too complex and slow to do without the use of a computer or many people doing calculations. In fact, the term "computer" originally described individuals who "computed." In some cases, like in British insurance companies, tens of thousands of these individuals did hand calculations, later augmented with electromechanical calculators. The 1950s and 1960s changed all that. For

Figure 1-5, Grace Murray Hopper and the UNIVAC

Courtesy of Computer History Museum

its scientific and business needs, Western society went from mostly analog models and human computers to the electronic computer. Suddenly, a single machine could both create software models of natural phenomena and technology and do the work of thousands of boring and repetitive rudimentary business calculators.

UNIVAC

Mauchly and Eckert went on to build the first commercially viable computer, the UNIVAC (Figure 1-5). First they formed a division of the old Remington Typewriter Company, then Remington Rand (later Sperry UNIVAC and then Unisys). Their first customer was the U.S. Census Bureau. The name UNIVAC became as synonymous with the computer in the 1950s as Kleenex became for paper tissues or Xerox for paper copies. Between 1951 and 1954, the company installed nineteen UNIVACs including ones at U.S. Steel and one at Pacific Mutual Life Insurance. Ironically, Howard Aiken, builder of the Mark I, felt there was a need for only five or six computers like the EDVAC in the United States and recommended that the U.S. Bureau of Standards not support Eckert and Mauchly's proposal to make commercial computers.

Grace Murray Hopper and the "bug"

Grace Murray Hopper made many contributions to programming. As part of the Mark I project at Harvard, she coined the term "bug" (referring to a problem in hardware or software) when she found an actual bug—a moth—in one of the Mark I's electromechanical relays and taped it to the logbook. She called the process of finding and solving these problems "debugging," and she spent much of the next 40 years doing it. She went on to work on the UNIVAC with Eckert and Mauchly. There she developed a compiler—a totally new concept—for a higher-level programming language. Later she created an even more powerful language called COBOL, one of the most widely used business programming languages.

The most celebrated use of the UNIVAC came during the 1952 presidential election. CBS News decided to include the machine's calculation of election results in their U.S. presidential election broadcast. Anchor Walter Cronkite learned that with a computer, it was definitely "garbage in—garbage out"! By 8:30 p.m. the night of the election, the UNIVAC calculated 100 to 1 odds in favor of Eisenhower. No one could believe the results and so CBS delayed reporting an Eisenhower win. Mauchly and Max Woodbury, another mathematician from the University of Pennsylvania, reentered the data (incorrectly, as it turns out), and CBS reported at 9 p.m. that UNIVAC gave Eisenhower 8 to 7 odds over Stevenson. The final electoral vote of 438 for Eisenhower and 93 for Stevenson proved the original data were closer to correct. In the end, CBS was first to call the race although not as soon or by the degree that they could have. They hadn't trusted the computer's calculations. By the end of the night they were convinced of the computer's usefulness, and four years later (and ever since) all the major U.S. television networks used computers in their election coverage.

IBM (Big Blue)

By 1955, Remington Rand's UNIVAC no longer dominated the computer marketplace. International Business Machines (IBM) took advantage of its long-standing ties to business to capture the hearts and minds of international businessmen. They had more than twice as many orders as Remington Rand that year. A saying developed: "You can't go wrong by buying IBM." Their salesmen's button-down shirts and blue suits became a familiar sight to anyone in the computer industry, and IBM became known as "Big Blue." It also became known as "Snow White" (as in "Snow White and the Seven Dwarfs") because by the 1960s IBM controlled over 70 percent of the market in computers. (Sperry Rand, with its UNIVAC, along with Control Data, Honeywell, Philco, Burroughs, RCA, General Electric, and NCR were the "dwarfs"). This arrangement actually lasted quite a long time, in fact, until the microcomputer (PC) arrived on the scene in the 1980s. More about that later.

mainframe – A large, expensive computer, often serving many terminals and used by large organizations; all first-generation computers were mainframes

While it is generally thought that IBM won the ***mainframe*** battle with superior salesmanship, a skill that founder Thomas Watson prided himself on, it is also the case that Remington Rand had many consumer products unrelated to office equipment and didn't have the focused vision of IBM in its drive to become *the* computer services company. That focus eventually led to superior products from IBM, starting with the 701 and the smaller 650 calculating machine in the mid 1950s. IBM's position grew even stronger with the introduction of the

Figure 1-6, IBM 360 mainframe computers were the size of refrigerators and required a full staff to manage them

Courtesy of IBM Archive

System/360 (Figure 1-6) in the 1960s. It was a scalable system, allowing companies to continue to add components as their businesses and computing needs increased. IBM usually leased the systems to the customer. Often IBM could recapture its investment in manufacturing the systems within a couple years. Meanwhile, most systems stayed in place for 10 or 15 years, or even longer. IBM made a lot of money during this period.

transistors in the second generation

The late 1950s and the first half of the 1960s might be considered the second-generation years. In software, higher-level languages like FORTRAN, COBOL, and LISP were developed. Assembly language, while easier to use than machine code, still had a one-to-one correspondence with the machine code. Each line of a high-level language could be far more powerful and might correspond to many lines of binary machine code. In one of these high-level languages, you might be able to write something like "FOR A = 1 TO 20 PRINT A" which would take numerous lines of assembly code.

transistor – A signal amplifier much smaller than a vacuum tube used to represent a one (on) or a zero (off), which are the rudiments of computer calculation, and often used as part of an integrated circuit (IC)

Hardware took a major leap forward as well. The *transistor* replaced the vacuum tube. It was far smaller, cooler (meaning cooler in temperature), cheaper to produce, and lasted longer. A form of random access memory (or RAM) also became available with the use of magnetic cores. With tape and drum, the magnetic read head could be easily positioned over the information in which you were interested. Now, information could be available instantaneously. The first magnetic disks, similar to ones in use today, also became available. Information that wasn't resident in memory could be accessed more quickly and efficiently.

circuit boards in the third generation

integrated circuit (IC) – A collection of transistors on a single piece of hardware (called a "chip") that greatly reduces its size and physical complexity

chip – A piece of encased silicon usually somewhere between the size of your fingernail to the palm of your hand that holds ICs

operating system (OS) – Software that allows applications to access hardware resources like printers or hard drives, and provides tools for managing and administering system resources and security

With the third generation, the second half of the 1960s saw the replacement of transistors with ***integrated circuits (IC)*** or ***chips*** on circuit boards. ICs are miniaturized transistors in solid silicon. They are called semiconductors because they have electronic conducting and nonconducting channels etched onto their surface. Cost and size were decreasing as speed and reliability took a leap in magnitude. Keyboards and screens were also introduced, giving the user a much easier way to communicate with the computer. Software saw the first ***operating system (OS)***, a program for managing all the jobs of the computer.

Operating systems had a number of advantages. First, the operating system could take care of utilizing all resources of the machine—printing or writing to files for example, so that each separate application program did not have to perform these tasks. Second, the OS enabled the machine to have multiple users or complete multiple tasks. Up to this point, the machine would do one job at a time for a single user.

Imagine what it was like in the days before operating systems: You carried your stack of IBM cards (Figure 1-7) over to the computer center in a shoebox. You stepped gingerly over your officemate who was picking up his stack of cards that had fallen in the parking lot and made your way down the long hall, handing your stack to the computer operator. Yes! You were "first in," which means

Figure 1-7, A very short stack of IBM punched cards

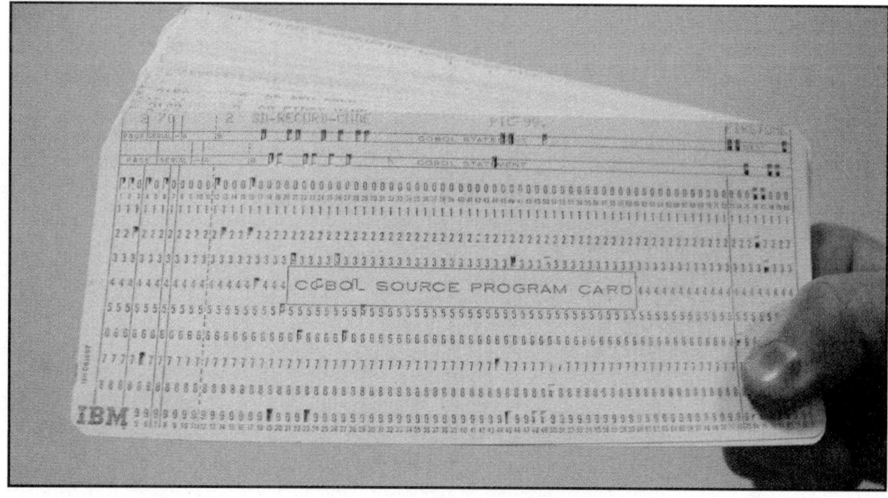

you would be "first out." Unfortunately, you were only first in this morning; there were at least five stacks of cards ahead of you from the previous day. Fortunately, you had brought the requisite coffee and donuts and somehow your stack ended up at the head of the line. The operator put the stack of cards in the card reader and after about 1000 "thip-thip-thips" as the cards went through the reader, the program had been input into the computer. If there was a problem in your code, you would have to go back and fix the card containing the problem, put the card back in the right place in the deck, and go through the process again. You might have picked up some more donuts while you were at it since you knew it was going to be a long night.

time-sharing

time-sharing – The ability of the computer to share its computing time with many users at the same time

Time-sharing solved the vicious "donut and card stack" cycle. Now, a number of users could sit at terminals—either screens or teletype-like consoles that used long paper rolls instead of punch cards to input instructions—and it looked like you had the computer to yourself. Of course, many times the system would get very slow, even if you were doing something very simple. That likely meant that there were a lot of other people "sharing" your time, or a few people doing some resource-intensive processes. It shouldn't be any surprise that people got excited about owning their own computer a few years later.

During this period the computer was beginning to be used by a broader population as a general-purpose machine, and many application programs were written—programs geared toward an end user rather than the programmer. Some programmers began to focus on writing code at the OS level, working on compilers and other tools that application programmers then used to create statistical or accounting programs, which would in turn be used by those end users, who generally knew little of programming and just wanted to use the application for a particular task. Now get out your silky shirt, disco shoes, and the suit with the wide lapels because we are heading into the '70s.

living in the '70s with the fourth generation

In computing, from the early 1970s on is known as the fourth generation of hardware and software, and is characterized by the continuing repackaging of circuits in smaller and smaller spaces. First came Large-Scale Integration (LSI) and then Very Large-Scale Integration (VLSI). Chips used in the '60s contained around 1000 circuits, LSI chips contained up to 15,000, and VLSI chips contained 100,000 to 1 million circuits. The number of circuits essentially doubled every 1.5 years. This process of fitting an ever increasing number of transistors and circuits on smaller and smaller chips is called miniaturization, and is one of the most important trends in computer hardware.

minicomputer – Mid-sized computer introduced in the mid to late '60s. It typically cost tens of thousands of dollars versus hundreds of thousands of dollars for a mainframe

The '70s saw the growth of *minicomputer* companies such as Digital Equipment Corporation (DEC) with its PDP and VAX machines, and Data General and its Nova. Minicomputers put a lot of power in a lot less physical space. One of these new computers could fit into the corner of a room, and software programs blossomed in this new environment.

The UNIX operating system was created by Ken Thompson and Dennis Ritchie in 1973 as an offshoot of a joint effort of AT&T, GE, and MIT. It was originally created on a DEC PDP-7 and written in B and later C (computer languages also invented by Thompson and Ritchie). Because of market limitations resulting from AT&T's monopoly status, AT&T couldn't sell UNIX and so distributed the software free to educational institutions. The real revolution of the '70s wasn't the minicomputer, however. By the end of the 1970s "ordinary" people were buying software game packages at the local Radio Shack and taking them home to play on something sitting on their desk called a "microcomputer."

the personal computer revolution

So, how, in less than ten years, did the world go from expensive, complicated machines (even the minicomputers required a great deal of room and expertise to operate), to the small plastic boxes that sat on desks at home entertaining kids (of all ages)? The culprits range from engineers forcing a hardware vision on their business managers, to software developers in it for the challenge, to electronic hobbyists realizing a dream, to software experts thumbing their noses at the establishment. In a few words: the time for a revolution was right. All the necessary hardware and software elements were at hand or being developed, and many different social, economic, and personal forces came together to support it. All that was needed was the will. Technically, practically everything needed was available right off the shelf.

note

David Ahl, formerly of Digital Equipment Corporation (DEC), noted "We [Digital] could have come out with a personal computer in January 1975. If we had taken that prototype, most of which was proven stuff, the PDP-8A could have been developed and put in production in that seven- or eight-month period."

Intel

One necessary element for the development of the PC came from a moderately sized company called Intel. In 1969, Intel had been creating semiconductors for electronic calculators, among other things. They had no intention of creating a computer. However, in contributing to the chip design of a calculator for a contract with the Busicom Company, Ted Hoth proposed putting more functionality on a single chip, essentially creating a ***central processing unit (CPU)***. That chip was named the 4004 for the number of transistors aboard. It was the precursor to the Intel 8008, then 8080, then 8086, then the 80286, 80386, 80486, Pentium, Pentium II, and Pentium 4 chips, and so on to today.

central processing unit (CPU) – The central controlling device inside of a computer that makes decisions at a very low level, such as what math functions or computer resources are to be used and when

microprocessor – A CPU on a single chip used in microcomputers

Intel, however, wasn't focused on trying to create a whole computer, never mind an industry. And even those in the company with vision mandated that the company would not get into end-user products (sold directly to the customer). When the programmer who created a little operating system for the Intel ***microprocessor*** asked if he might sell the combined chip and OS himself, Intel management told him he could do whatever he liked. That programmer was Gary Kildall and you'll hear about him again.

More than just the miniaturization of computing happened in the '70s and '80s. The whole computer marketplace changed. For the first time, software could be purchased as a commodity separate from the computer hardware. The story of that development involves a bunch of electronics hobbyists and a competition in an electronics magazine.

the Altair 8800

Hobbyists depended on magazines like *Popular Electronics* and *Radio Electronics* to learn about the latest advances in electronics. In addition, *Popular Electronics*, edited by Les Solomon, not only reported the latest advances, but also spurred their development. The hobbyist community was small enough that many knew each other, even if indirectly through publication in the magazine. In 1973, Solomon sought out the best contributors, asking for a story on "the first desktop computer kit." He received a number of designs, but felt they were not worthy of publication. A promising design by a Frenchman, Andre Thi Truong, actually did get created and sold in France that year but never made it to the pages of the magazine.

It wasn't until the January 1975 issue that Solomon published an article by Ed Roberts on the Altair 8800 (named after a planet in a Star Trek episode), a kit based on the Intel 8080. In 1974, Roberts faced the demise of his Albuquerque, New Mexico, MITS calculator company with competition from big players like

Texas Instruments and Hewlett Packard. He decided to bet the farm and take up Solomon's challenge—a bold decision given that, as far as anyone knew, there was no market for such a device beyond a few electronic hobbyists.

The results surprised almost everyone. Within three months of the *Popular Electronics* article, Roberts had 4000 orders for the Altair, at $397 each. Unfortunately, Roberts was a long way from fulfilling these orders. Parts were difficult to come by and they were not always reliable. Not only that, but the machine was completely disassembled, had no screen, keyboard, card reader, tape reader, disk drive, printer, or software. When complete, you had a box with a front panel that had switches and lights, each one for a binary bit. Data and program entry and the results were, in fact, very much like the original ENIAC, only in a much smaller package (Figure 1-8).

Figure 1-8, The MITS Altair 8800—assembled

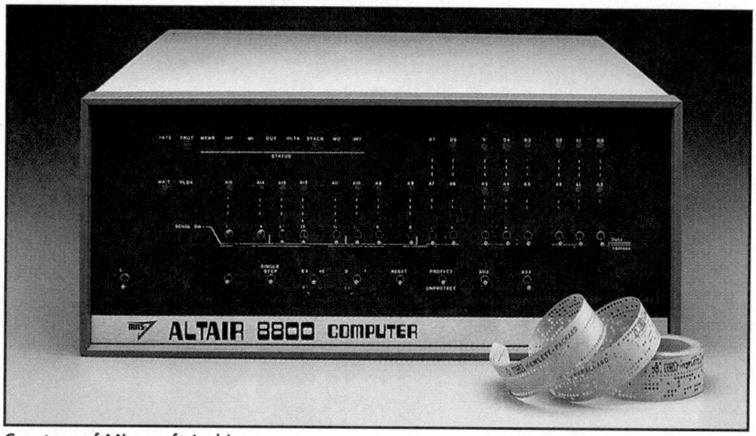

Courtesy of Microsoft Archives

Nevertheless, the orders kept pouring in. The hobby community was hungry for a machine that they could control, didn't have to wait in line to use, and was relatively portable. In addition, at its core, Roberts' machine had the goods—the capacity for input, storage, processing, and output—or at least the promise of the goods. Knowing that all the peripherals would have to be created later, Roberts created a machine with an ***open architecture***—a critical part of the microcomputer world even today. The machine had what would eventually be called a motherboard with expansion slots so that circuit boards for a computer screen or disk drive might be added. And, many of those interested hobbyists quickly moved to fill in the missing elements themselves.

***open architecture* – Computer hardware that is accessible for modification, and sometimes even documented**

enter Bill Gates, Paul Allen, and Microsoft

A couple of people who moved to fill the void were Paul Allen and Bill Gates. Gates and Allen were buddies living in Washington State. They were, essentially, technology hobbyists. While in high school they created a computer-like device called a Traf-O-Data. To gain experience with computers they worked for the automotive supplier TRW, and other companies, as programmers, mostly for free and for the fun of it. Gates was in college and Allen was working for Honeywell when Roberts' *Popular Electronics* article came out.

They called Ed Roberts, and the results of that call changed the world for both hardware and software. They told Roberts they had software, a BASIC programming language, already working—a claim not quite corresponding to reality. BASIC was an easy-to-use language that had been invented in the 1970s. Nevertheless, six weeks later Gates and Allen (Figure 1-9) demonstrated a rudimentary BASIC interpreter. This would be a huge leap over the machine code programming that the Altair required. Gates and Allen sold the BASIC software of their newly formed Micro-Soft company and Allen got the job of MITS Software Director—which meant that the newly formed corporate division of MITS now had one person in it. Soon after, Bill Gates left Harvard to join the fray. By 1981, Microsoft was on its way to becoming a multibillion-dollar company.

Figure 1-9, Paul Allen and Bill Gates in 1981

Courtesy of Microsoft Archives

the microcomputer begins to evolve

microcomputer – A desktop-sized computer with a microprocessor CPU designed to be used by one person at a time

Once it was shown that a ***microcomputer*** could be created and be profitable, a number of people got into the act. They also did so using Altair's techniques. Since the Altair bus (the mechanism through which the computer communicated with its various components) wasn't patented, hobbyists borrowed and renamed it the S100 bus, establishing a standard that any hardware/software company could use. A company called IMSAI started getting market share. Two companies, Southwest Technical Products and Sphere, both began building computers based on the more powerful Motorola 6800 chip. Another company was building the z80 processor. And, on the horizon, the Tandy Corporation, owner of Radio Shack, had a machine it was working on.

In general, MITS had its hand in so many efforts to both correct its startup flaws and compete at many levels that it was a victim of its own success. Problems continued to plague most of the hardware components. At one point the BASIC software had proven so much more popular than a flawed 4 K-memory board that MITS linked the prices to protect its hardware income. Buy the board and BASIC would cost around $150. Otherwise, you had to fork out $500 for BASIC, which in those days represented a tidy sum of money. Hobbyists countered by pirating the software and going to a third party for the board—possible since the bus was now a standard. The battle against the competition proved equally problematic. For example, MITS countered the Motorola chip by also building a 6800 Altair, but software and hardware were totally incompatible with the 8080 version. For distribution, MITS started to insist that the growing number of computer stores carry MITS products exclusively, an anathema to the hobbyist culture, and stores balked at the idea.

By the end of 1977, MITS was sold to Pertec Corporation, the beginning of the end for the Altair. Over 50 hardware companies had introduced competing models, including the PET from Commodore and another from a company named after a fruit, the Apple.

an Apple a day...

Apple Computer had its origins in Sunnyvale, California's Homestead High where Steve Jobs and Steve Wozniak met and shared a love of electronics and practical jokes (creating a bomblike ticking inside a friend's locker was one Wozniak "Woz" trick). They also shared a dream—to own a computer. In truth, Homestead High probably had a number of students who had that dream since many were the progeny of parents in the area's electronics industry, but it was a difficult dream to realize. Their first commercial product was a game idea from Nolan Bushnell at Atari: Breakout. Jobs and Woz (then at college and working at Hewlett-Packard, respectively) finished the game in four days. In 1975 Woz began working on his high school dream and successfully created a computer. It was a hobbyist's ideal, a simple design housed in a wooden box, but nowhere near being a commercial product. Nor was it ever intended to be. Jobs, however, convinced Woz the machine had a commercial future and dubbed it the Apple I. Their prankster spirits still alive, they began the company on April Fool's Day, 1976, and priced the machine at $666 (a biblical reference to the devil).

Apple might have remained a hobbyist machine, but Jobs could inspire people with his drive and enthusiasm. In 1976 they secured nearly $300,000 in funding. In 1977, Apple released the Apple II (Figure 1-10) based upon the Motorola 6502 processor, and made a profit by year's end, doubling production every few months. The Apple II was compact, reliable, and "talked up" in the industry. It was also adopted by many schools, and became many students' first experience with computers—making a lasting impression. But what really pushed it toward broad acceptance was the ease with which programmers could write applications for it.

To a large extent, microcomputers had so far been playthings for hobbyists. The most popular programs running on these machines were games. Games like MicroChess, Adventure, and Breakout put the machines in people's homes and introduced kids to computing. But the microcomputer wasn't recognized as a

Figure 1-10, The Apple II was the first popular PC

Courtesy Apple Computer, Inc.

business tool until Dan Bricklin and Bob Frankston, working in Frankston's Boston-area attic office, created VisiCalc for the Apple II.

VisiCalc was the first spreadsheet program where columns and rows that went far beyond the boundaries of the screen could have data values or equations. In its release year of 1979 it sold 500 copies a month. By 1981 it shipped 12,000 copies. The program was so flexible that customers used it for things it hadn't been intended for, like word processing, and it was powerful enough to become a tool, not just for home users, but for small businesses. It drove the sales of Apple IIs to such an extent that it created a whole new category of software: the ***killer app*** (short for killer application).

killer app – A software program that becomes so popular that it drives the popularity of the hardware it runs on

In 1983 another "killer app" called Lotus 1-2-3, based on the same spreadsheet principle as VisiCalc, pushed a different company's hardware. It had a huge marketing blitz behind it, had no ties to Apple, and seemed legitimate to the inhabitants of Wall Street. But, more importantly, the company that made the computer fairly screamed legitimacy among corporate executive types.

IBM offers the PC

When IBM realized that the Apple II had moved beyond the hobby and toy arena, they took a long view of the future and realized that the microcomputer might play a significant part in the traditional computer marketplace. IBM decided to enter the battle, intending to dominate the microcomputer market to the same extent they dominated the mainframe marketplace. Of course, in order to dominate the market, they needed to build the machine, and fast.

In order to get to market quickly, IBM approached the problem differently than they had for other hardware. Instead of building their own chip, the chip in the new machine was right off the shelf—the Intel 8088—similar to those used in other micros. Learning from the success of the Altair and recognizing that they needed the broad talents of the micro world to build the peripherals and software for their ***personal computer (PC)***, they did a few other things that never would have occurred in the mainframe world. The IBM PC used a nonproprietary CPU, had approachable documentation, and an open architecture similar to the Altair's. Recognizing the change in the market landscape, IBM also sold the machine through retail outlets instead of through their established commercial sales force.

personal computer (PC) – Originally, an IBM microcomputer; now generally refers to any microcomputer

MS-DOS

Searching for applications for its PC, IBM contacted Microsoft and arranged a meeting with Gates and his new business manager, Steve Ballmer. Gates and Ballmer put off a meeting with Atari (another fledgling home computer development company) and put on untypical suits and ties. In another first, they also signed a confidentiality agreement so that both Microsoft and IBM would be protected in future development.

IBM also needed an operating system and Gates sent them across town to meet with Gary Kildall at Digital Research Incorporated (DRI). Recall that Kildall had written the operating system for the Intel 4004. He had also written CP/M, an operating system for the IMSAI and other Altair-like computers that became quite popular. Before Kildall's CP/M, the closest thing to an operating system on the microcomputer had been Microsoft BASIC. CP/M was much more powerful and could work with any application designed for the machines. However, IBM hesitated at the $10 per copy cost of CP/M. Talking again with Gates they became convinced that they might be better off with a whole new operating system, because CP/M was an 8-bit OS and the 8088 was a 16-bit CPU. So, despite Microsoft not actually owning an operating system at the time, IBM chose Microsoft to develop its PC operating system.

note

A myth in the world of microcomputers persists that instead of meeting with IBM, Gary Kildall decided to go flying. The truth is that he had gone flying earlier that day for business. He did, in fact, meet with IBM.

Now all Microsoft had to do was create the operating system. Microsoft developed MS-DOS (for Microsoft Disk Operating System), which IBM called PC-DOS, to run on the Intel 8088. They accomplished this by reworking a program called SCP-DOS that imitated CP/M. Kildall, getting an early version of the program and discerning how similar it was to his, threatened to sue. Instead, he reached an agreement with IBM. IBM would offer his operating system as well as the Microsoft version. Unfortunately, when the product came out, IBM offered PC-DOS at $40 and CP/M-86 at $240. Which one would you have bought?

the Apple Macintosh raises the bar

With the IBM PC and DOS, Apple faced serious competition for the first time. Jobs, however, already had a response. As an operating system, DOS adequately controlled the machine's facilities, but few would call the user interface intuitive. Users had to type in commands (many of them cryptic) at the command line in order to get the machine to do anything. Jobs had a whole different idea for a user interface.

In late 1979, Steve Jobs had visited Xerox PARC (Palo Alto Research Center). Since the 1960s, its scientists and engineers had been at the cutting edge of computing science. There he saw a machine called the Alto that had graphics, menus, icons, windows, and a mouse. He also saw a technique for linking documents called hypertext, and something else called an Ethernet network that linked the machines on different engineers' desks. Many of Xerox's experiments implemented the ideas of Douglas Engelbart of Stanford Research Institute (SRI), a visionary inventor who also created the mouse. Unfortunately for Xerox, they had not successfully brought any of these products to market. The cost of one Alto—almost 2000 were built and installed—was about as much as a minicomputer. It's also possible that Xerox didn't want to commit wholeheartedly to ideas that might possibly threaten their core business of making paper copies. Jobs had no such worries and he aimed to put something on everyone's desk—paper or no paper.

Steve Jobs has said of his Apple I, "We didn't do three years of research and come up with this concept. What we did was follow our own instincts and construct a computer that was what we wanted." The same could be said of Job's next foray into computer development, and the effort again changed the industry. After several years and at least one commercial false start, a small "skunk works" team pushed by Jobs built a computer and small screen combination in a tan box together with keyboard and mouse: the Apple Macintosh (Figure 1-11). The operating system didn't look anything like DOS. The user moved an arrow on the screen with a mouse and clicked pictures (called icons) to get things done. To delete a file, for instance, the user would drag the file to a little icon of a trash can. The Macintosh had the first mass-produced ***graphical user interface (GUI)***.

graphical user interface (GUI) – An interface to the computer that uses graphical instead of text commands. This has come to mean windows, menus, and a mouse

Figure 1-11, Members of the Macintosh design team

Courtesy of Apple Computer, Inc.

The Macintosh's public unveiling was as dramatic a departure as the operating system itself. During the 1984 Super Bowl broadcast, a commercial came on that showed gray-clothed and ashen-skinned people trudging, zombie-like, into a large, bleak room. In the front of the room a huge television displayed a talking head of Big Brother droning on. An athletic and colorfully clothed woman chased by security forces ran into the room. She swung a sledgehammer into the television, which exploded. A message then came on the screen "On January 24th, 1984, Apple Computer will introduce Macintosh. And you'll see why 1984 won't be like *1984*." The commercial referred to George Orwell's apocalyptic visionary novel, *1984*, in which Big Brother is an omnipresent authoritarian power that tries to force everyone to do its bidding. It wasn't hard to guess whom Apple was likening to Big Brother; it was likely Apple's old nemesis, Big Blue (IBM).

In reality, the Macintosh, or "Mac" as it was affectionately called, was stymied by hardware limitations and an initial lack of software although it did sell well and changed the competitive landscape. However, in terms of competition for Apple, IBM didn't end up playing the role of Big Brother for long. In the early 1990s, that role went to the combination of Microsoft and Intel and has remained that way since.

other PCs (and one serious OS competitor) begin to emerge

In the early 1980s, Gates had persuasively argued that IBM should follow the direction of open architecture that they had begun in hardware by having it support any operating system as well. Successful third-party programs like VisiCalc drove hardware sales and helped make the case. Gates managed to convince IBM of something else: that Microsoft should be free to sell its operating system to other hardware manufacturers. With that one decision, IBM likely created the future of the PC world in which IBM would become a minority player. Because of its open architecture, third parties could essentially clone the IBM machine's hardware. And any hardware whose workings weren't covered by IBM's documentation were "reverse engineered" (reinvented to work exactly the same way). The mid 1980s through 1990s saw the slow descent of IBM's share of the PC market. Competing machines from Compaq, Dell, Gateway, Toshiba, and others, including hundreds of small shops, were first called "clones," but eventually co-opted the names "personal computer" and "PC" as well.

In this same time frame, Microsoft rose to dominance. Every clone had the Microsoft operating system on board. It turns out people needed a consistent user interface and operating system on which all the third-party software could run. Microsoft began to compete against Apple as well (despite writing application software for Apple machines). Microsoft worked to provide an OS that would incorporate the GUI features of the Mac. In 1988, four years after the Mac's introduction, Microsoft brought out the first commercially viable version of its Windows operating system, and came out with the first serious competition for the Mac GUI in 1991, with Windows 3.1, despite the fact it wasn't really a new operating system at all but a program that ran on top of DOS. IBM also developed a competing operating system called OS/2—actually written by Microsoft—but with few applications or users, it went nowhere.

In the 1990s, Microsoft took advantage of its position as almost sole supplier of operating systems to PCs. Software application companies began to lose market share. In 1990, Lotus 1-2-3 was the best-selling software package and WordPerfect was the best-selling word processor. Lotus had a gross revenue that wasn't much smaller than Microsoft's (only three years earlier Lotus had been the bigger company). By 2000, Lotus 1-2-3 and Word Perfect were blips on the software screen, replaced by Micro-soft's Excel and Word programs. Some flavor of Windows is now on over 90 percent of the personal computers in the world.

the latest generation (fifth)

From 1990 to today is generally labeled the fifth generation of hardware and software since the advent of the modern computer. In hardware this includes ***parallel computing*** (or parallel architectures) where a number of CPUs can be applied to the same task simultaneously.

parallel computing – The use of multiple computers or CPUs to simultaneously process a single task

One approach is single instruction, multiple data (SIMD) stream where a single command can operate on multiple sets of data simultaneously. Another approach is multiple instruction, multiple data (MIMD) stream (MIMD) where different parts of a program or different programs might be worked on simultaneously. A number of computers used to control Web pages, databases, and networks have two to four parallel processors in the same box and use these techniques. These are small enough and affordable enough that you can buy them and put on your desk. Larger and more expensive machines such as the Cray ***supercomputer*** can be used for complex modeling and scientific research. These supercomputers are at the extreme edge of computer processing power. A third approach for parallel processing uses another signature aspect of the fifth generation of computing: the network and its most spectacular realization, the Internet.

supercomputer – The fastest and usually most expensive computer available; often used in scientific and engineering research

the Internet

You can safely date the origins of the Internet back to a memo in 1962 by J.C.R. Licklider, where he proposed that different machines needed to communicate despite their different operating instructions. Licklider ran the Information Processing Techniques Office (IPTO) of the Advanced Research Projects Agency (ARPA; occasionally called the Defense Advanced Research Projects Agency or DARPA) of the U.S. Department of Defense. Four years later, Bob Taylor, who had inherited the position from Licklider, looked at the three terminals in his office that connected him to three different machines in three different parts of the country and decided to resurrect Licklider's idea—to create more office space if nothing else—and got Pentagon funding of $1 million.

Taylor argued that a communication system might help in three major ways:

- Research institutions working with the IPTO could share resources
- Computers the government was purchasing could be better utilized because incompatibility would not be a problem
- The system could be created so that it was robust: if one line went down the system would rechannel through another line

It is this last point that has led to the characterization of the development of the Internet as a product of the Cold War. Nor is the characterization far fetched, because ARPA itself was created by Eisenhower as a direct response to the possible threat posed by the Russian launch of Sputnik. Some have written that ARPANET was created so that it might survive a limited nuclear war or sabotage by dynamically rechanneling communication.

In fact, Paul Baran of the Rand Corporation had been working on this concept since 1960 concerning the U.S. telephone system, and the British had begun work along similar lines as well. Baran had ideas of a distributed network where each computer on the network would independently decide how to channel to the next computer. In addition, information could also be divided into blocks that were reassembled at their destination, with each block possibly following a different path. The ARPANET project did end up adopting these concepts (now called packets and packet switching), although arguably for reasons that had more to do with the system unreliability of the times than with any enemy threat.

Several months after the 1969 Apollo moon landing, the ARPANET was born, consisting of four computers at four locations: UCLA, UC at Santa Barbara, the Stanford Research Institute, and the University of Utah. The first message was the first three letters of "LOGIN" just before the system crashed. After that startup hiccup, however, the system expanded fairly rapidly. ARPA managed the feat of linking the different systems by having a computer (an Interface Message Processor or IMP) linked to the telephone or telegraph line and each mainframe having its own IMP. In addition, as long as you knew the communication protocols, you could build your own IMP. Professors and graduate students essentially built the beginnings of the Internet as part of their research or in their spare time.

You'll learn more about the Internet in Chapter 7, "The Internet."

By the mid '70s, scientists the world over were communicating by connecting their local networks via the protocols created for the ARPANET. By the mid '80s, the loose collection of networks was called "the Internet" (short for "internetwork") and by the early '90s, thousands of research institutions, U.S. government organizations such as the National Science Foundation, and corporations such as AT&T and GE made up the Internet. Agreed upon networking standards and international cooperation made the network a worldwide phenomenon. Another interesting development was that by the second year of operation, over two-thirds of the traffic on the network consisted of personal notes, similar to today's e-mail. It seems that despite the initial goal of sharing computer resources, the Internet was used mainly for communication.

LANs and WANs and other ANs

The Internet is a network of networks. It usually connects and works with local area networks (LANs) and wide area networks (WANs—which themselves can be made up of LANs). A WAN might be the network on your campus while a LAN connects the machines in your computer science building. These usually are controlled by a network technology called Ethernet and are physically linked by Ethernet cable. As fiber optics and various wireless technologies have improved, they also have become critical in adding computers to networks and have given rise to the terms WLAN (wireless LAN) and MAN (metropolitan area network) or UAN (urban area network).

When you share files with the guy in the next room, use a central printer, or use a program on a different machine in your building, you probably are not using the Internet per se; you're most likely using a LAN, maybe even a wireless LAN (WLAN). If the Internet is the "superhighway" of information, you might call the LANs and WANs the small town roads and freeways of information. A number of competing architectures for LANs and WANs arose in the 1970s, but by the late '70s, Ethernet was on its way to becoming the most popular standard for controlling network traffic. A company called Novell became a dominant player in networks in 1989 with their NetWare file server software.

You'll learn more about LANs, WANs, Ethernet, and networking standards in Chapter 6, "Networks."

super software and the Web

Paralleling the development of multiprocessors, networks, and the Internet, software also made great changes in the fifth generation. Programmers began to more widely adopt modular approaches, such as object-oriented programming (OOP), that facilitated larger, more complex, and more quickly and reliably delivered software products.

You'll see more about OOP in Chapter 12, "Software Engineering."

Another development was computer-aided software engineering (CASE) tools—tools that make the development of software easier and faster. While the promise of software programs writing other software pro-grams has yet to reach the point of replacing the programmer, a number of inroads toward automatic code generation have occurred. Today, object-oriented graphical programs such as Visio and Rational Rose can generate some code. With some fairly intuitive input, word-processing programs such as Word and WordPerfect and Web page development environments such as Macromedia Dreamweaver can practically automatically create Web pages—which brings us to what is probably the most monumental software development of the 1990s and beyond: the World Wide Web (WWW).

hypermedia – Different sorts of information (text, sound, pictures, video) that are linked in such a way that a user can move and see content easily from one link to another

hypertext – Hypermedia that is specifically text

browser – A program that accesses and displays files and other information or hypermedia available on a network or on the Internet

While you've seen how the Internet developed over the course of 40 years, it didn't really begin to develop into the powerful communication and economic system it is today until someone wrote the "killer app." A man named Tim Berners-Lee (Figure 1-12), working at the Centre European pour la Recherche Nucleaire (CERN), a laboratory for particle physics in France, created two software elements that would lead to making the Internet more accessible to the general public and commercial interests: the Web page and the browser. These two elements, combined with network access through the Internet, became known as the World Wide Web (WWW). Prior to the WWW, computer gurus in the know handled the communication between machines. Communicating required knowing the cryptic language of the machine protocols and didn't attract the casual user. The application of ***hypermedia*** (and ***hypertext***) to the Internet and a program to read that media (called a ***browser***) radically changed the equation.

Hypertext had its origins in a 1945 proposal by U.S. President Roosevelt's science advisor, Vannevar Bush. Bush imagined a machine that could store information and allow users to link text and illustrations, thus creating "infor-

Figure 1-12, Tim Berners-Lee, inventor of the World Wide Web

Courtesy of Massachusetts Institute of Technology

mation trails." A computer visionary in the 1960s, Ted Nelson, coined the word "hypertext" and spent years conceptualizing how this would work with the computer technology of his day.

The invention of the World Wide Web has been called a side effect of doing high-energy physics. A 1990 proposal by Berners-Lee to link and manage numerous documents includes the ideas of browsing links of documents kept on a server. In 1991 a prototype was created on a NeXT computer (NeXT is a Steve Jobs company started after he left Apple). In the next few years, using the Berners-Lee protocols, a number of simple browsers were created including one browser that had the most impact beyond the walls of academia: Mosaic. Written for the Mac and Windows systems by Marc Andreesen and released free of charge in August 1993, Mosaic had an extremely intuitive graphical interface. Now the cat was out to the bag. For while the general consumer didn't know it at the time, an easy-to-use browser interface was just what they had been waiting for. The proof: in six years, between 1992 and 1998, the number of Web sites went from 50 to approximately 2.5 million. Andreesen went on to found Netscape, and developed Mosaic into the Netscape browser, which dominated the marketplace in the 1990s and pushed Microsoft to develop its own browser.

the Microsoft era and more

By the mid '90s Microsoft was feeling the pressure from Netscape: Netscape had one of the most successful public stock offerings in the history of the stock market, and its browser was dominating the Web. Netscape was also operating system independent—it didn't require a particular operating system to run. Microsoft reacted by restructuring its products to be Internet compliant, and developing the Internet Explorer (IE) browser that it first gave away, then integrated into its Windows 98 OS. This integration of IE with the dominant operating system was the turning point in what came to be known as the "browser wars." In 1996, Internet Explorer's market share went from 7 percent to 29 percent—assisted by Microsoft becoming the promoted browser for AOL in exchange for an AOL icon appearing on every Windows desktop (competing with Microsoft's own MSN service). IE never stopped gaining users after that. In 1998, Netscape took a different tack, going totally *open source*, and released the source code for its browser.

open source - Software whose source code is accessible—and potentially even documented—for modification

In an antitrust suit filed against Microsoft in 1998, the U.S. government claimed that Microsoft's near monopoly in operating systems created an unfair advantage in competing against Netscape. Microsoft claimed that the Internet Explorer browser was an integral part of the operating system and could not be easily separated from the rest of the code. The 1998 sale of Netscape to AOL also muddied the legal waters.

The government case went even further back than the browser wars. It claimed that Microsoft's control over computer manufacturers in matters such as what third-party program icons might appear on the desktop was monopolistic. Microsoft's alleged practice of not releasing critical operating system information to third-party software vendors such as Lotus and WordPerfect (to the advantage Microsoft's own application software) was also claimed as monopolistic. In the end, however, Microsoft came out of the suit fairly well. Various parties settled separately and while a threat of breakup seemed possible, in 2001 under the Bush administration, most of the antitrust suit was dropped or lessened.

Today, the biggest threat to Microsoft in the personal computer market is the rise of Linux, a UNIX-based program written by Linus Torvalds while a student at the University of Helsinki. It is available, including source code, essentially for free. Many hobbyists have embraced Linux as their choice of operating system because of the low cost, available source code, and its reputed reliability. Although not originally written with this intention, it has been selected, and not without cost, by many corporations, large and small, as a viable operating system for servers for those very reasons as well. Corporate information technology experts cite eliminating dependence on a single vendor—Microsoft in this case—as appealing.

Operating systems on personal computers, however, are only part of the story in computing. Although it's true that a Microsoft operating system sits on more than 90 percent of Intel- (or an Intel clone-) based computers, only 10 percent of the software running on all the computing devices of the world comes from Microsoft—far from a monopoly. A fact like that puts the world of computing in perspective. For each personal computer, there are numerous mainframes, networked machines, handheld devices, and *embedded computers*, all requiring software. Where does this software come from? From large companies like Computer Associates, Oracle, Germany's SAG; small local firms and startups; and the hundreds of thousands of programmers worldwide. Perhaps from you.

embedded computers – Computers embedded into other devices: a phone, car, or thermometer, for example

what about the future?

A quick look at the future offers numerous tantalizing possibilities in computer development—and the social implications of that development. You've probably already noticed the first signs of these possibilities.

For more information on cutting-edge technologies and trends, see Chapter 14, "Emerging Technologies."

Parallel computing, for example, can create massive computing power. In 2003, Virginia Tech created the third fastest machine in the world by writing specialized software linking a collection of networked Macintosh computers. Parallel processing can work on the Internet as well. Today you can sign up for a scientific research project where, via the Web, you loan out some of your machine's processing power. Your machine can join hundreds or more machines working on a single scientific problem. With millions of machines on the Internet, imagine this as a model for problem solving.

With wireless networking you now can surf the Web without plugging into the wall. Soon, using wireless technologies such as Bluetooth, in addition to embedded computing (sometimes called *ubiquitous computing*), all the appliances in your home might be "talking." The water heater might hear from the furnace that it's on vacation mode and automatically adjust itself. Who knows, maybe your lost sock can tell you where it is! Medical equipment can be miniaturized and even implanted in our bodies, communicating to doctors via the Web.

ubiquitous computing – The possibility of computers being embedded into almost everything and potentially able to communicate as well

Everything is going digital as well. Will books, film, and photographs eventually disappear? Will music lovers no longer own CDs, but download what they want, when they want, from the Web? What of privacy? As increasing amounts of information about people are stored on computers, does everyone need to choose between invasion of their privacy and physical and fiscal security? Big questions also loom for the open model of computing. Will an open and essentially free operating system like Linux actually become commonplace? In any of these possible eventualities, you, as a computer professional, will have a significant role to play.

one last thought

Underlying all the developments in computer hardware and software that you've seen in this chapter is a larger context: societal and personal needs, wants, and desires shape the development of any technology, including computers and the programs that run them.

Perhaps there was market demand for the product because it fulfilled a physical and commercial requirement. For example, chip designers competed to cram ever more circuits in a smaller area so that hardware designers would choose their chips. Hardware designers then created physically smaller, faster, and less expensive computers that appealed to a larger and broader market, increasing hardware sales. Or perhaps the impetus behind an innovation was the drive to discover a solution to a problem—as with Babbage and his Analytical Engine, or the desire to create something new—like Woz and the Apple I. Perhaps it was the need for control exhibited by many early hobbyists who promoted getting away from centralized mainframes and owning their own machines. Perhaps it served a social or political need such as winning a war. Per-haps it served an ideal of what a computer should look like—such as Engelbart and his mouse—or, to stay ahead of the possible competition, like Bill Gates and his drive to succeed. In any event, needs, from the highest level to the most personal, play a complex role in the creation of computer hardware or a computer program.

Reinforce your understanding of chapter concepts and terms with the information and activities for Chapter 1 on the student CD.

While an arms-length view of history might suggest that technological development occurs in a seamlessly purposeful evolutionary direction, a closer look, as this chapter has shown, reveals the truth as being more complex. Perhaps the best idea wins, but it really depends on your definition of "best." As a computer scientist, only part of your job is to program or design. You need to be aware of the complex mix of requirements and historical forces affecting you. You should also be aware of the implications of what you create. That is how you will succeed. You will avoid the mistakes of the past and emulate the triumphs. You will share and appreciate a common heritage with those around you. And you'll tell a good story or two. Have fun!

chapter summary

- Understanding the evolution of computers and computer science will help you understand the broader context of the many different tasks you will undertake throughout your education and career.
- Computers are unique tools in that they can do different jobs depending on what software is running on them
- Today you can find computers everywhere from your desktop to your countertop
- At its core, every computer performs symbolic and mathematical manipulation
- The history of mathematical tools can be traced as far back as the Assyrians and their clay mathematical tables
- The punch card, a major development in the history of computing, owes its development to Jacquard's loom
- Charles Babbage is considered the father of modern computing because of his development of the Analytical Engine; Ada Lovelace Byron is considered the first programmer
- Herman Hollerith, later playing a part in what would become IBM, solved the U.S. Census problem of 1890 by use of a mechanical counting tool
- The ENIAC, attributed mainly to John Mauchly, J. Presper Eckert, and John Von Neumann, has been called the first electronic computer; it used vacuum tubes, had thousands of switches, and weighed tons
- Mauchly and Eckert went on to build the first commercial computer, the UNIVAC
- IBM dominated the mainframe marketplace in the late '50s, '60s, and '70s
- Transistors, and then integrated circuits, shrunk the size of the computer leading first to the minicomputer in the mid '60s and then to the microcomputer in the late '70s
- UNIX and BASIC were both invented in the early 1970s
- Hobbyists created the first microcomputers, the Altair was considered to be the very first
- Big business officially entered the microcomputer scene with the introduction of the IBM PC
- In the 1980s, with the microcomputer, for the first time, companies sold software directly to the end customers; prior to the microcomputer, software mostly came with the machine
- Apple computer introduced the small business community to inexpensive computing with the Apple II and VisiCalc, the first "killer app"
- Apple's MacIntosh introduced the first graphical user interface to the microcomputer world

- IBM lost market share in the late '80s and '90s because it had created an open system and had an agreement in which Microsoft could sell its operating system independent of IBM
- The Internet began with ARPANET built by the U.S. Department of Defense in the 1960s as a way to share computing resources, but the parties involved soon realized that it was more useful as a communication device
- The World Wide Web and the browser, especially Mosaic, permitted the use of the Internet to a broad audience, and consequently the use of the Internet via the Web exploded
- Wireless networks, ubiquitous and embedded computing, and parallel computing all promise to change the world you live in
- Societal and personal needs, wants, and desires shape the development of any technology, including computers and the programs that run them

key terms

abacus (6)

assembly language (13)

binary (machine) code (13)

Boolean logic (Boolean algebra) (10)

browser (32)

central processing unit (CPU) (20)

chip (17)

embedded computers (35)

graphical user interface (GUI) (27)

hardware (13)

hypermedia (32)

hypertext (32)

integrated circuit (IC) (17)

killer app(lication) (25)

mainframe (15)

microcomputer (23)

microprocessor (20)

minicomputer (19)

open architecture (21)

open source (34)

operating system (OS) (17)

parallel computing (29)

personal computer (PC) (25)

program loop (8)

slide rule (6)

software (13)

stored program concept (12)

supercomputer (29)

time-sharing (18)

transistor (16)

ubiquitous computing (35)

vacuum tube (10)

Von Neumann machine (11)

test yourself

1. Name two needs of society that led to the development of more complex mathematics.
2. What was the first mechanical device used for calculation?
3. How would you compare the early electronic computer to the player piano?
4. What technology did Herman Hollerith borrow from the Jacquard loom?
5. Who has been called the "first programmer"?
6. Name an important concept attributed to the person named in Question 5.
7. What innovation does the ENIAC appear to borrow from the Atanasoff-Berry Computer?
8. Name at least one computer other than ENIAC that developed independently and simultaneously during World War II.
9. What reason is given for the invention of assembly language?
10. What color can you attribute to IBM of the 1950s, and what significance did it have for IBM's eventual dominance of the marketplace?
11. Name two important hardware developments of the second generation of hardware.
12. What long-term memory storage device that computers have today did second generation computers often lack?
13. In what language was the first UNIX operating system written? What did Kernigan and Ritchie have to create to make the second version of UNIX?
14. On what kind of computer was the first UNIX operating system written?
15. Before the Altair, Ed Roberts made what?
16. What software did the Altair microcomputer get that later helped make Bill Gates rich?
17. Name the two people responsible for the first Apple computer. Name the "killer app" responsible for the Apple II's success.
18. What challenge to the IBM PC did Apple launch in 1984? What response did Microsoft launch against Apple a few years later?
19. One of the ideas used in the development of the ARPANET—splitting information into blocks and reassembling them at their destination—came from the Rand Corporation. The initial concept began in relation to what system?
20. To what decade can you trace the origins of the development of hypertext?

practice exercises

1. In 1642 Pascal created a mechanical device with gears and levers. This device was capable of what kind of calculation?

   a. Addition
   b. Addition and subtraction
   c. Addition, subtraction, and multiplication
   d. Addition, subtraction, multiplication, and division

2. Leibnitz built on Pascal's work by creating the Leibnitz Wheel. This device was capable of what kind of calculations in addition to the ones Pascal's could do?

   a. Subtraction
   b. Addition and multiplication
   c. Subtraction and multiplication
   d. Multiplication and division

3. The Jacquard loom is important in the history of computing for what innovation?

   a. It worked like a player piano
   b. Reusable cards with holes that held information
   c. The use of gears and wheels for calculation
   d. Paper rolls with holes that held information

4. IBM has some of its origins in what 1890 event?

   a. The U.S. census
   b. The first Jacquard loom in the United States
   c. Ada Lovelace's first program loop
   d. The introduction of electricity to the United States

5. Name the four important elements of Babbage's Engine that are a component of today's computer.

   a. The stored in memory program technique, an input device, an output device, and memory
   b. Mechanical calculation equipment, human powered mechanisms, punched cards, and an output device
   c. An input device, memory, a central processing unit, an output device
   d. An input device, the stored in memory program technique, a central processing unit, and an output device

6. What logical elements did Charles Sanders Peirce realize electrical switches could emulate in 1880?

   a. Epistemological calculus
   b. Ontological algebra
   c. Boolean algebra
   d. Metaphysical algebra

7. The U.S. military used the ENIAC computer for its intended purpose during World War II.

 a. True
 b. False

8. What important concept is attributed to John Von Neumann?

 a. The large memory concept
 b. The stored program concept
 c. The discrete variable automation concept
 d. The virtual memory concept

9. What company controlled 70 percent or more of the computer marketplace in the '60s and '70s?

 a. Sperry-Univac
 b. International Business Machines
 c. Hollerith Machines
 d. Microsoft

10. What features of transistors made them superior for computers compared to vacuum tubes?

 a. They were more expensive than tubes but lasted longer and were cooler in temperature
 b. They didn't last as long as tubes but were less expensive
 c. They were cheaper and smaller than tubes
 d. They were cheaper, smaller, and cooler than tubes and lasted longer

11. What important pastry helped move your job up in the queue in second generation software, and what software development made that pastry unnecessary?

 a. Donuts and integrated circuits
 b. Bear claws and multitasking
 c. Donuts and time-sharing
 d. Donuts and virtual memory

12. In hardware, the next step up from the transistor was the transmitter.

 a. True
 b. False

13. What magazines can we thank for the first microcomputer?

 a. *Science* and the *Wall Street Journal*
 b. *Popular Electronics* and *Radio Electronics*
 c. *Popular Electronics* and *Star Trek Monthly*
 d. *New Mexico Entrepreneur* and *Radio Electronics*

14. What important concept did the Altair use, which was borrowed by its competition, including the IBM personal computer?

 a. The computer came in kit form
 b. The computer's price was $666
 c. The machine had an open architecture
 d. The machine could be opened easily for repair

15. The Apple computer became very popular. What was its largest market and what software made it interesting to that market?

- **a.** The education market and the educational game "Shape Up"
- **b.** The games market and the game "The Big Race"
- **c.** The business market and the program Lotus 1-2-3
- **d.** The business market and the program VisiCalc

16. In 1990 what software company dominated the software market and what major product did it sell?

- **a.** Lotus and Lotus 1-2-3
- **b.** Bricklin and VisiCalc
- **c.** Apple and the Apple Operating System
- **d.** Microsoft and Word

17. Today, Microsoft considers its major competition in operating systems to be what system?

- **a.** Control Data Corporation OS
- **b.** Sega games operating system
- **c.** Linux operating system
- **d.** Mac OS X

18. ARPA was created in response to what major event in world history?

- **a.** World War II
- **b.** The Cold War
- **c.** The launch of Sputnik
- **d.** The inability of computers to communicate with one another

19. Name the three most critical large-scale developments of the fifth generation of software development from this list.

- **a.** Parallel computing, networking, and the multiple-data-stream approach
- **b.** The graphical user interface, networking, and computer-aided software engineering tools (CASE)
- **c.** Networking, the graphical user interface, and packet switching
- **d.** ARPANET, the Internet, and CASE

20. Marc Andreesen released what initial product that made browsers widespread?

- **a.** Netscape
- **b.** Mosaic
- **c.** Explorer
- **d.** Hypertext

digging deeper

1. How has the idea of open source changed the software industry?

2. How did the microcomputer revolution change how software became distributed? Who is partly responsible for this occurrence?

3. After selling MITS, Ed Roberts actually went on to get his medical degree and became a doctor. Why did his computer quickly lose its dominance in the microcomputer industry and his company eventually fold? What would you have done differently?
4. What critical agreement and what hardware decisions may have allowed Microsoft to monopolize the microcomputer world where IBM slowly lost market share?
5. Has Microsoft been unfairly labeled a monopoly? Would the demise of Linux change your opinion?

discussion topics

1. What values are there in having embedded computers talk to one another? What dangers?
2. Imagine that Microsoft didn't get to keep the rights to its software when it moved back to Seattle. What would the software world probably look like today?
3. Programming is now carried on 24 hours a day by having development teams stationed around the globe (U.S., Ireland, India, etc). Are these developments a threat or a benefit to programmers in the United States?
4. The beginning of this chapter mentioned that almost everyone is a computer user. What do you think would classify you as a computer scientist? What would likely classify you as a computer scientist in 1945?
5. Several schools in the United States and Western Europe have become concerned over the low numbers of women and minorities learning computer science. Recently, Carnegie Mellon focused on attracting women and minorities. How can society benefit by attracting higher numbers of these members of society to computer science? What would it mean for engineering culture, product design, management, or end users?

Internet research

1. Would the Internet in the United States survive a nuclear war? Who says what?
2. In the world of the Internet, what is an RFP? Who uses them and for how long have they been used?
3. Can you watch the Apple 1984 commercial? What color is the woman's shorts? What's on her shirt? Can you find the text of what "Big Brother" says?
4. Name seven pioneers of computing born in January.
5. Who is William Burroughs? What is his son known for back in the 1950s/60s?

chapter

2 software tools for techies

in this chapter you will:

- Learn what tasks you need to be prepared to accomplish within the computer industry and which tools can help you succeed in completing the tasks
- Learn how even computer scientists have to use word processors to create documents
- Learn what tools can be used to create a presentation
- Learn about the different types of graphics and what tools allow you to create and modify them
- Refresh your understanding of e-mail and how it benefits the computer industry
- Learn what tools are used to compress files
- Understand how files can be shared through the use of FTP
- Learn about creating spreadsheets to manage projects and which spreadsheet tools are best to use
- Realize that there are many different programming languages to choose from and that using a particular programming environment may make it easier to create an application
- Learn that Web development is an essential task to add to your skills
- Learn about database design and maintenance tools
- Learn that project management is essential to the success of a project

the lighter side of the lab

by spencer

Working with computers is not easy work, as some people might suppose. Sure, we get paid big bucks to sit in air-conditioned offices and do what we love all day. We always have the fastest computers and the newest versions of every program. And nobody appreciates the value of a game ending with the word "craft" like we do.

But it's not all fun and games. Nobody knows the pain associated with the word "geeks" like we do. It hurts, man. Come on, we're people too. (Well, at least those of us that aren't half-Klingon.)

As computer scientists, we need certain things in order to do our job properly. For example, how can a person be expected to survive on a 40 Gig hard drive? I mean, that only holds 13,321 MP3s. We could download that in our sleep.

Next, who is the "genius" that thought of the 8-ounce can of Mountain Dew? That's toddler size. Let's think this through: we have to spend five seconds every 10 minutes to open a new can. Here's an idea—how about a 384-ounce can of Mountain Dew? We would only have to open one can a day, which would increase our daily productivity by four minutes. In this business, time is money.

Finally, every computer science department should have a dating service. Sure, chat rooms have their perks, but, contrary to popular belief, we do venture out of the house every once in a while. We could really use a dating service. Or, better yet, prearranged marriages! We could have a company lotto to draw a spouse. I'm guessing the person who did away with prearranged marriages was probably the same genius who invented the 8-ounce Mountain Dew.

Just imagine how our productivity would skyrocket! Employers around the world, listen up—we're not asking a lot. These three requests are more like necessities, really. You would be wise to make us happy. If you play ball, you might one day find out that it really only takes about 10 seconds to get your e-mail back up and running.

why you need to know about...
software tools

You are sitting in your favorite chair in front of your computer monitor. Your mind is focused on saving the world from an alien race when suddenly a fly begins buzzing around your face. Your first reaction is to immediately get rid of the fly so you can get back to saving the world. The task has been defined! Your eyes lock onto the target as it hovers near the screen. At last, it takes a break from flying and lands on your monitor. You could use your hand to swat the fly, but you know from past experience that this approach usually ends up in failure. Instead, you deduce that you need a tool to increase your chances of sending this fly to Insect Heaven. You look around and settle for a tool that is lying next to the chair. Why did you select that specific tool? The tool was nearby, easy to reach, and you have used it before on other tasks. You slowly raise the tool above your head and focus on the fly's location. With the speed of a cheetah and the force of a rhinoceros you swat the fly. As the hammer comes crashing down upon the fly, you realize that you might have made a slight miscalculation in choosing this specific tool for this task. Then again, you always did want a new flat screen panel to replace your outdated monitor.

Whether it is in your personal life, school studies, or career, you have specific tasks that have to be completed. In many of these situations the outcome and time spent working on the task is improved through the use of a tool, or more descriptively, a software product. This chapter teaches you what tools you should have in your computer science toolbox. Choosing the right tool or software can enhance or hinder your progress in completing the task, so you need to be informed on what tasks might be lying ahead and which tools are most useful for certain tasks.

different tools for different rules

As a computer scientist you will be confronted with different tasks, and unless you have the knowledge and skill to choose the right tool and be able to properly use it, your successful and enjoyable experiences will be few and far between.

Consider yourself a worker with a box full of tools essential to getting your job done. To understand what tools are needed in the toolbox, you must first understand and recognize the tasks you will have to complete.

note

Be aware of the tools used in the industry. Choosing the right tool can help a project be a success.

The tasks you will encounter can be grouped into three main areas: office tasks, programming tasks, and Internet or Web tasks.

- Office tasks:
  - Creating documents
  - Creating presentations
  - Creating and using spreadsheets
  - Scheduling and managing projects
- Programming tasks:
  - Creating graphics
  - Diagramming and creating flowcharts
  - Creating programs
  - Creating and managing databases
  - Providing technical support
- Internet or Web tasks:
  - E-mailing files
  - Browsing the Internet
  - Uploading and downloading files
  - Developing Web sites and pages

Are you feeling overwhelmed yet? Computer scientists do not just sit around all day typing programs on the computer. Each task mentioned here could be more easily completed using the appropriate software tools. It is your decision to either learn the tools of the trade to assist you in your job or to struggle using the wrong tool, an outdated tool, or no tool at all.

The following sections examine the tools related to each of the task categories to help you determine which tool is best suited to the job at hand.

office tools

There are many tools you will use that are not directly involved in actually writing a program. These tools are support tools that help you as a computer scientist to build a strong foundation in your overall studies and career, as well as to support your programming tools. These office tools can assist you in creating documents, presentations, spreadsheets, budgets, and work schedules (Figure 2-1).

Figure 2-1, Office tools play a supporting role in computer science

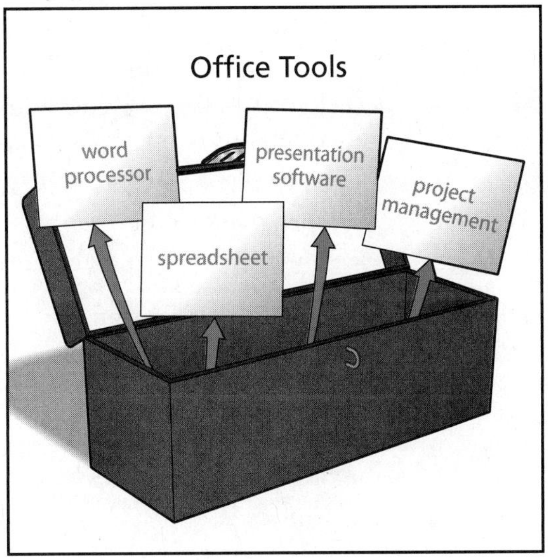

2

document tools

Creating documents will be an essential part of your studies and career no matter what field you decide to enter. Not only do you need to have a good document-creation tool to help you in your career, but you also need such a tool for your personal life and educational pursuits. Document tools include word processors, text editors, and desktop publishing software.

word processors

word processor – Text-editing and formatting software used to create a wide variety of documents

The ***word processor*** is an essential tool in your toolbox. The job of the word processor is to assist the writer in creating a wide variety of documents. Some of the documents you will create in the business world might include:

- letters
- resumes
- design documents
- project proposals
- faxes
- memos

Throughout your education you will need a word processor to create such documents as:

- Assignments
- Research projects
- Requests for letters of recommendation
- Resumes

A word processor is a multifunction tool that has the functionality of a screwdriver, hammer, pliers, and wrench all in one. A word processor can let you choose a font (style of lettering), format the characters (such as bold, underline, and so on), set margins, insert graphics, and use other formatting options that help you make the presentation of your document more professional and pleasing. Other tools that can be used within the word processor allow you to spell-check your words, view synonyms, and even determine if you are using proper grammar and vocabulary for your audience level. Some word processors also include tools to make simple drawings.

The most popular word processor on the market right now for the Windows and Mac operating systems is Microsoft Word (Figure 2-2).

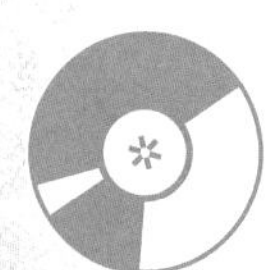

Try a step-by-step Microsoft Word tutorial on the student CD under Chapter 2, tutorials.

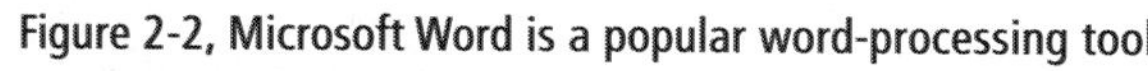

Figure 2-2, Microsoft Word is a popular word-processing tool

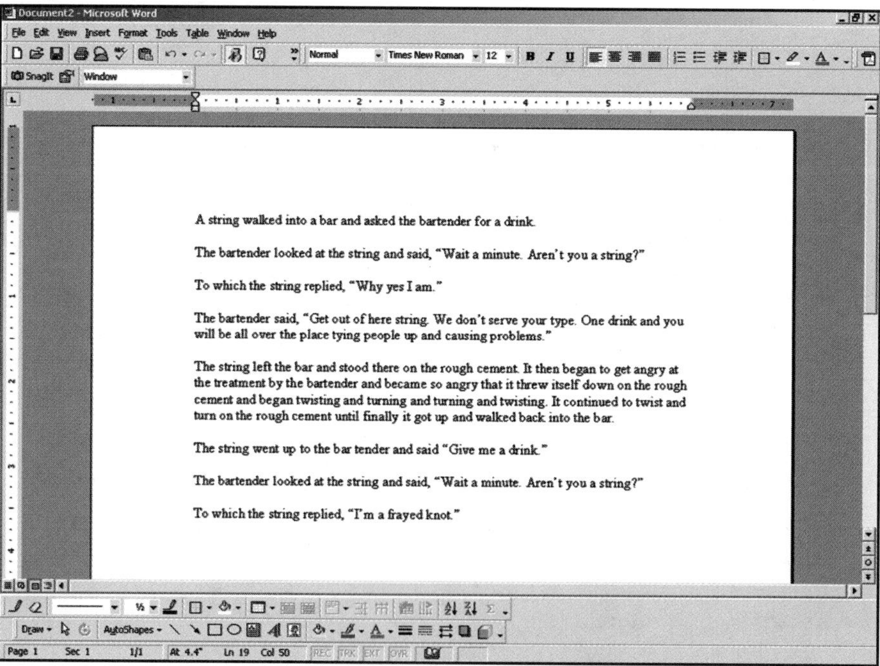

In the UNIX and Linux operating system environments, a popular word processor is StarOffice Writer, part of the StarOffice package (Figure 2-3).

Figure 2-3, StarOffice Writer is a word-processing tool used in UNIX and Linux

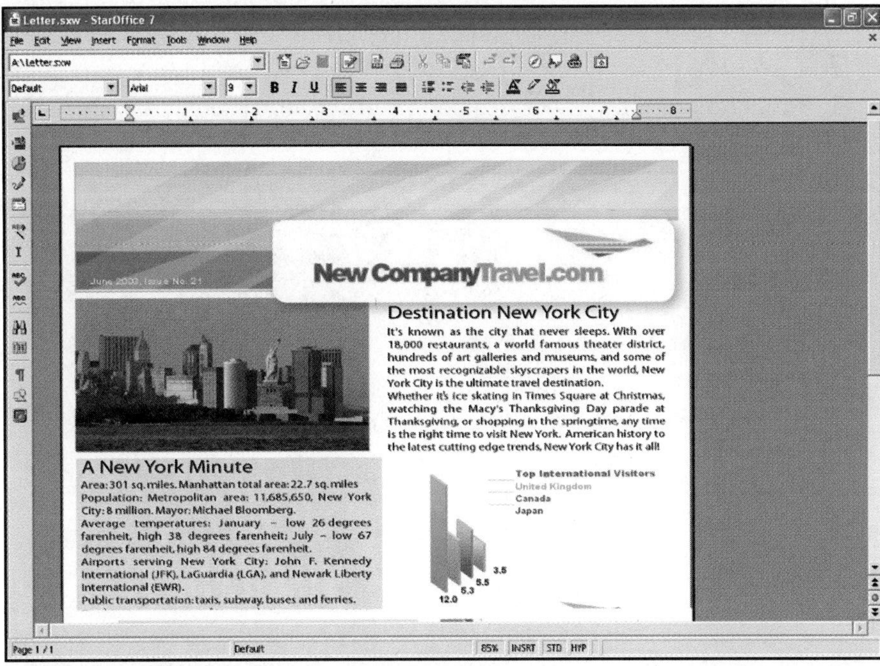

Courtesy of Sun Microsystems, Inc.

note Corel WordPerfect is another popular word processor.

text editors

text editor – *A program that contains basic functions for creating and editing text documents*

A text editor is a stripped-down version of a word processor in that it provides only very basic text entry and editing options and few or no formatting options. A ***text editor*** is a generic tool that allows you to do basic editing, although the finished document won't have a professional look. You cannot change the attributes of the characters you are typing into the document. However, a text editor is a handy tool, especially when you just want to input straight text without any added formatting, such as when you are entering programming commands.

You'll learn more about using a text editor to create programs in Chapter 11, "Programming."

Text editors are often included as part of a computer's operating system. For example, Windows includes the Notepad text editor (Figure 2-4). A text editor acts as a window where you can type text into a file, save it, and later edit the information.

The UNIX and Linux operating systems also have text editors. One of the more commonly used editors is called vi. As shown in Figure 2-5, the vi interface is text based. Instead of using your mouse and clicking menu items, vi requires you to manipulate the document through a series of keystrokes.

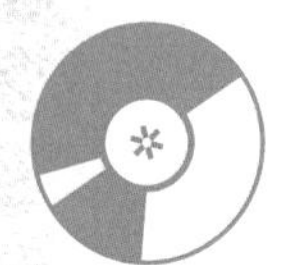

Try a step-by-step vi tutorial on the student CD under Chapter 2, tutorials.

Figure 2-4, Notepad is a simple text editor that comes with Windows

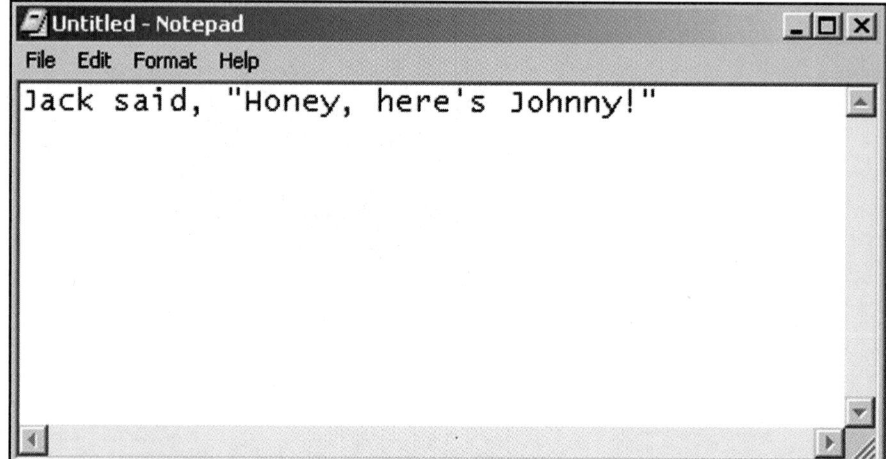

Figure 2-5, vi is a text editor used in UNIX and Linux operating systems

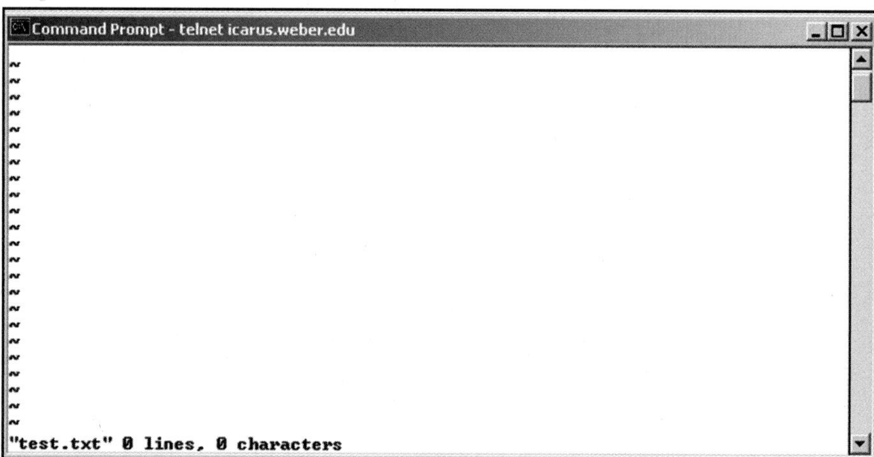

note

You can also use a full-functioned word processor to create and work with text files. Instead of saving the file as a Word document, for example, you would select the option to save the file as a text file. The file would then have a filename extension of ".txt".

desktop publishers

desktop publisher – *Software used to create documents that use pages laid out in brochure, magazine, newspaper, or book format*

Another tool used in creating documents is a ***desktop publisher***. This tool is used for creating more sophisticated documents such as brochures, magazines, books, and other published documents. A desktop publishing program might not have some features that a full-fledged word-processing tool would have, such as editing tools, grammar and spell-checking tools, or support for bullets or other formatting. (Then again, it might include these tools. As software gets more sophisticated, the lines between word-processing and desktop publishing tools are becoming blurred.) A desktop publisher can often take a word-processed document as input, and "pour" it into a layout or template that determines the final form, including embedded figures and photos.

The strength of a desktop publisher is that it allows you to use page-layout features to create documents such as magazines, newspapers, and books. For example, a word processor was used to create the text for this document and a desktop publisher was used to lay out the pages.

presentation tools

Adobe Reader

Adobe Reader is free software that lets you view and print Adobe Portable Document Format (PDF) files on just about any type of computer. Formerly known as Adobe Acrobat Reader, this popular tool (available for free download from *www.adobe.com*) is often used to view and exchange documents online across multiple hardware and software platforms.

There will come a day when you will be asked to make a presentation to a group of peers, clients, or management. This could be a request to present information on a researched topic, to give your opinion on a business change, to present your ideas on a new product, or any other request to communicate information to another person or group. Before you use a tool to create a presentation, you need to know when and how to use it.

In order to make your presentation informative and interesting, you want to create a format that catches the user's attention and at the same time presents the information in a concise, to-the-point format. You probably have been to a lecture with a monotone presenter in front of a room full of attendees who would rather listen to a cat scratching the chalkboard than sit another minute being bored to tears. Then again, maybe you have been the boring presenter. Or maybe you have attended a presentation that kept you sitting on the edge of your chair, hanging on the speaker's every word.

Dynamic speakers find a way to keep the audience's interest and present the information in a mode that is easy to understand. This is where you need to use a tool to help you deliver the content. It has been said, "A picture is worth a thousand words."

You could spend hours upon hours using a programming language to create a presentation or tutorial, but not only would you have to write the necessary computer statements to make the computer act like a slide projector, but you would also have to make sure you removed any glitches that might stop the system from working. Or, you could take an alternate route and create your entire presentation within a word processor, but you would not have the look and feel of a slide show. Why not use a tool that is specifically designed for creating presentations? This can save you time and money and help make your presentation robust and interesting.

presentation tool – Software that presents information in the form of a slide show

A widely used ***presentation tool*** is Microsoft PowerPoint. Microsoft PowerPoint allows you to create slides (screens) and combine them into presentations. Each slide is defined by the user and may contain text, images, sounds, or even video clips that are integrated through transitions that define how the slides are displayed. After the presentation is created, PowerPoint acts as a slide projector, displaying the presentation on your computer monitor or to larger audiences through the use of a data projector connected to your computer. Not only can you present interesting information but you can also make the mode of presentation entertaining. Figure 2-6 shows a PowerPoint slide.

Try a step-by-step Microsoft PowerPoint tutorial on the student CD under Chapter 2, tutorials.

Figure 2-6, A presentation tool helps you present information in an organized, attractive way

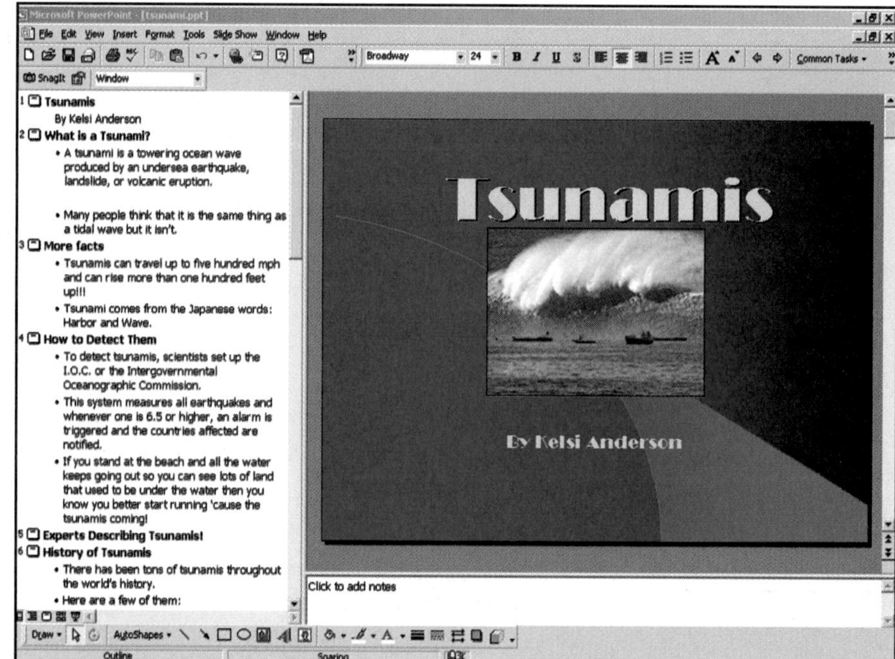

The primary purpose of a presentation tool such as PowerPoint is to help the speaker present the facts to the audience. One way a presentation tool helps spice up a presentation is through the use of slide transitions. A transition defines what happens between slides. For instance, one slide can dissolve from focus while the new slide is gradually displayed. You might have seen a presentation where a slide enters by flying onto the monitor display area. The transitions help keep the presentation interesting. You can even add a sound clip that is played as each slide is displayed.

You can also assign your own animation to each element on the slide (called custom animation). For example, custom animation allows you to have each line of a bulleted list appear separately on the screen when you press a key or button.

Using a tool such as Microsoft PowerPoint is the logical choice when creating a presentation. The next time you are given an assignment to explain the benefits of a particular piece of hardware or software, consider using a presentation tool to present your points clearly and attractively and to boost your credibility on the topic.

note StarOffice includes a presentation tool called Impress that is similar to Microsoft PowerPoint.

spreadsheet tools

spreadsheet – A document that consists of rows and columns that facilitates organizing information and making calculations

A *spreadsheet* is a document consisting of rows and columns that help you organize information into logical groupings. With all of the other tools you already need to learn how to use, why on earth would a computer scientist need to know how to use a spreadsheet? Spreadsheets are marvelous when you need to work with numbers such as budget figures. As a computer scientist there will probably come a time when you are a project leader or manager and need to know how to allocate money given to your group in order to be efficient and productive. You will need to work with dollar amounts and different categories of expenses. This type of information is often stored and manipulated in a spreadsheet.

how-to

There are many free tutorials on how to use Excel. Simply go to an Internet search engine (such as Google or Yahoo!) and search for "Excel tutorial". The skills you learn for one brand of spreadsheet are generally transferable to other brands of spreadsheets, with only some changes needed.

This tool accurately performs mathematical calculations (as long as you specify them correctly). Even better, most spreadsheets include graphing and charting capabilities so you can compare and contrast all of the numbers and double-check the results.

A popular spreadsheet tool is Microsoft Excel. It is a proven leader and very powerful. For example, if you want to create a budget, through the use of rows and cells you can define different budget categories, allocate dollar amounts, and then insert calculations to perform all of the mathematical operations and functions on the numbers. Excel even allows you to graph the information from your spreadsheet to make it more meaningful and descriptive. Figure 2-7 shows a sample Microsoft Excel spreadsheet.

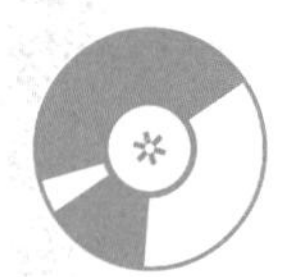

Try a step-by-step Microsoft Excel tutorial on the student CD under Chapter 2, tutorials.

Figure 2-7, With a spreadsheet you can organize information in rows and columns and perform calculations

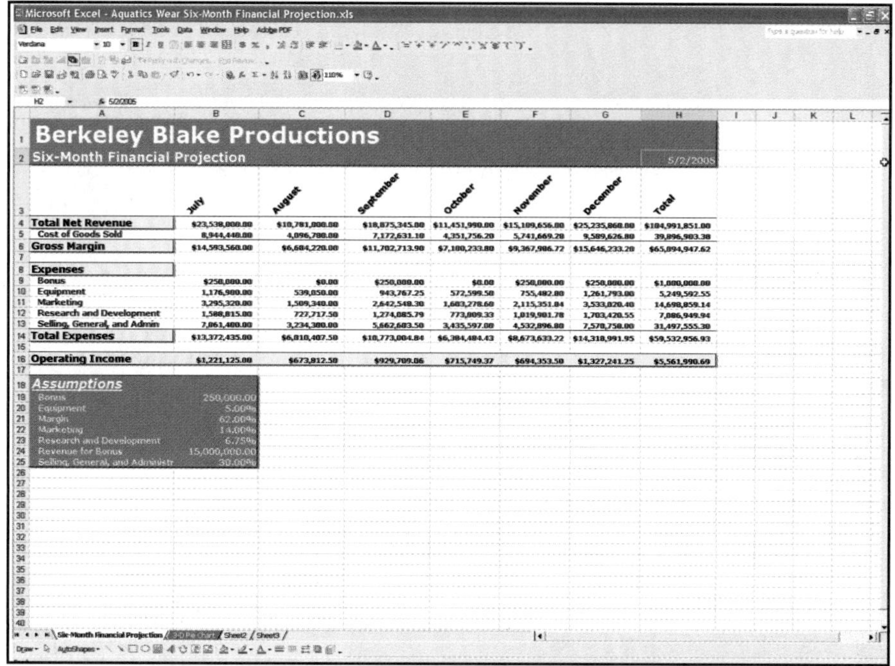

Berkeley Blake Productions							
Six-Month Financial Projection							5/2/2005
	July	August	September	October	November	December	Total
Total Net Revenue	$23,538,000.00	$10,781,000.00	$18,875,345.00	$11,451,990.00	$15,109,656.00	$25,235,860.00	$104,991,851.00
Cost of Goods Sold	8,944,440.00	4,096,780.00	7,172,631.10	4,351,756.20	5,741,669.28	9,589,626.80	39,896,903.38
Gross Margin	$14,593,560.00	$6,684,220.00	$11,702,713.90	$7,100,233.80	$9,367,986.72	$15,646,233.20	$65,094,947.62
Expenses							
Bonus	$250,000.00	$0.00	$250,000.00	$0.00	$250,000.00	$250,000.00	$1,000,000.00
Equipment	1,176,900.00	539,050.00	943,767.25	572,599.50	755,482.80	1,261,793.00	5,249,592.55
Marketing	3,295,320.00	1,509,340.00	2,642,548.30	1,603,278.60	2,115,351.84	3,533,020.40	14,698,859.14
Research and Development	1,588,815.00	727,717.50	1,274,085.79	773,009.33	1,019,901.78	1,703,420.55	7,086,949.94
Selling, General, and Admin	7,061,400.00	3,234,300.00	5,662,603.50	3,435,597.00	4,532,896.80	7,570,758.00	31,497,555.30
Total Expenses	$13,372,435.00	$6,010,407.50	$10,773,004.84	$6,384,484.43	$8,673,633.22	$14,318,991.95	$59,532,956.93
Operating Income	$1,221,125.00	$673,812.50	$929,709.06	$715,749.37	$694,353.50	$1,327,241.25	$5,561,990.69

Assumptions	
Bonus	250,000.00
Equipment	5.00%
Margin	62.00%
Marketing	14.00%
Research and Development	6.75%
Revenue for Bonus	15,000,000.00
Selling, General, and Administr	30.00%

note StarOffice for UNIX/Linux has a spreadsheet tool called Calc.

project scheduling and management tools

Although your toolbox is just about full and already has become quite heavy, there is one more essential tool that needs to be added. And as you progress through this book, you'll discover even more specialized tools that you can use. By now, you have probably realized that there is a lot of information you must learn in order to be an effective computer scientist. The more tools you become acquainted with, the more you will benefit in years to come.

One task you're highly likely to be involved with in computer science is developing software. The last tool discussed in this section is used to keep track of the status of a development project. For a project to succeed, you must first define and organize the major tasks to be completed. These tasks might include many of the ones discussed thus far in this chapter.

Project management is discussed in more detail in Chapter 13, "Software Engineering."

project management software *– Software used to keep track of project progress, schedule, and expenses*

If a project can be compared to a boat, then the project manager is the rudder that keeps the project on course. A project manager uses ***project management software*** to map the course the project must follow; this is done by defining tasks and milestones of a project and by tracking the progress towards completing those tasks and reaching those milestones.

The project manager or team uses project management software to help organize and motivate the developers, to ensure that the product meets the requirements set for it, and that the project stays on course, on time, and within budget. The project manager also keeps management abreast of the status and progress of the project. Time is money, and companies want to account for the time being spent on specific projects and to evaluate how productive the development effort has been. In this way they can learn from mistakes and become more efficient with each project that is completed.

One of the most popular project management tools is Microsoft Project. Microsoft Project also allows you to create various types of productivity charts showing how the project is or is not progressing.

Figure 2-8 shows a Microsoft Project window. Every task within a Microsoft Project file can be defined and assigned to a person responsible for seeing it completed. The amount of time needed to complete the project is also attached

Figure 2-8, Project management software tracks the schedule of tasks that need to be completed

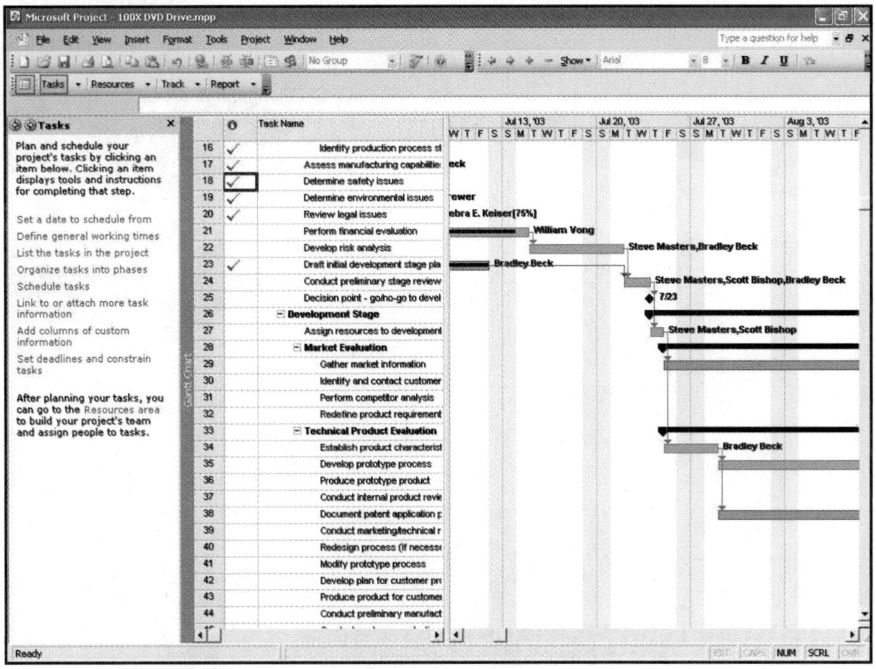

Courtesy of Microsoft Corp.

to the task. As status reports detail the work being accomplished, time and costs can be logged towards the tasks. Reports can then be created and distributed showing the efficiency of the project.

Learning and implementing project management software requires a large commitment. Not only must you divide a project into smaller tasks, but you must also keep accurate records regarding the work being completed. Project management software can be a powerful tool and may be quite expensive, but if at some time during your career you become the leader of a project or a group of developers, a basic knowledge of project management software will be essential.

programming tools

Your programming toolbox consists of many different tools that assist you in creating programs. A program consists of many different components, and each type of component may require a specific type of tool.

The programming tasks that are supported by the use of various tools include creating graphics, making diagrams and flowcharts, creating and managing databases, and technical support (Figure 2-9).

Figure 2-9, Programming tools play a supporting role in computer science

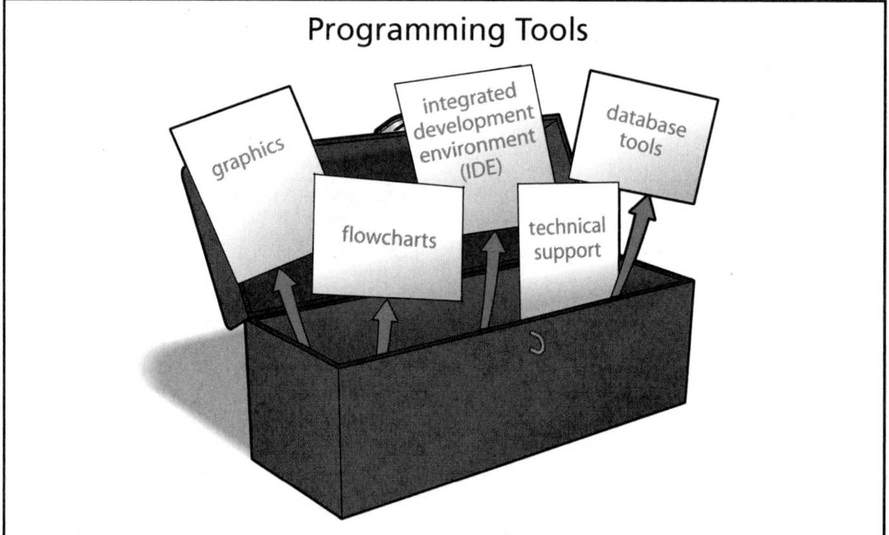

creating graphics

Many times you need a picture of a particular item or action. Whether it is a logo, a cartoon of a person using a computer, or a map of how to find your favorite computer store, graphics play a large part in the world of information sharing.

2

note There are many graphical images or pieces of predrawn artwork available for download or purchase known as "clip art."

The Internet provides access to many images that you can download and use within presentations, documents, programs, or Web sites. (Always be sure that you have permission for such use.) But what if the image doesn't exactly portray the subject you are representing? Unless you have a graphic design artist at your disposal, you have three options: draw the stick figure by hand, modify a graphic someone else has created, or create your own. For any of these options, you need a tool to help you accomplish this task. Drawing a figure by hand is like using a ball-peen hammer to tear down a building. Sure, it might accomplish the task someday, but it isn't going to be a good experience. You need to choose the right tool for the right task.

graphic formats

There are so many different images that are available either for purchase or through downloading from the Internet that it can be quite confusing to know the right image for the right task. There are also many different graphic formats, each having advantages and disadvantages for particular tasks. Using the right tool also implies that you use the right graphic format for the job. Some of the more popular formats are:

- BMP
- GIF
- JPG
- TIF

BMP (bitmap) – A Windows graphic format that is compact and used for images needing up to 16.7 million colors

The *BMP* (an acronym meaning "bitmap") format is the Microsoft Windows bitmap format. It is fairly compact and used for images that use up to 24 bits or 16.7 million colors and do not provide animation. Bitmap files tend to be very large and are not recommended for use on Web sites. A sensible use for a bitmap image is the background image of your Windows desktop.

GIF (Graphics Interchange Format) – A graphic format that supports up to 256 colors and is mainly used for buttons, banners, and both simple and animated images

GIF (pronounced "jif" or "gif") is the acronym for Graphics Interchange Format and was invented by CompuServe as a way to standardize graphic images. GIF images are mainly used for buttons, banners, simple images, and animated images. GIF images only allow 256 colors, but unlike other formats, they have a transparency feature. This means that you can specify an area on the GIF image to be transparent so that when it is displayed on a background, the background color comes through the GIF image. GIF images are unsuitable for photographs because of their limited number of colors.

note

A common mistake is to place animated GIFs on Web sites because they are cute. This tends to clutter the site and actually makes it less attractive and effective.

JPG or JPEG (Joint Photographic Experts Group) – A commonly used Internet graphic format that is the most efficient of all graphic formats and supports up to 16.7 million colors

JPG or **JPEG** (pronounced "jay-peg") is the acronym for Joint Photographic Experts Group and is the most efficient storage method of all graphic formats. This format is great for photos and when you want a small file, but the format loses quality each time it is changed and saved. JPGs are widely used on the Internet because of their small size and accurate color rendition but should be avoided if you want the image to have sharp edges. Sharp edges on a JPG tend to blur; instead, use the GIF file format.

TIF or TIFF (Tag Image File Format) – A graphic format that is widely used in professional photographic settings; the image is very realistic, but the files are very large

TIF or **TIFF** (pronounced "tiff") is the acronym for Tag Image File Format and is widely used in professional photographical settings. There is no loss or degradation of the image, which generates a lovely realistic image. The main problem is that the files are very large and are not usually suitable for sharing by e-mail.

graphic compression

lossless compression – A compression format used to remove redundant areas of an image without losing any image data; when the image is decompressed it returns to its original state

lossy compression – A compression format that eliminates redundant data and information that is not perceptible to the human eye; the image loses some of its quality when it is decompressed

Graphics can be compressed to reduce the size of a file. An image can be slightly altered depending on the data compression technique used. There are two types of compression:

- **Lossless compression**—Only redundant areas are removed so that no data is lost. If an image is compressed using lossless compression, then the image is the same when uncompressed.
- **Lossy compression**—Eliminates redundant information and information not perceptible by the human eye. If an image is compressed with lossy compression, then the image will be slightly different when decompressed, but often not detectably so. This usually creates a more compact file size for images but

has the penalty of losing some of the quality. Most video compression techniques (such as MPEG) and also the JPEG format use lossy compression.

working with graphics

As you have thus far learned, there is a lot more to images than meets the eye. Before you can intelligently select a graphics tool you need to know what options to look for. You need to know how to work with images so that they can be manipulated to present the desired output.

There are many different ways to modify or transform a graphic.
Some of these methods include:

- Scaling
- Rotating
- Cropping
- Converting from one format to another

scaling – Changing the display size of an image with or without changing the underlying size of the graphic

Scaling a graphic permits you to change the graphic's display size with or without changing the underlying size of the graphic. In other words, you can scale a graphic to resize it for display purposes only but leave the graphic in its original format. You can also scale a graphic to resize it and at the same time save the new format, thus losing its original format. Scaling is most commonly used when the graphic is not the correct size or does not fit in the desired output location. Figure 2-10 shows an example of scaling.

Figure 2-10, Scaling resizes an image

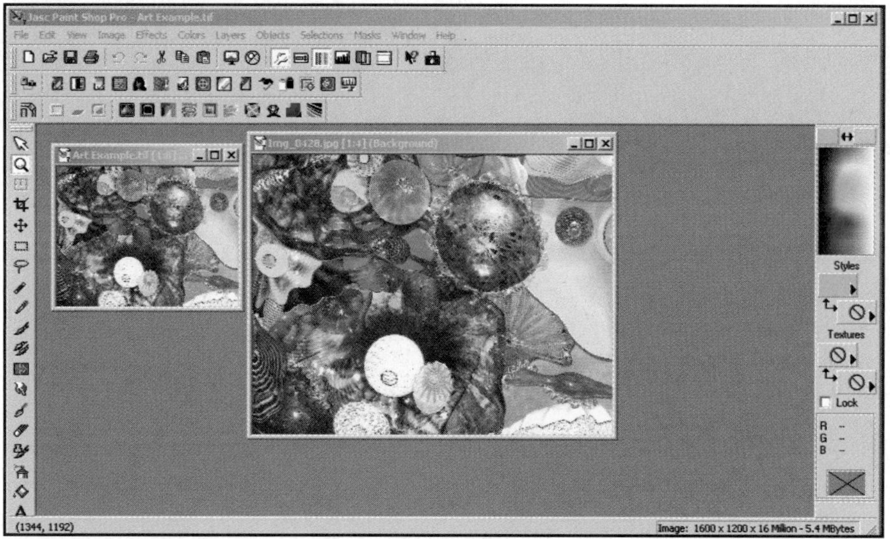

rotating – Modifying an image by moving the image from its current layout to a different position based upon a 360-degree circle

Rotating an image moves the image from its current layout to a different position based upon a 360-degree circle. For example, if the original picture is displayed on a document using portrait orientation (8 inches wide by 11 inches high) and you need to display the document using landscape orientation (11 inches wide by 8 inches high) you can rotate the image 90 degrees to the right. If needed, you can even flip the image upside down by rotating it 180 degrees. Figure 2-11 shows the image in Figure 2-10 rotated 90 degrees to the right.

Figure 2-11, Rotation

Figure 2-12, Cropping

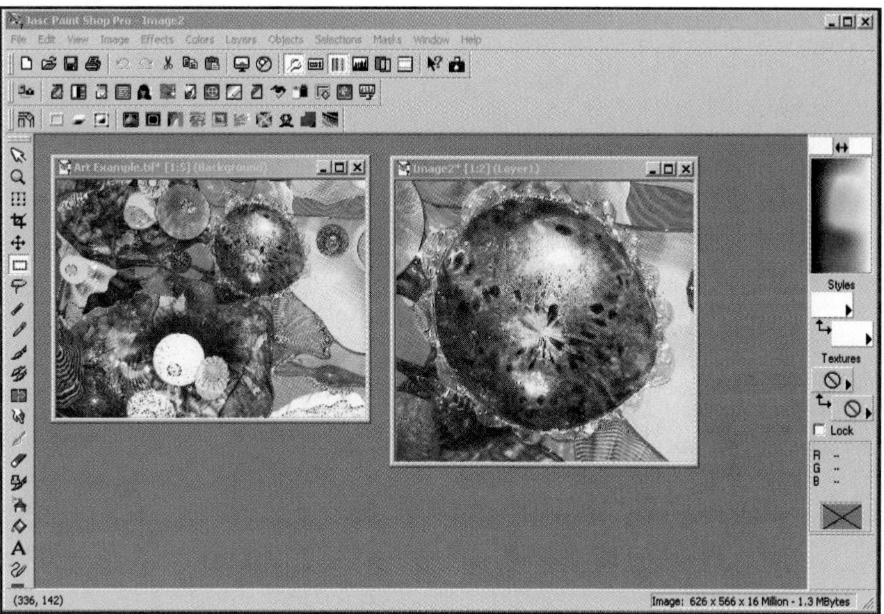

cropping – Modifying an image by cutting or trimming parts from the image

format conversion – Converting an image from one file format to another

Cropping allows you to cut or trim portions out of the image that are not needed (Figure 2-12). This is used to make the image more interesting and relevant. Why keep parts of an image that distract from the main idea? Make sure you choose a graphics tool that supports cropping.

Format conversion permits you to convert an image from one file format to another. Many of the available graphic tools support this feature, but you should confirm this. Saving an image stored in one format to a new format allows for greater flexibility in working with other types of programs. However, you need to be aware that there are some disadvantages associated with the process. With almost every conversion you perform, you lose some detail in an image.

There are many other ways to transform a graphic, and if you choose a good tool you can have complete control over how the image is displayed. Some of these other transformation methods allow you to blur the image, sharpen the image, enhance the edges, remove imperfections, add 3-D effects, and more.

freeware – Software that is offered to the user at no cost

shareware – Software distributed on a trial basis with the understanding that the user might want to pay for it later

There are many graphic tools available. Some are absolutely free (***freeware***). Some are ***shareware***, meaning you can use the software on a trial basis with the understanding that the user might want to pay for it later. Other tools are available for purchase. There are also products that provide a trial version that permit you to see if you like the product before you buy it.

Some popular graphic tools are:

· Macromedia Fireworks
· JASC Paint Shop Pro
· Adobe Photoshop

Each product has advantages and disadvantages. Each user has an opinion of the products; it's like asking your friends, "What's the best vehicle to buy?" The best way to decide which product is best for your needs is probably to download a trial version of the product and try it. You can also search magazines or the Internet for reviews of specific programs. You should also be aware that the more features a package offers, the steeper the learning curve for the product.

The different graphics programs are slanted toward certain tasks and users. Fireworks is a product you can purchase that is popular with Web designers. Paint Shop Pro is considered to be an inexpensive product with professional tools. It is priced well below other graphic packages and still performs many significant tasks needed by the computer scientist. Although it does not have as complete a selection of graphic tools as other packages, it can handle basic image creation and editing. Photoshop is the current standard professional graphics tool worldwide. It is geared toward the graphic designer or user wanting to make or modify images for use in applications and documents. Photoshop allows the user nearly complete control over the image properties. If you can't accomplish it in Photoshop, then you probably don't really need to do it.

note **StarOffice includes a drawing package called Draw.**

diagramming tools

Just as a builder needs a set of blueprints to construct a building, a computer scientist needs blueprints to construct a program. The blueprint is made up of diagrams and flowcharts created through the use of diagramming tools.

Figure 2-13, Microsoft Visio creates a wide variety of diagrams, including flowcharts

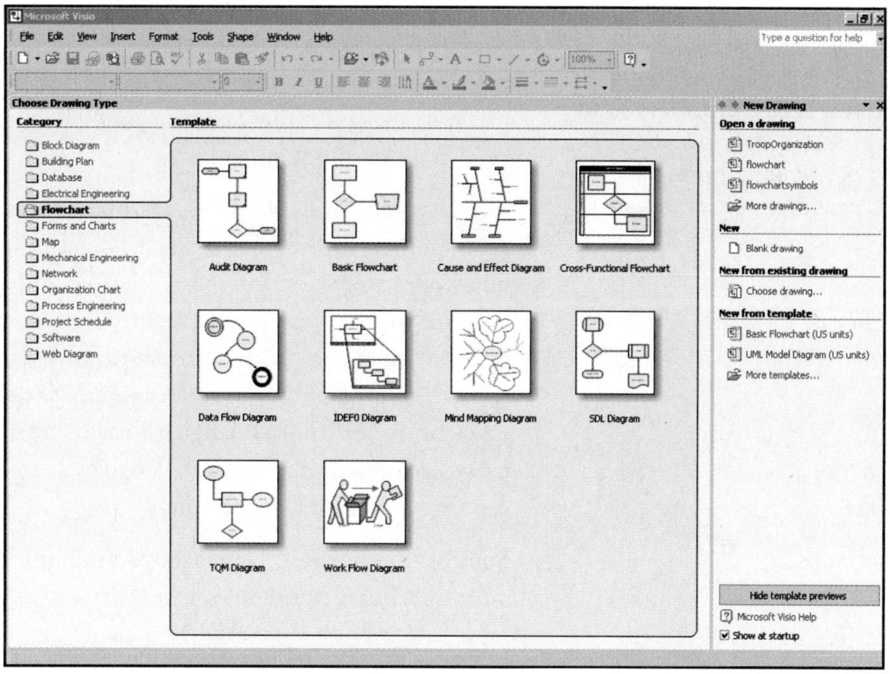

flowchart – A graphical diagram that uses geometric symbols to show the logical flow of a program or process

A *flowchart* is a graphical diagram consisting of standard geometric symbols that demonstrate the logical steps in creating a program. As shown in Figure 2-13, a programmer can use a flowchart as a roadmap to describe how a system should be developed.

Computer scientists use flowcharting for process design, and they create UML (Universal Modeling Language) diagrams used in developing object-oriented systems and programs. One diagramming tool that incorporates many of the diagramming features needed by computer scientists is Microsoft Visio. It not only allows you to create flowcharts but also a myriad of other diagrams that can all be used in the software-development process. Some of the diagrams you can make with Visio focus on networking, organizational hierarchies, charts and graphs, maps, engineering, database, Internet, and software-process design.

note

You can create flowcharts using Microsoft Excel by selecting the drawing toolbar and using the AutoShapes feature to create the geometric shapes.

integrated development environments

IDE (integrated development environment) – A workspace providing tools to support application development using a programming language

An *integrated development environment (IDE)* provides a set of programming tools in a single user interface. An IDE for a programming language, for example, might include a text editor, compiler, and debugger, all of which are started from a common menu.

Have you ever gone shopping for a particular item, and found yourself staring at rows upon rows of similar items, all claiming to be the best, unsure of which one would work best for you? Choosing a programming environment in which to write your programs can present a similar dilemma. There are so many different languages, each claiming to solve the problems of application development. Some claim they are easier to use while others claim they are more efficient. In reality, each language has its own strengths and weaknesses. Not every person will like the same languages, and some languages are better for certain types of tasks than others.

Some of the different languages you might learn or become familiar with in your career as a computer scientist are:

- ADA
- C
- C++
- C#
- Delphi
- Fortran
- Java
- Lisp
- .NET platform
- Pascal
- PERL
- Visual Basic

Many computer scientists learn more than one language, but often have a preferred language to write their programs. A lot of times you don't even get to choose the language to use for a project. Instead, either the client or the company dictates the programming environment.

An IDE is sometimes called a programming environment. An IDE or programming environment is the workspace and tools that support the language being used to write the program. Some of the supporting tools to consider when choosing an IDE are:

- Program editor
- Graphics editor
- Compiler
- Debugger
- Components or objects
- Compiler and linker
- Project manager
- Help system

It is essential to choose the right programming tool for the right project. Otherwise you might end up using an outdated or inappropriate tool that simply won't create a product that is acceptable to the end user.

Can you imagine using a hammer to remove a screw? Or what about using a handsaw to build a house? Wouldn't the right tool and tools using new technology help you get your job done more efficiently? One way to determine which programming languages you should learn is to take a look at the current jobs on the market. Find the languages that are most popular. This can be a good indicator of what you need to learn to make yourself marketable.

You'll learn more about choosing a programming environment in Chapter 11, "Programming."

There are programming tools everywhere. There are free ones, ones you can try before you buy, expensive packages that do every programming task imaginable, and those that are very basic. Throughout your computer science education you will learn to use some of these tools. This does not mean that those are the only ones you should ever learn. The world of software development is constantly changing. If you only learn one tool, you will soon find that your knowledge has stagnated and your skills will not be marketable.

Some popular programming environments include:

- Borland C++ Builder
- Borland Delphi
- Borland JBuilder
- Microsoft .NET platform (which includes VB .NET, C# .NET, and C++ .NET)
- Microsoft Visual Basic
- CodeWarrior (Mac and Linux)

Each has advantages and disadvantages, with developers staunchly supporting their preferred tool. Look at programming environments the way you would look at cars. You need to test drive quite a few before you know which is the one that makes you feel most comfortable.

database tools

database – A collection of data usually organized into tables

table – In a database, a collection of logically related information ordered by rows and columns

row – Represents a record of logically related information stored in a table

column – Represents a field within a row or record (e.g., First Name)

Another tool you need to add to your computer science toolbox is a tool to work with databases. A ***database*** is a collection of data usually organized into tables. A ***table*** is a collection of information ordered by rows and columns (much like a spreadsheet). A ***row*** represents a record of information while a ***column*** represents a field within the record. So what do all of these terms mean? It means that you can store information on your computer and have a database system help you maintain and organize it into something meaningful.

Databases are used in many different applications and Web sites. They are used to store such information as employee information, client purchase orders, inventory, and school grades. Databases are at the core of information collection and sharing. Can you imagine creating and maintaining the data in a telephone book as a text file? Every time a new subscriber was added, dropped, or changed their number, you would have to manually search for the subscriber's name or number, insert a line, type in the new name and save the document. The worst part would be when you wanted to retrieve specific data from the document. It wouldn't be easy to generate a report that only showed subscribers that live in a specific town or that have a common first name. This is where database tools shine. When you work with databases, you need a tool, usually a ***database management system (DBMS)***, to extract, organize, and maintain the data being stored.

database management system (DBMS) – A tool used to extract, organize, and maintain data stored in a database

Just as there is a wide variety of programming languages, there is a wide variety of database formats, each distinguished by popularity, price, and functionality. In many computer science programs and corporations, you will deal with databases using Oracle, SQL Server, or sometimes Microsoft Access. Oracle and SQL Server are the two most popular and widely used corporate DBMSs, with SQL Server being less expensive than Oracle. One other database format gaining a strong following for Web development is called MySQL.

Even though a database system itself is a tool, with each database package comes a list of additional tools that many developers feel are must-haves. Some come with the DBMS, but others are acquired separately. Oracle is perhaps the most popular database package and so it might be beneficial to look into a companion tool. For example, Toad is an Oracle database support tool created by Quest Software (Figure 2-14).

Figure 2-14, Toad is a support tool for Oracle

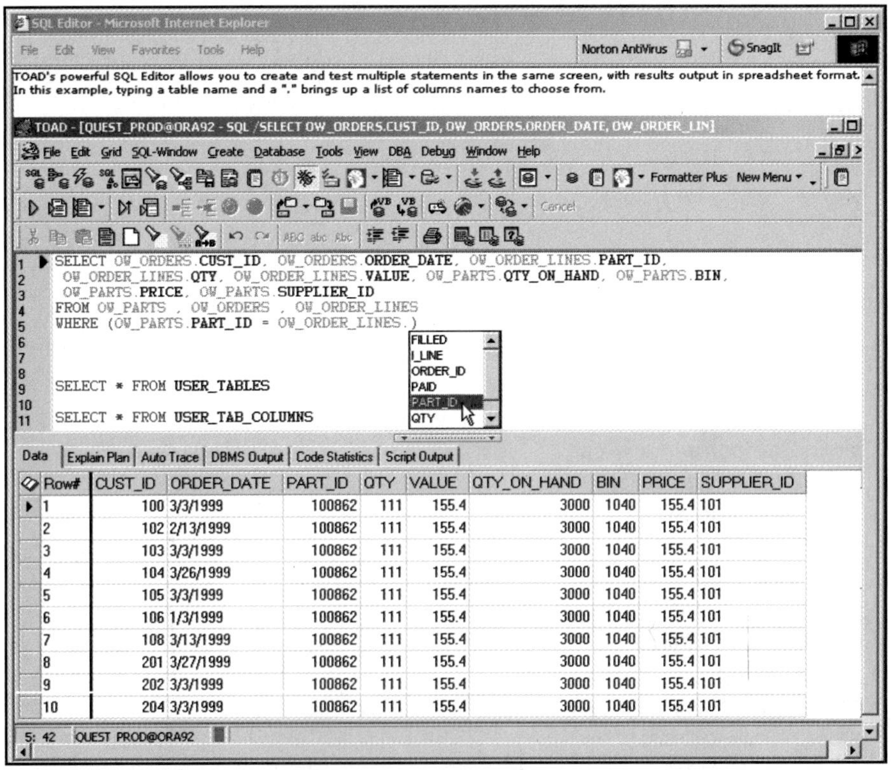

Row#	CUST_ID	ORDER_DATE	PART_ID	QTY	VALUE	QTY_ON_HAND	BIN	PRICE	SUPPLIER_ID
1	100	3/3/1999	100862	111	155.4	3000	1040	155.4	101
2	102	2/13/1999	100862	111	155.4	3000	1040	155.4	101
3	103	3/3/1999	100862	111	155.4	3000	1040	155.4	101
4	104	3/26/1999	100862	111	155.4	3000	1040	155.4	101
5	105	3/3/1999	100862	111	155.4	3000	1040	155.4	101
6	106	1/3/1999	100862	111	155.4	3000	1040	155.4	101
7	108	3/13/1999	100862	111	155.4	3000	1040	155.4	101
8	201	3/27/1999	100862	111	155.4	3000	1040	155.4	101
9	202	3/3/1999	100862	111	155.4	3000	1040	155.4	101
10	204	3/3/1999	100862	111	155.4	3000	1040	155.4	101

Courtesy of Quest Software

Toad provides a visual interface for working with data and file structures and is used in many corporations that implement Oracle databases. Instead of having to type in commands to create databases and tables or to view, alter, or maintain data, you can grab your mouse and click to your heart's content. Visual database creation is much more efficient than typing at the console. Toad works only with Oracle and is a little expensive, but many corporations use tools such as Toad to achieve greater worker productivity.

Another tool commonly used for small databases is Microsoft Access. It provides a visual interface for working with data (Figure 2-15).

Figure 2-15, Microsoft Access provides a visual interface for working with databases

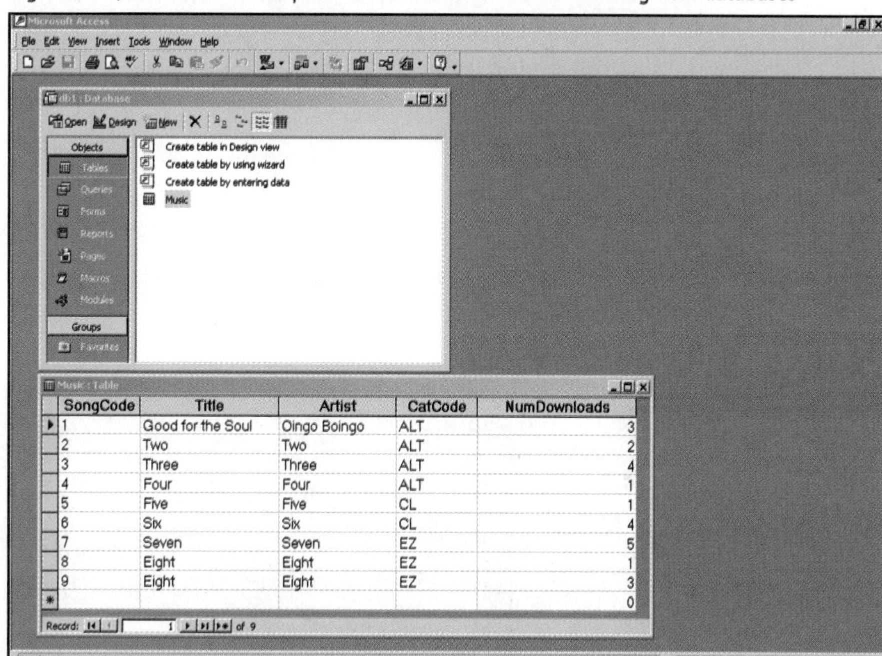

Microsoft Access is a relatively inexpensive database tool compared to some of the larger-scale database platforms such as Oracle and SQL Server, but it still provides a rich set of database tools that are simple and easy to use.

note StarOffice includes a database tool called Base.

technical support tools

If you write a program, you are most probably going to end up supporting it. If you do, you might want to use some type of remote access tool to support it. Perhaps the most popular such tool is pcAnywhere (Figure 2-16). It allows you to use your Internet connection or dial-up line to a remote computer and take control of it as if you were sitting in front of the remote computer. This means that you can sit at home and dial in to your PC at work, or connect to a user's machine and provide assistance by viewing and controlling that machine as if you were sitting at that machine.

All of the work that you do is displayed on your PC and also on the remote PC. As long as both computers have pcAnywhere installed, one can access the other. This is very advantageous when a support technician is trying to help an end user with a technical support issue. The support technician can actually take control of the remote PC to solve problems and even provide technical training.

note VNC is a free open source solution for remote access that can be downloaded from the Internet.

Figure 2-16, pcAnywhere allows you to remotely access another computer

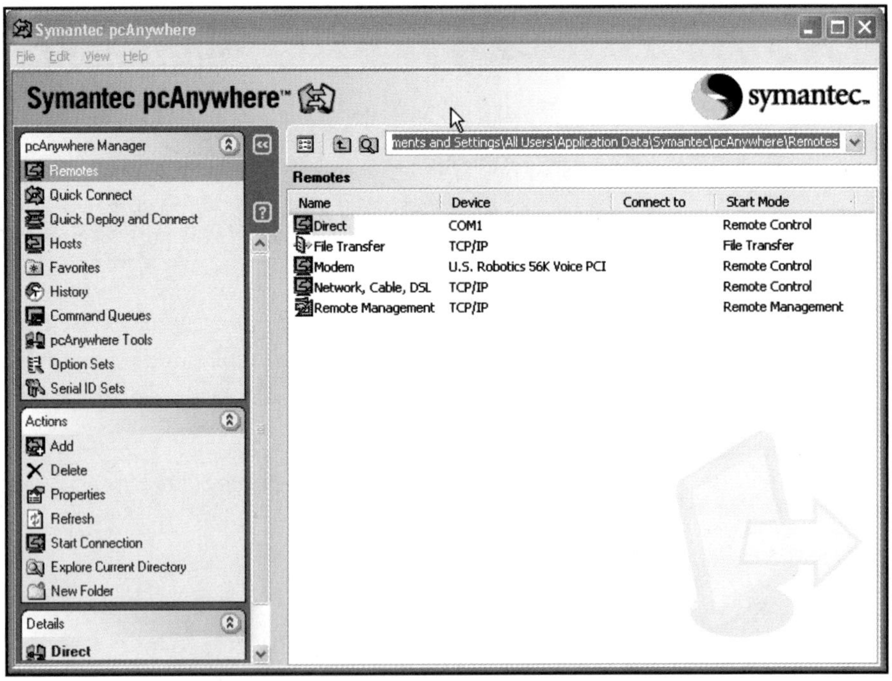

Internet tools

The Internet (also referred to as the Net) is dominating many aspects of modern life in both the personal and business arenas. Doing research on any topic has been revolutionized through the use of Web browsers. With e-mail and instant messaging, communication between people almost anywhere in the world can be instantaneous. Not only can you communicate by sending text in the form of e-mails, but you can also send files such as family photos, project specifications, music, data, assignments, or any type of file you would like to send.

note The world is connected and communicating! If you haven't already done so, the sooner you accept the fact that you need to "get connected," the sooner you can move along with the flow of technology.

Internet tools are playing an ever-larger role in the world of computer science as well (Figure 2-17). Internet tools include browsers, e-mail software, file transfer software, and remote access software.

Figure 2-17, Internet tools are increasingly important in computer science

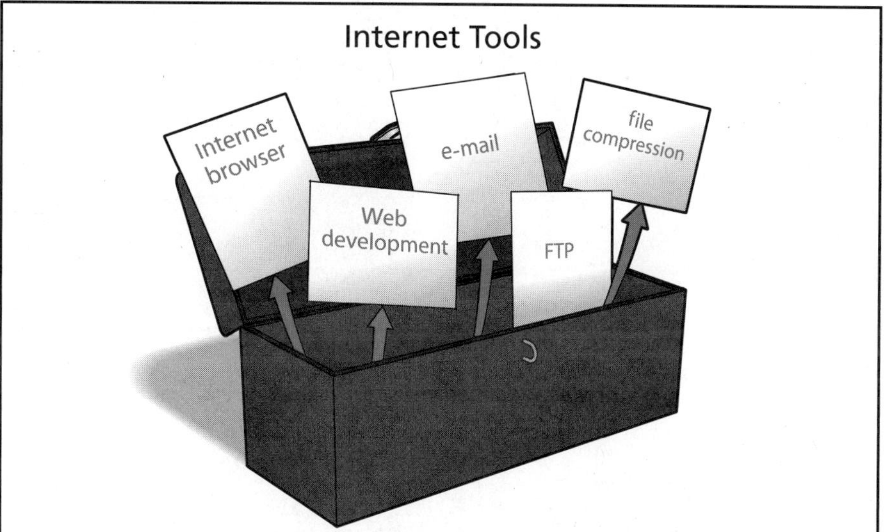

Web browsers

Browsing or surfing the Web is just another way of saying "I am connected to the Internet and am looking around at what it has to offer." The Internet is an amazing resource! No one person, although some would like to claim it, owns the Internet. It is a worldwide collection of linked computers that share information and files with other users.

browser – Software that allows you to view Web pages

In order to browse the Web you need a ***browser***. One popular browser is Microsoft Internet Explorer (Figure 2-18). Other browsers you might encounter are Netscape Navigator, Mozilla, Mosaic, Lynx, and Opera.

Figure 2-18, Microsoft Internet Explorer is a popular browser

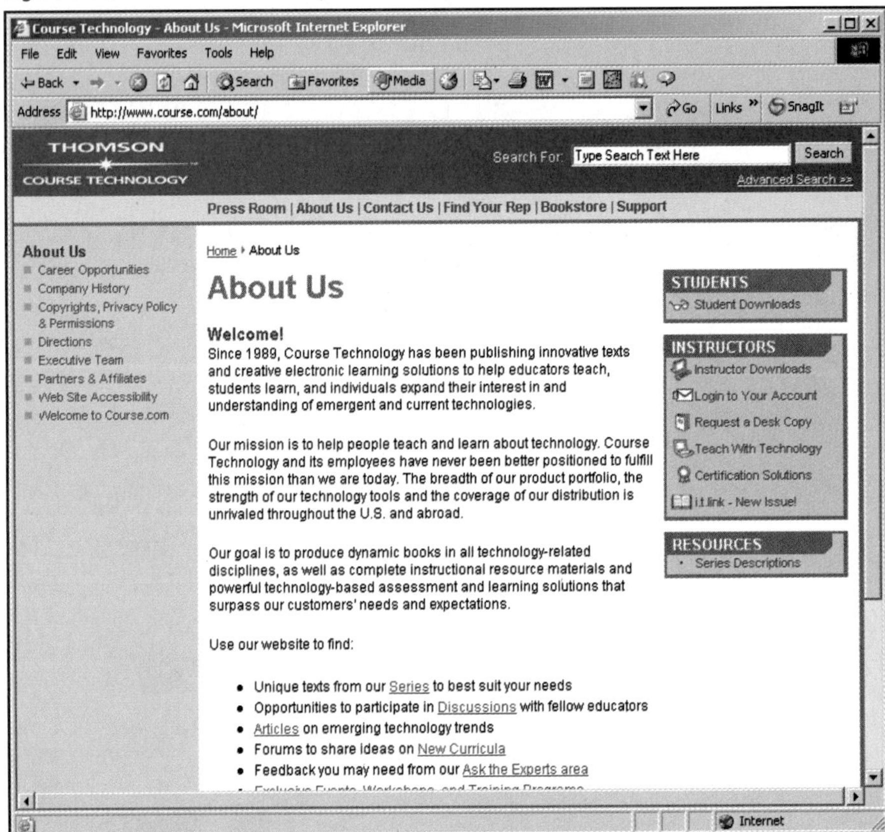

Each of the browsers is capable of viewing Web sites, downloading information, and providing a nice environment for surfing the Web.

e-mail tools

A first grader was filling out a form at school and came to the line where it required her to write down her home address. She looked at her mother for clarification and said, "Do they want my e-mail address?" E-mail has become a standard format of sharing information and data. You, no doubt, have been introduced to e-mail through an educational, professional, or social setting. It has become an essential tool for interacting with peers, colleagues, and family.

check that page

Your Web pages may be displayed differently depending on the browser the viewer is using. If you create Web pages, it is a good idea to test your browser both in Netscape Navigator and Microsoft Internet Explorer.

E-mail is opening new technological and business opportunities every day. Through the use of e-mail a student can complete an entire degree online from anywhere in the world. Business associates can use e-mail to communicate with a client even though the associate is located at a ski resort in Utah and the client is in New York. Through e-mail, a computer consultant can work with clients located all over the world. As the work is completed, the consultant e-mails the programs to the client to test. As long as they check their e-mail often, the line of communication remains open as if they were using a telephone or even face to face. E-mail opens the door to communicating worldwide without having to pay for a phone call, and in much less time than sending a letter through regular "snail mail."

You probably have already used e-mail, but if not, it is time to get connected! The tools you need to use are most likely already located on your PC.

note Make sure you have an antivirus software package loaded on your system before you begin to download e-mails.

Microsoft Outlook or Microsoft Outlook Express (Figure 2-19) are standard e-mail programs included with Windows operating systems and are used by millions of PC users all over the world. Another popular e-mail tool is Netscape Communicator. One other product called Novell GroupWise is very popular in educational and professional settings.

Figure 2-19, Microsoft Outlook Express

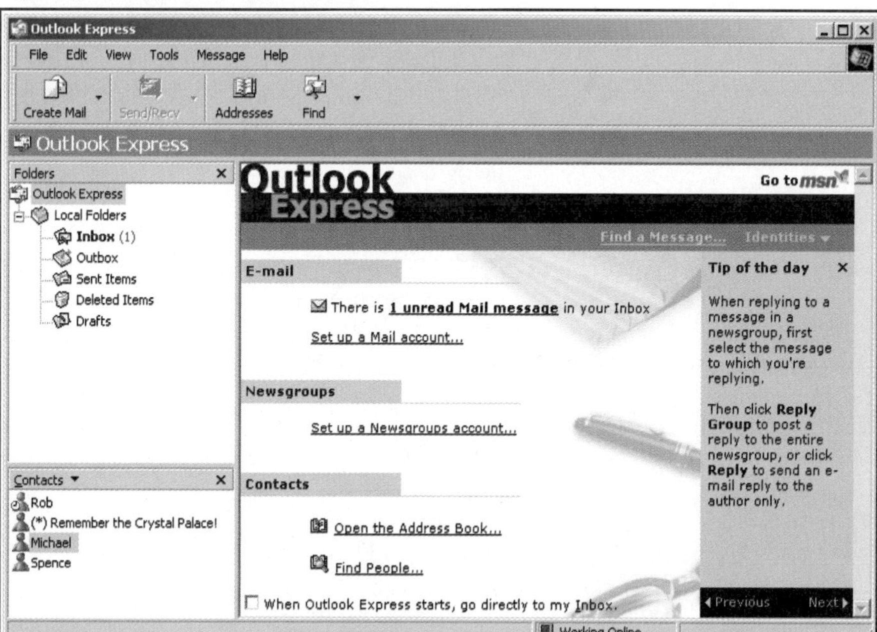

A dominant e-mail tool has not yet emerged for the UNIX and Linux operating systems but ELM (ELectronic Mail) and Pine (a spoof on ELM) are widely used. Pine (Figure 2-20) is easier to use for the novice.

Figure 2-20, Pine is a UNIX/Linux e-mail software product

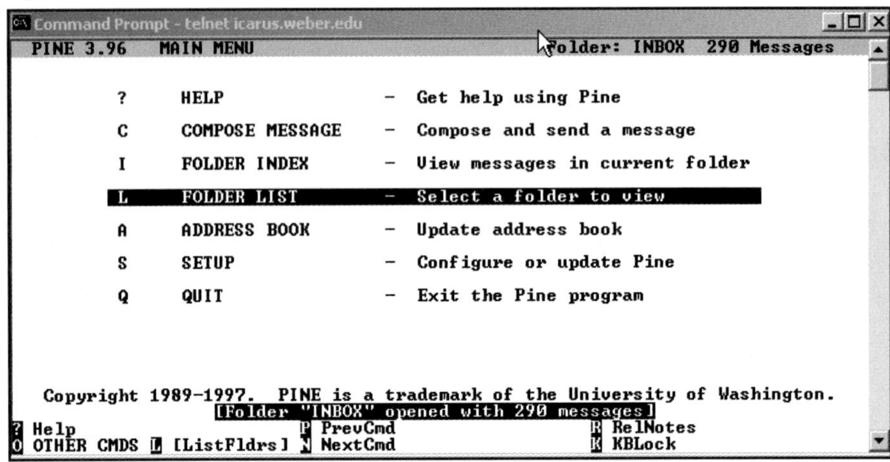

note Eudora is another popular e-mail software package.

compressing files

E-mail is not only a tool for sending text messages all over the world, but it can also be used to send documents, spreadsheets, programs, and images as attachments. Computer scientists use e-mail often to share files. Sometimes these files are quite large and the transmission and receipt of such files can take a long time and be quite annoying to users. This becomes even more evident when the user does not have high-speed access to the Internet or is paying for the time being used.

data compression – A method that uses a compression format to reduce the size of a file

decompression – Restoring a compressed file to its original format

Just as graphic images can be compressed, ***data compression*** can be used to reduce the size of a file and speed the transmission of the file through e-mail. Compression can also be used to reduce the file so that you can put it on a floppy disk, Zip drive, or another type of storage media. ***Decompression*** restores the compressed file to its original format.

There are many different compression algorithms. Some of the more popular formats for data and file compression are listed in Table 2-1.

Table 2-1, Popular data compression formats

name	compression format
RLE (run-length encoding)	Lossless
LZW (Lempel-Zif-Welch)	Lossless
Zip encoding	Lossless
Huffman	Lossless

Each compression algorithm is quite complex and has a mathematical foundation. Although many compression techniques have already been developed, there is still room for improvement. You may never have the need to create a new compression algorithm, but you will certainly use compression programs very often in your computer science career. Also, the common user will not know or care which compression algorithm a program is using, but the computer scientist can compare the advantages and disadvantages of the various methods and use the correct one for the job at hand.

Because of the wide variety of compression algorithms, many of the compression tools support their own type of file formatting. Some of the different compression formats are:

- zip
- tar
- lzh
- arj
- gz
- z
- sit
- mime

A popular tool for compressing and decompressing files in the Windows environment is called WinZip. Users can download an evaluation copy to see if they like the program. WinZip supports the formats: zip, tar, and mime. It is very easy to use, inexpensive, and very dependable. Windows XP has built-in file compression support. Using a compression tool allows you to easily create a new compressed file and then add the files to a list of files that need to be compressed. To decompress the zipped file you simply open up the file. A list of compressed files is displayed, as shown in Figure 2-21. You can choose to decompress one, many, or all of the files.

Figure 2-21, WinZip compresses and decompresses files

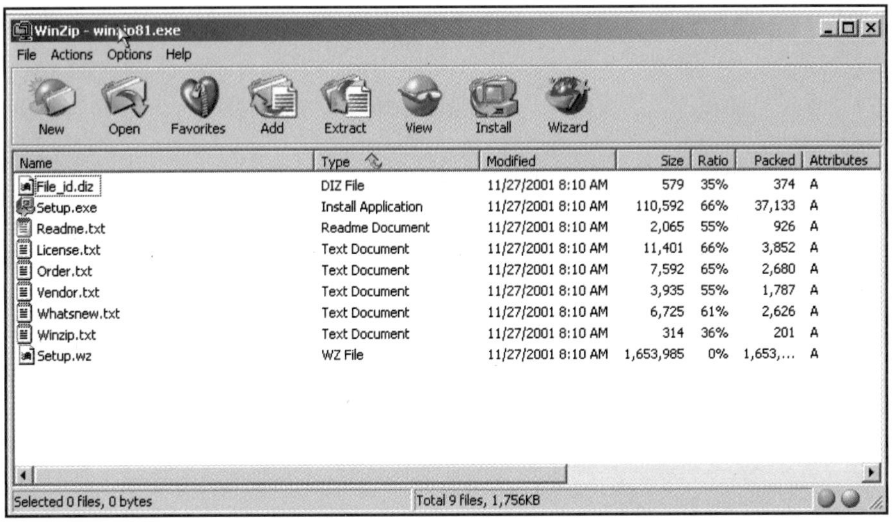

WinZip - winzip81.exe

File Actions Options Help

New Open Favorites Add Extract View Install Wizard

Name	Type	Modified	Size	Ratio	Packed	Attributes
File_id.diz	DIZ File	11/27/2001 8:10 AM	579	35%	374	A
Setup.exe	Install Application	11/27/2001 8:10 AM	110,592	66%	37,133	A
Readme.txt	Readme Document	11/27/2001 8:10 AM	2,065	55%	926	A
License.txt	Text Document	11/27/2001 8:10 AM	11,401	66%	3,852	A
Order.txt	Text Document	11/27/2001 8:10 AM	7,592	65%	2,680	A
Vendor.txt	Text Document	11/27/2001 8:10 AM	3,935	55%	1,787	A
Whatsnew.txt	Text Document	11/27/2001 8:10 AM	6,725	61%	2,626	A
Winzip.txt	Text Document	11/27/2001 8:10 AM	314	36%	201	A
Setup.wz	WZ File	11/27/2001 8:10 AM	1,653,985	0%	1,653,...	A

Selected 0 files, 0 bytes Total 9 files, 1,756KB

In UNIX and Linux, the process of file compression is slightly more cumbersome. If you want to combine more than one file into a larger file and then reduce its size you need to perform a series of steps. First you need to use the tar utility to combine files into one larger file. After the files have been combined, you can compress them using the compress or gzip utilities. The final result is a compressed file containing one or more files with the extension of tar.z. The uncompress or gunzip utilities decompress the file.

A file-compression tool is a must-have for your toolbox. Once you start compressing files you will ask yourself how you ever survived before data compression. Now if someone could just come up with a compression algorithm that reduces body fat!

file transfer tools

Sometimes e-mailing attachments just won't work. Either the e-mail account has a limit on the amount or type of data it can receive or it would be more beneficial to place the attachment in a common location so that many users can download and have access to it. This is a task where *File Transfer Protocol* (or *FTP*) software is the tool of choice.

FTP (File Transfer Protocol) – A transmission method used to send files across the Internet to a storage location defined by an FTP address

FTP is used to send files across an Internet connection to a storage location called an FTP site defined by a FTP address. The address would look similar to:

ftp://ftp.*mynewftpsite*.com/*filename*

where *mynewftpsite* is the FTP Web site location and *filename* is the name of the file you would like to access. Some FTP sites require you to log in with a username and password. Other sites don't restrict who can access the files.

Sending files via FTP is sometimes called "FTPing" files. You might need to FTP files from your machine to a central repository of files. For instance, many times a professor will post (or upload) files to a directory on the school network where students can access and download files to their own computers. This can include assignments, examples, tests, and other requirements. The students can then submit their homework, test answers, projects, and source code to the FTP site for the professor to then download and examine. Consider an FTP site as another directory on your PC that you have to access through the use of the Internet and an FTP tool. In this way, an FTP Web site can act as a network drive, giving you the ability to upload files to the network and download files to your PC.

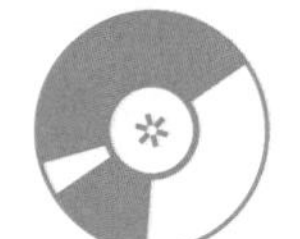

Try a step-by-step FTP tutorial on the student CD under Chapter 2, tutorials.

There are many different FTP software packages available. One widely used package is WS_FTP from Ipswitch, Inc. (see Figure 2-22). There are currently two different versions of WS_FTP. The Pro version is the professional version, and the LE version is for educational use.

Figure 2-22, WS_FTP Pro

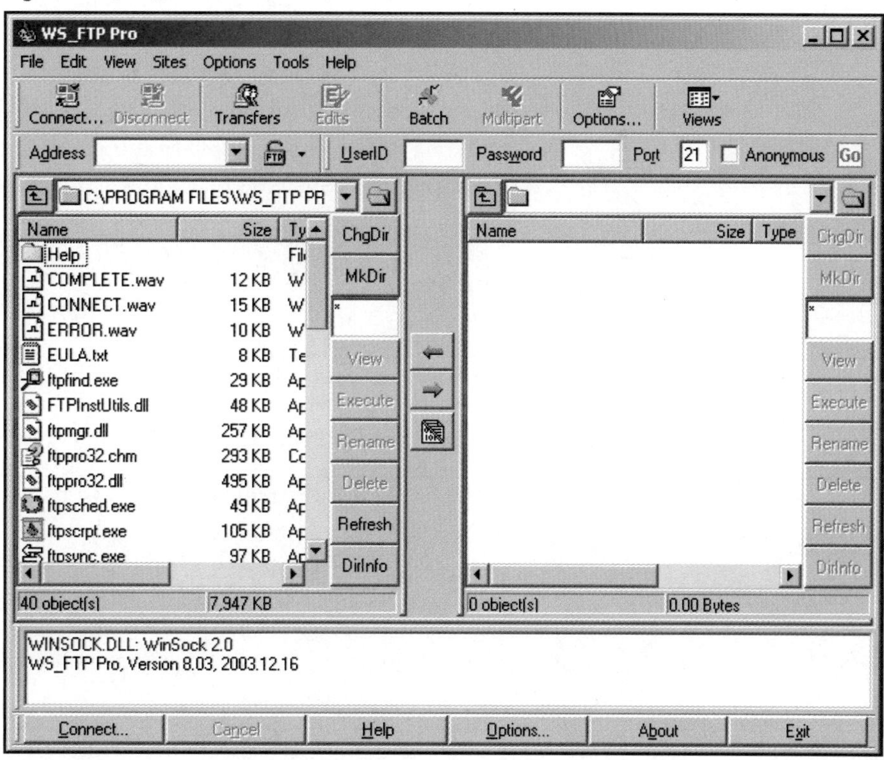

note Some operating systems come with built-in FTP tools, but these are generally not as user friendly as commercial tools.

In order to use an FTP tool you must know the FTP site address you wish to connect to so you can upload and download files. As with e-mail, transferring files using FTP can be expedited by compressing the files before sending them.

Instead of e-mailing files, worrying about viruses and attachments and blocked transfers, computer scientists use an FTP tool such as WS_FTP Pro to transfer files and to store programs, documents, and other files.

note UNIX/Linux has an ftp command that can be used to transfer files from one location to another.

Web development tools

One more tool for your toolbox is a tool to aid in creating and maintaining Web sites and Web pages. The Internet permits you to shop online, participate in auctions, research information, download software, play games, and keep yourself busy talking to strangers in chat rooms. Okay, so maybe there are some things that could distract you from more important tasks, but the point is that someone had to create all of these Internet sites. With the right education and tools, that someone could be you.

You will likely be faced someday with a request to create a business, personal, or educational Web site. It is best to know the tool you want to use before that time comes.

Oh what a tangled Web we weave when first we practice...writing Web pages. Well, Sir Walter Scott wasn't talking about Web pages, but if you choose the right Web development tool you can at least create Web pages that look good.

There are many different tools that can be used to build a Web site. Of course, using a tool that allows you to *visually* create a Web site is easier to use because seeing how your changes affect the appearance of a Web site is more efficient than having to run the site to see how it looks.

Some of the more popular tools for developing Web sites are:

- Adobe GoLive
- Macromedia Dreamweaver MX
- Microsoft FrontPage

As with all of the software mentioned in this chapter, each of these packages has advantages and disadvantages. FrontPage is geared more toward the novice user and is the least expensive, while Dreamweaver and GoLive are targeted more to professional Web designers. Macromedia Dreamweaver (Figure 2-23) is probably the most popular of the three at this writing and contains quite an array of supporting tools.

2

Those using Dreamweaver should have an understanding of the Web source code being generated. In fact, much of Dreamweaver's power comes from first designing your pages using a ***WYSIWYG*** (What You See Is What You Get) format and then enhancing the Web development environment and the pages by modifying the underlying code.

WYSIWYG – What You see Is What You Get. In word processing or Web design, the ability to output text and images onscreen exactly as they will appear in print or in a browser window

Figure 2-23, Dreamweaver incorporates WYSIWYG during Web development

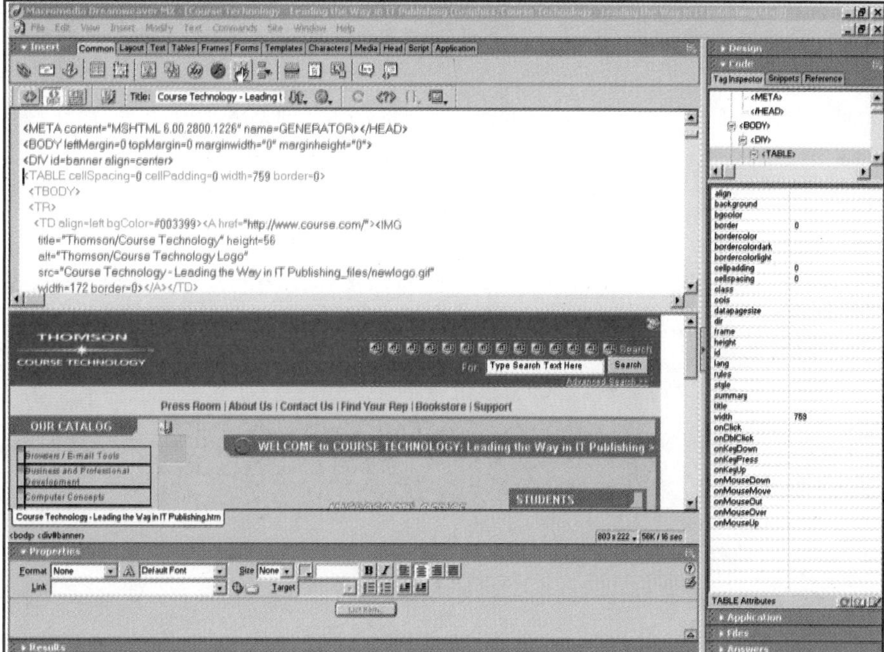

Figure 2-24, Microsoft FrontPage focuses on ease of use when creating Web pages

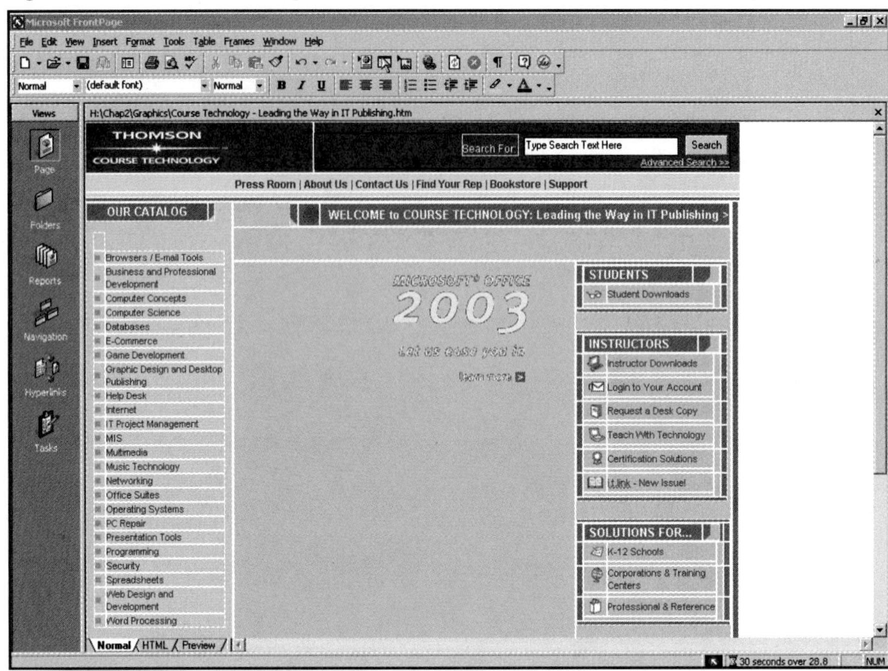

FrontPage is very easy to use but has not overtaken Dreamweaver as the most popular software product for business Web development. It also incorporates a WYSIWIG development environment. As shown in Figure 2-24, FrontPage is geared toward an environment where a user of any level can easily learn how to create a Web site.

So which package is the right one for you? It might not be any of these. Before you choose a Web development tool, you should first contact your Internet service provider and see what they recommend and support.

extra Web tools

In addition to Web development tools, there are other tools that can enhance the presentation of your Web site. Users like things that are pretty and fun, and through the use of Macromedia Flash MX you can really spice up how your site delivers the content to the visitor. Flash provides animation and interactivity that captures the visitor's attention and has them coming back for more.

As a Web developer, there are two goals on which you should focus. The first is getting users to visit your site. The second is to keep the visitor coming back. Adding interactivity through a medium such as Flash is one way to keep the user excited about the Web site. This is a required tool to have in your Web development toolbox if you want to gain an advantage over other Web developers.

one last thought

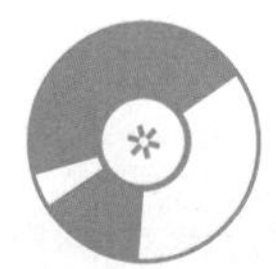

Reinforce your understanding of chapter concepts and terms with the information and activities for Chapter 2 on the student CD.

Now that you have been introduced to the different tasks you might be faced with as you enter the computer science field, and some of the tools you can use for each task, it's time to start using some of them. Just because you have been introduced to some of the tools doesn't make you an expert. You must now make a commitment to learn how to use these tools. Download the trial versions and discover for yourself which software you like. One of the keys to becoming a successful computer scientist is getting to know the tools that can help you do your job quickly and efficiently. Not only must you learn how to use the types of tools mentioned in this chapter but you must also stay on top of the new tools that are being introduced. If you are not learning something new, then your knowledge is becoming stagnant. In computer science you cannot afford to become stagnant without compromising your marketability.

chapter summary

- Computer science deals with more than writing programs. There are many different tasks you will undertake throughout your education and career
- Computer scientists need to create many documents through the use of a word processor such as Microsoft Word
- As a computer scientist, you can use presentation software to create presentations communicating information regarding projects, software, hardware, business changes, and so on
- As a computer scientist you might need to use a tool such as Microsoft Excel to create spreadsheets for budgets or other documents that need to perform calculations on numbers
- As a computer scientist, you most probably will have to manage projects using such tools as Microsoft Project, which include features that both define the tasks that need to be completed and track their progress
- As a computer scientist, you will work with different graphic formats, such as BMP, GIF, JPG, and TIF, for use within programs, documents, and Web sites
- Lossless compression removes redundant data and does not alter the image when decompressed
- Lossy compression eliminates redundant information but slightly alters the image when decompressed
- A programming environment or IDE (integrated development environment) is used to make application development easier and contains other tools that support the programming language being used to create an application
- The more commonly used database packages are Oracle, SQL Server, Microsoft Access, and MySQL
- E-mail clients such as ELM, PINE, and Microsoft Outlook are used to send information, documents, images, and files electronically
- Files can be compressed to reduce their file size resulting in shorter transmission times when being sent electronically
- Decompression is when a compressed file is returned to its original state and size
- Different types of compression methods are RLE, LZW, ZIP, and Huffman
- WinZip is one of the more popular compression tools
- WS_FTP is one of the more commonly used FTP (File Transfer Protocol) tools and is used to upload and download files to FTP Web sites
- As a computer scientist, you need to learn how to develop Web sites using tools such as FrontPage, Dreamweaver, and GoLive
- Flash is another Web tool that helps you spice up a Web site by adding animation and interactivity to capture the visitor's attention

key terms

BMP (bitmap) (59)

browser (72)

column (67)

cropping (63)

data compression (74)

database (67)

database management system (DBMS) (68)

decompression (74)

desktop publisher (53)

flowchart (65)

format conversion (63)

freeware (64)

FTP (File Transfer Protocol) (76)

GIF (Graphics Interchange Format) (60)

IDE (integrated development environment) (66)

JPG or JPEG (Joint Photographic Experts Group) (60)

lossless compression (60)

lossy compression (60)

presentation tool (54)

project management software (57)

rotating (62)

row (67)

scaling (61)

shareware (64)

spreadsheet (55)

table (67)

text editor (51)

TIF or TIFF (Tag Image File Format) (60)

word processor (49)

WYSIWYG (79)

test yourself

1. What tool is used to create documents?
2. What is an example of a current software tool used for creating documents?
3. What is an example of a current software tool used for creating presentations?
4. List four different graphic formats and describe their use.
5. What is the difference between lossless and lossy compression?
6. Describe scaling and how you might use it to change an image's display.
7. Describe rotation and how you might use it to change an image's display.
8. Describe cropping and how you might use it to change an image's display.
9. List three different current software tools that are used for working with graphics.

10. What is flowcharting and how can it help improve application development and communication?
11. What are some of the tools being used for flowcharting?
12. List six different current software tools that are used for e-mailing files.
13. List four different compression methods and the compression format being used.
14. What is an example of a current software tool used for compressing and decompressing files?
15. What is an example of a current software tool used for transferring files over an Internet connection?
16. What are some of the supporting tools that can be found in an IDE?
17. What is an example of a current software tool used for creating spreadsheets?
18. List three software tools used for creating Web sites.
19. What is the job of a project manager?
20. What is an example of a current software tool used for managing a project?

practice exercises

1. Which would *not* be considered a functionality of a word processor?
   - **a.** Spell check
   - **b.** Thesauruses
   - **c.** Grammar check
   - **d.** Programming environment
2. What is the primary purpose of a presentation software tool?
   - **a.** Help the speaker present information to the audience
   - **b.** Keep the audience awake
   - **c.** Provide a way for the speaker to speak less on the topic
   - **d.** Impress your audience with your newly found computer skills
3. Which graphic format is best suited for displaying images on the Internet?
   - **a.** BMP
   - **b.** GIF
   - **c.** JPG
   - **d.** TIF
4. Which graphic format is best suited for displaying animated images?
   - **a.** BMP
   - **b.** GIF
   - **c.** JPG
   - **d.** TIF

5. Which graphic format is best suited for displaying an image on the Windows desktop?
   - **a.** BMP
   - **b.** GIF
   - **c.** JPG
   - **d.** TIF

6. Which graphic format is best suited for professional, realistic images?
   - **a.** BMP
   - **b.** GIF
   - **c.** JPG
   - **d.** TIF
7. Which method to transform a graphic is used to change the image so that it can be displayed on a document that is in landscape orientation?
   - **a.** Scaling
   - **b.** Rotation
   - **c.** Cropping
   - **d.** Format conversion
8. Which method to transform a graphic is used to remove distracting items from an image?
   - **a.** Scaling
   - **b.** Rotation
   - **c.** Cropping
   - **d.** Format conversion
9. Which is *not* a valid file compression format extension?
   - **a.** zip
   - **b.** z
   - **c.** tar
   - **d.** gz
   - **e.** None of the above
10. Which file compression format is commonly used in UNIX and Linux?
    - **a.** zip
    - **b.** arc
    - **c.** tar
    - **d.** cab
11. FTP is used to:
    - **a.** Send messages to another user
    - **b.** Transmit files to another user
    - **c.** Transmit files to another location
    - **d.** Compress files so that they can be sent to another location
12. What is a common use of spreadsheets?
    - **a.** Creating a program
    - **b.** Creating a budget
    - **c.** Creating a resume
    - **d.** Managing a project's milestones

13. Which is *not* a programming language?

    a. C++
    b. Java
    c. WinZip
    d. Visual Basic

14. What is an advantage of using a Web development tool that incorporates WYSIWYG?

15. Write a short job description that you could use if you were going to hire a person to fill the job of project manager.

digging deeper

1. List as many features as possible that you feel a good word processor should contain.

2. What other graphic compression techniques are used besides lossless and lossy?

3. How many different compression formats are supported by WinZip?

4. Name some other graphic formats in addition to those mentioned in this chapter. How and when should they be used?

5. What tools could you use on Windows for:

    a. Presentations
    b. Creating graphics
    c. Uploading files
    d. Spreadsheets
    e. Web development
    f. Project management

discussion topics

1. If you could only have one tool discussed in this chapter, which would be the most beneficial to a computer professional?

2. What are the criteria for determining which is the best tool for a task?

3. What do you think will become an essential tool for computer professionals in the future?

4. Why is it important to continue to learn what tools are available to you as a computer professional?

5. What are some ways that a project manager can make sure that project deadlines are met?

Internet research

1. What are some good Web sites to download images?
2. What other graphic tools are being used, and how do they compare to the graphic tools listed in this chapter?
3. Can viruses be sent through e-mail? If so, what can be done to protect e-mail messages?
4. What is another compression tool being used, and how does it compare to WinZip?
5. What are some tools a user might use in Linux/UNIX to do:
    - **a.** Presentations
    - **b.** Creating graphics
    - **c.** Uploading files
    - **d.** Spreadsheets
    - **e.** Web development
    - **f.** Project management

chapter

3

computer architecture

in this chapter you will:

- Learn why you need to understand how computers work
- Learn what a CPU is, and what it is made of
- Learn how digital logic circuits are constructed
- Learn the basic Boolean operators
- Understand how the basic logic gates operate and are used to build complex computer circuits
- Learn the importance of Von Neumann architecture
- Understand how the computer uses memory
- Learn what a system bus is and what its purpose is
- Understand the difference between memory and storage
- Be able to describe basic input/output devices
- Understand how a computer uses interrupts and polling

the lighter side of the lab
by spencer

I recently got a call from a friend asking if I could "take a look" at his computer.

IMPORTANT NOTE TO COMPUTER SCIENCE MAJORS: If any friends or neighbors ask what you are studying, you are a History major. Trust me . . .

Any of you who have ever "taken a look" at someone's computer know that if you're going to "take a look" at someone's computer, you'd better not have anything planned for the next four days. I thought about telling my friend I had a date that night until I realized that he knew me well enough that he'd never buy it. So I told him I'd be right over. It turns out that he needed help setting up his brand new $1,500 computer.

IMPORTANT NOTE TO COMPUTER SCIENCE MAJORS: When upgrading your computer, it's important to take good notes—that way, when the time comes when you think you want to upgrade again, your notes will help to remind you that you'd rather eat fiberglass.

As we sat there copying files, my friend asked, "So, is this a good computer?"

"A good computer?" I replied.

He said, "Yeah. I've seen computers advertised for a lot cheaper, and $1500 just seemed like a lot of money to spend." (He had a good point—just imagine what you could do with $1500! You could buy groceries for almost three years, pay rent for almost five months, or buy a college textbook.)

So I asked him why he chose the computer he did. He described the painstaking decision process: He went to a computer store and told the salesperson he needed a computer. The salesperson pointed to a computer and said, "You want this one," so he bought it. Just imagine if the same method was used to decide on other purchases. Car Salesperson: "No, no, Mrs. Smith. You don't want a minivan. You want a Ferrari. It's much faster!" Mrs. Smith: "Who do I make the check to?"

In the end, we got everything but the printer working in just under four hours. That's a personal best. I guess all the practice is starting to pay off.

IMPORTANT NOTE TO COMPUTER SCIENCE MAJORS: I'd love to be able to help you when you get asked to "take a look" at someone's computer, but unfortunately I can't—I have a date.

why you need to know about...

computer architecture

Anyone can use a computer. Then again, there are more than a few people who have a hard time figuring out where the power button is. Most people, however, are able to use the computer for things such as e-mail, personal finance, or browsing the Web. Nearly every adult can drive a car, but how many can build one? How many know how to fix them? Would you take your car to be repaired by a person who only knew how to drive one?

To be a computer professional, you need to have an understanding of what goes on "under the hood" of a computer. When you write a computer program, you need to understand what happens inside the computer when it executes your instructions. When it breaks (and it will), you should have some idea of what might be the problem. Knowing how a computer works is not only interesting, but it can set you above other computer professionals who don't have this depth of knowledge.

A computer is a piece (or pieces) of hardware designed to run programs (software) and accomplish desired tasks. This chapter is primarily about hardware, and how that hardware is designed to work together as a computer system. In later chapters, you'll learn more about software.

inside the box

If someone asked to see your computer, what would you show him or her? A desktop computer normally consists of something you look at, something you type on, something you point with, and a big boxlike thing that does something, but you might not be sure exactly what.

Figure 3-1, Typical personal computer system

Courtesy of Fujitsu

Figure 3-1 shows a typical home computer, but what is the actual computer? Is it the thing you look at? Is it the big box thing? Or, is it all of them together? The answer is that it is all of the above, and it is also none of the above. The combination of the monitor (the thing you look at), the keyboard (the thing you type on), the mouse (the thing you point with), and the computer case (the big box) can be referred to as a computer system. For example, if you asked someone to move your computer to another desk, he would probably move all four items and the printer too. Everything together is often referred to as a computer, but the actual computer isn't the whole thing. The computer case is closer to being the actual computer, but it isn't either. The computer is actually just the CPU (central processing unit) inside of the case on the ***main board*** (sometimes called the ***motherboard***). Everything else on the board exists to support the CPU in its computing efforts. Figure 3-2 shows a main board and its primary components, and Table 3-1 describes the functions of these components.

main board or motherboard – The physical circuit board in a computer that contains the CPU and other basic circuitry and components

Figure 3-2, Main board with labeled components

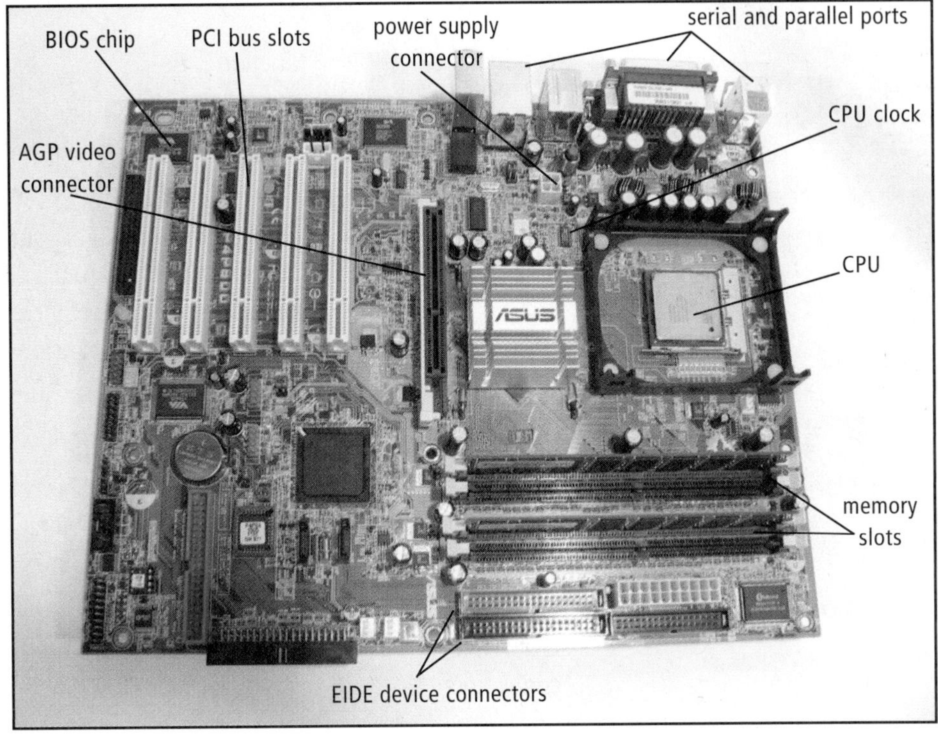

Table 3-1, Main board components

component	function
CPU (central processing unit)	The actual "computer" in the computer executes instructions to read from and write to memory and I/O devices and to perform math operations
memory slots	RAM (random access memory) DIMM (dual inline memory module) cards provide the main memory (RAM) of the computer; memory can be expanded by plugging additional DIMMs into the spare slots
I/O ports	Provide connections for input and output devices such as mice, printers, speakers, and I/O devices

(continued)

Table 3-1 (*continued*)

component	function
CMOS battery	Powers the small amount of CMOS memory that holds the system configuration while the main power is off
PCI expansion slots	Slots to connect PCI expansion cards to the motherboard that are used to add capabilities to the computer that are not included on the motherboard; examples of PCI expansion cards are sound, network, and modem
AGP slot	Allows a high-performance video card to be connected to a special expansion slot
power supply connector	Connection to the power supply that provides electricity to all components and expansion cards on the motherboard
EIDE drive connectors	Connectors for attaching hard drives and CD-ROM drives, or other EIDE (Enhanced Integrated Drive Electronics) devices

To begin exploring computer architecture, you can start with the CPU.

the CPU

The CPU *is* the computer. It contains the digital components that do the actual processing. It is made up of millions of transistors organized into specialized digital circuits that perform operations such as adding numbers and moving data. Transistors are simply small electronic switches that can be in either an on or an off state. The first Intel 8088 CPU had approximately 29,000 transistors. The Pentium IV has about 42 million. The transistors' ons and offs are treated as binary ones and zeros, and are used to accomplish everything that happens in a computer.

In Chapter 4, you'll learn how binary ones and zeros are used to represent data.

Inside the CPU, transistor circuits implement four basic functions:

- Adding
- Decoding
- Shifting
- Storing

Nearly everything that happens in a computer is done using these four specialized circuits. You'll see examples of each of these circuits later in the chapter.

- Adder circuits add numbers together. They are also used to perform other mathematical functions such as subtraction, multiplication, and division.
- Decoders are used to react to specific bit patterns by setting an output of 1 when the pattern is recognized. Decoders are often used to select a memory location based on a binary address.
- Shifters are used to move the bits in a memory location to the right or to the left. They are often used in conjunction with adders to implement multiplication and division.
- Flip-flops (also called latches) are used to store memory bits. Flip-flops provide a way to maintain the state of a bit without having to continue to provide input.

how transistors work

semiconductor – A medium that is neither a good insulator nor a good conductor of electricity, used to construct transistors

Because everything a CPU does happens by the process of transistors turning on and off, an explanation of how a transistor works might be a good place to start your quest to learn how a computer works. Transistors are made of ***semiconductor*** material such as altered silicon or germanium. A transistor consists of three parts, an emitter, a collector, and a base. A power source is placed across the collector and emitter, but the nature of the semiconductor doesn't allow electricity to flow between the two unless another voltage is placed between the base and the emitter. Therefore, the base of a transistor can be used to control the current through the transistor and also the voltage on the collector and emitter. Figure 3-3 shows a diagram of a transistor and how voltages are placed on it to switch it on and off. By switching on and off, the transistor can be used to represent the 1s and 0s that are the foundation of all that goes on in the computer. In the circuit shown, a positive voltage that is considered to be a binary 1 is the output when the transistor is not conducting. When a 1 is applied to the base, the transistor is switched on (conducts) and the output goes to 0.

Figure 3-3, Transistors are used to build logic circuits such as this NOT gate

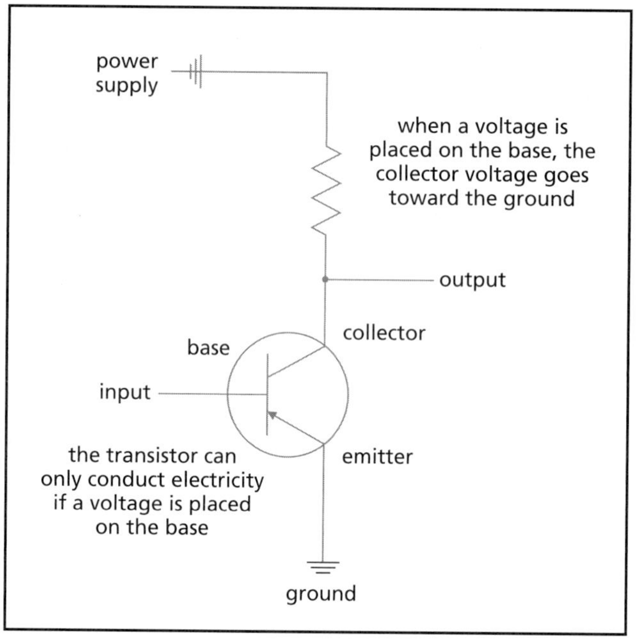

The size of each actual transistor circuit is very small. In the Pentium IV CPU, the transistors are 130 nanometers wide. A nanometer is one billionth of a meter. If you have a little time on your hands, you could think about dividing a meter into a billion parts.

digital logic circuits

Boolean operator – A word used in Boolean algebra expressions to logically test two values; the main Boolean operators are AND, OR, and NOT

Transistors are the smallest units in the computer; the only thing they can do is to turn on and off. They have to be grouped into specialized circuits in order to allow the actual computing to take place. The next level in the computer's design is the logic circuit. These circuits allow the computer to perform Boolean algebra. Boolean algebra is concerned with the logic of the ***Boolean operators***, AND, OR, and NOT.

You interact with devices using Boolean logic in much of what you do on a daily basis. Your microwave oven has circuitry that says, in effect, "When the door is closed AND the time has been set AND the start button is pushed, turn on the microwave." Or, you might have a light circuit in your house that uses this logic: "If the switch by the front door is on OR the switch by the back door is on, turn the overhead light on."

truth table – *A table representing the inputs and outputs of a logic circuit; truth tables can represent basic logic digital circuits as well as complex ones*

An understanding of Boolean algebra helps you understand logic circuits. Boolean algebra is a branch of mathematics that deals with expressing logical processes involving binary values. The binary values are 0 and 1, which happen to be ideal for using transistor circuits. Boolean algebra specifies expressions, or functions, that describe the relationship of binary inputs and outputs. Perhaps the best way to visualize these Boolean expressions is by using what is called a ***truth table***. Figure 3-4 shows a truth table for the Boolean operator, AND. The x, y, and z are simply variables that represent values that will be inserted in the truth table. Any letters could be substituted in place of the ones used in these examples. In this case, x and y are inputs, and z is the output.

Figure 3-4 Truth table for the AND operator

inputs		output
x	y	z
0	0	0
0	1	0
1	0	0
1	1	1

Truth tables are tabular representations of Boolean expressions. Truth tables always follow the same format. On the left are one or more columns representing inputs. On the right is usually one column representing the output, although sometimes multiple outputs are shown on the same truth table. A truth table should contain one row for each possible combination of the inputs. A truth table with two inputs would have four rows (2^2). A three-input truth table would have eight rows (2^3).

Boolean expressions are made up of Boolean variables and Boolean operators. Boolean variables are usually single letters that represent a value of 0 or 1. The variables are then connected with Boolean operators. For example, $z = (xy) + (x + y') + x'$ is a Boolean expression that can also be represented by a truth table. Boolean expressions such as this one will make a lot more sense as you learn more about truth tables and logic circuits.

note **Any Boolean expression can be represented by a truth table, and any truth table can be used to represent a Boolean expression.**

the basic Boolean operators

Three basic operators are used in Boolean expressions. They are AND, OR, and NOT.

AND

AND – Boolean operator that returns a true value only if both operands are true

The truth table in Figure 3-4 gives a tabular representation of the AND Boolean operator. The ***AND*** operator takes as input two values. As mentioned before, there is one row in the table for every possible combination of the two inputs. For each of the input combinations there is a specified output. As you can see, the AND operator has an output of 1 (true) only if both inputs are 1. Any other combination of inputs gives an output of 0. Later in this chapter you'll see when and why the AND operator is used in the computer. In Boolean algebra, the AND operator is sometimes represented by a dot, or, more commonly, by using no symbol at all between the letters. The truth table in Figure 3-4 can be represented by the Boolean expression, $xy = z$, which can be restated by saying, "x AND y results in z." In other words, the truth table describes what the output is for any set of inputs.

OR

OR – Boolean operator that returns a true value if either operand is true

Figure 3-5 shows the truth table for the Boolean OR operator. The Boolean ***OR*** operator returns a 1 only when either or both of the inputs are 1. The Boolean expression $x + y = z$ is equivalent to the information represented in the truth table for the OR operator. This expression can be restated to "x OR y results in z."

Figure 3-5, Truth table for the OR operator

inputs		output
x	y	z
0	0	0
0	1	1
1	0	1
1	1	1

NOT

NOT – Boolean operator that returns a false value if the operand is true and a true value if the operand is false

The ***NOT*** operator works with a single input and its purpose is to reverse the input. Figure 3-6 shows the truth table for the NOT operator. The Boolean expression for the NOT operator can be represented by either $x' = z$ or $\overline{x} = z$. This expression is stated as, "NOT x results in z."

Each of these basic Boolean operators can be combined with Boolean variables to form complex Boolean expressions. In addition, as you'll see later, Boolean

Figure 3-6, Truth table for the NOT operator

input	output
x	z
0	1
1	0

expressions can be used to describe a circuit that gives a desired output for a given set of inputs. That's just about all the computer does. It has millions of circuits that respond to particular inputs. Simple circuits are grouped together to form more complex circuits. These circuits in turn are grouped together to form circuits that are even more complex and have specialized purposes such as adding, decoding, and storing bits.

digital building blocks

gate – A transistor-based circuit in the computer that implements Boolean logic by creating a single output value for a given set of input values

Each of the basic Boolean operators can be implemented as a digital circuit made of one or more transistors. Each of the circuits is designed to carry out the function of the respective Boolean operator. These circuits are often referred to as *gates*. In the computer, the binary ones and zeros are actually different electrical voltage levels. The high voltage, which is typically a positive 3 to 5 volts, is treated as the 1. The low voltage, negative 3 to 5 volts, represents the 0. These voltages ultimately come from the power supply, but they are applied to the logic gates in the computer and the output of one gate becomes one of the inputs to another gate. The combinations of the gates then enable the computer to do all of the things that it does. Each gate in a circuit reacts in a completely predictable way. Gates can be combined to give a certain output when a specific input occurs. For example, a circuit could be easily designed to light up the correct elements of a 7-segment numeric display when a bit pattern representing the number is placed on the circuit inputs.

AND gate

Figure 3-7 shows the symbol and truth table for the AND gate.

Figure 3-7, Symbol and truth table for the AND gate

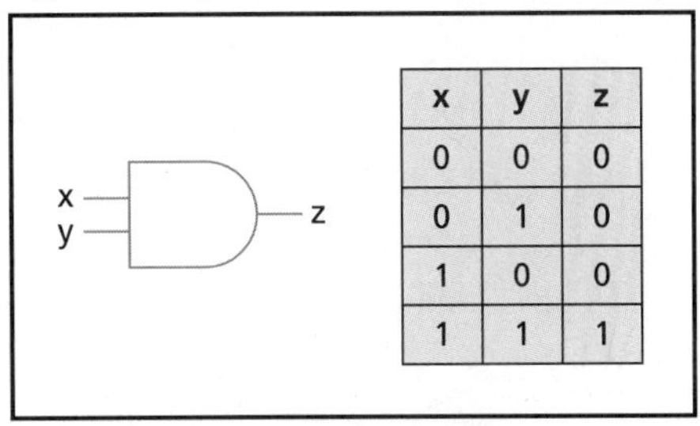

x	y	z
0	0	0
0	1	0
1	0	0
1	1	1

The AND gate allows for two inputs and has one output. The truth table gives the output values for all of the possible input scenarios. Note that the truth table for the AND gate is identical to the truth table for the AND Boolean operator.

OR gate

Figure 3-8 shows the symbol and truth table for the OR gate.

Figure 3-8, Symbol and truth table for the OR gate

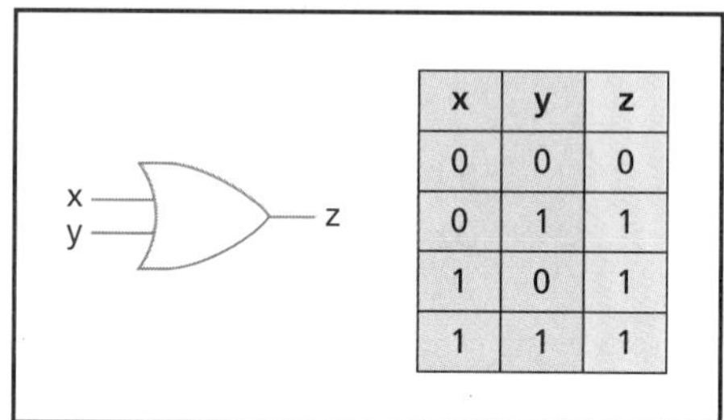

x	y	z
0	0	0
0	1	1
1	0	1
1	1	1

The OR gate also allows for two inputs and one output. The truth table for the OR gate again has output values for all possible combinations of input signals. The OR gate truth table matches the truth table for the OR Boolean operator.

NOT gate

Figure 3-9 shows the symbol and truth table for the NOT gate.

For a dynamic tour of the logic gates and circuits introduced in this chapter, check out the learning tools section under Chapter 3 on the student CD.

Figure 3-9, Symbol and truth table for the NOT gate

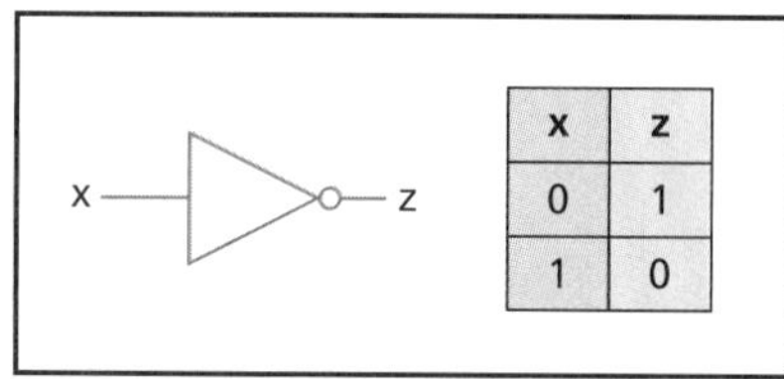

x	z
0	1
1	0

The NOT gate only has one input and one output. The truth table for the NOT gate just shows that the output is the opposite of the input. That is, the function of the NOT gate is to reverse the input. Again, this truth table is the same as its Boolean operator counterpart.

The AND, OR, and NOT gates are the basic building blocks of the CPU. There are also three additional gates that can be created using the basic gates. These additional three are NAND, NOR, and XOR. Sometimes they are grouped with the AND, OR, and NOT as basic gates.

NAND gate

NAND – A logical AND followed by a logical NOT that returns a false value only if both operands are true

Figure 3-10 shows the NAND gate and truth table. The ***NAND*** gate is a combination of an AND gate and a NOT gate. In effect, it takes the output of the AND gate and then reverses it with the NOT. The output on the truth table for the NAND is exactly the opposite of the output of the AND gate. The symbol for the NAND gate is an AND gate symbol with the addition of a small circle at the output to indicate the NOT.

Figure 3-10, Symbol and truth table for the NAND gate

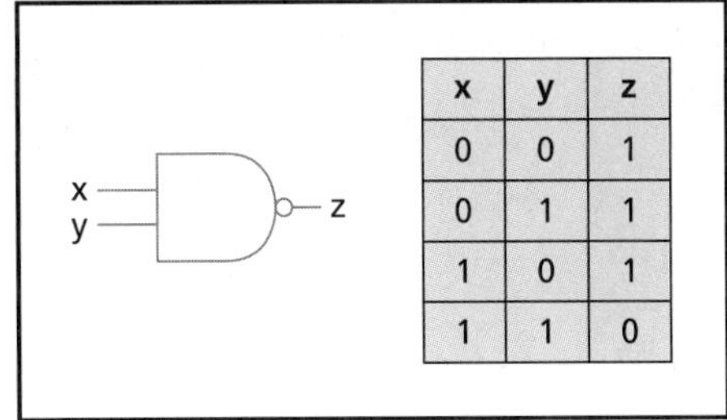

x	y	z
0	0	1
0	1	1
1	0	1
1	1	0

NOR gate

NOR – Logical OR followed by a logical NOT that returns a true value only if both operands are false

Figure 3-11 shows the NOR gate and truth table. The ***NOR*** gate is a combination of an OR gate and a NOT gate. The output of the OR is fed into the input of the NOT, effectively reversing the output of the OR. The symbol of the NOR gate is the same as the OR with the addition of the circle at the output, indicating the NOT.

Figure 3-11, Symbol and truth table for the NOR gate

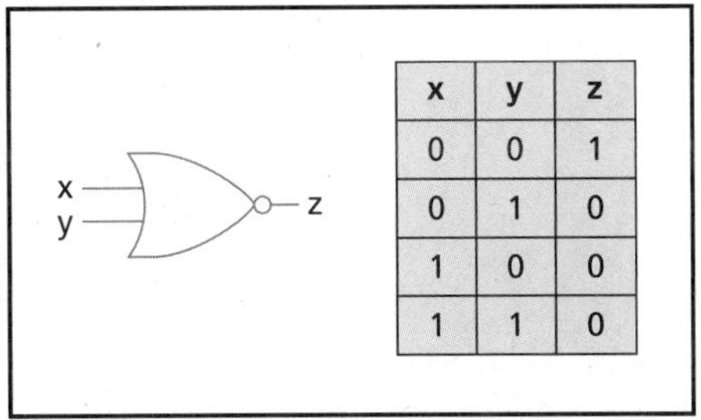

x	y	z
0	0	1
0	1	0
1	0	0
1	1	0

XOR gate

XOR – Logical operator that returns a true value if one, but not both, of its operands is true

In Figure 3-12, note that the truth table for the ***XOR*** (exclusive OR) gate indicates that the output is 1 only when the inputs are different. If both of the inputs are 0 or both are 1, then the output is 0. The symbol for an XOR gate is similar to the OR gate with the addition of the parallel curved line at the left.

Figure 3-12, Symbol and truth table for the XOR gate

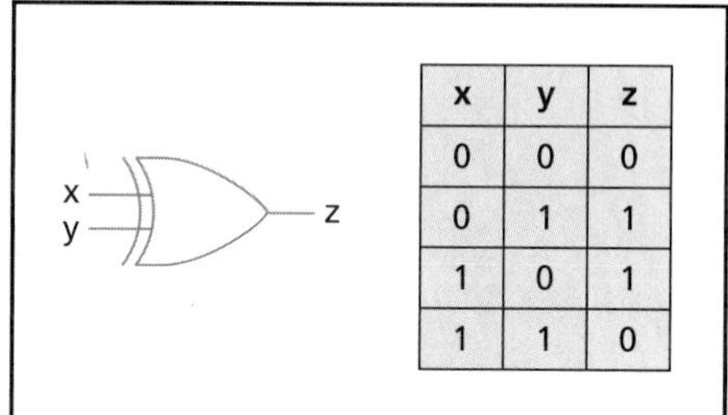

x	y	z
0	0	0
0	1	1
1	0	1
1	1	0

gate behavior

With any of the gates, you can predict the output for any given set of inputs. The gates are designed and built with transistors such that the output for any set of inputs follows the specifications given in the truth table. Therefore, if you were told the inputs to an XOR gate were 0 and 1, you could correctly predict that the output would be a 1. If the inputs were both 0, then the output would be 0.

It is also important to note that gates can be chained together to form specialized circuits that are more complex. The output from one gate is connected as an input to another gate. One of the first things you might notice from this capability is the ability to connect multiple gates of the same type to form a version of the basic gates that have more than two inputs. Figure 3-13 shows how a 3-input AND

Figure 3-13, Constructing a 3-input AND gate from two 2-input AND gates

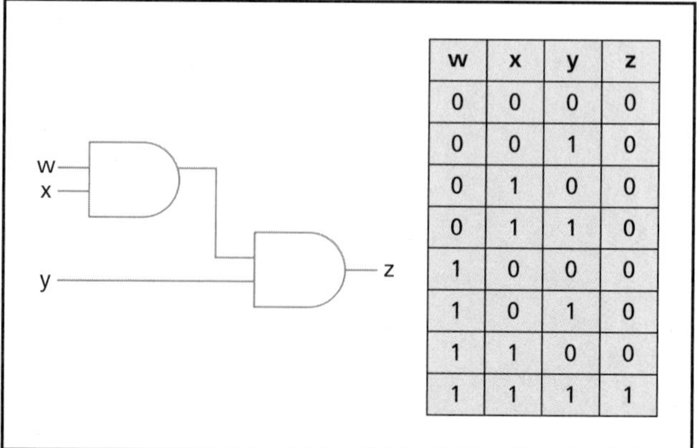

w	x	y	z
0	0	0	0
0	0	1	0
0	1	0	0
0	1	1	0
1	0	0	0
1	0	1	0
1	1	0	0
1	1	1	1

gate can be constructed from two 2-input AND gates. The figure also shows the truth table that would result from that construction. The output of the first AND gate is only 1 if both *w* and *x* are ones. The output of the second gate at *z* is 1 only if the output of the first gate is 1 and *y* is also 1. Therefore, the truth table for the entire circuit shows that the output is 1 only if all three inputs are 1s.

complex circuits

Now that you understand the basic gates and how truth tables work, you are ready to start combining the basic gates to form a few of the main circuits that make up the CPU. These circuits are the adder, decoder, shifter, and the flip-flop.

adder

One of the main functions of the arithmetic logic unit (ALU) portion of the computer's CPU is to add numbers. A circuit is needed that adds two binary numbers and gives the correct result. To build an ***adder*** circuit out of the basic logic circuits, start with the truth table showing the desired outcome for each set of circumstances. Figure 3-14 shows the truth table for adding two bits, including carry-in (ci) and carry-out (co). You might recognize that the terms carry-in and carry-out mean the same thing as borrow and carry in decimal addition and subtraction. In the adder, the bits are added according to the rules of the binary numbering system.

***adder* – The circuit in the CPU responsible for adding binary numbers**

Chapter 4, "Numbering Systems and Data Representation," has a full discussion of the rules for adding binary numbers.

Figure 3-14, Truth table for adding two bits with carry-in and carry-out

inputs			outputs	
x	y	ci	s	co
0	0	0	0	0
0	0	1	1	0
0	1	0	1	0
0	1	1	0	1
1	0	0	1	0
1	0	1	0	1
1	1	0	0	1
1	1	1	1	1

Note in this truth table that there are three inputs, the first bit to be added, *x*, the second bit, *y*, and the carry-in, *ci*, from a prior addition. Truth tables normally only have one output, but because both the sum, *s*, and the carry-out, *co*, work with the same set of inputs, they are shown on the same truth table in this case. The truth table indicates that for a given combination of the two bits you want to add, along with a carry-in from a prior addition, the sum bit has a fixed value, as does the carry-out bit.

The truth table for the adder circuit explains what needs to be done in the circuit. Figure 3-15 shows a circuit built out of the basic logic gates that implement the truth table for the adder. You can experiment with the circuit by putting combinations of ones and zeros on the three inputs and then follow the circuit through to see if it generates the correct outputs according to the truth table.

Figure 3-15, Adder circuit

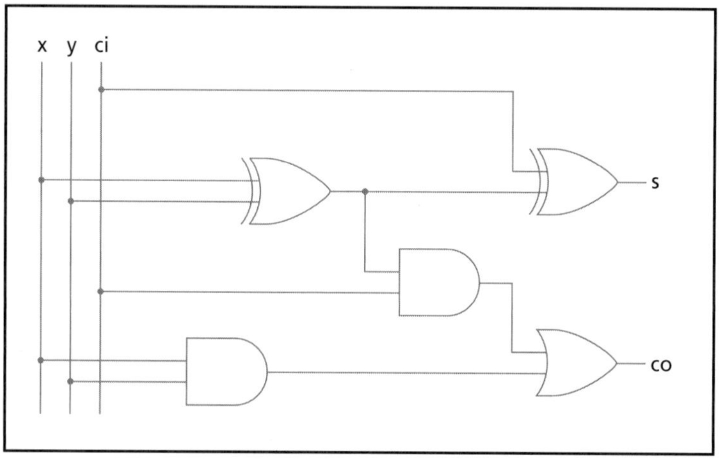

decoder

decoder – A digital circuit used in computers to select memory addresses and I/O devices

Decoder circuits are used heavily in the computer to perform functions such as addressing memory and selecting input or output devices. The idea behind decoders is that for a given input pattern of bits, an output line can be selected. Figure 3-16 shows a diagram of a 2-bit decoder along with the truth table for the circuit. Each of the output lines, *a*, *b*, *c*, and *d* can be selected, or set to 1, by a specific bit pattern on the input lines *x* and *y*. The circuit doesn't seem too impressive with just two inputs that can only control four lines, but a circuit with only 32 inputs could control 4 billion lines!

The truth table for the circuit in Figure 3-16 is best represented by showing all of the possible combinations of the two inputs on the left and showing all four possible outputs on the right. Remember that a basic truth table only has one output, so this truth table is actually four truth tables in one. It shows that for any of the four possible combinations of the two input bits, there is only one output line set to a 1 (selected).

Figure 3-16, Decoder with two input lines controlling four output lines

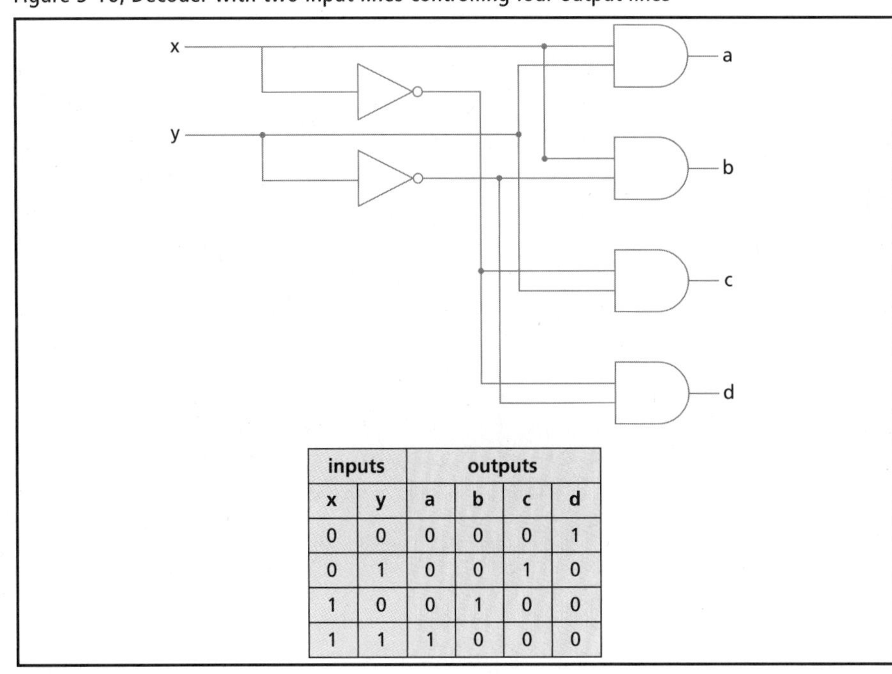

inputs		outputs			
x	y	a	b	c	d
0	0	0	0	0	1
0	1	0	0	1	0
1	0	0	1	0	0
1	1	1	0	0	0

flip-flop

flip-flop or latch – A digital circuit that has the ability to retain the binary value to which it was set after the input is removed; static RAM is constructed using flip-flop circuits

The ***flip-flop*** is not just footwear for the beach—it's also a special form of a digital circuit called a "latch." The ***latch*** is named because it latches onto a bit and maintains the output state until it is changed.

In the basic AND gate shown in Figure 3-7, the output of 1 is maintained only while both inputs are 1. In the case of the OR gate, one or both of the inputs must be a 1 before the output goes to 1. If both of the inputs are zero, the 1 at the output also changes to zero.

The flip-flop circuit, illustrated in Figure 3-17, holds the value at the output even if the input changes. There are two inputs to this type of circuit, *S* (set) and *R* (reset). The output is labeled *Q*. The designator *Q'* is the inverse of the value of *Q*.

Figure 3-17, A basic SR (set and reset) flip-flop circuit implemented using NOR gates

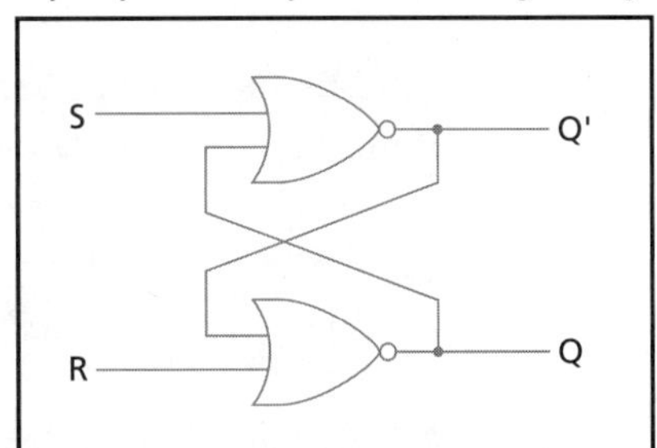

You can use the diagram shown in Figure 3-17 and the truth table for the NOR gate in Figure 3-11 to observe the operation of the flip-flop circuit. When the power is first turned on, all of the inputs and outputs start at logical 0. Because a NOR gate outputs 1 if both inputs are 0, both NOR gates begin to switch their outputs to 1. However, the first gate that switches to 1 sends that 1 to the feedback input of the other NOR gate and it then switches its output to 0. As that 0 is fed back to the input of the first NOR, the output stays at 1. The circuit is then stable with either $Q = 1$ and $Q' = 0$, or $Q = 0$ and $Q' = 1$. The circuit stays in that state until a 1 is placed on either S or R.

If a 1 is placed on the input S, the circuit flips to a state wherein the output Q goes to a 1. If the input S then returns to 0, the output Q remains 1. The circuit is now stable, and remains in that state until a 1 is placed on the R input. Placing the 1 on R flips the circuit to the opposite state wherein Q is 0. Then it stays in that state until 1 is again placed on the S input.

The ability of the flip-flop circuit to maintain a set state after the input voltage that set it goes away makes it ideal for storing bits. The high-speed cache memory in your computer is made of many thousands of flip-flop circuits. In fact, virtually all high-speed memory in the CPU or on video cards is made from flip-flop circuits. This type of memory is usually referred to as static RAM or *SRAM*.

SRAM – Static RAM, a type of high-speed memory constructed using the flip-flop circuit

shifter

shifter – Circuit that converts a fixed number of inputs to outputs that have bits shifted to the left or right, often used with adders to implement multiplication and division

Many operations in a computer benefit from the use of a shifter circuit. Shifters are used in math operations, such as multiply and divide. The ***shifter*** circuit takes a fixed number of inputs and converts them to outputs that have the bits shifted a fixed number to the left or right. Figure 3-18 shows the result of a shift right.

Figure 3-18, Inputs and outputs of a shifter circuit (one-bit right shift)

inputs	1	0	1	1	0	0	1	1
outputs	0	1	0	1	1	0	0	1

In Figure 3-18, you can see that each bit is copied to the bit to the right. A zero is moved into the leftmost bit and the rightmost bit is discarded. Shifter circuits can be designed that have the ability to shift any number of bits to the right or left and to carry bits in or out.

other circuits

There are other specialized circuits used in the computer, such as the multiplexer, parity generator, and counter. Building them involves the same process as described for the adder, decoder, and flip-flop circuits:

1. A truth table is constructed showing the desired output for each possible arrangement of inputs.
2. A Boolean algebra expression is created that is equivalent to the truth table. The expression might then be optimized using a set of mathematic rules governing Boolean expressions. These rules are called the ***Boolean basic identities***.
3. A circuit diagram is created to implement the finished Boolean expression.

Boolean basic identities – A set of laws that apply to Boolean expressions and define ways in which expressions may be simplified; they are similar to algebraic laws

Because a Boolean expression only contains AND, OR, and NOT operators, a circuit designed from an expression might ultimately only be made up of AND, OR, and NOT gates. The great thing about the whole process is that designers can use Boolean expressions to accurately predict what a circuit will do before spending a penny constructing the circuit.

In the early days of computers, computer scientists and electronic engineers had to spend many hours working with Boolean expressions and truth tables to design computer circuits. Now, current computers are used to design new computers. There are large and complicated software programs that do the majority of the work of designing and optimizing new logic circuits to complete desired tasks. Yet the basic building block of the computer has not changed: it's still the lowly transistor.

integrated circuits

The first computers were made to accomplish specific tasks in the same manner as described above, but the earliest computers used mechanical switches instead of transistors to represent the ones and zeros. Later, vacuum tubes were used for the switching. Vacuum tubes work in a similar manner to transistors, but they are much larger, use much more power, and generate tremendous heat. Early computers made from vacuum tubes filled whole rooms and required extensive air-conditioning to keep them cool. When vacuum tubes were replaced with transistors, computers became much smaller, but they still were nearly room size and also required air-conditioning. In the late 1960s, scientists learned how to put thousands of transistors, and thus logic circuits, on a single piece of semiconductor material. These were called integrated circuits (ICs). About 10 years later, scientists again found ways to make transistors even smaller and combined them into specialized complex circuits, which they called ***Very Large-Scale Integration (VLSI)***. The computers you use today are made up of VLSI chips that hold millions of circuits. With this technology, the millions of transistors that make up all of the specialized circuits in the CPU can be etched onto a single piece of silicon that is not much bigger than a pencil eraser.

Very Large-Scale Integration (VLSI) – The current point of evolution in the development of the integrated circuit; VLSI chips typically have more than 100,000 transistors

Von Neumann architecture

As you learned in Chapter 1, the first mechanical computers were special purpose computers—computers designed and built to accomplish a specific task, such as tabulating census information or calculating ballistic trajectory tables. These special-purpose computers could only do what they were designed to do and nothing else. Engineers searched for a way to design a computer that could be used for multiple purposes.

control unit (CU) – The part of the CPU that controls the flow of data and instructions in and out of the CPU

arithmetic logic unit (ALU) – The portion of the CPU responsible for mathematical operations, specifically addition

register – A small, very high-speed amount of memory located on the CPU; registers are used to store the data and instructions used by the CPU

The Von Neumann architecture described in earlier chapters had digital logic circuits that were designed to execute different types of tasks based on binary instructions that would be fetched from some type of storage device. Most computers today are still based on what has come to be called Von Neumann architecture, and are sometimes still called Von Neumann machines.

From a technical standpoint, Von Neumann architecture is defined by the following characteristics:

- Binary instructions are processed sequentially by fetching an instruction from memory, and then executing that instruction.
- Both instructions and data are stored in the main memory system.
- Instruction execution is carried out by a central processing unit (CPU) that contains a *control unit (CU)*, an *arithmetic logic unit (ALU)*, and *registers* (small storage areas).
- The CPU has the ability to accept input from and provide output to external devices.

Figure 3-19 shows a diagram of Von Neumann architecture.

Figure 3-19, Von Neumann architecture

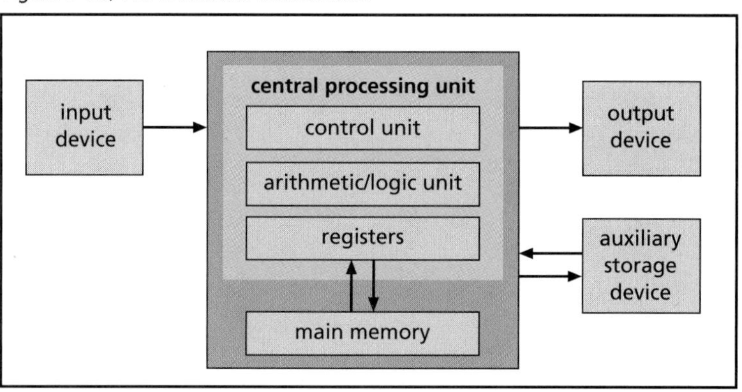

Try your hand at programming a Von Neumann machine in assembly/machine language in the learning tools section under Chapter 3 on the student CD.

At a basic level, a Von Neumann machine operates on what is called a "fetch-execute" cycle. Simply put, the CPU fetches an instruction from memory and then executes that instruction. The actual process can be slightly more complex. For example, the following is a typical fetch-execute cycle:

1. The control unit uses the address in a special register called a program counter to fetch an instruction from main memory.
2. The instruction is decoded to determine what, if any, data it needs to complete execution.
3. Any data that is needed is also fetched from memory and placed into other registers.
4. The ALU then executes the instruction using the data in the registers, if necessary.
5. Input or output operations required by the instruction are performed.

system clock – A crystal oscillator circuit on a computer motherboard that provides timing and synchronization for the operation of the CPU and other circuitry

The computer has a crystal clock called the *system clock* that times, or synchronizes, each of the steps in the fetch-execute cycle. A computer is often referred to by its clock speed. A Pentium IV, 3 GHz computer has a clock frequency of 3 billion clock pulses per second. That means that it can complete 3 billion fetch-execute steps each second. It makes you wonder why your computer ever seems slow!

This fetch-execute architecture on a general-purpose computer has been the mainstay of computer design for more than 60 years. By using increasingly faster clocks, computers have been able to get steadily faster. The first PC processor, using an Intel 8088, had a clock speed of 4.7 MHz. The next generation, the 80286, had a clock speed of up to 12 MHz and it ran about three times faster than the 8088 machine. The 80386 could clock up to 25 MHz and ran twice as fast as the 80286. The 80486 was four times as fast, with a clock speed of 100 MHz. This steadily increasing speed, however, hit a "wall" at around 100 MHz. Increasing the clock speed much beyond 100 MHz presented a problem. The processor still had to fetch instructions and data from memory over the electronic wires and circuitry of the bus that was limited to that speed by the laws and physics of electricity.

buses

bus – A collection of conductors, connectors, and protocols that facilitate communication between the CPU, memory, and I/O devices

system bus – The main bus that is used by the CPU to transfer data and instructions to and from memory and I/O devices

A *bus* in computer terminology is a set of wires and rules, or protocols, to facilitate data transfer. Von Neumann architecture involves using a *system bus* to get information from memory to the processor and back, and also to and from the input/output devices. The electrical signals are the ones and zeros used by the digital logic circuits that make up the various components in the computer. In order for this electrical signaling to be orderly, buses operate under a set of rules governing the level and the timing of all the signals on the bus. This set of rules

bus protocol – The set of rules governing the timing and transfer of data on a computer bus

is called the ***bus protocol***. The bus then is the combination of wires and a protocol.

Bus wires are divided into three separate signal groups:

· Control
· Address
· Data

The control group contains a clock-timing signal for the bus as well as other wires pertaining to timing and the protocol for the bus. The address wires, or lines, contain ones and zeros representing the binary address of either the main memory or an I/O device. All of the devices connected to the bus have an address. When the CPU puts an address onto the bus, the device responds by putting data on the data lines of the bus for the CPU to read. The logic circuit that is used to detect and respond to a particular address is a decoder similar to the one you learned about earlier in the chapter. The data wires contain the binary data that is being read from or written to memory and I/O.

PCI – A system bus to connect a microprocessor with memory and I/O devices; PCI is widely used in personal computers

Early PCs used buses with names like PC/XT, ISA, EISA, MCA, and VESA. Most PCs now use the ***PCI*** (Peripheral Component Interconnect) bus. As with all other buses, the PCI bus is a set of wires, protocols, and connectors that have been defined and standardized for use in computer systems. Everything that interacts with the CPU does so through a bus and most often via the PCI system bus.

Buses also allow external devices to have access to the CPU. Bus connectors on the motherboard allow video adapter cards, network adapter cards, sound cards, and other devices to be connected to the computer system.

peripheral buses

SCSI – A high-speed bus designed to allow personal computers to communicate with peripheral hardware such as disk drives, tape drives, CD-ROM drives, printers, and scanners

In addition to the main system bus in a computer, there are many other secondary buses. Many of these buses are used to connect storage and other peripheral devices to the main bus. Perhaps one of the most popular of these is the ***SCSI*** (Small Computer System Interface) bus. It is used to connect many different types of I/O devices to the computer. While it is known for its high performance and reliability, perhaps its most important characteristic is the ability to allow bus mastering. Bus mastering occurs when a device other than the normal controlling device (such as the CPU) has the ability to take control of the bus, directing and facilitating data transfers. Bus mastering allows the CPU to perform other tasks while two devices are communicating. This is especially important when copying the data on one device to another.

storage

A computer would be nearly useless if it didn't have the ability to retain programs and data when the power is turned off. In addition to needing the ability to read and write to electronic memory, memory contents need to be stored in a more permanent manner. The term storage is used to refer to the family of components used to store programs and data. Storage includes both primary storage (memory) and secondary or mass storage.

3

memory

As you've seen, one of the basics of Von Neumann architecture is the fetch-execute cycle. Each instruction is fetched from memory into the CPU for execution. Electronic memory is key to this architecture and to the speed of the execution of computer processing.

ROM (read-only memory) – A type of memory that retains its information without power; some types of ROM can be reprogrammed

RAM (random access memory) – A generic term for volatile memory in a computer; RAM is fast and can be randomly accessed, but requires power to retain its information

BIOS (basic input/output system) – A ROM (or programmable ROM) chip on the motherboard of a computer; the BIOS provides the initial startup (boot) program for the computer as well as the basic interrupt routines for I/O processing

Memory comes in two basic flavors, ***ROM*** (read-only memory) and ***RAM*** (random access memory). The name ROM indicates that it is memory that is permanently etched into the chip and cannot be modified; however, some special types of ROM can be rewritten under special conditions. ROM isn't erased when the computer power goes off. ROM responds to a set of addresses and places the requested data on the bus, but the CPU cannot write to it.

ROM is used in a chip on the motherboard called the ***BIOS*** (basic input/output system). The BIOS contains instructions and data that provide the startup program for the computer and basic input and output routines.

While the name, ROM, indicates that it cannot be written to, there are additional types of ROM that can be modified under special conditions. These ROM types usually have additional designators such as electrically erasable programmable read-only memory (EEPROM) and have the ability to rewrite all or portions of the memory on the chip.

RAM is called "random" because it does not have to be read sequentially, but rather any location in memory can be accessed by supplying an address. It is memory that can be read from or written to, unlike ROM. RAM is also volatile, meaning that it can be changed at will, and that it requires constant power to maintain the data stored in it.

Every program that runs on the computer is loaded into RAM, and the CPU fetches and executes the program from there. Program data is also stored in RAM. As you type your term paper into the word processor, the characters you type are written to RAM and stored there until you click save. RAM is volatile, meaning that when the power goes off, the RAM is cleared.

DRAM – Dynamic RAM, a generic term for a type of RAM that requires constant refreshing to maintain its information; various types of DRAM are used for the system main memory

RAM is a generic term for read/write memory. Actually, there are different types of RAM. In general, ***DRAM***, or dynamic RAM, is typically made of circuits that use just one transistor per bit. These DRAM circuits need to constantly be refreshed to maintain the data that is stored in them. This refreshing process takes time, which is the main reason why DRAM is so much slower than SRAM. Remember that the fetch-execute cycle of the CPU is dependent on the bus and on memory speed. Slower RAM could mean a slower computer.

A few companies have created improved versions of the standard DRAM. An ad for a computer might specify that it uses DDRRAM or SDRAM in main memory. These acronyms stand for special types of DRAM that are designed to be somewhat faster than normal RAM.

cache memory – High-speed memory used to hold frequently accessed instructions and data in a computer to avoid having to retrieve them from the slower-speed system DRAM

SRAM is made from flip-flop circuits. It is the fastest type of memory. It is normally only used in the registers of the CPU and in cache memory. ***Cache memory*** is a relatively small amount of static RAM that is used to speed up the computer. When CPU clock speeds began to exceed the maximum possible bus speed, computer designers needed to find a way to get around the problem. They came up with a technique that makes use of high-speed, expensive SRAM as a go-between for the CPU and the main DRAM. Instructions and data are initially fetched from DRAM into the SRAM at the slower bus speed, but when the CPU needs the instruction or data again, it can be fetched at the higher speed. Using high-speed memory and caching techniques allow the CPU speed to increase even though the system bus speed has topped out at around 133 MHz.

Personal computers typically have two levels of cache memory. These are referred to as Level 1 cache and Level 2 cache. Level 1 cache is manufactured as part of the CPU. Level 2 cache is a separate chip connected to the CPU via a high-speed local bus.

Conventional asynchronous DRAM chips have a rated speed in nanoseconds (ns), or billionths of a second, a speed which represents the minimum access time for reading from or writing to memory. This includes the entire access cycle. Memory speeds in modern systems range from 10–70 ns.

mass storage

Mass storage is named what it is because it uses devices such as hard drives or CD-ROMs that have much greater storage capacity than RAM or ROM. It is usually a much cheaper form of storage per megabyte, and its contents stick around after the power is turned off.

hard drives

The most commonly used form of mass storage is the hard disk drive. It's called a hard drive because the information is stored on metal platters. Floppy disk drives use the same magnetic technology, but the information is stored on removable flexible disks inside a plastic case.

Hard disks are made up of one or more metal platters (Figure 3-20) with a coating consisting of magnetic particles. These particles can be aligned in two different directions by an electromagnetic recording head, with the two different directions representing ones and zeros. The particles remain aligned in the same direction until the read/write head changes their direction.

Figure 3-20, Hard drive platters and read/write heads

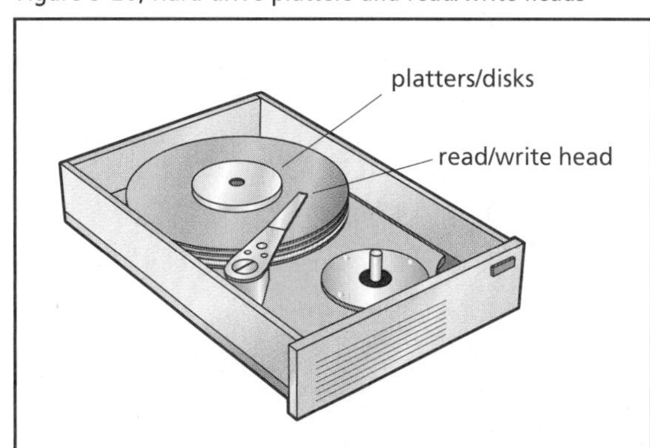

The platter spins very fast, usually in the neighborhood of 7200 revolutions per minute. As it spins, the read/write head moves horizontally across the surface of the disk, positioning over and writing on a specific area. A disk is formatted through the process of the read/write head recording marks on the surface of the disk in concentric circles, called tracks. Each of the tracks is further divided into portions called sectors. Organizing the surface of the disk in this way allows the hard drive to quickly find a specified track and sector on the disk for reading or writing. Hard disks can access data randomly, much like RAM. Hard drives are a standard in computers for storing large amounts of information. Hard disk drives can store hundreds of gigabytes of information relatively inexpensively.

When deciding on the type of mass storage, one factor to consider is the cost per megabyte. For example, a 200 gigabyte (GB) hard drive that costs $160 has a cost per megabyte of 8 cents. Compare that with a 512 MB SDRAM memory chip that sells for $120. That has a cost per megabyte of 23.4 cents. You can see that hard disk storage is much cheaper than RAM.

RAID (redundant array of independent disks) – A collection of connected hard drives that are arranged for increased access speed or high reliability

In situations where hard disk storage needs to be exceptionally fast and/or exceptionally reliable, multiple hard drives are connected to work together as a unit. These arrays of disks are called ***RAID*** systems (redundant array of independent disks). There are seven different types, or levels, of RAID. Each is designed to provide different levels of speed or reliability.

Hard drives can typically access information in a matter of milliseconds. That sounds quite fast, but the nanosecond speeds of the CPU and SRAM make hard drives seem like snails. Computer engineers are constantly striving to design computers and operating systems such that memory is used as much as possible.

note

One of the ways to drastically speed up a computer system is to increase the amount of memory so that the hard drive is used less during operation.

CD-ROM – A 120-mm disc used to store data, music, and video in a computer system using laser technology; CD-ROM discs are capable of holding up to 850 MB of information

DVD – A technology that uses laser and layering technology to store data, music, and video on 120-mm discs; DVD discs are capable of holding up to 9 GB of information

USB (universal serial bus) – A high-speed interface between a computer and I/O devices; multiple USB devices can be plugged into a computer without having to power off the computer

optical storage

Unlike hard disks, CDs and DVDs store data using optical (light) technologies. ***CD-ROM*** (compact disc read-only memory) has become a very popular form of mass storage. Most personal computer systems now have CD-RW (read/write) drives that use a laser to burn microscopic pits in the surface of a 120-mm compact disc (CD). These pits are then interpreted as ones and zeros when reading the disc. Like the hard disk, the CD spins and the laser head moves horizontally across the surface. Unlike the magnetic hard disk, the CD is written to in a continuous spiral from the inside to the outside of the disk. CD-ROM disks can store up to 850 MB of information. ***DVDs*** (digital video discs) are the same physical size as CDs, but can store many times more data. DVDs can hold nearly 9 GB of information, and are often used to store video data. Many personal computers are now equipped with DVD-RW drives.

flash drives

In the last few years, a device that plugs into the ***USB*** (universal serial bus) has replaced the floppy drive as the choice for portable storage. This device, known

flash drive – A small, thumb-size memory device that functions as if it were a disk drive; flash drives normally plug into the USB port of a personal computer

as a ***flash drive*** or thumb drive, plugs into a USB port on a computer and stores hundreds of megabytes of data in a package small enough to fit on a keychain. To the operating system of the computer, a flash drive appears as if it were a removable hard drive, but it really uses a special type of electronic memory, called flash memory. Flash memory is nonvolatile, meaning that the data stays when the power is removed.

input/output systems

Input and output (I/O) systems are the final component in the Von Neumann architecture of your computer system. The CPU fetches instructions and data from memory, and then executes the instruction. If the instruction is a math operation, then shifter and adder circuitry might perform the math, placing the new values in the CPU registers. The instruction might also transfer the binary value from the registers or memory to an I/O device. I/O devices make up a very important part of Von Neumann architecture and of the computer system. A computer without any I/O devices would be completely useless. The I/O devices are the computer's connection to the user.

input devices

port – In the context of I/O devices, a port is the physical connection on the computer to allow an I/O device to be plugged in

The main input device for most computer systems is the keyboard. The keyboard connects to the CPU through the keyboard controller circuit and through the system bus. Your keystrokes are translated in the keyboard to binary signals of ones and zeros that are interpreted by the CPU as letters, numbers, and control codes. Keyboards, and most other I/O devices, connect to the motherboard through a ***port*** (Figure 3-21). Ports are connectors on the outside of the computer that allow I/O devices to be plugged in to the system bus.

Figure 3-21, The motherboard provides numerous ports to connect peripheral devices

The mouse also serves as a primary input device. It works by sensing movement and translating that movement into binary codes. Other input devices include trackballs, styluses (pens), touch pads, and touch screens. Modems and network cards could be included in the list of input devices, although they are often categorized as networking or communication devices.

Networking and communication devices are covered in Chapter 7, "Networks."

CRT (cathode ray tube) – *The technology used in the conventional computer display monitor; CRTs use electron beams to light up phosphor displays on the screen*

RGB (red, green, and blue) – *A type of computer monitor that displays color as a function of these three colors*

resolution – *A measurement of the granularity of a computer monitor or printer; it is usually given as either a pair of numbers indicating the number of dots in a horizontal and vertical direction or as the number of dots per inch*

refresh rate – *The number of times per second an image is renewed on the screen of a display monitor; a higher refresh rate results in less flickering on the display*

LCD (liquid crystal display) – *A type of electronic device used as a computer display monitor; LCD displays have been popular in notebook computers and PDA devices, and have now also become used widely as desktop monitors*

output devices

It's obvious that a computer system would be of little worth if it didn't have the ability to communicate with the outside world.

monitors

The primary output device for home and business computer systems is, of course, the video display, or monitor. For years, monitors have been ***CRT*** (cathode ray tube) devices. In an ***RGB*** (red, green, blue) CRT, three electron streams (one for each color) are encoded with the color information and are then aimed from the back of the monitor to the front where they strike corresponding phosphor dots of each of the colors. When the beam hits one of these dots, it lights it up. The beams are swept horizontally and vertically over the face of the tube, varying the intensity to make up the different patterns and colors. This process is called raster scanning and has been used nearly as long as computers have been in existence. The quality of the display is defined by the resolution and the refresh rate.

Resolution is the number of dots (pixels) on the monitor screen. It is usually measured in terms of the number of pixels or dots horizontally and vertically. If a monitor is advertised as 1600 × 1200 / 68 Hz, it means that it is capable of displaying 1600 by 1200 (1,920,000) pixels, and its ***refresh rate*** (the number of times the screen image is renewed) is 68 times per second. (The faster the refresh rate, the less the image flickers.)

LCD (liquid crystal display) monitors are much thinner and run much cooler than CRT displays (Figure 3-22). Originally, they were just used in notebook computers, but they have become popular as desktop monitors as their prices have decreased. Rather than an electron beam, LCD displays use small transistors that block light when a voltage is applied. As with CRT displays, LCDs are rated in terms of their resolution and refresh rate.

Figure 3-22 Comparison of LCD and CRT monitors

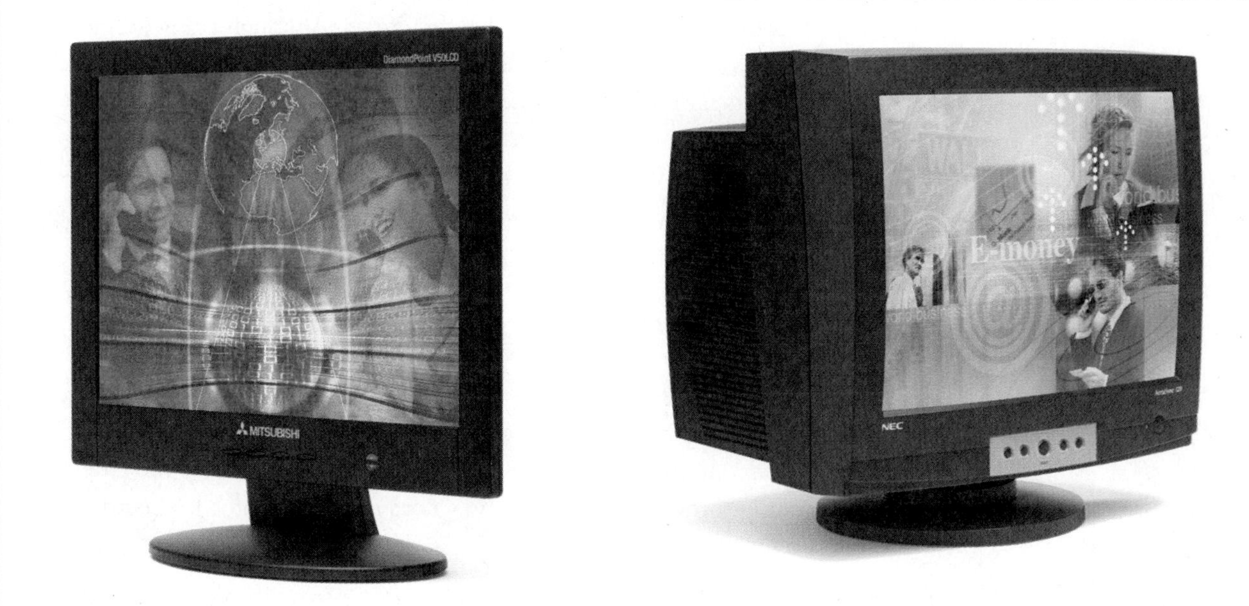

Courtesy of NEC Mitsubishi

printers

The printer is another main output device. Perhaps the most popular is the ink jet printer. It creates both pictures and text on the page by spraying tiny droplets of ink onto the paper as the print head moves back and forth.

Laser printers are also very popular, especially in business situations. They can typically print faster than ink jet printers at a smaller cost per page. Laser printers print by first scanning the print image onto an electrostatic drum. The drum then contacts a fine, black powder called toner and the toner sticks to the drum where the image has been drawn. The drum is then placed in contact with the paper and the toner is transferred to it. The last step is a heat fusing process that melts the toner into the surface of the paper.

The quality of printer output is measured in resolution (dots per inch or dpi) in both the horizontal and vertical directions. Resolution ranges from 300 dpi up to 2400 dpi for both inkjet and laser printers. Printers are also rated by the number of pages per minute that the printer is capable of printing. Laser printer ratings range from 6 to 15 ppm, inkjets are rated at 4 ppm and greater for black text, and photo-quality inkjets range from 0.3 to 12 ppm, depending on the type and quality of printing.

sound cards

Another common output device is the sound card. Although many motherboards have sound capability as part of the chipset, sound cards are still often used. The sound card fits into the PCI bus expansion slot on the main board. In the back of the sound card, there are connectors for audio input and output. Analog sounds can be converted to digital codes and stored in the memory or storage devices on the computer. The sound card is used to digitize sounds for storage or to read the binary sound files and convert them back into analog sounds.

interrupts and polling

As you have learned in this chapter, the CPU fetches and executes at a rate equal to the clock speed of the processor. Each clock pulse causes the CPU to fetch, decode, or execute a binary machine code instruction. As the CPU goes continuously through this process, how does it know when a keyboard key has been pressed?

For the keyboard and other I/O devices there are two techniques designed to process input and output information. The first is polling and the second is the use of interrupts.

polling – A technique wherein the CPU periodically interrogates I/O devices to see if they require attention; polling requires many more CPU resources than interrupt handling

interrupt handling – A process in computers wherein a signal is placed on the bus to interrupt the normal processing of instructions and transfer control to a special program designed to deal with events such as I/O requests

In *polling*, at regular intervals the processor asks each of the I/O devices if they have any requests for service pending. It's a bit like driving with small children who repeatedly ask, "Are we there yet?" "Are we there yet?" "Are we there yet?"

Polling works, but it is very inefficient because much of the CPU's time is spent asking the question (interrogating). *Interrupt handling* is a much more efficient method. The CPU has a companion chip that has a number of connections to wires in the control section of the system bus that are known as interrupt lines. When an I/O device places a voltage signal on one of these lines, the interrupt chip checks the priority of the interrupt and then passes it on to the CPU. The CPU then stops executing its current program and jumps to a special program designed to handle that specific interrupt.

choosing the best computer hardware

As you learn more about how the computer works, you are much better prepared to answer the question, "Which system or device is better?" Many times in your computer science career, you will need to make decisions on hardware and software purchases. For example, "Which is better, a Pentium IV / 2.6 GB or a Pentium IV / 4.0 GB?" Your answer to this and any other "Which is better?" question should be "It depends!" The question cannot be answered unless you know for what task the computer or device is going to be used. You have to know what the desired outcome is before you can say which computer or I/O device can best solve the problem.

For example, by now you should know that the speed of a computer depends on much more than just the CPU clock speed. Such factors as the memory type, bus speed, and even hard drive speed can impact overall speed much more than the CPU clock. Many people have purchased a new computer only to find that it didn't solve the problem they were trying to solve.

Reinforce your understanding of chapter concepts and terms with the information and activities for Chapter 3 on the student CD.

one last thought

Studying this book is just a beginning in your study of computer hardware and software. You should stay current on new technologies and see where they fit into your existing understanding of computers. Remember that having a greater understanding of how a computer works and how the parts of a computer system interact can give you much greater skill in whatever computer specialty you choose.

chapter summary

- It is important to understand the inner workings of a computer if you're planning a career in computers
- The CPU is the "real" computer in a computer system
- Transistors are the smallest hardware unit in a computer and are used to represent the ones and zeros in a computer
- Transistors are arranged into circuits that provide for basic Boolean logic
- The basic Boolean operators are AND, OR, and NOT
- The basic Boolean operators can be implemented as digital circuits or gates; simple gates can be combined to form complex circuits that perform specific desired functions
- The main circuits that make up the CPU are adders, decoders, and flip-flops
- Von Neumann architecture, characterized by a fetch-execute cycle and the three components, CPU, memory, and I/O devices, is the current standard for computers, and has been for over 60 years
- Buses transfer information between the parts of the Von Neumann architecture
- Memory consists of different varieties of ROM and RAM
- Mass storage is nonvolatile and is used to semipermanently store large amounts of data
- Input/output systems consist of input devices such as keyboards and mice, and output devices such as monitors and printers
- The CPU interfaces with I/O devices via techniques such as polling and interrupt processing

key terms

adder (103)

AND (98)

arithmetic logic unit (ALU) (108)

BIOS (basic input/output system) (111)

Boolean basic identities (107)

Boolean operator (96)

bus (109)

bus protocol (110)

cache memory (112)

CD-ROM (compact disc read-only memory) (114)

control unit (CU) (108)

CRT (cathode ray tube) (116)

decoder (104)

DRAM (dynamic RAM) (112)

DVD (digital video disc) (114)

flash drive (115)

flip-flop (105)

gate (99)

interrupt handling (118)

latch (105)

LCD (liquid crystal display) (116)

main board (92)

motherboard (92)

NAND (101)

NOR (101)

NOT (98)

OR (98)

PCI (Peripheral Component Interconnect) (110)

polling (118)

port (115)

RAID (redundant array of independent disks) (114)

RAM (random access memory) (111)

refresh rate (116)

register (108)

resolution (116)

RGB (red, green, blue) (116)

ROM (read-only memory) (111)

SCSI (Small Computer System Interface) (110)

semiconductor (95)

shifter (106)

SRAM (synchronous random access memory) (106)

system bus (109)

system clock (109)

truth table (97)

USB (Universal Serial Bus) (114)

Very Large-Scale Integration (VLSI) (107)

XOR (exclusive OR) (102)

test yourself

1. What is the purpose of a motherboard?
2. What does CPU stand for?
3. What are the four basic functions implemented inside the CPU?
4. What is the purpose of a decoder circuit?
5. What are the three parts of a transistor?
6. What are the main Boolean operators?
7. What type of table is used to represent the inputs and outputs of a logic circuit?
8. Which complex circuit is used to address memory?
9. What would be the output of an XOR gate if the inputs were both 0?
10. Which gate is combined with an AND to form the NAND gate?
11. What symbol is used for the OR Boolean operator in a Boolean expression?
12. Which of the complex digital circuits is used to construct SRAM?

13. Which memory type is faster, SRAM or DRAM?
14. What are the characteristics of Von Neumann architecture?
15. In computer terminology, what is a bus?
16. What are the three signal groups of a bus?
17. What is the purpose of cache memory?
18. What is polling?
19. Which is more efficient, polling or interrupt handling?
20. How is resolution measured?

practice exercises

1. Which of the following circuit types is used to create SRAM?
   - **a.** Decoder
   - **b.** Flip-flop
   - **c.** LCD
   - **d.** ROM
2. Which of the following is not one of the basic Boolean operators?
   - **a.** AND
   - **b.** OR
   - **c.** NOT
   - **d.** XOR
3. Transistors are made of ________________ material.
   - **a.** Semiconductor
   - **b.** Boolean
   - **c.** VLSI
   - **d.** Gate
4. Which of the following is not one of the bus signal groups?
   - **a.** Control
   - **b.** Address
   - **c.** Data
   - **d.** Fetch
5. Which type of memory cannot easily be written to?
   - **a.** RAM
   - **b.** SRAM
   - **c.** ROM
   - **d.** Flip-flop

6. Which of the following memory types is the fastest?
   - **a.** DRAM
   - **b.** ROM
   - **c.** XOR
   - **d.** SRAM
7. In a truth table, inputs are represented on which side?
   - **a.** Top
   - **b.** Bottom
   - **c.** Left
   - **d.** Right
8. Any Boolean expression can represented by a truth table.
   - **a.** True
   - **b.** False
9. Inputs of 1 and 0 to an XOR gate produce what output?
   - **a.** 0
   - **b.** 1
10. In a computer, what function does a decoder usually perform?
    - **a.** Adding
    - **b.** Shifting
    - **c.** Addressing memory
    - **d.** Multiplying
11. Boolean expressions are simplified through the use of:
    - **a.** Basic identities
    - **b.** Gate logic
    - **c.** Algebraic expressions
    - **d.** Specialized circuits
12. Which type of I/O processing is most efficient?
    - **a.** Boolean
    - **b.** Polling
    - **c.** Logic
    - **d.** Interrupt
13. Which of the following defines the quality of a video monitor?
    - **a.** Resolution
    - **b.** Flip rate
    - **c.** Beam strength
    - **d.** Inversion
14. Most computers today are based on
    - **a.** Von Neumann architecture
    - **b.** Upscale integration
    - **c.** Tabulation basics
    - **d.** Small-Scale Integration

15. Which part of the CPU is responsible for mathematical operations?

    a. CU
    b. ALU
    c. RLU
    d. VLSI

16. A ________________ in computer terminology is a set of wires and protocols designed to facilitate data transfer.

    a. Gate
    b. Bus
    c. Boolean circuit
    d. CPU

17. Most computers these days use the ________________ bus.

    a. VLSI
    b. ACM
    c. ASI
    d. PCI

18. The ________________ contains instructions and data that provides the startup program for the computer.

    a. RAM
    b. DRAM
    c. BIOS
    d. CPU

19. High-speed ________________ is used to speed processing in a computer system.

    a. Mass storage
    b. Cache memory
    c. ROM
    d. CD-ROM

20. The quality of printer output is measured in ________________.

    a. PPM
    b. CU
    c. DPI
    d. ROM

digging deeper

1. What are the Boolean basic identities and how are they used in reducing Boolean expressions?
2. How does the quality of laser printer output compare to that of an inkjet? Which has a lower cost per page?
3. What are the newest types of memory and how are they faster than prior memory technologies?

4. Compare the different storage media currently on the market. Which is fastest? Most cost effective? Most portable? Most durable?
5. What do you feel that standard monitor resolution should be and why?

discussion topics

1. If you could afford any computer, what would you have? Why? List the different hardware components you would include.
2. What new computer hardware technology do you think will have the largest effect on the computer industry in the next decade?
3. Why learn Boolean expressions and gate logic?
4. What could be some possible alternatives to Von Neumann architecture?
5. What are some of the ways logic gates are used in your everyday life?

Internet research

1. What is the fastest clock speed currently being used in desktop and notebook computers?
2. Who are the main vendors of CPUs? Which one appears to be the leading vendor and why?
3. Compare three desktop computers from different vendors. Describe the advantages and disadvantages of each.
4. What Internet sites display speed rankings for various hardware components?
5. List three manufacturers of motherboards and describe their products.

chapter 4

numbering systems and data representation

in this chapter you will:

- Learn why numbering systems are important to understand
- Refresh your knowledge of powers of numbers
- Learn how numbering systems are used to count
- Understand the significance of positional value in a numbering system
- Learn the differences and similarities between numbering system bases
- Learn how to convert numbers between bases
- Learn how to do binary and hexadecimal math
- Learn how data is represented as binary in the computer
- Learn how images and sounds are stored in the computer

the lighter side of the lab
by spencer

"Numbering systems." Now, this term is an excellent example of why computer scientists can have a hard time getting dates (at least, until they graduate and become gazillionaires). There might be more boring terms that could be used in place of "numbering systems." For example, they could use the term "Quantitative Analysis Protocols" or maybe "Algorithmic Processes for Deriving Alternative Radix Notation."

(If your eyes are lighting up and you're saying to yourself, "Yeah, they *should* use those terms instead!"—please seek professional help.) Why not just say "different ways to count things"? Or, better yet, "different ways to count doughnuts"? Just imagine you had opened to Chapter 4 to see the title "Different Ways to Count Doughnuts." Now that's a chapter you're going to read!

Sesame Street understands this principle. You never heard a conversation like this between Maria and Big Bird:

Big Bird: "Hi, Maria. What are you doing?"

Maria: "Oh, hi, Big Bird. I'm just executing conversions between numbering systems."

Big Bird: "Huh?"

Maria: "I'm converting this series of digits from the binary base 2 numbering system to the decimal base 10 numbering system by multiplying each individual digit's value in base 2 by its positional value in base 10 and calculating the total sum of all values."

Big Bird (running away): "Snuffyyyyyyyy!"

No, Sesame Street uses fun terms to teach. Everyone remembers The Count. ("One! One ball! Ah, ah, ah!") Give The Count five minutes and a dozen doughnuts, and he'd have the entire class counting in hexadecimal. ("C! C doughnuts! Ah, ah, ah!")

In conclusion, you shouldn't be intimidated by terms like "numbering systems" and "data representation." They're simply really, really boring terms for stuff that is actually pretty interesting. (If the computer scientists who make up terms like "numbering systems" took a lesson from The Count, they might be saying, "One! One Friday night spent with someone whose name isn't Pentium IV! Ah, ah, ah!")

We're just giving you a hard time, computer scientists. You know we love you. If Bill Gates had a dollar for every time someone made a joke about him . . . oh, wait—he does. Ah, ah, ah!

why you need to know about... numbering systems

Every computer game, program, picture, or sound is stored in the computer as a series of binary digits. Because humans don't normally talk binary, it means that if you want to be better able to tell a computer what to do, you must learn to understand binary and hexadecimal.

It might be that such terms as "data representation," "numbering systems," and "hexadecimal" are intimidating to you; however, like other things in life, you just have to become familiar with them to understand them. Most people are born with 10 fingers and 10 toes, so it's no accident that people are most familiar with the base 10 numbering system. You probably learned it watching Sesame Street and then again in elementary school. You might have counted on your fingers and even your toes. (Then again, you might still be counting on your fingers and toes.) Maybe if people were born with only two fingers and two toes this whole computer science binary thing would be much easier to understand. In any case, understanding numbering systems is really quite simple if you just take a deep breath, relax, and go through it one step at a time.

An understanding of numbering systems and data representation enables you to be more comfortable as you interact with the computer in later computer science courses and throughout your career. Many times, you will need to be able to read displays containing the contents of a computer's memory or the hard disk. These are often referred to as hexadecimal memory dumps. If you use a personal computer, you have probably experienced the dreaded "blue screen" fatal error message. It might have been something like:

```
an exception OE has occurred 0028:CICA38F1 in VXD MXECPV (02) +00000251.
This was called from 0028:C02A50EE in VXD VWIN32(05) +00001F16.
```

The hexadecimal numbers in this error message probably don't mean anything to you now, but as you continue your studies in computer science you will come to understand what these numbers mean and how they can be used to explain computer errors.

positive powers

Here's how a positive power is calculated:

$2^3 = 8$

that is,

2*2*2 = 8

powers of numbers—a refresher

Before you get into numbering systems and data representation, think back to something you learned in elementary school: the concept of powers of numbers.

You might remember that 2 squared equals 4. You might also remember that 2 squared is displayed with the power as a superscript, as in 2^2. Remember that raising a number to a positive power is just multiplying that number by itself the number of times specified by the power indicator (often called an exponent). The number 2^3 is just 2 * 2 * 2. The number 2 is multiplied by itself 3 times giving a value of 8. In working with computers, multiplication is represented by the use of the "*" (asterisk) character. Throughout the remainder of this chapter the asterisk is used to indicate multiplication.

That's all there is to positive powers—with the exception of two special cases. The two cases are when the exponents (powers) are 0 and 1. Raising a number to the 0 power always results in 1, no matter what the original number was. The number 10^0 is 1. The number 2^0 also has a value of 1. The other special case is that a number raised to the 1 power is always the number itself. So, 2^1 is always 2 and 16^1 is always 16.

note An important mathematical concept to note is that any number raised to the 0 power gives a value of 1.

Try it with base 10 numbers by raising 10 to the fourth power. The number 10^4 is just 10 * 10 * 10 * 10, or 10,000. The number 10^2 is 10 * 10, which equals 100.

Numbers can also be raised to negative powers. Negative powers are used to represent the fractional portion of numbers. Raising a number to a negative power is similar to raising it to a positive power with the exception of one final step. After you multiply the number the amount of times specified by the exponent, you take that result and divide it into 1. The number 2^{-3} is 1 divided by 2 cubed (2 * 2 * 2) and is equivalent to .125. For 10^{-4} the calculation would be 1 / (10 * 10 * 10 * 10) or .00001. In other words, you multiply 10 by itself 4 times, which gives you 10,000. Then divide that value into 1.

negative powers

In case you've forgotten, here's an example of how a negative power is calculated:

$2^{-3} = .125$

that is,

1 / (2 * 2 * 2) = .125

Understanding powers of numbers becomes very handy as you start to learn more about numbering systems.

counting things

When it comes right down to it, numbers are used to count things. Whether someone is dealing with money or miles, numbers are used to count how many things are represented. Whether negative, positive, whole numbers, or fractions, numbers are used to count. If your tuition was $2395, that indicates that it cost you two thousand, three hundred and ninety-five dollar units to attend school. You should be accustomed to that unit of measurement by now. But what does it mean? In elementary school you learned that $2395 really was 2 thousands plus 3 hundreds plus 9 tens and 5 ones. Right? But what does it *really* mean? The number 2395 really means $(2 * 10^3) + (3 * 10^2) + (9 * 10^1) + (5 * 10^0)$.

who's on base?

The base of a numbering system is the number of digits in that system.

Base 10 (decimal) has 10 digits, 0–9.

Base 2 (binary) has 2 digits, 0 and 1.

Base 16 (hexadecimal) has 16 digits, 0–F.

You are accustomed to counting in the decimal, or base 10, numbering system. You can also count in other numbering systems or bases. The computer uses a numbering base of 2, which is called ***binary***. That means that unlike base 10, which has 10 unique digits: 0, 1, 2, 3, 4, 5, 6, 7, 8, and 9, base 2 only has 2 unique digits, 0 and 1. Hexadecimal has 16 digits: 0, 1, 2, 3, 4, 5, 6, 7, 8, 9, A, B, C, D, E, and F. A base is identified by the number of digits a numbering system has, including zero.

When you count in base 10, you start with zero and count up to 9. Since there aren't any more digits after 9 you have to put a 1 in the tens column and then go back to 0 in the ones column. Again, this is something that you've been doing for years without even thinking about it.

binary – Numbering system with two digits, 0 and 1; the basis for modern computer systems. Also known as base 2

```
0, 1, 2, 3, 4, 5, 6, 7, 8, 9, 10, 11, 12, 13, 14, 15,
16, 17, 18, 19, 20, . . . , 99, 100
```

The process of counting in this manner is the same for any base.

In base 2 you start counting at 0 and then go to 1. When you get to 1, you have run out of digits as you did at 9 in base 10. So, you put a 1 in the twos column and go back to 0 in the ones column. When you get to 11, you have to go to 100 as you do with a 99 in decimal.

```
0, 1, 10, 11, 100, 101, 110, 111, 1000
```

hexadecimal (hex) – Numbering system with 16 digits, 0–9 and A–F. Often used as shorthand for binary (1 hex digit = 4 binary digits). Also known as base 16

Base 16 (***hexadecimal***) has more digits than either base 2 or base 10. Counting still starts at 0 and continues in the same column until you reach the highest possible value, F. Then you put a 1 in the sixteens column and set the ones column back to 0.

```
0, 1, 2, 3, 4, 5, 6, 7, 8, 9, A, B, C, D, E, F, 10, 11,
12, . . . , FF, 100
```

The important thing is to not stress over counting in other base numbering systems. Just realize that since you already know how to count in base 10, you actually also know how to count in the others.

positional value

positional value – The numerical value that each position in a number has; the value of a position is calculated by raising the base of the number to the power of the position

radix point – The point that divides the fractional portion from the whole portion of a number; in the decimal numbering system, it is referred to as a decimal point

A key principle of numbering systems is the concept of ***positional value***. In any numbering system, each position or digit in a number has a positional value. You're familiar with the base 10 positional values of ones, tens, hundreds, thousands, ten thousands, and so on. That same concept exists in all numbering bases. The value of each position in a number (positional value) is found by raising the base of the number to the power indicated by the position. The positions of a number start with a power of 0 in the rightmost place and then increase by 1 for each additional position going left. Negative powers begin with −1 at the right of the ***radix point***. The term "radix point" is used instead of decimal point because the number may not always be in decimal. Radix is synonymous with base.

For the number 436.95, the 4 is in position two, the 3 in position one, and the 6 is in position zero. To the right of the radix point the 9 is in position −1 with the 5 in position −2.

The positional value of each digit in a number specifies what multiplier that position gives to the overall number. For example, in the decimal (base 10) number, 4321, the digit 3 is multiplied by the positional value of the position it is in, which is 100 (10^2). The rest of the digits in the number are multiplied by their respective positional values. The 4 is in the position with a value of 1000, the 2 in the tens position and the 1 in the ones position. The digit in each position is multiplied by the value of the position. Then the result from each of the multiplications are added together giving you the total number of things being counted. Figure 4–1 shows how the positional values work in base 10 numbers.

Figure 4-1, Positional values for a base 10 number.

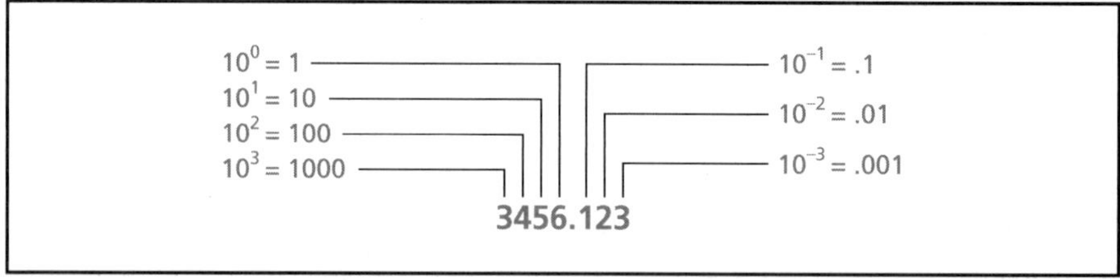

In Figure 4-1, the positional values for the number 3456.123 are shown. They are shown both as a power of 10, which is the base, and also as a number. From the figure you can see that there are 3 thousands, 4 hundreds, 5 tens, and 6 ones preceding the radix point. Following the point there is 1 tenth, 2 hundredths, and 3 thousandths.

Now consider a base 2 number such as 1011_2. (The subscripted 2 in the number 1011_2 indicates that the number is in base 2, or binary.) With binary numbers, each position also has a place value like that of base 10 numbers. Following the rule established above, the right-most position has a positional value of the base (2) raised to the 0 power. Again remember that any number raised to the 0 power has a value of 1. So, the positional value of the right-most digit is 1. The next position has a value of 2 raised to the power of 1. The next position is 2 squared and the next is 2 to the third. Figure 4–2 shows the positional values of a base 2 number.

Figure 4-2, Positional values for a base 2 number

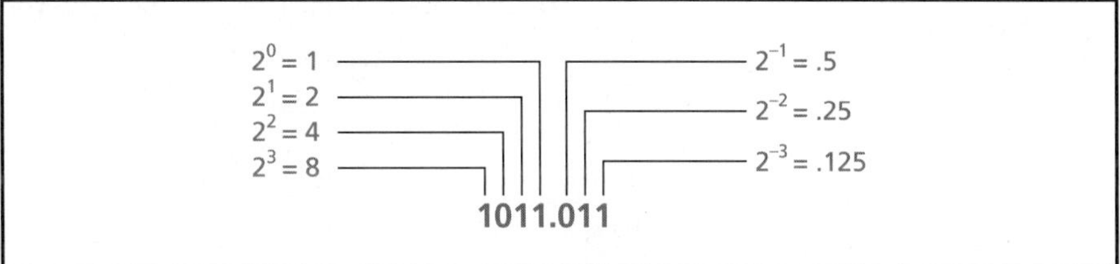

As has been demonstrated, the positional value of a number is significant because it gives the weight that each digit of the number contributes to the overall value of the number. You have probably never given this concept much thought as you have dealt with decimal numbers throughout your life. But as you begin to use numbers from other bases, you have to pay attention to and deal with positional values.

how many things does a number represent?

Positional values are used to calculate how many of something a given number represents. The process is to multiply each digit of the number by its positional value and then add all of those values together. So, the number 1001_2 is equivalent to nine things. The number 9 is calculated by taking $(1 * 2^0) + (0 * 2^1) + (0 * 2^2) + (1 * 2^3)$.

With a little practice you should begin to be comfortable evaluating numbers in any base using the following steps:

1. Calculate the value for each position of the number by raising the base value to the power of the position.
2. Multiply the positional value by the digit in that position.
3. Add each of the calculated values together.

Now try applying these steps to a decimal, binary, and hexadecimal number.

You can start with the number, 2345_{10}. It may seem a little redundant to do it this way with a base 10 number, but it will help make more sense when calculating the other bases.

1. Calculate the value for each position of the number by raising the base value to the power of the position.

$10^0 = 1$ (remember any number to the 0 power is 1)
$10^1 = 10$ (remember any number to the 1 power is the number itself)
$10^2 = 100$
$10^3 = 1000$

2. Multiply the positional value by the digit in that position.

$1 * 5 = 5$
$10 * 4 = 40$
$100 * 3 = 300$
$1000 * 2 = 2000$

3. Add each of the calculated values together.

$5 + 40 + 300 + 2000 = 2345$

Calculating the number of things represented by a base 2 number such as 10100110_2 may seem a bit more difficult, but the steps are the same as for a base 10 number.

1. Calculate the value for each position of the number by raising the base value to the power of the position.

$2^0 = 1$
$2^1 = 2$
$2^2 = 4$
$2^3 = 8$
$2^4 = 16$
$2^5 = 32$
$2^6 = 64$
$2^7 = 128$

2. Next multiply the positional value by the digit in that position.

$1 * 0 = 0$
$2 * 1 = 2$
$4 * 1 = 4$
$8 * 0 = 0$
$16 * 0 = 0$
$32 * 1 = 32$
$64 * 0 = 0$
$128 * 1 = 128$

3. Finally, add each of the calculated values together.

$0 + 2 + 4 + 0 + 0 + 32 + 0 + 128 = 166$

Performing the same process in base 16 (hexadecimal) may seem a bit more difficult because the numbers are larger, but it works exactly the same as the others. For the hex number 5678_{16}, the process goes like this:

1. Calculate the value for each position of the number by raising the base value to the power of the position.

$16^0 = 1$
$16^1 = 16$
$16^2 = 256$
$16^3 = 4096$

2. Next multiply the positional value by the digit in that position.

   1 * 8 = 8
   16 * 7 = 112
   256 * 6 = 1536
   4096 * 5 = 20,480

3. Finally, add each of the calculated values together.

   8 + 112 + 1536 + 20,480 = 22,136

Remember that base 16 (hexadecimal) has digits larger than nine. Remember also that the digits beyond nine are A–F. These digits have (decimal) values of 10–15. Otherwise, the process is exactly the same as before. For the hex number $ABCD_{16}$ the process goes like this:

1. Calculate the value for each position of the number by raising the base value to the power of the position.

   $16^0 = 1$
   $16^1 = 16$
   $16^2 = 256$
   $16^3 = 4096$

2. Next multiply the positional value by the digit in that position.

   1 * D (13) = 13
   16 * C (12) = 192
   256 * B (11) = 2816
   4096 * A (10) = 40,960

3. Finally, add each of the calculated values together.

   13 + 192 + 2816 + 40,960 = 43,981

converting numbers between bases

Since all numbering system bases are just a way of counting things, it stands to reason that for any quantity, there is a number in any base to represent it. Table 4-1 illustrates how quantities from 0 to 20 are represented in bases 2, 10, and 16. Also note that as you're counting, when you reach the highest digit for a base, you must add 1 to the next higher position to the left and return to 0 in the position you're working with. The base 2 counting starts with 0 then goes to 1. Because there are no more digits to work with in base 2, you add a 1 to the column to the left and return to 0. There wasn't already a value in the column to the left, so in effect you added 1 to 0 to get the next value, 10. Base 10 runs out of digits at 9 and doesn't need to go to 10 until then. Base 16 doesn't run out of digits until F. When F is reached, the next value is 10.

Table 4-1, Counting in different bases

base 10	base 2	base 16
0	0	0
1	1	1
2	10	2
3	11	3
4	100	4
5	101	5
6	110	6
7	111	7
8	1000	8
9	1001	9
10	1010	A
11	1011	B
12	1100	C
13	1101	D
14	1110	E
15	1111	F
16	10000	10
17	10001	11
18	10010	12
19	10011	13
20	10100	14

If you created a giant counting table that went from zero to a really big number, you could convert numbers from one base to another by looking up the number in the column for one base and looking across to find its counterpart in another column. But no one wants to carry around a really big book containing a really big table. Fortunately there's an easier way. You can use some simple mathematics to convert from one base to another.

converting to base 10

Converting to base 10 from any other base follows the same process you learned in the last section. This process makes use of what you have learned about the positional value of numbers.

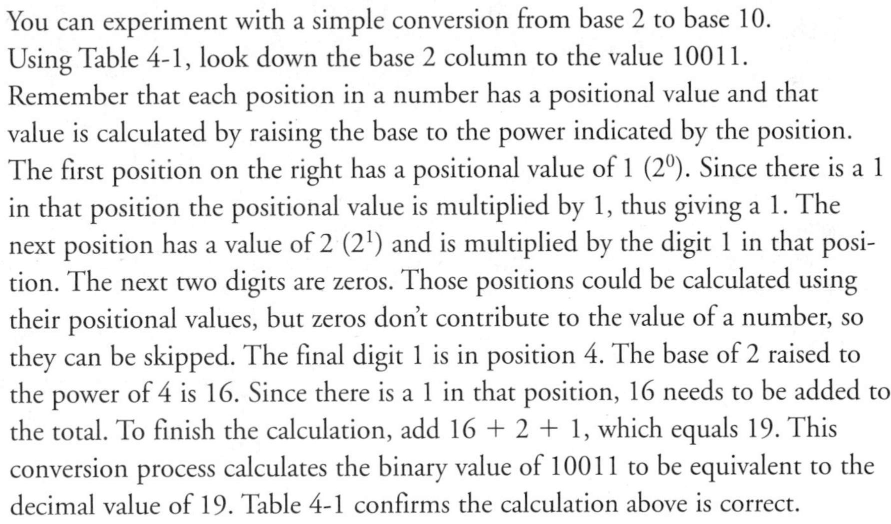

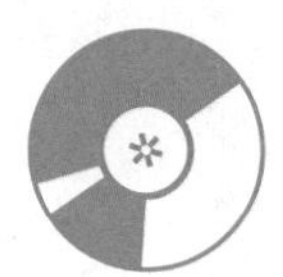

For a visual walk-through of converting between number bases, check out the learning tools section under Chapter 4 on the student CD.

You can experiment with a simple conversion from base 2 to base 10. Using Table 4-1, look down the base 2 column to the value 10011. Remember that each position in a number has a positional value and that value is calculated by raising the base to the power indicated by the position. The first position on the right has a positional value of 1 (2^0). Since there is a 1 in that position the positional value is multiplied by 1, thus giving a 1. The next position has a value of 2 (2^1) and is multiplied by the digit 1 in that position. The next two digits are zeros. Those positions could be calculated using their positional values, but zeros don't contribute to the value of a number, so they can be skipped. The final digit 1 is in position 4. The base of 2 raised to the power of 4 is 16. Since there is a 1 in that position, 16 needs to be added to the total. To finish the calculation, add 16 + 2 + 1, which equals 19. This conversion process calculates the binary value of 10011 to be equivalent to the decimal value of 19. Table 4-1 confirms the calculation above is correct.

Converting base 16 (hexadecimal) to base 10 follows the same process. (Note that hexadecimal has 16 possible digits, 0–F.) The alphabetic letters A–F are still part of the normal alphabet, but they're also used in hexadecimal to represent the numeric values above 9.

To convert the hexadecimal value 13_{16} to its decimal counterpart, multiply the digit in each position by its positional value, and add the results together. The first digit on the right is a 3 and is in position 0. Since position 0 always has a value of 1 in any base (16^0), the 3 in that position is multiplied by 1 resulting in 3. The next digit to the left, 1, is in position 1. Raising the base 16 to the power of 1 gives 16. Multiply the positional value of 16 by the digit in that position (16 * 1 = 16). Adding the calculated values for each position (16+3) results in 19. See Table 4-1 to verify your answer.

Although larger numbers result in larger total values, the process is the same. Converting from any base to decimal always follow the steps given above.

converting from base 10

Converting from base 10 to any other base is nearly as simple, but it follows a different process. To convert from decimal to another base, you can use the following steps:

1. Divide the decimal number by the number of the base to which you're converting.

2. Write down the remainder.
3. Divide the whole number result of the prior division by the base again.
4. Write the remainder to the left of the last remainder written.
5. Repeat Steps 3 and 4 until the whole number result is 0.

For a step-by-step tutorial on number conversion, try the tutorials section under Chapter 4 on the student CD.

After completing the steps above, you will have written down the equivalent number to the base 10 number.

Try this example. The decimal number 19 can be converted to the hexadecimal counterpart using the outlined steps.

1. 19 / 16 = 1 with a remainder of 3 (write down 3).
2. 1 / 16 = 0 with a remainder of 1 (write down 1 to the left of the 3 so that you have 13).
3. The whole number result of the last division was 0, so the process is stopped.
4. The decimal value 19 therefore has a hexadecimal equivalent of 13.

Converting the decimal 19 to binary works the same way, except you have a few more divisions to do.

1. 19 / 2 = 9 with a remainder of 1(write down 1)
2. 9 / 2 = 4 with a remainder of 1 (write down 1 to the left of the first 1)
3. 4 / 2 = 2 with a remainder of 0 (write it to the left of the second 1)
4. 2 / 2 = 1 with a remainder of 0 (write it left of the previous 0)
5. 1 / 2 = 0 with a remainder of 1 (continue by writing it to the left)
6. The whole number result of the last division was 0, so the process is stopped.
7. The decimal value of 19 therefore has a binary equivalent of 10011.

Working through a few more of these conversions can help you to be comfortable with them. It's important that you know how it works. Of course, you can always use a calculator that converts from one base to another. Many calculators have the ability to convert between bases.

note

The calculator built into Windows (Start, [All] Programs, Accessories) has the ability to convert between hex, binary, and decimal. Try a few examples manually and then use the Windows calculator to check your work. Make sure the calculator is in the Scientific view.

binary and hexadecimal math

Adding decimal numbers together is easy for most people. You have been adding and subtracting decimal numbers for most of your life. You probably haven't given much thought to exactly what you were doing, though. Try adding the decimal numbers 685 and 925. Did you get a result of 1610? What process did you go through to get that result? The process is important because you use the same process for any base.

You started by adding the right-most digits of the number together (5 + 5 = 10). Because 10 is larger than 9, you put a 0 in that position and carried the 10 as a 1 to the next position. Then you added the carried 1 to the 8 and 2 as the next values from the numbers you were adding. Adding 8 + 2 + 1 results in 11, so again a 10 was carried as a 1 to the next position to the left. Finally 6 and 9 were added to the carried 1, resulting in 16. The 6 was placed in that position and the 10 carried as 1 to the next position. The result of the process was the number 1610.

Adding numbers in other bases follows nearly the same steps as in adding decimal numbers. The only difference is the carry process. In decimal, you carry ten to the next column. What you are actually doing is carrying the base to the next column. So, when you add numbers in other bases you still carry the base to the next column.

Look at Figure 4-3 for an example of how two binary numbers are added together using the process described above. Note that in binary, 1 + 1 doesn't equal 2. In binary, there isn't a digit 2, so 1 + 1 equals 10.

Figure 4-3, Adding numbers in binary

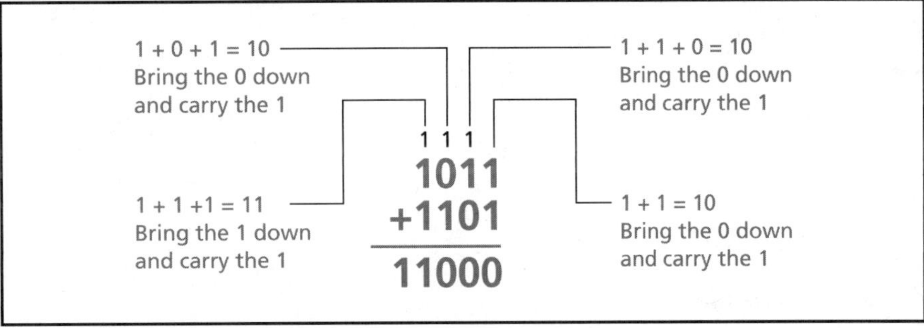

Subtraction in other bases also follows the same process as is used in subtracting base 10 numbers. When the top number is smaller than the bottom, you borrow an amount equal to the base from the column to the left. In decimal you borrow 10s. In binary you borrow 2s. Borrowing from the column to the left reduces it by 1. Figure 4-4 shows an example of subtraction using base 2 numbers.

Figure 4-4, Subtraction using base 2 numbers

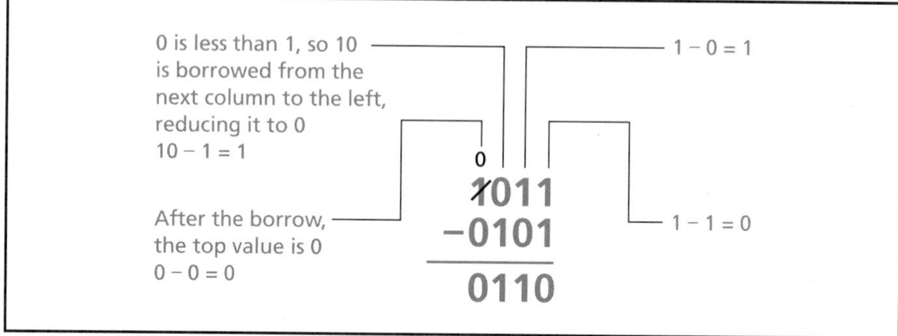

Although it is beyond the scope of this text, you can also multiply and divide in any base in a manner very similar to what you do with decimal numbers.

bit – The abbreviation for a binary digit; a bit is either a one or a zero, and is the smallest unit of representation in a common computer system

byte – A group of eight bits that are considered as one unit and is used as the basic unit of measurement in a computer system; memory is measured in the number of bytes the computer has

word – A group of bits in a computer system; the number of bits in a word is machine dependent, although common word sizes are 16, 32, and 64 bits; a typical computer system manipulates bits in word increments

nibble – A term sometimes used to refer to four bits

data representation in binary

Remember, computers are only capable of storing binary information. The transistors that make up the computer can only exist in either of two states, on or off. This means that everything that takes place in the computer and everything that is stored in the computer has to be stored as base 2 values. Thus, an understanding of binary is necessary to examine and analyze the contents of memory, hard disk data, or Internet packets.

Each of the ones and zeros (ons and offs) in the computer are referred to as ***bits*** (*b*inary dig*its*). A ***byte*** is a grouping of eight bits. Individual computer systems have larger groupings that are referred to as ***words***. Half of a byte is four bits and is sometimes referred to as a ***nibble***. This term was no doubt invented by a very comedic computer scientist.

Humans have a very difficult time dealing with the large binary numbers that computers use. To make it easier, computer scientists sometimes use hexadecimal as a shorthand method to represent binary values. Each hexadecimal digit relates directly to a 4-bit binary pattern. Therefore, a long binary value can be represented by hexadecimal equivalent using one-fourth as many digits. For example, the binary number 1111101011001110 is equivalent to the hexadecimal number,

FACE. Test it out for yourself by taking the binary number and grouping the individual bits into groups of four, beginning on the right. The groups are 1111, 1010, 1100 and 1110. Then look in Table 4-1 to get the hexadecimal counterpart to each 4-bit binary number. When separating these binary digits into groups of four, it is absolutely essential to begin grouping on the right. Grouping from the left gives you an erroneous value if the number of binary digits is not an even multiple of four.

4

note

Each hexadecimal digit corresponds to a 4-bit binary pattern. Table 4-1 shows the relationship between hex and binary.

You can also create an equivalent binary number for a hexadecimal value by taking each of the hexadecimal digits and replacing it with the 4-bit counterpart for that hexadecimal digit. The hex value C2D4 is equivalent to the binary value 1100001011010100. Again, you can use Table 4-1 to do this conversion.

Now you should begin to understand some of what is displayed in blue screen errors and other messages. The error message shown at the beginning of this chapter contains hexadecimal values that represent the actual binary information stored in the computer at the time the error occurred. Computer programmers can use the information displayed to pinpoint the exact location of the error.

Everything that's stored in or displayed on a computer is in binary. The next time you play a game on your computer, you might ponder the fact that everything you're seeing—and even everything the computer is doing that you don't see—is the result of little transistors turning on and off to form binary bit patterns. Or, you might concentrate on the game so you can win.

representing whole numbers

whole (integer) numbers – A number (positive, zero, or negative) that has no fractional portion; also referred to as an integer number

Whole numbers, or ***integer numbers***, can be represented internally in the computer as a simple binary integer similar to the ones you worked with earlier in the chapter. These whole numbers are always stored in a fixed number of bits. For example, the year 2004 might be stored in the computer as a 16-bit integer value of 0000011111010100. This binary value is displayed as the equivalent hex value of 07D4.

There are also negative numbers that need to be represented in the computer. The binary numbering system only contains the value of the number, or its magnitude. It doesn't contain the sign of the number. So techniques need to be devised to allow for the storage of both the sign and the magnitude of a number. Various ways of storing signed numbers in binary have been devised, but the most commonly used is a method referred to as "two's complement." In this

two's complement – A method of representing negative numbers in a computer system; a binary number is converted to two's complement format by flipping, or reversing the state of each bit and then adding 1 to the entire word

method the left-most bit of the binary number is reserved as a sign bit to indicate the sign of the number. Zero is used to indicate positive and 1 indicates that the number is negative. The remaining bits are used to store the absolute value, or magnitude of the number. ***Two's complement*** involves a process of starting with a number and then performing a conversion on the binary digits if the number is negative. If the number is positive, then it is left as is.

The process of performing a two's complement operation on a number to store it as a negative value takes place in the following manner. The number is first converted from decimal to binary as described earlier in the chapter. Then, each of the bits of the number are reversed or flipped to the opposite state. Finally, a binary 1 is added to the complete binary number.

Your checkbook might have a negative balance of $124. In a 16-bit signed integer field, this is represented as 1111111110000100_2 ($FF84_{16}$). This value is arrived at through the following process:

1. Convert the decimal value 124 to binary

   124_{10} = 1111100

2. Place it into a fixed length field of 16 bits, extending leading zeros to the left

   0000000001111100

3. Then the bits are flipped or reversed

   1111111110000011

4. Then a 1 is added to the entire number using binary addition

   1111111110000100

The final result containing the two's complement, negative binary number can also be represented in hex as FF84.

Figure 4-5 shows the process of converting both positive and negative numbers to the two's complement format.

Figure 4-5, Storing numbers in a two's complement, 8-bit field

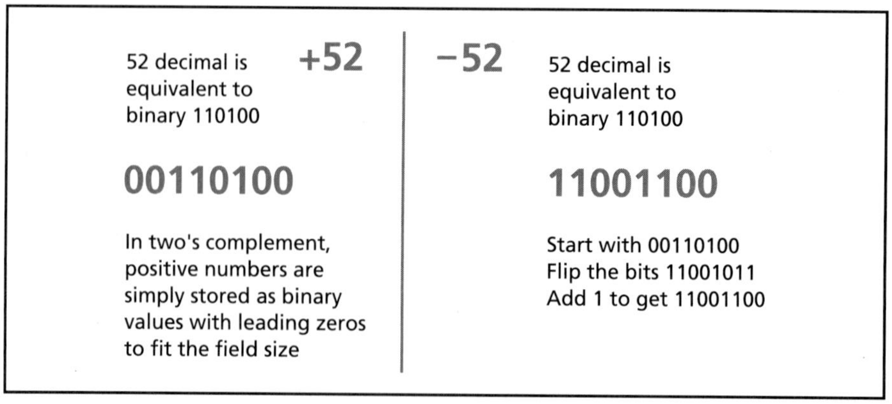

+52	−52
52 decimal is equivalent to binary 110100	52 decimal is equivalent to binary 110100
00110100	**11001100**
In two's complement, positive numbers are simply stored as binary values with leading zeros to fit the field size	Start with 00110100 Flip the bits 11001011 Add 1 to get 11001100

Computers distinguish between signed binary numbers and unsigned binary numbers. They do so by examining the first bit of the number. If the first bit is a 1, the number is treated as a two's complement negative number. If there is a 0 in the first bit, the number is positive and is left as it is.

To ensure that the sign of the number is always in the first bit, both signed and unsigned numbers in the computer are designed to always take up the same number of bits. Having a 32-bit, signed integer field indicates that a positive or negative number stored in that field always has 31 bits with the sign being in the remaining bit. Positive numbers have leading zeros to fill the 31 bits. Negative numbers have leading zeros prior to the two's complement process.

Note that having a fixed number of bits reserved to hold a number also limits the maximum value that can be represented by the number. A number placed in a 32-bit field cannot exceed the binary value that can be represented by the 31 available bits.

representing fractional numbers

Institute of Electrical and Electronics Engineers (IEEE) – An organization involved in the formulation of networking and electronics standards

mantissa – In scientific notation, the mantissa contains the actual digits of the number and is placed before the exponent

exponent – In scientific notation, the exponent is the power of the base that is multiplied by the mantissa to give the actual number

floating point or scientific notation – A method of representing numbers that have fractional values in a consistent manner; the numbers are represented as a mantissa and an exponent, such as 3.144543E+8

In the real world, numbers other than whole integer numbers need to be represented. The amount in your bank account, as small as it might be, is stored in a computer somewhere. When you're standing at the ATM looking at that $1.53 balance, think how the computer might store the 53 cents. You've learned how the computer stores integers, both positive and negative. How does it store fractional portions of numbers? How does it store the numbers to the right of the decimal place?

Mathematically, fractional values are calculated as shown in Figures 4-1 and 4-2. In addition to positive fractional numbers, computers must also be able to store negative fractional numbers.

Computer designers were faced with the question of how to store fractional numbers years ago, and came up with a technique that has been adopted by the *Institute of Electrical and Electronics Engineers (IEEE)*.

You may already be familiar with *floating point*, or *scientific notation* of numbers. You might have seen a number such as 1.345E+5 on a calculator display. This method of displaying numbers uses a *mantissa* and an *exponent*. The mantissa (1.345) contains the actual digits of the number while the exponent (+5) describes where to place the decimal point. The E in base 10 notation means "ten to the power of." The number 1.345E+5 indicates that the actual number is 134,500.

IEEE-754 – A standard for the binary representation of floating-point numbers; it is the 754th standard proposed by the IEEE

The ***IEEE-754*** specification, which dictates how floating-point numbers are stored in most Intel-based computers, uses binary mantissas and exponents. The details of the IEEE-754 specification and other floating-point storage techniques will come later in your educational program. For now, you just need to understand that they exist and you may have to interpret them at some point in your career.

representing characters

Numbers need to be stored in such a way that they can be manipulated mathematically. In addition to numbers, computers also need to be able to store characters. Characters have no mathematical relationship between them and so the method of storing them is different than numbers.

American National Standards Institute (ANSI) – An organization that works with industry groups in the formulation and publication of standards

American Standard Code for Information Interchange (ASCII) – A standard for storing text characters in computers; the ASCII standard allows for 128 possible characters to be represented by seven bits

Early in the history of computers, the ***American National Standards Institute (ANSI)*** met to standardize the way characters would be represented in computers. This group formulated a character set coding scheme of 7-bit patterns that provided a standard way of representing characters with specific bit patterns. This scheme is called ***American Standard Code for Information Interchange (ASCII).***

Table 4-2 shows a partial listing of the ASCII character set. The ASCII character set provides for uppercase and lowercase English characters, numeric characters, punctuation, and additional special characters. It also has bit patterns set aside to represent control characters for video displays and printers. In total, ASCII provides for 128 (2^7) different characters.

Table 4-2, Sample standard ASCII characters

symbol	decimal representation	hex representation	binary representation
Space	32	20	00100000
$	36	24	00100100
1	49	31	00110001
9	57	39	00111001
A	65	41	01000001
Z	90	5A	01011010
a	97	61	01100001
z	122	7A	01111010
}	125	7D	01111101

Extended ASCII – A method for storing characters using an 8-bit code; extended ASCII is an extension of 128 characters beyond the original 7-bit ASCII code that was developed by the American National Standards Institute

As computers became more global, the need arose to support additional characters. The original ASCII specification was limited to 128, so a new code set was defined that used eight bits instead of seven. This new code was named ***Extended ASCII*** and allowed for 128 additional characters, bringing the total number of characters to 256.

Still, for language scripts such as Asian and Arabic, Extended ASCII did not allow for sufficient characters. Another group met and proposed a new standard, which they named ***Unicode***. Unicode provides for 34,168 unique characters and is compatible with ASCII. Unicode is becoming the standard method of character representation.

Unicode – The Unicode Worldwide Character Standard is a 16-bit standard for storing text or script information, and it defines 34,168 unique characters and control codes

When you are typing characters into your computer, those characters are being stored as binary patterns, either in the format of ASCII, Extended ASCII, or Unicode. All character data, such as the data contained in databases, is stored on the hard disk in this format also.

representing images

You've learned now that everything that goes on in a computer is done in binary. Video displays and printers are no exception.

If you look closely at your computer monitor you can see that what's being displayed on the computer screen is not a solid image. The images on your screen are made up of small dots of colored light. Each of these dots is referred to as a "pixel" (picture element). A ***pixel*** is the smallest unit that can be displayed on a computer monitor. Pixels are arranged in rows and columns. The number of pixels in each row and column defines the resolution of your display. A common resolution on a personal computer monitor is 1024 × 768. This resolution indicates that your monitor is displaying 768 rows with 1024 dots, or pixels on each row. As the resolution numbers get larger for a monitor, the size of each pixel gets smaller.

pixel (picture element) – The basic unit of programmable color on a computer display or in a computer image; the physical size of a pixel is dependent on the resolution of the display device

As you might have guessed by now, each pixel is stored in the computer as a binary pattern. The binary pattern contains information about the color and brightness of each pixel. This binary pattern may be eight bits and allow for up to 256 different levels of color and brightness. Or, it might be 24 bits per pixel, giving the possibility of over 16 million different colors. One common way of encoding pixel information is by assigning a value to each of the colors, red, blue, and green, with each color using eight of the 24 bits. This is referred to as ***RGB encoding***. If all of the 24 bits are ones, the pixel is displayed as a bright white. If all of the bits are zeros, the pixel is perceived as black. Values other than all zeros or all ones are perceived as a color made up of the amount of red, green, and blue specified in each of the 8-bit sections.

RGB encoding – A method of defining the color and brightness of a pixel in terms of the intensity of each of the colors: red, green, and blue

Images, such as photos, can also be stored in the computer in the same manner. When a pattern of bits is stored for each pixel or dot, these bitmap (BMP) files can be very large. A photo with 1024 × 768 resolution consists of 786,432 pixels. If each pixel uses 24 bits to store the color information, the size of the file is more than 2 million bytes (2 megabytes or MB). Large image files such as this can be a problem when sending them over the Internet. Because of this, various compression techniques have been devised to allow the same image information to be stored in a smaller file. The formats JPG, GIF, and others are examples of compressed image formats. Various techniques are used in these formats to take advantage of repeating patterns and colors and to replace the pixels that they consist of with special codes.

Moving images are stored in a similar manner. The DVDs that you watch are just a series of still images that are displayed one after another at a rate of nearly 30 images per second. Compression is essential to store and display images at that rate. Examples of video compression formats are MPEG (MPG), QuickTime (MOV) and Windows Media Video (WMV).

representing sounds

Sounds are stored in the computer in a manner very similar to images. A sound consists of a waveform that has amplitude (volume) and a frequency (pitch). The computer samples sounds at fixed intervals and each sample is assigned a binary value according to its amplitude. This process is illustrated in Figure 4-6. The number of bits used for each sample determines how many unique amplitude levels can be represented. You may have noticed on a multimedia program or in the properties for one of your audio files information about the sampling rate and size of the file. To achieve CD-quality audio, the sound must be sampled over 44,000 times a second, and each sample must be 16 bits, allowing for more than 65,000 different amplitudes.

Figure 4-6, Digital sampling of a sound wave

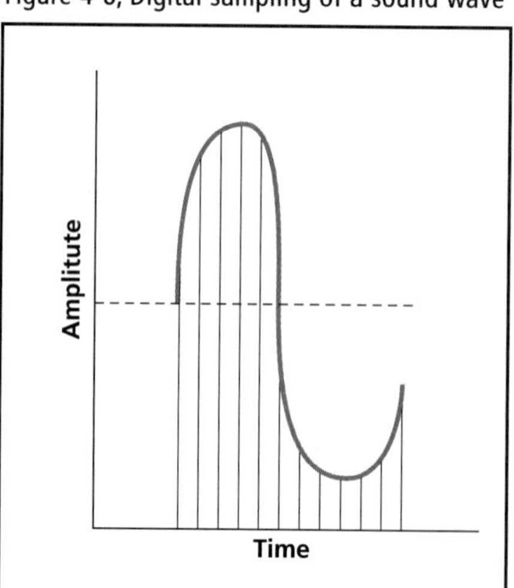

WAV – An audio file format that has become a standard for everything from PC system and game sounds to CD-quality audio

MP3 (MPEG-1 Audio Layer-3) – A standard technology and format for compressing a sound sequence into a small file as compared to an uncompressed sound file such as a WAV file

Raw audio samples are stored in files such as *WAV* files. Sound files can also be quite large and thus benefit from compression techniques such as *MP3*.

The representation of sounds and images is an evolving science. Computer scientists are constantly striving to make sound and image files smaller. It might be that you will be the one to come up with a new method of compression that will revolutionize the multimedia industry. Detailed information about each of the image and sound formats is readily available on the Internet.

one last thought

Having an understanding of number conversion and data representation is vital to excelling in the computer field. Since everything that is stored in or takes place on a computer is ultimately done in binary, someone has to be able to "talk" binary in order to create new ways of executing instructions and storing data.

Reinforce your understanding of chapter concepts and terms with the information and activities for Chapter 4 on the student CD.

Although it is possible to learn to program or to manage a database without understanding binary and hexadecimal, having this understanding will give you a depth that others without it will not have. It seems that there's always one person in an organization whom everyone else goes to for help in solving the difficult problems. That person is vital to the organization. Wouldn't you want to be that person?

chapter summary

- The powers of a number can be calculated by multiplying the base, or radix, of a number by the exponent
- Numbering systems are used to count things
- The positional value of each digit in a number can be calculated by raising the radix of the number to the position of the specific digit
- Numbers in one numbering system can be converted to any other numbering system
- Converting to and from base 10 and any other base follows a set procedure
- The hexadecimal numbering system is used as shorthand for binary values
- Whole numbers can be represented in binary using either signed or unsigned techniques
- Fractional numbers can also be represented using binary
- Binary values can also be made to represent characters, images, and sounds

key terms

American National Standards Institute (ANSI) (144)

American Standard Code for Information Interchange (ASCII) (144)

binary (131)

bit (140)

byte (140)

exponent (143)

Extended ASCII (145)

floating point notation (143)

hexadecimal (hex) (131)

Institute of Electrical and Electronics Engineers (IEEE) (143)

IEEE-754 (144)

integer number (141)

mantissa (143)

MP3 (147)

nibble (140)

pixel (145)

positional value (132)

radix point (132)

RGB encoding (145)

scientific notation (143)

two's complement (142)

Unicode (145)

WAV (147)

whole number (141)

word (140)

test yourself

1. What does the subscript 10 indicate in the number 3456_{10}?
2. What does the superscript 10 indicate in the number 2^{10}?
3. What is the value of 2^8?
4. What is the positional value of the first digit on the left of the binary number 10110?
5. What is the largest number of items that can be represented with four binary bits?
6. What is the positional value of the A in the hexadecimal number CAFE?
7. What numeric value in base 10 does the binary number 10101010 represent?
8. What is the binary equivalent of the decimal number 345?
9. What base 10 value is equivalent to $1C4B_{16}$?
10. What hexadecimal value is equivalent to 2576_{10}?
11. What numeric value in hexadecimal is equivalent to the binary number 1011111010101101?
12. What binary value is equivalent to the hex number C43A?
13. What is the binary result of adding the binary numbers 1001 + 1111?
14. What is the two's complement value of the binary number 01110110?
15. How many unique characters does extended ASCII allow?
16. How many pixels is a computer monitor with a resolution of 1024×768 capable of displaying?
17. What is the ASCII code (in hex) for the capital letter A?
18. How many different colors can be represented with a 24-bit pixel?
19. Which of these image formats—BMP, JPG, GIF—is not compressed?
20. Any number, raised to the zero power returns a value of what?

practice exercises

1. What does the subscript 16 indicate in the number $C4A6_{16}$?
   - **a.** An exponent of 16
   - **b.** A positional value of 16
   - **c.** The number is a base 16 number
   - **d.** None of the above
2. What does the superscript 3 indicate in the number 16^3?
   - **a.** An exponent of 3
   - **b.** A positional value of 3
   - **c.** The number is a base 3 number
   - **d.** None of the above
3. What is the value of 16^3?
   - **a.** 163
   - **b.** 48
   - **c.** 4096
   - **d.** 256
4. What is the positional value of the 1 in the binary number 100000?
   - **a.** 64
   - **b.** 32
   - **c.** 16
   - **d.** 8
5. What is the largest number of items that can be represented with four hexadecimal digits?
   - **a.** 4096
   - **b.** 40960
   - **c.** 65536
   - **d.** None of the above
6. What is the positional value of the A in the hexadecimal number BEAD?
   - **a.** 2
   - **b.** 10
   - **c.** 16
   - **d.** 32
7. What numeric value in base 10 does the binary number 10000001 represent?
   - **a.** 129
   - **b.** 10,000,001
   - **c.** 65
   - **d.** None of the above

8. What is the binary equivalent of the decimal number 543?

a. 11111011110111
b. 101100111
c. 1011010011
d. 1000011111

9. What base 10 value is equivalent to $3C0D_{16}$?

a. 15,373
b. 32,767
c. 68,536
d. 10,125

10. What hexadecimal value is equivalent to 1234_{10}?

a. ABC
b. 4D2
c. C34
d. A65

11. What numeric value in hexadecimal is equivalent to the binary number 1101111010101101?

a. BCAF
b. BE6C
c. 6FAD
d. DEAD

12. What binary value is equivalent to the hex number C43A?

a. 1100100100010110
b. 1100110101111010
c. 1100010000111010
d. 1100001101011101

13. What is the binary result of adding the binary numbers 0110 + 1101?

a. 10011
b. 1111
c. 01101101
d. 101001

14. What is the two's complement value of the binary number 010100110?

a. 101011001
b. 101011010
c. 010100111
d. None of the above

15. How many unique characters does ASCII allow?

a. 16
b. 32
c. 128
d. 255

16. How many total bits are required to store 24-bit color information for a 1024 × 768 display?

    a. 18,874,368
    b. 786,432
    c. 1024
    d. 24

17. What is the ASCII code (in hex) for the lowercase letter "z"?

    a. 7A
    b. 80
    c. 32
    d. AB

18. What is the minimum number of bits required to represent 256 colors in a pixel?

    a. 4
    b. 8
    c. 16
    d. 32

19. What color is represented if the pixel bits are all ones?

    a. Red
    b. Black
    c. Cyan
    d. White

20. Any number raised to the power of 1 is what?

    a. 1
    b. The positional value times the digit
    c. The number itself
    d. None of the above

digging deeper

1. Can all numbering system bases be used as shorthand for binary? If not all bases, then which bases can?
2. What other image formats are there? What are the strengths and weaknesses of each?
3. How would you calculate the value of a number with a fractional power?
4. What are some alternative methods of converting from base 10 to other numbering system bases?
5. What is the purpose of the ASCII codes from 0_{10} to 26_{10}?

discussion topics

1. What would be the implications for computing if a transistor-type device could be created with 10 stable states?
2. In working with computers, what types of situations require knowledge of numbering systems?
3. What types of compression techniques can be used to make images and sounds smaller?
4. What are the word sizes of the major computers? What is the significance of a word size?
5. How can a Hex Editor be used to examine the contents of memory and disks?

Internet research

1. Where are standards, such as IEEE-754, available for downloading or printing on the Internet?
2. What is the history of numbering systems?
3. What are some examples of Web pages and downloadable programs that can convert between the various forms of data representation and numbering systems?
4. What are the advantages and disadvantages of each of the different image and sound formats listed in the text?
5. What do the hexadecimal values represent in a typical "blue screen" fatal error message?

5

chapter

operating systems

in this chapter you will:

- Learn what an operating system is
- Become familiar with the different types of operating systems
- Identify the major functions of an operating system
- Understand how operating systems manage processes
- Understand how operating systems manage resources
- Understand how operating systems provide security
- Learn how to perform basic operating system file management functions in Windows, UNIX, and DOS

the lighter side of the lab
by spencer

My first car was a 1982 Toyota Tercel. It was a lovely two-tone color. (The first tone was the original tan, and the second tone was added to the driver-side door when I got in a wreck a week after I got my license.)

There wasn't any A/C in the car. If I wanted to turn up the heat in the winter, I had to crawl underneath the dash and pry the lever over with a screwdriver. The horn only worked if the steering wheel was turned at a certain angle. For much of the time I was driving the car, I had to make sure to park it on a hill so I could pop the clutch to start it.

But that little car ran and ran and ran. When I finally sold it, it had well over 200,000 miles. To my surprise, I saw it drive past at an intersection a few years later. (I'd recognize that custom paint job anywhere.) I was so impressed with the reliability of that car that, when the time came, I decided to buy another Toyota.

Which brand of car to purchase is no joking matter for many people. The rivalry between Ford fans and Chevy fans gets pretty heated! But when I got into the CS department, I realized that the Ford/Chevy rivalry is nothing compared to the Windows/UNIX rivalry.

I personally believe there is a simple solution to settle the debate between UNIX and Windows once and for all: Let's get the two in the ring. It would be a good fight. UNIX takes a lot more time to "train for the fight," while Windows is ready to "jump into the ring." On the other hand, Windows demands a much heftier prize for fighting than UNIX. (Then again, you have to pay the "trainers" to fix UNIX when its "arms and legs" fall off.)

But as the UNIX "trainers" will tell you, once you get the "arms and legs reattached," UNIX can "go all 15 rounds." Windows starts quickly, but tends to "freeze in fear" (most often when I'm working on a major assignment due the next day.)

I'm not sure who will come out on top in the end. But I think there is one thing that we can all agree on: it's a good thing that computers don't have ears or teeth, because the fight could get messy.

why you need to know about...
operating systems

Just try to run a program on a computer without an operating system. See if you can save a file without an operating system. Try to print a file without using an operating system. In fact, try to do anything on a computer that doesn't have an operating system. As they say in the movies, "It just ain't gonna happen!"

Operating systems are essential to the operation of the modern computer. Everything that takes place on a computer goes through, uses, or gets permission from the operating system. Inside the computer, the operating system is king. Outside the computer, you can be king—if you know how to control the operating system. This chapter will help you to understand what an operating system is, what it does, and how it works. This chapter also explains how to perform some basic folder and file functions in Windows, UNIX, and DOS, the major operating systems in use today. Armed with a better understanding of what the operating system is doing and how it works, you and your computer can be much more efficient. If you learn how to use operating systems now, everything else becomes much easier as you can concentrate on the new material in future courses and not have to spend time trying to find your files. Your professors have heard the "I lost my file" story many times and are not very impressed by it.

what is an operating system?

operating system (OS) – The program on a computer system responsible for managing the user interface, system resources, and processes

An *operating system (OS)* is the software "control center" of the modern computer system. The operating system is the first program loaded into memory when the computer is started up (booted). The OS then remains resident in memory to load and supervise all other programs that execute on the computer. Both people and application software interface with the CPU and I/O devices through the OS (Figure 5-1).

how does a computer boot?

The process of starting up a computer system is most commonly referred to as ***booting*** the system. The term "boot" comes from the idea of using bootstraps to pull on boots. Each computer comes hardwired with a small program called a bootstrap loader that checks the status of all of the hardware devices of the computer, then goes to a storage device, and loads the OS into memory so that it can be executed. The process of checking the hardware is called the ***POST***, which stands for power-on self test. You have probably watched the lights flash, and messages displayed on the monitor as the POST was performed when you booted your computer.

Figure 5-1, An operating system provides an interface between the user, applications, and hardware

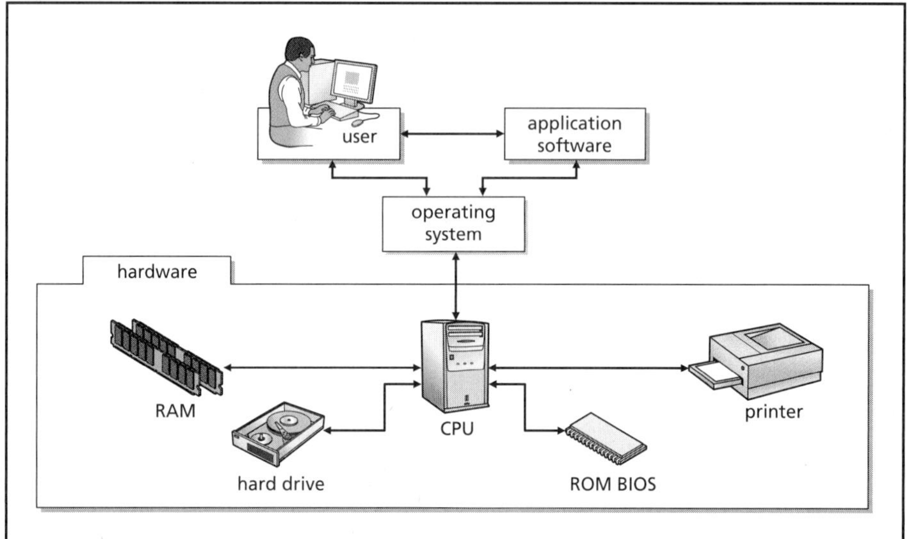

booting – The process of starting up a computer system

POST – power-on self test; a procedure performed by the computer boot routine

driver – A special program designed to provide an interface to a specific I/O device

The OS provides a way for application programs, such as a word processor or Web browser, to interact with the computer hardware. The OS also contains special interfaces that allow the computer to interact with peripheral devices. These interface programs are called ***drivers***, short for device drivers. For example, when you click the Print icon while working in your word processor, the word-processing application signals the operating system that a document needs to be sent to the printer. The operating system then communicates the document data to the device driver for the printer, and the device driver controls the printer as it prints out your document.

note **Many problems on a computer are caused by outdated device drivers, especially video drivers. Check the Web site of your device's manufacturer for updated drivers. These updates can be freely downloaded and installed.**

Operating systems come with the ability to connect with standard default devices such as the keyboard and screen. For most other I/O devices, such as printers, scanners, or cameras, device drivers must be installed. These drivers are often written by the manufacturers of the devices. Although they usually ship with the I/O device, it's always a good idea to check the manufacturer's Internet site for an updated driver. Many problems can be avoided by downloading and installing the most current driver for a device.

before the OS

Early computers didn't have operating systems. The desired program had to be entered bit by bit, using switches on a front panel. The program was the only thing running on the computer and would remain in memory only as long as the computer had power.

***kernel* – The core of an operating system that controls processor, disk, memory, and other central functions**

An operating system is just a computer program, although it is a very important one. Operating systems, as with other programs, are written in programming languages such as Assembler, C, and C++. Operating systems generally consist of two parts, the core program (called the ***kernel***) and various other system programs that serve to support and extend the kernel (Figure 5-2). The kernel is the basis of the OS. It is a relatively small program that is loaded first and remains in memory for the entire time the computer is on. The program responsible for loading the kernel is contained in the BIOS chip located on the motherboard of the computer. When power is turned on, the CPU begins executing the instructions located in the BIOS chip. These instructions perform the power-on self test (POST) and then load the kernel of the operating system from the boot device specified in the CMOS RAM. Once the kernel is loaded into memory, the BIOS program transfers control to the kernel.

The BIOS and CMOS are also described in Chapter 3, "Computer Architecture."

Figure 5-2, Various components support the operating system kernel

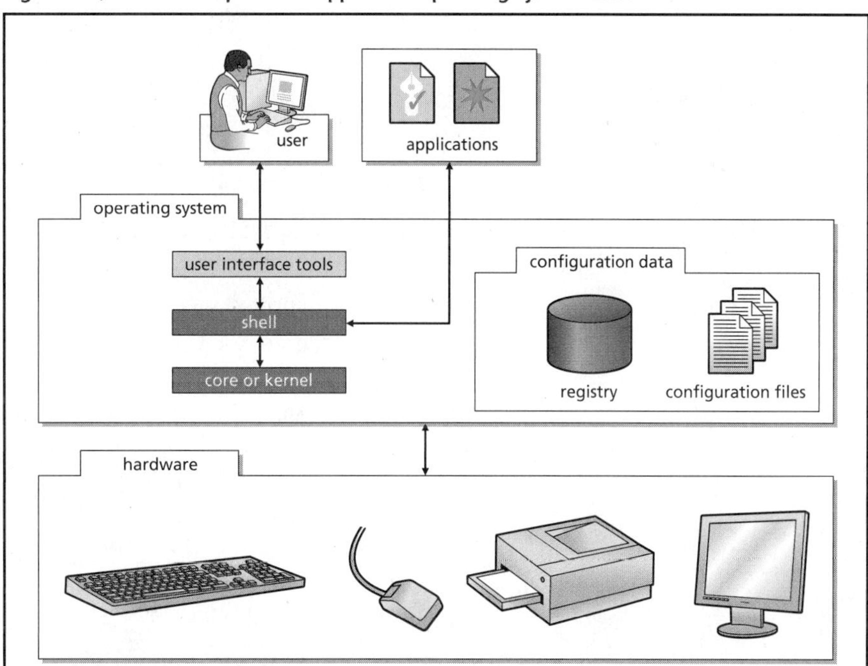

Windows – A popular Microsoft GUI operating system for Intel-based processors

DOS – disk operating system; a single-user, single-tasking, command-line operating system that was the Microsoft predecessor to Windows

Linux – A multitasking, multiuser, open-source operating system patterned after the popular UNIX operating system

UNIX – A multitasking, multiuser command-line operating system that is known for its stability and reliability

The other components are called system components, or modules. The main module is the program responsible for the user interface. In Windows, this module provides the graphical desktop that you use to perform computer functions. Drivers are other modules that interface with I/O devices such as printers, monitors, and network cards. All of these modules work together to provide both the user and program with access to the CPU (central processing unit) and other connected devices.

If you have used a computer, you have used an operating system. Most operating systems are loaded on the computer's hard disk, though on smaller handheld computers and personal digital assistants (PDAs), the OS can reside on a ROM chip. Currently, Microsoft *Windows* is the most widely used operating system. Years ago, you might have used *DOS*. (Yes, the OS in DOS stands for "operating system." The "D" in DOS is for "disk," indicating that this operating system had support for disk drives, a novel feature at the time.) The company you work for now might be converting to the *Linux* or *UNIX* operating system on their Web servers. You might have used the Macintosh operating system (Mac OS) at school. Operating systems vary in style and special features, but they all perform basically the same functions. Table 5-1 shows how each of the main operating systems fits into the overall scheme of operating system development.

note

References to UNIX in this chapter also apply to Linux. Linux is an open-source operating system patterned after UNIX. Commands and features in Linux are very similar to those of UNIX.

Table 5-1, Operating system summary

operating system	approx. date	description
UNIX (Bell AT&T)	1968	First widely used multiuser, multitasking OS, initially for midrange computers
CP/M	1975	First OS that allowed business work on personal computers, with the associated VisiCalc spreadsheet software
MS-DOS	1980	First OS for the IBM PC
PC DOS	1981	IBM version of Microsoft MS-DOS
Mac OS	1984	First widely distributed OS to use a graphical user interface (GUI) and a mouse, for Apple PCs; Mac OS X is closely related to UNIX, but runs only on Apple computers

open source – Computer programs, including operating systems, that have been developed as a public collaboration and made freely available for use or modification

operating system	approx. date	description
Windows 3.x	1990	Early Microsoft Windows versions, including Windows 3.1 and Windows 3.11 (collectively referred to as Windows 3.x) provided a graphical interface to what was essentially still DOS "under the hood"
Linux	1990	An *open-source* OS, meaning that it was developed, tested, and enhanced by many people as a collaborative effort. Based on UNIX, Linux was initially developed by Finnish computer science student Linus Torvalds in 1990. Its development has expanded to include a graphical interface and many other modules. Those participating in its development make the operating system freely available to everyone, although some companies charge to package or support Linux. Because of its low cost, availability for many types of computers, and stability, Linux has become very popular in the last few years.
Windows NT	1993	Included more advanced security features, network support, and user administration features than Windows 3.x. Windows NT came in two versions: Windows NT Workstation for end-user computers and Windows NT Server to manage and maintain a network. Primarily designed for businesses and technical users, as opposed to home users.
Windows 9x	1995	The Windows 9x operating systems—Windows 95, Windows 98, and Windows Me (Millennium Edition)—rely on a DOS core, but provide a more user-friendly interface and advanced features such as automatic recognition and configuration of I/O devices (Plug and Play), more integrated Internet capabilities, and support for hardware devices such as DVDs.
Windows 2000	2000	An upgrade of Windows NT, Windows 2000 provides additional features including greater network support and increased speed and stability. There are several versions of Windows 2000: Windows 2000 Professional is popular for the corporate desktop, while Windows 2000 Server, Windows 2000 Advanced Server, and Windows 2000 Datacenter Server are network operating systems.

(continued)

Table 5-1 (*continued*)

operating system	approx. date	description
Windows XP	2001	Windows XP combined the user-friendly features of Windows 98 and Windows Me with the strengths of Windows 2000. Windows XP provides an upgraded user interface, support for multiple users, better performance, and more support for multimedia such as audio and video. Windows XP is available in three versions: Home Edition, Professional, and Tablet PC Edition.
Windows Server 2003	2003	Windows Server 2003 is a network operating system with additional features for managing and maintaining a network. It provides increased security, enhanced file and print server support, support for remote access, and more. Windows Server 2003 comes in several versions including Standard Edition, Enterprise Edition, Datacenter Edition, Web Edition, and Small Business Server 2003.
Windows "Longhorn"	2006 (exp.)	The newest version of Windows is currently code named "Longhorn." This version of Windows is a radical departure from the prior architectures, especially in the area of the file management system. Longhorn has a task-based user interface and new security enhancements.

note

Versions of Microsoft Windows are installed on over 90% of desktop computers worldwide.

platform – The operating system running on a computer

The operating system running on a computer is often called its *platform* and is typically tied to a particular CPU. Application software that runs on one platform will not run on another platform without modification. For example, the Microsoft Word application that runs on a Windows XP platform cannot run on an iMac computer running Mac OS. Applications that have been converted to run on multiple platforms are referred to as "cross-platform" applications and should run nearly identically in either OS.

types of operating systems

single-tasking – An operating system that only allows one process (task) to be running at a time

multitasking – The ability of a computer operating system to effectively support more than one process running at a time

network operating system – An operating system designed to provide strong network services

multiprocessing – The coordinated processing of a process by more than one processor at the same time

Operating systems can be classified by their features or intended uses. For example, DOS and Windows 3.*x* are considered ***single-tasking*** operating systems, meaning that only one program or task could be open at a time. Current versions of Windows and Mac OS are examples of multitasking operating systems. They are referred to as ***multitasking*** because they can service many different program tasks at a time. Most of today's operating systems are multitasking. Some operating systems, such as NetWare, UNIX, Windows 2000 Server, and Windows Server 2003 are designed as ***network operating systems***, with capabilities to configure and manage networks of computers.

Each operating system has been designed to be strong in a particular area. For example, recent versions of Microsoft Windows and Mac OS have been designed to have an easy-to-use interface and to incorporate multimedia capabilities, to appeal to home and small-business users. UNIX is designed to be very strong in the areas of multitasking, security, and ***multiprocessing*** (using more than one CPU). UNIX is known for its stability. Windows is installed on the overwhelming majority of desktops, but UNIX is often the operating system of choice in the server environment. Servers are computers that are used to service many different users, particularly in the areas of database and Internet Web servers.

running backwards?

In the world of computers it is very important that older hardware and software be compatible with newer computers. This concept is referred to as "backward compatibility" and is crucial to the success of a new operating system or CPU. Many failures in the history of personal computers can be traced to the fact that they were not backward compatible.

There are many other operating systems running on equipment such as PDAs and cell phones. In some cases, the operating system is just a scaled down version of a larger operating system. This is the case with the Windows CE operating system that is used in the Pocket PC and other compatible PDAs. Palm-compatible PDAs use an operating system called Palm OS. It's important to remember that every multipurpose device with a CPU must also have an operating system.

functions of an operating system

Although they have different features and strengths, all operating systems perform the same basic functions. For example, they provide a user interface, schedule and manage the execution of programs, manage memory, configure devices, provide file management and security, provide basic networking capability and monitor performance. The basic functions that all operating systems perform can be classified into four main categories:

- Provide a user interface
- Manage processes
- Manage resources
- Provide security

5

command-line interface – A method of communicating with the operating system by typing commands and receiving responses in plain text

graphical user interface (GUI) – A method of interacting with the operating system wherein information is displayed in a graphical format and the user can select items using a pointer object such as a mouse

command prompt – Words and symbols displayed on the monitor that indicate to the user of a command-line operating system that it is waiting for user input

provide a user interface

As a computer user, you are no doubt familiar with the first function, the user interface. The user interface is a program that provides you with the ability to communicate with the computer. Operating systems provide for input from devices such as the keyboard, mouse, touch screen, and audio.

There are two basic types of user interfaces: the *command-line interface* and the *graphical user interface (GUI)*. These are shown in Figure 5-3. DOS and UNIX use a command-line interface, and are sometimes called console operating systems. In these operating systems, users interact with the operating system by typing commands at a *command prompt*, with the output displayed as characters and numbers. Windows and Mac operating systems use a graphical user interface (GUI). Users interact with GUI operating systems via the keyboard and mouse or other pointing device by clicking icons and buttons, opening graphical windows, and making menu selections as opposed to typing in text commands.

Figure 5-3, The Windows command prompt emulates a DOS environment (top); the default GUI interface of Windows XP (bottom)

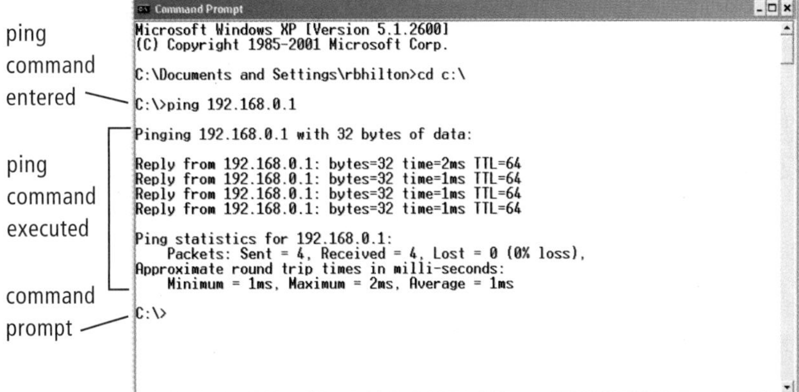

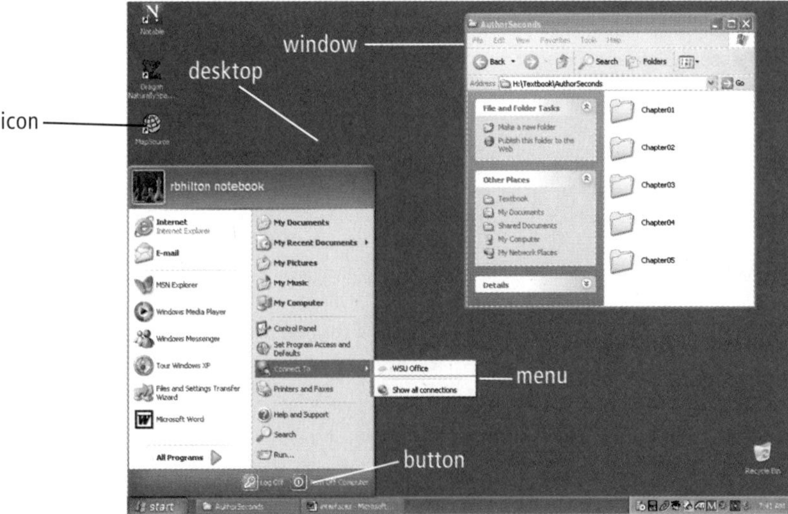

the first GUI

The graphical user interface was invented by scientists at the Xerox Corporation in 1970. It was adopted later by Apple Computer and used extensively in the Macintosh family of computers before being adopted by Microsoft for its Windows product. Now, virtually all home and business operating systems have a GUI option.

Although Windows is primarily a graphical OS, within Windows you can also access a command prompt. This command prompt is normally located in the Accessories program group. The command prompt emulates a DOS environment. DOS, the first Microsoft operating system, is a command-line operating system with no graphical interface. Graphical interfaces can be added to the UNIX operating system, but standard UNIX uses a command-line interface. To provide for backward compatibility, Windows has always included the ability to interface to the computer via the command prompt. Many classes in computers require that you have some knowledge of the command prompt interface in Windows in order to run UNIX or DOS programs and to back up your files in a console environment.

manage processes

process – A small program running on a computer that may be part of a larger program

Operating systems are responsible for loading, starting, running, and stopping processes—or programs—on the computer. Each program that you run is a *process*. Processes might then start (sometimes called spawn) other processes to support them. In Windows, for example, you can view the processes that are running by pressing the Ctrl+Alt+Del key combination to open the Task Manager window, then select the Processes tab to display information on the processes currently running. Figure 5-4 shows an example of the Windows Task Manager screen.

Figure 5-4, Windows XP Task Manager

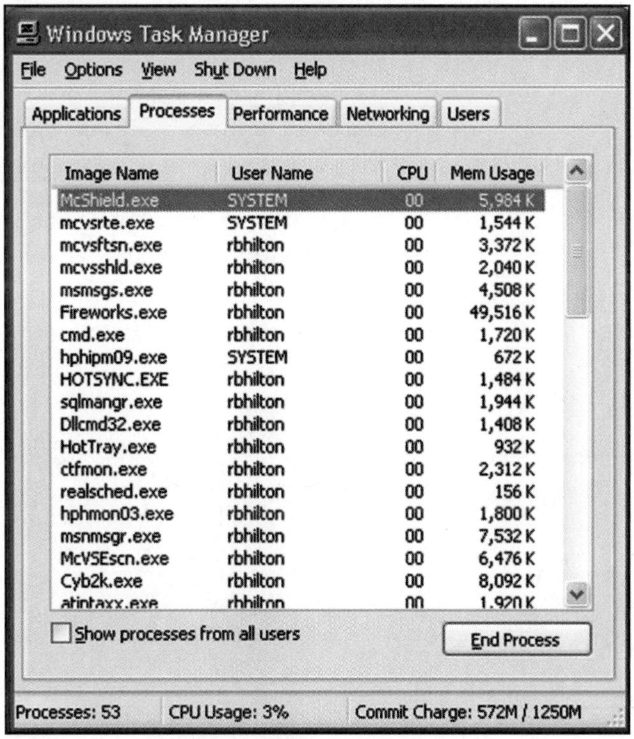

Windows Task Manager

File Options View Shut Down Help

Applications | Processes | Performance | Networking | Users

Image Name	User Name	CPU	Mem Usage
McShield.exe	SYSTEM	00	5,984 K
mcvsrte.exe	SYSTEM	00	1,544 K
mcvsftsn.exe	rbhilton	00	3,372 K
mcvsshld.exe	rbhilton	00	2,040 K
msmsgs.exe	rbhilton	00	4,508 K
Fireworks.exe	rbhilton	00	49,516 K
cmd.exe	rbhilton	00	1,720 K
hphipm09.exe	SYSTEM	00	672 K
HOTSYNC.EXE	rbhilton	00	1,484 K
sqlmangr.exe	rbhilton	00	1,944 K
Dllcmd32.exe	rbhilton	00	1,408 K
HotTray.exe	rbhilton	00	932 K
ctfmon.exe	rbhilton	00	2,312 K
realsched.exe	rbhilton	00	156 K
hphmon03.exe	rbhilton	00	1,800 K
msnmsgr.exe	rbhilton	00	7,532 K
McVSEscn.exe	rbhilton	00	6,476 K
Cyb2k.exe	rbhilton	00	8,092 K
atintaxx.exe	rbhilton	00	1,920 K

Show processes from all users

End Process

Processes: 53 | CPU Usage: 3% | Commit Charge: 572M / 1250M

The UNIX/Linux operating system has a similar function to display information on active processes. At the console prompt, you can type the command, *ps -aux* to get a list of all running processes along with resource usage information. Figure 5-5 shows an example of the output of the *ps* command. There is no command in DOS to list currently running processes because in DOS only one process can be running at a time. DOS was designed to be used by a single user, completing one task at a time. UNIX, on the other hand, was designed to accommodate multiple users and multiple tasks.

Figure 5-5, Viewing processes in UNIX using the *ps* command

```
Command Prompt - telnet icarus.weber.edu
<icarus.weber.edu>$ ps
   PID TTY        TIME CMD
 23612 pts/5      0:00 bash
 23638 pts/5      0:00 more
 23637 pts/5      0:00 sh
 23622 pts/5      0:00 man
<icarus.weber.edu>$
```

In reality, only one process can run at a time on all single CPU systems. For example, in Windows you might be listening to a CD while you are downloading a file, and at the same time using the word processor to write your term paper. If you were to run the Task Manager and look at active processes, you would probably see even more processes running than that. It would seem that you are running many processes at once; however, the computer is actually only executing one process at a time. Von Neumann architecture supports only the serial execution of instructions; during any given clock cycle, only one instruction from one single program can be executed.

The parts of a computer system, such as the CPU, memory, keyboard, monitor, and network adapter, all function at different speeds. The CPU is the fastest and can execute billions of instructions per second. Main memory is slower and can only be accessed millions of times per second. Since memory and other devices are slower than the CPU, the CPU has time to spare. It uses this spare time to execute a few instructions at a time for each of the processes running. Of course, the CPU is also much faster than the user. Consider a typist who types at 60 words per minute. In the time between each keystroke, the CPU can execute billions of instructions.

time slicing

Computers can effectively run many programs with only one process through effective time management. (College students also have to be good at time management—or at least those who want good grades *and* a social life. You have probably observed students talking on the cell phone while eating breakfast while studying for a history assignment and maybe even putting on makeup. Actually, maybe that was you.)

time slicing – A method of allocating fixed time units to processes running on a computer such that it appears to the user that all of the processes are running simultaneously

The method that allows multiple processes to share the CPU is called ***time slicing***. This is a very important responsibility of the operating system. It works by allocating small segments of CPU time to each of the processes that are running, one after another. It appears to the user that multiple processes are all running at the same time, but in reality the processor is just using its time very efficiently. Time slicing works because often the CPU is waiting for I/O devices to return information.

interrupt handling – A method of allowing processes and hardware I/O devices to interrupt the processor's normal executing in order to handle specific tasks

Time slicing, managed by the operating system, allows computers to accomplish much more work than they would otherwise, but it is a very complicated process. The operating system must be able to decide which process is ready for execution and which process is waiting for some I/O to take place. Sometimes, processes need to have CPU time immediately, such as to process special keystrokes like Ctrl+Alt+Del, which can be used in the Windows environment to view and terminate processes. Since the operating system might be allocating time to other processes when the keystrokes come in, the operating system must also give processes the ability to interrupt the CPU and jump to the head of the line of processes that are requesting CPU time. This takes place through something called ***interrupt handling***.

To see demonstrations of time slicing and interrupts, check out the learning tools section under Chapter 5 on the student CD.

Interrupts can be initiated by programs or devices. When an interrupt occurs, the CPU stops what it is doing and goes to a program in memory called an interrupt handler. There are multiple interrupt handlers in memory waiting for their number to be called. The main interrupt handler is part of the operating system and is executed when the time slice timer ticks. This interrupt routine is coded to decide which processes are ready for more execution time and which of the processes is next in the execution schedule.

manage resources

resources – Devices connected to the CPU of a computer such as main memory, hard disk, and CD-ROM drive; all running processes have to share these devices

Devices such as main memory, hard disk, and the CD-ROM drive are the computer's ***resources***. They are used by the CPU to accomplish the tasks required by the program. Each process that is running on the computer may need to access and use these resources. Therefore, another responsibility of the operating system is to manage the resources of the computer.

I/O devices have to be configured to work properly within the environment in which they are installed. Historically, the process of configuration was performed by computer users through the process of setting physical switches or jumpers or through the use of special software utilities. In 1995 a new technology was introduced with the Windows 95 operating system. This technology was referred to as ***Plug and Play (PnP)***. The goal of Plug and Play was to create a computer whose hardware and software would work together to automatically configure devices and assign resources, allowing for easier hardware changes and additions. Plug and Play has been a feature of all subsequent versions of Windows and has been implemented in other operating systems, as well.

PnP (Plug and Play) – A technology that allows the operating system and hardware to work together to automatically detect and configure I/O devices

It is theoretically possible for each of the programs or processes running on a computer to directly access I/O devices. For example, sometimes DOS-based games directly access the video card to try to improve performance. Having individual processes access I/O directly is not a good idea. Each program that directly accesses I/O devices would need to have drivers for the specific I/O devices attached to the computer. It makes much more sense to have the operating system be responsible for all interfacing with the I/O devices. That way any program could simply request the operating system to perform the I/O and only the operating system would have to be set up to recognize and interface with the I/O devices.

Managing the resources of the computer is tricky in that the operating system must assign and keep track of priorities for each of the devices and for each of the running processes. Things are made even more difficult when a process is waiting for a resource that is allocated to another process, and that second process is waiting for a resource allocated to the first. This rare situation is called ***deadlock***. Unless the operating system is able to break the deadlock, by recognizing it and releasing one of the resources, the processing ceases and the system freezes up. While deadlock rarely occurs, if the operating system didn't provide a remedy for it, the system wouldn't be able to continue processing without a reboot.

deadlock – A rare situation where I/O devices and/or processes are waiting on each other for the use of resources; this situation would continue indefinitely without intervention by the OS

manage memory

Another important function of the operating system is managing memory. All of the programs and processes running on a computer are stored in main memory, or RAM. The data for the programs is also stored there. When a user issues a command to run a program, the operating system determines the location of free space in memory and loads the program from the disk to the memory location. As processes and programs come and go, the operating system must constantly manage memory and communicate with the CPU as to where to begin executing a program.

provide security

Some of the processes running on a computer are programs that the user has initiated. Others processes are initiated by the user programs that are running on the system. Still others are part of the operating system itself. All of these processes theoretically could have access to all of memory and to all of the system resources. Problems could arise if one process wrote into the memory area of another process. Operating systems are responsible for the protection of memory and other resources. Operating systems serve as the "resource police," ensuring that resources are distributed evenly among the competing processes.

floppy disk to the rescue

Most major operating systems allow for the creation of a recovery disk. This disk can be used in the event that you cannot boot your system.

It is also dangerous to allow an unauthorized user to access programs or devices on the computer. Most computer systems contain sensitive data, and access to that data needs to be controlled. The operating system provides a means for allowing only authorized users to access programs or devices, to keep the computer and its resources secure. One way that operating systems provide security is to allow system administrators to set up user accounts that are password protected. Many operating systems also allow administrators to set up group policies. These policies are rules governing which resources a class or group of users are allowed to access. When a new user is created and attached to a group, the user automatically gains the rights and permissions of that group. The system administrator saves time by not having to list all of the individual permissions each new user will have.

using an operating system

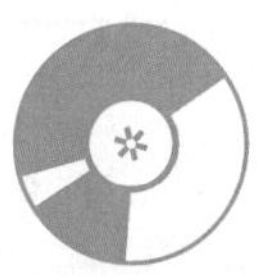

To learn how commands are typically entered in DOS, UNIX, and Windows, see the tutorials section under Chapter 5 on the student CD.

As you embark on your education and future career in the computer industry, you will have to use and interact with many different operating systems. Although it is helpful to understand how an operating system works, it may be just as important to know how to perform basic tasks you'll be required to do. Much of your interaction with the operating system will simply be starting programs and running them. At other times you will need to know how to use the operating system to manage the resources of your computer. In this section you will learn how to perform some basic file management tasks with several different operating systems.

managing disk files

From the user's point of view, one of the main functions of an operating system is to organize the files on the drives in the computer system. In order for the user to be able to manage files, the operating system needs to have a formal filing structure. Nearly all operating systems allow the user to give names to files,

folder – *Structure on a formatted disk that enables storage and organization of files; also known as directory or subdirectory*

directory – *Same as folder; folder terminology is often used in Windows, while directory/subdirectory is more often used in DOS and UNIX*

root level – *The main or base folder/directory level on a drive*

as they are stored. To better organize the files, operating systems allow you to organize files into structures called ***folders*** or ***directories***. Folders are organized into a treelike structure with a single ***root level*** and one or more branches. The files can then be viewed as leaves, or nodes on the tree structure. Figure 5-6 shows an example of the tree structure of folders and files in the Windows operating system.

Figure 5-6, Windows Explorer graphical interface for manipulating files

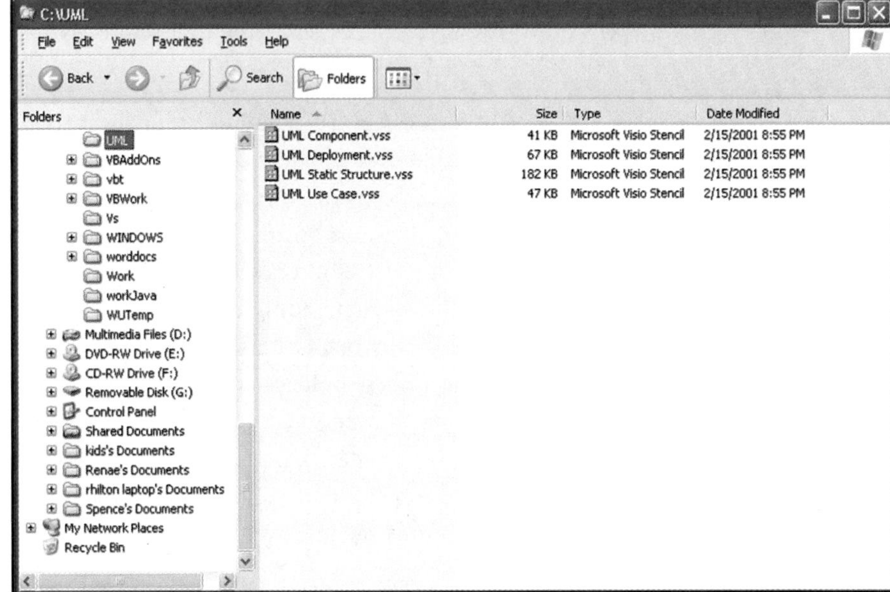

In command-line operating systems such as UNIX and DOS, a similar structure is used, but it can't be directly viewed as a tree structure and must be manipulated with operating system commands entered into the console window. Figure 5-7 shows how files and folders can be viewed by using the UNIX

Figure 5-7, UNIX command-line interface for displaying files and folders

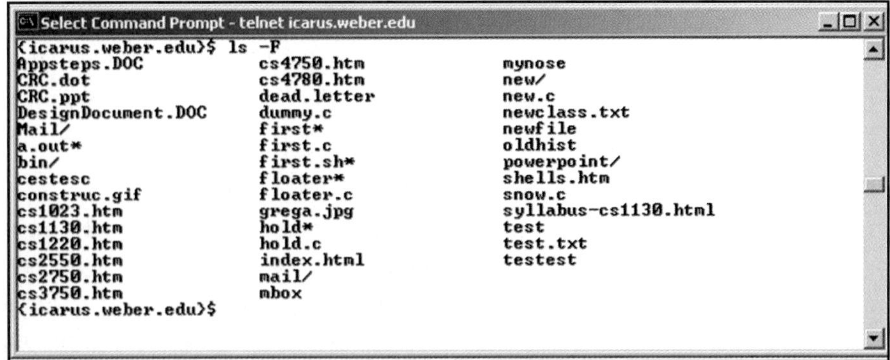

how are files organized on CDs?

CDs have their own filing system, but each operating system translates the filing system of the CD into a format common to the operating system so that the user can treat it the same as any other drive on the system.

command-line prompt, and the command *ls*. Figure 5-8 shows how folders and files can be viewed using the DIR command in a DOS environment.

Figure 5-8, DOS command-line interface showing the results of the DIR command

```
Command Prompt

C:\UML>dir *.* /p
 Volume in drive C has no label.
 Volume Serial Number is F0C6-A78D

 Directory of C:\UML

12/10/2003  04:00 PM    <DIR>          .
12/10/2003  04:00 PM    <DIR>          ..
02/15/2001  08:55 PM            41,472 UML Component.vss
02/15/2001  08:55 PM            68,608 UML Deployment.vss
02/15/2001  08:55 PM           186,368 UML Static Structure.vss
02/15/2001  08:55 PM            47,616 UML Use Case.vss
               4 File(s)        344,064 bytes
               2 Dir(s)  21,612,748,800 bytes free

C:\UML>_
```

DOS in Windows

You can practice your DOS commands in Windows by opening a Command Prompt window: Click Start, click Run, type *cmd* and click OK. To close the window, type *exit* at the command prompt and press Enter.

The graphical interface of Windows makes it easy for users to view and manipulate the folder structure. The Windows Explorer program, which is the program shown in Figure 5-6, is one way of viewing and managing files in Windows. In this Explorer view, the drives and folders of the system are shown in the left pane, and subfolders and files are shown in the right pane. The right pane can be set to view the folders and files in different ways. The files in the right pane of Figure 5-6 are shown in the Details format, which displays information concerning the file size, type, and date. Graphical interfaces can drastically improve user productivity when working with computers.

The next sections show you how to perform some basic file-management functions using Windows XP, DOS, and UNIX. If you can become familiar with these, you will be able to get along with your computer and be more effective in everything else you do in the computer field.

UNIX and DOS natively use a command-line interface, so the commands listed for them are the commands that you would enter on the command line. There are many graphical user interfaces available for UNIX/Linux, but they aren't used here.

The commands for UNIX and DOS have what are called command-line switches (sometimes called command-line parameters or flags). In DOS, these appear in the format:

```
DIR  C:\*.*  /P
```

just in case

Remember that commands in DOS are not case sensitive (for example, DIR, dir, or Dir work the same), but UNIX commands are case sensitive (*LS* or *Ls* will not work for *ls*)

The command DIR is a DOS command that lists the files in a specified directory or subdirectory. The command shown causes the operating system to list all of the files located at the root level of the C hard drive. The /P is a switch that modifies the operation of the DIR command. Without it, the DIR command continually lists files until all files are listed. Placing the /P switch in the command causes the DIR command to pause when the screen is filled and wait for you to press a key to continue. Then another screen full is displayed in the same manner until all the files have been displayed. This gives you a chance to see all of the files listed at that level of the disk drive.

Although the syntax for the commands will be shown, you'll need to consult each operating system's Help feature to find detailed information concerning the switches. In DOS, you can enter HELP <*command*> to get more details. In UNIX or Linux, entering *man* <*command*> gives you the manual on the command. Note that nearly all of the switches are optional, and you don't need to worry about them most of the time.

The basic operations for creating and managing folders and files that will be explained here for each of the operating systems are:

- Partitioning disks
- Formatting disks
- Creating folders (subdirectories)
- Listing folders and files
- Renaming folders and files
- Deleting folders and files
- Copying folders and files
- Moving folders and files

partitioning disks

partition – *An area of a hard disk that has been reserved to hold files of a particular operating system type*

format – *Organizing the disk surface in such a manner as to be able to have folders and files written to it*

Before a disk can be used, it must be divided into ***partitions*** and ***formatted***. Both of these are accomplished by running a program that is part of the operating system. Partitioning a disk prepares it to be formatted by dividing the surface of the disk into areas called partitions. The partitions are simply broad divisions of the total capacity of the disk into specific OS areas. Partitions are not yet prepared to receive folders and files. That requires formatting.

Windows and DOS use the FDISK command to partition the drives, and UNIX uses *fdisk*. Partitioning commands like FDISK should be executed only when needed. It is somewhat complicated to use and can easily erase your entire hard drive. If you have any fondness for the files on your hard drive, you'll stay away from the FDISK command unless you really know what you're doing.

note

CAUTION: The FDISK command completely and irreversibly erases disk drives. Never run FDISK unless you are sure of what you are doing.

command syntax

In the command syntax in the tables in this chapter, words in bold are required, and italic words are replaced with the specified information. Items in square brackets are optional and may be omitted.

formatting disks

After a disk has been partitioned, it can be formatted by the operating system. The process of formatting arranges the disk surface into addressable areas and sets up the basic directory tree structure on the disk. Formatting can also be used to place a copy of the operating system on the disk so that it can be used as a boot disk for starting the computer. Table 5-2 shows the commands for formatting in Windows XP, DOS, and UNIX.

note

CAUTION: Formatting a disk completely erases the contents of the disk. Never format a disk unless you are certain that you don't need any files that are on the disk.

Table 5-2, Formatting disks in various operating systems

operating system	commands/procedures to format disks
Windows	Nearly all types of disks (floppy disks, hard disks, removable disks) can be formatted in Windows through the Windows Explorer application. Some specialized removable disks have their own format program, but most can be formatted directly through the operating system format program. The disk can be formatted in Windows by right-clicking on the drive that needs to be formatted, and selecting Format from the drop-down menu. In the Format window, various options can be set. Most of them are defaults and should not be changed. You can do either a full format or a quick format. The full format marks the tracks and sectors on the disk and puts the basic tree structure on the disk. The quick format just puts an empty tree structure on the disk. There is also an option to put the system startup files on the disk. Once the options have been selected and the Start button has been clicked, the disk is formatted. The OS informs you when the format is complete and the disk is ready to use.

(continued)

Table 5-2 (*continued*)

operating system	commands/procedures to format disks
DOS	Disks are formatted in DOS via the FORMAT command at the command line. The command can have one of the following forms: **FORMAT** *volume* [/FS:*file-system*] [/V:*label*] [/Q] [/A:*size*] [/C] [/X] **FORMAT** *volume* [/V:*label*] [/Q] [/F:*size*] **FORMAT** *volume* [/V:*label*] [/Q] [/T:*tracks* /N:*sectors*] **FORMAT** *volume* [/V:*label*] [/Q] **FORMAT** *volume* [/Q] Following the FORMAT command and the volume (drive), are various switches that give additional direction to the format process. You can type HELP FORMAT at the DOS prompt to get additional help on the FORMAT command.
UNIX	In UNIX, you can use the *fdformat* command to format a disk. The command takes the form: **fdformat** [-dDeEfHlLmMUqvx] [-b *label*] [-B *filename*] [-t *dostype*] [*devname*] The items in the brackets are optional switches that modify the command. You can get more detail on the *fdformat* command by entering *man fdformat* at the UNIX console prompt. UNIX also has the *format* command to format hard disks. Enter *man format* at the UNIX prompt for more help on formatting hard drives.

note CDs and DVDs are usually formatted only as they are written. Exceptions are rewritable CDs and DVDs.

creating folders (subdirectories)

After a disk has been partitioned and formatted, files can be stored on it. To provide for better organization, operating systems allow for the disk to be further divided into folders or directories, which themselves can contain folders or subdirectories. There is one main level called the root level. At this level, the user can create one or more folders. Each folder is within the root folder, or within another folder level. Folders inside another folder are called child folders, or subdirectories, and the folder containing them is called a parent folder or parent directory. A folder that is a child to one folder could also be parent to another folder. Any of the folders on a disk can contain files and/or additional child folders.

The parent-child structure has nearly unlimited depth, but as a practical matter you should avoid creating more than 5–10 levels in the structure. Nesting more than 10 folders results in excessive file path names and makes the files in those folders difficult to find.

In order for the user to be able to create this structure, the operating system needs to provide a method of creating folders. Folders are given names and each of the operating systems has specific rules on how they may be named. In general, folder names must start with a letter and may include additional numbers or letters and some special characters up to a length of 255 characters, though DOS has a limitation of eight characters for the name and three characters for the file extension. UNIX is case sensitive, meaning that it treats uppercase and lowercase letters as different letters. DOS and Windows are not case sensitive.

note

Windows uses the term "folder," whereas DOS and UNIX use the terms "directory" and "subdirectory." In most of the discussion in this text, the terms are used interchangeably.

Table 5-3 shows commands and procedures for creating folders in Windows, DOS, and UNIX.

Table 5-3, Creating folders

operating system	commands/procedures to create folders
Windows	Folders can be created in Windows in two ways: • Right-click the blank area of the far-right pane of Windows Explorer when you have already selected a drive or folder. After right-clicking, select New from the drop-down menu and then select Folder. A folder called New Folder is now appended to list of files and/or folders in the right pane. You can then click that folder and rename it to whatever name you like. • Select the folder you want to be parent to the new folder and then select File, New, Folder from the top menu of Windows Explorer

DOS	In DOS, the command to make a folder is MKDIR or MD, which stands for "make subdirectory." The syntax for the MD command is:
	`MD [drive:] path`
	In this syntax, the drive is optional and path refers to either a single folder name or an entire parent-child structure.
	In a command-line interface such as DOS, you need to be aware of the concept of current directory. Since there isn't a graphical representation of the parent-child structure, the user has to be able to navigate the structure by typing commands instead of clicking on a particular folder. The DOS command to move to a particular level is CHDIR or CD. The path in both the MD and CD syntax is the folder structure.
	If the command
	`MD \F1\F2\F3`
	were typed at the DOS prompt, a folder structure would be created with the folder named F1 created as a child to the root. F2 would be created as a child to F1 and F3 as a child to F2.
	You could then move the current directory (or folder) to F2 by entering "CD \F1\F2." If your current folder were the root folder, you would get an error if you tried to make F2 your current folder by entering "CD F2," because F2 is not a child of the root.
	If you just enter a folder name with the MD command, such as "MD F4," the F4 folder would be created as a child to your current folder. Therefore, when using the MD command, you need to either use the entire tree structure, or use the CD command to move the current folder to the parent and then use the MD command with the name of the folder you want to create at that level.

operating system	commands/procedures to create folders
UNIX	UNIX and DOS are very similar in many respects. The UNIX *mkdir* command works like the DOS MKDIR/MD command. UNIX also uses *mkdir* to create subdirectories (folders). In addition, the current subdirectory concept holds true in UNIX. You can change your current subdirectory by using the *cd* command, which is the same as the CD command in DOS.

5

listing the contents of drives and folders

Table 5-4 shows the procedures and commands to list the contents of drives and folders in Windows, DOS, and UNIX.

Table 5-4, Listing the contents of drives and folders

operating system	commands/procedures to list contents of folders or drives
Windows	The main program for viewing drives, folders, and files in Windows is Windows Explorer. It can be executed by clicking Start, All Programs, Accessories, Windows Explorer. On your system, Windows Explorer also might be on the desktop as an icon. You can also start Windows Explorer by holding down the Windows (flag) key and pressing the letter e. In Windows Explorer, you can browse the tree structures of your disk drives. If you click on the plus symbol next to a folder, it opens up the contents of the folder. In general, folders are on the left and files on the right, although you can also see folders on the right at times. If you right-click a file or folder and select Properties from the drop-down menu, you can view the details about the object that you've selected.
DOS	The DOS command to list the files of a drive or folder is DIR. The syntax is: `DIR [drive:][path][filename] [/A[[:]attributes]] [/B] [/C] [/D] [/L] [/N] [/O[[:]sortorder]] [/P] [/Q] [/S] [/T[[:]timefield]] [/W] [/X] [/4]` As you can see, there are many switches that can be used to modify the way the DIR command displays the output. You specify the drive letter, folders (path), and file specification of the drive or folder you want to list.

(continued)

Table 5-4 (*continued*)

operating system	commands/procedures to list contents of folders or drives
UNIX	The UNIX command to list files and folders is *ls*, for "list," and it operates in a similar manner to the DOS DIR command. The syntax is: `ls [-a] [-A] [-b] [-c] [-C] [-d] [-f] [-F] [-g] [-i] [-l] [-L] [-m] [-o] [-p] [-q] [-r] [-R] [-s] [-t] [-u] [-x] [pathnames]` Like its DOS counterpart, the *ls* command has many switches to modify the manner in which files are displayed. You can find information about the switches by entering *man ls* at the command prompt.

renaming folders and files

Once you have created folders, the operating system also provides for renaming them, as shown in Table 5-5.

Table 5-5, Renaming folders and files

operating system	commands/procedures to rename folders or files
Windows	Folders and files are renamed in Windows Explorer by right-clicking the folder or file and then selecting Rename from the drop-down menu. The cursor moves to the highlighted folder or file name and you can type in the new name. You can also rename a folder in Windows by clicking a folder to select it, and then pressing F2 and entering the new name.
DOS	The command syntax for renaming folders in DOS is the same for renaming files: `RENAME [drive:][path]oldfilename newfilename` The full path is required for the path (folder structure) and name, but only the new name is required, without repeating the path.
UNIX	The UNIX syntax for renaming a file or directory is the same as for moving it: `mv directory newname` Where *directory* is the full path specification to the subdirectory or file, and *newname* is the desired new name.

deleting folders and files

An operating system must also provide the ability to delete folders. Note that deleting folders requires care because deleting folders also deletes all of the files and child folders contained within the deleted folder. DOS and UNIX don't allow for recovery of folders and files after they have been deleted. In Windows, deleted files and folders reside in the Recycle Bin folder until it is emptied.

5

wildcard – A symbol that stands for one or more characters, used in selecting files or directories

All of these OSs allow the use of wildcards. ***Wildcards*** are characters that are used to match any character, much like the joker can match any card in many card games. In DOS, Windows, and UNIX, wildcard characters are the asterisk (*) and the question mark (?). The asterisk matches any group of characters and the question mark matches a single character. For example, the path

```
c:\windows\system32\drivers\*.inf
```

includes all files in the c:\windows\system32\drivers folder tree that have .inf as a file extension.

Here are some more examples of wildcards:

*.exe	All .exe files	?xyz	Files such as 1xyz, 2xyz, etc.
a*.bat	All .bat files beginning with "a"	??xyz	Files such as 10xyz, abxyz, etc.

Wildcards can be used with many DOS and UNIX commands, and with Windows command-line commands, to include groups of files and/or folders in the file manipulation commands. As with other commands, wildcard specifications are case sensitive in UNIX, but not in DOS.

Table 5-6 shows various OS commands to delete folders and files.

Table 5-6, Deleting folders and files

operating system	commands/procedures to delete folders and files
Windows	In Windows there are two ways to delete a folder: • Right-click the folder you want to delete, then select Delete from the drop-down menu. • Left-click the desired folder and then press Delete. In both cases you see a message asking if you're sure you want to delete; you must click Yes or press Enter to confirm. Note that in Windows deleting a folder also deletes all files and folders contained in the deleted folder. *(continued)*

Table 5-6 (*continued*)

operating system	commands/procedures to delete folders and files

DOS	DOS has different commands for deleting folders and files. The DOS command to delete a folder is:
	`RD [/S] [/Q] [drive:]path`
	where *path* is the folder tree with the folder you want to delete at the end.
	The folder has to be empty before it can be deleted in DOS unless the /S switch is specified.
	The DEL command is used to delete files in DOS:
	`DEL [/P] [/F] [/S] [/Q] [/A[[:]attributes]] filenames`
	You can use wildcards (? for a single character or * for any character) in the *filenames* specification to delete more than one file at a time and, as you can see, there are many switches that modify the way that the DEL command executes.
	The DEL command doesn't send files to a holding area, like the Recycle Bin in Windows. When you issue the DEL command, the file is marked as deleted and only a special recovery program can get it back.
	The DEL command doesn't actually delete the data in the file. It remains on the disk until some other file uses that space.

UNIX	In UNIX, the *rm* command is used to delete folders (subdirectories) or files. For subdirectories, the *–r* switch has to be used to indicate that a subdirectory, rather than a file, is being deleted: `rm filename [-i]` The *rm* command deletes the file or files specified by filename. The optional switch *-i* causes the *rm* command to prompt you before each file is deleted. You can use the UNIX wildcards to specify groups of files to be deleted. More information on the *rm* command can be found by entering *man rm* at the command prompt.

5

copying files and folders

After the basic folder and file structures have been set up on the computer's hard drives, files can be copied into the folders or stored at the root. One of the most essential functions of an operating system is to allow for saving files to the disk drives. Partitioning, formatting, and folder creation are all done to prepare the drive to receive files. As a user, learning how to manipulate files and folders on the computer is one of the most important things that can be learned. There are few things more frustrating than losing a file on the hard drive, or losing all of your unsaved work when the power goes out. Knowing how to copy files and folders and how to organize drives into folders gives you the ability to be more effective in your work and help you to perform proper backups. Table 5-7 shows you how to copy files in Windows, DOS, and UNIX.

Table 5-7, Copying files and folders

operating system	commands/procedures to copy folders and files
Windows	As with other functions, there is more than one way to copy files from one location to another. Windows Explorer is once again the graphical tool used to perform the file copying. The easiest, safest, and most consistent way to copy files is by using the copy and paste functions. Simply right-click a file and select Copy from the drop-down menu. Next, right-click on the folder or drive you want to copy the file into and click Paste. A copy of the file is placed at the selected location. You can also copy files by holding down Ctrl while left-clicking the file and, while holding the left mouse button down, dragging the file to the desired folder and/or drive. This process is risky in that if you accidentally let go of the key or button before you get to your destination, you may end up with the file in a location that you didn't plan, and you might also delete the file at its original destination. Folders can be copied in the same manner as files. Any files or child folders in the copied folder are also copied. Note that multiple files and/or folders can be selected for copying by using the left mouse button and either Shift or Ctrl. Shift is used to select contiguous files: holding Shift and clicking the first and then the last file in a series selects the whole group. If Ctrl is held down, each click on a file or folder adds it to the selection.

(continued)

Table 5-7 (*continued*)

operating system	commands/procedures to copy folders and files
DOS	As with Windows, DOS also has more than one way to copy files. They are similar, but one copies child folders and the other does not. The COPY command can be use to copy either individual files or groups of files. The syntax for the COPY command is: **COPY** [/D] [/V] [/N] [/Y | /-Y] [/Z] [/A | /B] *source* [/A | /B] [+ *source* [/A | /B] [+ ...]] [*destination* [/A | /B]] There are a lot of optional switches that can be used with the COPY command, but normally the COPY command is used by specifying just the source and destination, separated by a space. Because a space separates the source and destination, the file or folder paths must be enclosed in quotes if there are any spaces in them. For example: COPY c:\windows\win.ini "c:\program files\common\win.ini" For help with the additional capabilities of the COPY command, enter HELP COPY at the DOS prompt. Another copying command available in DOS is the XCOPY command. The syntax for XCOPY is very similar to the COPY command except that it has considerably more switches: **XCOPY** *source* [*destination*] [/A | /M] [/D[:*date*]] [/P] [/S [/E]] [/V] [/W] [/C] [/I] [/Q] [/F] [/L] [/G] [/H] [/R] [/T] [/U] [/K] [/N] [/O] [/X] [/Y] [/-Y] [/Z] [/EXCLUDE:*file1*[+*file2*] [+*file3*]...] The main difference between the two commands is that XCOPY can copy folders and subfolders in addition to copying files, although the XCOPY command has many extended capabilities such as being able to copy files within a specific date range.

operating system	commands/procedures to copy folders and files
UNIX	The *cp* command is used in UNIX to copy files. The syntax for *cp* is: `cp filefrom fileto` *filefrom* and *fileto* are full path specifications to the "from file" location and the "to file" location. UNIX has a greater set of wildcards, but still uses the asterisk and question mark in the same manner as in DOS. The use of the asterisk wildcard following a *filefrom* or *fileto* specification instructs the *cp* command to include all of the files and subdirectories contained in the main subdirectory specification.

5

moving files and folders

Moving files is similar to copying the files except that the original file is deleted after it is copied. The command to move a file is actually a copy command followed by a delete command. Table 5-8 shows procedures and commands to move files and folders.

Table 5-8, Moving files and folders

operating system	commands/procedures to move folders and files
Windows	Moving files in Windows follows nearly the same process as copying them. The safest way is to right-click the folder or file you desire to move, then select Cut from the drop-down menu. Next, go to the location that you want to move the folder or file into, right-click and select Paste from the drop-down menu. You can also move a file by clicking it and then, while holding down the left mouse button, dragging the selected file or folder to the folder or drive you want to move it to and releasing the mouse button. This is called "drag and drop," and is not as reliable a method as cutting and pasting.
DOS	The MOVE command is used in DOS to move files. The syntax for MOVE is: `MOVE [/Y	/-Y] [drive:][path]filename1[,...] destination` MOVE works like COPY, except that it deletes the original file after it is copied to the destination. Note that the MOVE command doesn't work with folders. There's no single command in DOS to move a folder; however, folders can be copied, and then deleted from the original location using the commands described in Table 5-6.

(continued)

Table 5-8 (*continued*)

operating system	commands/procedures to move folders and files
UNIX	In UNIX the *mv* command is used to move subdirectories as well as files. The syntax is: `mv oldname newname -r` The *-r* switch is used to include all child subdirectories and files in the move process.

one last thought

Reinforce your understanding of chapter concepts and terms with the information and activities for Chapter 5 on the student CD.

Because operating systems are a central part of computing, it is essential that you learn the basic operating system concepts as well as how to use them. In later computer science courses, you will expand your knowledge of the theory of operating systems. In virtually all of your later courses, you will have to interact with operating systems to complete your studies and assignments. The coverage of operating systems in this chapter is not exhaustive by any means, but it gives you some common OS tools for managing files and folders.

chapter summary

- Operating systems are essential to the operation of the modern computer
- Operating systems are special programs designed to manage overall computer operation
- An operating system is the software control center of the modern computer system
- Application programs interface with the hardware of a computer through the operating system
- Operating systems consist of a core program called a kernel and various other system programs
- Operating systems provide a user interface. The two main OS interface types are graphical and command line (console)
- The operating system is loaded as a result of the loader program contained in the system BIOS
- The operating system normally resides on the system hard drive and is loaded into memory
- The operating system running on a computer is often referred to as the system's platform
- Operating systems may be single-tasking or multitasking
- Operating systems provide a user interface, manage processes, manage resources, and provide security for the system
- Operating systems are responsible for loading, starting, running, and stopping processes
- Operating systems allow multiple processes to share the CPU through a process called time slicing
- Some operating systems use Plug and Play (PnP) technology to automatically detect and configure I/O devices
- The most popular operating systems are Windows, UNIX, and DOS
- Operating systems also provide for the management and organization of disk folders and files
- Console commands can be modified by using command switches or parameters
- Disks can be organized into folders (subdirectories) and files
- Learning to use operating system disk management functions can make your work as a computer scientist more efficient

key terms

booting (158)
command-line interface (164)
command prompt (164)
deadlock (168)
directory (170)
DOS (160)
driver (158)
folder (170)
format (172)
graphical user interface (GUI) (164)
interrupt handling (167)
kernel (159)
Linux (160)
multiprocessing (163)
multitasking (163)
network operating system (163)
open source (161)
operating system (OS) (157)
partition (172)
platform (162)
PnP (Plug and Play) (168)
POST (158)
process (165)
resources (167)
root level (170)
single-tasking (163)
time slicing (167)
UNIX (160)
wildcard (179)
Windows (160)

test yourself

1. What is the first program loaded into memory when a computer is started up?
2. Special programs designed to allow the computer to communicate with peripheral devices are called what?
3. What is the core program of the operating system called?
4. What is multitasking?
5. What is multiprocessing?
6. What are the four main categories of operating system functions?
7. What are the two basic types of user interfaces in an operating system?

8. What is a process in an operating system?
9. What method allows multiple processes to share the CPU?
10. What is the purpose of an interrupt handler?
11. Folders and files in an operating system are organized into what type of structure?
12. In UNIX, how can information on OS commands be accessed?
13. What is the purpose of formatting a disk?
14. Give an example of a case-sensitive operating system.
15. What command would be used in DOS to create a folder?
16. What command in UNIX would be used to list the folders and files on a drive?
17. In an operating system, what is a wildcard?
18. In Windows, what key can be used to rename a file?
19. For what task is Plug and Play used in an operating system?
20. Do PDA devices require an operating system?

practice exercises

1. DOS stands for:
    - **a.** Demand open sources
    - **b.** Disk operating system
    - **c.** Device outer shell
    - **d.** Direct operating system
2. Multitasking operating systems can service many different ____________ at once.
    - **a.** Users
    - **b.** Program tasks
    - **c.** User interfaces
    - **d.** Operating systems
3. The ____________ portion of an operating system remains in memory for the entire time the computer is on.
    - **a.** CPU
    - **b.** Overlay
    - **c.** Interrupt
    - **d.** Kernel

4. Which of the following is not a multitasking operating system?

    a. Linux
    b. UNIX
    c. Windows
    d. DOS

5. An operating system method of allowing multiple processes to share the CPU is:

    a. Time slicing
    b. Multiuser
    c. I/O
    d. Command line

6. Deadlocks are resolved by:

    a. Interrupts
    b. Time slicing
    c. Memory segments
    d. The operating system

7. Graphical interfaces can be added to the UNIX operating system.

    a. True
    b. False

8. Command-line switches are used to:

    a. Modify the operation of the command
    b. Disable the operating system
    c. Enable the graphical interface
    d. Remove folders

9. Before a disk can be used it must be:

    a. Erased and locked
    b. Partitioned and formatted
    c. Filled with folders and files
    d. Time sliced

10. The process of ____________ arranges the disk surface into addressable areas and additionally sets up the basic directory tree structure of the disk.

    a. Partitioning
    b. Time slicing
    c. Booting
    d. Formatting

11. The main level of a disk is called the:

    a. Root
    b. Platform
    c. Head
    d. Subdirectory

12. DOS is case sensitive.

    a. True
    b. False

13. Which operating system(s) uses MD to create folders?

  a. DOS
  b. UNIX
  c. Windows
  d. Both DOS and UNIX

14. What is the command in DOS to list the files and folders on a disk volume?

  a. LS
  b. DIR
  c. CHDIR
  d. LIST

15. Which of the following is the command used in UNIX to rename files?

  a. rename
  b. F11
  c. mv
  d. ls

16. The command for deleting a folder in DOS is:

  a. DEL
  b. RM
  c. RMDIR
  d. RD

17. In Windows Explorer, multiple folders and files can be selected by using the left mouse button and:

  a. Right mouse button
  b. Shift
  c. Alt
  d. Double-clicking

18. The UNIX wildcard _______________ can be used to match multiple characters.

  a. ? (question mark)
  b. – (hyphen)
  c. / (forward slash)
  d. * (asterisk)

19. The UNIX command to delete a file is:

  a. del
  b. delfile
  c. rm
  d. filedel

20. Windows Explorer can be used to drag and drop both files and folders.

  a. True
  b. False

digging deeper

1. What functions are performed by the kernel of an operating system?
2. What is a thread and how does it relate to a process?
3. Who is responsible for developing device drivers for an operating system?
4. What is spooling and what function does it perform in an operating system?
5. What shells are used in conjunction with Linux to provide a GUI? What is the strength of each?

discussion topics

1. Could there be a computer system that doesn't have an operating system?
2. What other functions could an operating system perform?
3. What techniques other than time slicing could be used for process management?
4. Which is better, a graphical user interface or command-line interface?
5. What makes an operating system stable?

Internet research

1. What is the most popular graphical interface available for Linux and how does it compare to Windows?
2. What is the next version of Windows called and what new features will it have?
3. Who created Linux and for what purpose was it created?
4. What is the process for locating and downloading device drivers for the major operating systems.
5. What is the difference between Linux and UNIX?

chapter 6

networks

in this chapter you will:

- Learn how computers are connected
- Become familiar with different types of transmission media
- Learn the differences between guided and unguided media
- Learn how protocols enable networking
- Learn about the ISO/OSI reference model
- Understand the differences between network types
- Learn about local area networks (LANs)
- Learn about wide area networks (WANs)
- Learn about wireless local area networks (WLANs)
- Learn about network communication devices
- Learn how WANs use switched networks to communicate
- Learn how devices can share a communication medium
- Learn about DSL, cable modems, and satellite communications

the lighter side of the lab

by spencer

Growing up with a father who works in computers is an interesting experience. For example, we currently have eight computers hooked up on our home network. (Four people currently live in our home.) We're never more than 30 feet away from being able to check our e-mail.

So you can imagine how I felt when my family and I recently took a trip across the U.S. in a motor home. During the weeklong trip, we only had access to the Internet four times, and two of those times were on a—brace yourself—dial-up connection.

Four days into the trip, I was huddled over the only computer at the KOA campground like a dog over his food bowl, waiting for my e-mails to download at 56K. (Luckily, only two days had passed since I last checked my e-mail, so I only had 326 junk mails.)

Before you come to the conclusion that my social life is completely dependent on e-mail, let me assure you it is not—I also spend a lot of time on instant messenger.

Instant messaging has taken my life hostage. As I write this, I've got three conversations going. I currently have 41 contacts on my IM. Here's how they break down: 8 family members; 4 close friends; 12 friends; 5 old StarCraft buddies; 2 old coworkers; 2 people I met once; 8 acquaintances of friends that I've never actually met; 1 partridge in a pear tree.

It's always fun to guess who will IM me the quickest after I log on. I honestly think that one of my contacts must sit with her hand on the mouse, staring at the screen, waiting for me to log on. She would be a gold medalist in Speed Instant Messaging.

I could probably compete in the Instant Message Juggling event. I've had as many as nine conversations going at the same time. It's actually more dangerous than it sounds. Just imagine if a message like "Dave is such a loser!" fell into the wrong window (i.e., Dave's).

It's funny to think that something as simple as instant messaging can be so scary, but I've gotten myself in trouble before by typing in the wrong window. It's just a good thing that those kinds of mix-ups don't happen too often.

k dave, i'm back. i was just trying to finish up this chapter foreword I was writing for some computer geeks.

why you need to know about... networks

Imagine life without e-mail, Web browsers, and file sharing. Picture a bored teenager with no instant messaging, having to resort to using the telephone or (heaven forbid) snail mail to communicate with friends. Networking is the glue that connects computers together. Without networking, computer users couldn't share printers. Online shopping, banking, and research would be impossible. Soon after the computer was invented, computer scientists realized that computers would need to be connected to other computers and peripheral devices, and began working on technologies and standards that would make networking possible.

Networking has now moved from government research centers, universities, and large corporations to home computing. As people began to have more than one computer at home, they needed to share resources such as printers and Internet connections. Networking has indeed become central to computing. The network has effectively become an extension of the computer's system bus.

Now that networking has become an integral part of computing for homes and enterprises, designing, implementing, and maintaining networks has become increasingly important. Many types of security management and performance tuning can only be done by trained professionals. In your computer science education, you will learn more about networks and networking. You will use networks in nearly all that you do. Networks, including the Internet, are becoming an integral part of personal computers, and as a computer scientist you will have to incorporate network technologies into nearly everything you develop for computers. This chapter gives you a basic understanding of how networks operate, and introduces you to the TCP/IP protocol, which is at the heart of the Internet.

connecting computers

As you know, computers are binary devices. Instructions, numbers, pictures, and sounds are all stored and transferred using ones and zeros, which are actually electrical voltage signals. Computers could be connected to each other to share information by just extending the bus signals—if the computers were right next to each other. Buses consist of many wires. The PCI system bus has 98 of them. A cable to extend the PCI bus to another computer would have to be very thick and wouldn't be practical at all. Because of the difficulties of extending the system bus in order to connect computers, new technologies had to be developed. Although computers next to each other are sometimes connected, the greater need is to connect computers that are physically farther apart. In all situations, connecting computers requires a medium, such as wire, to carry electrical signals, and a communications protocol, such as TCP, to control and manage the process.

transmission media

transmission medium – A material with the capability to conduct electrical and/or electromagnetic signals

Sending ones and zeros from one computer to another requires a ***transmission medium***. A transmission medium is some type of material that is a conductor of electrical and/or electromagnetic signals. Perhaps the most popular medium has been copper wire. Copper wire is a good conductor of electricity and is relatively inexpensive. It is also quite flexible and thus easy to work with.

note

More than one transmission medium is referred to in the plural form as transmission media.

bandwidth – A measurement of how much information can be carried in a given time period over a wired or wireless communications medium, usually measured in bits per second (bps)

signal to noise ratio – A measure of the quality of a communications channel

bit error rate – The percentage of bits that have errors relative to the total number of bits received in a transmission; a measure of the quality of a communication line

attenuation — A reduction in the strength of an electrical signal as it travels along a medium

Transmission media are rated in four different ways:

- ***Bandwidth***—The speed the medium is able to handle, measured in bits per second. Bandwidth is a function of how much the medium is affected by outside electrical influences, referred to as noise.
- ***Signal-to-noise ratio***—The proportion of signal compared to noise, which is calculated by the formula stnR $= 10 \log_{10}$ (signal/noise). High ratios are better than low ratios because a high ratio indicates that the signal is stronger than the noise.
- ***Bit error rate***—The ratio of the number of incorrectly received bits to the total number of bits in a specified time period. The ability of a medium to transmit binary information usually drops off (the error rate increases) as the transfer rate increases.
- ***Attenuation***—The tendency of a signal to become weaker over distance. Because of resistance to electrical flow, an electrical signal gets weaker as it travels, especially on copper wire. All transmission media have limitations on the distance that the signal can travel because of attenuation.

guided media – Physical transmission media such as wire or cable

unguided media – Transmission media that you can't see, such as air or space, which carry radio or light signals

Transmission media are classed as two general types: guided and unguided. ***Guided media*** are physical media such as copper wire or fiber-optic cable. ***Unguided media*** describes the air and space that carries radio frequencies (RF) or infrared (IR) light signals.

guided media

The most common guided medium is copper wire in the form of either twisted pair or coaxial cable. Another type of guided medium is fiber-optic cable, which uses glass and light to transmit data. Figure 6-1 shows these common types of cables.

Figure 6-1, Coax, twisted pair, and fiber-optic cable are guided media

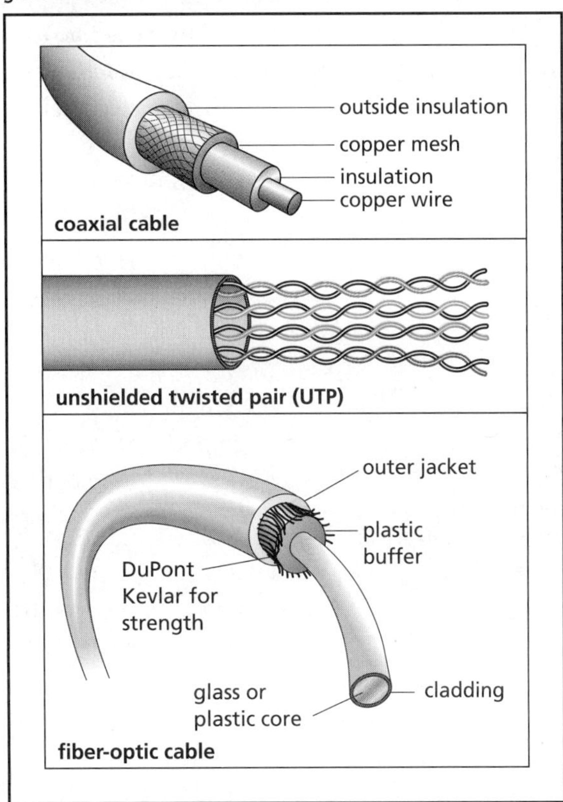

coaxial – Communication cable that consists of a center wire surrounded by insulation and then a grounded foil shield that is wrapped in steel or copper braid

twisted pair – A pair (sometimes pairs) of insulated wires twisted together and used as a transmission medium in networking

copper wire: coax and twisted pair

Copper wire has been the network conductor of choice for many years. It is also used to carry satellite or cable TV signals inside your house. Copper wire is manufactured in two basic formats: ***coaxial*** (sometimes just called coax) and ***twisted pair.***

Transmitting data requires two wires, one to carry the signal, and one for the ground, or return line. Two copper wires could be used to connect computers together. Just using two simple wires has problems however. There is

10Base5 – An Ethernet networking cable made up of a thick coax cable capable of transmitting at rates up to 10 Mbps

10Base2 – An Ethernet networking cable made up of a thin coax cable capable of transmitting at rates up to 10 Mbps

electronic noise all around. It is emitted by all electronic wiring and equipment. It is even emitted by the sun. Since copper is affected by this noise, one way to increase the bandwidth of a copper wire is to protect it from the noise by surrounding it with a metal shield. Cable manufactured in this way is called coaxial cable. It has a high signal to noise ratio and can support bandwidths up to 600 MHz. Different types of coaxial cable have been used over the years to network computers together. The cable types are usually given such names as ***10Base5*** and ***10Base2***. Coaxial cable has been a very popular medium in the past, but it is being replaced in most instances by twisted pair cables that are less expensive to produce and that have even higher bandwidths. Coax is still used when computers connect to the Internet through a cable television service using a cable modem.

inductance – The magnetic field around a conductor that opposes changes in current flow

impedance – The opposition that a transmission medium has toward the flow of alternating electrical currents

The main copper transmission medium currently in use is called twisted pair. The reason that it is called twisted pair is because it consists of pairs of copper wires that are twisted. The reason that the wires are twisted has to do with the electrical property of ***inductance***. When metal wires run parallel to each other in close proximity, electrical current in one wire induces an electrical signal in the wire or wires next to it. In motors and generators, this is a good thing, but in computers and networking, inductance is a big problem. Because the electrical signals on the wires are treated as ones and zeros, and because ones and zeros make up the data being transmitted, it would be bad if a zero were changed to a one or vice versa by some type of interference on the line. It would especially be a problem if the bit error involved a substantial decrease in your checking account balance! Twisting the wires nearly eliminates inductance, enabling higher bandwidth and longer wires. All copper wires are also subject to ***impedance***. This impedance makes the electrical signals weaken as they travel along the wire. The reduction in signal is called attenuation, as mentioned earlier.

Twisted pair cable comes in two configurations, shielded and unshielded. Like coaxial, the twisted pair can be wrapped in an aluminum foil-like shield to protect the wires from outside interference. Shielded twisted pair is designed to be faster and more reliable than unshielded cable, but it is more expensive and less flexible. The less expensive unshielded twisted pair (UTP) cable continues to be the more popular of the two.

Twisted pair cables have been rated by the standards organizations EIA/TIA (Electronic Industry Alliance/Telecommunications Industry Association) according to the maximum frequency the cable can reliably support. Table 6-1 indicates the category ratings of twisted pair cable. Categories above 2 normally have four pairs of twisted wire.

6

Table 6-1, EIA/TIA twisted pair cable categories

category	maximum frequency
1	4–9 KHz
2	1 Mbps or less
3	10 MHz
4	20 MHz
5	100 MHz
6	250 MHz
7	600 MHz

Cat 5 – A popular Ethernet twisted pair communication cable capable of carrying data at rates up to 100 Mbps

10BaseT – A twisted pair Ethernet networking cable capable of transmitting at rates up to 10 Mbps

100BaseT – A fast Ethernet networking cable made up of four twisted pairs of wire and capable of transmitting at 100 Mbps

fiber optic – Guided network cable consisting of bundles of thin glass strands surrounded by a protective plastic sheath

You might have heard the term Cat 5 used when referring to networking cable. ***Cat 5***, or Category 5, is the most common twisted pair cable in use for homes and businesses. The maximum frequency of 100 MHz for the Cat 5 cable is sufficiently fast for most home and business networks. Twisted pair cables are also known by names such as ***10BaseT*** and ***100BaseT***.

Copper has been used for many years in coaxial and twisted pair configurations, but as the need for faster data transmission has increased, the computer industry has turned to optical media.

fiber-optic cable

Copper wire "guides" electrical signals along the wire. ***Fiber-optic*** cables use glass fibers to guide light pulses along a cable in a similar manner. Fiber-optic cables are made of a thin strand of nearly pure glass surrounded by a reflective material and a tough outer coating. Fiber-optic cables can transmit binary information in the form of light pulses. Transmission speeds of fiber-optic cable are much higher than copper because fiber-optic cables are much less susceptible to attenuation and inductance. In fact, the principle of induction doesn't apply to fiber-optic cables at all. Light, unlike electricity, is immune to induction and other electronic noise on the cable. Because induction isn't a problem at high frequencies, as it is in copper cable, fiber-optic cables have bandwidths hundreds of times faster than copper.

So, if fiber optic is faster, why hasn't the world switched to it? In the past the problem has been the cost. Fiber-optic cable is complicated to manufacture and the glass used in the cable has to be very pure. In the early days of fiber-optic development, the cables were very expensive. But, as more and more businesses have chosen the speed and reliability of fiber-optic cable, economies of scale have brought the price down. In some cases, fiber-optic cable is becoming even cheaper than copper. As the price of fiber continues to drop and as the quality increases, you can expect fiber optics to become the most widely used guided medium. Although fiber optics will continue in popularity, many factors are contributing to the increase in the use of the unguided media of wireless technologies.

unguided media: wireless technologies

Wouldn't it be nice if you could skip the wires and use radio waves to connect your computers? Well, you can. The convenience and low price of wireless networking is allowing the computing industry to make inroads into many businesses and nearly all home networks. The main benefit of wireless technologies is that there is no need to run cables between computers. Cabling is expensive in both material and labor. Another benefit is that computers can be mobile, rather than having to be attached to the network at a single location. Table 6-2 lists some wireless technologies, many of which are illustrated in Figure 6-2.

Table 6-2 Wireless technologies

wireless technology	transmission distance	speed
Bluetooth	33 feet (10 meters)	1 Mbps
WLAN 802.11b	375 feet (112 meters)	11 Mbps
WLAN 802.11a	300 feet (90 meters)	54 Mbps
WLAN 802.11g	375 feet (112 meters)	54 Mbps
Satellite	Worldwide	1 Mbps
Fixed broadband	35 miles (56 kilometers)	1 Gbps
WAP (cell phones)	Nationwide	384 Kbps

To understand wireless technologies, you need to understand how radio transmissions work. You use the technology behind wireless networking all the time—cell phones, walkie-talkies, garage door openers, microwave ovens, and, of

Figure 6-2, Wireless technologies

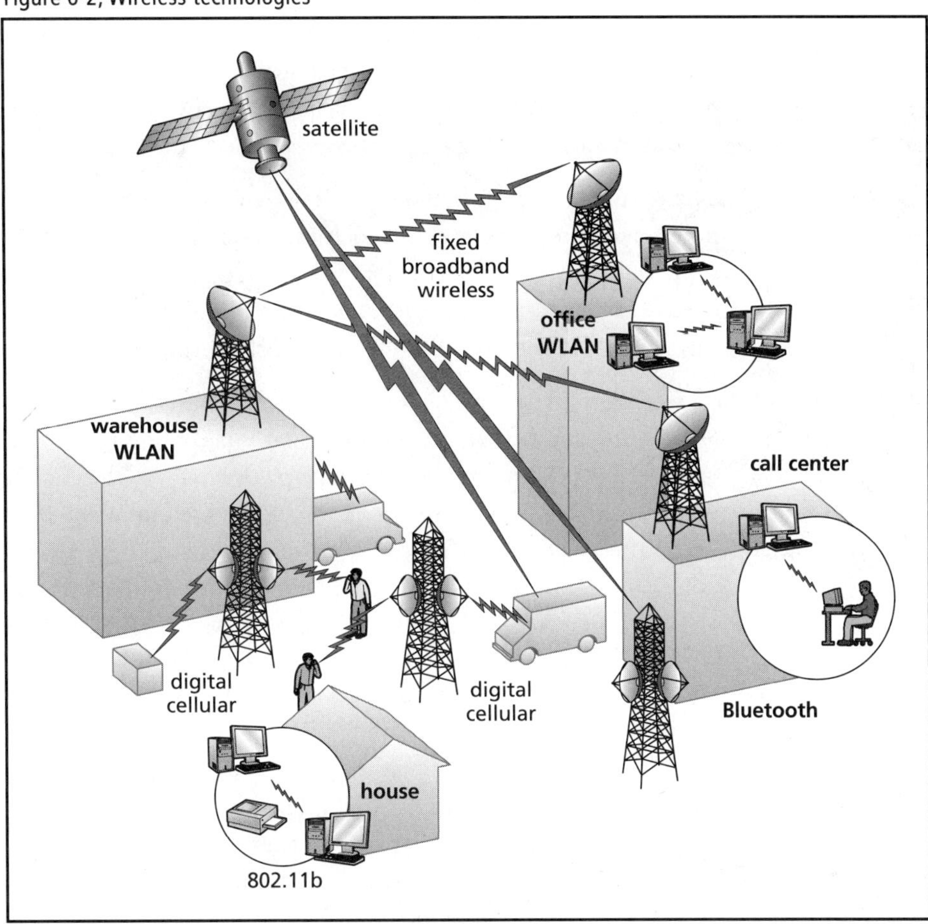

course, radio. In all of these products, an electronic signal is amplified and then radiated from an antenna as electromagnetic waves. These waves travel through the air and sometimes through outer space and are picked up by another antenna and converted back to an electronic signal. Electromagnetic waves can be transmitted at many different frequencies. The difference between a low-pitched sound and a high-pitched sound is the frequency of the sound waves, or vibrations. The frequency of radio waves works in much the same way, except that radio waves deal with electromagnetic waves instead of vibrations. Each time you tune to a new radio station, you are actually changing frequencies.

hotspots

802.11 wireless connections are being installed in airports, bookstores, coffee shops, and other commercial locations to enable people to access the Internet with their wireless-enabled notebook computers or PDAs. These locations are known as "hotspots."

Wireless networking uses the same technology as the radio in your car and the cell phone in your pocket. The complete possible range of radio frequencies, or spectrum, has been divided up by international governing bodies into bands of frequencies. Each of these bands is allocated toward a specific industry or purpose. The frequency band at the 2.4 GHz range has been allocated for unlicensed amateur use. That makes it a perfect fit for wireless networking for home and businesses.

IEEE (Institute of Electrical and Electronics Engineers) – An organization involved in the formulation of networking standards

802.11 – A family of specifications for WLANs developed by IEEE; there are currently four specifications in the family: 802.11, 802.11a, 802.11b, and 802.11g

Bluetooth – A specification for short-range radio links between mobile computers, mobile phones, digital cameras, and other portable devices

The Institute of Electrical and Electronics Engineers (***IEEE***) formulated a standard for wireless networking using the 2.4 GHz range. They numbered this standard ***802.11***. Later variations have included 802.11b, 802.11a, and 802.11g, which have been used heavily in wireless networking. If you have a wireless home networking system, it is most probably using one of the 802.11 wireless standards.

These wireless standards allow wireless networks to transmit data between computers and wireless devices in much the same manner as guided media such as copper and fiber optics. The goal in both is to transmit binary information between computer systems. Selecting the proper medium, however, is only part of the problem. There's a lot more to networking computers than just choosing a transmission medium.

Bluetooth is another wireless protocol that is becoming very popular for connecting keyboards, mice, printers, and other I/O devices to the computer. Bluetooth is not really a networking protocol, but can be used to interface to a LAN. The Bluetooth specification allows for maximum distances between devices to range from 3 inches to 328 feet, depending on the power of the transmitter.

light transmission

For short distances, infrared light is also used to send and receive information through the transmission medium of the air. For infrared to work, there must be a clear line of sight between the sending device and the receiving device. Portable devices such as PDAs, cell phones, and notebook computers often have this capability. Many types of wireless keyboards and mice also use infrared technology. Pulses of infrared light are used to represent the ones and zeros of binary transmission. Infrared transmissions are capable of transmission rates up to 4 Mbps.

note

Remote controls for home entertainment devices also use infrared transmission.

protocols

protocol – A set of rules designed to facilitate communication; protocols are heavily used in networking

A ***protocol*** is a set of rules designed to facilitate communication. In both human and computer interactions, protocols are essential.

You deal with protocols in your life every day. For example, you deal with classroom protocol each day you attend class (for some of you, that's less often than it should be!). When you're in a classroom with the professor talking and you have a question, the normal protocol is for you to raise your hand and keep it up until the professor acknowledges you. At some point, the professor indicates to you that you may ask your question. When you have finished your question, the professor answers it and then asks if the question was resolved. If so, the professor resumes the lecture.

note Networking would be impossible without the use of protocols.

The classroom protocol used in this example is designed to facilitate communication and understanding in the classroom. This protocol provides for an orderly flow of information transfer. The description above was simple, but classroom protocol is actually quite a bit more complex. Protocols are often represented with a timing diagram. A timing diagram shows the protocol interactions between two entities.

Table 6-3, is an example of timing for the classroom scenario.

Table 6-3, Protocol timing diagram

time period	professor	student
1	Lecturing	
2		Raises hand to show desire to ask question
3	Notices student's hand and finishes thought	
4	Tells student to proceed	
5		Lowers hand to acknowledge professor's recognition
6		Asks question
7		Stops talking to indicate question is complete
8	Answers question	
9	Continues lecturing	

A very similar process to the one above occurs throughout computer communications and especially in networking. If you designed a circuit to put a binary signal on a transmission medium, you would have to take into consideration the protocol for communicating data from one machine to another. It isn't enough to just put voltages on the line. You must also provide for an orderly flow of information from one machine to the other. This happens through a transmission protocol. In fact, there are many protocols in use in your computer. One example is that of Web pages, which will be covered in a later chapter. You have probably typed "HTTP" into the address line on your browser. The letter "P" in "HTTP" stands for protocol. The same goes for TCP/IP and FTP. In those cases also, the letter "P" stands for protocol. Without protocols, there would be no Internet. Actually, without protocols, computers would not function.

You'll learn a lot more about protocols such as HTTP, FTP, and TCP/IP in Chapter 7, "The Internet."

Communication protocols such as TCP (Transmission Control Protocol) provide for two computers to establish a communication connection, transfer the data, and terminate the connection.

A timing diagram for a protocol such as TCP (Table 6-4) might look similar to the one for the classroom protocol. Instead of the actual words, computers use special codes to facilitate the communication process.

Table 6-4, Timing diagram for a communication protocol

time period	computer 1	computer 2
1	Listening	Listening
2	Are you ready?	
3		Yes I am
4	Here comes part 1	
5		I received part 1
6	Here comes part 2	
7		I received part 2
8	I'm finished	
9		Terminate

TCP is actually a little more complicated than that, but the process is similar. Computers use a protocol such as the one shown above to ensure that the information gets from the sender to the receiver exactly as it was sent. That means that the protocol must have provisions to check for errors and to retransmit parts of the information if necessary. This process happens all of the time you are browsing the Internet, playing streaming files, or chatting over an instant messenger. You haven't had to worry about the process because of something that was done in 1984. That year, two standards groups, the

ISO (International Organization for Standardization) – An organization that coordinates worldwide standards development

CCITT (Comite Consultatif International de Telegraphique et Telephonique or International Telegraph and Telephone Consultative Committee) – A standards group that was involved in the development of the ISO/OSI networking model

ISO/OSI RM – A data communications model consisting of seven application layers

datagram – A packet of information used in a connectionless network service that is routed to its destination using an address included in the datagram's header

International Organization for Standardization (***ISO***) and the Comite Consultatif International de Telegraphique et Telephonique (International Telegraph and Telephone Consultative Committee, or ***CCITT***) got together to formulate what is now known as the ISO Open Systems Interconnect reference model (***ISO/OSI RM***), or sometimes just the OSI model.

ISO/OSI reference model

The OSI reference model was designed to formulate a standard to enable different types and brands of computers to communicate with one another. It is a conceptual model for the communication process that has seven discrete layers, each with a specific responsibility or function:

1. *Physical*—The Physical layer defines the electrical, mechanical, procedural, and functional specifications for activating and maintaining the physical link (such as the cable) between end systems.
2. *Data Link*—The Data Link layer provides for reliable transit of data across the physical link. The Data Link layer is also responsible for the physical addressing of the data and for their notification, ordered delivery of frames, and flow control.
3. *Network*—The Network layer provides connectivity and path selection between two end systems. The Network layer uses routing protocols to select optimal paths to the series of interconnected subnetworks. The Network layer is also responsible for assigning addresses to messages.
4. *Transport*—The Transport layer is responsible for a guaranteed delivery of data. It uses data units called ***datagrams***. The Transport layer is also responsible for fault detection, error recovery, and flow control. This layer manages virtual circuits by setting them up, maintaining them, and shutting them down.
5. *Session*—The Session layer is responsible for establishing, maintaining, and terminating the session between applications.
6. *Presentation*—The Presentation layer is responsible for formatting data in such a way that it is ready for presentation to the application. The Presentation layer is responsible for translation, formatting, and syntax selection.
7. *Application*—The Application layer is responsible for giving applications access to the network.

note Networking protocols and topologies don't always use all seven layers of the OSI model.

PDU (protocol data unit) – *A data communications packet that contains protocol information in addition to a data payload*

Each layer is defined in terms of a header and a protocol data unit (*PDU*). The headers for each layer contain fields of information related to the function of each layer and the message data that is being sent. The sending side of the communication creates the header and then the corresponding layer on the receiving side uses that header. The PDU is used to communicate information about the message to the next layer on the same side. Figure 6-3 shows the communication process of the OSI layers.

Figure 6-3, How the OSI model processes data

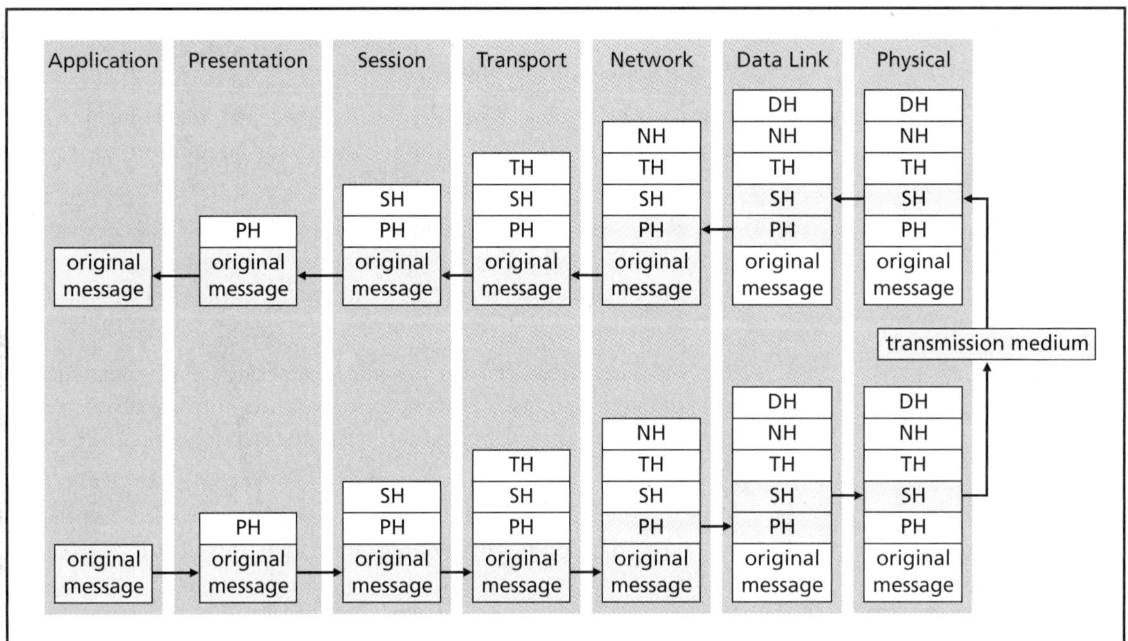

Note in Figure 6-3 how the layers function as a message is transmitted. The message originates at an application such as your Internet browser. The message is then passed down to the Presentation layer. The Presentation layer adds a header pertaining to the message and the responsibilities of that layer. It is then passed to the Session layer and another header, specific to the Session layer, is added to the message and the presentation header. That same process continues down to the Physical layer. The Physical layer places the new message, which consists of the original message along with all of the headers from the prior layers, on to the transmission medium. When the receiving side gets the message, each layer examines its header and acts on the information contained in it. Normally, each layer passes the message, minus the header for that layer, up to the next layer. If a layer detects a problem, it may request retransmission of the message.

You can see that layers in the OSI model are defined and designed to provide services for the process of communicating between computers. The description here is brief, but provides sufficient information about what each layer's responsibilities are. The actual ISO/OSI definition consists of many pages of specific information about the responsibilities of each layer. The effect of breaking down a communication process into layers is that each layer can be programmed and designed independently of the others. Once a layer works, it can be plugged into the other layers. Different types of networks can use the same programming code for all of the layers except the one specifically responsible for that type of network. For example, if all of the layers have been programmed to handle Internet communication over copper wire, a change to a wireless technology will require modifications to the physical layer only. The rest of the layers could remain as they were for the network on copper wire.

You might be noticing that learning about networks requires you to learn a whole new vocabulary—and you're barely started. Learning these new terms, however, will help you in interviewing for jobs and in communicating with other computer professionals.

network types

LAN (local area network) – A network of computers within a single building or in close proximity

WAN (wide area network) – A network in which the computer devices are physically distant from each other, typically spanning cities, states, or even continents

One way of classifying networks is in terms of the proximity and size of the network. A ***LAN*** (local area network) is a relatively small number of computers connected together in close proximity, usually within a building or complex, typically over copper wire. A ***WAN*** (wide area network) consists of a large number of computers spread over a large geographical area, such as a state or a continent. Sometimes you will also hear the term MAN (metropolitan area network) used to describe a network that spans a city or metropolitan area. Deciding whether to use the term LAN or WAN to describe a network is not always easy. There is no standardized definition, although typically if the network is confined to a single building it is usually called a LAN. If multiple physical locations are connected together through a combination of copper wire and/or telephone or other communication services, it is normally referred to as a WAN. The Internet is the largest example of a WAN. Figure 6-4 shows an example of how a WAN can be composed of a combination of LANs and/or WLANs.

WLAN (Wireless LAN) – A local network that uses wireless transmission instead of wires; the IEEE 802.11 protocol family is often used in WLANs

Because of the increasing popularity of wireless networking, especially in home and small businesses, a new term has entered into the vocabulary. ***WLAN*** (wireless local area network) is used to describe a LAN that uses wireless as a transmission medium, instead of copper wire or fiber optics.

Figure 6-4, Example WAN configuration

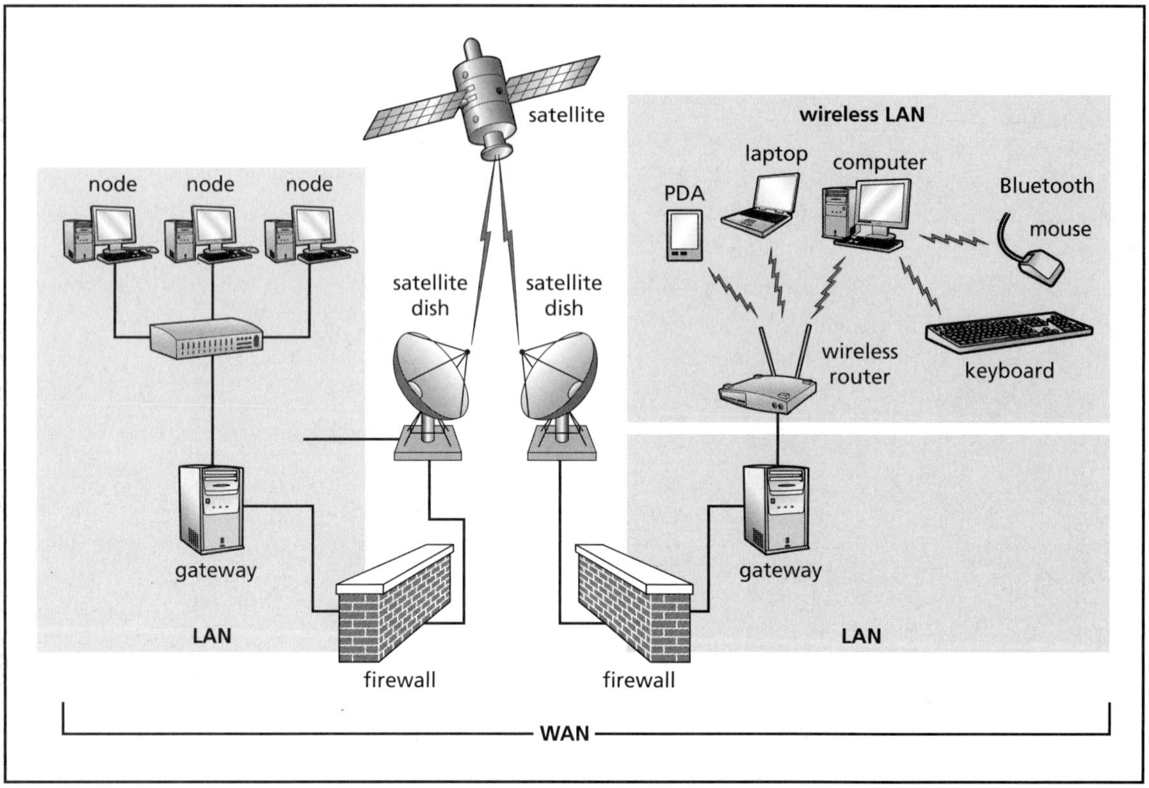

LAN topologies

network topology – *A schematic description of the arrangement of a network, including its nodes and connecting lines*

node – *Any addressable device attached to a network that can recognize, process, or forward data transmissions*

Once the transmission medium and protocols are in place, the computers can be connected in a number of different configurations. These network configurations are often referred to as ***network topologies***. The computers attached to a network are often referred to as ***nodes***.

There are three basic topologies, or ways of connecting computers in a LAN:

- *Ring topology*—This method connects all of the computers in a ring, or loop, with a cable going from one computer to another until it connects back to the first computer. When a computer wishes to send a message or data to another computer on a ring network, it sends the message to the next computer in the ring. Each computer on the ring network has an address. If the message is not addressed to the computer receiving it, the computer forwards the message to the next computer. This process repeats itself until the message reaches the correct computer.

- *Star topology*—In a star topology, one of the computers or a network device such as a hub or switch in the network serves as a central point, or hub, for all messages. When a computer in this configuration wants to send a message to another computer, it sends the message to the central node. The central computer or device then forwards the message to the computer it is addressed to. Once again, all computers on the network must have a unique address.
- *Bus topology*—A network in a bus topology is configured much like a system bus on a computer. Each computer, or node, on the network is connected to a main communication line, or bus. Any of the computers attached to this bus can place a message on the bus that is addressed to any other computer on the bus. All of the computers "listen" to the bus, but only the one with the desired address will respond. The bus line requires a special terminator at the end of the line to absorb signals so that they do not reflect back down the line.

To see the main network topologies in action, check out the learning tools section under Chapter 6 on the student CD.

The bus topology has emerged as the most popular method of connecting computers in a LAN configuration. Figure 6-5 illustrates these three network topologies.

Figure 6-5, LAN topologies

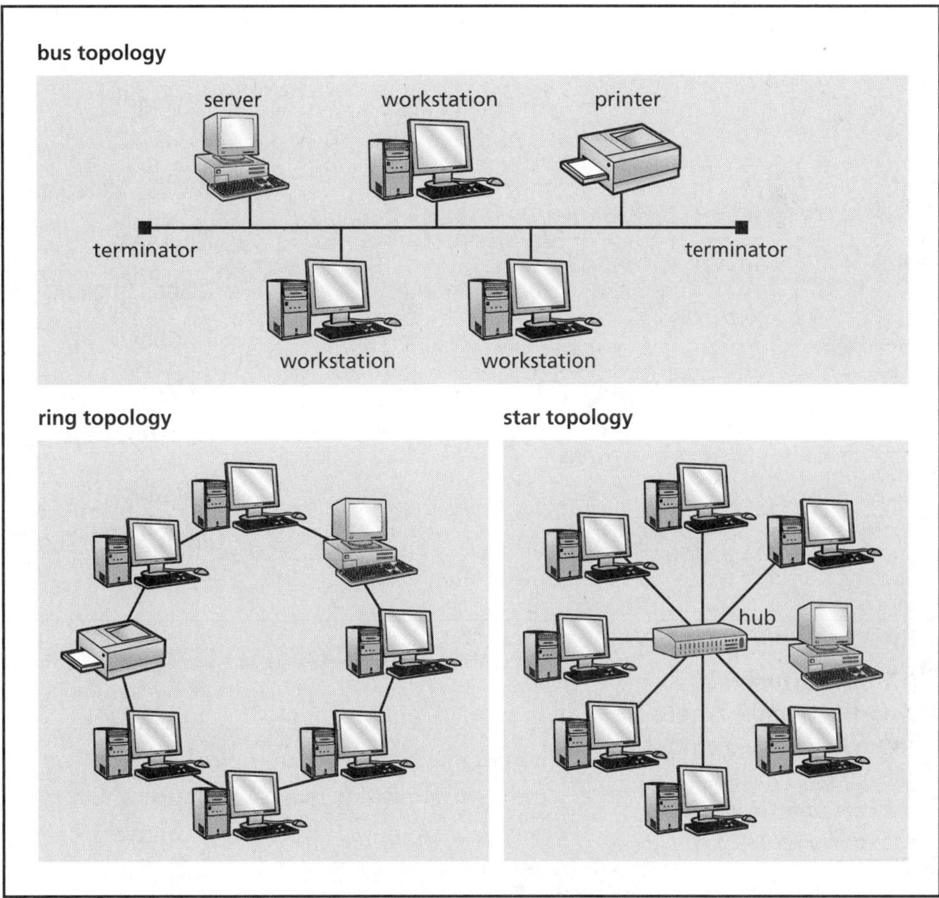

Ethernet – A common method of networking computers in a LAN using copper cabling at speeds up to 100 Mbps

token ring – A LAN technology that has stations wired in a ring, in which each station constantly passes a special message token on to the next; whichever station has the token can send a message

FDDI (Fiber Distributed Data Interface) – A token-passing, fiber-optic cable protocol with support for data rates of up to 100 Mbps; FDDI networks are typically used as the main lines for wide area networks

LAN communication technologies

LANs can also be classified according to the technology used to connect nodes to the network. A widely used technology that has become the industry standard for LANs is ***Ethernet***. Ethernet is based on a bus topology, but it can be wired in a star pattern, sometimes called a star/bus topology. Today, Ethernet is the most popular LAN technology because it is relatively inexpensive and easy to install and maintain. The original Ethernet transferred data at 10 Mbps, and a more recent standard, Fast Ethernet, transfers data at 100 Mbps. Many PCs come with built-in Ethernet 10/100 ports to accommodate both speeds. Gigabit Ethernet provides even faster transfer rates of up to 1 Gbps (1 billion bits per second), and recently 10 Gigabit Ethernet appeared on the scene.

The second most popular LAN technology is ***token ring***, which uses a ring topology and controls access to the network by passing around a special signal called a token. Standard token ring networks support data transfer of 4 or 16 Mbps. Other LAN technologies that are generally faster and more expensive are ***FDDI*** and ***ATM***. Table 6-5 summarizes the bandwidth of various LAN technologies.

Table 6-5, Bandwidth of LAN technologies

LAN technology	bandwidth
Ethernet	10 Mbps (megabits per second)
Fast Ethernet	100 Mbps
Gigabit Ethernet	1 Gbps (gigabits per second)
10 Gigabit Ethernet	10 Gbps
Token ring	4 Mbps, 16 Mbps
Fast token ring	100 Mbps, 128 Mbps
FDDI	100 Mbps
ATM	Up to 2.488 Gbps

ATM (Asynchronous Transfer Mode) – A network technology based on transferring data in cells or packets of a fixed size at speeds up to 2.488 Gbps

network communication devices

LANs, WANs, and WLANs can be connected together to form larger, more complex WANs. These larger WANs might consist of LANs of different types, located physically far apart. To connect them together, various communication devices are employed. In order to connect to a network, a computer or network device needs a network interface card. Networks also often use repeaters, hubs, switches, bridges, gateways, routers, and firewalls to solve networking issues.

NIC (network interface card)

NIC (network interface card) – A circuit board that connects a network medium to the system bus of a computer device and converts the binary information of a computer into a format suitable for the transmission medium in use; each NIC has a unique, 48-bit address

Each physical device connected to a network must have a network interface card (***NIC***). This card is usually in an expansion slot on the motherboard, or in a card slot on a notebook computer, and includes an external port for attaching network cable or an antenna for wireless connection. Each NIC has a unique, 48-bit address called the MAC address or physical address, that is given by the NIC manufacturer and that is used to identify it on the network (by the OSI Physical layer). The NIC becomes the interface between the physical network and your computer and as such it normally connects to your main system bus.

repeater

repeater – A network device that is used to amplify signals on long cables between nodes

As mentioned earlier, signals decrease (attenuate) as they travel through a transmission medium. Attenuation limits the distance between computers in a network. ***Repeaters*** alleviate this problem by amplifying the signal along the cable between nodes. Repeaters don't alter the content of the data in any way. They just boost the signal.

hub

hub – A network device that functions as a multiport repeater; signals received on any port are immediately retransmitted to all other ports of the hub

A ***hub*** is a special type of repeater that has multiple inputs and outputs, unlike the standard repeater that has just one input and one output. The inputs and outputs are all connected together. The hub allows multiple nodes to share the same repeater.

switch

switch – A network repeater with multiple inputs and outputs; each input can be switched to any of the outputs creating a point-to-point circuit

A ***switch*** is similar to a hub in that it is a repeater with many input and output ports. A switch differs from a hub in that the inputs and outputs are not all connected together. Instead, the switch examines the header of the packet of the input and switches a point-to-point connection to the output that is addressed by the packet. Because it is not just a passive device like a hub, it has the OSI Layer 2 (Data Link) responsibilities of examining headers for addresses.

bridge

bridge – A special type of network switch that can be configured to allow only specific network traffic through, based on destination address

A ***bridge*** is similar to a switch in that it amplifies the signals that it receives and can connect inputs with outputs, but it differs in that it can allow a network to be divided into segments to reduce overall traffic on the entire network. Recall that on a bus network, all of the messages are presented to all of the computers on the network. That places a heavy load on each computer, as it has to examine every message to see if it needs to respond. In a large network, this traffic can significantly slow the network. A bridge has intelligence. It can read the address of each message it receives and then forward it to just the segment of the network containing the addressed computer.

gateway

gateway – A network component, similar to a bridge, that allows networks of different types to be connected

A *gateway* is similar to a bridge, but has the additional capability to interpret and translate differing network protocols. Gateways can be used to connect networks of different types, or to connect mainframe computers to PCs. Your PC no doubt connects to the Internet through a gateway. Most gateways are simply a computer with software that provides the functionality of a gateway.

router

router – A network device, similar to a gateway, that directs network traffic based on its logical address

Routers are small, special-purpose devices or computers that are used to connect two or more networks. Routers are similar to bridges and gateways, but they function at a higher OSI layer. Because they can "route" the network traffic based on the logical (IP) addresses assigned at Layer 3 (the Network layer), they are not dependent on the physical (Layer 1) MAC address of the network interface on the computer. Routers can also understand the protocol information placed onto the message by the Network layer and make decisions based on it. Routers are at the heart of the Internet. You'll learn more about the Internet and IP addresses in another chapter, but routers are essential to the process of getting your Web page request to its intended destination.

firewall

firewall – A network device that protects a network by filtering out potentially harmful incoming and outgoing traffic

A *firewall* is a device designed to protect an internal network or node from intentional or unintentional damage from an external network. Firewalls limit access to networks. Many firewalls are router based, meaning that the firewall functionality is added to the router. The firewall can examine inbound and outbound network traffic and restrict traffic based on programmed parameters and lists. A well-designed firewall can do much toward protecting an internal network from unwanted or malicious traffic. Although most firewalls are separate hardware devices, many operating systems, such as Windows XP, have built-in software firewalls.

The use of firewalls and other network security techniques are discussed in more detail in Chapter 13, "Security and Ethics."

note A network firewall is named after the physical firewall in buildings that is designed to slow the spread of a fire through the building.

6

switched networks

So far you have read about computers being connected in LAN and WAN configurations. You might have pictured these computers being connected via copper cable such as coaxial and twisted pair, or via wireless networks. If you had two computers that you wanted to connect together, you could run a Cat 5 wire between them—if they were close to each other. What if one computer was in San Francisco and the other was in New York? You could get a really large spool of wire and start walking, or you could try to find someone who already had a wire running from San Francisco to New York and try to share that wire.

Well, someone already does have a wire going from nearly any location in the world to any other location. That someone is typically the telephone company. By the time computers were invented, and more importantly, by the time people wanted to network them, the telephone companies already had cables all over the place. It was natural to want to use this existing network of wires to connect computers. The problem, however, was that the phone system was designed to carry analog voices, not digital data. The first hurdle of using the phone system to transmit data was finding a way to convert bits into sounds. Engineers came up with a device called a ***modem*** (modulator/demodulator). Modems convert binary digits into sounds by modulating, or modifying, a tone such that one tone can indicate a zero bit and another tone can indicate a one. If you have connected to the Internet using a modem, you have heard the different tones as the sending and receiving modems begin to communicate with each other.

modem – A device that converts binary signals into audio signals for transmission over standard voice-grade telephone lines and also converts the audio signals back into binary

Voices require only a small frequency range in order to be understood. Because of this, the telephone companies could split the bandwidth of a copper conductor into multiple ranges or bands and then let homes and businesses share the total bandwidth. Doing so made it more cost effective to run the wires. The small bandwidth required for voice presented a new problem for engineers. The standard voice-grade telephone line is designed to carry frequencies in the range of 300 to 3300 Hz. That meant that the highest data range would be 3300 bits per second. So how does your 56K (56,000 bps) modem go faster than that? Modem manufacturers achieved higher speeds by coming up with some tricks.

AM (amplitude modulation) – A technique of placing data onto an alternating carrier wave by varying the amplitude of the signal; this technique is often used in modems

FM (frequency modulation) – A technique of placing data onto an alternating carrier wave by varying the frequency of the signal; this technique is often used in modems

First, they realized they could modulate not only the frequency of a sound (how fast it vibrates), using a technique called frequency modulation or ***FM***, but at the same time, they could modulate the volume (amplitude) of the sound waves (amplitude modulation or ***AM***) as well. The combination of the two allows more bits to fit into the same frequency range. Additionally, it is possible to shift the starting point, or phase, of an audio waveform and measure that shift

PM (phase modulation) – A technique of placing data unto an alternating carrier wave by varying the phase of the signal; PM is the most often used modulation type in modems

on the other end. This is called phase modulation (*PM*). Figure 6-6 illustrates FM, AM, and PM. Using a combination of all three allows transmissions at approximately 30,000 bps. To get the additional speed and approach 56,000 bps, the data has to be modified so it doesn't take up so much bandwidth and different rates are used for sending and receiving.

Figure 6-6, Frequency modulation, amplitude modulation, and phase modulation

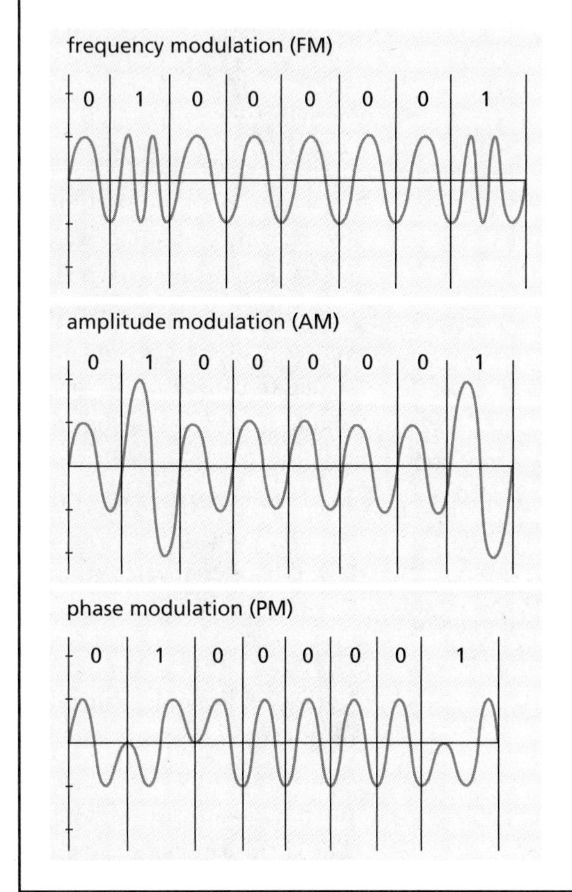

AM and FM

AM and FM radio station carrier signals are modulated in the same manner as in wireless networking. FM is better for music because it is less susceptible to signal noise.

A radio station's frequency (such as 1160 AM or 102.7 FM) indicates the carrier frequency of the station. From that frequency the signal is modulated with either AM or FM.

The main method for modifying data to take up less bandwidth is to compress it. You've already read about compression techniques in other chapters, but as a review, remember that you can compress information by replacing repeating patterns with a code. For example, as you've been reading this chapter, you might have noticed that words such as "protocol," "bandwidth," "frequency," and "network" have been repeated over and over (and over and over). That might be a bit annoying for you to read, but it's great for transmitting over a modem. The compression capabilities of the modem can take repeating patterns of letters and/or numbers and replace them with a much shorter code. The word "bandwidth" has nine letters in it. If it was replaced with a 2-byte code, that would save seven bytes for every occurrence of the word in a text, and allow more data to be sent within the limits of the telephone frequency range.

Finally, frequency is a function of the number of transitions from a sound wave's high point to low point in a second. If the bits in a message could be rearranged so that the ones and zeros were grouped together better, the number of transitions would be less and more bits could be sent in the same amount of time.

The combination of these three techniques has pushed modems to their 56K limit, but a 56K modem is probably not fast enough for you.

high-speed wide area networks

Because most WAN networks use the telephone company's existing wires, they have to live within the constraints established by the phone companies. With standard voice-grade lines, the maximum data rate for modem dialup is 56 Kbps. For most network applications, this rate is painfully slow. Since networking is becoming an extension of the system bus, it stands to reason that there is a need for high-speed network connections. The normal copper wire that comes into your home or business is actually capable of speeds of over 1.5 Mbps. The telephone company limits the bandwidth so that more subscribers can share the cost of the wiring between the home or business and the phone company. One way of getting a faster connection is by leasing all of the bandwidth on the wire. The normal copper wire is capable of carrying 24 voice channels. You can lease all 24 channels on the wire. This dedicated line is referred to as a *T1 line*. As you might imagine, leasing a T1 line can be quite expensive.

T1 line – A digital transmission link with a capacity of 1.544 Mbps; T1 uses two pairs of normal twisted wires, the same as found in most residences

If you needed a faster connection, you could lease one of the higher-speed lines that the telephone company offers. The T3 line consists of 28 T1 lines. For speeds greater than what a T3 can offer, fiber-optic lines are used. These fiber-optic lines are given OC (optical carrier) designations. Table 6-6 lists the various high-speed WAN options available from the telephone companies.

Table 6-6, High-speed WAN connections

connection	speed	equivalent
T1	1.544 Mbps (megabits per second)	24 voice lines
T3	43.232 Mbps	28 T1 lines
OC3	155 Mbps	84 T1 lines
OC12	622 Mbps	four OC3 lines
OC48	2.5 Gbps (gigabits per second)	four OC12 lines
OC192	9.6 Gbps	four OC48 lines

multiple access

FDM - A technique for combining many signals on a single circuit by dividing the available transmission bandwidth by frequency into narrower bands, each used for a separate communication channel

Most WAN connections use one of two techniques to divide the bandwidth of the connection among multiple users. Normal telephone voice-grade lines use what is called frequency-division multiplexing (***FDM***) to divide up the bandwidth among subscribers, so that each has a certain frequency or channel for the duration of the communication session. For example, in the case of the T1 line, the total bandwidth or frequency range of the copper is divided up among the 24 possible users as voice-grade lines.

FDM is inefficient because in most cases many of the subscribers sharing a line are not using it. Think right now of what your phone line is doing. We hope you're not talking while you're reading. How about while you're working or at school? At any given instant, much of the bandwidth is not being used. Even in a normal telephone conversation or Internet session, the bandwidth is effectively being wasted when you're not talking or sending data.

TDM – A technique for combining many signals on a single circuit by allocating each of the signals a fixed amount of time, but allowing each of the signals the full bandwidth during the allotted time

A better way of dividing the bandwidth of a medium might be dividing it up based on time instead of frequency. You could allow each user the entire bandwidth, but just for small amounts of time. By managing this process, each user could have an effective speed that would exceed the speed that could be achieved via FDM. This technique is called time-division multiplexing (***TDM***). Figure 6-7 compares how bandwidth is shared by FDM as opposed to TDM.

DSL

DSL (digital subscriber line) – A method of sending and receiving data over regular phone lines using a combination of FDM and TDM

Many homes and businesses use a high-speed Internet connection called digital subscriber line (***DSL***). DSL is a combination of FDM and TDM, incorporating the best features of both. In DSL the total bandwidth of the copper phone wire is divided up into 247 different frequency bands. Your voice travels over the lower 4 KHz band and the remaining bands are used in various combinations for uploading and downloading data. DSL uses a special "modem" to place voice communications into the frequency band reserved for it and data in the area above the voice band. That composite signal is then digitized and combined with the signals from other customers using TDM and placed on a high-speed medium and sent to the central office (telephone switching station) to be redirected to its ultimate location. These techniques allow DSL speeds to range from 256 Kbps up to 1.5 Mbps, with an ability to have upload speeds different from download speeds. Because of attenuation, a DSL subscriber is required to be no more than 18,000 feet away from the nearest telephone company switching office. Much effort, however, is being put into developing new DSL techniques that can overcome this distance barrier.

when is a modem not a modem?

The DSL modem isn't really a modem, it's a transceiver. It doesn't modulate the signal from analog to digital and vice versa in the way that a regular dial-up modem does.

Figure 6-7, FDM and TDM

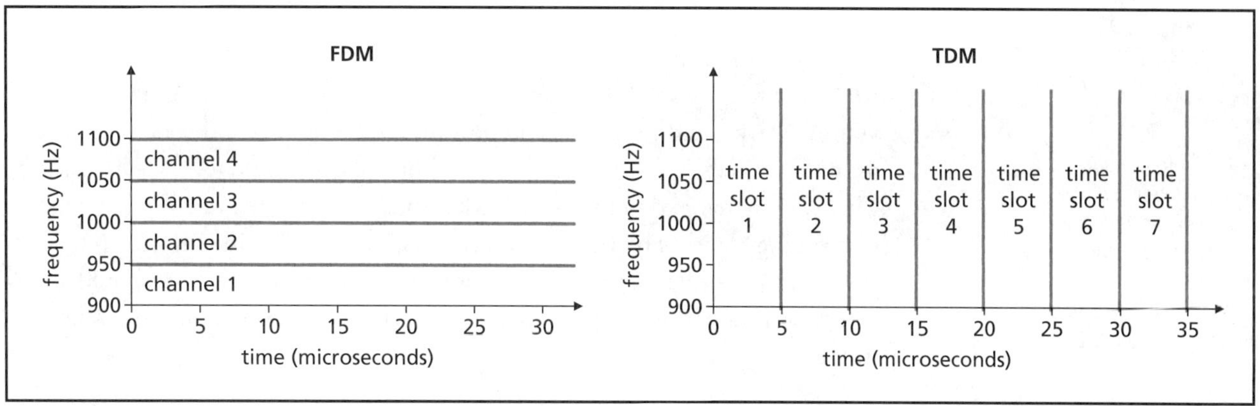

cable modems

cable modem – A type of digital modem that connects to a local cable TV line to provide a continuous connection to the Internet

Another popular method of implementing a WAN, especially for home Internet connections, is through a ***cable modem***. The coax cable that comes into a home for cable television (CATV) can carry hundreds of channels. Each of the channels is allocated a 6 MHz bandwidth. One or more of the channels is reserved for data transmission, though these channels might not be used if you only use cable TV. When you subscribe to a cable Internet service, the cable company connects the Ethernet connector on your computer to a cable modem which is connected to the CATV cable. Downstream from each home is a device that takes the signals from all of the nearby homes and uses TDM to combine them into one signal for transmission to the Internet provider. Cable modems are capable of speeds up to 42 Mbps, but normally speeds are limited by the provider to less than 1 Mbps. This limitation allows more customers to share a single cable line. Cable modems also provide for differing upload and download speeds.

satellite technologies

Wireless WAN technologies are becoming more widely used as the technology improves and the price comes down. Many homes and businesses cannot be connected to a WAN other than by a dial-up connection because they are located out of range of DSL, cable, and other wired or short-range wireless technologies. One of the few options is satellite. Either the same satellite dish used for television broadcasts or one much like it is placed outside to receive and send signals to an orbiting satellite. As wireless technology improves, it may surpass guided media, especially copper cable, as the most widely used transmission medium.

Reinforce your understanding of the chapter concepts and terms with the information and activities for Chapter 6 on the student CD.

one last thought

As networks become more tightly integrated with computers and computing, computer scientists will have an ever greater need to program for and interact with networks, and to understand networking topologies and protocols. The list of key words in this chapter is long, but it barely scratches the surface. There are many textbooks much thicker than this one that detail just a single networking topic. The IEEE specifications for the 802.11a wireless protocol alone consists of 91 pages! There's a lot to learn, but this chapter should serve as a good foundation for your future networking and other computer science studies.

chapter summary

- Networking is essential to modern computing
- Networking requires a transmission medium to carry the transmitted information from one computer device to another
- Transmission media are rated in terms of their bandwidth, signal-to-noise ratio, bit error rate and attenuation
- Copper wire has been the most widely used network conductor, primarily in the form of coaxial and twisted pair cable
- Fiber-optic cable has a much higher bandwidth than copper conductors
- Cat 5 is a twisted pair copper cable that is most commonly used in Ethernet networks; it has a throughput of up to 100 Mbps
- Wireless technologies allow networking to be conducted using electromagnetic waves or light
- The IEEE 802.11 family of standards applies to wireless networking
- A protocol is a set of rules designed to facilitate communications and is essential to networking
- The ISO/OSI reference model defines a set of protocols necessary for data communications; the seven protocol layers are (1) Physical, (2) Data Link, (3) Network, (4) Transport, (5) Session, (6) Presentation, and (7) Application
- The main network types are WAN, LAN, and WLAN
- LAN topologies are ring, star, and bus
- The most popular LAN technology is Ethernet, and token ring is another LAN technology
- Various hardware devices are used in networking such as NICs, repeaters, hubs, switches, bridges, gateways, routers, and firewalls
- Voice telephone service is widely used to extend networks, and modems provide the conversion from digital binary to analog audio to make the use of voice networks possible
- Transmission media is shared among users by using FDM and TDM techniques
- DSL, cable modems, and satellite are popular broadband WAN solutions

key terms

10Base2 (198)

10Base5 (198)

10BaseT (199)

100BaseT (199)

802.11 (202)

AM (amplitude modulation) (213)

ATM (Asynchronous Transfer Mode) (210)

attenuation (196)

bandwidth (196)

bit error rate (196)

Bluetooth (202)

bridge (211)

cable modem (217)

Cat 5 (199)

CCITT (Comite Consultatif International de Telegraphique et Telephonique (205)

coaxial (197)

datagram (205)

DSL (digital subscriber line) (216)

Ethernet (210)

FDDI (Fiber Distributed Data Interface) (210)

FDM (216)

fiber optic (199)

firewall (212)

FM (frequency modulation) (213)

gateway (212)

guided media (197)

hub (211)

IEEE (Institute of Electrical and Electronics Engineers) (202)

impedance (198)

inductance (198)

ISO (International Organization for Standardization) (205)

ISO/OSI RM (reference model) (205)

LAN (207)

modem (213)

network topology (208)

NIC (network interface card) (211)

node (208)

PDU (protocol data unit) (206)

PM (phase modulation) (214)

protocol (202)

repeater (211)

router (212)

signal-to-noise ratio (196)

switch (211)

T1 line (215)

TDM (216)

token ring (210)

transmission medium (196)

twisted pair (197)

unguided media (197)

WAN (wide area network) (207)

WLAN (wireless LAN) (207)

test yourself

1. What are the two general types of transmission media?
2. What are the four ways that transmission media are rated?
3. What are the two basic copper wire formats?
4. What is the maximum frequency of Cat 5 cable?
5. What are examples of networking protocols?
6. How many layers are there in the ISO/OSI reference model?
7. What is a WAN?
8. What are the three LAN topologies?
9. Which of the three LAN topologies has emerged as the most popular?
10. What is a NIC?
11. Which network device can interpret and translate differing network protocols?
12. What is the difference between a hub and a switch?
13. Which network device is designed to prevent damage to an inside network from an outside source?
14. What frequency range are voice-grade telephone lines designed to carry?
15. What is the speed range of DSL?
16. What is bandwidth?
17. How does a WLAN differ from a LAN?
18. What is the difference between AM and FM?
19. How many standard voices lines are equivalent to a T1 line?
20. Which type of multiplexing combines signals on a circuit by dividing the available transmission bandwidth into narrower bands?

practice exercises

1. Which is a better signal to noise ratio?

   a. High
   b. Low
   c. Guided
   d. Unguided

2. Fiber-optic cable is made of:

   a. Glass
   b. Nylon
   c. Braided copper
   d. Copper

3. Which is a faster networking cable?

   a. 10BaseT
   b. 100BaseT

4. Which of the following standards is used in wireless networking?

   a. Cat 5
   b. ISO/OSI
   c. 802.11
   d. TCP

5. Which of the following is not one of the ISO/OSI reference model layers?

   a. Physical
   b. Wireless
   c. Transport
   d. Application

6. Which of the ISO/OSI protocol layers is responsible for a guaranteed delivery of data?

   a. Transport
   b. Network
   c. Data Link
   d. Presentation

7. Which of the ISO/OSI protocol layers is involved with the electrical specifications of a network?

   a. Physical
   b. Network
   c. Session
   d. Transport

8. Which of the following is a LAN topology?

   a. Cat 5
   b. Coaxial
   c. Star
   d. Repeater

9. A hub has a single input and a single output.

   a. True
   b. False

10. Normal speeds of a cable modem are in the area of:

a. 56 KHz
b. 1 Mbps
c. 10 Mbps
d. 100 Mbps

11. DSL speeds range from:

a. 256 Kbps to 1.5 Mbps
b. 256 Mbps to 15 Mbps
c. 56 Kbps to 256 Kbps
d. 100 Kbps to 156 Kbps

12. Standard voice-grade lines are designed to carry frequencies in the range of:

a. 1.5 MHz to is 15 MHz
b. 500 MHz to 1 MHz
c. 56 KHz to 100 KHz
d. 300 Hz to 3300 Hz

13. Modems convert binary digits into sounds by modulating tones.

a. True
b. False

14. Which of the following is not a network device?

a. Router
b. Gateway
c. Ramp
d. Hub

15. Which of the following is used to connect the computer to the network?

a. Gateway
b. NIC
c. Ramp
d. Router

16. What factor reduces the strength of an electrical signal as it travels along a transmission medium?

a. Bandwidth
b. Signal-to-noise ratio
c. Bit error rate
d. Attenuation

17. Which of the following is the most commonly used twisted pair cable category?

a. Cat 1
b. Cat 5
c. 10Base2
d. 10Base5

18. Which type of guided medium is the least susceptible to attenuation and inductance?

    a. Coaxial cable
    b. Twisted pair cable
    c. Fiber-optic cable
    d. They are all the same

19. Which bus topology has emerged as the most popular method of connecting computers in a LAN configuration?

    a. Token ring
    b. Star
    c. Bus
    d. Loop

20. DSL is a combination of what two types of multiplexing?

    a. FDM and TDM
    b. FDM and FM
    c. AM and TDM
    d. AM and FM

digging deeper

1. What is a TCP packet? How is it used? What does it look like?
2. How many of the seven ISO/OSI layers are implemented in the TCP/IP protocol?
3. What is a connection-oriented protocol?
4. How can a bus topology handle more than one computer transmitting at the same time?
5. What are the characteristics of each of the IEEE 802.11 wireless standards?

discussion topics

1. What are the advantages of wireless networking? What are the disadvantages?
2. What are examples of protocols in your everyday life?
3. Why is it necessary for a computer scientist to have a knowledge of networking?
4. What are the advantages of using twisted pair cable for networking? What are the disadvantages?
5. How do you think the ISO/OSI model helped further networking progress?

Internet research

1. What other standards have the ISO, IEEE, and CCITT groups formulated?
2. Where is the ISO standards group located and who are the members of the group?
3. What are the costs of setting up a wireless home network as opposed to a wired home network?
4. What types of jobs are available in the field of networking?
5. What is the history and evolution of the network topologies ring, star, and bus?

chapter

7

the Internet

in this chapter you will:

- Learn what the Internet really is
- Become familiar with the architecture of the Internet
- Become familiar with Internet-related protocols
- Understand how the TCP/IP protocols relate to the Internet
- Learn how IP addresses identify devices connected to the Internet
- Learn how DHCP can be used to assign IP addresses
- Learn how routers are used throughout the Internet
- Learn how a DNS server translates a URL into an IP address
- Learn how port numbers are used with IP addresses to expand Internet capabilities
- Learn how NAT is used in networking
- Learn how to determine your own TCP/IP configuration
- Learn how HTML and XML are used with the World Wide Web
- Learn how to develop a simple Web page using HTML
- Learn how search engines make the World Wide Web more usable

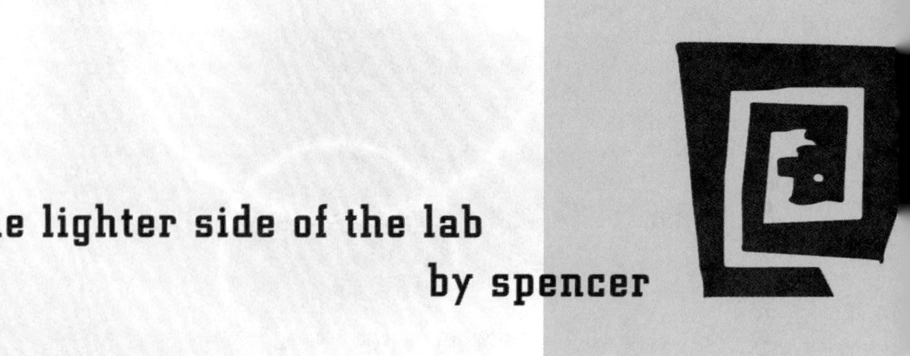

the lighter side of the lab
by spencer

Our power went out not too long ago. Because we live on such a reliable (and by "reliable," I mean completely unreliable) power grid, we're experts at dealing with power outages. We simply lit the 450 scented candles located throughout the house, compliments of my mom. Soon the house was well lit and smelling very good.

The real crisis came when my parents, who were fixing dinner when the power went out, tried to finish cooking. Fortunately, we have a gas range that isn't dependent on electricity. But nobody could remember how to heat a can of refried beans without a microwave.

I can remember buying our first microwave oven. It was the size of a small Buick and a little bit heavier. Little did I know that 20 years later as a college student, I would depend on the microwave to do any cooking that Taco Bell and Pizza Hut didn't do for me.

Luckily, we eventually got dinner figured out. But I realized how many things we depend on every day that have been invented during my lifetime. I can remember getting our first VCR, camcorder, video game, and cell phone, just to name a few.

I can also remember logging onto the Internet for the first time. Talk about a life-changing event! I now spend approximately 36 hours a day surfing the Net (which I believe is slightly below the national average).

A good chunk of that time is spent shopping on eBay, which is a lot more fun than normal shopping. It's like shopping mixed with fighting. Right after I first signed up, I bid on a set of golf clubs. I had responsibly set a personal bidding limit for myself of $200.

With only a minute to go, I noticed someone had outbid me. Now I was really mad. "I'll show you!" I threatened. I bid, then he bid. The bids flew back and forth until the time expired.

I stared at the screen as it reloaded for the last time, holding my breath in anticipation. Suddenly the words appeared: "You are the winner." "Yes!" I yelled, "Take that, sucker!" (I was extremely excited until I noticed I'd spent $25 more than I wanted.)

In summary, I don't know how I'm going to survive if the power goes out and I can't use the Internet. I think it's time to buy a generator. Maybe I can find one on eBay.

why you need to know about... the Internet

You may have heard of the Industrial Revolution in your history classes. The world was forever altered by the invention of powered machinery and mass production. The computer revolution has also changed the world. Nearly everything you use is in some way related to computers. Either it has a computer embedded in it, like your car, or its design was made possible by computers.

You are now living through one of the world's greatest technological revolutions, one that is changing the way we think and act. Computers and the Internet are changing the face of nearly every industry. There was a time when all workers had to be located at their place of business. Now workers in many fields can perform their jobs from home just as easily as at the office or plant. Education is certainly benefiting from this revolution. It might be that you're reading this text as part of an online course where all of your interaction is via the Internet.

Perhaps the greatest change is in the areas of knowledge and learning. Now, anyone with access to a computer has nearly all the world's knowledge at their disposal. And in the United States, that is nearly everyone, because computers are in most homes, and are widely available in public libraries. You can sit at home and check the news and weather, compare prices, and shop online. You can do your banking, renew your car registration, and apply for a student loan. You probably registered for your college courses online.

In your studies, you will be required to do much research on various topics. While you may spend time in the library, much of your research will take place online (or online at the library). This chapter will show you how the Internet can help you to do research.

The field of computer science is heavily involved in all aspects of this Internet revolution. Nearly all of the networks, protocols, and server and client programs have been programmed and are maintained by computer science professionals. That's why the focus of this chapter is to help you to gain a basic understanding of not only how the Internet works but also of the technologies involved in its everyday use. You, as a computer scientist, are on the leading edge of the knowledge and information revolution. You may be involved in formulating new uses for the Internet and perhaps also with regulating and providing ways to limit misuse.

what is the Internet?

ISP (Internet service provider) – A company that provides access to the Internet and other related services such as Web site building and virtual hosting

In an earlier chapter, you learned about LANs and WANs. The Internet is actually just a collection of LANs and WANs that are connected together to form a giant WAN. When you connect your computer to your Internet service provider (***ISP***), you become part of this WAN. You have already learned much of the history of the Internet. From small beginnings, the Internet has evolved into this massive network that involves nearly every computer in the world.

You might be surprised to learn that the Internet is not just one thing, but rather is a collection of many things. You might also be surprised to know that nobody owns the Internet. There are a few groups that propose rules for the Internet and other entities that manage the way it works, but no one owns the whole Internet. Everyone who is connected to, or provides communication to, the other computers on the Internet owns a part of it. The Internet is very interesting in that everyone involved in it is doing it for his or her own purposes, but in doing so, they benefit many others. The companies providing the communication lines do it for profit. Companies providing content on the Internet also do it for profit. Many institutions and individuals provide information for the good of society and to disseminate information, but it all benefits everyone.

note **It is estimated that there are nearly a billion Internet users in the world.**

Understanding the Internet requires an understanding of many of the individual technologies that make up the whole. These individual technologies build upon one another in such a way that they are best presented in sequential fashion, starting with the general structure or architecture of the Internet.

the architecture of the Internet

POP (point of presence) – An access point to the Internet

NBP (national backbone provider) – A provider of high-speed network communication lines for use by ISPs

Your computer might be part of an existing LAN, or it might be a stand-alone computer. Either way, it is likely connected to the Internet. Your LAN is connected to the Internet through communication lines, normally leased from the phone company to an ISP. If you connect using a modem through a telephone line, you are connecting through the existing voice system to the LAN of your ISP. If you connect using a cable modem, you are connecting to your ISP through the cable TV system. Your Internet provider maintains a switching center called a point-of-presence (***POP***). That POP might be connected to a larger ISP with a larger POP and connections to communication lines with much higher speeds. That larger ISP is probably connected to national or international ISPs that are often called national backbone providers (***NBP***s), as shown

Figure 7-1, Internet data can pass through several levels of ISPs

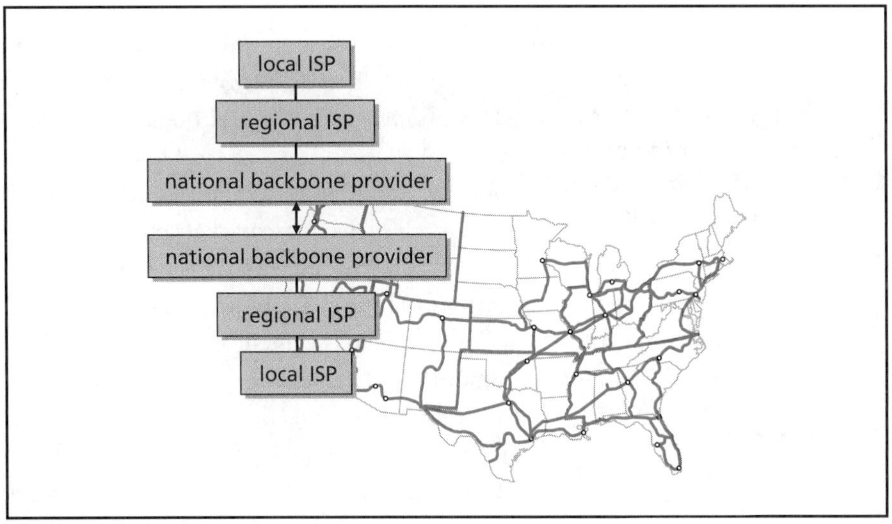

local ISP
regional ISP
national backbone provider
national backbone provider
regional ISP
local ISP

in Figure 7-1. All of these ISPs, from large to small, have network-switching circuitry such as routers and gateways and are eventually connected to optical cables that are capable of transmitting many billions of bits per second.

After reading the networking chapter, you have an understanding of LANs and WANs. You also have a basic understanding of the specialized equipment such as NICs, routers, gateways, and firewalls that are used to control the flow of information between computers on a network. The components you have already read about are the components that make up the hardware of the Internet. To really understand how the Internet works at a hardware level, you need to learn a little more about these pieces of equipment. But, before you can really understand each of these specialized network devices, you need to understand protocols and addressing.

protocols

HTTP (Hypertext Transfer Protocol) – A protocol designed for transferring files (primarily content files) on the World Wide Web

SMTP (Simple Mail Transfer Protocol) – A TCP/IP related, high-level protocol used in sending e-mail

FTP (File Transfer Protocol) – A protocol designed to exchange text and binary files via the Internet

Hardware is only part of what makes the Internet work. As you have studied before, a protocol is a set of rules established to facilitate communication. In the context of the Internet, the importance of protocols cannot be overstated. There are many protocols involved with the Internet. You have probably typed HTTP at the front of a Web address many times. The acronym ***HTTP*** stands for Hypertext Transfer Protocol. You most certainly have used e-mail, which uses ***SMTP*** (Simple Mail Transfer Protocol). You might also have sent or received a file via ***FTP***, which stands for File Transfer Protocol. Computing in general, and networking in particular, is made possible by protocols.

A more thorough explanation of protocols is contained in Chapter 6, "Networks."

TCP and IP

TCP/IP (Transmission Control Protocol/Internet Protocol) – The suite of communications protocols used to connect hosts on the Internet

TCP (Transmission Control Protocol) – An OSI transport level, connection-oriented protocol designed to exchange messages between network devices

The basic networking protocols for the Internet are a pair of protocols that work together to deliver binary information from one computer to another. This protocol pair is called ***TCP/IP***. The first protocol, ***TCP*** (Transmission Control Protocol), is responsible for the reliable delivery of data from one computer to another. It accomplishes this task by first separating the data into manageable, fixed-size packets and then establishing a virtual circuit with the destination computer to transmit them. TCP also manages the sequencing of each of the packets and provides for retransmitting packets that are received in error. Each data segment is appended to a header that contains information about the total packet, including information such as the sequence number and a checksum for detecting errors in the transmission of the packet. Table 7-1 illustrates the sections of a TCP header. The header is at the beginning of every TCP data packet. Although it's not necessary for you to know all of the details of the TCP header, a few of the fields will be used in the explanations that follow.

Table 7-1, TCP header fields

header field	size in bits
Source port	16
Destination port	16
Sequence number	32
Acknowledgment (ACK) number	32
Data offset	4
Reserved	6
Flags	6
Window	16
Checksum	16
Urgent pointer	16
Options	32

IP (Internet Protocol) – The protocol that provides for the addressing and routing of Internet packets from one computer to another

The TCP protocol ensures reliable delivery of packets, but it has no provision for addressing the packets to ensure that they get to the correct place. That is the job of the Internet Protocol, or ***IP***. The TCP packets are sent to the IP layer

For an illustration of how packets move through a network, see the learning tools section under Chapter 7 on the student CD.

software, where another header is added containing addressing information. Table 7-2 shows the fields contained in an IP header. As with the TCP header, you don't need to be concerned with all of the details of the header.

Table 7-2, IP version 4 datagram header

header field	size in bits
Version	4
Header length	4
Type of service	8
Total length of datagram	16
Packet identification	16
Flags	4
Fragment offset	12
Time to live (TTL)	8
Protocol number	8
Header checksum	16
Source IP address	32
Destination IP address	32
IP options	32

IP addresses

IP address – A unique, 32-bit number assigned to network devices that use the Internet Protocol

IPv4 – Version 4 of the Internet Protocol, the most widely used version of IP

IPv6 – Version 6 of the Internet Protocol has greater capability than IPv4, including the provision for a much greater number of IP addresses

Central to the operation of this protocol is the ***IP address*** of both the source and destination. During the initial design of the Internet Protocol, it was established that every computer (or device) attached to the Internet would have a unique identifying number. This number, or address, is a 32-bit binary value. Having a 32-bit address allows for 4,294,967,296 (2^32) different addresses. You'd think that would be plenty, but the addresses are in danger of running out. The most widespread version of IP, ***IPv4***, uses 32-bit addresses. A new version of IP (***IPv6***) has been designed and has 128-bit addresses, allowing for 2^128 possible addresses. Considering that the world has (only?) 6.5 billion people, there should be plenty of addresses to spare if IPv6 is used. Converting every device to support the new IPv6 will take some time, but eventually all devices connected to the Internet will support the new standard.

It's difficult for humans to deal with the 32-bit binary numbers that the computer equipment uses, so an IP address is normally represented as a set of four decimal numbers, separated by periods. A typical IP address looks like 192.168.0.12. Each of the decimal numbers in an IP address represents eight bits (an octet) of the overall 32-bit address. That means that each of the decimal values can range from 0 to 255. The address above is actually 11000000101010000000000000001100 in binary. See how much easier it is to remember 192.168.0.12 than a long binary number?

The total pool of IPv4 addresses is separated into groups, called classes. These classes are designated by the letters A, B, C, D, and E (Figure 7-2). The idea behind the classes is that some entities such as large corporations and universities need to have and manage more IP addresses than small companies. The first part of the IP address identifies the network class, the middle part identifies the host on the network, and the final part identifies the node connected to the host.

Figure 7-2, IP address classes

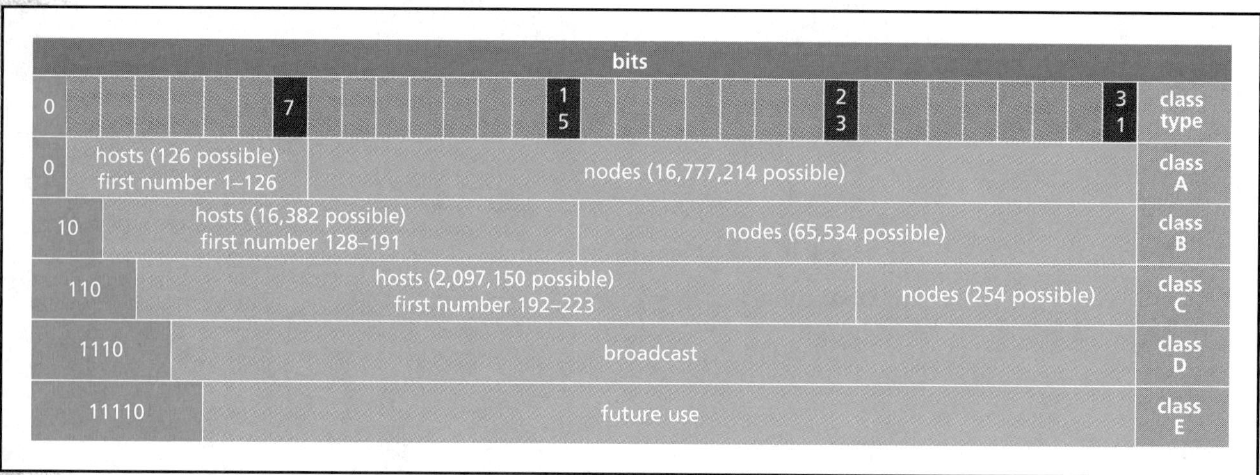

There are some special reserved addresses:

- Address 0.0.0.0 is reserved for the default network.
- Address 127.0.0.1 is used for testing as a loopback address (the local computer).
- Address 255.255.255.255 is reserved for network broadcasts (sending the same data to every computer on the network).
- Address range 10.0.0.0–10.255.255.255 is reserved for private networks.
- Address range 172.16.0.0–172.31.255.255 is reserved for private networks.
- Address range 192.168.0.0–192.168.255.255 is reserved for private networks.

Looking at the IP address classes shown in Figure 7-2, you can see how the range of IP addresses has been divided. In the figure, a host corresponds to a corporation, university, or some other entity that has a need for IP addresses.

Nodes are the number of devices with unique IP addresses that each host can have. Notice that Class A addresses are designed for very large entities with a need for up to 16 million nodes, but only 126 entities in the entire world can have a class A network. An entity with a class B license can have up to 65,534 IP addresses for their nodes, and there is only room for 16,382 class B hosts in the world. There are over two million class C hosts possible, but each of them can only have up to 254 nodes.

IANA (Internet Assigned Numbers Authority) – The organization under contract with the U.S. government to oversee the allocation of IP addresses to ISPs

ARIN (American Registry of Internet Numbers) – The organization in the United States that manages IP address numbers for the country and assigned territories

You can tell from the first number of your IP address what class of license your institution has. At home, you receive a node address from your ISP, who in turn may receive it from a larger ISP or NBP.

So, who is in charge of allocating these addresses? The *IANA* (Internet Assigned Numbers Authority) maintains a high-level registry of IP addresses for the entire world. The IP addresses are actually assigned by regional agencies. *ARIN* (American Registry for Internet Numbers) is a nonprofit agency that allocates IP addresses in North America, among other areas.

The IP address is the key part of the Internet Protocol. If a computer "knows" the IP address of another computer, the components of the network, from computer to router to router to computer, can respond to the address and direct the packet to the correct communication line.

subnet – A portion of a network that shares part of an address with other portions of the network and is distinguished by a subnet number

IP addressing also supports the concept of a *subnet*. A subnet consists of a block of IP addresses that form a separate network from a routing standpoint. Subnets are defined through the use of a subnet mask. The subnet mask looks very much like an IP address. For example, the subnet mask of 255.255.255.0 defines a subnet in which all of the devices on the subnet are the same in the first three parts of the IP address. The zero in the last position of the subnet mask indicates that each device on the subnet has a different last number in the range from 0 to 255.

DHCP

DHCP (Dynamic Host Configuration Protocol) – A communications protocol that automates the assignment of IP addresses in an organization's network

Another protocol that is a key part of the Internet is *DHCP* (Dynamic Host Configuration Protocol). This is a protocol that is used between a computer and a router. Usually, institutions are given a block of IP addresses that they can use for their own networking purposes. These institutions could configure each computer and manually set an IP address for each computer. DHCP, however, allows each computer to automatically be assigned an IP address each time it is started up. This dynamic allocation of IP addresses saves the network administrator time. Each computer that is configured for DHCP uses that protocol to communicate with the router and get an IP address. That way, the network administrator only has to set up the DHCP server to allocate a block of addresses. After it is configured, the individual nodes can be moved around and new computers can be added without having to try to decide what IP addresses are available.

hold that address

Static (fixed) IP addresses are often used in addition to DHCP to ensure that a particular network device, such as a printer, is always accessible by the same address.

router – A device or software in a computer that determines the next network point to which a packet should be forwarded toward its destination

routers

The network hardware component that makes the Internet work is the ***router***. The key to the Internet is the fact that IP packets can be routed to the correct destination via a number of different routes. The Internet was originally designed to be immune to problems on a particular network. Using routers, a packet can just be sent on an alternate line if the desired line is damaged or busy (Figure 7-3).

A router is actually a specialized computer that is connected to many different communication lines and is programmed to examine the packets that it receives on one line and route them to the communication line that can get the packet closer to its final destination. Routers are used to join networks together. The Internet, as mentioned, is a collection of many different networks. Routers, therefore, make the Internet possible by connecting all of these networks together, and by forwarding the IP packets to either another router or to their final destination.

Figure 7-3, Routers provide many alternate routes for packets

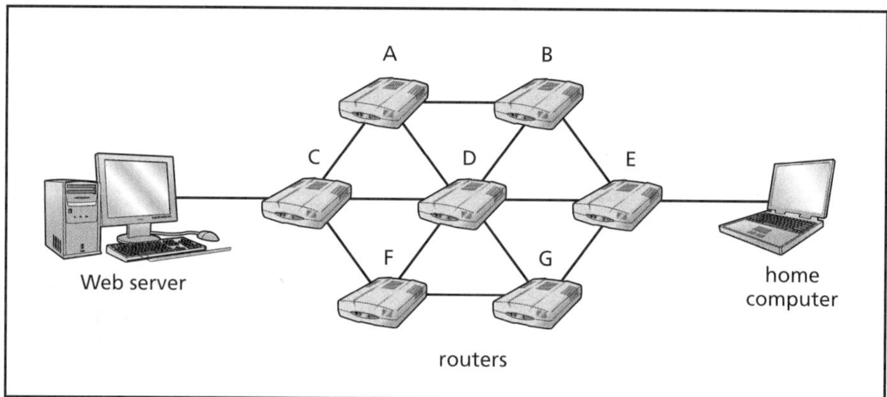

note **The Internet would not exist without the capability of routers.**

Routers work in a manner similar to the way mail is delivered. Consider a package with the address:

Course Technology
25 Thompson Place
Boston, MA 02210

The postal service examines the ZIP code of this address and puts the package on a truck that takes the package either to another truck, or to the airport. The postal workers, or machines in some cases, do what's necessary to get the package closer to its ultimate destination. All along the trip to Boston, various workers examine the ZIP code and place the package on some type of transportation that gets it closer to its destination. When the package arrives at the post office in Boston, another worker places the package on a truck that is driven to the street address for final delivery.

Now consider the IP address, 12.129.23.63, which is the IP address for the Course Technology Web site. If you were sending some data to that IP address from your home computer, the first packet that leaves your computer is sent to a router at your ISP. The router examines the destination address in the packet header to see if the address is within your ISP's LAN. If so, it forwards your data packet on a communication line that takes it to the computer within the ISP. Because your packet is probably on a different LAN than Course Technology, the router checks its internal tables and places the packet on a communication line that takes the packet to another router that is closer to the ultimate destination.

how much is that router?

Prices of routers vary widely. Large commercial routers can cost over $100,000; small routers for home use can sell for under $50.

When the next router gets the packet, it follows the same process. First, it examines the address to see if it is part of the LAN to which the router is connected. If not, a table lookup occurs and the packet is placed again on a communication line that takes the packet to another router that is even closer to the specified address.

Finally, the packet is forwarded to a router on the Course Technology LAN. This router notes that the destination address is within the LAN and places the packet on the communication line connected to the specified computer.

Each of the packets that make up your message is sent in this same manner and not all take the same path. Routers have the ability to communicate with each other using another special protocol. They share information concerning the amount of traffic on the lines to which they are connected. If the communication line that the router normally uses is down or heavily congested, the router sends the packet out on another line, usually one that is still close to the destination specified by the IP address.

time to live (TTL) – A field in the IP header that enables routers to discard packets that have been traversing the network for too long

So that packets do not keep bouncing from router to router forever, one of the fields in the IP header is the ***time to live (TTL)*** field. This field is initialized to a value (normally 40–60) and each time a packet passes through a router, the field is decremented by one. When the count reaches zero, the packet is discarded.

Because packets can be discarded and some may never reach the specified destination, how can you be certain that the data you sent is received just as you sent it? Also, because of the way routers work, the packets that make up your complete message may take many different routes to the final destination. How can you guarantee that your packets are received in the correct order? As mentioned earlier, TCP ensures reliable delivery of data from one computer to another and checks that the data received in the packet is identical to the data that was sent. TCP also includes information about the order in which the packets were originally sent, and uses this sequence number to order the packets once it has received all of them. If any of the packets are missing, the receiving TCP layer sends a message back to the sending TCP layer requesting a retransmission of the missing packet. Any packets containing data errors are also requested for retransmission. Errors are detected when the receiving side detects that the checksum doesn't match the sent packet.

The combination of TCP and IP ensure that data sent from one computer to another gets there in a fast, orderly, and reliable manner. Without TCP/IP and routers, there would be no Internet.

UDP

UDP (User Datagram Protocol) is another protocol that works with IP to broadcast data. UDP differs from TCP in that UDP doesn't have the ability to guarantee delivery or recover from errors in transmission. UDP is often used for streaming audio or video.

high-level protocols

In your reading on networking, you learned about the OSI networking model and its seven layers of protocols. The suite of protocols that work with TCP/IP can be compared to the OSI layers (Figure 7-4). TCP and IP span the Session,

Figure 7-4, TCP/IP protocols compared to the OSI model

network user

OSI model	TCP/IP
7 Application layer type of communication; e-mail, file transfer, Web page	FTP SMTP HTTP Telnet
6 Presentation layer encryption, data conversion: ASCII to EBCDIC, BCD to binary, etc.	
5 Session layer starts, stops session; maintains order	
4 Transport layer ensures delivery of entire file or message	TCP (delivery ensured) UDP (delivery *not* ensured)
3 Network layer routes data to different LANs and WANs based on network address	IP
2 Data Link (MAC) layer transmits packets from node to node based on station address	
1 Physical layer electrical signals and cabling	

Transport, and Network layers. SMTP, HTTP, FTP, and Telnet are called "high-level protocols" because they are "above" TCP and IP in the networking model. It is important to remember that these high-level protocols use TCP/IP over the Internet to accomplish their specific tasks. Messages are passed from the high-level protocol to the TCP layer, which splits the messages into packets, if necessary, and adds the TCP header and forwards it down to the IP layer for addressing. From there, the packets are sent down to the Data Link and Physical layers for transmission across the communication medium. These high-level protocols can also be used in environments other than the Internet. In that case, the messages from these protocols are passed down to some other lower protocol for transmission and error detection and correction.

7

SMTP

The Simple Mail Transport Protocol (SMTP) is used to send e-mail messages over the Internet. This protocol establishes a link from an e-mail client, such as Microsoft Outlook, to a mail server such as Microsoft Exchange and then transfers a message according to the details of the protocol. This protocol, like all others, exchanges a series of messages, called handshaking, to establish the parameters of the intended communication of data. The receipt of e-mail is handled by another protocol, either ***POP3*** (Post Office Protocol version 3) or ***IMAP*** (Internet Message Access Protocol).

POP3 (Post Office Protocol version 3) – The most recent version of a standard protocol for receiving e-mail from a mail server

IMAP (Internet Message Access Protocol) – A standard protocol for accessing e-mail from a mail server

FTP

The File Transfer Protocol is used to provide the reliable and efficient transmission of data files, especially large files. FTP has been in use for many years. As with SMTP, FTP requires both a client program and a server program in order to be able to transfer files. Most operating systems include a default command-line FTP client. In Windows you can get to the command-line client by opening a command prompt window and typing FTP at the prompt. You can also use Internet Explorer to connect to an FTP server by specifying the address of the server in the IE address bar. For example, you could enter *ftp://ftp.aol.com* to connect to the AOL FTP site as shown in Figure 7-5.

FTP clients are an important tool for computer scientists, as described in Chapter 2, "Software Tools for Techies."

note

PING is a commonly used command-line utility to test communication between two IP devices.

Figure 7-5, Command-line FTP session

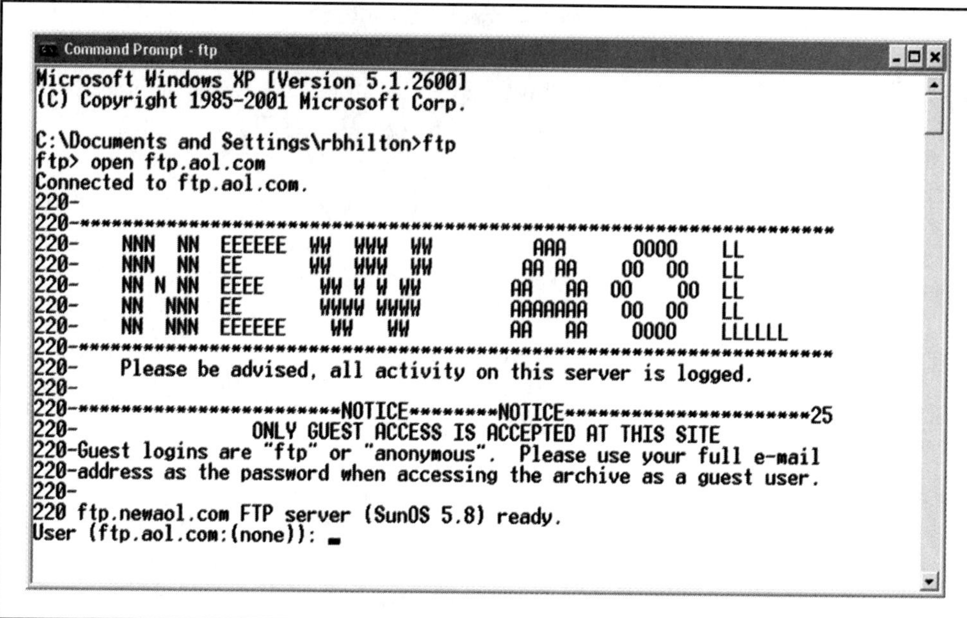

Telnet

Telnet has been the Internet standard protocol for remote login to a UNIX host. Telnet runs on top of TCP/IP and allows the client computer to log on to the host computer and perform most of the same functions that could be performed if the user were sitting at the host computer. Figure 7-6 shows an example of a Telnet session. Most operating systems include a command-line Telnet client.

Figure 7-6, Command-line Telnet session

```
Command Prompt - telnet
Microsoft (R) Windows 2000 (TM) Version 5.00 (Build 2195)
Welcome to Microsoft Telnet Client
Telnet Client Build 5.00.99206.1

Escape Character is 'CTRL+]'

Microsoft Telnet> open icarus.weber.edu
```

secure HTTP

A Web address that begins with *https* instead of *http* is a secure Web site that is capable of sending Web pages back in an encrypted format. Internet Explorer and Netscape show a small closed padlock icon on the lower status bar to indicate that a page is secure. If the padlock is open, the page is not secure.

HTTP

Although all of the protocols discussed so far are used in conjunction with the Internet, the Hypertext Transfer Protocol (HTTP) is the protocol that makes the Web possible. In the early days of the Internet, files were transferred between computers using FTP and other older protocols. Researchers and scientists wanted a better way to be able to present data, and so in 1990, Tim Berners-Lee came up with the idea of the World Wide Web and built the first rudimentary browser program. Central to the idea of the World Wide Web was a Web server, a Web browser, and a protocol that allowed the two to communicate. HTTP is the protocol that allows Web browsers and Web servers to talk to each other. When you type in a Web address such as *http://www.course.com*, the *http* tells the browser that you are using the Hypertext Transfer Protocol to get the Web page that you're looking for.

URLs and DNS

domain name – A name used to locate the IP address of an organization or other entity on the Internet, such as www.course.com

DNS (Domain Name System) – A method of translating Internet domain names into IP addresses (DNS servers are servers that are used in the process)

URL (Uniform Resource Locator)—The Englishlike address of a file accessible on the Internet

It would be very difficult to have to try to remember the IP address of every Web site that you would like to visit. When there were only a few computers on the Internet, the IP address was the way that Web pages were accessed. As the Internet grew, the problem of having to remember IP addresses was solved by allowing Web servers to have ***domain names*** and by the development of the Domain Name System (***DNS***). Now, to locate a Web page or to send an e-mail message, you use what is called a Uniform Resource Locator (***URL***). A URL consists of the domain name followed by specific folder and/or filenames, as shown in Figure 7-7. The domain names are mapped to IP addresses by another special computer called a DNS server. This computer's job is to translate domain names from URLs into IP addresses.

If there were only one DNS server for the entire Internet, it would get overwhelmed very quickly. Instead, there are many thousands of DNS servers distributed throughout the Internet. Your ISP maintains a DNS server, but it doesn't have to contain all of the existing domains in the world. Instead, each DNS server is responsible for just a portion of the world's domains.

Figure 7-7, Structure of a URL

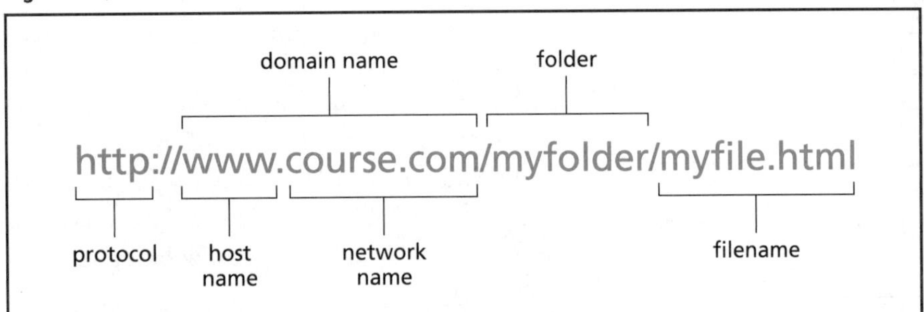

A domain has levels (Table 7-3). You are probably familiar with the original top-level domains (TLDs) of .com, .edu, .gov, .net, .org, and .mil. You might also have heard of some of the newer ones such as .biz and .info. There are also top-level, two-character domains for every country. There is a top-level DNS server for each of the top-level domains. Each of these servers has information about all the DNS servers within that domain.

Table 7-3, Top-level domain names used on the Internet

TLD	meaning
.aero	Air-transport industry
.arpa	Address and Routing Parameter Area
.biz	Business
.com	Commercial
.coop	Cooperative
.edu	U.S. educational
.gov	U.S. government
.info	Information
.int	International organization
.mil	U.S. military
.museum	Museum
.name	Individuals, by name
.net	Network
.org	Organization
.pro	Profession
.ca, .mx	Canada and Mexico and other countries are represented by two-letter codes

For example, there is a top-level .edu server. That server has information on the IP addresses of all of the lower-level servers managing domains within .edu. An educational institution, such as Weber State University, has a domain server containing information on all the domains under *weber.edu*. There may be additional servers under that domain, such as *faculty.weber.edu*. The server at each level has knowledge of a lower-level server that may have better knowledge of finding the IP address you're looking for.

When you type in a URL in the address bar of your browser, you send a DNS lookup request to the DNS server at your ISP. If the URL is outside of the domain of your ISP, the DNS server contacts a top-level DNS. That DNS might then give the address of another DNS server, and that one to another until your ISP's DNS server has contacted the DNS server that knows the correct IP address and can return it to your browser. Once the DNS server at your ISP has located an IP address for a URL, it saves, or caches, the address in case there's another request for the same URL.

DNS servers are smart, in that they can communicate (using a protocol, of course!) to other domain name servers and stay updated with the correct IP address for any URL. Each of the domain name servers is maintained by the network administrators of that domain. This is another example of how people acting for their own purposes on the Internet actually benefit all.

port numbers

There was another problem that existed in the early days of the Internet that needed to be solved. That problem was that one computer with one IP address needed to be able to use multiple protocols at the same time. In addition, people wanted to be able to have multiple browsers open simultaneously. You can compare this to having multiple chat windows open so that you can chat with a dozen of your closest friends at once.

port number – An addressing mechanism used in TCP/IP as a way for a client program to specify a particular server program on a computer in a network and to facilitate Network Address Translation

To solve the problem, the concept of a *port number* was established. In the context of the Transfer Control Protocol (TCP), there is the ability to specify beyond the IP address of the Internet Protocol (IP) by specifying a unique port number (sometimes just called a port) for each application. A port number can be specified for both the sending and receiving computers in the TCP header. The combination of IP address and port number is much like a street address and apartment number. The street address gets you to the building, and then the apartment number takes you to the correct apartment.

Most protocols have a standard port number. The standard port number for HTTP is 80, and for FTP it is 21. There are a possible 65,636 port numbers that can be used with each IP address. You can specify a particular port by appending a colon and the port number following the domain or IP address. For example http://192.168.2.33:8080 specifies the IP address of 192.168.2.33 and the port number of 8080. Only the specific program set to "listen" on port 8080 can respond to the IP packets coming in to that address. Table 7-4 lists some of the more commonly used port numbers.

Table 7-4, Commonly used TCP/IP port number assignments

port number	protocol
21	21 FTP (File Transfer Protocol)
23	Telnet
25	SMTP (Simple Mail Transfer Protocol)
53	DNS (Domain Name System service)
68	DHCP (Dynamic Host Control Protocol)
80	HTTP (Hypertext Transfer Protocol)
110	POP3 (Post Office Protocol version 3)
139	NetBIOS

NAT

NAT (Network Address Translation) – The translation of an inside IP address to an outside IP address; NAT is often used to allow multiple computers to share one Internet connection

Now that you have an understanding of how TCP/IP, routers, and port numbers work, you are ready to learn a new term, ***NAT*** (Network Address Translation). If you set up a home network, you might use a wireless router using NAT. There's also a high probability that your school labs also use routers and NAT. With NAT, multiple computers can share one Internet connection.

NAT is dependent on DHCP and port numbers. A range of IP addresses that is reserved for internal LAN use is 192.168.0.0 to 192.168.255.255 (subnet mask 255.255.0.0). This IP address range is often used for internal LANs that are connected to a DHCP router. On the Internet side of the router, one IP address is presented to the Internet. That way, many computers can share one IP address. Because the 192.168 subnet is never presented to the outside Internet, all LANs can use the same addresses if they are behind a DHCP, NAT router.

All of the computers using the DHCP assigned IP addresses can share the same Internet connection through one IP address because of ports. Each internal IP address is assigned a port number to be used in conjunction with the main IP address. When HTTP or other messages come to the router from the Internet, they are routed by the TCP protocol to the computer with the corresponding port number.

checking your configuration

IPCONFIG – A Windows command-line utility that can be used to display the network settings currently assigned and given by a network

You can check the network configuration of your computer in Windows by using the ***IPCONFIG*** command at a command prompt window. You do this by clicking Start, Programs, Accessories, then Command Prompt. At the command prompt, type the command IPCONFIG and then press Enter. On the screen you will see your current IP address, your subnet mask, and the address of your gateway to the Internet. The IP address is the one that has been assigned to your computer by either your network administrator or your ISP. The subnet mask is a set of numbers that identify the subnet to which you're connected. The gateway address is the IP address of either a computer or router that serves as your gateway to the next level in the Internet. Figure 7-8 shows the result of typing the IPCONFIG command. You can get even more information about your network connections by typing IPCONFIG /ALL at the command prompt.

7

Figure 7-8, Executing the IPCONFIG command at the command prompt

Command Prompt - ftp

```
Microsoft Windows XP [Version 5.1.2600]
(C) Copyright 1985-2001 Microsoft Corp.

C:\Windows>IPCONFIG

Windows IP Configuration


Ethernet adapter Belkin Connect Ethernet:

        Connection-specific DNS Suffix  . :
        IP Address. . . . . . . . . . . . : 192.168.0.33
        Subnet Mask . . . . . . . . . . . : 255.255.255.0
        Default Gateway . . . . . . . . . : 192.168.0.1

C:\Windows>
```

note

You can get help on all of the available IPCONFIG options by entering IPCONFIG /H at the command prompt.

www

The www (for Worldwide Web) in front of many domain names is part of the URL. The URLs *www.foxnews.com* and *foxnews.com* are not the same. Web site URLs are not required to start with www.

Web server *– A program running on a computer that responds to HTTP requests for Web pages and returns the pages to the requesting client*

HTML (Hypertext Markup Language) *– A set of markup symbols or codes inserted in a file that specify how the material is displayed on a Web browser page*

HTML

You have discovered the network aspects of what goes on when you type a URL into the address bar of a browser, but you might still have the question, "What exactly is a Web page?"

When you type *http://www.course.com* into your browser's address bar, what happens? As described above, first the URL is sent to the DNS server of your ISP and you receive back the actual IP address corresponding to the domain you entered. Your browser then sends an HTTP request to that IP address. When the HTTP request gets through all the routers to the Web server you addressed, the ***Web server***, which is just a computer that is programmed to respond to HTTP requests, sends back the requested Web page. In this case, only a domain was specified, so the server sends back a default page. Default pages have names such as index.htm, default.htm, or in this case default.cfm. The person responsible for the Web server, sometimes referred to as the Webmaster, can specify the default Web page.

What is a Web page? There are a few possible answers to this question, but the majority of Web pages are simply text files containing the textual information of the page and ***HTML*** (Hypertext Markup Language) tags. HTML tags are formatting commands that enable the browser to display the content of the page in a graphical, easy-to-read format. Table 7-5 lists some of the most commonly used HTML tags.

note

HTML tags are enclosed in less-than signs (<) and greater-than signs (>) and most of the tags come in pairs, with an opening and closing tag.

Table 7-5, Common HTML tags

tag	purpose
<HTML> </HTML>	Used to provide a boundary for the HTML document; everything between the <HTML> and the </HTML> is considered to be part of the Web page
<HEAD> </HEAD>	The <HEAD> tags are placed inside the <HTML> tags; the <HEAD> tags provide a boundary for items that are not part of the document, but are used to direct the browser to do certain things

Table 7-5 (*continued*)

tag	purpose
<TITLE> </TITLE>	The <TITLE> tags are used to surround the Web document's title. This is the title that appears in the title bar of the browsers when the page is displayed. The <TITLE> tags go inside of the <HEAD> tags.
<BODY> </BODY>	The <BODY> tags enclose the part of the Web page document that is to be displayed in the browser; the <BODY> tags are placed inside of the <HTML> tags, but not inside the <HEAD> tags
 	 is used to force the browser display area to go to a new line. Note that the is a single tag. There is no closing tag for the tag.
<P> </P>	The <P> tags are used to define a paragraph in the Web document and to cause a paragraph break to take place.
<FONT></FONT>	The <FONT> tags are used to specify the font for the text between the tags; the opening <FONT> tag has special arguments that are used to specify the type, size, and color of the font for the included text
<A> </A>	The <A> tag pair is used to specify a link to another Web page or a specific location on the current page; the opening <A> tag has arguments that reference the linked page or position
<IMG>	The <IMG> tag is used to insert an image in the document; the <IMG> tag has arguments that are used to specify the location and size of the image to be displayed

Table 7-5 (*continued*)

tag	purpose
<FORM> </FORM>	The <FORM> tags are used to provide the boundaries for an input form on the Web page; other tags are placed inside of the <FORM> tag to create items such as input boxes and buttons on the Web page
<INPUT>	The <INPUT> tag is used to specify data input objects inside of the <FORM> tags; these tags allow data input to take place on a Web page
<TABLE> </TABLE>	The <TABLE> tags are used to define an area on the Web page that displays tabular data in rows and columns
<TR> </TR>	The <TR> tags are placed inside of the <TABLE> tags to signify the start of a table row
<TD> </TD>	The <TD> tags are placed inside of the <TR> tags to define a column within the row of a table

There are many more tags available in HTML. If you are going to design Web pages, you will have to know how to use HTML, even if you use a Web page design tool such as Microsoft Front Page or Macromedia Dreamweaver.

HTML requirements

These eight HTML tags are required for every Web page:

<HTML>

<HEAD>

<TITLE>

</TITLE>

</HEAD>

<BODY>

</BODY>

</HTML>

creating a simple Web page

You can create a simple Web page on your own computer and test it using your browser. Others won't be able to get to your Web page because your computer is probably not set up to be a Web server, but you can test Web pages that you create without having a Web server. Simply open a Notepad window and type in the HTML document shown in Figure 7-9. After you have entered the HTML tags exactly as shown, save it to your hard drive or other storage media. HTML files should normally have a file extension of .htm or html. Then use Windows Explorer to find the document where you saved it and double-click it. That opens your browser and displays the document as you have specified it to be formatted in your HTML code (Figure 7-10).

To save some typing, the Notepad files shown in Figure 7-9 and Figure 7-11 are available in the source code section under Chapter 7 on the student CD.

Figure 7-9, HTML tags for a simple Web page

```
<html>
<head>
<title>My First Web Page</title>
</head>
<body>
<p>My First Web Text<br>
 <b><font size="3" face="Arial">My First Table</font></b></p>
<table width="30%" border="1">
  <tr>
    <td><b>Protocol</b></td><td><b>Purpose</b></td>
  </tr>
  <tr>
    <td>TCP</td><td>Reliable Delivery</td>
  </tr>
  <tr>
    <td>IP</td><td>Addressing</td>
  </tr>
  <tr>
    <td>HTTP</td><td>Web Pages</td>
  </tr>
</table>
</body>
</html>
```

Figure 7-10, Simple Web page as displayed on the browser screen

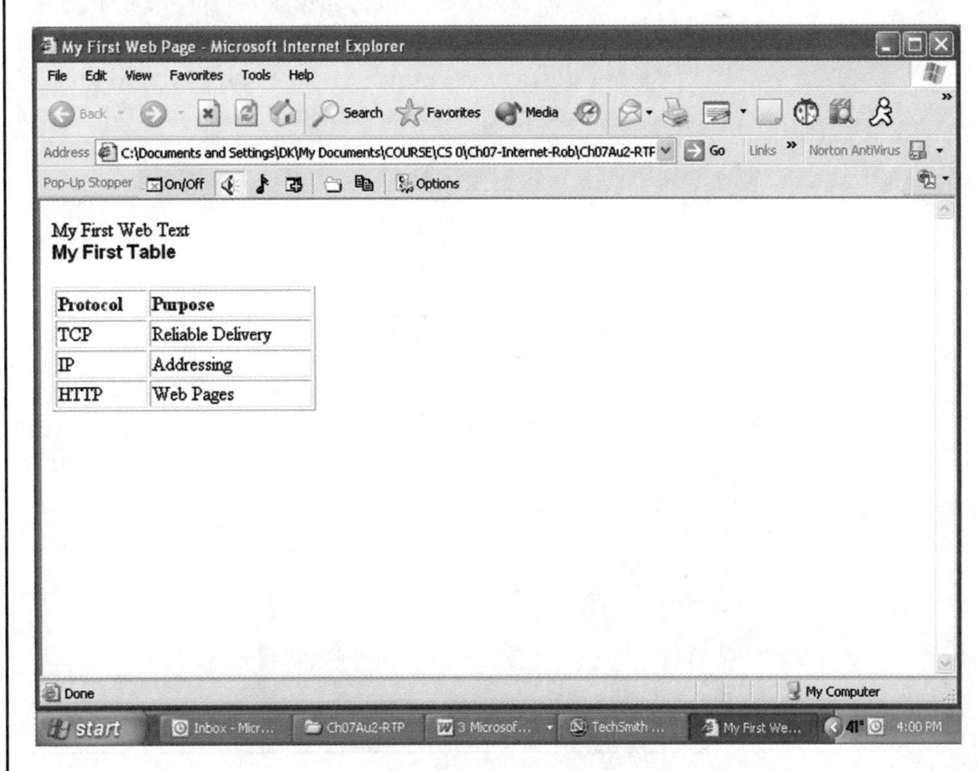

For step-by-step instructions on HTML, see the tutorials section under Chapter 7 on the student CD. For additional HTML exercises, see the learning tools section under Chapter 7.

HTML is not case sensitive. Even though Table 7-5 shows the tags as uppercase, the browser accepts them as upper- or lowercase. It's also important to note that HTML is free form and ignores white space, such as excess spaces, tabs, or lines. The HTML tags in Figure 7-9 could all be on the same line and the browser would still display it correctly. However, formatting HTML tags as shown in the example makes it easier for you, the HTML developer, to create and maintain the page.

Creating Web pages in HTML is very tedious. Therefore, most Web designers don't create Web pages using straight HTML. They create the pages visually using a Web design tool. You need to know HTML, however, because many times the design tools don't do exactly what you want, and you have to go into the HTML code to fix it.

hyperlinks

***hyperlink** – A link that allows the user to select a connection from one word, picture, or information object to another*

One of the most powerful aspects of the Web and HTML is the ability to provide links on a page to other pages. The HTML <A></A> tags are used for this purpose. The format of the ***hyperlink*** tag pair is shown in Figure 7-11, and its result in a browser window is shown in Figure 7-12. The user can click on the underlined hyperlinks and then be taken to the specified URL.

Web server programs

HTML is the language used by Web browsers to display Web pages. Normally, HTML pages are static; they never change from one request to another. To make the information on a Web page dynamic, that is, to give it the ability to be different each time it is accessed, you need to have a technology that has greater programming capability than that of the simple formatting available in standard HTML.

Figure 7-11, Using the <A> tag to create hyperlinks in a Web document

```
<html>
<head>
<title>My Second Web Page</title>
</head>
<body>
<p><b>My Set of Hyperlinks to News Sources</b><br>
<a href="http://cnn.com">CNN</a><br>
  <a href="http://foxnews.com">FOX NEWS</a> <br>
  <a href="http://www.nbc.com/nbc/NBC_News/">NBC</a><br>
  <a href="http://abcnews.go.com/">ABC</a><br>
  <a href="http://www.cbsnews.com/sections/home/main100.shtml">CBS</a></p>
</body>
</html>
```

Figure 7-12, Browser view of example hyperlink Web page

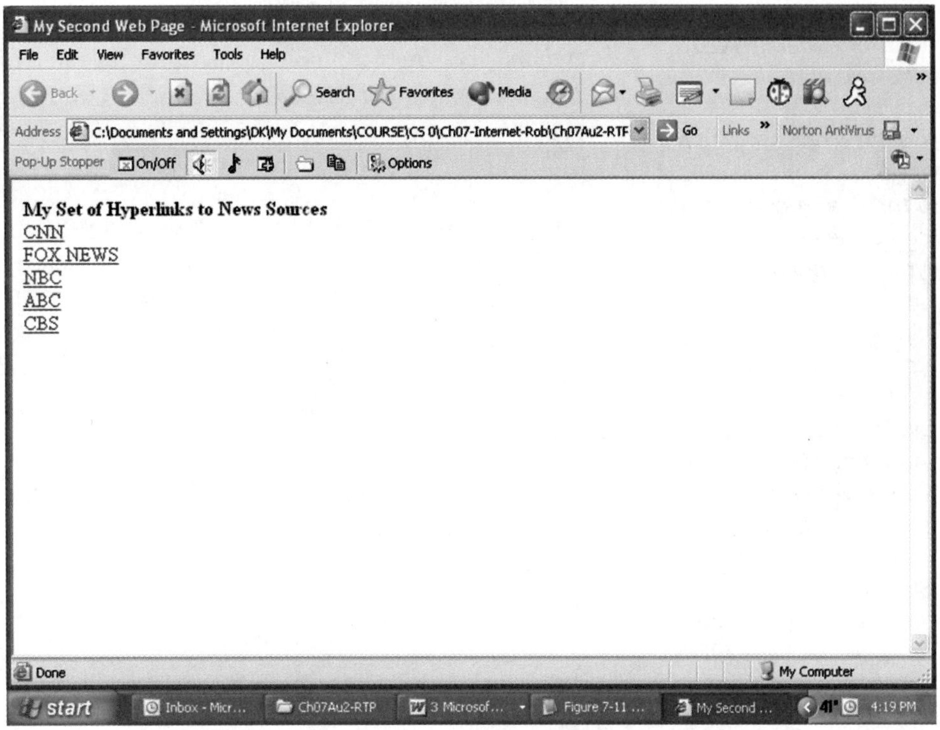

DHTML (Dynamic HTML) – An extension to HTML tags and options that allow for Web pages that are responsive to user interaction

JavaScript – An interpreted programming or script language from Netscape; is somewhat similar in capability to Microsoft VBScript

VBScript – An interpreted script language from Microsoft that is a subset of the Visual Basic programming language often used by Web browsers and ASP servers

Web browsers allow for dynamic Web pages in the form of ***DHTML*** (Dynamic Hypertext Markup Language). DHTML provides for Web page animation and for more responsive user interactions. Therefore, both HTML and DHTML also allow for the inclusion of scripting code, such as ***JavaScript*** or ***VBScript***. These scripting languages allow a Web page developer to include dynamic properties, such as changes to an area of the Web page based on keystrokes or mouse movement or clicks and timers. The Web page is still static in that the page stored on the Web server doesn't change between accesses, but once it is displayed in the browser, items can be dynamically altered in response to various events.

To allow a Web page to be *completely* dynamic—to have the ability to be different each time it is accessed—the page has to be created at the time it is accessed. There are Web server technologies available that allow this to take place. ***CGI*** is an older technology that allows older programming languages, such as ***Perl***, to be used to dynamically create Web pages as they are requested. CGI/Perl is being replaced by newer technologies such as ***ASP***, ***JSP***, ***PHP***, and ***Python***. These new technologies perform the same function: they are used to create programs that reside on a Web server, and when they are accessed via HTTP and a browser, they dynamically create an HTML or DHTML Web page and return it to the browser as if it were a static page.

Server-side Web technologies are used heavily on the Internet now for everything from Internet banking and shopping to television program guides. There is a good chance that if you choose a career in computer programming, you will be doing server-side dynamic Web page programming.

CGI (Common Gateway Interface) – An older Web server technology that provides for dynamic Web page creation

Perl – A script programming language similar in syntax to the C language, often used to develop CGI dynamic Web pages

ASP (Active Server Page) – A page that combines features of HTML and JavaScript or VBScript programming code used on a Web server to dynamically create Web pages

JSP (Java Server Pages) – Comparable to Microsoft's Active Server Page (ASP) technology, except that it runs only programs written in Java

PHP – In Web programming, a script language and interpreter that is freely available and used primarily on Linux Web servers

Python – An interpreted, object-oriented programming language similar to Perl that has gained popularity in recent years

Web service – Programming and data on a Web server that is designed to make that data available to other Web programs

SGML (Standard Generalized Markup Language) – A standard for how to specify a document markup language or tag set

Web services

An outgrowth of dynamic server-side Web page programming is a relatively new technology called Web services. A ***Web service*** is a server-based Web program that contains data to be used by other programs or Web pages, rather than being viewed. Web services are becoming very popular in business to provide information such as stock quotes to other programs. For example, Amazon.com provides Web services that allow other Web sites to include information from Amazon.com on their sites.

XML

The original specification for HTML was derived from a document specification for ***SGML*** (Standard Generalized Markup Language). SGML is not a markup language like HTML; rather, it is a specification as to what a markup language should consist of. HTML has been enormously popular because it allows people to format Web pages in appealing ways. However, HTML deals only with the *form* of a Web page, not its content.

XML (Extensible Markup Language) – A markup language designed to create common information formats and share both the format and the data on the World Wide Web

metadata – In XML and in database systems, information about the characteristics of the data contained in the data file; sometimes referred to as "data about data"

Another implementation of SGML that has become very popular is *XML* (Extensible Markup Language). XML is similar to HTML in structure, but it serves a different purpose. HTML is used only to format content for display in a browser, XML goes beyond that and provides data and information *about* that data; such information is called *metadata*. XML can be used to display Web pages, but its greater use is in its ability to transfer data. XML has become the standard for transferring data via the Internet. Figure 7-13 shows an example of an XML dataset. You can see that XML is similar to HTML. The main difference is that HTML is mainly used to format the output of a text document, whereas XML is mainly used to transfer data via the Web.

Figure 7-13, Sample XML data document

```
<?xml version="1.0" encoding="ISO-8859-1"?>
<?xml-stylesheet type="text/xsl" href="sample.xsl"?>
<dvd_library>
  <dvd>
    <id>D0146</id>
    <title>The Lord of the Rings: The Return of the King</title>
    <rating>PG-13</rating>
    <price>24.95</price>
    <review>****</review>
  </dvd>
  <dvd>
    <id>D3218</id>
    <title>Dumb and Dumber</title>
    <rating>PG-13</rating>
    <price>14.95</price>
    <review>****</review>
  </dvd>
  <dvd>
    <id>D4482</id>
    <title>Mom and Dad Save The World</title>
    <rating>PG</rating>
    <price>8.95</price>
    <review>*****</review>
  </dvd>
</dvd_library>
```

using the Internet

While you're in school, you will often need to research assigned topics. The Internet has become a tremendous resource for performing research. Spending time developing skills in searching the Internet can aid you in all your educational pursuits. In the early days of the Internet, newsgroups were the primary method of research.

The widespread use of the Internet has opened up many new security concerns and ethical issues, covered in Chapter 13, "Security and Ethics."

search engines

The World Wide Web has hundreds of millions of Web pages. Many of them are useless for research, but many are very relevant and accurate. As the number of pages on the Internet has grown, it has become obvious that there is a need to be able to search the Web for the needed information. Many indexing methods have been tried, but the search engine has emerged as the preferred method for finding information on the Web. Figure 7-14 shows an example of the teoma.com search engine running in Internet Explorer.

Figure 7-14, A search engine provides various capabilities for Web searching

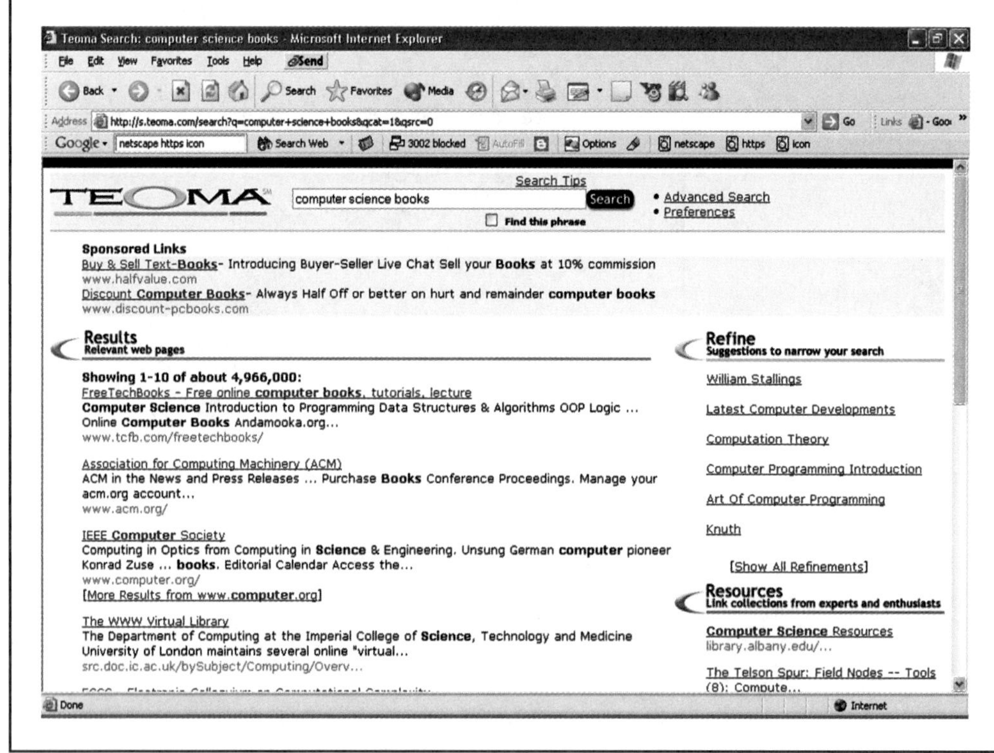

search engine – A program, usually accessed on the Web, that gathers and reports information available on the Internet

bot – A small program, also called a spider or a crawler, that accesses Web sites to gather their content for search engine indexes

spider – Also called bot or crawler, a program that visits Web sites and reads their pages and other information in order to create entries for a search engine index

Search engines use many different methods to build a database of Web sites that people can search, but probably the most widely used method is called "crawling." Crawling makes use of a special program called a ***bot*** (for robot) or a ***spider***. A bot starts with a few Web pages that have been submitted for indexing, and then scans those pages for links to other Web pages. The program then follows the links to those Web pages and repeats the process for every page it finds.

7

As the program identifies each page, it retrieves the relevant words on the page and uses them to create an index to each page based on the words on the page and on a special section of the HTML header called the <META> tag. This tag contains keywords that describe the contents of the Web page.

Most search engines make use of crawlers, while others consist of human-created directories. Some search engines, such as Dogpile.com, aren't actually search engines at all, but rather compilations of results from other search engines in a relevant format. Table 7-6 lists some of the more popular search engines.

Table 7-6, Some popular Web search engines

search engine	URL
Google	*www.google.com*
AllTheWeb	*www.alltheweb.com*
Yahoo	*www.yahoo.com*
MSNSearch	*search.msn.com*
Teoma	*teoma.com*

As you might imagine, search engines get millions of hits per day. The search sites have to be well designed from the standpoint of both hardware and software in order to maintain quick response with such a high hit rate. All aspects of designing and maintaining a search site require high technical skills of the type learned in a computer science program.

As a computer science student and as a professional, you will have many opportunities to benefit from the power of search engines. You will do well to spend some time and learn how to enter keywords for searches so that you can maximize your productivity when using one of these search engines.

one last thought

From a humble start, the Internet has grown into perhaps the most widely used medium for information gathering. From research to entertainment, the Internet has become part of nearly everyone's life. Even third-world countries are beginning to use and benefit from the Internet and its use. There are very many good things that have come about as a result of the growth and acceptance of the Internet; however, there are also problems with the Internet.

Reinforce your understanding of chapter concepts and terms with the information and activities for Chapter 7 on the student CD.

Perhaps the biggest problem with the Internet is its anonymity. When you go to a Web page, you don't know where it is. When you type your user ID, account number, or password into an input field on an Internet form, you can't be completely sure where you are sending it. It is difficult to tell if the information on a page is reliable. Identity theft and virus replication are just two of the many ethical and societal problems related to Internet usage.

New technologies related to the Internet are described in Chapter 14, "Emerging Technologies."

One thing is for sure—the Internet is here to stay. As time goes on, the Internet will become more and more a part of everyday life. As the Internet grows in usage, computer scientists will continually be required to develop and use new Internet related technologies.

chapter summary

- The Internet has revolutionized the world
- The Internet is just a giant collection of LANs and WANs
- The Internet is not owned by any single person or entity
- You connect to the Internet through ISPs and NBPs
- Protocols are vital to the operation of the Internet
- TCP/IP is the protocol set that makes the Internet possible
- TCP is used for accurate delivery of data packets
- Every device connected to the Internet has a unique IP address
- IP is used for addressing and routing of data packets
- IP addresses are organized into classes for block allocation
- DHCP is a protocol that can assign IP addresses to devices
- Internet networks are organized into subnets
- Routers are key to the operation of the Internet
- SMTP, POP3, and IMAP are protocols for sending and receiving e-mail
- FTP is widely used to send and receive files of various types
- HTTP is the protocol for sending and receiving data on the Web
- A URL is translated into an IP address by the DNS
- Port numbers are used to extend the capability of IP addressing
- NAT is widely used in home networking
- You can check your computer configuration with the IPCONFIG command
- HTML is the language of the World Wide Web
- XML is used to transfer data via the Internet
- Web pages consist of information surrounded by HTML formatting tags
- Scripting languages can be used on Web pages to make them dynamic
- Hyperlinks are used on Web pages to connect to other pages
- Web services make data available to other programs
- Search engines are used to find pages on the Internet

key terms

ARIN (235)
ASP (252)
bot (255)
CGI (252)
DHCP (235)
DHTML (251)
DNS (241)
domain name (241)
FTP (231)
HTML (246)
HTTP (231)
hyperlink (250)
IANA (235)
IMAP (239)
IP (232)
IP address (233)
IPCONFIG (245)
IPv4 (233)
IPv6 (233)
ISP (230)
JavaScript (251)
JSP (252)
metadata (253)
NAT (244)
NBP (230)
Perl (252)
PHP (252)
POP (230)
POP3 (239)
port number (243)
Python (252)
router (236)
search engine (255)
SGML (252)
SMTP (231)
spider (255)
subnet (235)
TCP (232)
TCP/IP (232)
time to live (TTL) (237)
URL (241)
VBScript (251)
Web server (246)
Web service (252)
XML (253)

test yourself

1. The Internet is a collection of __________ and __________.
2. Who owns the Internet?

3. What does the acronym ISP stand for?
4. What is an NBP?
5. What is the protocol SMTP used for?
6. Which Internet protocol is responsible for the reliable delivery of data from one computer to another?
7. Which Internet protocol manages the sequencing of data packets?
8. Which Internet protocol maintains port information?
9. What is the size, in bits, of an IP version 4 address?
10. Which IPv4 class allows for the greatest number of hosts?
11. What is the IP address 255.255.255.255 reserved for?
12. What is the regional agency that assigns IP addresses for North America?
13. What is the function of DHCP in networking?
14. What is a router?
15. What limits TCP/IP packets from bouncing from router to router forever?
16. What is the purpose of the FTP protocol?
17. Which network device is used to resolve domain names into IP addresses?
18. What is the Windows command-line command to check the network configuration of your computer?
19. What is the language of the World Wide Web?
20. What programs are used to "crawl" the Web?

practice exercises

1. The Internet is owned by:
   - **a.** ARIN
   - **b.** The FCC
   - **c.** The United Nations
   - **d.** None of the above
2. Internet providers maintain a switching center called a:
   - **a.** Point of presence
   - **b.** Backbone
   - **c.** Router
   - **d.** None of the above

3. The purpose of HTTP is to:
   - **a.** Format Web pages
   - **b.** Transfer Web pages
   - **c.** Route addresses
   - **d.** None of the above
4. Which of the following is not an Internet-related protocol?
   - **a.** HTTP
   - **b.** HTML
   - **c.** TCP
   - **d.** FTP
5. How many possible ports are allowed in TCP?
   - **a.** 8
   - **b.** 16
   - **c.** 65,536
   - **d.** 16,137,285
6. Which portion of the TCP/IP protocol stack provides for error detection and correction?
   - **a.** TCP
   - **b.** IP
   - **c.** Both
   - **d.** Neither
7. How many different hosts can be granted a Class A IP address allocation?
   - **a.** 16,137,285
   - **b.** 65,536
   - **c.** 16,382
   - **d.** 126
8. Which Internet protocol is used to dynamically assign IP addresses?
   - **a.** TCP
   - **b.** DHCP
   - **c.** HTTP
   - **d.** DNS
9. Routers are critical to the operation of the Internet.
   - **a.** True
   - **b.** False
10. Which Internet component is responsible for decrementing the TTL?
    - **a.** Router
    - **b.** Switch
    - **c.** DNS
    - **d.** Packet

11. Which of the following is an example of a high-level protocol?

- **a.** TCP
- **b.** IP
- **c.** DHCP
- **d.** SMTP

12. Which of the following protocols makes the Web possible?

- **a.** FTP
- **b.** Telnet
- **c.** HTTP
- **d.** None of the above

13. Which of the following is an example of a URL?

- **a.** www.course.com
- **b.** 192.168.0.22
- **c.** 1110111010111010110101
- **d.** HTTP

14. How many domain name servers does the Internet have?

- **a.** 1
- **b.** 2
- **c.** Thousands
- **d.** Millions

15. What is the standard port number for HTTP?

- **a.** 1
- **b.** 21
- **c.** 50
- **d.** 80

16. How many IP addresses are presented to the Internet when NAT is used?

- **a.** 1
- **b.** 21
- **c.** Thousands
- **d.** Unlimited

17. Which of the following is an example of an HTML tag?

- **a.** <HTTP>
- **b.** <HTML>
- **c.** <TCP>
- **d.** <DHCP>

18. Which HTML tag is used to provide links to other pages?

- **a.** <HTTP>
- **b.** <LINK>
- **c.** <A>
- **d.** <P>

19. XML is just another name for HTML.

   a. True
   b. False

20. Bots are used by ______________ to crawl the World Wide Web.

   a. Routers
   b. Search engines
   c. XML
   d. TCP/IP

digging deeper

1. What is the purpose of each of the fields in a TCP packet header?
2. What is the purpose of each of the fields in an IP packet header?
3. How are routers programmed?
4. What is the difference between a router, a gateway, and a switch, as applied to the Internet?
5. What is the process for obtaining a block of IP addresses for your business?

discussion topics

1. In what ways has the Internet impacted society?
2. What is meant by the term "digital divide"?
3. What are the security issues related to the Internet and how are they being addressed?
4. What are the individual steps involved in an HTTP request?
5. How does your department computer lab connect to the Internet?

Internet research

1. What are the major search engines and what are the strengths of each?
2. Find a map of Internet backbone communication lines. Where are the main lines located?
3. What are the major Web browsers? What are their strengths and weaknesses?
4. What is the membership makeup of the ARIN organization?
5. Research some domain names of your choosing to see if they are available.

chapter 8

database fundamentals

in this chapter you will:

- Consider the widespread use of databases
- Take a brief tour of database development history
- Learn basic database concepts
- Be introduced to popular database management software
- See how normalization makes your data more organized
- Explore the database design process
- Understand data relationships
- Gain an understanding of Structured Query Language (SQL)
- Learn some common SQL commands

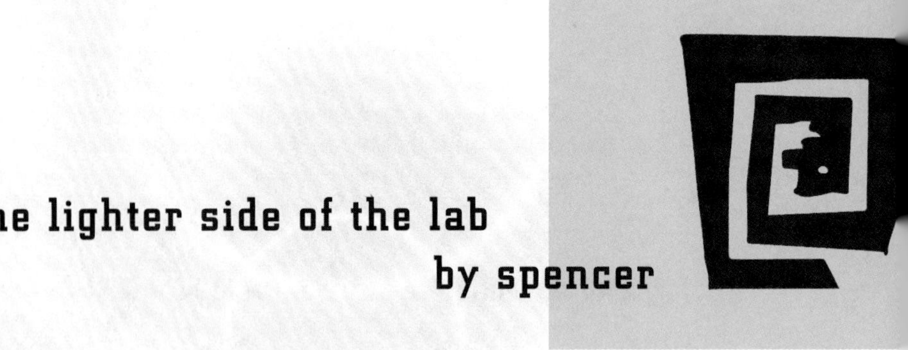

the lighter side of the lab

by spencer

I don't know of any two words that make me cringe like the words "corrupted data." I've spent the last four years working in technical support for a local software company. For those who haven't had the opportunity to work in technical support, here is how a typical call goes:

ME: Hi, you've reached technical support. This is Spencer. CUSTOMER: Hi. I got some error message yesterday when I did something in the program. What do I do to fix it?

ME: All right, do you remember what the message said? CUSTOMER: No.

ME: Do you remember what you were doing when you got the error message? CUSTOMER: Who am I? Einstein?

ME: All right, let's try opening the program. CUSTOMER: Oh! Here we go! It says the data is corrupted. What do I do now?

ME (cringing): We'll need to restore from one of your backups. CUSTOMER: Okay. Is that something I need to order?

(Brief pause) ME: Backups. You know—the thing you're prompted to do every time you leave the program. CUSTOMER: Oh, yeah! That message is so annoying! I always click "No." Is there any way to turn that message off?

(Brief pause) ME: All right, let's search your computer to see if we can find a recent backup. Click on "Start." CUSTOMER: Is that a right-click or a left-click? ME: Left-click. Now click on "Search." CUSTOMER: Is that a right-click or a left-click? ME: Left-click. It will always be a left-click, unless I say it's a right-click. CUSTOMER: Okay.

ME: Now click on "All Files and Folders." CUSTOMER: That's a left-click, right? ME: Yes! Now, do you see where it says "All or part of file name"? CUSTOMER: My computer doesn't have that. ME: Okay, it should be the first thing on the "Search" screen. CUSTOMER: No. It's not here.

(Brief pause) ME: Okay, it has to be there somewhere. CUSTOMER: Nope . . . nope . . . oh, wait! You mean right here in the middle of the screen? ME: (Sigh)

. . . and so on for the next 40 minutes. But the good news is that I've discovered that my head supports bus mastering: my mouth handles the support with absolutely no communication to or from my brain! I sometimes catch myself 20 minutes into a technical support call and not recalling a word anybody has said. This is good, because it frees up brain cycles to think about more important things . . . like the day I won't have to take another support call.

why you need to know about... databases

Can you imagine a world where none of the data was organized? How could a baseball announcer know that the batter hits .357 every other Thursday against this right-handed pitcher when the temperature is below 60 degrees, the moon is full, and the umpire ate tacos for dinner? Who would ever think to relate information like that to someone listening to a baseball game? The baseball announcers have a myriad of facts at their fingertips because someone has entered information into a database allowing the announcer to extract it based upon any criteria desired.

Without databases, how could a shopper find that very rare DVD of Godzilla versus the Centrino processor when there are so many other DVDs to choose from? It would be like finding a needle in a haystack! Instead of searching through all the DVD titles by name, you would have to start at the first DVD being offered for sale and scan through each item one at a time hoping that you encounter the DVD you want.

In order to be an effective computer scientist, you must know the proper way to design databases. The process of designing databases is called normalization and consists of several different steps. You should also know the basics of how information is retrieved from databases through a series of statements called Structured Query Language or SQL (pronounced "sequel" or sometimes S-Q-L), and be familiar with the major players in the database management software arena.

database applications

database – Data that has been organized and logically related into a file or set of files to allow access and usage

Data that has been organized and logically related to allow access, retrieval, and use of that data is called a ***database***. The database is a storage mechanism that allows you to logically relate data so that you can extract it at a later time with little effort, and even "query" the data to create new information.

Many software applications use some type of database as the data repository. Think of what would happen if applications had no way to track information. How could a bank keep track of your account? How could a healthcare provider keep track of your health history? How could the government keep track of criminals? Without a database most applications would be useless and would send the technical world spiraling back decades into the past. The paper trails would be endless and trees all over the world would have shivers of fright running up their bark. It is amazing to think of all the places where databases are being used and how they make your life simpler.

What type of database applications have you seen today? If you can't think of any, reflect on the last time you went to the grocery store. Information about all of the food items is stored in a database. How else would the store know how much to charge for the item? At the same time you are purchasing the item, there is probably a column in the food item database called "Quantity" which is automatically being updated within a database file. Or consider another common example: where did that last telemarketing salesperson get your telephone number? Probably it was purchased from a vendor who supplied a database that included your name, phone number, address, and other pertinent information. Here are other examples of activities that use database applications:

- Student grading
- Library book inventory
- Genealogy
- Social Security information
- Realty estate sales
- Video store rentals
- Retail business sales
- Space shuttle missions

Database applications are everywhere! This implies that database development is an essential part of your daily life. And, as a computer scientist, working with databases will most likely be an important part of your professional life.

Before diving into the fundamentals of databases and the systems developed to manage them, let's take a short historical tour.

brief history of database management systems

Back in the mid 1970s kids were frantically searching the neighborhood for empty pop bottles. Each unbroken bottle retrieved a nice return of at least five cents that could be applied toward a pack of sports trading cards. Although that hard stick of bubble gum that came with the sports card lost its flavor within minutes, kids spent hours upon hours reading the information on the cards and sorting them in different orders. Some liked their cards sorted by team name while others sorted the cards by position. In fact, some cards were even sorted by sport, team, and name. Then again, some kids sorted their cards by sport and card number. In other words, the information could be sorted in many different ways, with each owner determining the sort order.

In recent years, there has been a craze to swap and share music files over the Internet. Users have organized their music files by artist, song title, music category, or other attributes. Like baseball card collectors, music lovers spend hours upon hours organizing their music files. Whether it's baseball cards or music files, things are collected and organized according to a person's preference.

8

So what does this have to do with databases? Back in the early 1970s, while many thoughts turned to impeachment of the United States 37th President, Richard Nixon, the end of the Cold War, and watching the movie *The Exorcist*, E.F. Codd and C.J. Date were hard at work for IBM creating a theoretical model for designing data structures. This model became the foundation upon which database applications have been designed for the past two and a half decades. Believe it or not, those kids collecting sports cards and users collecting music files and then sorting them were putting into practice some of the database theories conceived by Codd and Date.

Structured Query Language (SQL) – A special language used to maintain the structure of a database and also modify, query, or extract information

database management system (DBMS) – A program used for managing storage, access, and modifications to a database

The development of software for organizing and sorting large amounts of data began with two mainframe products: System R by IBM and Ingres, created at the University of California, Berkeley. Both of these systems used a special language called ***Structured Query Language (SQL)*** to query or extract information from the databases. This language became a standard database feature. As PCs became more and more popular in businesses, PC users clamored for the type of software packages they were accustomed to using on the large mainframes. Thus the road was paved for other software vendors to create ***database management system (DBMS)*** packages.

In 1975 while working for Martin-Marietta and managing the database for the Viking spacecraft ground support system, Wayne Ratliff developed a database program called Vulcan. In 1980 the program was renamed dBASE II and was marketed for PCs by a company called Ashton-Tate. (There never was a dBASE I, but the name dBASE II was chosen to give consumers greater confidence in a product that seemed to have been already tested on the market.) dBASE II was such a success that soon Ashton-Tate dominated the PC DBMS market. The popularity of dBASE opened the door for other companies to bring out PC database products such as Paradox, Microsoft Access, or FoxPro, trying to provide features dBASE II lacked or improve on areas where dBASE II was weak.

note In 1991 Borland International acquired Ashton-Tate and their dBASE products. Today, dBASE is not a serious contender in the PC database market.

distributed data

Databases were originally created to act as a central data repository, but today a database might be stored on several computers that can be in different physical locations. This is called a distributed database. The primary advantages of a distributed database are flexibility, reliability, expandability, and efficiency. Disadvantages are cost and complexity.

As mainframe database systems such as System R and Ingres and PC systems such as dBASE became widespread, it became evident just how powerful databases were in providing essential information for corporate decision making, as well as enhancing almost all business systems from inventory management to customer support. Since then, databases have become an essential and critical part of business, and therefore of software development.

In today's computer industry, every company that wants to use a database must decide which DBMS package to use. There is a wide variety of databases on the market (see a sample in Table 8-1), each with its own strengths and weaknesses.

Table 8-1, Popular database management systems

DMBS name	vendor	computer type
Access	Microsoft	PC, server, PDA
DB2	IBM	PC, midrange server, mainframe
InterBase	Borland Software	PC, server
MySQL	MySQL AB (public domain)	PC, midrange server
Oracle	Oracle	PC, midrange server, mainframe, PDA
Paradox	Corel	PC, server
SQL Server	Microsoft	Server
Sybase	Sybase	PC, midrange server, PDA
Visual FoxPro	Microsoft	PC, server

note Microsoft Access was developed in the early 1990s and is included in the Microsoft Office Professional software package.

note MySQL is one of the most popular open source databases, often used on Internet Web sites.

take a test drive

As a researcher, you might have to recommend a specific DBMS to use as the company standard. What will you recommend? If you look at the advertisements and literature, all the DBMSs look good. One thing you can do now to prepare yourself is to start trying out and learning popular DBMS packages. Take them for a test spin and formulate your own opinions as to what you like and dislike about the products. Many database vendors have trial versions you can download and test to see if you like what the package has to offer.

database management system fundamentals

8

A database management system (DBMS) helps manage data and extract information from it using a query language. A DBMS manages the database structure and controls access to the data stored in the database, thus guaranteeing data integrity and data consistency.

The main functions of a DBMS are to:

- Manage database security
- Manage access of multiple users to the database
- Manage database backup and recovery
- Ensure data integrity
- Provide an end-user interface with the database
- Provide or interface with a query language to extract information from the database

note The person that maintains the database in a company is called the database administrator or DBA.

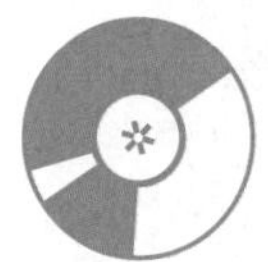

For a quick tutorial on using Microsoft Access, see the tutorials section under Chapter 8 on the student CD.

table or entity – Data arranged in rows and columns much like a spreadsheet

column, field, or attribute – A specific piece of information in a table row

row, record, or tuple – A collection of columns

database concepts

In order to understand the functionality of the DBMS you must first understand the basic elements of a database. Within a database, there can be one or more tables. Each ***table*** or ***entity*** is divided into rows and columns much like a spreadsheet. Figure 8-1 shows a database table with information about a music collection. Each ***column*** (called a ***field*** or ***attribute***) represents a specific piece of information (Song_Name, Track_Num, Album_Num, Album_Name, and so on) and the ***row*** (***record*** or ***tuple***) represents the collection of columns. Each song is considered to be a record or row in the database and contains information that can be arranged in columns describing the row.

Figure 8-1, A database table consists of rows and columns

Songs-orig : Table

	Song_Name	Artist_Code	Album_Num	Track_Num	Album_Name	Artist_Name	Media_Type	Genre_Code
▶	American Soldier	TK	911	3	Shock'n Y'all	Toby Keith	MP3	CW
	Beer For My Horses	TK	826	5	Unleashed	Toby Keith	MP3	CW
	Big Time	PG	10	14	Shaking the Tree	Peter Gabriel	CD	POP
	Come As You Are	NIRV	24	3	Nevermind	Nirvana	MP3	NW
	Lithium	NIRV	24	5	Nevermind	Nirvana	MP3	NW
	One Tree Hill	U2	146	9	The Joshua Tree	U2	CD	NW
	Only a Lad	OB	78	16	Best O Boingo	Oingo Boingo	CD	NW
	Sledgehammer	PG	10	3	Shaking the Tree	Peter Gabriel	CD	POP
	Sloop John B	BB	45	7	Pet Sounds	The Beach Boys	Vinyl	CLA
	The Thrill is Gone	BBK	98	8	The Best of B.B. King	B.B. King	MP3	BLU
	With or Without You	U2	146	3	The Joshua Tree	U2	CD	NW
*			0	0				

Record: 1 of 11

domain – Set of possible values for a column

The set of possible values for each column is called the *domain* of that column. For instance, the domain for the column labeled Genre_Code in Figure 8-1 is: ALT, BLU, CLA, CW, EL, GOS, HR, JAZ, NW, POP, RAP, and RB.

- ALT - Alternative
- BLU - Blues
- CLA - Classic Rock
- CW - Country Western
- EL - Easy Listening
- GOS - Gospel
- HR - Hard Rock
- JAZ - Jazz
- NW - New Wave
- POP - Pop
- RAP - Rap
- RB - R & B

the real stuff

Many companies have one database for their real, working data and another database with a similar structure that uses fake data for their test environment. This way, the company can test the validity of the data and confirm that changes to the database structure or software that supports the data does indeed function properly without affecting the "live" work environment.

note

Sometimes a program developer designs the software so a drop-down list box displays all of the domain values from which the user can select. This helps to keep the data consistent and avoids user entry errors.

A collection of columns referring to one item is called a row or tuple. The collection of rows comprises the contents of the table. A collection of one or more tables makes up a database. A database can contain one or more related tables that are kept in an organized structure, which allows easy access by software developers. The information within each table can be organized and more quickly accessed through the use of indexes or orders.

***index* – A special type of file that occupies its own space and specifies that one or more columns in a table determines how the information stored in the table is organized**

indexes

An ***index*** is a special type of file that occupies its own space and specifies one or more columns that determine how the information stored in a table is organized. For example, the table consisting of rows and columns can represent music in your music database. The rows represent songs while the columns contain more specific detailed information such as Song_Name, Track_Num, and Album_Num. In fact, many different types of information you encounter everyday are sorted by an index. Can you imagine a phone book with the information ordered sequentially? In other words, as a new phone number is created it is placed in the back of the phone book. You would have to search for hours in order to find a specific phone number. Instead, the information in the table (or phone book) is organized into an index or order by choosing specific columns. For instance, the Last Name and First Name columns can organize the phone book. Now you can retrieve phone numbers simply by knowing the alphabet.

tables vs. databases

How do tables and databases relate to each other? This point is very important. In many database packages, the terms database and table are *not* synonymous. The *database* refers to the file that stores the information about the tables while the *table* is the data file with the rows and columns of information.

Think of all of the mp3 music files you can download that are stored on your favorite Web site. What if the songs were stored in a table in a random order? Would you want to spend all night searching row-by-row trying to find a particular song? Definitely not! You have better things to do like reading this textbook and excelling in your computer science courses.

note The primary advantage of using an index is the ability to find data in a table without scanning the entire table.

By using an index, all of the songs can be sorted in a myriad of ways simply by specifying on which columns you want to sort. For instance, you can sort the songs by artist in ascending order with the "A"s at the top and the "Z"s at the bottom. Or you can sort the songs alphabetically in descending order with the "Z"s at the top and the "A"s at the bottom. You could even have an index that sorts the songs using a combination of two columns, such as artist and song title. The disadvantage of using indexes is that they require more storage space in the database, and the operations for updating the data take a little longer because the indexes must also be updated.

more's company

A company can (and usually does) have many databases, with each database acting as a virtual filing cabinet for related information.

Every table within a database should have some type of index defined to make searching quicker and the retrieval of data more organized.

an example of indexing

Imagine you are walking down the aisle in a grocery store pushing the food cart with the wobbly wheels. The cart acts like a database because it holds the food items you wish to purchase and store at your home. As you pass the frozen foods section you open one of the freezer doors and grab the cheap one-item frozen pizza with simulated cheese (an essential substance for serious developers!). You take note of the UPC, brand name, amount, description, and price and throw it in your cart. You wobble over to the drink aisle and pick up a six-pack of your favorite beverage loaded with plenty of caffeine in order to finish that project on time. Once again you notice the UPC, brand name, amount, description, and price and hook it on the side of the cart. The process of gathering food items continues until either your cart is full or you have bought all of the essential developer food items. You might not have realized it, but you have actually created your own database by placing food items in your shopping cart. Your database of food items is compared against the store's database when you purchase the items at the checkout stand. Each item can be related to a row in the database. Figure 8-2 demonstrates how some items purchased at the grocery might appear in a database.

Figure 8-2, You use database concepts in your everyday life

Food : Table

	UPC	Brand_Name	Amount	Description	Price
▶	020188081029	Beefies	1	Frozen Pizza	$3.25
	993059377373	Pure Juice	6	Electrify Soda	$2.29
	768498522313	Popper	6	Microwave Popcorn	$2.59
	869488263567	SugarD	12	Sweet Cakes	$3.79
	896746255671	Beefies	2	Chimichanga	$0.79
	233254518898	CoolQ	1	Root Beer Ice Cream	$4.25
	574827764671	CheesePleeze	6	Macaroni and Cheese	$0.49
	985183848511	CoolQ	1	Cookie Dough Ice Cream	$4.25
	372883718232	Popper	3	Grandma Goose Popcorn	$1.79
*			0		$0.00

Record: 1 of 9

Each row in the database has similar attributes that might have different information describing the product. Notice that each food item purchased has information that is shared by the other food items, such as a brand name, amount, description, and price.

As stated earlier, columns can be used to create an index that determines how the row items are sorted. When the columns are used to determine the sort order of information they are called ***keys***. There can be one key or a combination of keys determining the sort order.

key – In a database table, one or more columns used to determine the sort order of the data

The information kept in a database is kept in natural or sequential order. This means that the first record you see in the database is the very first record you created and stored in the database file. Using keys to sort the database information allows you to view the data in any desired order. To illustrate how keys are used to determine the sort order, refer back to the grocery shopping cart data listed in Figure 8-2. The order in which the records are displayed was the order in which they were entered. For example, if the UPC column were the key, the records in the database would be sorted in ascending order using the value stored in the UPC column. The view of the database would be the same as that shown in Figure 8-3.

Figure 8-3, Database records sorted using the UPC column as a key

Food_by_UPC : Table

UPC	Brand_Name	Amount	Description	Price
020188081029	Beefies	1	Frozen Pizza	$3.25
233254518898	CoolQ	1	Root Beer Ice Cream	$4.25
372883718232	Popper	3	Grandma Goose Popcorn	$1.79
574827764671	CheesePleeze	6	Macaroni and Cheese	$0.49
768498522313	Popper	6	Microwave Popcorn	$2.59
869488263567	SugarD	12	Sweet Cakes	$3.79
896746255671	Beefies	2	Chimichanga	$0.79
985183848511	CoolQ	1	Cookie Dough Ice Cream	$4.25
993059377373	Pure Juice	6	Electrify Soda	$2.29
*		0		$0.00

Record: 1 of 9

You can also combine keys to further organize the data. For example, Figure 8-4 shows the data ordered by Brand_Name and Description. That is, first it is sorted by Brand_Name, and then within Brand_Name by Description, in ascending alphabetical order.

Figure 8-4, Database records sorted by Brand_Name and Description

Food_by_Brand_Desc : Table

UPC	Brand_Name	Amount	Description	Price
896746255671	Beefies	2	Chimichanga	$0.79
020188081029	Beefies	1	Frozen Pizza	$3.25
574827764671	CheesePleeze	6	Macaroni and Cheese	$0.49
985183848511	CoolQ	1	Cookie Dough Ice Cream	$4.25
233254518898	CoolQ	1	Root Beer Ice Cream	$4.25
372883718232	Popper	3	Grandma Goose Popcorn	$1.79
768498522313	Popper	6	Microwave Popcorn	$2.59
993059377373	Pure Juice	6	Electrify Soda	$2.29
869488263567	SugarD	12	Sweet Cakes	$3.79
*		0		$0.00

Record: 1 of 9

All of the information for the database is kept in the database file. This file acts as a repository of information and can be viewed or manipulated through a wide variety of media such as reports, forms, labels, low-level file I/O, and source code, to name a few.

normalization

normalization – A process of database design that structures tables to eliminate duplication and inconsistencies in the data structure

With all of the information that is being stored around the world, a set of database standards evolved to ensure that information is properly retrieved and stored. The set of rules that dictates how databases are designed is called ***normalization***. Normalization is the process of structuring tables to eliminate duplication and inconsistencies in the data structure. In plain language, normalization tells you how to organize the data stored in the database so that not only does the application function properly, but the amount of duplicate and unwanted information being stored is minimized. The process of normalization works through a sequence of stages called normal forms, such as first normal form, second normal form, and third normal form. From a database design point of view, second normal form is better than first normal form, and third normal form is better than second normal form. There are five normal forms (or six, if you count a refinement called Boyce-Codd normal form, BCNF) but for most database applications, third normal form is as high as you need to go.

note

The rules of normalization have been standardized and accepted by the computer industry. By following standards that are in place, the database work that computer scientists perform is consistent no matter what the company or project.

don't forget the end user

When designing a database you should always consider the needs of the end users (the people using the data). In fact, end users can help design the database and reports! They know the type of data that needs to be collected and how that data will be used to help them do their jobs. The more you include the end user in the design of the database the greater probability of the success of a project.

Normalization solves three problems that often occur when designing databases. The first problem is that if a database is not properly normalized, it cannot represent certain real-world information items. The second problem occurs when the database contains redundancies (repetitions) in the data. This simply wastes time and storage space. The third problem occurs when important information has been excluded during the design of the data structures. By following the rules of normalization, your tables will be accurately defined to ensure the integrity and stability of your database application.

preparing for normalization: gathering columns

Before you begin creating the database and following the normalization process, you need to make a list of all of the pertinent fields (columns or attributes) that you think are needed in the database application. Often you can create this list by looking at the reports the end user has given you, such as the Song inventory report shown in Figure 8-5.

Figure 8-5, End-user report with table columns highlighted

Songs

Artist_Name	Song_Name	Track_Num	Album_Name	Media_Type	Genre_Code
B.B. King	The Thrill is Gone	8	The Best of B.B. King	MP3	BLU
Nirvana	Come As You Are	3	Nevermind	MP3	NW
Nirvana	Lithium	5	Nevermind	MP3	NW
Oingo Boingo	Only a Lad	16	Best O Boingo	CD	NW
Peter Gabriel	Big Time	14	Shaking the Tree	CD	POP
Peter Gabriel	Sledgehammer	3	Shaking the Tree	CD	POP
The Beach Boys	Sloop John B	7	Pet Sounds	Vinyl	CLA
Toby Keith	American Soldier	3	Shock'n Y'all	MP3	CW
Toby Keith	Beer For My Horses	5	Unleashed	MP3	CW
U2	One Tree Hill	9	The Joshua Tree	CD	NW
U2	With or Without You	3	The Joshua Tree	CD	NW

Often enough, each field on a report is a field or column in a table or consists of one or more combined table fields. Write these fields on your column list and continue this process for each of the reports supplied by the end user.

The next step is to review the input forms that the user has specified. Each field on an input form used within an application (Figure 8-6) should be a column in a table. Add these columns to your master column list and

Figure 8-6, Additional table columns can be gleaned from input forms

Songs

Song_Name	Sledgehammer
Track_Num	3
Album_Num	10
Album_Name	Shaking the Tree
Media_Type	CD
Artist_Code	PG
Artist_Name	Peter Gabriel
Genre_Code	POP

Record: 1 of 11

continue the process for each of the forms found in the approved program you are creating.

The next step is to review all of the documentation for any fields that do not appear on the end-user reports or forms. In the example, these fields might include:

· Song_Name
· Track_Num
· Album_Num
· Album_Name
· Media_Type
· Artist_Code
· Artist_Name
· Genre_Code

getting ready for normalization

1. Create a list of all the columns or fields you need in the database application by reviewing the specifications and forms supplied by the end user.

2. Create tables of columns by logically grouping associated fields.

3. Continue grouping the fields until all of the columns have been assigned to one big table.

Once all of the columns have been gathered and documented on your master column list, you are ready to move to the next step: creating tables of columns by combining associated fields.

This is accomplished by logically grouping information that is dependent upon other information. An example of this could be information pertaining to an artist and all of his or her associated song files. To create the music database you need to gather all of the data for the rows and columns that relate to each other, such as those shown in Figure 8-7.

Figure 8-7, Columns relating to the song files are placed in one table

Song_Name	Track_Num	Album_Num	Album_Name	Media_Type	Artist_Code	Artist_Name	Genre_Code
Sledgehammer Big Time	3 14	10	Shaking the Tree	CD CD	PG PG	Peter Gabriel Peter Gabriel	POP POP
Lithium Come As You Are	5 3	24	Nevermind	MP3 MP3	NIRV NIRV	Nirvana Nirvana	NW NW
Sloop John B	7	45	Pet Sounds	Vinyl	BB	The Beach Boys	CLA
Only a Lad	16	78	Best O Boingo	CD	OB	Oingo Boingo	NW
The Thrill is Gone	8	98	The Best of B.B. King	MP3	BBK	B.B. King	BLU
With or Without You One Tree Hill	3 9	146	The Joshua Tree	CD CD	U2 U2	U2 U2	NW NW
Beer For My Horses American Soldier	5 3	826 911	Unleashed Shock'n Y'all	MP3 MP3	TK TK	Toby Keith Toby Keith	CW CW

For an animated view of how normalization works, see the learning tools section under Chapter 8 on the student CD.

These are all fields that relate to each other and describe the song files. Continue this process until all of the columns/fields have been assigned to one table. With all of the fields defined and placed in one table you are ready to begin the normalization process of refining your database design.

8

first normal form

Once you have the data in column and row format, you have what is known as an unnormalized table. At this point you could define a database table based on this design, but redundancies and dependencies may cause problems once the table is in use. The table needs to be normalized to a stable state in order to prevent these problems.

The first step in the normalization process is to modify the rows and/or columns of the tables to ensure that each row-column intersection has only one value. As each new row is created to accommodate the repeating groups, cell data from the original row need to be copied into each column.

first normal form (1NF) – Eliminating repeating fields or groups of fields from the table and confirming that every column has only one value by creating a new record in the table

In the unnormalized table of Figure 8-8, the Song_Name column has two values in the first row. Note that some of the columns of the first row have one value and some have two values. To put the table into *first normal form (1NF)*, a separate row needs to be created for each of the two values in the fields that have two values.

Figure 8-8, Columns with duplicate data need to be simplified

Unnormalized Data

Artist_Code	Song_Name	Artist_Name	Album_Num	Album_Name	Track_Num	Media_Type	Genre_Code
TK	American Soldier	Toby Keith	911	Shock'n Y'all	3	MP3	CW
	Beer For My Horses		826	Unleashed	5		
PG	Big Time	Peter Gabriel	10	Shaking the Tree	14	CD	POP
	Sledgehammer				3		
NIRV	Come As You Are	Nirvana	24	Nevermind	3	MP3	NW
	Lithium				5		
U2	One Tree Hill	U2	146	The Joshua Tree	9	CD	NW
	With or Without You				3		
OB	Only a Lad	Oingo Boingo	78	Best O Boingo	16	CD	NW
BB	Sloop John B	The Beach Boys	45	Pet Sounds	7	Vinyl	CLA
BBK	The Thrill is Gone	B.B. King	98	The Best of B.B. King	8	MP3	BLU

You can see that the Songs table shown in Figure 8-8 is not in first normal form because the Album_Num, Album_Name, Artist_Code, Artist_Name, Media_Type, and Genre_Code columns contain duplicate values. First normal form requires that columns contain only single values, as shown in Figure 8-9. This is resolved by creating a new record for the duplicated column values and then filling in the blanks so that the columns in the record all have a value.

first normal form

Eliminate column values that are repeated by making a new record in the table and copying the common data to the column values

Notice that there is still redundant (repeated) data in some of the columns. This will be addressed during a later stage of normalization.

Figure 8-9, Songs table in 1NF

First Normal Form Data

Artist_Code	Song_Name	Artist_Name	Album_Num	Album_Name	Track_Num	Media_Type	Genre_Code
TK	American Soldier	Toby Keith	911	Shock'n Y'all	3	MP3	CW
TK	Beer For My Horses	Toby Keith	826	Unleashed	5	MP3	CW
PG	Big Time	Peter Gabriel	10	Shaking the Tree	14	CD	POP
PG	Sledgehammer	Peter Gabriel	10	Shaking the Tree	3	CD	POP
NIRV	Come As You Are	Nirvana	24	Nevermind	3	MP3	NW
NIRV	Lithium	Nirvana	24	Nevermind	5	MP3	NW
U2	One Tree Hill	U2	146	The Joshua Tree	9	CD	NW
U2	With or Without You	U2	146	The Joshua Tree	3	CD	NW
OB	Only a Lad	Oingo Boingo	78	Best O Boingo	16	CD	NW
BB	Sloop John B	The Beach Boys	45	Pet Sounds	7	Vinyl	CLA
BBK	The Thrill is Gone	B.B. King	98	The Best of B.B.King	8	MP3	BLU

second normal form

primary key (PK) – A column or combination of columns that uniquely identifies a row within a table

The next step requires you to assign a primary key to the table and identify the functional dependencies within the table. A ***primary key (PK)*** is simply a column or combination of columns that uniquely identifies a row within a table. For instance, if you consider all of the students in one of your computer science courses, you could see that the primary key could be the Student ID as there are no repeating IDs in the entire university. Every student has a unique number that identifies that person or makes one person unique. Other examples of primary keys that make a record unique might be:

- Car VIN (Vehicle Identification Number)
- SSN (Social Security Number)
- Driver's license number
- Purchase order
- Tax ID
- Bank account number

determinant – A determinant in a database is any column or columns you can use to determine the value assigned to another column (or columns) in the same row

Before you learn the second step to normalization, it is essential that you understand the concept of a ***determinant.*** A determinant in a database is any column or columns you can use to determine the value assigned to another column (or columns) in the same row. In simpler terms, the column Artist_Code is a determinant for the Artist_Name column. The value "PG" determines that the Artist_Name is Peter Gabriel.

note By default, a primary key is a determinant.

second normal form

Apply to tables with multiple keys and eliminate redundant data.

A functional dependency is the combination of a determinant and the columns that it determines. Consider the column Artist_Name. It is functionally dependent upon the column Artist_Code. The artist name "Peter Gabriel" is dependent upon the code "PG."

Still confused? Here's another example. You probably have a student ID number. In a database, your ID number can be used to determine your name, address, and other information. Your name, however, couldn't be used to determine your student ID because it's possible that multiple students can have the same name.

second normal form (2NF) – First normal form has already been applied to the table and every column that is not part of the key is fully dependent upon the primary key

functional dependency – When a column's single value is dependent upon another column's value

A table is in ***second normal form (2NF)*** if it is in first normal form and every column that is not part of the primary key is fully dependent upon the entire primary key. This concept is called ***functional dependency***. A column is functionally dependent upon another column if for each value of the first column there is only one value for the second column.

Note that the primary key for the Songs table in Figure 8-9 is a composite key of Artist_Code, Song_Name, and Album_Num. Those three fields combined account for unique song records as the song title could be duplicated by multiple artists, but adding the Album_Num makes each record unique.

composite key – A key that is made up of more than one column

Looking at the Songs table you can see that the Artist_Code, Song_Name, and Album_Num columns make up the primary key. This type of combined key is called a ***composite key*** because there is more than one column that makes up the key. To put a table in second normal form you must determine which columns in the table are not dependent upon the primary key.

note

If a table does not have a composite key then it is, by default, in second normal form.

For example, the Track_Num column is dependent upon the Song_Name, Artist_Code, and Album_Num columns because there is one and only one track number for a distinctive song, artist, and album. On the other hand, the Album_Name column is not dependent upon the entire primary key. Values such as Album_Name that are not dependent upon the complete primary key should be removed to a separate table. Figure 8-10 shows how the Songs table is split into three tables: a Songs table with Album_Num dependent on the Song_Name and Artist_Code PKs; an Album table with Album_Name dependent on the key Album_Num; and an Artist table, where the Artist_Name is not dependent upon the complete primary key. The Artist_Name was also removed from the Songs table and put into its own table using the Artist_Code as the primary key and the Artist_Name as a dependent column.

Figure 8-10, 2NF: Remove any columns that are not dependent upon the primary key and create a new table

Second Normal Form Data

Songs Table

Artist_Code	Song_Name	Album_Num	Track_Num	Media_Type	Genre_Code
BB	Sloop John B	45	7	Vinyl	CLA
BBK	The Thrill is Gone	98	8	MP3	BLU
NIRV	Come As You Are	24	3	MP3	NW
NIRV	Lithium	24	5	MP3	NW
OB	Only a Lad	78	16	CD	NW
PG	Big Time	10	14	CD	POP
PG	Sledgehammer	10	3	CD	POP
TK	American Soldier	911	3	MP3	CW
TK	Beer For My Horses	826	5	MP3	CW
U2	One Tree Hill	146	9	CD	NW
U2	With or Without You	146	3	CD	NW

Artists Table

Artist_Code	Artist_Name
BB	The Beach Boys
BBK	B.B. King
NIRV	Nirvana
OB	Oingo Boingo
PG	Peter Gabriel
TK	Toby Keith
U2	U2

Album Table

Album_Num	Album_Name
10	Shaking the Tree
24	Nevermind
45	Pet Sounds
78	Best O Boingo
98	The Best of B.B. King
146	The Joshua Tree
826	Unleashed
911	Shock'n Y'all

There are many advantages in placing a table into second normal form. The main advantage is that it eliminates repetition of data, which can amass into a large quantity of wasted disk space.

third normal form (3NF) – *Eliminate columns that are not dependent only on the primary key*

transitive dependency – *When one column is dependent upon another column that is not part of the primary key*

third normal form

Third normal form (3NF) eliminates columns that are not dependent only on the primary key. In database parlance, putting a database in 3NF eliminates transitive dependencies. A *transitive dependency* exists when one column is dependent upon another column that is not the primary key.

8

For example, the Songs table shown in Figure 8-11 has added a field to the Songs table called Genre_Desc. This column describes the Genre_Code column.

Figure 8-11, Songs table with the Genre_Desc column added

Songs table

Artist_Code	Song_Name	Album_Num	Track_Num	Media_Type	Genre_Code	Genre_Desc
BB	Sloop John B	45	7	Vinyl	CLA	Classic Rock
BBK	The Thrill is Gone	98	8	MP3	BLU	Blues
NIRV	Come As You Are	24	3	MP3	NW	NewWave
NIRV	Lithium	24	5	MP3	NW	NewWave
OB	Only a Lad	78	16	CD	NW	NewWave
PG	Big Time	10	14	CD	POP	Popular
PG	Sledgehammer	10	3	CD	POP	Popular
TK	American Soldier	911	3	MP3	CW	Country Western
TK	Beer For My Horses	826	5	MP3	CW	Country Western
U2	One Tree Hill	146	9	CD	NW	NewWave
U2	With or Without You	146	3	CD	NW	NewWave

third normal form

Eliminate columns that are not dependent only on the PK. 3NF is the same concept as 2NF but it applies only to those tables that have single primary keys.

Each nonkey field in the table should be a fact about the primary key. The Genre_Desc column is dependent upon the Genre_Code column, which is not part of the primary key for the Songs table. In this case, the Genre_Desc has nothing to do with any part of the Songs table's primary key. It instead is a fact about the Genre_Code.

Figure 8-12, Songs and Genre tables in 3NF

Third Normal Form Data

Songs table

Artist_Code	Song_Name	Album_Num	Track_Num	Media_Type	Genre_Code
BB	Sloop John B	45	7	Vinyl	CLA
BBK	The Thrill is Gone	98	8	MP3	BLU
NIRV	Come As You Are	24	3	MP3	NW
NIRV	Lithium	24	5	MP3	NW
OB	Only a Lad	78	16	CD	NW
PG	Big Time	10	14	CD	POP
PG	Sledgehammer	10	3	CD	POP
TK	American Soldier	911	3	MP3	CW
TK	Beer For My Horses	826	5	MP3	CW
U2	One Tree Hill	146	9	CD	NW
U2	With or Without You	146	3	CD	NW

Genre Table

Genre_Code	Genre_Desc
BLU	Blues
CLA	Classic Rock
CW	Country Western
NW	NewWave
POP	Popular

To put the Songs table into third normal form, you create a Genre table containing the Genre_Code and Genre_Desc columns, with Genre_Code as the primary key, as shown in Figure 8-12.

As shown in Figure 8-13, by putting the database in 3NF, the repetition of the Genre_Desc, Artist_Name, and Album_Name columns in the Songs table can be eliminated, thus saving disk space.

note The fourth and fifth normalization forms break the data down into smaller pieces to eliminate redundancy. These forms apply only in rare situations and are not often used.

Figure 8-13, Eliminating repetition saves storage space

Third Normal Form Data

Songs Table

Artist_Code	Song_Name	Album_Num	Track_Num	Media_Type	Genre_Code
BB	Sloop John B	45	7	Vinyl	CLA
BBK	The Thrill is Gone	98	8	MP3	BLU
NIRV	Come As You Are	24	3	MP3	NW
NIRV	Lithium	24	5	MP3	NW
OB	Only a Lad	78	16	CD	NW
PG	Big Time	10	14	CD	POP
PG	Sledgehammer	10	3	CD	POP
TK	American Soldier	911	3	MP3	CW
TK	Beer For My Horses	826	5	MP3	CW
U2	One Tree Hill	146	9	CD	NW
U2	With or Without You	146	3	CD	NW

Genre Table

Genre_Code	Genre_Desc
BLU	Blues
CLA	Classic Rock
CW	Country Western
NW	New Wave
POP	Popular

Artists Table

Artist_Code	Artist_Name
BB	The Beach Boys
BBK	B.B. King
NIRV	Nirvana
OB	Oingo Boingo
PG	Peter Gabriel
TK	Toby Keith
U2	U2

Album Table

Album_Num	Album_Name
10	Shaking the Tree
24	Nevermind
45	Pet Sounds
78	Best O Boingo
98	The Best of B.B. King
146	The Joshua Tree
826	Unleashed
911	Shock'n Y'all

the database design process

Trying to understand each of the normal forms and then normalizing the tables you have designed can be quite cumbersome. However, your goal in normalization should be moderation: to reach a balance between redundant data and redundant keys. There are six steps you can follow to make designing data structures easier while adhering to the basic normalization forms. Here's an example of the database design and normalization process based upon the creation of a student grading system.

step 1—investigate and define

The first step in the database design process is to investigate and research the information you will model. Define the purpose of the database and how it will be used. Use any documents the end user currently uses to complete his or her job. These documents can be a basis to help define the database and tables needed to create the forms and reports. The more you involve the end user, the greater your chances of more accurately designing the database. The student-grading system will be based upon a course syllabus that defines all of the items for which a student can receive a grade.

step 2—make a master column list

Create a list of all the fields for which you need to store information along with their properties. The properties might include such items as:

- Field Name
- Data type (char, varchar, number, date, etc.)
- Length
- Number of decimal places (if any)

Once again, review the user's document(s). The forms and reports are good indicators of the fields you need so that you can manipulate and manage the data. For this example, you might have fields such as Student ID, First Name, Last Name, E-Mail, Grade Level, Grade Level Description, Homework Average, Quiz Average, Test Average, Final Exam, Final Grade, Letter Grade, Course ID, Course Description.

step 3—create the tables

Once all of the fields or columns have been defined it is time to logically group them into tables. This is the heart of the design process and relies heavily upon the normalization rules. The main rules used in database design are the first through third normal forms. Once a table is in 3NF, for the most part it has been accurately defined. Use your common sense. The task of normalizing databases can be compared to that of cleaning up a toy closet. At first, the job looks monumental, but if you take one shelf at a time, the project's mammoth scope slowly dwindles. Organize the toy shelves by first cleaning out the closet into one big pile of toys. Then decide which types of toys go on which shelves. Now you are ready to begin placing one toy at a time on the appropriate shelf.

This process applies to database design. Logically organize the columns into their appropriate "shelves." As you are organizing the columns, look for any duplicates or ways you can save "shelf" space. Why keep two games that are exactly the same when they both have all of their pieces? You can only play one game at a time so get rid of one and keep the other on the toy shelf. Why keep two copies of the same column when they both represent the same data? Get rid of one and keep the other in the table. Figure 8-14 shows the tables that are created for the student-grading system.

Figure 8-14, Tables created for the student-grading system

Student : Table

Student_ID	First_Name	Last_Name	E_Mail	Grade_Level
111111111	SpongeBob	SquarePants	SpongeBob@wsu.edu	Fr
223212578	Squidward	Tentacles	Squidward@wsu.edu	So
543768893	Yosemite	Sam	Yosemite@wsu.edu	Ju
984367183	Bugs	Bunny	Bugs@wsu.edu	Sr

Record: 1 of 4

Grades : Table

Course_ID	Student_ID	Homework_Ave	Quiz_Ave	Test_Ave	Final_Exam	Final_Grade	Letter_Grade
1829388133	111111111	70	65	60	72	67	D+
1829388133	223212578	80	85	90	86	85	B
1829388133	984367183	96	92	94	98	95	A
2731288812	543768893	84	82	86	78	83	B-
3712883828	223212578	100	90	88	92	93	A-
3712883828	984367183	100	98	98	96	98	A
4311223112	111111111	60	70	82	80	73	C-
4311223112	223212578	82	84	78	90	84	B
		0	0	0	0	0	

Record: 1 of 8

Grade_Level : Table

Grade_Level	Grade_Desc
Fr	Freshman
Ju	Junior
So	Sophomore
Sr	Senior

Record: 1 of 4

Courses : Table

Course_ID	Course_Desc
1829388133	Underwater Programming
2731288812	Intro to Computer Science
3712883828	Software Engineering for Cartoons
4311223112	Database Design in a Toon Environment

Record: 4 of 4

step 4—work on relationships

After the database is normalized, it is time to move on to relationships. As in your everyday life, a relationship defines how one entity works with or relates to another. If you do not work on your personal relationships, then your life will likely be a mess. This concept also applies to table relationships. If you do not spend time working on the table relationships, your database design will be a mess.

relationship – How one entity or table works with another

In database design, a ***relationship*** defines how one table relates to another. Two types of relationships are discussed in this chapter:

- One-to-many (1:M)
- One-to-one (1:1)

foreign key (FK) – A column in one table that is a primary key in another table

Each relationship determines what type of data is stored in each of the tables. Relationships need to have primary and foreign keys defined in each of the tables. The primary key was discussed earlier in this chapter. A ***foreign key (FK)*** is defined as a column in one table that is part of the primary key in another table. For instance, the Genre_Code column in the Genre table (Figure 8-12) is the primary key in the Genre table, so it is considered to be a foreign key in the Songs table. The same applies to the Artist_Code and Album_Num. They are both considered to be foreign keys in the Songs table because they are primary keys in other tables.

The following sections show how primary keys and foreign keys function in the types of relationships between tables.

one-to-many

one-to-many (1:M) relationship – One instance of an entity (parent table) is associated with zero to many instances of another table (child table)

The ***one-to-many (1:M) relationship*** is the most common relationship and states that each record in Table A (such as the Grades table in Figure 8-15), relates to multiple records in Table B (such as the Student table). In other words, for each (1) course being taught, there can be many (M) students.

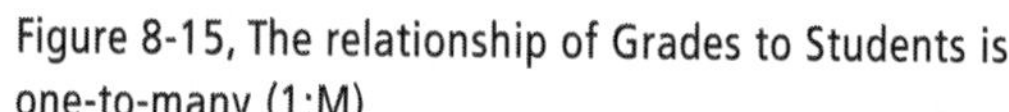

Figure 8-15, The relationship of Grades to Students is one-to-many (1:M)

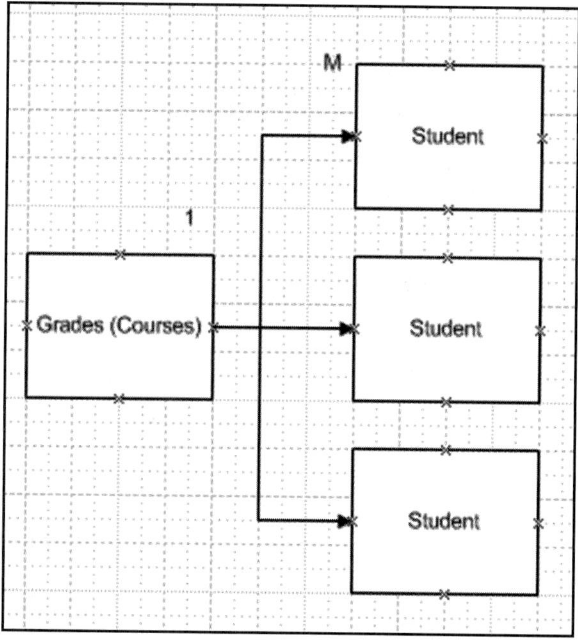

The one-to-many relationship requires that a foreign key column or columns in the "many" table have a value that refers back to the primary key column(s) in the "one" table. Referring back to Figure 8-14, you can see that the Student_ID column is a foreign key in the Grades table and a primary key in the Student table.

one-to-one

one-to-one (1:1) relationship – One instance of one entity (parent table) is associated with only one instance of another entity (child table)

The ***one-to-one (1:1) relationship*** dictates that for every record in Table A there can be one and only one matching record in Table B. This type of relationship is quite unusual and many times indicates that the two entities actually belong in the same table.

M:M

Although some consider it poor data design, another relationship is the ***many-to-many (M:M) relationship***, in which Table A can have more than one matching record in Table B and Table B can have more than one matching record in Table A. Many-to-many relationships are often decomposed into several one-to-many relationships.

many-to-many (M:M) relationship – Many instances of one entity or table (parent table) are associated with many instance of another entity (child table)

Figure 8-16, The relationship of Student to Grade Level is one-to-one (1:1)

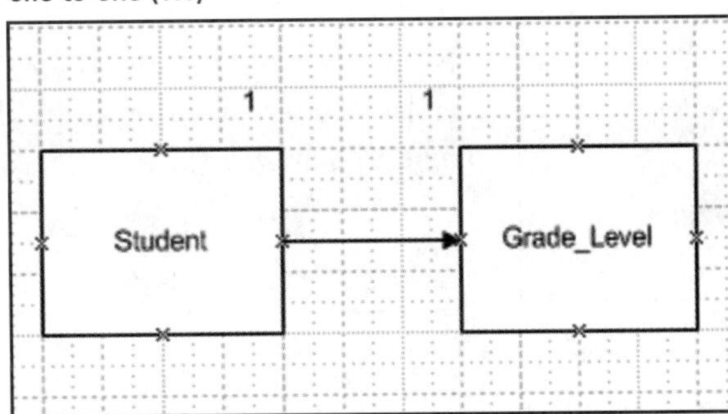

The first thing you should consider if you find a 1:1 relationship is whether you can combine these into one table. However, there are many times when 1:1 relationships are appropriate. For example, each student can have only one grade level (Figure 8-16).

The one-to-one relationship requires that a foreign key column(s) in "one" table have a value that refers back to the primary key column in the other "one" table. Looking back at Figure 8-14 you can see that the Grade_Level column is a foreign key in the Student table and a primary key in the Grade_Level table.

step 5—analyze the design

With all of the data pieces in place it is time to analyze the work completed. Search for design errors and refine the tables as needed. Follow the normalization forms (ideally to third normal form) and correct any violations that might hamper the performance of the database.

ER modeling

At this point it is wise to create a data model to give a visual representation of how all of the tables or entities interact and relate to each other within the database. This model is called an ***entity relationship (ER) model***.

entity relationship (ER) model – A data model that visually represents how all of the tables interact and relate to each other within the database

cardinality – Shows the numeric occurrences between entities in an ER model

An ER model is comprised of entities (tables) and relationships. The entities represent the database tables while the relationships show how each table relates to another table. The model can also include cardinality to visually describe the type of relationship between tables. ***Cardinality*** shows the numeric occurrences between entities in an ER model. The different types of cardinality, along with their standard notations, include:

- 0..1, 0:1 (zero to one)
- 0..M, 0:N, 0..*, 0..n (zero to many)
- 1..1, 1:1 (one to one)
- 1..M, 1:M, 1:N, 1..*, 1..n (one to many)

the first ER model

Dr. Peter Chen, recognized as a software pioneer, derived the mathematical formulations and graphic notations to build ER diagrams and first introduced ER modeling in 1976.

· M..1, M:1, N:1, *..1, n..1 (many to one)
· M..M, M:M, N:N, *..*, n..n (many to many)

For example, an ER model for the student-grading system would show the four tables (Student, Grades, Grade_Level, and Courses) and how they relate to each other (Figure 8-17).

Figure 8-17, The student-grading system ER model in Visio

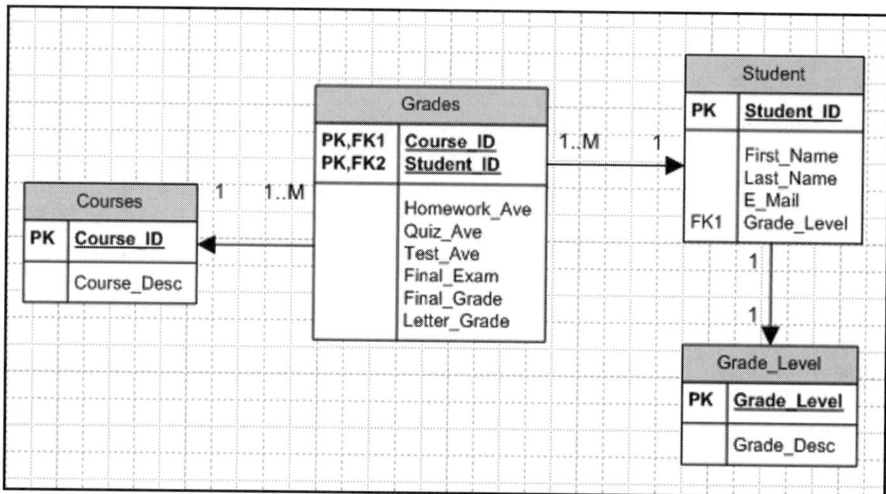

ER tools

There are many data-diagramming tools you can use to create an ER model, such as Microsoft Visio (introduced in Chapter 2 and used in this chapter).

The PK and FK symbols in Figure 8-17 represent the defined primary and foreign keys within each table. The numbers next to the foreign key are created by Microsoft Visio and are simply a way the system informs you that one foreign key is different from another within that table entity.

step 6—reevaluate

Reevaluate database performance and ensure that it meets all of your reporting and form needs. Include the end user and explain each of the tables and fields being used. Make sure that the fields have been properly defined to the end user's requirements. Have you ever played the gossip game where one person starts a rumor and whispers it along to the next person? The next person quietly passes it on and the process continues until it reaches the last person. The last person vocally announces the gossip and everyone laughs at the fact that it usually isn't even close to the original rumor. The end user might not have the same way of thinking or expressing himself or herself as you do, so it's always a good idea to reevaluate and check with the end user to see that the database design meets the user's goals.

If you find your database "toy closet" is not designed to hold all of the toys, you will either have to leave some toys out of the closet or make the closet a mess by stuffing in as many toys as possible. In other words, spend the time and effort to get the database design right the first time, so you don't have to backtrack to get your design process on the right road.

Once you have properly designed a database, you will want to manipulate the data structure. You do this by using the commands found in SQL.

Structured Query Language (SQL)

As mentioned earlier in this chapter, Structured Query Language (SQL) is a powerful database language used for defining, querying, modifying, and controlling the data in a database. SQL provides a means to:

- Manipulate data
- Define data
- Administer data

Manipulating data involves retrieving the data and modifying the data. Retrieving the data involves SQL statements that become part of a query; their intent is to search a database and retrieve information.

There are many different "dialects" of SQL on the market, but once you learn the basic statements in one version, in most cases you can transfer this knowledge to other SQL versions.

note

Only the basics of SQL are discussed here. For more information on SQL, please review the many available book options from Course Technology at *www.course.com*.

SQL provides the following advantages:

- Reduces training time—Because SQL is English based, it is easy to understand and to learn
- Makes applications portable—SQL is standardized and works similarly on many different databases. This means that if you learn SQL once and move to a different database, you should still be able to use your SQL knowledge you previously acquired.
- Reduces the amount of data being transferred—Instead of transferring all of the data stored in the table, SQL just deals with the data you want to see, thus reducing how much data is sent to the user.
- Increases application speed—SQL only sends you the data you want to see instead of sending the entire set of data; this results in a faster transfer of information.

Figure 8-18, A sample SQL statement and results

SQL statement:

```
SELECT Song_Name, Artist_Code, Album_Num, Track_Num, Media_Type
FROM Songs
WHERE Genre_Code ="NW";
```

Result:

Songs Query : Select Query

Song_Name	Artist_Code	Album_Num	Track_Num	Media_Type
With or Without You	U2	146	3	CD
One Tree Hill	U2	146	9	CD
Only a Lad	OB	78	16	CD
Lithium	NIRV	24	5	MP3
Come As You Are	NIRV	24	3	MP3
*		0	0	

Record: 5 of 5

SQL is not a hard language to learn because it uses simple descriptive statements, such as CREATE TABLE, INSERT, and SELECT. For example, Figure 8-18 shows a SQL statement that produces a list of all the songs in your music database that are in the "NW" (New Wave) category.

The following sections show the basic SQL commands for creating tables, adding (inserting) rows of data, and querying the table to select certain information from the table.

CREATE TABLE statement

A great feature of SQL is that the statements are fairly easy to figure out. For instance, the CREATE TABLE statement is used to . . . create a table!

The syntax is:

```
CREATE TABLE table_name
( column_name datatype [NULL | NOT NULL]
[, column_name datatype [NULL | NOT NULL] . . . );
```

The CREATE TABLE statement is straightforward. Its job is to create a new table within a database. The table_name is the name of the table you want to create. Make sure that this name is descriptive of the data being stored. For example, you could call a table of information about songs in your music database Songs.

The next line begins with an open parenthesis and is the clause that permits you to define the table's columns/fields. Once again, make sure you use descriptive names for the data being represented. Type the name of the first column in the table (e.g., Song_Name), followed by a space and the name of its data type (int for integer, char for character, currency, datetime, and so on). Some of the data types such as char need a length specified. This is accomplished by adding opening and closing parentheses with the length in between, such as char(10).

The data types used in this CREATE TABLE statement are described in Table 8-2.

Table 8-2, Common SQL data types

type	description
char	Fixed number of characters
int	Whole numbers
varchar	Variable number of characters used when the length is not known
date/time	Calendar dates
number	Numbers that include decimals; when using this data type you must specify the total length of the data area and also the number of decimal positions

Anything declared with square brackets is considered optional. The square brackets should *not* be considered part of the statement that you would enter. The keywords NULL and NOT NULL are optional and indicate whether data is required for the specified column. The vertical bar separating them means you can use one or the other.

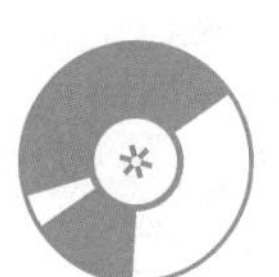

A Microsoft Access database My_Music that contains the Songs table is available under the source code section of Chapter 8 on the student CD.

The third line of the statement is also optional, meaning that you can have a table with one column if desired. If there are more columns, then you continue the input process by separating each column with a comma. The last thing to do when writing a SQL statement is to make sure that you close it with a semicolon (;). It tells the system that the statement is completed.

The following SQL statement creates a table called Songs. There are six columns created in the table structure: Song_Name, Album_Num, Artist_Code, Track_Num, Media_Type, and Genre_Code. Some columns require data (NOT NULL) while others do not (NULL). Note that SQL commands can be uppercase or lowercase, but the convention is to use uppercase for SQL keywords.

```
CREATE TABLE Songs
(Song_Name char(50) NOT NULL,
Album_Num number NOT NULL,
Track_Num number NULL,
Media_Type char(5) NULL,
Artist_Code char(5) NOT NULL,
Genre_Code char(5) NOT NULL
);
```

note

Some database developers like to precede each column name with an acronym for the table. For example, the SQL to create the Songs table could have included the character "s" representing the songs table name: s_Song_Name char(50) NOT NULL. When you are creating several tables, it helps readability and understanding to use this convention.

Executing this code creates a table called Songs in the current database.

SQL scripts

SQL statements are often stored in a text file that can be used to run a series of SQL statements as a SQL script. This saves a lot of time in retyping SQL commands in case you need to regenerate table structures or modify data. Simply create a text file using Notepad and type or paste in your SQL command(s).

INSERT statement

The INSERT statement allows you to add new rows of data to the table. The syntax is:

```
INSERT INTO table_name [(column1, column2, . . . )]
VALUES (constant1, constant2, . . . )
```

The syntax for the INSERT statement requires a table name so that the system knows into which table to insert data. If you are not entering data for every column in the table you need to specify which columns are receiving the data. The square brackets ([..]) specify that the column listings (column1, column2, and so on) are optional.

The only fields that are required to have data in the Songs table are the Song_Name, Album_Num, Artist_Code, and Genre_Code fields, because they were declared as being NOT NULL in the CREATE TABLE statement. The rest of the fields are not required to have data when you add a new record to the table. To add information about the song "Where the Streets Have No Name" by U2, you use the statement shown in Figure 8-19.

Figure 8-19, SQL INSERT statement to add a record to the Songs table and its result

SQL statement:

```
INSERT INTO Songs (Song_Name, Album_Num, Artist_Code, Genre_Code)
VALUES ("Where the Streets Have No Name", 146, "U2", "POP");
```

Result:

Songs : Table

Song_Name	Album_Num	Track_Num	Media_Type	Artist_Code	Genre_Code
American Soldier	911	3	MP3	TK	CW
Beer For My Horses	826	5	MP3	TK	CW
Big Time	10	14	CD	PG	POP
Come As You Are	24	3	MP3	NIRV	NW
Lithium	24	5	MP3	NIRV	NW
One Tree Hill	146	9	CD	U2	NW
Only a Lad	78	16	CD	OB	NW
Sledgehammer	10	3	CD	PG	POP
Sloop John B	45	7	Vinyl	BB	CLA
The Thrill is Gone	98	8	MP3	BBK	BLU
Where the Streets Have No Name	146	0		U2	POP
With or Without You	146	3	CD	U2	NW
*	0	0			

Record: 11 of 12

You do not have to put each column and column value on a separate line but many developers do so to make the script more readable and easier to maintain. Every column did not need to be initialized with data (included in the INSERT statement). The columns defined as NULL, such as Track_Num, could be omitted from the SQL script in both the column list and the value list as it was defined as being able to accept a NULL value.

If you do not supply the column names, then SQL assumes you are inserting a row into the table using the order of the columns as they are defined in the table structure:

```
INSERT INTO Songs
VALUES (
"Where the Streets Have No Name",
146,
NULL,
NULL,
"U2",
"POP");
```

If you do not specify the column list then you *must* enter in data for the columns defined as NULL in order to gain access to the NOT NULL columns that follow the NULL column. The statement above implies that there are two fields in front of the field receiving the "U2" Artist_Code data. The previous

SQL statement that listed the columns did not need to specify NULL values because the SQL statement listed each column that was receiving data.

note Make sure you know the format of the table. This means that you need to know the order of the columns.

SELECT statement

The SELECT statement is the most commonly used SQL statement and is responsible for retrieving data from one or more tables within a database. The syntax for the SELECT statement is:

```
SELECT [DISTINCT] column_list
FROM table_reference
[WHERE search_condition]
[ORDER BY order_list]
```

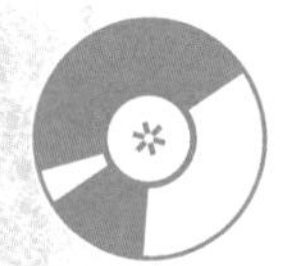

For an animated illustration of the SQL SELECT statement, check out the learning tools section under Chapter 8 on the student CD.

For example, Figure 8-20 shows the statement to select the Song_Name, Media_Type, and Track_Num fields from the Songs table, and its result in Microsoft Access.

Figure 8-20, SQL SELECT statement to return song's name, media type, and track number

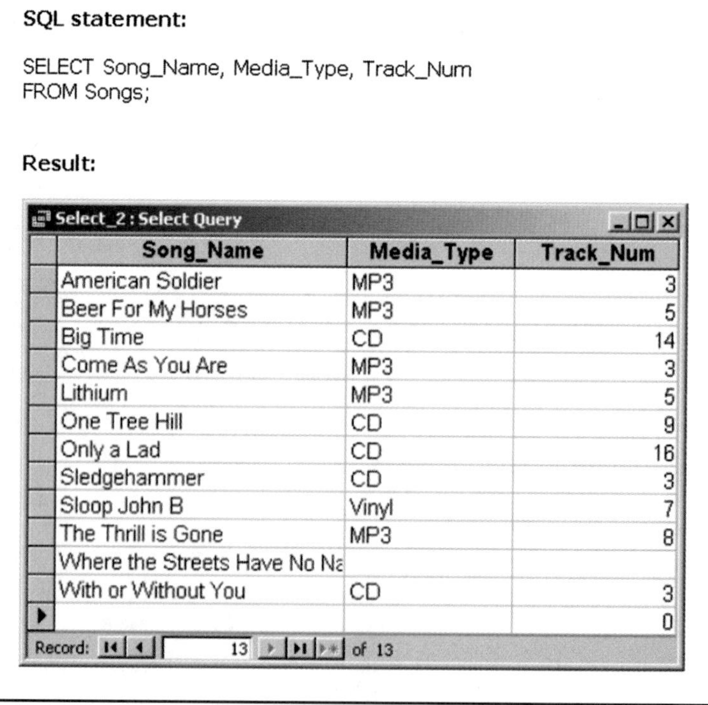

SQL statement:

```
SELECT Song_Name, Media_Type, Track_Num
FROM Songs;
```

Result:

Select_2 : Select Query

Song_Name	Media_Type	Track_Num
American Soldier	MP3	3
Beer For My Horses	MP3	5
Big Time	CD	14
Come As You Are	MP3	3
Lithium	MP3	5
One Tree Hill	CD	9
Only a Lad	CD	16
Sledgehammer	CD	3
Sloop John B	Vinyl	7
The Thrill is Gone	MP3	8
Where the Streets Have No Na		
With or Without You	CD	3
		0

Record: 13 of 13

Looking at Figure 8-20, notice that in the SQL statement, the desired columns from the table are separated with commas, and the statement ends with a semicolon. The order of the fields does not have to match that of the defined table structure. The order that you specify in the SELECT statement determines the order in which the data is retrieved and displayed.

WHERE clause

The WHERE clause in the SQL SELECT statement specifies additional criteria for retrieving data from a table. Think of the WHERE clause as being the search criteria, in that you can exclude or include specific types of rows depending on their column values. Figure 8-21 shows a SQL SELECT statement with a WHERE clause that searches for and retrieves the Song_Name and Track_Num for songs that have a media type of "CD".

Figure 8-21, SQL SELECT statement using a WHERE clause and its result

SQL statement:

```
SELECT Song_Name, Track_Num
FROM Songs
WHERE Media_Type="CD";
```

Result:

Query1 : Select Query

Song_Name	Track_Num
With or Without You	3
One Tree Hill	9
Only a Lad	16
Sledgehammer	3
Big Time	14
	0

Record: 5 of 5

Notice that the Media_Type column did not have to be specified as part of the SELECT column list. When you are using a field in a WHERE statement, it is usually wise to include it in the fields selected, just to make sure the data being retrieved is accurate. Figure 8-22 shows a more descriptive version of the SELECT statement in Figure 8-21.

Figure 8-22, More descriptive SQL SELECT statement using a WHERE clause

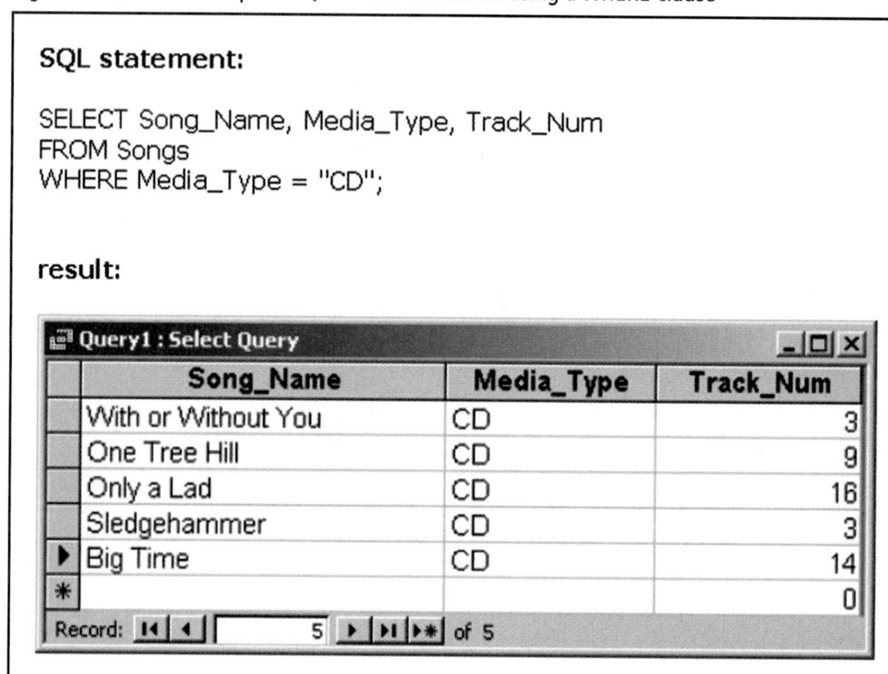

SQL statement:

```
SELECT Song_Name, Media_Type, Track_Num
FROM Songs
WHERE Media_Type = "CD";
```

result:

Query1 : Select Query

Song_Name	Media_Type	Track_Num
With or Without You	CD	3
One Tree Hill	CD	9
Only a Lad	CD	16
Sledgehammer	CD	3
Big Time	CD	14
		0

Record: 5 of 5

You can also specify more than one search criterion through the use of the AND and OR keywords. AND indicates that all criteria *must* be met, and OR is more flexible, indicating only one criterion needs to be met. Try this next query. What do you think the results will be?

```
SELECT Song_Name, Media_Type, Track_Num
FROM Songs
WHERE Media_Type = "CD" AND
Track_Num > 6 ;
```

If you guessed that the results would be the rows "Only a Lad," "Big Time," and "One Tree Hill," you were right: all of these songs' Media_Type is "CD" AND the Track_Num is greater than 6. Now, what do you think the results of the following SELECT statement will be?

```
SELECT Song_Name, Media_Type, Track_Num
FROM Songs
WHERE(Media_Type = "CD" OR Media_Type = "MP3")
AND
Track_Num > 6 ;
```

Figure 8-23 shows the results of these two SELECT statements, one using AND and one using OR. As you can see, the OR result contains more entries, because it selects songs that are either "CD" OR "MP3" AND have a track number that is greater than 6.

Figure 8-23, SQL SELECT statement using a WHERE clause with AND versus OR

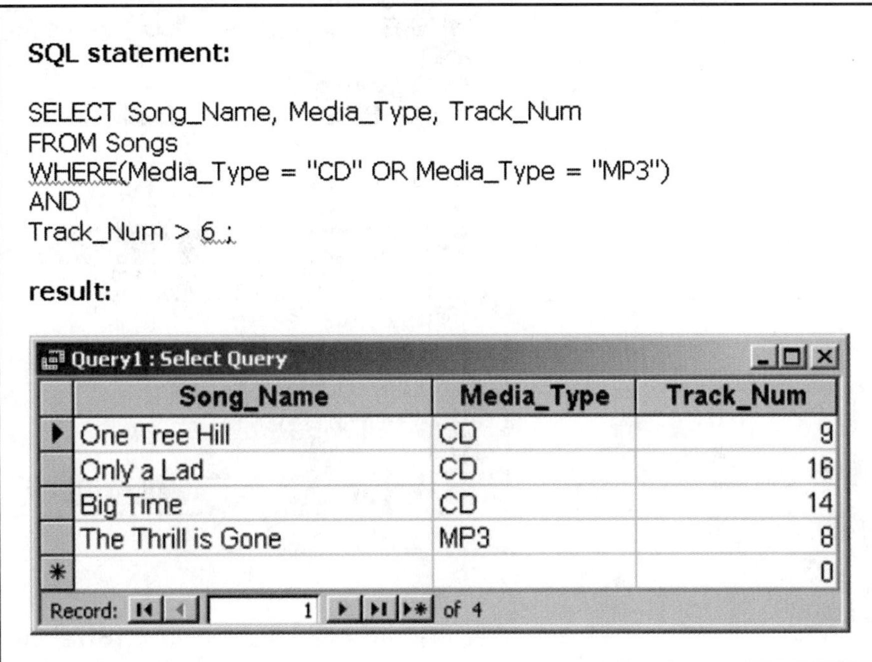

ORDER BY clause

Now that you have seen how to specify search criteria, you are ready to specify the order in which the rows of data are returned.

The ORDER BY clause permits you to change how the data is returned from the SELECT statement. By default, the data is returned in sequential order, meaning that the rows are kept in the order in which they are entered. Thus, the first row of data returned is the first record that matches the search criteria and the first record entered into the table.

If you want to arrange the data into a more meaningful representation, you can specify the ORDER BY column name(s). For example, Figure 8-24 shows the SQL statement and results to select songs that have a track number greater than 6, arranged in order by Song_Name and then by Track_Num.

Figure 8-24, SQL SELECT statement using an ORDER BY clause and its result

SQL statement:

```
SELECT Song_Name, Track_Num, Media_Type
FROM Songs
WHERE (Media_Type = "CD" OR Media_Type = "MP3")
AND
Track_Num > 6
ORDER BY Song_Name, Track_Num;
```

result:

Query1 : Select Query

Song_Name	Track_Num	Media_Type
Big Time	14	CD
One Tree Hill	9	CD
Only a Lad	16	CD
The Thrill is Gone	8	MP3
*	0	

Record: 1 of 4

The first time this script was executed without the ORDER BY clause (Figure 8-23), the results were a little different. The same number of records were returned but they were in a different order. The first record was "One Tree Hill" which implies that out of the four records returned, it was the first record entered into the table that satisfied the search criteria. Applying the ORDER BY clause allows the data to be rearranged and presented in a more meaningful order. Now the first record that you see is "Big Time."

note

Notice that when more than one field is used in the ORDER BY clause they are separated by a comma.

8

The ORDER BY clause also allows the SQL statement to return the data in ascending (default) or descending order. Figure 8-25 shows a SQL SELECT statement that displays the Song_Name and Track_Num for all Media_Type columns that are "CD" OR "MP3" AND have Track_Num column values greater than 6. The information is in ascending order by Track_Num and Song_Name with the smallest Track_Num value at the top of the list and the greatest value at the bottom of the list.

Figure 8-25, SQL SELECT statement using an ORDER BY clause with the default ascending option

SQL statement:

```
SELECT Song_Name, Track_Num, Media_Type
FROM Songs
WHERE (Media_Type = "CD" OR Media_Type = "MP3")
AND
Track_Num > 6
ORDER BY Track_Num, Song_Name;
```

result:

Query1 : Select Query

Song_Name	Track_Num	Media_Type
The Thrill is Gone	8	MP3
One Tree Hill	9	CD
Big Time	14	CD
Only a Lad	16	CD
*	0	

Record: 1 of 4

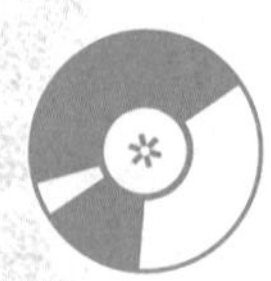

Reinforce your understanding of chapter concepts and terms with the information and activities for Chapter 8 on the student CD.

Figure 8-26 SQL SELECT statement using an ORDER BY clause with the DESC option

SQL statement:

```
SELECT Song_Name, Track_Num, Media_Type
FROM Songs
WHERE (Media_Type = "CD" OR Media_Type = "MP3")
AND
Track_Num > 6
ORDER BY Track_Num DESC, Song_Name;
```

result:

Query1 : Select Query

Song_Name	Track_Num	Media_Type
The Thrill is Gone	8	MP3
One Tree Hill	9	CD
Big Time	14	CD
Only a Lad	16	CD
	0	

Record: 1 of 4

If you would like to see the data returned in descending order, you simply place the word DESC next to the column on the ORDER BY clause. Figure 8-26 shows the SQL statement to order the songs by Track_Num and Song_Name using Track_Num in descending order, and its result.

You have barely scratched the surface of SQL power. There are more options you can specify on the SELECT statement that allow you to be more specific on the search criteria or more specific on the format of the returned results. Also, there are many more SQL commands that can be used to maintain, define, and administer the data found within a database.

one last thought

A database that is not properly organized can be more of a hinderance than a benefit. You have to carefully plan the structure of the data and how it will be stored, apply normalization rules, and use the right SQL statements to extract the kinds of information you want. With these structures, a database becomes a powerful tool used in many arenas, including business and computer science.

chapter summary

- A database is a collection of logically related information used in an application to create meaningful output for the end user
- Normalization is the process of decomposing tables to eliminate unwanted redundancies and dependencies in a data structure
- Database information is kept in sequential order but you can view the order of the records in different formats by creating indexes and assigning keys
- Primary keys are used to uniquely identify table entries while foreign keys are primary keys in other tables
- The manner in which one table relates to another table is called a relationship
- The two types of relationships discussed are one-to-many (1:M) and one-to-one (1.1)
- First normal form eliminates repeated fields
- Second normal form dictates that every column that is not part of the key is fully dependent upon the primary key
- Third normal form states that no nonkey columns depend on another nonkey column
- Fourth and fifth normal forms are rarely used, but further break down tables into nondependent, nonredundant forms
- The six steps for designing a database are: investigate, create a master column list, create the tables, work the relationships, analyze the design, and reevaluate
- Structured Query Language (SQL) is a powerful database language that allows you to define, maintain, query, and administer data

key terms

cardinality (289)

column (field or attribute) (271)

composite key (281)

database (267)

database management system (DBMS) (269)

determinant (280)

domain (272)

entity relationship (ER) model (289)

first normal form (1NF) (279)

foreign key (FK) (287)

functional dependency (281)

index (273)

key (274)

many-to-many (M:M) relationship (288)

normalization (276)

one-to-many (1:M) relationship (289)

one-to-one (1:1) relationship (288)

primary key (PK) (280)

relationship (287)

row (record or tuple) (271)

second normal form (2NF) (281)

Structured Query Language (SQL) (269)

table (or entity) (271)

third normal form (3NF) (283)

transitive dependency (283)

test yourself

1. What is a database? Give an example of a database in current use that affects you.

Use the following table for Questions 2–7

record #	team	wins	losses
1	Anteaters	10	2
2	Byrds	8	0
3	Monkeys	6	6
4	Admirals	10	2
5	Sapsuckers	5	7

2. The table is listed in what order (primary key)?
3. Write a SQL SELECT statement to list the contents of the table in order of wins.
4. Write a SQL SELECT statement to list the contents of the table in order of wins and team.
5. Write a SQL INSERT statement to add the team Bears. The Bears have 3 wins and 9 losses.
6. Write a SQL INSERT statement to add the team Lions. The Lions have 9 wins and 3 losses.
7. Write a SQL SELECT statement to list all of the contents of the table.
8. What is normalization and what problems does it solve?
9. Explain the first three normalization forms.
10. List and explain the six steps for designing a database.
11. Create a normalized database to support a space shuttle launching application. The government wants to keep track of astronauts, space shuttles, and launch history. Define the tables, primary and foreign keys, and indexes. Make sure that the tables are finalized in the third normalized state.

12. Draw an ER model to represent the space shuttle launching application designed in Question 11. Make sure you show the relationships and label the cardinality. Also show the primary and foreign keys.

Use the following table for Questions 13–20

field name	field size	field type	sample data
Error_Log_Date		Date	12/15/2004
Error_Log_Time		Time	2:24:32 PM
User_Code	8	Text	KATIE
User_First	15	Text	KAYTLEN
User_Last	25	Text	ANDERSON
Error_Code	4	Text	LOG
Error_Code_Desc	40	Text	INCORRECT LOGIN
User_Password	10	Text	MONK
Error_Log_Desc	80	Text	USER INPUT WAS BAD
Error_Status_Code	1 if Text	Yes/No or Text	C—Completed, U—Unresolved, I—In Process of Being Fixed
Error_Priority_Code		Number	May contain a number from 1 to 5 with 1—Very High, 2—High, 3—Medium, 4—Low, 5—Very Low

13. Using the fields listed above, normalize the data by organizing the fields into tables. HINT: You should end up with at least three tables.

14. Write a SQL CREATE statement to create each of the tables. Make sure you identify which fields you feel should or should not allow NULL values.

15. Write a SQL INSERT statement to add at least 3 records to each table created.

16. Using the normalized tables, write a SQL SELECT statement to show all of the users (User_Code, User_First, and User_Last). Sort the information by the User_Last and User_First columns.

17. Using the normalized tables, write a SQL SELECT statement to show all of the errors (Error_Log_Date, Error_Log_Time, Error_Code, Error_Status_Code, Error_Priority_Code, Error_Code_Desc, and Error_Log_Desc). Sort the information by the Error_Log_Date and Error_Log_Time columns.

18. Using the normalized tables, write a SQL SELECT statement to show all of the information regarding each error along with the first and last name of the user who created the error.

19. Review the Error_Status_Code column in the normalized tables. The user wants to see the description be displayed for the Error_Status_Code column. This description will also be used in a drop down list box when the user is entering in information on the screen for the error. What can you as the database designer do to enhance the current design of the tables and make the structure of the database more flexible in handling more Error_Status_Codes being added to the system?

20. Review the Error_Priority_Code column in the normalized tables. The user wants to see the description be displayed for the Error_Priority_Code column. This description will also be used in a drop down list box when the user is entering in information on the screen for the error. What can you as the database designer do to enhance the current design of the tables and make the structure of the database more flexible in handling more Error_Priority_Codes being added to the system?

practice exercises

1. Which of the following is *not* a valid DBMS?

   a. SQL Server
   b. C++
   c. Oracle
   d. DB2

2. A table is divided into databases.

   a. True
   b. False

3. A column is divided into tables.

   a. True
   b. False

4. What is the set of possible values for a column?
   - a. Domain
   - b. Table
   - c. SQL
   - d. Index

5. What specifies how the information within an entity is organized?
   - a. Domain
   - b. Table
   - c. SQL
   - d. Index

6. First normal form says:
   - a. No nonkey columns depend on another nonkey column
   - b. Every column that is not part of the key is fully dependent upon the primary key
   - c. Eliminate repeated fields
   - d. None of the above

7. Second normal form says:
   - a. No nonkey columns depend on another nonkey column
   - b. Every column that is not part of the key is fully dependent upon the primary key
   - c. Eliminate repeated fields
   - d. None of the above

8. Third normal form says:
   - a. No nonkey columns depend on another nonkey column
   - b. Every column that is not part of the key is fully dependent upon the primary key
   - c. Eliminate repeated fields
   - d. None of the above

9. What uniquely identifies a row within a table?
   - a. Index
   - b. Column
   - c. Primary Key
   - d. Tuple

10. A composite key is a column that contains unique information.
    - a. True
    - b. False

11. Which is *not* a step of the database design process?
    - a. Create the tables
    - b. Create the relationships
    - c. Investigate
    - d. Add the data

12. When creating a table using SQL, you *must* specify whether the column will be NULL or NOT NULL.

    a. True
    b. False

13. The INSERT SQL statement allows you to add multiple records in one statement.

    a. True
    b. False

14. By default, the data returned by the SQL SELECT statement are in descending order.

    a. True
    b. False

15. Which of the following SQL SELECT options are used to organize the data being returned?

    a. ORDER BY
    b. SORT BY
    c. WHERE
    d. None of the above

digging deeper

1. Talk to at least three different companies that use databases and find out which DBMS package they use. Ask them why they selected that particular DBMS and report your findings.
2. List at least five SQL statements that have not been discussed in this chapter. Describe what they do, and give an example of each.
3. Research the fourth and fifth normal forms. Describe each, and demonstrate in an example how they are applied to a database.
4. Are there any other database relationships besides 1:M and 1:1? If so, describe the relationship and use tables that you have defined to show how it is implemented.
5. What are the advantages and disadvantages of using Oracle versus SQL Server?

discussion topics

1. What are some of the times you have encountered databases being used?
2. If you could create a database to make some aspect of your life easier, what type of information would it contain?

3. If you were creating a database registration system for your university, what tables would it contain? What columns would be found in the tables?
4. If you were creating a database system to hold all of your music files, what tables would it contain? What columns would be found in the tables?
5. What are some possible negative effects on privacy and citizens' rights that the use of databases might have?

Internet research

1. List and describe at least five Web sites that give SQL tutorials. Share this information with your class and professor.
2. Choose a particular database format (such as Oracle, SQL Server, or whatever) and research the following information: current version, current price, training options, certifications available, company information, and company stock price. Create a spreadsheet or word-processed table to display your results.
3. What type of computer jobs requires knowledge of a DBMS package? Search the Internet using sites such as Dice, Monster, CareerBuilder, and so on, and write down the jobs and the types of DBMS packages, and the tasks or skills required.
4. List at least five Web sites that use databases to store information. Describe the information they are storing. Try to identify some of the tables they might have created to use within their Web site.
5. Using the DBMS packages listed in this chapter, identify the advantages and disadvantages of each. Use the Internet to search for opinions, reviews, and other articles.
6. List and describe three different modeling tools (other than Microsoft Visio) that allow you to do ER modeling.

data structures

in this chapter you will:

- Learn what a data structure is and how it is used
- Learn about single- and multidimensional arrays and how they work
- Learn what a pointer is and how it is used in data structures
- Learn that a linked list allows you to work with dynamic information
- Understand that a stack is a linked list and how it is used
- Learn that a queue is another form of a linked list and how it is used
- Learn that a binary tree is a data structure that stores information in a hierarchical order
- Be introduced to several sorting routines

the lighter side of the lab

by spencer

As soon as you flip this page, you're going to be bombarded with a list of words with which you're probably not familiar, words such as "pointers," "arrays," "stacks," and "queues." Don't stress out! Calmly pick up your textbook, slowly walk toward the nearest open window, gently hurl the textbook through the open window, and change your major to Art. I'm kidding, of course—change it to Sociology.

Actually, these concepts aren't as complicated as they might seem at first. There are examples all around us. For example, you see an example of a pointer whenever you go to a commencement speech where somebody has a laser pen. That person uses the laser pen as the address used to "point" out to the rest the audience where the speaker's forehead is.

Arrays can be extremely useful to keep track of information when all of the entries are of the same type. This technology has given NASA scientists the ability to keep track of which Baldwin brother is which.

Stacks are found all around us. In fact, I was near the bottom of a stack just the other day. This stack consisted of my two cousins, my three brothers and myself, and was created when my brother initialized the command, "Doggypile!" *Note*: FIFO does *not* work with doggypile stacks, as demonstrated by my cracked ribs. (Feel free to return and laugh at that statement after you've read through the chapter.)

Most of us stand in at least one queue on a daily basis, whether it is in the supermarket, at a restaurant, or for the shower in the morning as everybody tries to get ready for school at the same time. (We know queues better as "lines.") In fact, I almost had a little "buffer overflow" as I stood in the extremely long queue for the restroom at a football game recently.

You see—data structures really aren't that difficult. By applying these technical terms to aspects of everyday life, learning these principles becomes easy enough that anybody can do it—even an Art major.

why you need to know about...

data structures

A doctor, an engineer, and a computer scientist were discussing which of their professions had been around the longest. The doctor, said, "In the beginning there was Adam and Eve. Someone had to know medicine to create Adam and Eve." The engineer turned to the doctor and said, "Before Adam and Eve could live on the earth it had to be created. Someone had to know engineering to create the earth." The computer scientist just laughed and said, "You are both wrong! In the beginning, there was chaos. Who do you think created all that chaos?"

In order for a computer to be effective there must be some type of organization. Without it, chaos would run rampant. The computer would not access and retrieve memory effectively. System response time would be outrageous. In fact, computers would perform so horribly that they would be worthless. Data structures organize the data in a computer and make it possible to access and process that data in an efficient and meaningful way.

All programs use some form of data and in order to be able to write effective computer programs you must understand the basics of what a data structure is and how it is used. As you learn more about programming and begin writing computer programs, you will find many occasions for using the kinds of data structures introduced in this chapter.

data structures

Why worry about organizing your data on a computer? Think of your bedroom. How hard is it to find something you are looking for? If your room is organized and clean, it is a lot easier and quicker to find an item. If it is messy and disorganized you have to look through everything to try and find it, thus taking a longer amount of time and expending more energy.

A ***data structure*** can be defined as a way of organizing data. There are different types of data structures in memory, such as arrays, lists, stacks, queues, and trees. There are also ways of organizing data on storage media, such as file structures.

data structure – A way of organizing data in memory, such as arrays, lists, stacks, queues, and trees, or on storage media, such as file structures

Chapter 10 focuses on "File Structures," while this chapter focuses on memory structures.

A computer's memory is organized into cells. Each memory cell has a memory address, through which the contents of the cell can be accessed. As shown in Figure 9-1, memory addresses are organized consecutively: if the first memory cell has an address of zero, the next memory cell has an address of one.

Figure 9-1, Consecutive memory locations

position	value
0	Mercury
1	Venus
2	Earth
3	Mars
4	Jupiter

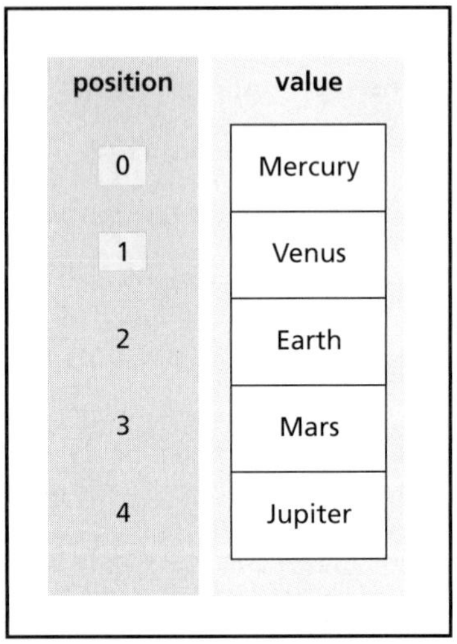

For a quick walk-through on data structures, see the tutorials section under Chapter 9 on the student CD.

Luckily for you, data structures make it possible to use a computer without having to worry about the details of how information is stored in consecutive memory locations. The most common data structures are arrays and lists.

arrays

array – A set of contiguous memory cells used for storing the same type of data

An ***array*** is the simplest memory data structure and consists of a set of contiguous memory cells. The group of contiguous memory cells must store the same type of data. This means that if the first memory cell contains a number, then all of the memory cells associated with the array must also contain numbers.

Arrays are used for storing similar kinds of information in memory. This information can then be sorted or left in the order it was entered into the array. Arrays can be used to store student grades, book titles, names of college courses, a space shuttle launch checklist, and on and on. As long as the information is of the same type and you want to store it in memory, an array may be the data structure to use.

For example if you wanted to write a computer program that asks the user to enter five different numbers, print them back to the screen in reverse order, and then calculate the sum of the numbers, you can create an array of five positions to temporarily hold the number values. The number values can be accessed

Figure 9-2, Arrays make the logic of a program easier to understand and use

array name: aNumbers

position	value		value
0	95	0 Variable1	95
1	88	1 Variable2	88
2	92	2 Variable3	92
3	78	3 Variable4	78
4	85	4 Variable5	85

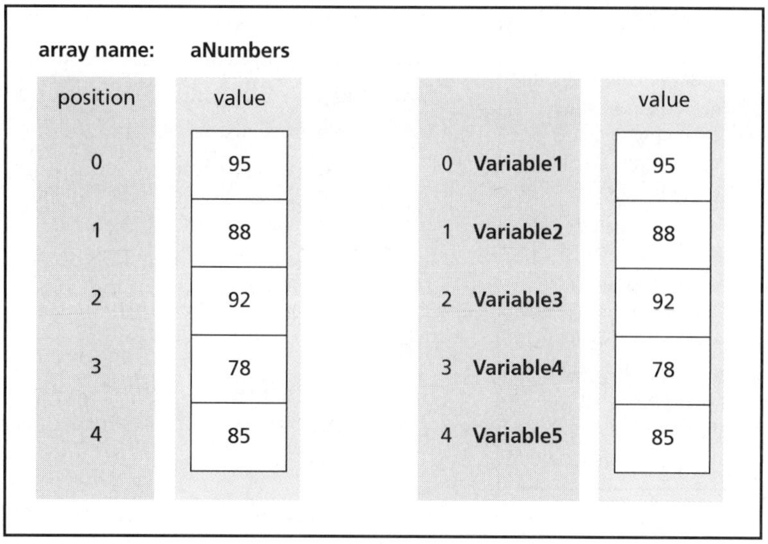

through the use of the array. As shown in Figure 9-2 if you did not use an array then you would have to create five different holding areas or variable names with each area having its own name. Using the array makes the logic of the program easier to understand and use. Instead of having to worry about five different memory variables or names, using an array requires you to only remember the array name.

how an array works

When an array is first defined, you must tell the computer system what type of data will be stored and how many memory cells you would like to use. For example, in the Java programming language, you create a new array and specify the type and the size of the array by using the "new" keyword. You also specify a name for the array, which is used to access the contents of the cells in the array. Consider this statement:

```
int[ ] aGrades = new int[5];
```

- The int[ ] part of the statement tells the computer that the array will hold integer (numeric) values. If the array was going to hold character values, it would say char[ ].
- The word "aGrades" is the name of the array, the name by which the memory contents will be accessed.
- The "new" keyword tells the computer that a new array is being created.

Hungarian notation

In this convention, the first letter of a variable name represents the type of data being stored. For example, an integer variable name would be preceded with the letter "i" as in "iGrade." This way of naming variables is not a requirement of programming languages, and doesn't affect how the computer deals with variables, but it helps programmers to easily see what type of data should be found in a memory location.

element – A memory cell in an array

- The int[5] part of the statement tells the computer to reserve five memory locations to store the numeric (int) values for the array.
- The "=" sign (equals sign, called an assignment operator) takes the newly created array of five memory cells and assigns aGrades as the "manager" of those memory cells.
- The ";" (semicolon) tells the computer that the end of the statement has been reached.

Note that the name of the array includes a lowercase letter "a" in front of the text "Grades." This is called Hungarian notation, a variable-naming standard devised to make a program's statements more readable.

The five contiguous memory cells are reserved in memory and can be referenced through the use of the word that has been set up as the manager, in this case, aGrades.

The aGrades array is considered a single-dimensional array because it contains only one row or column of elements (Figure 9-3). (An ***element*** is another name for a memory cell in an array.) The dimension of an array is how many levels are created to hold the array elements.

Figure 9-3, Five contiguous memory cells managed by aGrades in a single-dimensional array

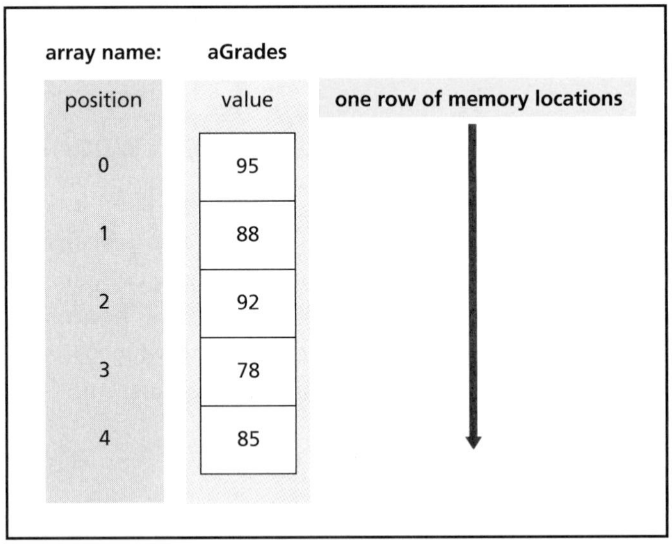

Think of a single-dimensional array as a row of mailboxes on a street (Figure 9-4). Each mailbox has an address associated with it. For this example, say that the street name is aGrades. There are five property locations on the street, each of them having its own unique mailing address. All of the mailboxes are lined up in a row on the street so the postal carrier can easily organize and deliver the mail.

Figure 9-4, A row of mailboxes is similar to a row of contiguous memory (an array)

Also, there are strict rules for the postal carrier. The only type of items that can be delivered to the mailboxes on the street have to be defined when the mailboxes are first built. In this example, the mailboxes only allow the receipt of letters containing numbers. As the postal carrier drives up to the mailboxes, the address on each of the letters determines which mailbox receives the information being mailed.

So how is the process of putting values into the cells of an array accomplished in a computer? The first address or position in the array starts with the number zero (0). Arrays start at element zero because they are implemented through the use of memory addresses. When you create a new array and assign it to a name the computer reserves some memory locations to accommodate the size of the array. The name is actually assigned the memory location of where the array begins in memory. This memory location is used just like a postal carrier would use an address to find a specific mailbox. Once the memory location (or mailbox) is found, the computer knows that the next element in the array is one position or ***offset*** over from the starting address. The offset is used to specify the distance between memory locations. The computer has been told that to locate the next element within the array it must use the array's starting memory location stored in the first position of the array and then move over the number of offsets representing different positions within the array.

offset – Used to specify the distance between memory locations

For example, the first position of the array, referenced as position zero, could be found by using the starting memory location of the array plus zero offsets. In other words, it is equal to the starting position of the array. The next location of the array, referenced as position one, is found by using the starting memory location plus one offset. The third position of the array, referenced as position two, is found by using the starting memory location plus two offsets (Figure 9-5).

Figure 9-5, Arrays start at position 0 and use an offset to know where the next element is located in memory

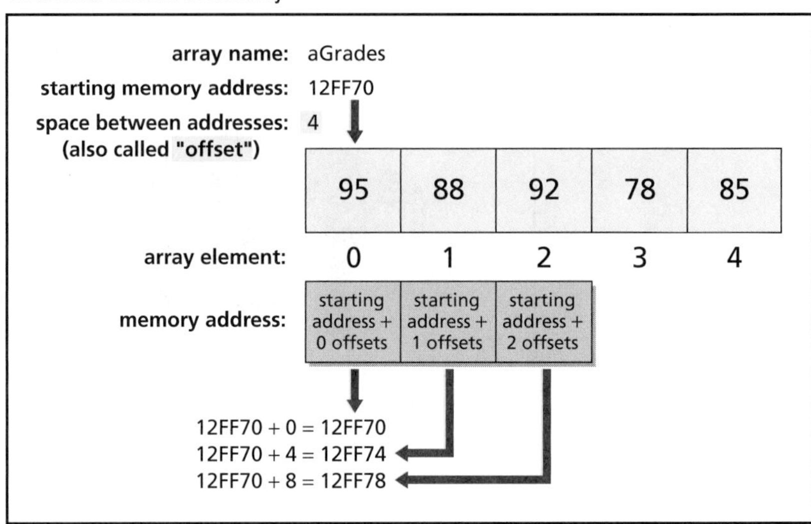

index (subscript) – How an array accesses each element stored in its data structure

To more easily use an array, the array uses an *index* or a *subscript*. It tells the computer which memory cell to access in the array by looking at the position of the element. The index is placed between the square brackets "[ ]" and next to the array name. To store a value of 50 in the first element you use the statement:

```
aGrades[0] = 50;
```

When the array was created it was specified that the array had five contiguous memory locations. The preceding statement just placed the value 50 in the first position. Remember that position 0 is the first position, so when an array has positions 0–4, there are actually five memory cells or addresses. If you wanted to store a value in the fifth element, then you would need to access position four.

```
aGrades[4] = 100;
```

If you were to store a value in every element of the array, it might appear as shown in Figure 9-6:

```
aGrades[0] = 50;
aGrades[1] = 30;
aGrades[2] = 25;
aGrades[3] = 85;
aGrades[4] = 100;
```

upper bound – The highest position in an array

lower bound – The lowest position in an array

The *upper bound* of the array is the element with the highest position (4) while the *lower bound* of the array is the lowest position being used (0). These bounds can be used in conjunction with the length of the array to process through the array element by element until all elements have been processed.

Figure 9-6, The array with all elements stored

position	value
0	50
1	30
2	25
3	85
4	100

multidimensional arrays

multidimensional array – An array consisting of two or more single-dimensional arrays

Besides single-dimensional arrays, there are ***multidimensional arrays***. A multidimensional array consists of two or more single-dimensional arrays. Refer back to the example of an array being a row of mailboxes. In a single-dimensional array, there is just one row of mailboxes. In a multidimensional array, there are multiple rows of mailboxes stacked on top of each other, as shown in Figure 9-7.

Figure 9-7, A multidimensional array is like apartment mailboxes stacked on top of each other

floor \ apartment #:	0	1	2	3	4
0	floor 0 apartment 0	floor 0 apartment 1	floor 0 apartment 2		
1	floor 1 apartment 0				
2					

Think of a multidimensional array as being like stacks of mailboxes you might find in an apartment building. The apartment building has a mailbox for each tenant. The apartment building floor numbering starts on floor zero because it is ground level. Each floor is offset by the number of flights of stairs above ground level so the second floor in the apartment building is floor one or one flight of stairs above ground level or floor zero. The address of each mailbox is the combination of the floor number plus the apartment number. For example, the first mailbox has the address of floor zero, apartment number zero. The last mailbox has the address of floor two, apartment number four. On each floor there are five apartments numbered zero through four. The only way the postal carrier will know which apartment receives the letter is by also knowing the floor.

Are you officially confused? You can make it even simpler by starting with the simplest multidimensional array. Almost everyone has played tic-tac-toe. A tic-tac-toe board (Figure 9-8) is actually a two-dimensional array, that is, an array within an array.

Figure 9-8, Tic-tac-toe board

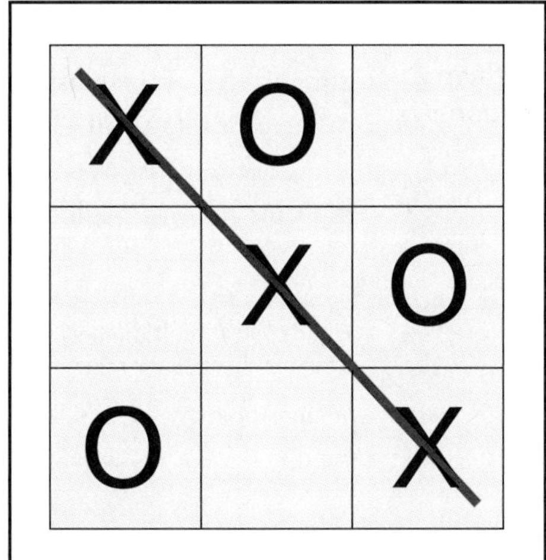

The tic-tac-toe board array consists of three positions in the first row, three in the second, and three in the third. The first row contains an array of three positions, as shown in Figure 9-9. The rows are numbered from zero to two, and the columns are numbered from zero to two. All of the array elements in the first row have a row value of zero with a column value of zero, one, or two.

The second and third rows are also arrays (Figure 9-10). All of the array elements in the second row have a row value of one with a column value of zero, one, or two, and all of the array elements in the third row have a row value of two with a column value of zero, one, or two.

Figure 9-9, First row of the tic-tac-toe board

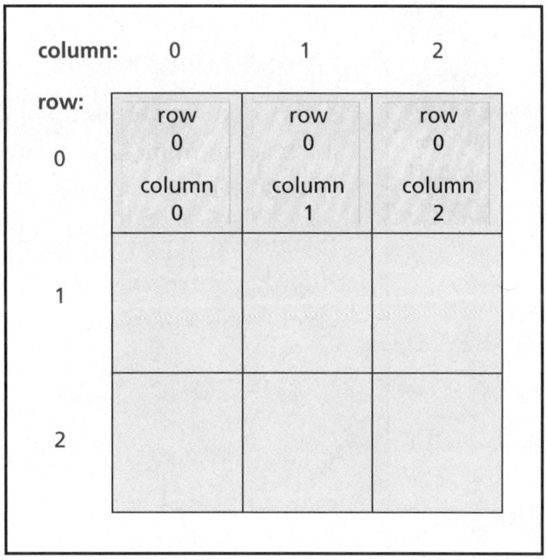

row: \ column:	0	1	2
0	row 0 column 0	row 0 column 1	row 0 column 2
1			
2			

Figure 9-10, Second and third rows of the tic-tac-toe board

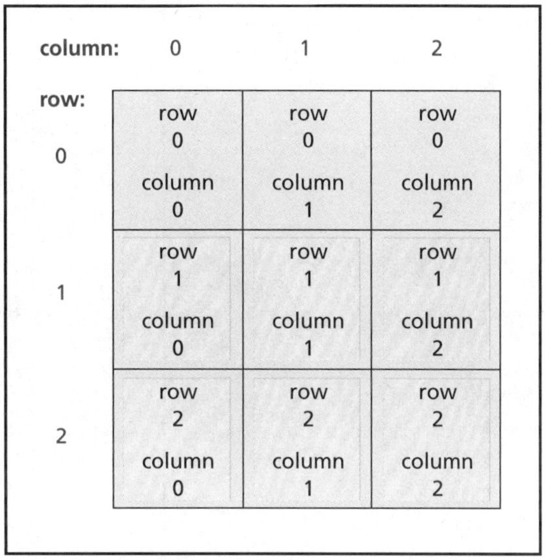

row: \ column:	0	1	2
0	row 0 column 0	row 0 column 1	row 0 column 2
1	row 1 column 0	row 1 column 1	row 1 column 2
2	row 2 column 0	row 2 column 1	row 2 column 2

It is easy create the tic-tac-toe board as a multidimensional array in memory. Using the array syntax defined earlier in the chapter, the statement appears as:

```
char[ ][ ] aTicTacToe = new char[3][3];
```

Don't get confused in thinking that you would declare a three-by-three array as [2][2] since arrays are zero-based. In declaring an array size, you do not need to worry about the fact that arrays start at zero. You only need to remember that

multidimensional arrays

In C++ you create a multidimensional array and store a value in one of the array elements using the statements:

```
char aTicTacToe[3][3];
aTicTacToe[1][1] = 'X';
```

In Delphi (Pascal) you create a multidimensional array and store a value in one of the array elements using the statements:

```
var aTicTacToe : array[0..2,0..2] of char;
aTicTacToe[1,1] := 'X';
```

arrays are zero-based when you begin accessing the elements. Simply remember that when you are declaring the size of the array you need to think of how many elements are needed.

This statement creates three arrays, each having three storage locations. It is a lot easier to think of it as having three rows and three columns (much like a spreadsheet).

If you were to play a game of tic-tac-toe you might want to start by putting an X in the center position (Figure 9-11). To place the character X in the second row of the second column, you use the following statement:

```
aTicTacToe[1][1] = 'X';
```

Why wasn't the location shown as [2][2]? That's right—because arrays are always zero-based, so the first row is index row zero, and the second row is index row one, and so on.

Figure 9-11, Storing a value to a location of an array

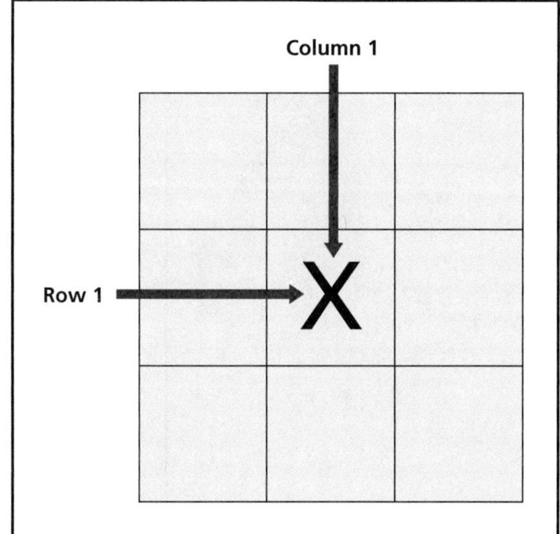

Take a look at Figure 9-12.This is an example of a three-dimensional array. It can be explained as having three arrays or levels. On each level (array) there is a two-dimensional array containing rows and columns.

Are you ready to try a four-dimensional array? Actually, many programmers suggest that you go no further than three levels deep on an array because the more levels you have, the more complicated the array becomes. Remember, simplicity makes writing and maintaining data structures a lot easier.

Figure 9-12, Three-dimensional array

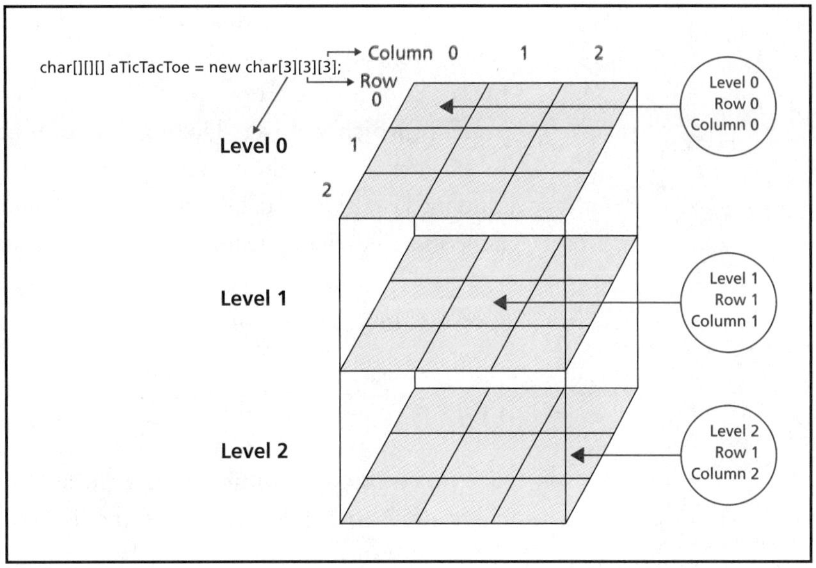

uses of arrays

Arrays are an excellent data structure for storing information in memory because they can be sequentially accessed without any knowledge of the memory cell contents. As long as you know the name of the array and the data type for the elements, you can retrieve and store data to the array. Arrays are also easy to implement and are a great benefit to people who write computer programs. Consider a program that stores 20 student names. Instead of creating 20 separate storage locations each with its own name, you would only have to create one array that contains 20 storage locations, accessed by a single name plus an index. That is a lot easier to remember and implement.

You have learned that an array is a collection of homogeneous data items. In Chapter 11, "Programming," you will be introduced to a data structure called a class. It is a collection of heterogeneous data items.

A disadvantage of using arrays is that there is a lot of overhead or computer power that can be expended when trying to insert new elements into the defined array structure. The array is a contiguous list data structure, which means that memory cells are located one after the other in memory. What if you defined an array to hold 20 student names but then one more registered for the course? Now you have run out of room in the array. You would have to redefine the size of the array and make sure that all of the information in the first array is copied correctly to the second array. This is quite inefficient and cumbersome.

Another disadvantage of arrays is that the data in the memory cells can only be accessed sequentially—that is, one at a time, in order. This means that if you wanted to find a specific value stored in an array you would have to start at the first position in the array and look at every single position until you found the value for which you were looking. You cannot randomly search the data stored in the elements based on search criteria. Once again, if you are using arrays for random searching of data then the computer is performing work that can be done more efficiently using a different data structure.

The real benefits of arrays become more apparent when you learn how to program loops, which are discussed in Chapter 11.

lists

The process to dynamically change the size of an array is quite inefficient and daunting. Another data structure, the list, was developed to overcome some of the disadvantages of arrays. This data structure holds lists of data that are dynamic, that is, they vary in size. Examples of lists that grow or shrink include class enrollment, cars that are brought in for repairs, and e-mail boxes. In fact, any type of data where the amount of data is unknown or could change is a good candidate for a list data structure. The amount of storage needed to store the list is unknown and needs to be flexible so that it can accept new items or remove present items from the list.

The forms of lists that can be implemented to work efficiently with dynamic data are:

· Linked lists
· Queues
· Stacks

Each of these data structures is introduced in the following sections.

linked lists

linked list – A data structure that uses noncontiguous memory locations to store data; each element in the linked list points to the next element in line and does not have to be contiguous to the previous element

A *linked list* is used when the exact number of items is unknown or there is a possibility that the length of the structure might change. For example, a linked list could be used to store students' names who visit a professor's office in a day, points you have scored against an opponent in your favorite video game, or companies that have sent you spam e-mail. You use the logic behind a linked list every day!

A linked list differs in use from an array in the fact that it stores the data noncontiguously (not in order). Instead of allocating a block of memory with array cells contiguously following each other, the linked list maintains the data and the address of where to go next. Remember that each cell of an array uses an address as a reference to access the data. The linked list also uses addresses, but implements them as "What memory location is next in line that I should jump to, because the memory locations I am using can be stored anywhere in memory?"

Linked lists are the basic constructs for other more advanced data structures such as queues and stacks. All of these structures use pointers. Learning how pointers work is not rocket science, but it tends to be a topic that beginning computer science students can get phobic about. In fact, you have already used pointers and maybe didn't even realize it! All you have to know is that a ***pointer*** is a memory cell that contains the address of another memory cell as its data. Just think "address" and it becomes no big deal. You have already worked with addresses while learning about arrays. An address is simply a location in memory.

pointer – A memory variable that points to a memory location

For example, consider a game where students sit in a circle. Each student has a piece of paper that has a box in the upper left corner and another box located in the center of the paper. The centered box is divided into two boxes (Figure 9-13). The box on the left indicates a student number. The students are told to write down their favorite color in the first box and leave the second box alone as it already has a number printed in it.

Figure 9-13, The piece of paper used in the linked list game

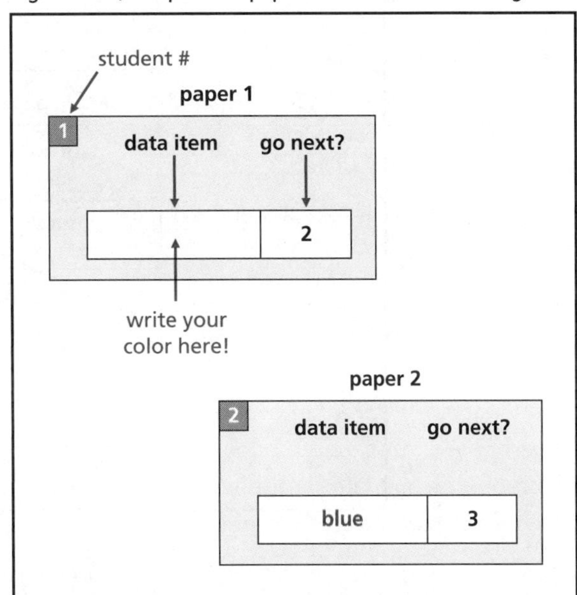

The professor also has a piece of paper, but it only contains a number. The professor starts the game by reading aloud the first number and pointing to the student whose piece of paper contains that number. The pointed-to student then reads aloud the color written in the first box, and then reads the student number in the second box printed on his piece of paper. The student with this number then reads her color and calls out the student number written on her paper. This process continues until all of the students have had a turn to read the color they wrote on the paper, and to call out the number in the second box. How does this end? The last student does not have a number printed in the second (ID) section on the piece of paper. Instead, the last student's "Go Next" box contains a null (also called a ***null value***).

null value – The absence of a value meaning that there is no value stored; null is not the same as blank or zero

head pointer – A pointer that points to the beginning of the first element in a data structure

This game demonstrates how a linked list is used in memory and how a pointer is used to tell the system which memory location is the next one in the list. Each piece of paper represents the structure of a linked list: it contains both data (the first part, the color) and a pointer to where to go next (the student ID number) (Figure 9-14). The professor's piece of paper represents the ***head pointer*** or the beginning of the linked list that indicates where to get the first piece of information.

Figure 9-14, Structure of a linked list

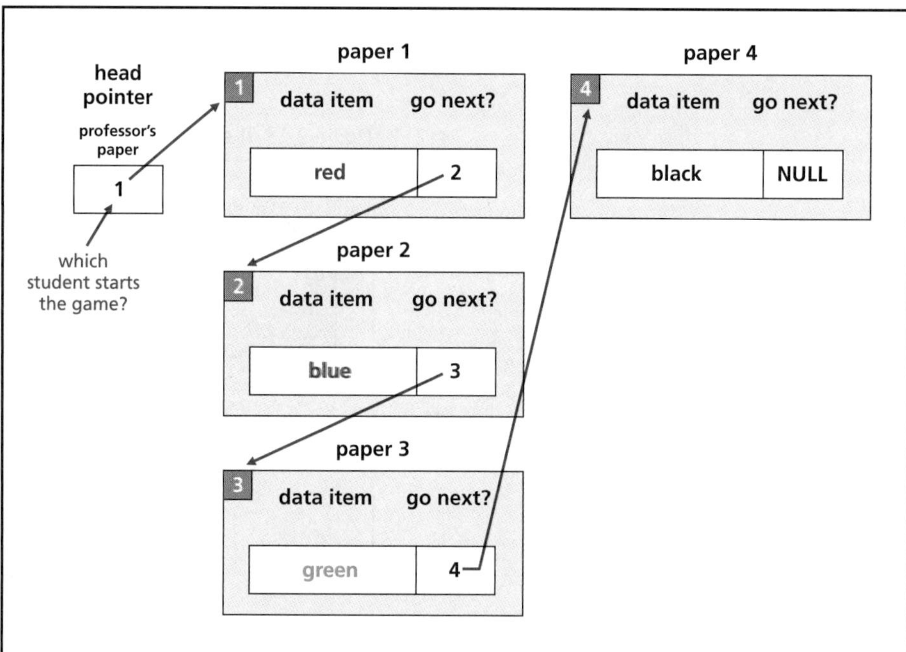

What would happen if you wanted to insert a new element into the list? If this was an array, you would have to resize the array, which would cause the system to allocate a new block of memory big enough for the entire array, and then the contents of the old array would need to be copied to the memory cells of the new array. This is not a very efficient way of storing data in memory if you are adding and deleting elements.

A linked list on the other hand, simply creates a new "piece of paper" with one location for the data and another for the "where to go" pointer address. Then the pointer on the piece of paper prior to where the new paper is to be inserted is changed to point to the new paper. The pointer on the new paper is made to point to the next paper in the sequence. Assume that a new student joins the class. The professor hands a piece of paper with the number five on it to the new student and tells the student to sit at the end of the line and to write a favorite color in the left box of the paper. The professor then tells the student to follow student three in telling the class the color, and then the new student should point to student four (Figure 9-15).

Figure 9-15, Inserting an element into a linked list

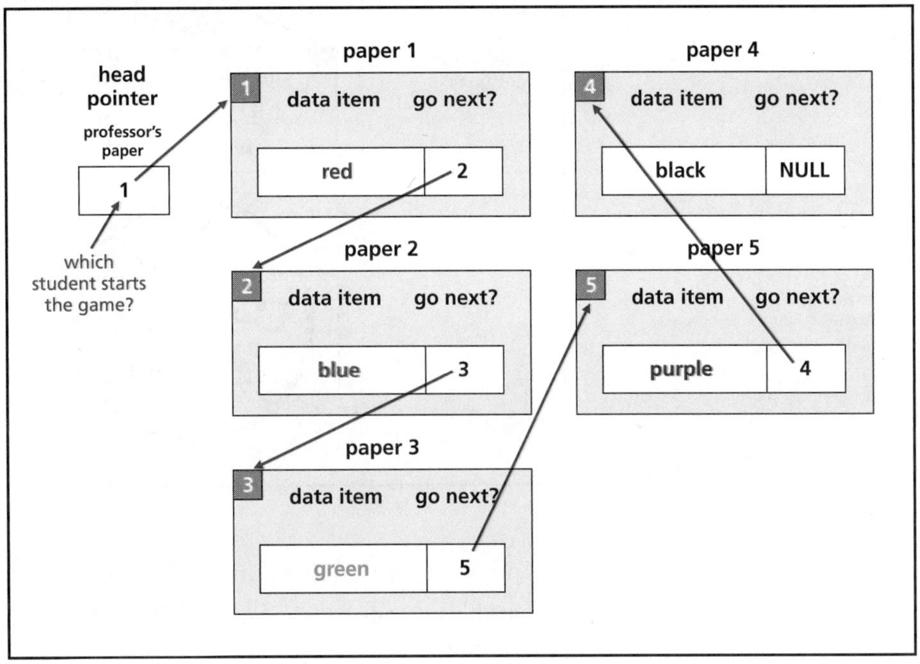

A linked list does not have to work with contiguous memory, thus making it more efficient for dynamic structures. The professor could have even put the new student at the beginning of the line and it still would not have affected how the information was processed. Why? Because the professor would have still told student number one to start. Student one would have read off the color "red" and then called on student two who would have read the color "blue." This process would continue until after student three read the color "green" and then called on the new student, which is number five. Student five would read "purple" and then call on student four who would read "black" and then stop.

The same concept applies when you want to delete an element from the linked list. The element that points to the item that is being deleted must have its pointer modified to point to the item that the deleted item used to point to (Figure 9-16).

Figure 9-16, Deleting an element from a linked list

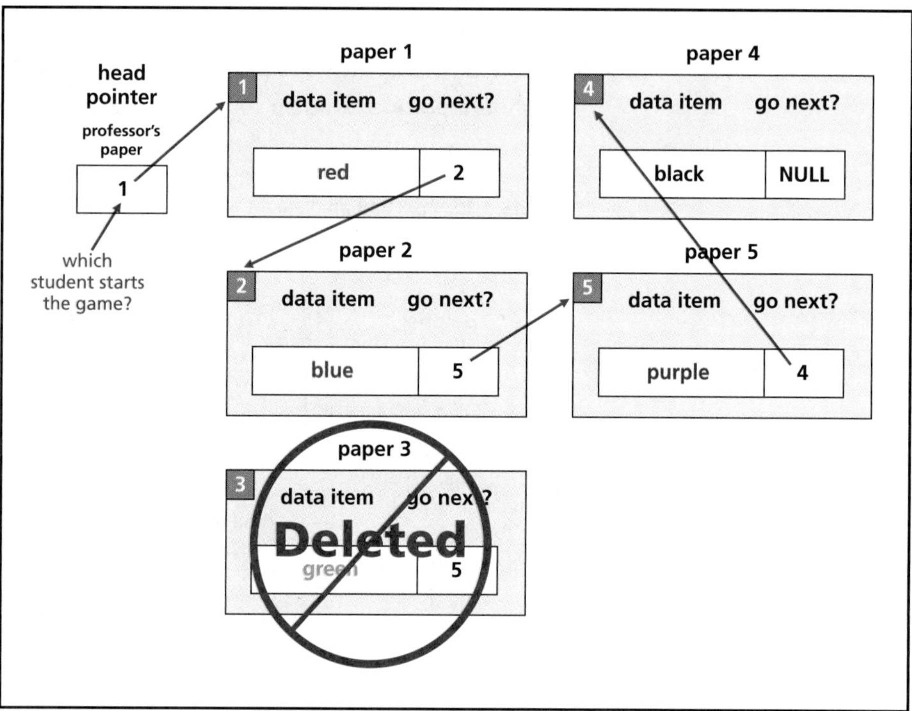

Without having to move any of the students in the class, a student can be deleted from the game. All that has to happen is that whichever student was pointing to the deleted student needs to change their "Go Next?" to point to the student that followed the deleted student. In other words, before the item is deleted in a linked list, the "Go Next?" value is saved so that the previous item can be updated to skip the deleted item.

stacks

stack – A list in which the next item to be removed is the item most recently stored

A *stack* is a special form of a list that allows you to "push" new items onto the list and "pop" current items off the list. It is very similar to how some all-you-can-eat buffet restaurants provide plates to their customers (Figure 9-17). The plate holder is spring loaded and as a customer removes a plate from the stack, every plate moves up one position. As clean plates are added to the stacks, the current plates move down away from the top of the stack. The kitchen employee pushes the plates onto the stack while the customers pop

peeking – Looking at the top item in the stack without removing it from the stack

the plates from the stack. Looking at the top plate to inspect it without removing it from the stack is called ***peeking***.

Figure 9-17, The stack concept

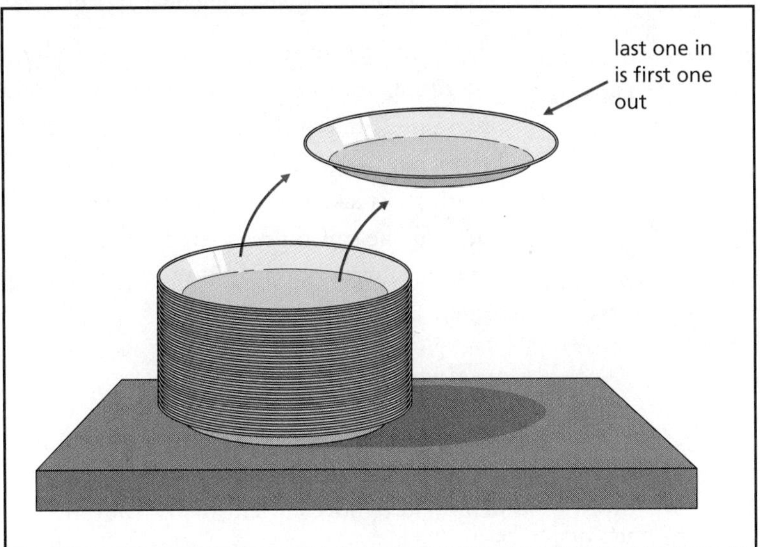

last in, first out (LIFO) – The last item placed on the stack is the first item removed from the stack

push – Place an item on the stack

pop – Remove an item from the stack

A stack is considered a ***last in, first out (LIFO)*** data structure. A LIFO data structure is like a stack of plates. The last or most recent plate ***pushed*** (put) onto the stack is the first plate ***popped*** (removed) from the stack. Another example of the last in, first out data structure is a text editor. As you type in characters, the character insertion pointer resides at the end of the last character typed in. If you press the backspace key the last character typed is removed. Or, think of a can of Pringles potato chips. The factory pushes the chips into the cylinder containing the chips. The first chip pushed into the cylinder sits at the very bottom and will be the last one to come out.

Notice that in this stack, items are added or taken away only from the top of the stack. In other words, the first value that is popped from the stack is the value that has remained on the stack for the shortest amount of time. The very last item popped from the stack will have remained on the stack for the longest time.

uses of a stack

How a stack is used can best be explained by understanding how a computer processes the lines of source code within a computer program. As the computer executes a computer program it understands the tasks it is supposed to accomplish through the use of source code. A line of source code is simply a command to do some work. This work might include storing a value into memory, performing a mathematical calculation, displaying a value to the monitor, sending information to the printer, or a myriad of other tasks.

procedure – A group of one or more computer statements that perform a task

The source code is logically organized into ***procedures*** or groups of related computer commands that perform a task. Another line of source code might call the procedure and tell it to execute its lines of source code. The called procedure might in turn call another procedure and so on until there is a long list of procedures that have called each other.

The computer must keep track of the calling procedure so that when the called procedure's source code is completed, it can return to where it left off in the program. Think of this as the computer creating a "lifeline" so that it always knows how to get back where it came from. This backtracking is accomplished by using a stack. The computer pushes the address of a procedure call onto the stack. As the called procedure finishes executing its source code, the address of the procedure is popped off the stack, and the computer proceeds to the next statement in the program.

back to pointers

stack pointer – A pointer that keeps track of where to either remove or add an item to the list in a data structure

In most stack implementations there is a pointer that keeps track of the top of the stack (called the ***stack pointer***). The computer knows where to push new items and remove current items from the data structure by using the memory location pointed to by its stack pointer. Remember that stacks, like linked lists and arrays, are just memory locations that have been organized into structures to facilitate reading from them and writing to them.

Figure 9-18 shows how the stack pointer is adjusted when an item is popped off the stack.

Figure 9-18, Stack pointer is decremented when item is popped

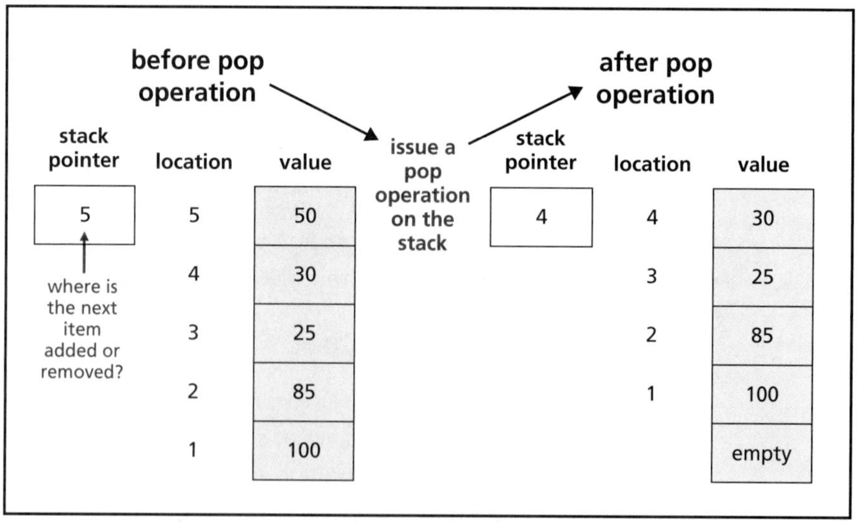

Before an item is popped from the stack, the status of the stack must be checked to make sure that there is an item to pop. Before an item is pushed onto the stack, the computer must check to make sure there is room for the new item. Otherwise, pushing or popping could cause an error.

queues

queue – A list in which the next item to be removed is the item that has been in the list the longest

first in, first out (FIFO) – The last item placed on the stack is the last item removed from the stack, and the first item removed from the stack is the first item placed onto the stack

A ***queue*** is another type of linked list that implements a ***first in, first out (FIFO)*** storage system. Insertions are made at the end of the stack while deletions are made at the beginning. The implementation of this data structure is similar to that of a waiting line. For example, the first customer in line is the first one to leave the line. The last customer in the line will be in line the longest. You have encountered FIFO when you have gone to a bank, bought food at the supermarket, driven your car on and off a ferry, or lined up at the school bookstore to buy this textbook.

uses of a queue

A queue is used in many situations within a computer system and you will hear it referenced by people who work with computer task management. For example, as you print documents, they are placed into a print queue. The first item to be printed is the document that has been in the queue the longest. As the item is printed, it is deleted from the queue and the next item is printed. If you request to print another document, it is placed at the end of the queue. This process continues until the queue is emptied. The queue is a "worker bee" that simply accepts what is given and pushes it out if it can. It keeps pushing out the oldest items and putting the newer items at the end of the list.

In a queue, all of the insertions of new data occur at the rear of the queue while the removal of data occurs at the front of the queue.

pointers again

tail pointer – Keeps track of the end or rear position of the data structure

dequeue – To remove an item from a queue

A queue uses a head pointer and a tail pointer. The head pointer keeps track of the beginning of the queue. As you might have guessed, the ***tail pointer*** keeps track of the end of the queue (Figure 9-19). If the queue contains no items then both the head and tail pointer point to the same location.

When an item is removed from the queue (to ***dequeue*** an item), the head pointer is changed to point to the next item in the list following the item recently removed. Consider the queue shown in Figure 9-20. If you were to dequeue an item from the queue, the oldest entry (which is stored in location one) would be removed. The head pointer would then be updated to point to location two signifying that it is currently the oldest entry in the queue.

Figure 9-19, A queue uses a FIFO structure

head pointer
1
queue front
tail pointer
5
queue rear
location
value
5 50 newest entry
4 30
3 25
2 85
1 100 oldest entry

Figure 9-20, Removing an item from the queue

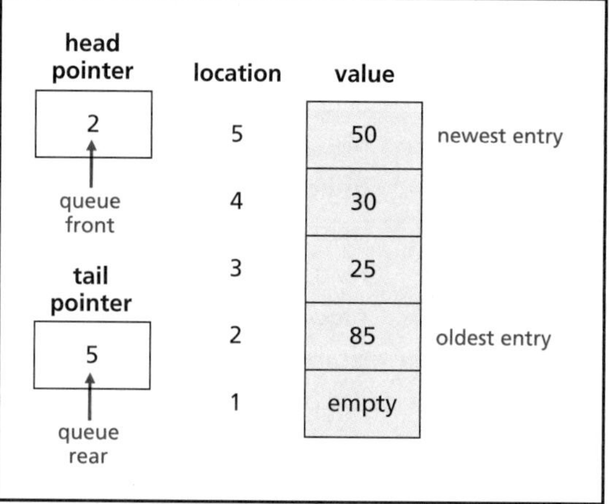

enqueue – To insert an item into a queue

When an item is inserted into the queue (to ***enqueue*** an item), the item is placed at the end of the list and the tail pointer is updated. As shown in Figure 9-21, a new entry containing the value of 18 is enqueued into the queue, thus adding a new item to the list and updating the tail pointer to point to the newest item added to the queue.

note There are many different ways to implement data structures in programming, depending on how the programmer wants to do it.

As you can see, both stacks and queues use pointers to keep track of the items in their data structures.

Figure 9-21, Inserting an item into the queue

head pointer	location	value	
2 (queue front)	6	18	newest entry
	5	50	
tail pointer	4	30	
6 (queue rear)	3	25	
	2	85	oldest entry
	1	empty	

trees

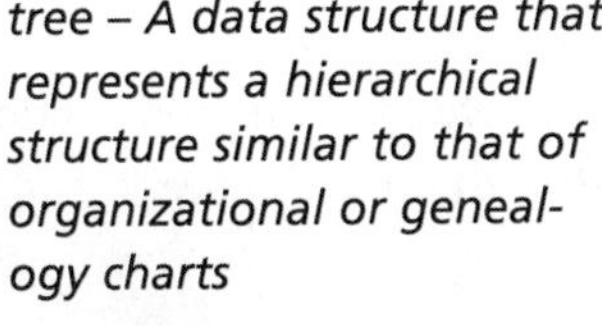

tree – A data structure that represents a hierarchical structure similar to that of organizational or genealogy charts

Another data structure that uses pointers to manipulate the storage of information, but is not a list, is a binary tree. A ***tree*** represents a hierarchical structure similar to that of organizational or genealogy charts and is useful for keeping the list of data in a hierarchy and for speeding up searches (Figure 9-22).

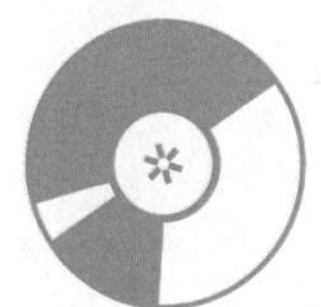

For an animated view of stacks, queues, linked lists, and binary trees, see the learning tools section under Chapter 9 on the student CD.

Figure 9-22, Tree data structure

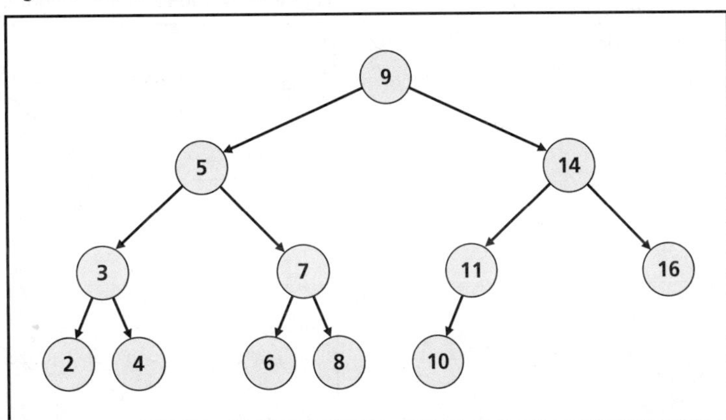

node or vertex – Each position in the tree

right child – The child node to the right of the parent node

left child – The child node to the left of the parent node

Each position in the tree is called a ***node*** or ***vertex***. The tree is binary because each node has at most two child nodes. A node in the tree can have zero, one, or two child nodes. The child node to the left of the parent node is called the ***left child***. The child node to the right of the parent node is called the ***right child***.

root – *The node that begins the tree*

leaf node – *A node that does not have any children nodes*

The node that begins the tree is called the ***root***. It is not a child of any node. A node that does not have any children is called a ***leaf node*** (Figure 9-23).

Figure 9-23, Tree nodes

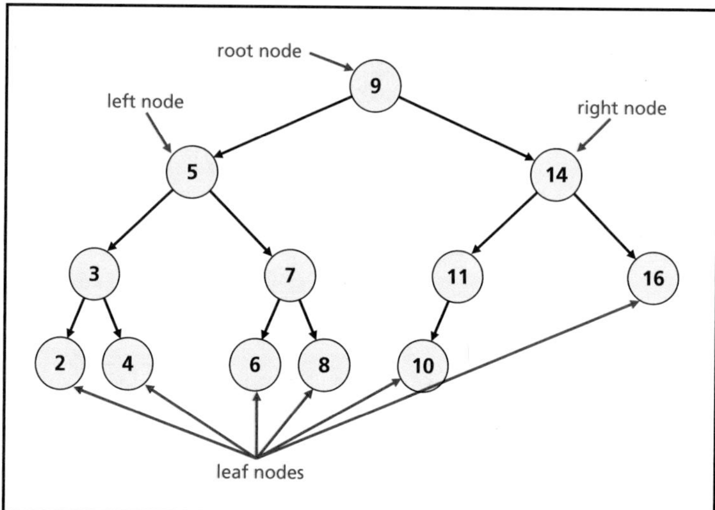

depth or level – *The distance from the node to the root node. The root's depth or level is 0*

height – *The longest path length in the tree*

The ***depth*** or ***level*** of the binary tree refers to the distance from the root node. The maximum number of levels is called the ***height*** of the tree (Figure 9-24).

Figure 9-24, The level and height of a binary tree

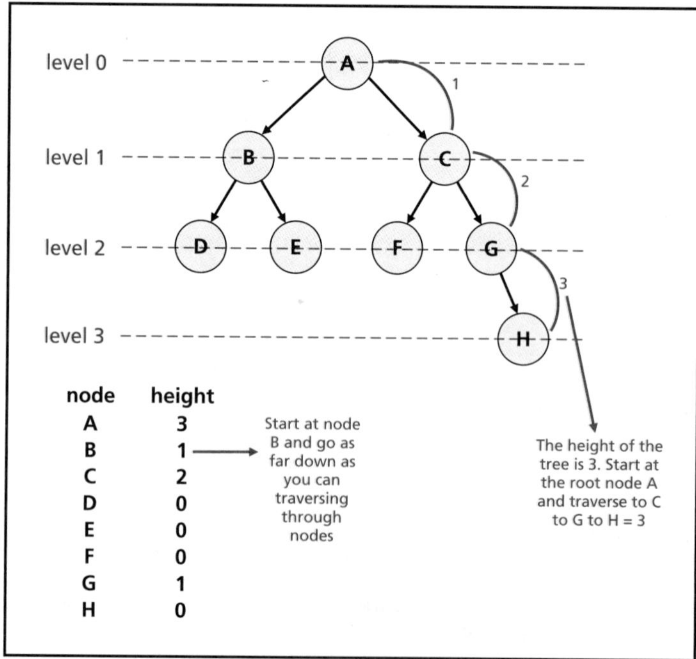

node	height
A	3
B	1
C	2
D	0
E	0
F	0
G	1
H	0

uses of binary trees

binary search tree (BST) – A binary tree where the left child's data is less than the parent node and the right child's data is greater than the value of the parent node

Binary trees can also be called *binary search trees (BST)* as long as the tree follows two rules:

1. The data value of the left child of a node is less than the value of the parent node.
2. The data value of the right child of a node is greater than the value of the parent node.

Binary search trees, when properly arranged, are a useful data structure for searching through stored data. One of the uses could be storing information in a hierarchical representation such as the file system shown in Figure 9-25.

Huffman coding

David A. Huffman, a student at MIT in 1952, constructed an encoding method that implements binary search trees to be used in file compression algorithms. The method is called the Huffman Coding Tree.

You'll learn more about file systems in Chapter 10.

Figure 9-25, File system structure can be stored as a binary search tree

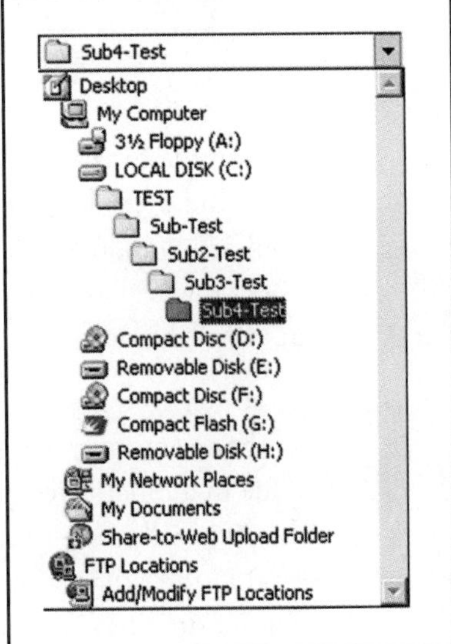

searching a binary tree

A binary search tree contains three components.

- Left child pointer
- Right child pointer
- Data

As shown in Figure 9-26 a node contains the data, a left pointer, and a right pointer.

Figure 9-26, Binary tree node

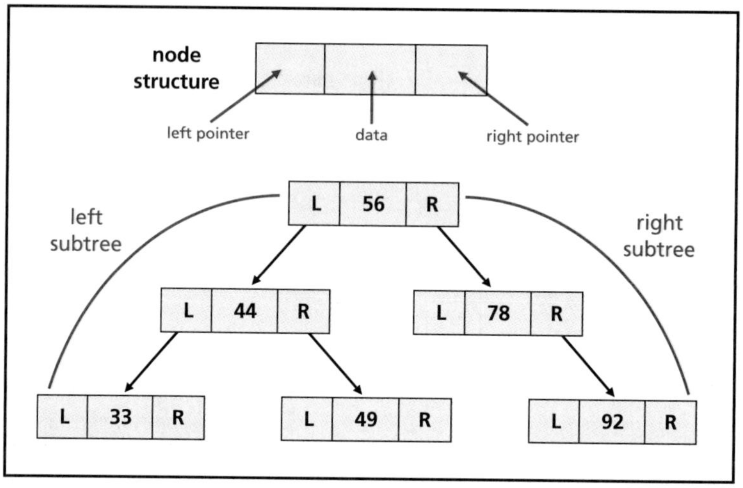

Within the binary tree there is a root pointer. It contains the address of the root node and provides the initial starting access to the tree. If the left or right child pointers contain a null (or empty) value then the node is not a parent to other nodes down that specific path. If both left and right pointers contain null values then the node is not a parent down either path.

To search a binary tree, it must first be defined properly. In a binary tree, the left node always has a value less than the right node. Searching for a particular value in a binary tree requires you to start at the root position and determine if the path will move to the left child or the right child. If the left pointer is NULL, then there is not a node to traverse down the left side. If the left pointer does have a value, then the path continues down that side. If you have found the value you are looking for, then you stop at that node.

Searching for a value of 8 in Figure 9-27 requires the following steps:

1. Start at the root node.
2. Does the value of 8 = the root value (9)? No. Then is the value of 8 > the root value (9)? No. Move to the left child (5).
3. Does the value of 8 = 5? No. Then is the value of 8 > 5? Yes. Move to the right child (7).
4. Does the value of 8 = 7? No. Then is the value of 8 > 7? Yes. Move to the right child (8).
5. Does the value of 8 = 8? Yes. Stop traversing the tree.

Figure 9-27, Searching the binary tree for the value of 8

Searching for a value of 10 in Figure 9-28 requires the following steps:

1. Start at the root node.
2. Does the value of 10 = the root value (9)? No. Then is the value of 10 > the root value (9)? Yes. Move to the right child (14).
3. Does the value of 10 = 14? No. Then is the value of 10 > 14? No. Move to the left child (11).
4. Does the value of 10 = 11? No. Then is the value of 10 > 11? No. Move to the left child (10).
5. Does the value of 10 = 10? Yes. Stop traversing the tree.

Figure 9-28, Searching the binary tree for the value of 10

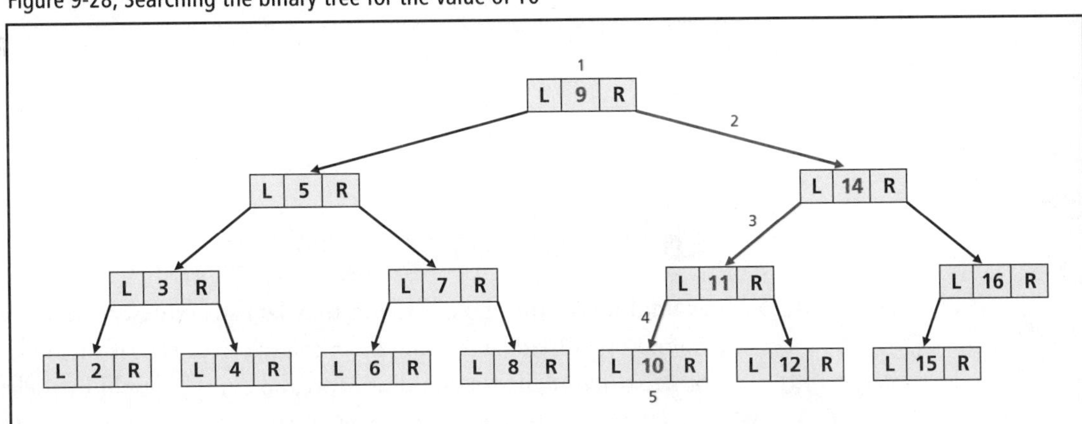

Searching for a value of 1 in Figure 9-29 requires the following steps:

1. Start at the root node.
2. Does the value of 1 = the root value (9)? No. Then is the value of 1 > the root value (9)? No. Move to the left child (5).
3. Does the value of 1 = 5? No. Then is the value of 1 > 5? No. Move to the left child (3).
4. Does the value of 1 = 3? No. Then is the value of 1 > 3? No. Move to the left child (2).
5. Does the value of 1 = 2? No. Then is the value of 1 > 2? No. Attempt to move to the left child, but stop traversing the tree because the left child pointer (2) is NULL.

Figure 9-29, Searching the binary tree for the value of 1

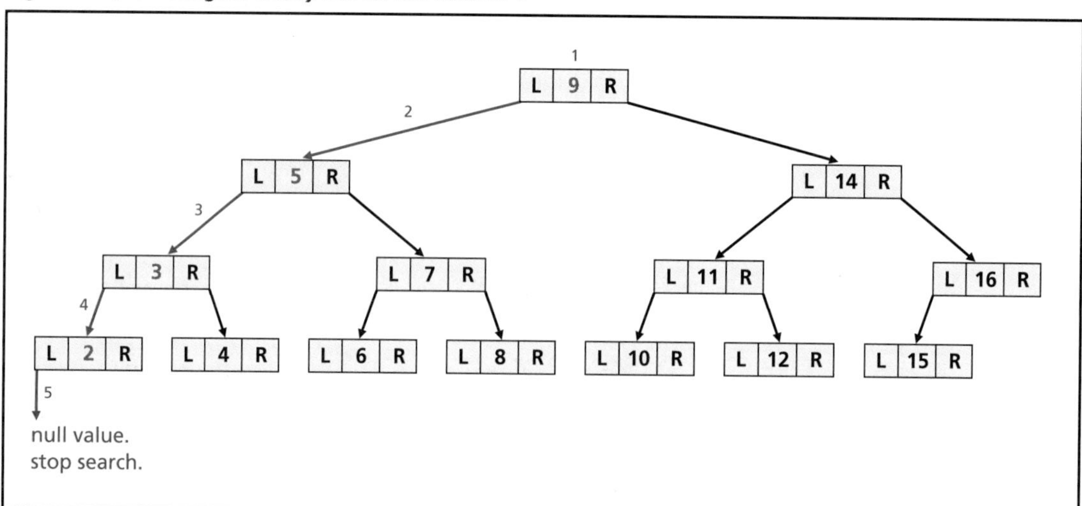

You can perform these same searches for any number, with the result being either the value is found or not found.

sorting algorithms

In addition to the array, list, and tree data structures, there is another essential way to organize data: sorting it. In many cases, even if that data were in a list or other structure, if you could not sort the data, it would be useless. Can you imagine a phone book that simply entered the data sequentially in order of new phone numbers assigned to customers? The last person in the phone book would be the last person to sign up for a phone number from the telephone company. It would take you forever (or longer) to find the phone number of a person who lived in New York City!

Almost any type of output from the computer is in some type of sort order so that the reader can easily interpret it. Here are some other examples of data being sorted:

- Words in a dictionary
- Files in a directory
- Index of a book
- Course offerings at the university

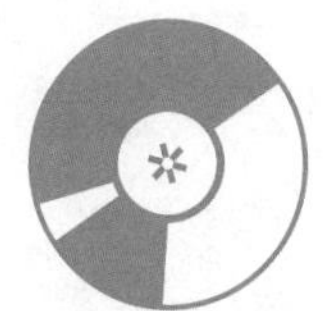

To compare different sorting algorithms, check out the learning tools section on the student CD under Chapter 9.

Think back to the previous chapter that discussed databases. The Songs table contained a list of all of the songs stored in the music inventory. Sorting the songs by title made finding a song easier. If the data were not sorted, then you would have to look through each song record until you found the one for which you were looking If you have five songs then the search takes no time at all. If you had over 2000 songs then you might as well start canceling all of your extracurricular activities while you spend your time searching through music records.

Remember that an algorithm is a procedure or formula for solving a problem. In order to sort data you first need to create an algorithm that defines the process for sorting. There are many algorithms for sorting sort data; each one has advantages and disadvantages. In fact, the list of sorting algorithms continues to grow as more computer scientists try to improve on sort routines already established. Two of the sorting routines that are covered in this chapter are the selection and bubble sorts.

selection sort

selection sort – Selects the smallest unsorted item remaining in the list, and then swaps it with the item in the next position to be filled

The ***selection sort*** is a simple sorting routine in that it mimics very closely how you might sort a list of values. The selection sort starts at the first value in the list and then processes each element looking for the smallest value. Once it is found it uses that smallest value and places it in the first position of the list and at the same time moves the value that was in the first position to the location that used to contain the smallest value. Then the sort moves on to the next position looking for the next smallest value. It continues to "swap places" with the current position and the position where it found the smallest value. Perhaps it would be easier to explain this using an example. Consider an array that contains the following list of numbers: 14, 8, 2, 4, and 10. Follow the example of the selection sort shown in Figure 9-30.

In a selection sort, the computer starts processing through the list until it finds the smallest value. In this example, the number 2 in element 2 is the smallest value, so the value of 2 is moved into element 0 (or the first location) and the value of 14 is moved to element 2 (Step 2 in Figure 9-30).

The computer accepts the fact that the value in element 0 is the smallest and ignores looking at that position for the rest of the sort. Instead, it moves on to

Figure 9-30, The selection sort

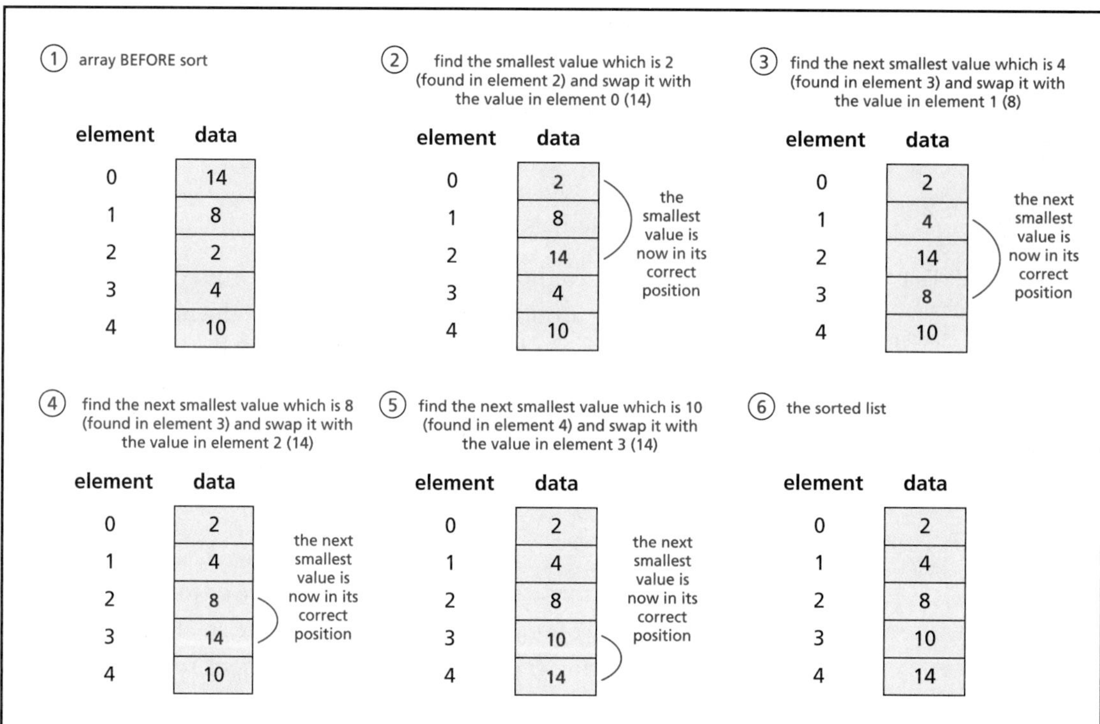

the next element (1) and begins searching again for the next smallest value. It finds the number 4 located in element 3. It moves the value of 4 up to element 1 and moves the value of 8 to element 3 (Step 3 in Figure 9-30).

Once again, the computer knows that memory location 1 now has the next smallest value stored and moves on to element 2. This process of searching for the smallest value and swapping it with the current location continues. It finds the number 8 located in element 3. It moves the value of 8 up to element 2 and moves the value of 14 to element 3 (Step 4 in Figure 9-30).

This process of searching for the smallest value and swapping it with the current location continues. It finds the number 10 located in element 4. It moves the value of 10 up to element 3 and moves the value of 14 to element 4 (Step 5 in Figure 9-30). This list is finally sorted (Step 6 in Figure 9-30).

bubble sort – Compares each item in the list with the item next to it. If the first item is greater than the second, then it swaps them. The algorithm repeats this process until it makes a pass all the way through the list without swapping any items

The selection sort is simple to use and implement but is not very efficient for large lists.

bubble sort

The ***bubble sort*** is one of the older and slower sort methods. It works by starting with the last element in the list and comparing its value to that of the item just above it in the list order. If it is smaller, then it changes positions and continues up the list comparing to the other items until it does not pass the "I am smaller so I move up" test. If it is not smaller, then the next item is compared to the item above it and swapped if it is smaller. The system continues checking the values until the smallest value "bubbles" up to the top. Then the entire process starts all over again but stops at the second item because it already knows that the first item contains the smallest value.

Consider an array that contains the following list of numbers: 14, 8, 2, 4, and 10. Follow the example of the bubble sort shown in Figure 9-31.

Figure 9-31, The bubble sort

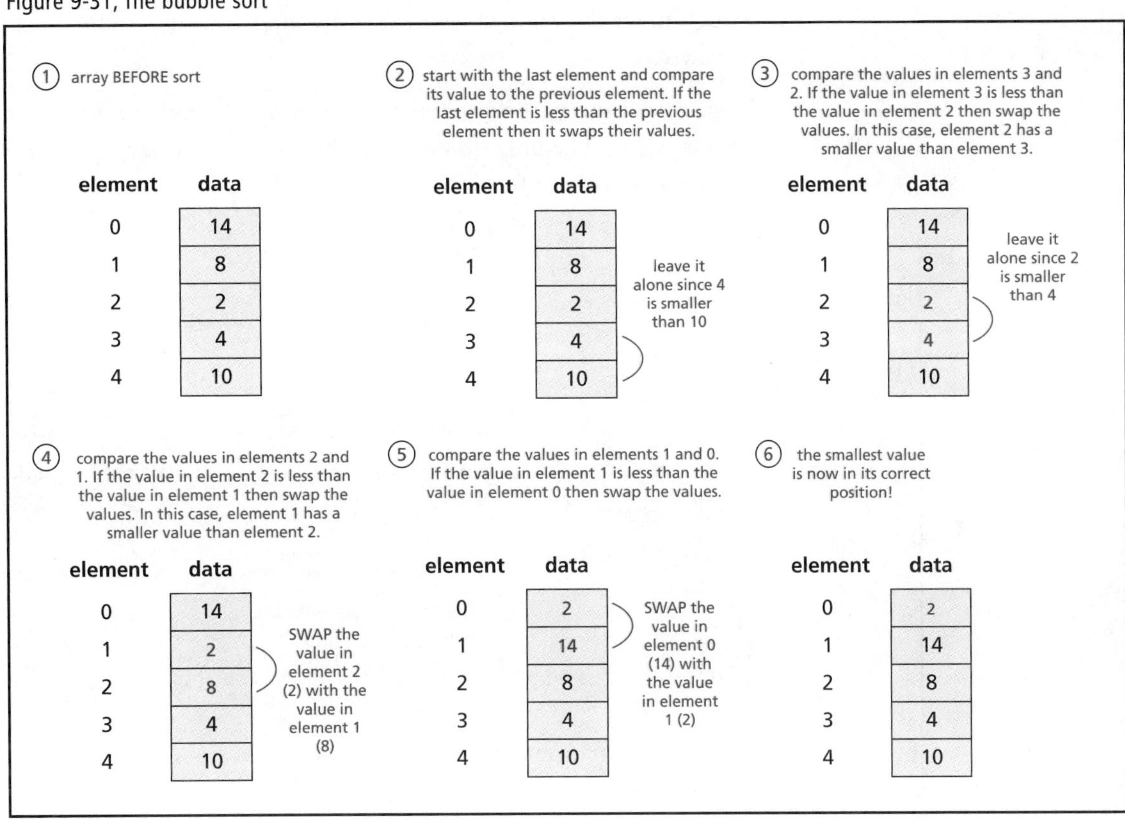

The computer starts the processing with element 4. It compares the value of 10 with the value of 4 in element 3. Because the value in element 3 (4) is smaller than the value in element 4 (10) it leaves the 10 alone and uses the value in element 3 (4) for the next comparison (Step 2 in Figure 9-31). Next, the value of 4 in element 3 is compared with the value of 2 found in element 2. Because the value of 2 is smaller than 4 and because it is already higher up in the list, it leaves them alone (Step 3 in Figure 9-31).

Next, the value in element 2 (2) is compared with the value in element 1 (8). Because 2 is less than 8, the values are swapped so that the value of 2 is now in element 1 and the value of 8 is in element 2 (Step 4 in Figure 9-31).

Now compare the value in element 1 (2) with the value in element 0 (14). Because 2 is less than 14, the values are swapped so that the value of 2 is now in element 0 and the value of 14 is in element 1 (Step 5 in Figure 9-31).

After all that work, the smallest value has "bubbled" up to the top of the sorted list (Step 6 in Figure 9-31). Now you only have to continue that process with the remaining four elements in the array! The only nice thing about the bubble sort, besides the fact that it is easy to implement, is that you do not have to worry about the value in element 0 any more as you already know that it is the smallest.

Figure 9-32 shows the entire process starting all over with the bottom position and its value. The only difference is that you do not have to worry about the element in position 0.

Figure 9-32, The bubble sort continues

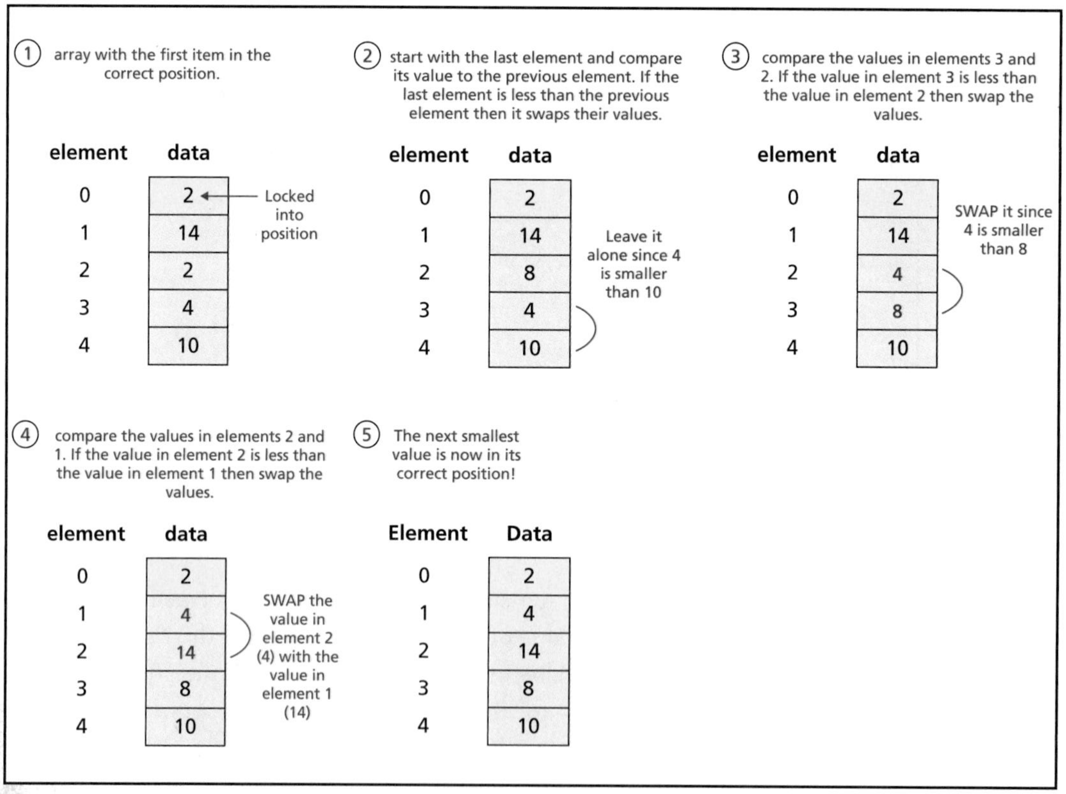

Element 4 has a value of 10 and it is compared to the value in element 3 (4) (Step 2 in Figure 9-32). No change occurs so the computer moves on to comparing elements 3 and 2. The value in element 3 (4) is smaller than that in element 2 (8) so it is swapped (Step 3 in Figure 9-32).

On you go by checking the value in element 2 (now 4) to the value stored in element 1 (14). As the value in element 2 is smaller, it is swapped (Step 4 in Figure 9-32). The second smallest value has now bubbled its way to the second position in the list (Step 5 in Figure 9-32).

The process continues as shown in Step 1 in Figure 9-33 with the first two elements now locked into place. Element 4 still has a value of 10 and it is compared to the value in element 3 (now 8). As element 3 has a value that is smaller than element 4, no change occurs (Step 2 in Figure 9-33). Element 3 (8) is compared with element 2 (14). As element 3 (8) has a value that is smaller than element 2 (14), the values are swapped (Step 3 in Figure 9-33). The third smallest value has now bubbled its way to the third position in the list (Step 4 in Figure 9-33).

Figure 9-33, The bubble sort still swapping along

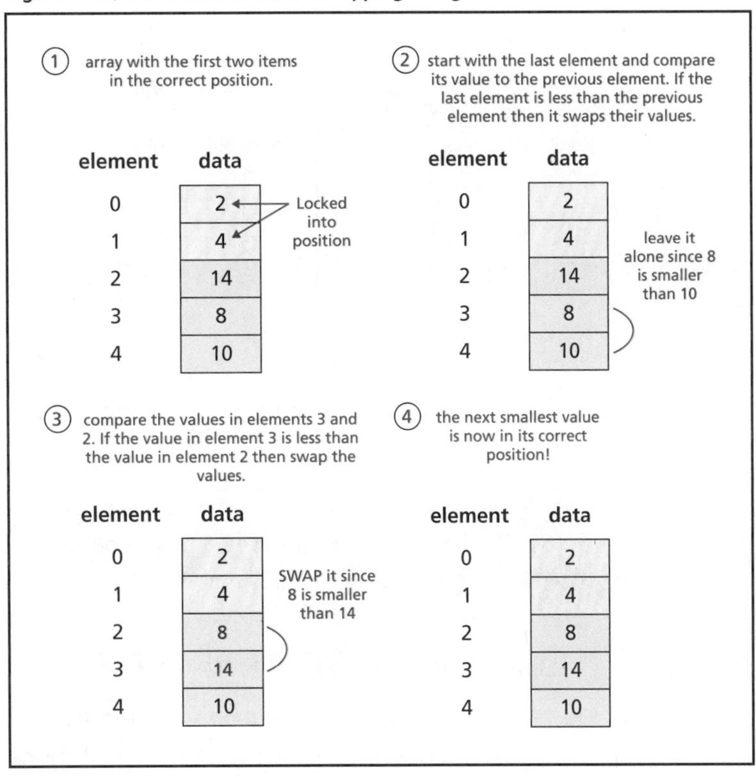

Hang in there because you are almost done! The process continues as shown in Step 1 of Figure 9-34 with the first three elements now locked into place. Element 4 still has a value of 10 and it is compared to the value in element 3 (now 14). As element 4 (10) has a value that is smaller than element 3 (14), the values are swapped (Step 2 in Figure 9-34). The fourth smallest value has now bubbled its way to the fourth position in the list (Step 3 in Figure 9-34). And as there is only one element left and there is nothing to compare it against; that element 4 *must* have the largest value in the entire list of values.

Figure 9-34, The bubble sort's last comparison

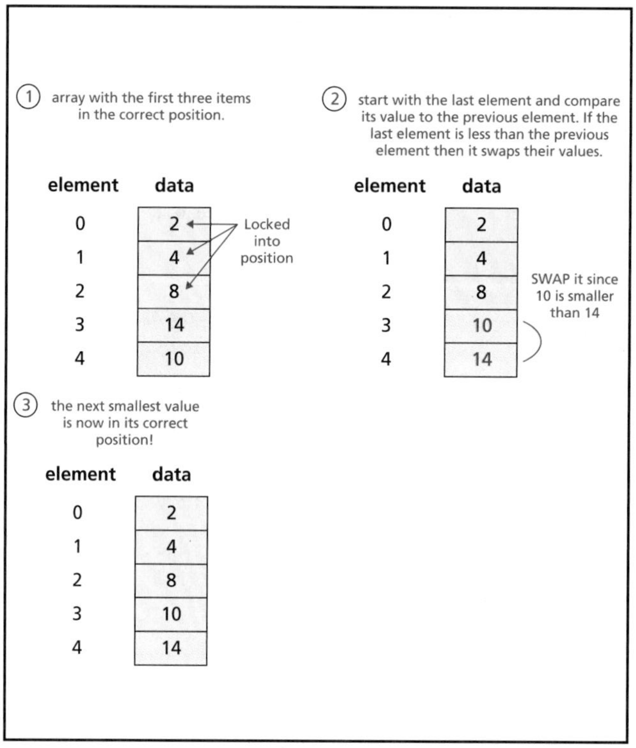

As you can see, a bubble sort involves a lot of comparisons—and this list has only five values in it! The bubble sort is simple to use, but it requires many comparisons, thus making it quite inefficient in terms of processing speed.

other types of sorts

Selection sorts and bubble sorts are easy to implement but run too slowly because they make too many comparisons for large lists of information. For this reason, other sort routines have been created with the specific purpose of sorting data in a shorter amount of time with fewer comparisons.

Some of these other routines that are popular are:

- Quicksort—This routine incorporates the logic that it is easier and faster to sort two small lists than one large list (divide and conquer). It is very fast and useful when there is a large amount of information to be sorted. The routine keeps breaking down the data into smaller lists until they are quite manageable to sort. It does this by calling itself over and over until each list is sorted. The process of calling one self is called ***recursion***. After the lists are sorted, the sorted sets are simply combined into one big sorted set. Believe it or not, you have already encountered the basics of a quicksort through the knowledge you have obtained with a binary search tree. The quicksort is very fast but it is also very difficult to comprehend.

recursion – The process of calling one self

note

Do you suppose if you looked up recursion in a dictionary it would say, "See recursion"?

- Merge sort—Similar to the quicksort, the merge sort splits the data into sets. Instead of continually splitting the data over and over into small sets, the merge sort splits the data into two equal halves. Each half is sorted and then merged back together into one list. This sort also implements recursion by calling itself over and over until the data is sorted. It is fast but not as efficient as the quicksort because it uses twice the memory to perform its sorting algorithm.
- Insertion sort—An insertion sort requires two list structures into which sorted items are inserted. The first list is the data structure containing the information and the second list is the sorted data structure. It simulates having a group of cards in your hand. As you select a card, it is put in its proper place in the sorted list. You continue this process of moving cards around until all of the cards are in their properly sorted location. This sort is not very complex and still offers the advantage of efficiency with lists fewer than 1000 elements.
- Shell sort—This is an efficient routine that makes multiple passes through the list grabbing a set of values to sort. It then uses the insertion sort routine to sort the data. For each pass, the system grabs a larger set of data. As the size of the set increases, the number of sets that need to be sorted decreases until the entire list is sorted.

There are other sort routines available with each having its own advantages and disadvantages. One of these advantages or disadvantages might be the complexity of programming code needed to implement the sort. Another might be the amount of memory the routine needs to complete the sort.

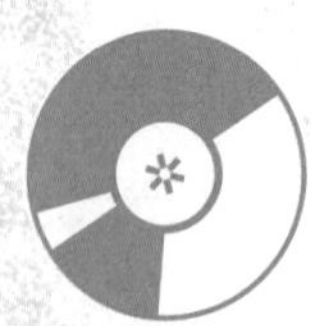

Reinforce your understanding of chapter concepts and terms with the information and activities for Chapter 9 on the student CD.

one last thought

Algorithms are used everywhere in the computer science industry. They are used for creating and working with data structures, searching for information, and sorting the data. As you progress through your computer science program you might even be the person who develops the fastest sorting algorithm ever known in the computer industry!

Knowing how to work with data structures and sorting algorithms will be a necessity when you begin to write computer programs. Many of the algorithms have already been written and are available for your use. You must have a foundation of data structures in order to write a computer program. Also, by knowing what tools are available you will be able to save a lot of time by not reinventing the sort routine.

chapter summary

- Data structures are used to organize data
- Arrays are stored in contiguous memory cells (one right after the other)
- To define an array, you must specify the array name, type, and size
- A single-dimensional array is a structure that consists of one level of array elements
- A multidimensional array is a structure that consists of more than one level, and each level consists of an array
- The size of the array is stored internally through the use of an upper and lower bound of the array
- A pointer is a memory cell that points to another memory cell location
- A linked list is a data structure that can be used when the size of the information to be stored is unknown or will change. Stacks and queues are forms of linked lists
- A stack implements a last in, first out (LIFO) storage method
- A queue implements a first in, first out (FIFO) storage method
- A tree data structure represents a hierarchical storage method
- Each position in the tree is called a node
- Binary search trees are very efficient for searching information
- There is a wide variety of sorting algorithms, including: selection, bubble, quicksort, merge, insertion, and shell sorts

key terms

array (314)

binary search tree (BST) (335)

bubble sort (340)

data structure (313)

depth (334)

dequeue (331)

element (316)

enqueue (332)

first in, first out (FIFO) (331)

head pointer (326)

height (334)

index (subscript) (318)

last in, first out (LIFO) (329)

leaf node (334)

left child (333)

level (334)

linked list (324)

lower bound (318)

multidimensional array (319)

node (vertex) (333)

null value (326)

offset (317)

peeking (329)

pointer (325)

pop (329)

procedure (330)

push (329)

queue (331)

recursion (345)

right child (333)

root (334)

selection sort (339)

stack (328)

stack pointer (330)

tail pointer (331)

tree (333)

upper bound (318)

test yourself

1. Describe the uses of an array.
2. How would you define an array to keep track of five students' student number (integer value) and their final average rounded to the nearest whole number (integer value)?
3. Using the array defined in question #2, write the necessary statements to store information for the five students' student number and final average in each of the array elements.
4. Describe in your own words how a stack works.
5. Describe in your own words how a queue works.
6. Describe in your own words how a binary tree works.

For questions 7 and 8, use Figure 9-35.

Figure 9-35, Sample data for questions 7 and 8

element	data
0	32
1	4
2	7
3	2
4	25
5	10

7. Show each step to sort the data using a bubble sort.
8. Show each step to sort the data using a selection sort.

For questions 9 and 10, use the Figure 9-36.

Figure 9-36, Sample data for questions 9 and 10

element	data
0	5
1	32
2	30
3	1
4	2
5	20

9. Show each step to sort the data using a bubble sort.
10. Show each step to sort the data using a selection sort.

For questions 11–15, use Figure 9-37.

Figure 9-37, Sample data for questions 11–15

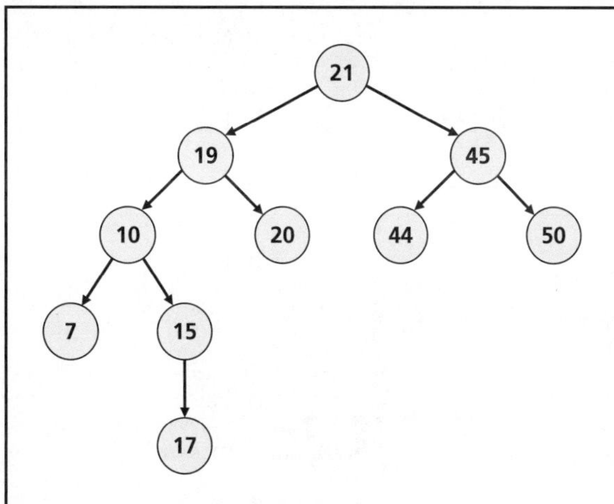

11. Label the root and leaf nodes.
12. What is the maximum height of the tree?
13. On what level is the node with the value 15?

14. Show the steps followed to find the value of 7.
15. Show the steps followed to find the value of 17.

practice exercises

1. A(n) __________ is a data structure that consists of contiguous memory locations.
    - **a.** Array
    - **b.** Stack
    - **c.** Queue
    - **d.** Tree
2. A(n) __________ is used within an array to access each element.
    - **a.** Index
    - **b.** Subscript
    - **c.** Both a and b
    - **d.** None of the above
3. Elements of a given array may contain information of different data types (integers, characters, decimals, etc.).
    - **a.** True
    - **b.** False
4. The statement char[] aAnswers = new char[5] declares an array that has memory locations of 1 through 5.
    - **a.** True
    - **b.** False
5. The offset is used to specify the distance between memory locations.
    - **a.** True
    - **b.** False
6. Arrays are a good data structure to use with dynamic data.
    - **a.** True
    - **b.** False
7. A stack uses LIFO.
    - **a.** True
    - **b.** False
8. A queue uses FIFO.
    - **a.** True
    - **b.** False

9. LIFO is an acronym for:
   - **a.** List in, first order
   - **b.** Last in, first out
   - **c.** Last in, first order
   - **d.** List in, first out

10. FIFO is an acronym for:
    - **a.** First in, first out
    - **b.** First in, first order
    - **c.** First in, final out
    - **d.** First in, final order

Use Figure 9-38 to answer questions 11–15

Figure 9-38, Sample data for questions 11–15

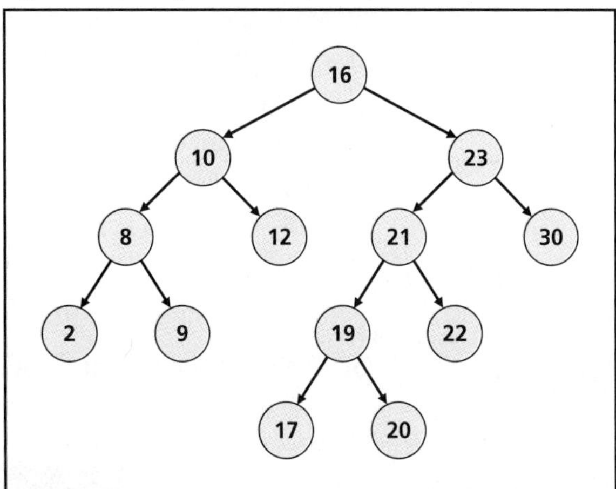

11. How many comparisons does it take to find the following numbers?
    - **a.** 8
    - **b.** 2
    - **c.** 23
    - **d.** 30
    - **e.** 17

12. What is the number of nodes on level 3?

13. What is the number of nodes on level 4?

14. What is the maximum height of the tree?

15. How many right and left child nodes are there?

Given the following numbers: 1, 2, 3, 4, 5, 6, 7, 8, 9, 10, 11, and 12, answer questions 16 through 20.

16. Draw a binary search tree for these numbers. Make sure that proper binary search tree rules are applied.
17. How many comparisons does it take to find the number 4?
18. How many comparisons does it take to find the number 11?
19. What is the maximum height?
20. On what level is the number 6?

digging deeper

1. Write a sorting routine different from those presented in the chapter to organize information and explain how it is implemented.
2. Using six different numbers in any order draw a diagram that demonstrates how the merge sort works.
3. Draw a diagram that demonstrates how the insertion sort works using six different numbers in any order.
4. Draw a diagram that demonstrates how the quicksort works using six different numbers in any order.
5. Draw a diagram that demonstrates how the shell sort works using six different numbers in any order.

discussion topics

1. Which sorting routine do you think is best to use when sorting the information you might find in a phone book for a large city? Why?
2. List five scenarios for using an array.
3. List five scenarios for using a stack.
4. List five scenarios for using a queue.
5. Write the necessary statements to define an array for a three-dimensional tic-tac-toe board and then play the game with other class members by specifying the array location where you would like to place an X or an O.

Internet research

1. What are some sorting routines currently being used that have not been mentioned in this book? What are the advantages and disadvantages of using them?
2. Find a Web site that visually demonstrates the different sorting algorithms and share it with the class.
3. Find at least three Web sites that demonstrate how a stack and queue work.
4. Find at least three Web sites that explain binary trees and share them with the class.
5. Describe how a binary search works using the pre-order, post-order, and in-order traversal.

chapter

10

file structures

in this chapter you will:

- Learn what a file system does
- Understand the FAT file system and its advantages and disadvantages
- Understand the NTFS file system and its advantages and disadvantages
- Compare various file systems
- Learn how sequential and random file access work
- See how hashing is used
- Understand how hashing algorithms are created

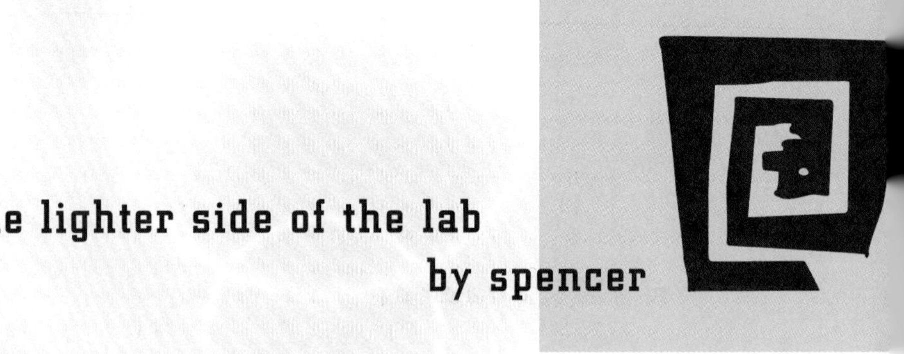

the lighter side of the lab

by spencer

I was recently hired to work at the university newspaper. I was really excited until it came time to get paid. No, that's not just a lame reporter joke. (I'd have to actually get paid to be able to joke about it.)

Not long after they hired me, I received an e-mail instructing me to stop by the payroll office to fill out some forms for tax purposes. Sounds easy enough, doesn't it?

The form was one of the IRS' more simple forms, so I only had to ask for help 30 times. Within just six or seven hours, I was done. After completing the two forms, I walked up to the counter to hand them in. The nice person behind the desk said, "Okay, I'll just need to see your Social Security card."

Now I'm pretty sure that I had a Social Security card at some point in my life. I can picture what it looks like. It's popped up here and there, but has now disappeared from existence (much like my dating life).

I explained that I would have to return when I found my Social Security card. She informed me that they would hold my checks until I did. (Judging by how well I did with holding onto my Social Security card, the checks were probably safer in their hands anyway.)

I began the search in my bedroom. Unfortunately, my room needs a little "defragmentation," if you know what I mean. I checked the stack-o'-junk on my dresser, despite the risk of avalanche. I checked the pile-o'-clothes, but didn't find anything other than a pair of pants I'd completely forgotten about that had probably been there since the late '90s.

At this point I was completely out of ideas, so I pulled out the big guns—I asked my mom. (This is a luxury that all of you smarty-pants who moved out of your house before you were 25 don't have. Who's laughing now?) Unfortunately, she couldn't find it either.

I've now worked for the university newspaper for nine weeks without getting paid. I can't help but think that none of this would have happened if I had used better file structures. I could have created a linked list using yellow sticky-notes beginning in my baby book. Defragging would be fun—almost like a scavenger hunt. It would be impossible to lose anything!

Once again, we see that computers hold the answer to any question: "Nothing is easy."

why you need to know about... file structures

Have you ever thought what it would be like if you were listening to your favorite musical selection and a third of the way through the song the system prompted you to go find a file containing the next part because not all of the song was in one location? Or what if you were reading a book and had to check out five different books because each one contained a couple of chapters? In either situation, you would be frustrated. Instead of being able to complete the task without interruption, you would be distracted by having to spend time just locating the resources being used. It would be more productive and enjoyable if you could simply listen to a song or read a book from start to finish.

Files that contain information (such as songs or books) are commonly used in everyday computer tasks. The computer operating system is responsible for managing the files and making sure tasks are uninterrupted. This involves the use of a file manager and file management system. By understanding how an operating system stores and maintains data in a computer, you can gain a greater comprehension of how a computer handles files, learn how you can manipulate files, and help to keep your computer running as efficiently as possible.

what does a file system do?

file system – Responsible for creating, manipulating, renaming, copying, and removing files to and from a storage device

One of the functions of an operating system is to organize and maintain files on secondary storage media such as hard drives, CD-ROMs, and removable media. A ***file system*** is the part of the operating system responsible for creating, manipulating, renaming, copying, and removing files to and from these storage devices. A hard disk, also called a hard drive, is the most common place to store files. Besides being a place to store all of your documents, music files, and movies, the hard disk is the central location for storing the operating system, applications, and user files.

In this text you have learned about many operating systems you might someday use (or already be using), and you were also introduced to many different applications or tools that are available to make your life as a computer science student easier. Each one of those operating systems and applications uses files in accomplishing its tasks.

note While working at Intel, Dr. Gary A. Kildall introduced the first personal computer (PC) operating system in 1974, called CP/M.

note Microsoft Windows was not Microsoft's first software product. Microsoft was formed in 1975 and began working on their first product, Microsoft BASIC.

Microsoft OSs

Microsoft introduced its first operating system, MS-DOS, in 1981. Microsoft introduced its first widely used graphically based operating system in 1990 (Windows 3.0). Since then, it has regularly upgraded the Windows operating system:

Windows 3.11 (1993)

Windows NT (1993)

Windows 95 (1995)

Windows 98 (1998)

Windows ME (2000)

Windows XP (2001)

Windows Server 2003 (2003)

directory – An organizational unit within a storage medium that stores files, folders, and subdirectories

random access – Reading or writing data directly anywhere on disk

sequential access – Reading and writing in order from the beginning

User files are those files that you create for your own use. These files might include things such as:

- Word-processing documents
- Source code for programs that you have written
- Music files
- Movie files
- Spreadsheets
- Pictures

The list could go on and on because there are so many different computer programs and tools available. Each of these files takes up some storage space on a hard disk or other medium, and the file system must keep track of the files. One way the file system does this is to organize files into common storage areas called ***directories***. In fact, the file system acts very much like a filing cabinet with each piece of paper representing a file and each file folder representing a directory or subdirectory (Figure 10-1). In fact, the Mac OS and Windows both use a file folder icon to represent a directory, and call directories "folders." As you saw in Chapter 6, the operating system uses a similar treelike hierarchical structure to organize files into directories and subdirectories (folders) (Figure 10-2).

The job of the file system is to keep track of where the files and directories are located and assist the computer user by relating these files and folders to the physical structure of the storage medium, such as a hard disk. Hard disks are physically organized into tracks and sectors, and read/write heads move over specified areas of the hard disks to store (write) or retrieve (read) data (Figure 10-3).

A hard disk is a ***random access*** device, meaning that you can read or write data directly anywhere on the disk. (Another type of access is ***sequential access***, where you must start at the beginning of the data and read until you get to the data you want. You'll learn more about access methods later in the chapter.) Random access is a faster way to access data, but computer users want to be able to store and organize their information in a more orderly (less random)

Figure 10-1, Files and directories in a file system are similar to documents and folders in a filing cabinet

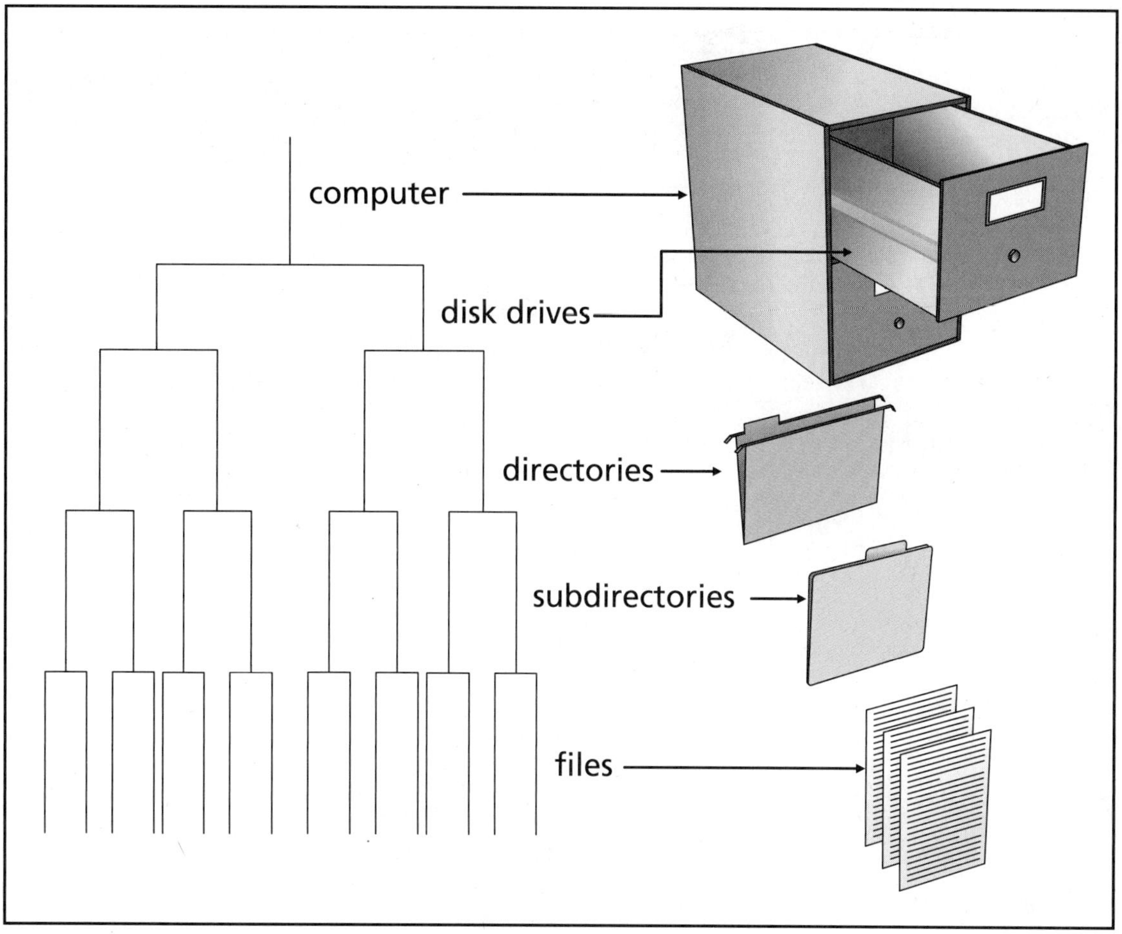

fashion. That's where the file system comes in. Various file systems have been developed to allow users to organize their files as they would like, while at the same time being able to take advantage of the speed of random access (sometimes called relative access).

FAT (file allocation table) – File management system used to locate files on a storage medium

NTFS (New Technology File System) – File management system implemented with Windows NT and incorporated into Windows 2000, XP, and 2003; used to locate files on a storage medium

file systems and operating systems

The type of file management system being used depends on the operating system version. The first Microsoft file system was called the file allocation table (*FAT*). Different versions of FAT were used from MS-DOS in the 1980s through Windows 95, 98, and ME. Beginning with Windows NT, the default Windows file system changed to ***NTFS*** (New Technology File System), though FAT was still supported. Windows 2000, XP, and 2003 use NTFS by default. UNIX and Linux systems support several different file systems, including XFS, JFS, ReiserFS, ext3, and others. The original Macintosh Filing System (MFS)

UNIX/Linux

UNIX was introduced in 1969 under a product named UNICS. Some of the more common UNIX operating system names are: IBM AIX, Sun Solaris, HP-UX, SCO UNIX, and FreeBSD. Linux is a popular PC type of UNIX first developed by Linus Torvalds in 1991.

Apple

In 1978, Apple introduced its first operating system, Apple DOS (unrelated to MS-DOS). In 1984 the Macintosh was the first PC to use a graphical operating environment. The current version of the operating system is Mac OS X.

Figure 10-2, Folders and files in Windows XP

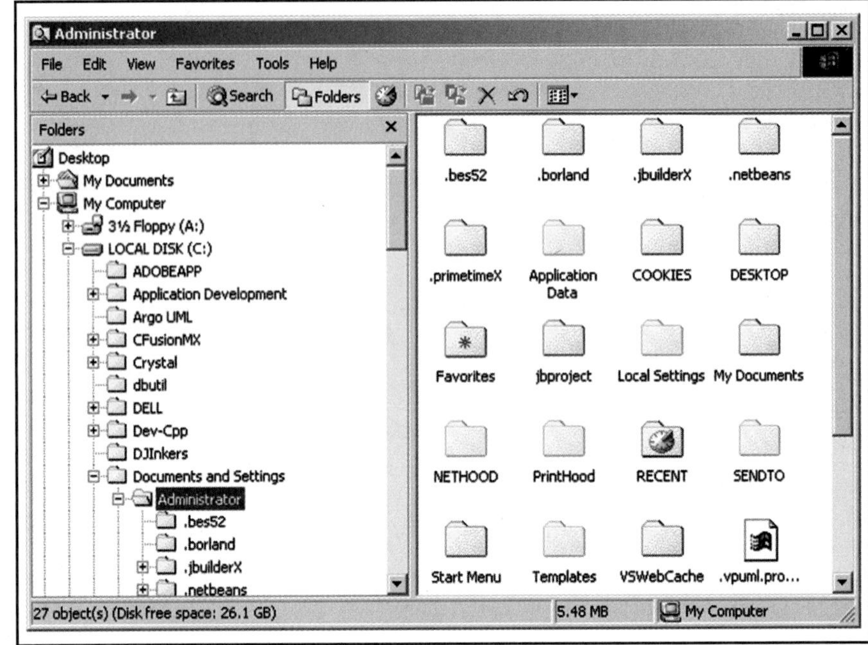

Figure 10-3, Hard disk platters are divided into tracks and sectors, and read/write heads store and retrieve data

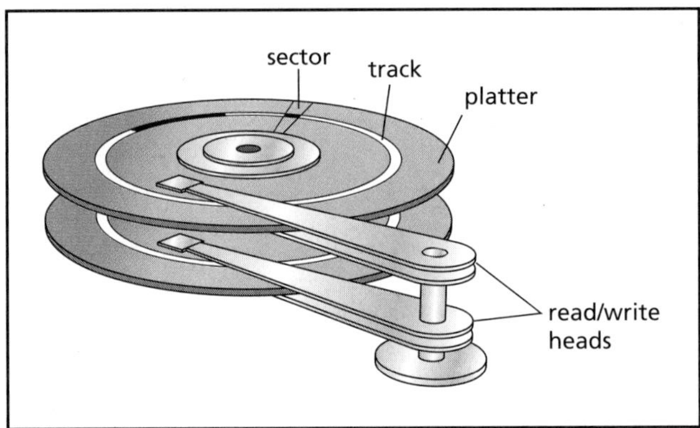

evolved into the Hierarchical Filing System (HFS) and then the Hierarchical Filing System Extended Format (HFS+), the current Mac OS X file system.

Each of these file management systems was suitable at the time it was developed to handle storing and maintaining the operating system's file structure, but unlike fine wine, filing systems become outdated and new ideas and methods are discovered. The newest Windows file management system—NTFS—has many advantages over the older FAT file management system. But before you can appreciate NTFS you need to first understand how FAT came to be and what it accomplished.

what's your file system?

To see which file system a hard drive in your Windows computer uses, open My Computer, right-click the drive, and click Properties. The file system is listed near the top of the General tab.

FAT

At first glance, you might think you have found the reason why the health and exercise industry in the United States is so popular. Many people are out of shape and worrying about being overweight. Even the computers we use are weight conscious. They incorporate FAT into their system and try their best to manage it!

Actually, FAT was introduced back in the days of the first PC operating system, MS-DOS. In those days, you could actually store the entire operating system on a single floppy disk. As you learned earlier, a hard drive stores information in sectors. The sectors are contained within tracks. In many file management systems, including FAT, sectors are grouped together to form ***clusters*** (also called allocation units) (Figure 10-4).

cluster – Contains a group of the smallest units that can be accessed on a disk (sectors)

Figure 10-4, Sectors are grouped into clusters on a hard disk

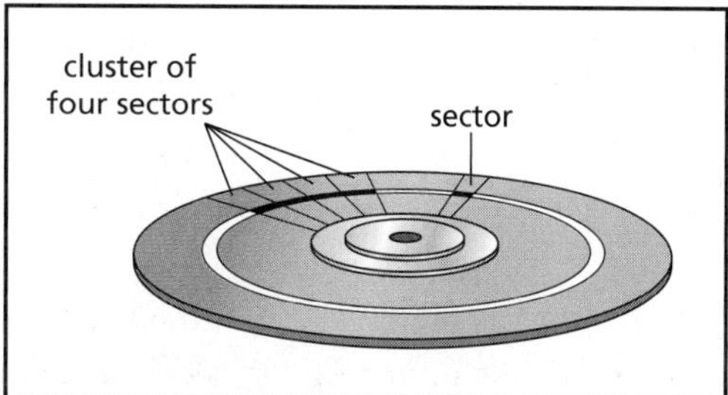

Data is stored in 512-byte sectors on the hard drive, and depending on the size of the file, the data might occupy one or more sectors. For performance reasons, sectors are organized into clusters. The clusters are organized in contiguous (one after the other in order) blocks of sectors on the disk. So in reality, a file might occupy one or more clusters which in turn consist of one or more sectors. The file allocation table simply keeps track of which files are using which clusters. It keeps track of the files and where they are located through the use of entries in the file allocation table.

The FAT file management system organizes the hard drive into several areas, as shown in Figure 10-5:

- Partition boot sector
- Main file allocation table (FAT)
- Backup FAT
- Root directory or folder
- Data area (measured in clusters)

Figure 10-5, Typical FAT file system

Partition boot record (1 sector)
Main FAT (size is up to two clusters)
Backup FAT (same size as main FAT)
Root directory
Data area (size varies). Here all other files and directories are stored. Size measured in clusters, which are composed of groups of sectors.

The partition boot sector contains the information needed for the system to be able to know how to access the volume. (A volume is a drive or partition on a drive that is formatted with a file system. A hard disk can have more than one volume, or one volume can span several disks.) There are two file allocation tables stored in fixed locations: the main FAT and a backup FAT. If an error occurs in reading the main FAT then the other can be copied back to the first table to ensure system stability. The root folder keeps an entry for every file and folder stored in the root directory. Each of these entries contains information on the file or folder including the name and size of the folder. The root entries also contain the number of the cluster holding the beginning of the file.

The FAT format progressed from FAT12 through FAT16 to FAT32. The three numbers refer to the number of bits in each file allocation table entry. As the number of bits for FAT entries increased, so did the size of partitions and files that could be used with FAT.

Every file and folder on a drive is made up of clusters. The clusters are made up of sectors. The computer needs to know which clusters are used for each file. The FAT table contains this information. It maintains the relationship between the files and clusters being used for the file. Each of the clusters has two entries in the FAT: the first shows the current cluster information and the second contains a link to the next cluster to use.

note

Flash memory devices such as SmartMedia, Compact Flash, and memory sticks emulate popular file management schemes such as FAT.

Because the clusters are linked together this way in the file allocation table, the FAT is a form of a linked list. The process of linking all of the clusters of a file together continues until the last of the file is placed in the final cluster. It is marked with a special code so when the system is looking for all the pieces of the file it knows when it has reached the last cluster and does not need to find any more of the file.

The FAT system keeps track of which clusters it can use for writing information and which are already in use holding file data. The system also keeps track of which clusters are bad and no longer usable. It marks these clusters so that it does not attempt to use the bad clusters.

VFAT

VFAT (or virtual FAT) was a type of file management created by Microsoft in the mid 1990s to interface between the system and the FAT so that the operating system could handle long file names (longer than eight characters).

When you first format your hard drive there are many clusters available for use. There could also be some that have already been marked as bad. If you store a file on a newly formatted hard drive the system most probably stores the information in a contiguous block of clusters. As time goes by and you store, delete, and move files, the contiguous blocks might not be contiguous any more. The system then puts the data into the clusters wherever they can best fit, which are more often than not noncontiguous blocks. Having data scattered all over the disk can create some problems.

defragging XP

To access Disk Defragmenter in Windows XP, click Start, All Programs, Accessories, System Tools, Disk Defragmenter. In order to defragment the drive properly, you might need to turn off virus checkers, screen savers, and other programs that are running.

disk fragmentation

disk fragmentation – Occurs when files have clusters scattered in different locations on the storage medium rather than in contiguous locations

As more and more files are stored on the hard drive and the clusters of a file become less and less contiguous, the system begins to slow down because it is moving the hard drive read/write heads all around trying to locate the clusters for a particular file. Every time a new file is stored, the system tries to recover open space. Eventually, a file can have its clusters stored in every corner of the hard drive. This state of affairs is called *disk fragmentation* (Figure 10-6). Fragmentation can occur in NTFS as well, but it is a much greater problem with FAT. To compensate for this unorganized storage method, Windows provides a tool to reorganize the clusters on the hard drive so that they are once again contiguous. The Disk Defragmenter system utility acts like the computer system's mother: it comes into the hard drive, takes a look at how messy it is, and cleans everything up. It is a wonderful tool that should be used regularly to ensure your system runs at peak performance. Disk Defragmenter improves performance by minimizing movement of the read/write heads.

Figure 10-6, Files become fragmented as they are stored in noncontiguous clusters; a defragmenting utility moves files to contiguous clusters and improves disk performance

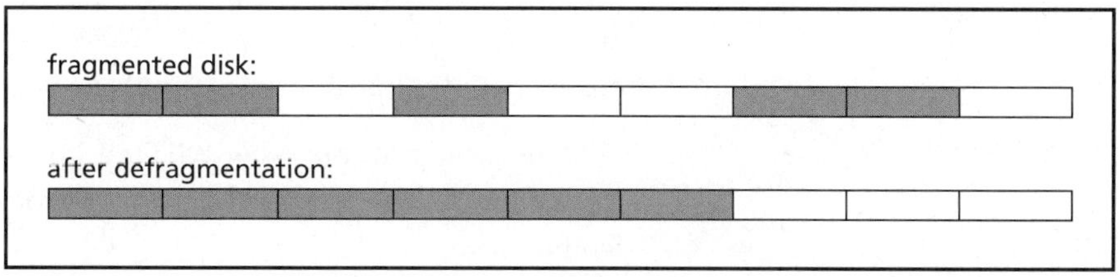

undelete that file!

Windows makes the process of undeleting a file relatively easy. All you have to do is open the Recycle Bin icon on the desktop, right-click the file that was deleted, and click Restore to restore the file to its original location.

advantages of FAT

The main advantage of the FAT system is its efficient use of disk space. Because large files don't have to have contiguous clusters, the FAT system can place the parts of the file wherever they fit.

Another great advantage is that file names can have up to 255 characters. File names were limited under FAT16 to eight characters for the name and three for the file extension. FAT32 supports the 255 character file names.

One more advantage of using the FAT file management system is how easy it is to undelete files that have been deleted. When a file is deleted the system does not actually remove it from the hard drive but instead places a hex value of E5h in the first position of the file name. The actual file and its contents remain on the drive and can be easily undeleted by providing the correct first letter of the file during the undelete process. In fact, unless you do a low-level format where the system formats the drive by removing all of the stored data, you can usually recover deleted files.

disadvantages of FAT

There are many disadvantages of using FAT when comparing it to NTFS. One of these disadvantages is that overall performance slows down as more files are stored on the partition. Another problem that already has been alluded to is the fact that the drive can quite easily become fragmented.

Another disadvantage is the lack of security. FAT32 lacks many security features, whereas NTFS provides the ability to assign access rights to files and directories. FAT32 also can have file integrity problems such as lost clusters, invalid files and directories, and allocation errors. All of these problems are addressed through the implementation of NTFS.

NTFS

The goal of the New Technology File System (NTFS) was to overcome the limitations of the FAT file management system. It was introduced with Windows NT and is the default file system on Windows 2000, XP, and Server 2003 operating systems. NTFS is often referred to as a "journaling" file system as it keeps track of transactions performed when working with files and directories. If any errors are encountered, the system "rolls back" the transactions found in the journaling file system until it is satisfied that the system is once again stable. This is a great benefit to using the file system under NTFS as it is less likely to become corrupt; but if it does, it is usually smart enough to fix itself.

master file table (MFT) – Table used in NTFS to store data about every file and directory on the volume

NTFS uses a ***master file table (MFT)*** to store data about every file and directory on the volume. It is very similar to a table of information detailing facts about each file.

from FAT to NTFS

If you are converting a FAT drive to an NTFS drive, the reserved blocks of space are usually located somewhere in the middle of the partition, resulting in slower performance. It is always recommended to do a clean install on a new drive when converting.

The MFT is similar to a database table containing various attributes about different files and resembles a table of contents for the files and folders in the volume. When a file or directory is created on the volume a record is also created in the MFT. Like the FAT file management system, NFTS uses clusters (allocation units) for storing data. It reserves blocks of space to allow the MFT to grow.

All of the hard drives in a computer do not have to use the same file management system. One could use FAT while another uses NTFS.

advantages of NTFS

The structure of the NTFS makes file access very fast and reliable. When you wanted to view a file under the FAT file system, the system first had to read the entry in the FAT and make sure it was a valid entry. Then it accessed the file by searching for the clusters assigned to the file. In NTFS, the system simply goes right to the file as soon as you request it.

Through the use of the MFT, the system can recover from problems without losing significant amounts of data. The journaling or auditing of transactions permits easy restoration to a stable system state.

Security has been greatly increased over FAT. Under NTFS, an administrator can specify which individual users or groups of users can perform certain operations on files and directories (also called file and directory permissions). This includes both the reading and writing of data to the files and folders. FAT was designed during the single-user era, while NTFS is geared more toward a networked environment.

Encrypting File System (EFS) – Encryption technology that converts the data within a file using an encryption algorithm and key value to nonreadable information; in order to make the information understandable again you must decrypt it using another key value

NTFS also supports file encryption through the *Encrypting File System (EFS)* and file attributes. You have the ability to encrypt files so as to protect them from unauthorized access. Even if another user accesses a file owned by a different user they are not able to view the data and receive an "Access Denied" error message.

file compression – Process of reducing file size and thus taking up less disk space

The last advantage discussed is another file attribute that controls file compression. A user can set a file to be compressed and save disk space. *File compression* is the process of reducing the size of a file or a folder. The entire process is transparent to the user, meaning that the file does not have to be decompressed before it can be read. The system handles the compressing and decompressing for you. You simply sit back and reap the benefits of saving disk space through the use of file compression.

note

There are many different types of file compression, but hard drives have become so inexpensive that many computer users do not want to sacrifice performance for disk space.

why not compress?

There are two disadvantages to using file compression:

- It slows performance
- You cannot encrypt a compressed file

disadvantages of NTFS

There are also disadvantages of using NTFS on a volume. Because NTFS has a larger overhead than FAT it is not recommended to use it as a file management system on volumes that are less than 4 GB. For example, the system file needs of NTFS on a 100 MB drive are about 4 MB. This also means that you cannot format a floppy disk and use NTFS as the file management system as it would not fit on the disk.

Another disadvantage is that you cannot access NTFS volumes from MS-DOS, Windows 95, or Windows 98.

comparing file systems

Table 10-1 compares the features of FAT16, FAT32, and NTFS. Which file system you use depends on the operating system you are using, and what features you need or want. For example, if you are using Windows 9*x* as an operating system then you use FAT; whereas, if you are using Windows 2000 or XP you use NTFS. Choosing the correct file system is not so much hardware dependent as it is operating system dependent.

Table 10-1, Fat16, FAT32, and NTFS compared

feature	FAT16	FAT32	NTFS
Total volume size	4 GB	2 GB to 2 TB	2 TB
Maximum file size	2 GB	4 GB	Size of drive (theoretical limit of 2^{64} bytes)
OS support	DOS, Windows 3.*x*, 9*x*, NT, 2000, XP, 2003	Windows 95 (OSR2), 98, NT, 2000, XP, 2003	Windows NT (service pack 4), 2000, XP, 2003
Compatible with floppy disks	Yes	Yes	No
Security	Limited security	Limited security	Extensive security and auditing options
File compression	Supported with extra utilities	Supported with extra utilities	Supported as part of NTFS

Table 10-1 (*continued*)

feature	FAT16	FAT32	NTFS
Journaling (file activity tracking)	None	None	Yes
Large database support	Limited	Yes	Yes
Multiple disk drives in one volume	No	No	Yes

10

If your hard disk drive is 10 GB or less then you may want to use FAT because it is more efficient in handling smaller volumes of data. Otherwise, for Windows systems that support it, NTFS is recommended, especially in today's networked environment where security is important. Also, these days 10 GB hard drives just don't go very far after you have loaded the operating system, a word processor, spreadsheet, programming tools, graphic editors, and all of the other tools you need as a computer scientist. It's more likely that you'll be using 40 GB and larger hard drives, and will need a file system equipped to deal more easily with large volumes, such as NTFS.

In the UNIX/Linux environment you also have many file system choices. Table 10-2 shows some of the file systems used with UNIX and Linux. As with the file systems available for use in Windows, some of the Linux file systems support journaling, some support long filenames, and all have specified maximum file sizes.

Table 10-2, Some file systems supported by UNIX/Linux

file system	description
ext (extended file system) and the newer versions, ext2 and ext3	File system that comes with Linux by default; the current version, ext3, supports journaling
ufs (UNIX file system)	Original file system for UNIX that is compatible with virtually all UNIX systems and most Linux systems

(*continued*)

Table 10-2 (*continued*)

file system	description
MS-DOS	File system that offers compatibility with FAT12 and FAT16 (does not support long filenames); typically installed to enable UNIX to read floppy disks made in MS-DOS or Windows
Network file system (NFS)	File system developed by Sun Microsystems for UNIX systems to support network access and sharing of files (such as uploading and downloading files) and supported on virtually all UNIX/Linux versions as well as by many other operating systems
UmsMS/DOS	File system that is compatible with extended FAT16 as used by Windows NT, 2000, XP, and Server 2003, but it also supports security permissions, file ownership, and long filenames

The best way to determine which file system to use, barring any specific hardware requirements, is by asking yourself what type of file system environment do you want to work in and what is your current operating system. Then evaluate the advantages and disadvantages of each of the possible file systems and you should have your answer.

file organization

Now that you have an idea of what a file system does and the different types of file systems that are out there, take a closer look at the characteristics of the files themselves and how they are stored on disks or other media.

binary or text

A file is a storage location that contains data that is treated as either binary or text. All files are stored as binary files, and as you learned in Chapter 5, all data on the disk is actually stored as ones and zeros. The difference between text files and binary files is that text files consist of ASCII or Unicode characters. Each time you type in a character the system stores a byte to the file. This includes all characters including hyphenation, punctuation, spaces, and so forth. Text files are readable by using programs such as word processors or text editors and are easy to view and modify. Some examples of text files are those that are created with editors like Notepad in Windows or vi in UNIX/Linux.

Binary files are not readable with these programs and are often used to refer to a file that is not a text file. They are computer readable but not human readable and contain coded and numeric information. Binary files are more compact and faster to access (read and write) than text files because the system does not have to convert the data. The data can remain in the binary language that the computer understands rather than converting it to text we can read and understand. Some examples of binary files are executable programs, applications, sound files, and image files.

sequential or random access

Data is usually stored either sequentially or randomly. Sequential storage means that data is accessed one chunk after the other in order, and random storage dictates that there is no specified order to the stored data. Instead, random access (also called direct or relative access) allows data to be accessed in any order (Figure 10-7).

Figure 10-7, Sequential vs. random access

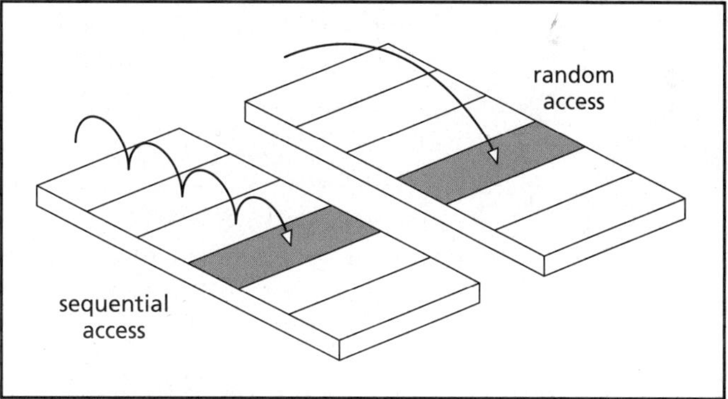

sequential access

A sequential file is accessed starting at the beginning of the file and processed to the end of the file. The data stored in the file can be thought of as one long row of information. An example of a sequential file might be an audio file or a video file. When you add new data, it is written at the end of the file. Because data is appended to the end of the file, the writing process is very fast. On the other hand, retrieving data can be extremely slow depending on the location of the data.

Sequential file access allows you to mimic the look of a database table by storing information in the file row by row like a database table record. Each line of the sequential file can be organized or logically grouped as if you were describing a record. For example, a line in a sequential file might consist of a student ID, first name, last name, and letter grade. As shown in Figure 10-8, a comma (or another character such as a tab) can be used as a row delimiter to separate each of the fields in the line.

Figure 10-8, A comma can be used as a row delimiter

```
1234,Joseph,Blow,C
2452,Mary,Lamb,A–
5839,Alexander,Roma,B
8983,Marissa,Anderson,A
7738,Miles,Gregory,A
8442,John,Jones,C+
```

Instead of using a character as a delimiter you could also use a fixed size for each of the fields. Data that is not long enough to fill the entire field could be padded with spaces. Figure 10-9 shows the layout of student records in fixed format:

- Student ID—4 characters long
- First name—10 characters long
- Last name—15 characters long
- Grade—2 characters long

Figure 10-9, Data can also have a fixed size

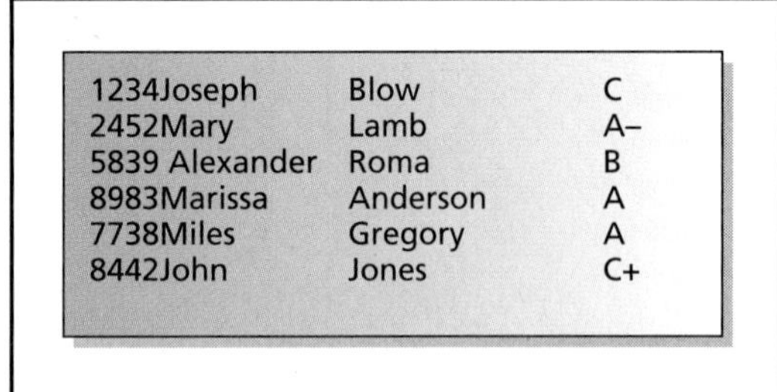

```
1234Joseph    Blow           C
2452Mary      Lamb           A–
5839 Alexander Roma          B
8983Marissa   Anderson       A
7738Miles     Gregory        A
8442John      Jones          C+
```

By the time you are done creating a sequential file you have stored one or many rows of data in order.

A major drawback to sequential access occurs when you insert, delete, or modify existing records. This requires you to process the entire file by writing all of the information with the changes to a new file.

random access

Although sequential access is often used in computer systems, it has a serious drawback in that the only way to get to a specific record in a file is by starting at the beginning of the sequential file and reading through the file until you get to the record you want. If the file has a small number of records, this isn't much of a problem. When files contain a large number of records, or the records are very large, sequential access of a file can become a real problem. It takes time to read each of the records, especially when the disk read/write head has to be moved. Therefore, to deal with large amounts of data, another method needed to be formulated.

Accessing a particular record in a file could be very fast if you could directly position the read/write head on the desired record without having to read all of the records in front of it. If all of the individual records were the same size, you could mathematically calculate the position of the record on the disk surface and go right to it. This is the principle behind random (also called relative or direct) access. Relative records are fixed in length, while sequential records vary in size (Figure 10-10).

Figure 10-10, Sequential records vary in size; relative records are all the same size

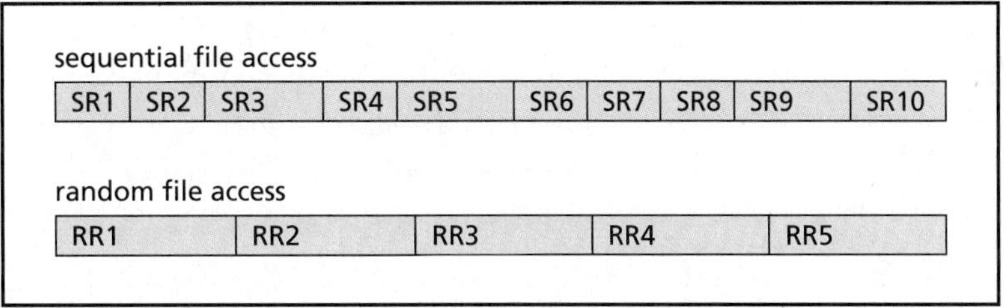

For example: Consider a file of 1000 records where each record is 100 bytes in size. If you want to access record number 538, you multiply the record number by the record size (538 * 100) and calculate that the record you're looking for is 53,800 bytes into the file. Depending on how many bytes per sector and per track on the disk, you can then position the read/write head at that exact point.

An added benefit of relative file access is that records can be updated in place. If you want to make a change in a record, you calculate the position of the record and then write directly to the record. Sequential access does not allow for this as each of the records can be a different size. Updating a sequential file requires the entire file to be copied to a new file, modifying the record as it is written to the new file.

The advantages of relative file access are the speed of getting to a particular record and being able to update the record in place. The disadvantage is that disk space can be wasted if data does not fill the entire record or if some of the relative record numbers do not have data. Relative file access works well when a sequential record number can easily identify records.

hashing

hashing – A common method used for accessing data either in a file or a database table through the use of a unique value called the hash key

hash key – Unique value used in hashing algorithms and identifying records

In situations where records cannot be identified by a sequential numeric value, or in situations where the numeric identifying value is not in sequential order beginning with one, another technique has been developed that allows nonnumeric record keys to be used to access relative record files. This technique is called ***hashing*** and is widely used in database management systems. Hashing involves using a hashing algorithm to generate unique values for each of the records. The ***hash key*** is then used as a key value within a list of rows or records of information. Combined together, the hash keys establish an index similar to what you learned in the database chapter.

why hash?

The goal of hashing is to create an algorithm that allows a key field such as a phone number that is not suited for relative file access to be converted into a relative record number that can be used. Even ASCII character fields can be converted using an appropriate hashing technique.

For example, if you are storing customer information, you could use the telephone number as the identifying key in a relative access file, but your file would have large blocks of unused spaces reserved for unused telephone numbers. For example, if you lived in area code 702, you would have to waste the space for relative records 0 through 7019999999. That, of course, is unacceptable.

To solve the problem you employ a simple hashing technique. You subtract 701999999 from the customer's phone number and use that result as the relative key. Doing so solves the problem of the wasted space of relative record numbers of phone numbers less than 702-000-0000. This still isn't the most efficient hashing technique, however, because you still waste many blocks of space that lie between the ranges of phone numbers of your customers, as it is very unlikely that customer phone numbers are in order beginning with 701-000-0001. You need to come up with a better hashing technique. Although an efficient ***hashing algorithm*** might be difficult to come up with, there are a few basic techniques that you can use to formulate it.

hashing algorithm – A routine of logic used for determining how hash values are created

A moderately simple technique for hashing a number such as a phone number is to first determine the maximum number of records you might have. The records in the relative file should have a key value from 0 to the highest number possible, minus 1. This range is then used to allocate space for the file to store all of the records it might end up using. Once you know how many records you need to store, you can create an algorithm that converts the customer's phone number into a number in the specified relative record range.

A simple way to accomplish this is to divide the highest possible phone number by the expected number of customers, with the result being an algorithm key. Once you have this key, it can be used on customer phone numbers to calculate an associated relative record number.

For example, a telephone number in the United States is made up of 10 numeric digits (999-999-9999, not including parentheses or dashes). A rough estimate is made and it is decided that you could have approximately 2000 customers. So, you divide 9999999999 by 2000 to come up with the algorithm key, which, rounded, is 5,000,000. If your first customer had a phone number of 702-555-1234, the relative record is calculated to be 7025551234 / 5000000, or 1045. The record for this customer is then stored in relative record 1045.

This hashing technique might be useful if the 2000 customer phone numbers were evenly spread throughout the range of 0000000000–9999999999. In a normal situation, however, the phone numbers are more likely to be grouped in a single area code and in just a few three-digit prefixes. In this case the algorithm generates a large quantity of collisions.

collision – In hashing, when the hashing algorithm generates the same relative key for more than one original key value

Collisions, in a hashing algorithm, are when the algorithm generates the same relative key for more than one original key value. In the example above, the same relative key is generated for the phone numbers 522-500-5000 through 522-999-9500. That, of course, isn't acceptable. A better algorithm needs to be developed.

A simple remedy for the collision problem might be to expand the algorithm. For example, the algorithm above could be expanded to include the sum of the digits in the phone number, with the hope that doing so lessens the chances of collision. Again, using the phone number 702-555-1234 gives you the relative key of 1045. Add to that the sum of the digits of the phone number, or 34 (7 + 0 + 2 + 5 + 5 + 5 + 1 + 2 + 3 + 4), giving 1045+34, or 1079. Now, another number such as 702-555-5678 would have a relative record number of 1045 + 50 or 1095, and a collision is avoided. Using this technique does not avoid collisions altogether, but it does lessen them. Note that if one customer has a phone number of 702-555-1234 and another has a number of 702-555-4321, a collision would occur.

With a little skill and mathematical ability, an algorithm can be developed that is the most efficient possible for the range of customer telephone numbers and collisions would be nearly eliminated.

dealing with collisions

overflow area – Area in a file that is used in case a collision occurs during the hashing algorithm

Even the best hashing algorithm occasionally will have collisions. Some provisions must be made for dealing with them. One common way is to create an ***overflow area*** in the relative file that holds records with duplicate relative record numbers.

The overflow area works in this manner (shown in Figure 10-11). The first record with a specific relative key calculated by the hashing algorithm is placed in the specified place on the disk. When the hashing algorithm generates the same key for a different phone number, the system goes to the specified relative location on the disk file, and checks to see if the phone number of the record there matches the phone number of the customer. If not, the second record is written to the overflow area at end of the file.

Figure 10-11, An overflow area helps resolve collisions

When a record is to be retrieved, the process is similar. The hash key is calculated from the phone number and the record at the calculated position is retrieved. If the record at that location isn't the desired one, then the overflow area is searched sequentially until the matching record is found.

hashing and computer science

In the past, creating hashing algorithms has been the focus of computer science contests. The most efficient hashing algorithm for a given key was awarded the prize—maybe something like a new, deluxe pocket protector.

Reinforce your understanding of chapter concepts and terms with the information and activities for Chapter 10 on the student CD.

Hashing is of great benefit to companies that produce database management systems. Each company wants the most efficient storage and lookup routines so that their systems outperform the competition.

There are many different hashing algorithms that are used in computer science. Some are based upon encryption and decryption while others focus on indexing. Many programming languages now have specialized libraries of hashing routines built into the language, but don't be surprised if one day you have the need to create your own hashing routine.

chapter summary

- A hard drive is an example of a random access device that stores information in tracks and sectors, and accesses data through read/write heads
- A file system is responsible for creating, manipulating, renaming, copying, and removing files from a storage device
- Windows uses either FAT or NTFS as the file system
- The FAT (file allocation table) file system keeps track of which files are using specific clusters
- FAT is vulnerable to disk fragmentation
- NTFS (New Technology Filing System) is commonly used with Windows 2000, Windows XP, and Windows 2003 and uses a master file table (MFT) to keep track of the files and directories on a volume
- NTFS has many advantages over FAT, such as better reliability and security, journaling, file encryption, and file compression
- Linux can be used with many file systems, such as XFS, JFS, ReiserFS, and ext3
- A file contains data that is either binary or text (ASCII)
- Data is usually stored and accessed either sequentially or randomly (relative access)
- Hashing is a common method for accessing a relative file and involves a hashing algorithm to generate a hash key value used to identify a record location
- Collisions occur when the hash key is duplicated for more than one relative record location
- The goal of hashing is to create an algorithm that allows a key field to be converted into a relative record number with a small number of collisions

key terms

cluster (361)

collision (373)

directory (358)

disk fragmentation (363)

Encrypting File System (365)

FAT (359)

file compression (365)

file system (357)

hash key (372)

hashing (372)

hashing algorithm (372)

master file table (MFT) (364)

NTFS (359)

overflow area (373)

random access (358)

sequential access (358)

test yourself

1. Describe what a file system does.
2. Describe how FAT is implemented.
3. Describe how a drive becomes fragmented.
4. Explain how defragmentation works and how it can improve system performance.
5. How does FAT differ from NTFS and when are both used?
6. What are the advantages and disadvantages of FAT?
7. Describe how NTFS is implemented.
8. What are the advantages and disadvantages of NTFS?
9. Describe the master file table (MFT) and how it works.
10. What are the advantages and disadvantages of file compression?
11. What is the difference between a text file and a binary file?
12. How does sequential file access differ from random file access?
13. What are the strengths and weaknesses of sequential file access and random file access?
14. Explain how hashing works.
15. Assume you are trying to create a hashing algorithm to work with information stored for a student registration system. The student information is identified by the student ID which is seven characters long. The numbers range from 1000000 to 9999999. Write a hashing algorithm that minimizes collisions.

practice exercises

1. Which of the following is *not* a responsibility of the file system?
    - **a.** Creating files
    - **b.** Manipulating files
    - **c.** Renaming files
    - **d.** Copying files
    - **e.** None of the above
2. Sectors are made up of clusters.
    - **a.** True
    - **b.** False
3. Under the FAT file system, files do not need to be stored in a contiguous block of memory.
    - **a.** True
    - **b.** False
4. Which of the following FAT formats allows for the largest volume size?
    - **a.** FAT12
    - **b.** FAT16
    - **c.** FAT32
    - **d.** None of the above; they all have the same maximum volume size
5. Which tool is used to reorganize the clusters so as to minimize head movement?
    - **a.** Disk Defragmenter
    - **b.** Sequential access
    - **c.** FAT
    - **d.** NTFS
6. FAT32 provides the ability to assign access rights to a file and directory.
    - **a.** True
    - **b.** False
7. Which is *not* an advantage of using NTFS?
    - **a.** Journaling
    - **b.** File encryption
    - **c.** Efficient disk usage on small volumes
    - **d.** Security

8. Which is *not* a file system implemented on Linux?
   - a. Overflow area
   - b. XFS
   - c. JFS
   - d. ext3

9. Assume you are tracking information on rocket launches. Each launch is assigned a number from 1000 to 100000. There will most probably be around 5000 launches, and you are using a hashing algorithm that divides the highest possible number of launches by the expected number of launches. What would the hashing algorithm key be?
   - a. 200
   - b. 20
   - c. 500000
   - d. 5000000

10. Using the information from problem 9, if you had a rocket launch number of 80000, what would the relative record be?
   - a. 4000
   - b. 400
   - c. 50
   - d. 5000

digging deeper

1. What is a journal file system?
2. Are there any other types of file systems besides journal, FAT, and NFTS? If so, please describe them.
3. Does disk defragmenting really make a difference in the overall performance of your system? Why or why not?
4. What is a hash table and how is it used?
5. Create a hashing algorithm you could use to uniquely identify records. Make sure you describe how it works.

discussion topics

1. Using problem 12 from the Test Yourself section, discuss and determine which hashing algorithm is best suited for reducing the number of collisions.
2. What situations are best for using sequential file access?
3. What situations are best for using relative file access?
4. Why would you want to convert your FAT32 file system running under Windows 2000 to NTFS? What problems could arise? Should you always convert to NTFS from FAT?
5. If your current system were using FAT for the file management system, what would you need to consider before switching to NTFS? Include specific details along with what things you need to confirm before making the switch.

Internet research

1. What are the most current file systems being used under Windows? Describe the differences.
2. What are the most current file systems being used under Linux? Describe the differences.
3. Find five Web sites that discuss and explain hashing. The Web sites should also demonstrate a hashing algorithm. Share your findings.
4. How would you convert a FAT file system to NTFS?
5. How does FAT organize a hard drive?
6. How does NTFS organize a hard drive?

chapter

11

programming

in this chapter you will:

- Learn what a program is and how it can be developed
- Understand the difference between a low-level and high-level language
- Be introduced to low-level languages using the Assembly programming language as an example
- Learn about the structure of a program, including algorithms and pseudocode
- Gain an understanding of the basics of high-level programming languages using Java as an example
- Learn about variables and how they are used
- Be introduced to the Java operators
- Explore the different control structures used in programming
- Understand the terms associated with object-oriented programming

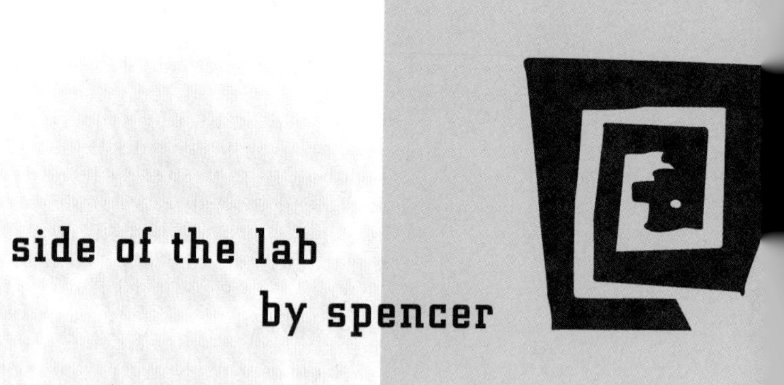

the lighter side of the lab
by spencer

I wrote my first program when I was 12. My dad showed me how to fire up Basic in DOS, and I followed the instructions of a sample program in a book. After just three or four hours, I had a program that asked, "Hello. What is your name?" The user could then enter a name like "Spencer," and the program would then display, "Hi, Spencer!" Needless to say, I gave up programming for a number of years.

Then one day my dad offered to pay me to program some reports for him. If I hadn't had the brain of a teenager, I might have been smart enough to realize that there must be a reason my dad didn't want to program the reports himself. But because I did have the brain of a teenager, I probably thought he wanted me to do it because he couldn't figure it out himself.

I spent the next few weeks converting between inches and twips in order to program in the correct X and Y coordinates. I suppose there are probably more tedious things in this world—like maybe searching for a grain of salt in a bag of sugar. I might have hung up my programming hat altogether, if it weren't for the encouraging words of my dad . . . and the paycheck.

I started reading how-to books on programming and taking lessons from my dad. Pretty soon, I was promoted from programming reports to working on the actual functionality of the program. I've been programming ever since. Those who haven't ever programmed just can't comprehend the feelings that accompany compiling the program that you wrote with your own two hands for the first time, and receiving 162 compile error messages. It brings tears to my eyes just thinking about it.

But then you start to debug the program. You and your coworkers laugh at the level of stupidity that went into making the errors you did. One by one, you fix the errors. And then one day, it happens: You compile the program and no errors come up. (This event is usually accompanied by wild cheering and occasional jumping up and down that we lovingly refer to as the Compile Dance.)

Of course, now that the program compiles, it is time to run it. If it compiled it must work. Four days and 20 hours later you decide that maybe there is a problem with the program. You would think that the computer could have known it wasn't going to work right. After many bags of microwave popcorn and caffeinated sodas, the program not only compiles but also does what it was supposed to do.

Programming is a great job that I would recommend to anyone. In fact, if you're interested in programming work, give me a call—I've got some reports that need to be programmed.

why you need to know about... programming

You've probably heard the story about the foolish man and the wise man that each wanted to build a house. The wise man built his house upon the rock while the foolish man built his house upon the sand. When the rain came down and the floods came up, the house that was built upon the sand was washed away. However, the house that was built upon the rock was still intact because it was built upon a firm foundation.

This same concept applies to programming. Programs are used all of the time and you might not even realize it. They can be found in your microwave, the space shuttle, an ATM, and even your car. If these programs were not built upon a firm foundation of structured logic, consider the possibilities: your microwave would burn your food, the space shuttle would never launch, the ATM would give your money away to other people, and your car would sit in the driveway gathering dust!

Learning solid programming practices is essential in your career as a computer scientist, and to the people and organizations that will (it is hoped) benefit from the programs you produce.

Building a strong foundation is based upon how well you learn the basic language constructs and how to implement them in writing a program. If you can learn how to write structured and logically written programs that are readable and understandable by other software developers, you can become a great asset to any organization. Good programming skills are acquired through diligent practice, trial, and error. In fact, it can be related to learning a foreign language. You can learn all of the language basics but if you do not practice using it you can never thoroughly learn the language. Learning a programming language comes from practice, practice, and even more practice!

what is a program?

There are so many programs being used every day that it would be mind boggling to try to list all the programs that have been written. So, if the world is so dependent on programs, wouldn't it be nice to know what a program is and what it can do?

program – A collection of statements or steps that solve a problem and need to be converted into a language that the computer understands to perform one or more tasks

A ***program*** is simply a collection of statements or steps that solve a problem and need to be converted into a language that the computer understands to perform one or more tasks. The statements are usually written in a language that is understood by humans but not by computers. The statements are entered as a logical ordered set (also called an ***algorithm***). In order for the computer to execute the algorithm, the set of statements needs to be converted into a language the computer understands. This conversion process uses an interpreter or a compiler.

note **The only language the computer understands is called "binary," and consists of ones and zeros.**

algorithm – A logically ordered set of statements used to solve a problem

interpreter – A program included with an executable application that acts as the translator between the program and the computer by converting program statements one by one into a language the computer understands

compiler – A program that reads all of the statements from a program and converts them into a computer language

An ***interpreter*** is a separate program that is needed in order for a program to run. It performs exactly as its name implies—it interprets the program's statements one by one into a language that the computer can understand and acts as the translator between the program and the computer.

A ***compiler***, on the other hand, reads all of the statements from the program and converts them into a computer language. Thus the finished compiled program stands on its own and does not need an interpreter. It is already fluent in "computer-ese."

A program is developed to assist someone in accomplishing a task. To meet the requirements of the task, the developer should communicate with the program user to confirm what is really needed. The program might perform calculations, gather information, or process the information and display the results. Programs are used to make vehicles run efficiently, operate an appliance, or even map out your next family vacation. They are used everywhere and relied upon to function properly.

When a program does not perform accurately there can be two possible causes. Either a piece of logical functionality was left out of the program, or the program has one or more statements that are logical errors.

A program that does not have full functionality can be corrected by proper software engineering. Think of writing a program as being analogous with putting together all of the pieces of a puzzle. In order to successfully put all of the pieces in their right spot you need to first know what pieces are available to use and recognize how they fit with other pieces.

You'll learn more about putting programs together in Chapter 12, "Software Engineering."

eastern roots

The word algorithm came from Mohammed ibn-Musa al-Khwarizmi (approximately AD 780 to 850), a mathematician and part of the Baghdad royal court. He wrote a book that eventually introduced algebra to the West.

I speak computer

The first step in programming is to determine what language you want to use to communicate with the computer. As stated earlier, your computer speaks only one language—binary. All of the other programming languages that are used by humans to create computer programs end up in binary, so in actuality you can choose whatever programming language suits your needs and meets your preferences.

Choosing a programming language is like trying to choose your favorite ice-cream flavor. There are just so many to choose from, and all of them can satisfy your need for ice cream. How do you choose a specific flavor? It is based upon your individual taste.

Welcome to the world of computer languages. Here are a few of the programming flavors from which you can choose:

- ADA
- Assembly
- C
- C++
- C#
- COBOL
- FORTRAN
- Delphi (Pascal)
- Java (and JavaScript)
- Lisp
- Perl
- Smalltalk
- Visual Basic

Lady Ada

ADA was named after Ada Byron (1815–1852), daughter of the poet Lord Byron. She was a mathematician and is considered the first computer programmer. She wrote to Charles Babbage regarding his new calculating engine and expressed her ideas for a plan that could calculate Bernoulli numbers.

No single language is considered to be the "king" of programming languages. Each has its own strengths and weaknesses. What it boils down to is preference of the programmer, appropriateness for the task at hand, or perhaps corporate standards. For example:

- Assembly works well when you want to control hardware.
- COBOL got its start and continues to be popular in business.
- FORTRAN is geared toward engineering and scientific projects.
- Java and JavaScript are well suited for Internet applications.
- Lisp is well known for working with artificial intelligence.
- Pascal was created to teach people how to write computer programs.
- Smalltalk was created to assist developers in creating programs that mimicked human thinking.
- Visual Basic was produced to provide a simple yet powerful GUI programming environment.

The following are examples from each of the languages as they would appear in a simple program that prints, "Computer Scientists Are Wired!"

ADA:

```
with TEXT_IO; use TEXT_IO;
procedure Wired is
        pragma MAIN;
begin
        PUT ("Computer Scientists Are Wired!");
end Wired;
```

assembly:

```
mov ah,13h
mov dx,0C00H
mov cx,30
mov al,00
mov bh,00
mov bl,1fH
mov ah,13H
lea bp,[Msg]
int 10H
int 20H

Msg:    db 'Computer Scientists Are Wired!'

EXE_End
```

C:

```
#include <stdio.h>

main()
{
        printf("Computer Scientists Are Wired!\n");
}
```

note Dennis Ritchie developed C in the early 1970s for UNIX while working at AT&T Bell Labs. Its predecessor was called B, which was built upon the BCPL language.

C++:

```
#include <iostream>

int main(int argc, char *argv[])
{
        cout << "Computer Scientists Are Wired!\n" ;
}
```

note C++ was written by Bjarne Stroustrup at Bell Labs between 1983–1985 and is an extension of C.

COBOL:

```
000100 IDENTIFICATION DIVISION.
000200 PROGRAM-ID.  WIRED.
000300 DATE-WRITTEN. 12/15/03  16:09.
000400*  AUTHOR GREG ANDERSON
000500 ENVIRONMENT DIVISION.
000600 CONFIGURATION SECTION.
000700 SOURCE-COMPUTER. RM-COBOL.
000800 OBJECT-COMPUTER. RM-COBOL.
000900
001000 DATA DIVISION.
001100 FILE SECTION.
001200
100000 PROCEDURE DIVISION.
100100
100200 MAIN-LOGIC SECTION.
100300 BEGIN.
100400  DISPLAY "Computer Scientists Are Wired!"
        LINE 12 POSITION 25.
100500  STOP RUN.
100600 MAIN-LOGIC-EXIT.
100700  EXIT.
```

note COBOL is an acronym for Common Business Oriented Language and was developed in 1959 by a group of computer professionals called the Conference on Data Systems Languages or CODASYL.

Delphi (Pascal):

```
Program Hello (Input, Output);
Begin
     Writeln ('Computer Scientists Are Wired!');
End.
```

note Delphi is object-oriented Turbo Pascal and was released by Borland in 1995. Pascal was developed in the early 1970s by Niklaus Wirth to provide more structure in programming and also to serve as a method for learning the concepts of computer programming.

FORTRAN:

```
PROGRAM WIRED
PRINT *,'Computer Scientists Are Wired!'
STOP
END
```

note

A team of programmers at IBM led by John Backus developed FORTRAN in 1957. It is an acronym for FORmula TRANslation.

Java:

```
class Wired {
    public static void main (String args[]) {
      System.out.print("Computer Scientists Are Wired!");
    }
}
```

note

Java evolved from a language named Oak which was developed in the early 1990s at Sun Microsystems. It was created as a platform-independent language.

Lisp:

```
;;; Common LISP
(defun wired ()
      (print "Computer Scientists Are Wired!")
)
```

note

Lisp (List Processing Language) was based upon the work of John McCarthy while working at IBM. It was created to support artificial intelligence and was released in the mid 1960s.

Smalltalk:

```
Transcript show:'Computer Scientists Are Wired!';cr
```

note

Smalltalk is an object-oriented programming language designed at Xerox PARC by Alan Kay, Dan Ingalls, Ted Kaehler, Adele Goldberg, and others during the 1970s.

Before you decide in which language you prefer to program, you need to research them a little more and decide whether a low-level or high-level language is right for you.

low-level language – *Programming language that resembles more what a computer can understand rather than a human*

machine language – *The lowest-level language, which is directly understood by a computer*

assembly language – *A language that resides in between the lowest-level language and a higher-level language; it assigns letter codes to each machine language instruction*

assembler – *Reads the assembly language code and converts it into machine language*

high-level language – *Programming language that is more human-friendly or more natural for humans to read*

A ***low-level language*** is a programming language that gives direct instructions to a particular CPU or piece of hardware in binary code understood by computers, but not so easily understood by humans. The lowest-level language is ***machine language***, in which instructions are encoded as straight binary bit patterns. In fact, the only instructions that a computer actually ever carries out are in machine language. An ***assembly language*** program is one step up from machine language in that it assigns letter codes to each machine language instruction. A program called an ***assembler*** reads assembly-language code and translates it into machine language. A ***high-level language*** is one that is more human-friendly, using more natural (to humans, anyway) language (Figure 11-1). A high-level language such as C++ or Java requires a compiler or interpreter to translate it into machine language. High-level languages can also be used on many different types of computers, making them more platform independent.

Figure 11-1, Different types of programming languages

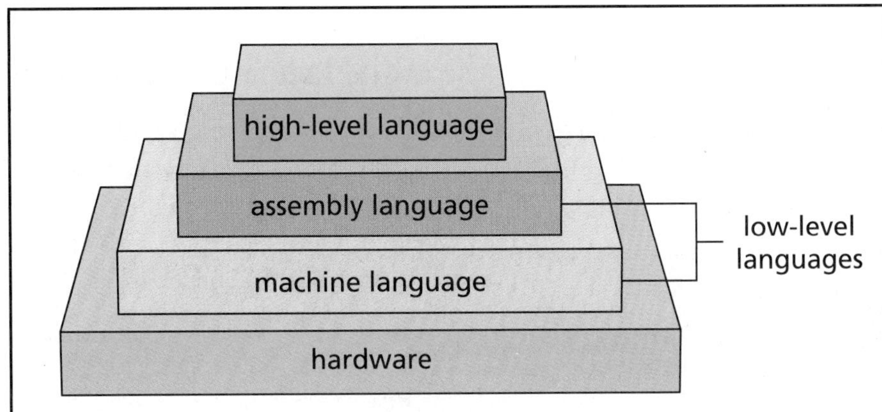

go for a drive

Many of these languages offer free versions or trial versions that you can take for a test drive. Make sure you do before you make a commitment!

The sections that follow give you a taste of how a low-level language works using assembly language as an example, then a general introduction to how high-level languages work, followed by a section that uses the Java language to illustrate the principles of high-level languages. To introduce you to all the programming languages would take an entire library full of books! As a computer scientist, you'll likely work with many different languages, and discover for yourself what "flavor" you prefer.

low-level languages

As mentioned earlier, machine language is the lowest-level language, which includes only series of binary numbers. Very few people actually ever code in machine language (machines are trained to do that), so this chapter won't go into detail on how it works. Assembly language (sometimes called Assembler because an assembler converts the assembly language into machine language) is close to machine language, but is written using more Englishlike statements. As with machine language, each assembly language statement corresponds to one machine instruction. Assembly language produces programs that are usually smaller and run faster than programs in higher-level languages. It is very powerful. In fact, almost anything you can do on a computer can be done in Assembler. This is not always the case for other languages. Assembly language is closely tied to the particular CPU type, and Assemblers have been written for every type of CPU.

note

The 808X architecture of early Intel processors is used to illustrate the use of Assembler in this chapter because it is fairly simple.

assembly language statements

In an earlier chapter, you read about computer registers. Nearly everything that happens within a computer goes through and uses the CPU registers. Registers are special memory locations in the CPU that are used to hold information that the program can use. The registers AX, BX, CX, and DX are called general-purpose registers (GPRs) and are mainly used for arithmetic operations or accessing an element within an array. Under the 808X architecture there are also the special-purpose registers. The special-purpose registers consist of pointer registers, segment registers, and a flag register.

The assembly programming language consists of alphabetic instructions (or instructions written in a text format) that are converted into machine instructions. There is a one-to-one relationship between the assembly instruction and the actual instruction the machine understands.

Consider the following example. As you read the assembly code you might feel that it is very cryptic. One of the disadvantages of assembly language is that it can be hard to read and understand.

```
;NASM-IDE ASM Assistant Assembler Project File
[BITS 16]    ;Set code generation to 16 bit mode
%include 'exebin.mac'
EXE_Begin
[ORG 100H]        ;set addressing to begin at 100H
cls:    mov ah,06
        mov cx,0000
        mov dx,184fH
        mov al,00
        mov bh,1fH
        int 10H
        mov dx,0C22H
        lea bp,[Hi]
        mov cx,12
wst:    mov al,00
        mov bh,00
        mov bl,1fH
        mov ah,13H
        int 10H
        cmp dh,0Ch
        jnz stop
        inc dh
        lea bp,[Bye]
        mov cx,8
        jmp wst
stop:   int 20H

Data:
Hi:  db 'How Are You?'
Bye:       db 'Goodbye!'
EXE_End
```

syntax – Refers to the spelling and grammar used within a programming language's statements

get on your case

Some assembler languages are case sensitive, meaning that a lowercase "a" is regarded differently than an uppercase "A". For example, the word "wst" is *not* recognized as also being "WST". You need to determine whether or not your assembler is case sensitive.

Clear as mud? Now you understand why the biggest disadvantage of the assembly programming language is readability. Then again, once you know and understand the ***syntax*** of the language, it is not as cryptic as you might think, and you reap the rewards of fast executing code and the power to do anything you want within the computer system. The main problem with using assembly language is that it takes a lot of programming to accomplish very little. Also, the assembler for a particular CPU can only be used on that CPU and the assemblers for different CPUs have very different syntax.

In assembly language, each programming statement performs a task. Some of these instructions or statements are explained in the following sections.

mov

The mov statement moves values around. For example,

```
mov cx, 8
```

tells the assembler to move the value of 8 into the cx register.

note **Assembly statements are read from right to left.**

You can move a value from memory to a register, from register to memory, or from register to register.

```
mov dx, cx
```

This tells the assembler to move the value stored in the cx register to the dx register. You need to understand that it does not wipe out the value that is stored in cx. It still has the value of 8, but now dx also has that value of 8. In reality, the mov statement copies values rather than moving them.

Some other commonly used assembly statements are:

- add—Add one value to another value.
- inc—Increment a value in the register.
- sub—Subtract one value from another.
- cmp—Compare two values.
- jnz—Jump to a specific location in the program (similar to a "go to" in other languages)

add

The add instruction takes a value on the right and adds it to the value on the left.

```
mov cx, 3
mov dx, 8
add dx, cx
```

The first statement moves a value of 3 into the cx register. The second statement moves the value of 8 into the dx register. The last statement takes the value in the cx register (3) and adds it to the value stored in the dx register (8) resulting in the value of 11 now being stored in the dx register.

inc

The inc instruction adds one (1) to the register being used.

```
inc dx
```

This statement takes the value contained in the dx register, which is currently 11 from the previously executed add instruction, and increases (or increments) it by 1. The register dx now contains the value of 12.

sub

The sub instruction tells the assembler to subtract one number from another number.

```
mov cx, 4
mov dx, 7
sub dx, cx
```

The first statement moves a value of 4 into the cx register. The second statement moves the value of 7 into the dx register. The last statement takes the value in the cx register (4) and subtracts it from the value in the dx register (7) and places the result back into the dx register (3).

At the conclusion of execution for those three statements, the cx register still contains the value of 4, but the dx register now contains the value of 3 (similar to dx = dx – cx).

cmp

The cmp instruction tells the assembler to compare two values. It works like a subtract instruction but does *not* store the result in a register. Instead, the result is used to set flag bits in the flags register (FL). If the result of the compare equals zero, the zero flag (ZR) is set to a binary one and the sign flag is set to zero (plus). If the result of the compare is a negative, the zero flag bit is set to zero and the sign flag is set to 1 (negative).

```
mov cx, 4
mov dx, 7
cmp dx, cx
```

The first statement moves a value of 4 into the cx register. The second statement moves the value of 7 into the dx register. The last statement compares the value of register dx to the value of register cx. If dx – cx = 0 then the zero flag is set. You can now use this comparison to determine whether or not to jump to a different location in the program using a conditional jump instruction such as the jnz instruction.

jnz

The jnz instruction tests the value of the zero flag maintained by the system. If the zero flag (ZR) is set to a value of 1, then it tells the system to jump somewhere else in the program. If the zero flag is not set, then it continues to process through the code on the next line.

```
mov cx, 4
mov dx, 7
cmp dx, cx
jnz stop
```

Building upon the previous example, the jnz instruction checks the zero flag that might have been set during the cmp instruction. If the zero flag has a value of 1 then it tells the system that the previous cmp instruction evaluated to a 0 value and that it should now jump or pass control to a section in the program labeled "stop." If the value of the zero flag is 0 then it means that the previous cmp instruction did not evaluate to a zero when the two registers being used were compared.

Are you a master assembly programmer yet? Don't worry. It takes practice to learn a new language, and low-level languages are harder to understand and learn because they are more hardware oriented rather than human speech oriented. Now that you have seen how a low-level language works, it is time to take an overall look at high-level languages, and then some specific examples using Java.

high-level languages

High-level programming languages allow you to write programs that are less dependent upon the type of computer/CPU, and their programming statements are more easily understood by humans than those of low-level languages. High-level languages are easier to write, read, and maintain than low-level languages. Also, high-level languages can accomplish much more with a single statement. With a high-level language, unlike Assembler, there is not a one-to-one relationship between the language statements and the underlying binary instructions. However, high-level language programs are generally slower, because they must either be compiled or interpreted.

Some currently popular high-level languages include:

- ADA
- C
- C++
- C#
- COBOL
- Delphi
- Java
- JavaScript
- Pascal
- Perl
- Visual Basic

integrated development environment (IDE) – An interface provided with software development languages that incorporates all of the necessary tools needed to write, compile, and distribute programs; these tools often include an editor, compiler, graphic designer, and more

Over the years, these languages have developed and have become more and more powerful while maintaining an environment that promotes productivity and flexibility. Many of these languages (as well as some assemblers) incorporate some form of ***integrated development environment (IDE)*** with their programming package. The IDE acts as a working desktop from which the programmer can more easily write applications (Figure 11-2).

Figure 11-2, Microsoft Visual Studio .NET makes software development easier

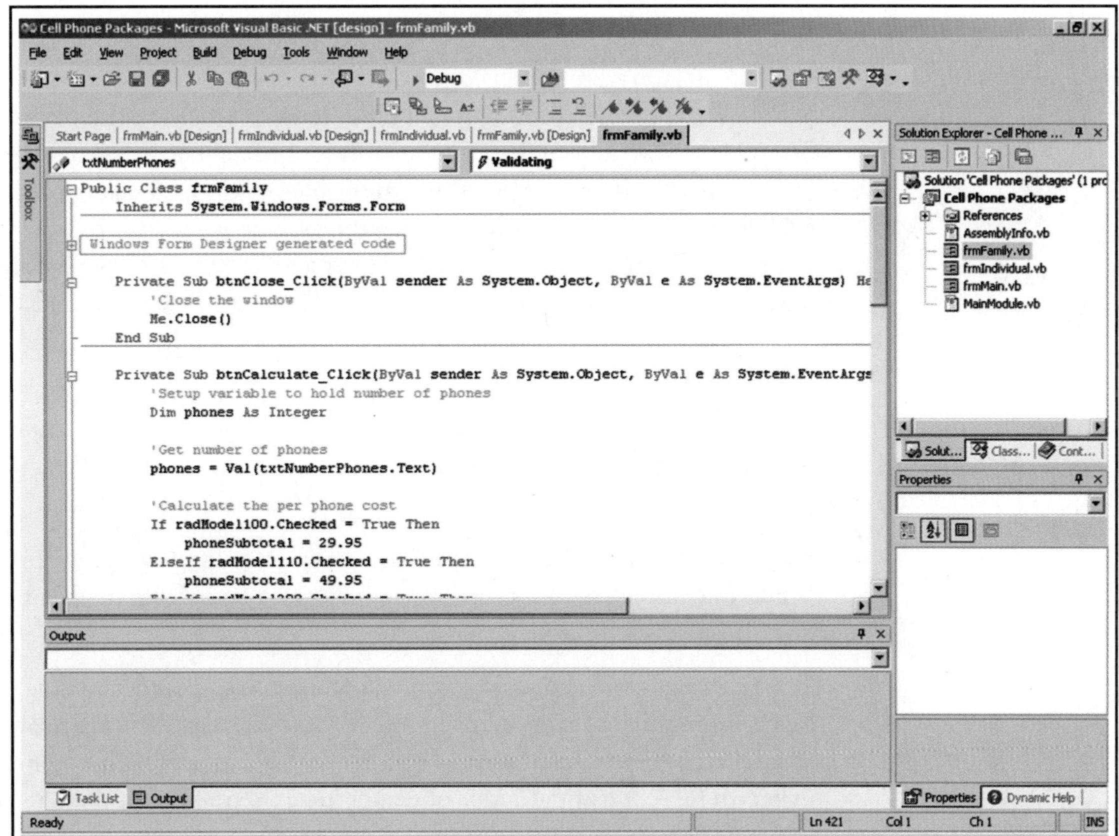

that (inter)face is familiar

Companies that develop programming language packages are working to create standard interfaces to their programming languages. For example, Microsoft Visual Studio .NET incorporates an IDE that allows the software engineer to write programming statements in C++, Visual Basic (VB), or C# within the .NET environment using the same IDE interface. This saves time and money because developers only have to learn to use one software development tool.

structure of a program

Before you begin to write a program in any programming language, you must first determine how the program should work and how the language syntax should be incorporated. As stated earlier, syntax is a formal definition of the rules and grammar for the language. Just as in any spoken language, you must not only learn the vocabulary, but you must also learn the rules for implementing the vocabulary.

When you learn a foreign language, you must start at the beginning. You learn a little about the culture in which the language is used, the alphabet, numbers, simple phrases, and then move on to grammatical rules and conjugation of verbs. This same process can be applied to learning a programming language. Before you implement the syntax of a programming language you need to first understand how a program is structured. The structure of a program is based upon algorithms, and is often represented using pseudocode.

algorithms

When you are presented with any kind of problem, you figure out what method you're going to use to solve it. For example, if you were trying to get an A in an introductory computer science course you would need to follow some type of plan. Your plan might include: attending lectures, taking notes, reading the chapters, doing the assignments, studying, taking the quizzes and tests, and completing the final exam.

Within each of those tasks you might break it down into smaller subtasks. For example, how would you describe the process of taking notes? First, you ensure you receive a good night's sleep the night before class. Ok, so that's probably not going to happen, but you could do such things as be prepared with paper and a couple of pencils. If the professor emphasizes a topic you take more detailed notes. If the professor says that the next part of the lecture is not included on the test, you might feel inclined to put your pencil down and rest your eyes.

For many things you do in your life, you might logically plan out a series of steps in order to accomplish that which you are trying to do. Plain and simple, it all boils down to thinking logically about the solution to a problem.

In programming, an algorithm is a method for solving a problem. The algorithm consists of executable steps that you need to follow to solve the problem. When you encounter a problem, you define a list of steps that need to be followed to successfully solve the problem.

To take an algorithm and convert it into a program using a programming language, it must first be represented in some type of language. Whether that language is in a human form, picture form, a combination of both or some other unknown form, it has to describe or demonstrate a series of steps that should be accomplished. Programmers often use a form of representation called pseudocode.

pseudocode

pseudocode – A readable description of an algorithm written in human language

Pseudocode is a detailed yet readable description in human language that describes an algorithm that needs to be converted into a programming language. The text is in a human-understandable format, but following the steps of a program. Pseudocode can be considered a template for what needs to be converted into programming language syntax.

Consider the following pseudocode for entering grades for a student and calculating the final average:

```
FIND/ADD STUDENT:
Search for a student
If the student is not found, add student
Display the student information

INPUT GRADES:
Prompt the user to select which grade to enter
(assignment, quiz, or test)
Accept the input and store to the database
Prompt the user to see if they need to enter more grades
If so, return back to the first prompt asking for a
grade
Continue this process until there are no more grades to
be entered for the student

CALCULATE FINAL GRADE:
Calculate the final grade
     First calculate the assignment average
     Apply the appropriate weighting
     Calculate the quiz average
     Apply the appropriate weighting
     Calculate the test average
     Apply the appropriate weighting
     Add up all of the weighted averages
     Compare to the grading scale
     Print the student final average
     Store the average grade and letter grade to the
     database
```

Do you see how the task is logically broken into smaller subtasks? It is then easier to define the necessary steps involved in each of the subtasks.

There are no formal rules regarding pseudocode and how it should be written. When writing pseudocode you need to consider whether or not the information you are providing is enough to explain the process to someone who has never been introduced to the type of problem being solved.

How do you learn how to write pseudocode and to think logically? Once again, it all refers back to the same concept you use when trying to learn a new language because if you think about it, pseudocode *is* a new language. The answer is *practice!* Many times a professor has students write the pseudocode algorithm to a program before the student can begin typing in programming statements. Why? Is it because the professor loves to assign busywork? No. It is because the professor knows that you need to practice thinking logically and then putting that logic (the necessary steps in solving the problem) down on a piece of paper before you start programming.

Here's another example of how to start defining an algorithm using pseudocode. Suppose you want to write a program to accurately convert the temperature in degrees Celsius to Fahrenheit or vice versa (Figure 11-3). In this instance, as in many programming instances, you need to determine what formulas need to be used in your algorithms.

note

Make sure any formulas you use in an algorithm are accurate! Any mistakes could at best make the program worthless, and at worst prove disastrous.

Start with the formulas needed in the algorithm:

- Fahrenheit to Celsius: Celsius Temp = (5/9) * (Fahrenheit Temp – 32)
- Celsius to Fahrenheit: Fahrenheit Temp = ((9/5) * Celsius Temp) + 32

Once the formulas have been proven to be correct, you can begin detailing the steps needed in order to write a program to get input from the user, make the conversions, and then display the results back to the user.

Here is the pseudocode that you can implement to solve this problem:

```
Menu:
     Do you want to perform a conversion?
             If Yes then
                  Which conversion do you want to perform?
                      If Celsius to Fahrenheit then
                          Go to the Fahrenheit section
                      If Fahrenheit to Celsius then
                          Go to the Celsius section
             Else If No then
                  Exit the program

Celsius:
     Ask the user for a temperature in Fahrenheit
     Apply the entered temperature to the formula Celsius
```

Figure 11-3, Temperature conversion chart

Temperature Conversion Chart	
Celsius	Fahrenheit
0 C	32.0 F
1 C	33.8 F
2 C	35.6 F
3 C	37.4 F
4 C	39.2 F
5 C	41.0 F
6 C	42.8 F
7 C	44.6 F
8 C	46.4 F
9 C	48.2 F
10 C	50.0 F
11 C	51.8 F
12 C	53.6 F
13 C	55.4 F
14 C	57.2 F
15 C	59.0 F
16 C	60.8 F
17 C	62.6 F
18 C	64.4 F
19 C	66.2 F
20 C	68.0 F
21 C	69.8 F
22 C	71.6 F
23 C	73.4 F
24 C	75.2 F
25 C	77.0 F
26 C	78.8 F
27 C	80.6 F
28 C	82.4 F
29 C	84.2 F
30 C	86.0 F

```
      Temp = (5/9) * (Fahrenheit Temp - 32)
      Display the result saying Fahrenheit Temp ##
      converted to Celsius is XX
      Return to the Menu section

 Fahrenheit:
      Ask the user for a temperature in Celsius
      Apply the entered temperature to the formula
      Fahrenheit Temp = ((9/5) * Celsius Temp) + 32
      Display the result saying Celsius Temp ## converted
      to Fahrenheit is XX
      Return to the Menu section
```

By the time you have completed the pseudocode, the program is basically written using a human-understandable language.

choosing the algorithm

There can be many different ways to perform a task or accomplish a goal. But one way can be more effective than the others. Your job as the programmer/designer is to determine which algorithm is the best one to use for the project. For example, assume that you want to go to Disney World during spring break, and are trying to decide the best way to get there. What are some of the algorithms you could use for solving this problem? You could always fly, with the advantage being that you would arrive in a relatively short time. The disadvantage is cost. You could drive, with the advantage being lower cost but the disadvantage being greater time and wear and tear on the vehicle. You could hitchhike, with the advantage being even lower cost but the disadvantage being greater time and lower safety. You could walk, with the advantage being cost and the disadvantage being time.

Each of the algorithms or solutions to the problem of getting to Disney World solves the problem, and each has advantages and disadvantages. The critical issue is selecting the right algorithm.

note **The selection of a particular algorithm can be based on a myriad of deciding factors. It is wise to spend time investigating all of the options before you begin implementing the algorithm.**

testing the algorithm

Before you get too excited and start typing your program, you still have to perform one more suggested step. You should always test the algorithm and pseudocode you have written. Pretend that you are the end user and that you are trying to run the program.

note

Make sure you write your pseudocode and test the algorithm before you begin writing the source code.

When you test an algorithm, you should always put yourself in the user's situation. The user might not know anything about temperature conversions. A good rule to follow is to plan for the best but expect the worst. In other words, pretend that you are the most computer-illiterate person on the planet trying to run this program. What mistakes could you make?

note

When writing a program you should always consider yourself the end user not knowing anything about how a computer system should work. This allows you to create a program that is easier to use.

Look at the part of the algorithm that takes the temperature value the user entered. A very large assumption is being made. What if the user does not enter a numeric value? What if instead, the user enters the letter "A"? There could be trouble right here in pseudocode city!

Maybe the pseudocode needs to be altered to confirm the user entered a valid numerical value.

```
Celsius:
     Ask the user for a temperature in Fahrenheit
     If the value entered is numerical
            Apply the entered temperature to the formula
            Celsius Temp = (5/9) * (Fahrenheit Temp - 32)
            Display the result saying Fahrenheit Temp ##
            converted to Celsius is XX
     Else
            Display a message stating that the value
            entered is NOT allowed
     Return to the Menu section

Fahrenheit:
     Ask the user for a temperature in Celsius
     If the value entered is numerical
            Apply the entered temperature to the formula
            Fahrenheit Temp = ((9/5) * Celsius Temp) + 32
            Display the result saying Celsius Temp ##
```

```
        converted to Fahrenheit is XX
    Else
        Display a message stating that the value
        entered is NOT allowed
    Return to the Menu section
```

This can be taken one step further. Instead of the Celsius and Fahrenheit routines each displaying an error message you can have a new section that handles any errors that occur. If an error occurs then you send control to that new section. When it is done displaying the error message and doing anything else it might need to do, it returns back to where it left off.


```
Celsius:
    Ask the user for a temperature in Fahrenheit
    If the value entered is numerical
        Apply the entered temperature to the formula
        Celsius Temp = (5/9) * (Fahrenheit Temp - 32)
        Display the result saying Fahrenheit Temp ##
        converted to Celsius is XX
    Else
        Go to Error
    Return to the Menu section

Fahrenheit:
    Ask the user for a temperature in Celsius
    If the value entered is numerical
        Apply the entered temperature to the formula
        Fahrenheit Temp = ((9/5) * Celsius Temp) + 32
        Display the result saying Celsius Temp ##
        converted to Fahrenheit is XX
    Else
        Go to Error
    Return to the Menu section

Error:
    Display a message stating that the value entered is
    not allowed
    Return back to either the Celsius or Fahrenheit
    section depending on which section was currently in
    use
```

Testing the algorithm and expecting the worst to happen can help ensure that you create proper pseudocode from correct logic.

make it meaningful

When displaying an error message, make sure it is descriptive of the problem that occurred. For example, instead of saying "Hey, there is a problem," you could say "The value entered is not a valid number. Please choose between 0 and 100."

syntax of a programming language

Once you have defined the algorithm to use in creating your program and have given the logic behind solving the problem a thorough test, you can begin translating the algorithm into statements in a specific programming language.

Writing a program can be compared to following a recipe (the algorithm and pseudocode) to correctly combine all of the ingredients in the correct order to produce a super masterpiece (a program). A programming language consists of many different "ingredients" that can be used to make your application, and you as the programming "chef" need to know what ingredients are available and how they should be combined.

Some of the different ingredients you can use are:

- Variables
- Operators
- Control structures
- Objects

Using these ingredients allows you to build a program, but you need to know why and when to use them. Otherwise, it is like throwing a random bunch of ingredients from your refrigerator into a pot and hoping that something turns out that is edible.

The next few sections use the Java language to explain and illustrate how these building blocks of programs are used to construct a program.

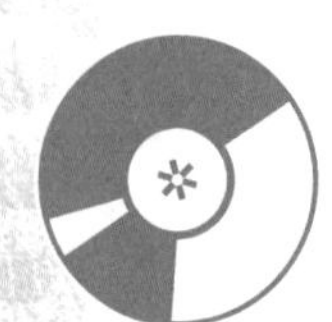

The Java programs in this chapter are included on the student CD under Chapter 11. You can also find examples of these programs in C and C++ for comparison.

learning to cook with Java

Java is a high-level programming language specifically designed for use with the World Wide Web (or Internet). Java was first introduced by Sun Corporation in 1995, and since then, with the support of many other corporations, its popularity has continued to rise. When it first came out, Java was intended to be used to perform little tasks or small applications (applets) without having to write an entire program. Today, Java has become a full-blown programming language, as well as the language of choice for developing applications for communications devices and media such as PDAs, cell phones, the Internet, and networks.

The main advantages of using Java over other languages are:

- *It uses familiar syntax*—Its syntax is similar to the popular C++ language but easier to use.
- *It is very portable*—A program written for one computer can be run on others without recompiling.
- *It is powerful*—The language has a rich library (classes) of routines to do most of the necessary programming tasks.

- *It is popular*—Java is widely used in many different computing environments, and is presently one of the most popular languages.

The most common reason a developer might choose to use Java over other high-level languages is portability. You can write one application that can run on a Windows operating system, and if it is correctly programmed it can also run on a UNIX operating system. Because Java is such a popular and widespread language, and because it is often used in colleges and universities to teach programming skills, Java is used here to illustrate basic programming concepts in this book. Also, it is a language that is in high demand because so many companies are using it. However, the building blocks you learn about here will also be used in just about any other high-level language.

Now you learn what ingredients are available when "cooking" with Java.

variables

Remember the old saying "Different strokes for different folks"? This same concept is applied in everyday programming. There is no single way to write a program. Every person has a different style or preference. But every programmer uses variables, no matter what their style or preference.

variable – Name used to identify a certain location and value in the computer memory

Imagine a pizza without any toppings! Who would want a pizza like that? A program needs variables just like a pizza needs toppings. A ***variable*** is a name used to identify a certain location in your computer's memory. Some programmers like to use variables to hold running totals while others might use variables to keep track of a company name. The type of application being written determines what type of variables need to be created, modified, and maintained. It is possible that a program can be written that does not incorporate variables, but for the most part you will see and use variables in all of your programs.

When the variable is defined, the type of data that can be stored in that memory location is specified. By using the variable name, you can access the contents of the specified memory location and use its value in your application. A variable name is simply an easy way to access your computer memory without having to know the actual hardware address.

For example, assume you are trying to change the oil in a car engine. You need to find the oil plug, so you pull out your handy-dandy engine drawing and attempt to locate something that looks like an oil plug. The engine drawing does not have descriptive labels for each item. Instead, part numbers are used. There are two items that appear to be plugs, so you take a guess which one is the oil plug and dive under the car engine. As you remove the plug and the fluid begins draining, you notice that instead of the usually dirty black color your oil usually has, it is a majestic purple color.

What started off being an oil change has unexpectedly turned into a transmission fluid replacement. This mistake happened because the plugs had numbers instead of names. If you think of the plugs as variables, you can see why using the variable's name (instead of its hardware address) avoids the ambiguity of accessing the wrong memory location and using a value that doesn't apply to the current programming situation. In a high-level language, the variable name can also be called an ***identifier***.

identifier – Name of a variable

When you associate an identifier with a variable, it is called *declaring* that variable. A ***declaration*** is a statement that associates an identifier with a variable (or an action, or some other element of the programming language that can be given a name).

declaration – A statement that associates an identifier with a variable (or an action, or some other element of the programming language that can be given a name)

When you declare a variable, you specify its different attributes, which define how it is processed. Some of those attributes are:

· Identifier (name)
· Type (character, numeric, boolean, etc.)
· Content

For example, the statement

```
int numTicketsBought;
```

can be used to declare a variable used to hold the integer number of tickets bought.

note Java is a case-sensitive language. Make sure that you are consistent in your naming conventions. For example, the word "Amount" is not the same as the word "amount." Every letter has to match.

identifiers and naming conventions

As mentioned above, the identifier is the name of the variable or tag used to access the contents in memory associated with the variable. The rules for declaring a variable in Java are as follows:

· Use only letters, underscores, and numbers
· Begin the name with a letter
· Avoid Java ***reserved words*** that have specific programming meanings

reserved word – A key word that has a specific instructional meaning; the name cannot be redefined as it is already being used by the programming language as an instruction

When deciding upon an identifier, be sure to devise a name that is descriptive of the data being stored. For instance, if you are storing a person's salary you do not want to use a variable labeled "x". It does nothing for the understandability of the program and destroys the ease of maintenance. For instance, some companies have not implemented variable naming standards, which allows their programmers free rein to choose whatever variable names they desire to use. One such company comes to mind. The data-processing staff thought it was clever to use variable labels that were humorous but nondescriptive of their contents such as: Fred, Wilma, Barney, Tally, Rally, Sally, and so on. Although it made the sometimes tedious job of programming a little lighter through the use of humor, it also caused some problems when trying to debug and maintain the applications. Because the variable names were not descriptive, each variable had to be monitored to determine its contents. When choosing a name make sure the name is not already being used by the programming language as part of the instruction set, and at the same time choose a descriptive name. For instance, you cannot use the word "int" as it is already being used by Java as a variable type declaration.

note **Be sure to use a descriptive name for a variable identifier.**

If desired, you can use more than one word for the variable's identifier. One standard (created by Sun Microsystems, the inventor of Java) suggests that you lowercase the first character of the first word but then uppercase the first character of subsequent words:

```
int numCookiesBought;
```

Using the Sun standard, it is best that you do not use an underscore for the first character, although it is legal to do so. One-character names (e.g., i, j, k, x, etc.) should not be used unless they are for variables where you simply discard the value. Overall, it is best to *always* give your variables meaningful names.

note **Many developers separate words with an underscore (_). For example:**

int num_Cookies_Bought;

variable types

All variables in Java are strongly typed. In other words, you must declare the type of data each variable can hold. There are eight different types of data that can be used in Java with each type defining the type of data being accessed. Six of them are number related, one is character related, and the last is for true and false (Boolean). The syntax for declaring a variable is

```
type variableName;
```

integer data types

The integer data types are used for positive and negative whole numbers (Table 11-1).

Table 11-1, Java integer data types

data type	storage requirement	values
int	4 bytes	−2,147483,648 to 2,147483647
short	2 bytes	−32,768 to 32,767
long	8 bytes	−9,223,372,036,854,775,808L to 9,223,372,036,854,775,807L Long integers have the suffix of L
byte	1 byte	−128 to 127

Some examples in Java are:

```
int studentTickets;
short studentFees;
long studentTuition;
byte studentGrade;
```

floating-point data types

Floating-point data types are used for positive and negative numbers that may also have decimals (Table 11-2).

Table 11-2, Java floating-point data types

data type	storage requirement	values
float	4 bytes	±3.40282347E+38F (approx. 6–7 decimal digits)
double	8 bytes	±1.79769313486231570E+308 (15 significant digits)

Some examples are:

```
float salary;
double bGatesSalary;
```

character data type

The character (char) data type is used for variables that hold only one character (Table 11-3).

Table 11-3, Java character data type

data type	storage requirement	values
char	2 bytes	Character is stored using single quotes and stored as Unicode

An example of the char type is:

```
char studentMiddleInit;
```

Unicode

Unicode was mentioned earlier in the book. Recall that it is a 16-bit character set that uniquely identifies all characters

boolean data type

The Boolean data type is used for only one of two values: true or false. In Java you cannot associate a number with a Boolean value. In other languages such as Visual Basic, you use a numeric value of 1 to mean true and a value of 0 to mean false. Java simply relies upon a "true" or "false" value (Table 11-4).

Table 11-4, Java Boolean data type

data type	storage requirement	values
boolean	1 byte	true or false

An example is:

```
boolean deserveRaise;
```

when is a quote not a quote?

In Java, 'a' is *not* the same as "a". The value within the single quotes is a character, and the value between the double quotes is a string.

String data type

The char data type allows one character to be recognized and is contained within a single quotation mark. If you want more than one character then you need to use the string data type. For example, a variable of type string can be used to store a student's name, address, city, or other piece of information that is not a number and contains more than one character.

Strings are declared using double quotes. Even if there is only one character inside of a pair of double quotes, it is still considered a string.

String variables are declared using the String keyword:

```
String sName;
```

note

Notice that the String keyword has the first character capitalized while the other data types are all lowercase.

This statement declares a string variable called sName that contains no character but is considered an empty string.

```
String sName = "Joe Blow";
```

This statement declares a String variable called sName, which contains the string "Joe Blow".

concatenation – The process of combining or joining strings into one value

The plus(+) operator works a little differently with strings than it does with numeric values. It is a string ***concatenation*** operator, meaning that it takes one string and combines it with another:

```
String sFirstName = "Joe";
String sLastName = "Blow";
String sFullName;

sFullName = sLastName + ", " + sFirstName;
```

This statement takes the value stored in sFirstName (Joe) and adds it onto the string ", " and then adds it onto the value stored in sLastName (Blow) resulting in the variable sFullName containing "Blow, Joe".

Hungarian notation

Hungarian notation – Variable naming method that gives each variable an identifier at the beginning of the variable name describing the data type of the variable

Another standard exists for variable identifiers. It is called ***Hungarian notation,*** developed by Microsoft programmer, Charles Simonyi. He decided it would be helpful if the identifier contained a character at the beginning that described the data type contents. For instance, a variable named "bBirth" would be a Boolean value representing birth date. Table 11-5 shows Hungarian notation using Java.

Table 11-5, Java Hungarian notation

notation	data type	example
c	char	cMiddleInit
f	float	fSalary
i	int	iStudentCount
li	long	liSecondsLived
si	short	siStudentsPaid

Just because a variable is using Hungarian notation doesn't mean it has to contain the specified data value. It is only for the sake of readability! The Java compiler completely ignores the name when determining whether or not the programming instruction statements are valid. The only things it worries about are the naming rules, that reserved words are not used within a variable name, and that the variable is used correctly.

variable content

variable initialization or initializing – Providing an initial value when the variable is first declared

When a variable is declared you can immediately assign it a value through the use of the "=" sign. Assigning a value to a variable at declaration is called ***variable initialization*** or ***initializing*** that variable. You don't always have to initialize a variable (but sometimes if you don't, the programming language assigns it a default value).

better safe . . .

No matter which programming language you use, it is often wise to initialize your variables to some starting value rather than wondering if the system is going to initialize them. Whenever you program you should incorporate the principle, "Better safe than sorry."

For example, the following two statements use Hungarian notation to declare a variable called iStudentCount and then assign it a value of 456.

```
int iStudentCount;
iStudentCount = 456;
```

This can also be done on one line:

```
int iStudentCount = 456;
```

When you assign a value to a character variable, it should be enclosed in single quotes:

```
char cMiddleInit;
cMiddleInit = 'S';
```

Or if you prefer, you can combine them on one line:

```
char cMiddleInit = 'S';
```

When you assign a value to a String variable, it should be enclosed in double quotes:

```
String sMiddleName;
sMiddleName = "S";
```

Or if you prefer, you can combine them on one line:

```
String sMiddleName = "S";
```

note

Make sure you use blank lines and spaces to help make your source code more readable.

operators

operators – Symbols used to manipulate the data

In many high-level languages ***operators*** are used to manipulate the data contained in variables. The operators are classified by data type. One operator might work with numbers while another operator might be specifically designed to work with Boolean values.

math operators

The mathematical operators are: + – * / % for addition, subtraction, multiplication, division, and modulus. The % (modulus) operator returns the remainder when performing division. Figure 11-4 shows the results of statements using the addition, subtraction, multiplication, division, and modulus operators in Java.

mathematical shortcuts

There are also shortcuts you can use in Java for the binary arithmetic operators: +=, –=, *=, /=, and %=.

Table 11-6 shows all of the mathematical operators.

Figure 11-4, Java operators and results

Java statements	Results

int iFirstNum = 15;
int iSecondNum = 10;
int iResult = 0;
 	
iResult = iFirstNum + iSecondNum;
	iResult =
	25

int iFirstNum = 15;
int iSecondNum = 10;
int iResult = 0;
 	
iResult = iFirstNum - iSecondNum;
	iResult =
	5

int iFirstNum = 15;
int iSecondNum = 10;
int iResult = 0;
 	
iResult = iFirstNum * iSecondNum;
	iResult =
	150

int iFirstNum = 15;
int iSecondNum = 10;
int iResult = 0;
 	
iResult = iFirstNum / iSecondNum;
	iResult =
	1

int iFirstNum = 15;
int iSecondNum = 10;
int iResult = 0;
 	
iResult = iFirstNum % iSecondNum;
	iResult =
	5

Table 11-6, Mathematical operators

operator	description
+	addition
–	subtraction
/	division
%	modulus or remainder
*	multiplication
+=	addition and then assignment
–=	subtraction and then assignment
*=	multiplication and then assignment
/=	division and then assignment
%=	modulus and then assignment

For example,

```
int iFirstNum = 15;
int iSecondNum = 10;

iFirstNum += iSecondNum;
```

results in the variable iFirstNum receiving a value of 25. It is the same as typing:

```
iFirstNum = iFirstNum + iSecondNum;
```

The shortcuts perform the first symbol's action and then assigns the result to the variable listed on the left side of the symbol. The statement,

```
iFirstNum += iSecondNum;
```

takes the value of iFirstNum and adds it to the value of iSecondNum. That is the plus (+) sign of the shortcut. The equals (=) sign informs the system to take the result of the addition operation and assign it back to the variable on the left side of the symbol. In this example, the variable iFirstNum receives the result of the two values added.

The shortcuts are handy because they cut down on keystrokes, but some programmers do not like them because they feel it can hurt the readability of the source code.

increment and decrement operators

Two of the most common programming instructions you use are incrementing or decrementing the value in a variable. Java provides increment and decrement operators that perform this task without having to type out the entire statement.

For example, the ++ operator takes the value of a variable and adds 1 to it (called "incrementing"). The -- operator, or decrement, subtracts 1 from the value of the variable.

```
int iCount = 5;
int iResult;

iResult = ++iCount;
```

The increment operator takes the value stored in the iCount variable and adds 1 to it and stores the value of 6 in the iResult variable.

The decrement operator takes the value stored in the iCount variable and subtracts 1 from it and stores the value of 4 in the iResult variable:

```
int iCount = 5;
int iResult;

iResult = --iCount;
```

There are two types of increment and decrement operators: pre- and post-.

The pre- operator places the ++ or -- operator before the variable name. Having the operator in front of the variable name informs the system that the first thing that should happen on that line of source code is the increment or decrement:

· Preincrement: ++variable
· Predecrement: --variable

The post- operator places the ++ or -- operator after the variable name. Having the operator after the variable name informs the system that the very last thing that should happen on that line of source code is the increment or decrement:

· Postincrement: variable++
· Postdecrement: variable--

See how this works. Consider the following preincrement example:

```
int iCount = 5;
int iResult = 0;

iResult = ++iCount;
```

"pre" is rude

Remember that pre has the letter "r" in it, which stands for "rude"—meaning that it always goes first. No matter where it is located in the line of source code, the pre- operator is executed first. It butts in front of anything else on the line.

"post" is polite

Remember that post has the letters "po" in it which stand for "polite," meaning that it always lets everything else on the line of source code go first. No matter where it is located in the line of source code, the post- operator is executed last.

In this example, the variables are initialized, and then the variable iCount is incremented to the value of 6, which is then assigned to the variable iResult. Here's another example of the pre- operator:

```
int iCount = 5;
int iResult = 0;

iResult = ++iCount + 10;
```

In this example, after the variables are initialized the very next thing that happens, because the pre- operator is being used, is the preincrement of the variable iCount to 6, which is then added to 10 and stored to iResult (16).

Now consider this postincrement example:

```
int iCount = 5;
int iResult = 0;

iResult = iCount++ + 10;
```

Since the post- operator is being used, the first thing that happens is the addition between the variable iCount with the value of 5 and the number 10. This sum of 15 is then stored in the variable iResult. After everything else is completed on the line, the postincrement of the variable iCount occurs, thus changing it to a value of 6.

relational operators

The main functionality of relational operators is to compare values. The Java relational operators are listed in Table 11-7.

Table 11-7, Java relational operators

operator	meaning
!=	not equal to
<	less than
>	greater than
<=	less than or equal to
>=	greater than or equal to
= =	equals

> **no strings attached**
>
> The == operator is a comparison operator, but it should *never* be used to compare one string to another. If you use the == operator on strings, it compares whether one string points to the same memory location as another string. Instead, use the equals() method associated with any variable that you have declared as a string, as in this example:
>
> String sFirst = "Math";
>
> String sSecond = "Physics";
>
> Results:
>
> sFirst.equals(sSecond) would result in a false

***expression** – A programming statement that returns a value when executed*

To illustrate these operators, assume the following variable declarations and initializations:

```
int iFirstNum = 15;
int iSecondNum = 10;
```

iFirstNum > iSecondNum would result in a true

iFirstNum < iSecondNum would result in a false

iFirstNum != iSecondNum would result in a true

After making these comparisons or relations, you can use the result to determine what other action you want to take within the program. You will learn more about the flow of the program later in this chapter.

logical operators

The main function of logical operators is to build a truth table when comparing expressions. An ***expression*** is simply a programming statement that when executed returns a value. The expressions usually also use relational operators to compare variable contents or values. The Java logical operators are provided in Table 11-8.

Table 11-8, Java logical operators

operator	meaning
!	not
&&	and
||	or

You learned about truth tables in Chapter 3, "Computer Architecture."

Table 11-9 shows how the logical operators might be implemented within a program given the following variables:

```
int iFirstNum = 15;
int iSecondNum = 10;
int iThirdNum = 20;
int iFourthNum = 15;
```

Table 11-9, Sample Boolean expressions

expression	value	explanation
(iFirstNum >= iSecondNum) && (iThirdNum >= iFourthNum)	T and T equals T	(15 >= 10) and (20 >= 15)
(iFirstNum <= iSecondNum) && (iThirdNum >= iFourthNum)	F and T equals F	(15 <= 10) and (20 >= 15)
(iFirstNum == iSecondNum) && (iThirdNum == iFourthNum)	F and F equals F	(15 == 10) and (20 == 15)
(iFirstNum != iSecondNum) && (iThirdNum != iFourthNum)	T and T equals T	(15 != 10) and (20 != 15)
(iFirstNum >= iSecondNum) || (iThirdNum >= iFourthNum)	T or T equals T	(15 >= 10) or (20 >= 15)
(iFirstNum <= iSecondNum) || (iThirdNum >= iFourthNum)	F or T equals T	(15 <= 10) or (20 >= 15)
(iFirstNum == iSecondNum) || (iThirdNum == iFourthNum)	F or F equals F	(15 == 10) or (20 == 15)
(iFirstNum != iSecondNum) || (iThirdNum != iFourthNum)	T or T equals T	(15 != 10) or (20 != 15)

precedence

The order in which the operators appear can determine the output. For instance:

```
2 + 3 * 4
```

outputs 14, *not* 20!

precedence – The order in which something is executed; those symbols that have a higher precedence are executed before those with a lower precedence

Even though it would seem that 2 + 3 (or 5) times 4 results in the answer 20, the answer is really 3 * 4 (12) + 2, which is 14. Why? It is because the operators have a ***precedence*** or level of hierarchy. In other words, certain operations are performed before other operations. In this case, multiplication takes precedence and is performed before addition. Figure 11-5 shows the order of precedence of the operators discussed, with the highest (first performed) at the top of the pyramid.

Figure 11-5, Order of relational and mathematical precedence

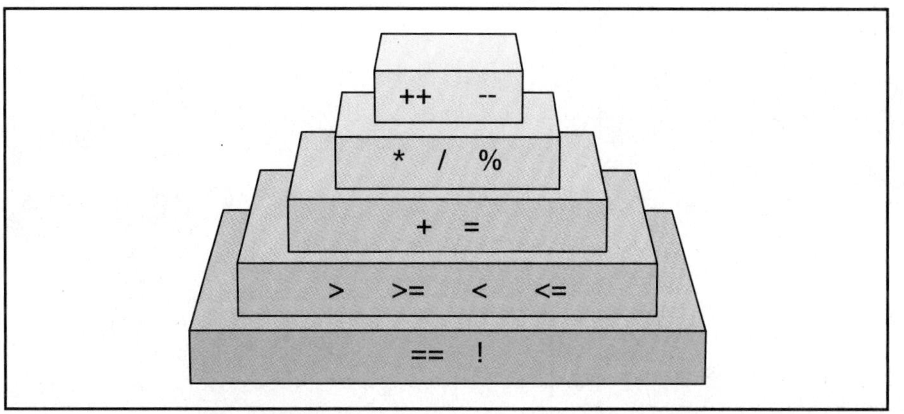

note Remember that parentheses have the highest precedence and should be evaluated before any other operator.

Using the order of precedence, look at the following examples:

(2 + 3) * 4	outputs 20
2 − 5 * 2	outputs −8

Java control structures and program flow

control structure – An instruction that dictates the order in which the statements in a program are executed

All high-level languages including Java use a variety of control structures. A *control structure* is an element that dictates the flow of the program and enforces modular structured programming.

If you don't follow proper structured programming practices, your programs can end up looking like "spaghetti code," that is, source code that breaks the modular structure and flow of the application (Figure 11-6). Instead of a controlled flow of execution, the program flow leaps from one area to another area and is extremely hard to follow. In fact, trying to maintain a spaghetti code application is like trying to empty a bathtub full of water using a sieve. Just imagine trying to find the beginning and ending part of a spaghetti noodle in a bowl without moving the noodles. You can't follow the flow!

one bite at a time

Modular structured programming requires that you break down a project into smaller, more manageable pieces. Why? Because it makes the program easier to design, maintain, and debug. Just remember the old saying "How do you eat an elephant? One bite at a time." If you try to digest the whole thing at one sitting you will be unsuccessful.

There are four types of control structures found in high-level programming languages. They are:

- Invocation
- Top down
- Selection
- Repetition

eliminate the "go to"

Bud the programmer was hired by a medical software company to maintain an in-house report-writing program. After two weeks of trying to unravel the source code, he still could not figure out the flow of the application because of the many "go to"s that jumped from one place in the program to another in a tangled mess. He finally went to his supervisor, who looked at the program and decided that the best solution was to rewrite the application. Had the original programmer(s) properly used programming control structures, the company could have saved a great deal of money and time in application development and maintenance.

Figure 11-6, Spaghetti code makes your program harder to maintain and debug

Each control structure performs a specific task and is commonly used throughout an application. In fact, the control structures work together and can be nested within other control structures.

Java and other high-level languages support these basic control structures. If implemented correctly, these structures provide the tools to create a program that incorporates good control flow. Even with all of the tools available, the programmer can still abuse the flow of control and write a horrible program.

invocation

Invocation is the act of calling something. Every Java program has a block of code called "main" that tells the operating system it is the starting point. The block of code is called a *function*. A function performs a task and can, if needed, return one value.

function – A block of source code that performs a task and can return a value

Consider the following source code saved in a file called Save_Ferris.java:

```
public class Save_Ferris {
     public static void main(String[] args) {
            System.out.println("I could have been the
            Walrus!");
     }
}
```

note Make sure you use the standard Java naming convention by capitalizing the first character of each word in the function name (except for function *main*).

The first line of the program

```
public class Save_Ferris {
```

is a statement to the compiler declaring that the following source code is all part of the Save_Ferris Java program. The curly brace "{" indicates that there is a block of code associated with the Save_Ferris Java program. If there is a beginning curly brace then there should be an ending curly brace. The word "public" tells the Java compiler that this source code can be seen by any other source code that wants to use it and is included in the same program. The term "class" identifies what type of source code is being used.

note You will learn more about classes later in this chapter but for now, it will suffice to say it is a program.

The next line of code promotes modular programming by breaking down parts of the program into areas.

```
public static void main(String[] args) {
```

scope – Where something can be seen and what other source code can see and use it

This area of code or name of the function is called "main" and is the starting point for any Java program. Once again, the word public indicates the *scope* of the source code. Scope refers to where something can be seen. Public scope means that it is visible for any other source code to use.

The word "static" indicates that the function belongs to a class. In this example, the main() function belongs to the Save_Ferris class.

note As you learn more about object-oriented programming you will come to realize that the functions in a class are really called "methods." But for now, use the term "functions."

the Java *main* function

The Java *main* function does not return a value and must be declared to return *void*. Other languages such as C allow *main* to return a value back to the operating system.

The keyword "void" indicates that the main source code is not going to return anything to the operating system when it has completed executing. It still prints things on the screen, but it does not return anything back to the operating system to use.

parameter – *A received value assigned to a variable that is used by a block of source code*

The words inside of the parentheses "String[] args" is used as a receiver when the program is executed. Whenever a Java program is executed it can receive *parameters* or values. The parameters are passed as values simply by typing them on the same line after the Java program name. For example, if you wanted to pass the number 10 to a Java program called "hello" you type

```
C:\>hello 10
```

This executes the Java program and passes the value of 10 to the variable called args of type String.

top down (also called sequence)

The top-down control structure is implemented when the program statements are executed in series, from the top line to the bottom line one at a time. The execution of the statements is carried out one after another.

For instance, look at the following source code in the file Add_It_Up.java for an example of the top-down control structure.

```
public class Add_It_Up {
     public static void main(String[] args) {
            int iFirstNum = 15;
            int iSecondNum = 10;
            int iThirdNum = 20;
            int iFourthNum = 15;
            int iResult = 0;

            iResult = iFirstNum + iSecondNum;
            System.out.print("15 + 10 = ");
            System.out.println(iResult);

            iResult = iThirdNum - iFourthNum;
            System.out.print("20 - 15 = ");
            System.out.println(iResult);

            System.out.println("Have a nice day!");
            }
}
```

note Don't forget to always close the block of code with the curly brace "}"! For each opening brace you need a closing brace.

compiling the program

In order to compile and run your Java programs, make sure that the public class name matches your file name where you are saving the source code and has a file extension of "java." To make matters simpler, you can use the following statements on the Java programs you create in this book's exercises.

public class *Java_Name*{

public static void main(String[] args) {

put your source code here}

}

Whatever name you use for "Java_Name" should be the same name as your source code file. After typing in the source code, you compile the Java program by typing

javac *Java_Name*.java

where Java_Name is the name of the source code file. You can now execute the program by typing in "java" and the name of the source code file without the file extension.

java Java_Name

The output generated by this Java code is:

```
15 + 10 = 25
20 - 15 = 5
Have a nice day!
```

In a top-down sequence, the first statement to be executed is the first line in the program.

In the example, the "int iFirstNum = 15;" statement is the first statement executed. Next, control is passed on to the next line that declares and initializes the variable iSecondNum. This process continues until all of the variables are declared and initialized. Then the mathematical operations begin. First, the contents of iFirstNum are added to iSecondNum and stored to iResult through the line "iResult = iFirstNum + iSecondNum;". Second, the system then prints a string of characters to the output device (usually the monitor) through the line "System.out.print("15 + 10 = ");". The flow of the program continues downward until there are no more lines left to process.

Each of the statements is executed in sequential order starting with the first line and continuing until the last line is processed. This is the most common form of programming control structure, found in every programming language.

The top-down control structure is implemented by typing in statements that do not call other pieces of source code but simply execute the current line and proceed to the next line.

Before continuing with the other control structures, it is important to show you how control statements or other blocks of code can be set off so they are easier to identify, and introduce a couple Java statements (output and input) that can make the code in the rest of the sections easier to understand.

blocks of code

A sequence of several statements can be enclosed with an opening and closing brace. This forms a single block statement meaning that the enclosed statements are related to each other in functionality. This helps make your program more readable and also more accurate. You will read later in this chapter that leaving out braces can cause your program to function incorrectly.

```
{
statement 1;
statement 2;
}
```

There are other times when the braces are required. They are most often used when working with control structures such as invocation, selection, and repetition.

output data

As you can probably surmise, you can output data to the current output device (i.e., monitor) through the use of the System.out.print() statement. System.out has two methods to output ("print") data to the output device:

```
System.out.print(expression);
System.out.println(expression);
```

insertion point – Where the cursor is ready to display data

The print() method prints the evaluated expression or string but leaves the current *insertion point* at the end of the data being output. In other words, it is like writing words on a piece of paper but keeping the pencil ready to write more on the same line if told to do so.

The println() method prints the evaluated expression or string and when completed, moves the insertion point to the next line. This method is like writing a line, then picking up the pencil and moving it to the beginning of the next available line on the paper.

note Remember the word "method"! You will soon realize how appropriately this word is used as you learn about objects and classes.

You can output all types of data. Consider the statements listed in Table 11-10.

Table 11-10, Sample Java output statements

statement	output
System.out.println(15 + 10);	25
System.out.println(15 + iFirstNum);	30
System.out.println("Computer Scientists have better memory!");	Computer Scientists have better memory!
System.out.println("Computer Scientists \nhave better memory!");	Computer Scientists have better memory!
System.out.println("iFirstNum + 15 = " + (15 + iFirstNum));	IFirstNum + 15 = 30

There are a couple of things you need to notice. The first thing is the "\n". In Java, this is called the newline escape sequence. It tells the system to move to the next line and acts as if someone pressed Enter on the keyboard. It moves down a line and to the far left. Whatever follows the sequence continues to print starting at the new location.

Notice that you can concatenate or join values. The last statement joins a string with an expression in the line "(iFirstNum + 15 = " + (15 + iFirstNum)). System.out is very flexible in printing data to the output device and will most definitely become a useful tool throughout your Java programs.

input data

Displaying data is great, but wouldn't it be nice to also get data from the user so that you do not have to manually change values of a variable within your program? Java provides input statements to read data from the current input device (usually the keyboard). As System.out provides several methods to display data, it only makes sense that there is a System.in to provide methods for retrieving data from the current input device.

In order to get input from System.in, you must first create some new variables. These variables are not explained here, but just trust that you need them if you want to read strings from the keyboard. The variables are responsible for reading characters from the input stream (keyboard) and then putting all of the characters read one by one into another variable that acts as a memory buffer holding the newly entered string. This value can then be assigned to your string variable that you have declared by making a call to the readLine() method. Consider the following program written using Sun's Java environment. The file that contains all of this information is called MyProg1.java. You can create your Java program source code files using any text editor. After typing in your program, save the file with the name of MyProg1.java to distinguish it as a Java program and to ensure that the file name is the same as the class name. (You learn more about classes later in the chapter.)

typical typos

One of the biggest mistakes programmers make is typing wrong characters or misspelling words. Whenever a program does not compile successfully, start by checking that words are spelled correctly and that the case matches.

```
//Sample Java Program #1
//Lines that start with // are comment lines
//The Java compiler ignores comment lines
//Normally you should put information about the program
//including your name in the top comment section

//Java has many class libraries for performing common
//tasks
// java.io is the library for the input and output
import java.io.*;

//the class statement defines this program class
//the name here MUST match the file name, ie.
//MyProg1.java
public class MyProg1 {
```

```
//this statement is required exactly as written
public static void main(String[] args) {

      //these two lines establish objects
      //to allow input from the keyboard and output
      //to the console
      InputStreamReader charReader = new
      InputStreamReader(System.in);
      BufferedReader keyboard = new
      BufferedReader(charReader);

      //declare strings to hold the names that are
      //input and output
      String sFirstName = "";
      String sLastName = "";
      String sFullName = "";

      //program statements should always be
      //included in
      //a "try/catch" block
      try
      {
            //this statement prompts the user to
            //enter a first name
            System.out.print("Enter the first
            name: ");

            //and then reads the name entered from
            //the keyboard
            sFirstName = keyboard.readLine();

            //same thing for the last name
            System.out.print("Enter the last
            name: ");
            sLastName = keyboard.readLine();

            //this statement combines the first and
            //last names and puts the combined
            //names into a new field
            sFullName = sFirstName + " " +
            sLastName;

            //These statements display the entered
            //names and the concatenated names
            System.out.println("Firstname is: "
            + sFirstName);
```

```
                    System.out.println("Lastname is: "
                    + sLastName);
                    System.out.println("Full name is: "
                    + sFullName);
            }
            //this section catches and displays
            //any errors that occur when the program is
            //running
            catch (IOException e){
                    System.out.println("Error " +
                    e.getMessage());
            }
    }
}
```

Java 5 offers the Scanner class which can be used to gather input from the keyboard.

This source code reads two string values from the keyboard and assigns them to two different variables. Then it combines or concatenates those variables with a space " " between them and prints all of the variables to the output device.

This and the other Java programs shown in this chapter contain many new elements that you have not seen thus far in Java. A brief explanation is given in the program listing, but detailed coverage is beyond the scope of this introductory text. For those of you "chomping at the bit" to become Java experts, there are a plethora of Web sites with free Java tutorials that open the doors to a vast knowledge of Java programming. Just go to your favorite search engine and enter "Java tutorial."

Now, back to the control structures. The rest of the control structures do something to change the flow of your basic top-down program. That is, instead of just executing statements one after the other, the invocation, selection, and repetition structures direct the flow of execution to another block of code or location in the program, and generally provide for a way to return control back to the top-down structure.

more on invocation

Invocation is the act of calling something or someone. Java implements invocation through the use of calling functions and methods. You have already learned that a function performs a task and can return a value. A method is a glorified name for a function that belongs to a piece of code called a class. Methods will be discussed later in this chapter, but suffice it to say that the invocation control structure executes the statements contained in a function or method. In other words, when a function name is encountered, the system passes control to the first line of source code contained within that function. The function completes the execution of all of its statements and returns control to the original calling point.

For example, the equals() method associated with String variables returns a Boolean value determining whether two strings are equal. When used, the system passes control (although you don't see it happen) to the source code associated with the equals() method, executes the statements, does the comparison and then returns the Boolean value.

The following source listing combines the top-down and invocation control structures. The variable declaration and initialization statements are executed in sequential order (top-down), and the statement "bCompare = sName.equals(sNewName);" is an example of invocation, because it calls the equals() method.

```
public class Combining_Strings {
    public static void main(String[] args) {
        String sName;
        String sNewName;
        boolean bCompare;

        sName = "Mary Lamb";
        sNewName = "Joe Blow";

        bCompare = sName.equals(sNewName);

        System.out.println(sName);
        System.out.println(sNewName);
        System.out.println(bCompare);
    }
}
```

Once all of the statements have been executed in the equals() method, control is returned to the assignment statement placing the value returned from the method in the variable called "bCompare." Control is then passed to the next statement, continuing the top-down control structure.

As in this example, more than one control structure can be combined in your source code. In fact, it is common to see all four control structures in a program.

The invocation control structure is implemented whenever the same module of code is executed more than once in an application. The code that is repetitively executed should be placed in a function or method and then called whenever it is needed. The reason for this is to cut down on the amount of code a programmer would have to type thus saving time and money. It also makes the program more modular and structured.

Learning more about functions, procedures, and methods will be an important part of learning Java and continuing your education in computer science.

selection

Up to now, you have learned that statements can be executed from one line to the next in sequential order. You have also learned that you can execute other statements kept in other areas of the application by making a call (invocation) to the area name. Sometimes, however, you need the program to make a choice (selection) depending on a value or situation.

Making and evaluating selections in a program is a standard part of most programs that you will write. They are used all of the time! In this example, if the job level of the employee is equal to "Manager" then the salary increase is equal to the salary times .08. If the job level is not equal to "Manager", then use a .03 salary factor. The program has to determine what the job level is and then perform specific code based upon that job level.

Salary Increase:

```
If Job Level = "Manager" then
     salary = salary * 1.08
else
     salary = salary * 1.03
```

Remember the algorithm for allowing a user to convert Fahrenheit to Celsius and Celsius to Fahrenheit? This also involves selection: if the user selects Celsius, one thing happens; if the user selects Fahrenheit, something else happens.

```
Convert to Celsius:

     Ask the user for a temperature in Fahrenheit
             Apply the entered temperature to the formula
             Celsius Temp = (5/9) * (Fahrenheit Temp - 32)
             Display the result saying Fahrenheit Temp
             ## converted to Celsius is XX

Convert to Fahrenheit:

             Ask the user for a temperature in Celsius
             If the Value entered is numerical
                     Apply the entered temperature to the
                     formula Fahrenheit Temp = ((9/5) *
                     Celsius Temp) + 32
                     Display the result saying Celsius Temp
                     ## converted to Fahrenheit is XX
```

If this pseudocode were implemented using Java, it would look something like this:

```
//Converting_Temps
//Lines that start with // are comment lines
//The Java compiler ignores comment lines
//Normally you should put information about the program
//including your name in the top comment section

//Java has many class libraries for performing common
//tasks
//java.io is the library for the input and output
//so in order to do keyboard I/O the library must be
//imported

import java.io.*;

//the class statement defines this program class
//the name here MUST match the file name, ie.
//MyProg2.java
public class Converting_Temps {

//this statement is required exactly as written
public static void main(String[] args) {

     //these two lines establish objects
     //to allow input from the keyboard and output to the
     //console
     InputStreamReader charReader = new
     InputStreamReader(System.in);
     BufferedReader keyboard = new
     BufferedReader(charReader);

     //declare strings to hold the input from the
     //keyboard
     //and double precision floating point variables
     //to hold the temperatures
     String sInput = "";
     double dCelsius = 0.0;
     double dFahrenheit = 0.0;
     String sChoice = "";

     //program statements should always be included in
     //a "try/catch" block
     try
     {
            //this statement prompts the user to choose
            //which conversion to perform
```

```
System.out.print("Enter F for Fahrenheit to
Celsius OR ");
System.out.print("Enter C for Celsius to
Fahrenheit: ");
sChoice = keyboard.readLine();

if (sChoice.equals("F"))
{
       //this statement prompts the user to
       //enter a Fahrenheit temperature
       //input from the keyboard comes in as a
       //text string
       System.out.print("Enter the Fahrenheit
       temperature: ");
       sInput = keyboard.readLine();

       //and must be converted into a floating
       //point number
       //so that it can be used in a
       //calculation
       dFahrenheit =
       Double.parseDouble(sInput);

       //this statement calculates the Celsius
       //temperature
       dCelsius = (5.0/9.0) * (dFahrenheit -
       32.0);

       System.out.println(sInput + " converted
       from F to C is " + dCelsius);
}
else
{
       //this statement prompts the user to
       //enter a Celsius temperature
       //input from the keyboard comes in as a
       //text string
       System.out.print("Enter the Celsius
       temperature: ");
       sInput = keyboard.readLine();

       //and must be converted into a floating
       //point number so that it can be
       //used in a calculation
       dCelsius = Double.parseDouble(sInput);
```

```
                    //this statement calculates the
                    //Fahrenheit temperature
                    dFahrenheit = ((9.0/5.0) *
                    dCelsius) + 32.0;

                    System.out.println(sInput + " converted
                    from C to F is " + dFahrenheit);
            }
        }
        //this section catches and displays
        //any errors that occur when the program is running
        catch (IOException e){
        System.out.println("Error " + e.getMessage());
        }
        }
}
```

note

The variable dTemp is of type Double. Because the readLine only reads strings, the input value in the variable sTemp needs to be converted to a double. This is accomplished using the Double.parseDouble() method which accepts a string value and returns a double value.

Java implements the selection control structure through the use of the *if*, *if-else*, *if-else-if*, and *switch* statements.

if statement

You implement the *if* and *if-else* statement every day of your life. There is always a situation where a decision must be made. Depending on your decision, certain results occur. If you choose what is behind door number one, you win a new car. If you choose what is behind door number two, you win a donkey. For every choice there is a result.

The syntax for the *if* statement is:

```
if (condition)
    {
    one or more statements;
    }
```

You do not have to put the statements within a block if there is only one statement associated with the *if* control structure, but it is better to be safe than sorry.

ABCs of blocks

One big mistake new programmers often make is having more than one statement associated with an *if* control structure, but forgetting to group the statements together in a block. The result is the first statement is dependent upon the *if* control structure and the rest always execute.

note

A good rule to follow is to always use blocks when working with selection control structures!

11

The condition in the syntax is an expression that returns either a true or a false value. If needed, you can add an *else* part to the control structure to perform some other functionality if the *if* control structure evaluates to a value of false.

```
if (condition)
      {
      one or more statements;
      }
else
      {
      one or more statements;
      }
```

If the expression evaluates to true then the system executes the nested series of commands located below the *if* statement up to the *else* keyword. If the expression evaluates to false then the system executes the nested statement listed below the *else* statement up to the closing brace "}".

In the program just shown (Converting_Temps), the system checks to see what type of value the user entered and stored in the sChoice variable. The contents of the variable are compared against the string "F". If the user entered a "F" then the system asks the user to enter in the temperature in Fahrenheit. *else*, if the user did not enter an "F" it prompts for Celsius.

```
if (sChoice.equals("F"))
{
      //this statement prompts the user to enter a
      //Fahrenheit temperature
      //input from the keyboard comes in as a text string
      System.out.print("Enter the Fahrenheit
      temperature: ");
      sInput = keyboard.readLine();

      //and must be converted into a floating point number
      //so that it can be used in a calculation
      dFahrenheit = Double.parseDouble(sInput);

      //this statement calcuates the Celsius temperature
      dCelsius = (5.0/9.0) * (dFahrenheit - 32.0);
```

```
        System.out.println(sInput + " converted from F to C
        is " + dCelsius);
    }
    else
    {
        //this statement prompts the user to enter a Celsius
        //temperature
        //input from the keyboard comes in as a text string
        System.out.print("Enter the Celsius temperature: ");
        sInput = keyboard.readLine();

        //and must be converted into a floating point number
        //so that it can be used in a calculation
        dCelsius = Double.parseDouble(sInput);

        //this statement calcuates the Fahrenheit
        //temperature
        dFahrenheit = ((9.0/5.0) * dCelsius) + 32.0;

        System.out.println(sInput + " converted from C to F
        is " + dFahrenheit);
    }
```

The *if* statement is implemented anytime you need a series of statements to be executed depending on a certain expression.

There is a problem with the *if* control structure listed above. What if the user presses the "G" key? Then the system assumes that you want to convert from Celsius to Fahrenheit. Is that what the user wanted to do? Is that what you prompted the user to enter?

Remember that whenever you write a program you should imagine the end user as computer illiterate. Plan for the worst. In this situation, the user could enter whatever they wanted instead of the "F" or "C". The program should *only* perform the calculations if the user enters the correct choice. The way to resolve this dilemma is by adding an *else-if* to the *if* control structure. In fact, this also provides a way to inform the user that the valid choices are "F" or "C".

```
    if (sChoice.equals("F"))
    {
        //this statement prompts the user to enter a
        //Fahrenheit temperature
        //input from the keyboard comes in as a text string
        System.out.print("Enter the Fahrenheit
        temperature: ");
        sInput = keyboard.readLine();
```

```
        //and must be converted into a floating point number
        //so that it can be used in a calculation
        dFahrenheit = Double.parseDouble(sInput);

        //this statement calculates the Celsius temperature
        dCelsius = (5.0/9.0) * (dFahrenheit - 32.0);

    System.out.println(sInput + " converted from F to C is
    " + dCelsius);
    }
    else if (sChoice.equals("C"))
    {
        //this statement prompts the user to enter a Celsius
        //temperature
        //input from the keyboard comes in as a text string
        System.out.print("Enter the Celsius temperature: ");
        sInput = keyboard.readLine();

        //and must be converted into a floating point number
        //so that it can be used in a calculation
        dCelsius = Double.parseDouble(sInput);

        //this statement calcuates the Fahrenheit
        //temperature
        dFahrenheit = ((9.0/5.0) * dCelsius) + 32.0;

        System.out.println(sInput + " converted from C to F
        is " + dFahrenheit);
    }
    else
    {
        System.out.println("Your valid choices are F or C");
    }
```

The *if-else-if* provides a way to perform certain blocks of code depending on the state of a variable within the program while it is running. It is very easy to implement and makes your program more flexible in handling data and processing information.

switch statement

nesting – Putting one control structure inside of another

As you can see in the previous program listing, putting one *if* control structure inside of another *if* can decrease the readability of the source code. Putting one control structure inside of another is called ***nesting***.

There is a need for a statement that allows many options to be tested but at the same time group blocks of code to be executed depending on the results. In Java this statement is the *switch* statement.

The syntax for the *switch* statement is:

```
switch (expression)
{
case value_1 :
     statement_1;
     break;
case value_2 :
     statement_2;
     break;
case value_3 :
     statement_3;
     break;
default :
     statement_4;
}
```

A *switch* statement allows you to test the value of an expression and, depending on that value, to jump to some location within the *switch* statement. The expression must be either integer or character based and is evaluated and then the system begins searching down all of the *case* statement values trying to find a match. If it finds a match then all of the *case* statements are executed. That is why you need to put a *break* statement at the end of each case. This tells the system to quit processing all of the *case* statements and send control to the end of the *switch.* Through the use of the *break* statement you can make sure the system only performs the case that it matches.

note You should not use the *switch* statement to compare string data types.

```
//Java has many class libraries for performing common
//tasks
//java.io is the library for the input and output
//so in order to do keyboard I/O the library must be
//imported

import java.io.*;

public class Switch_Statement {
```

```
//this statement is required exactly as written
public static void main(String[] args) {

     //these two lines establish objects
     //to allow input from the keyboard and output to the
     //console
     InputStreamReader charReader = new
     InputStreamReader(System.in);
     BufferedReader keyboard = new
     BufferedReader(charReader);

     //character variable to hold the input
     char cInput = '';

     //program statements should always be included in
     //a "try/catch" block
     try
     {
            //this statement prompts the user to choose
            //which conversion to perform
            System.out.print("Enter the letter grade: ");

            //the (char) statement converts the data
            //coming back from the keyboard
            //to a character value
            cInput = (char) keyboard.read();

            System.out.println("");

            switch (cInput)
            {
            case 'A' :
                   System.out.println("You get an A");
                   System.out.println("Great job!");
                   break;
            case 'B' :
                   System.out.println("You get a B");
                   System.out.println("Nice job!");
                   break;
            case 'C' :
                   System.out.println("You get a C");
                   System.out.println("Good enough!");
                   break;
            default :
```

```
                    System.out.println("You get a D");
                    System.out.println("See you next
                    semester!");
               }
          //this section catches and displays
          //any errors that occur when the program is running
          catch (IOException e){
          System.out.println("Error " + e.getMessage());
          }
     }
}
```

If no match is found then the statement(s) for the default section are executed. The default section is optional, but it is wise to have some message be displayed stating that no match was found.

If more than two values execute the same block of code you can simply place them one on top of the other in a top-down structure. For example, if you wanted to perform the same code if the value was "A" or "B" or "C" then you could do:

```
switch (cInput)
{
case 'A' :
case 'B' :
case 'C' :
               System.out.println("You get a(n) " + cInput);
               System.out.println("You passed!");
               break;
default :
               System.out.println("You get a " + cInput);
               System.out.println("Do NOT pass go and go
               directly to jail!");
}
```

The *switch* statement makes your source code more readable and maintainable as compared to a convoluted *if-else-if* statement.

```
if (cInput == 'A')
{
     System.out.println("You get an A");
     System.out.println("Great job!");
}
else if (cInput == 'B')
{
     System.out.println("You get a B");
     System.out.println("Nice job!");
}
```

```
else if (cInput == 'C')
{
     System.out.println("You get a C");
     System.out.println("Good enough!");
}
else
{
     System.out.println("You get a D");
     System.out.println("See you next semester!");
}
```


note Note that by using the *if* statement, you did not need to also use *break* statements to stop the testing of conditions.

Just like the *if* statement, the *switch* statement is implemented anytime you need a series of statements to be executed depending on a certain expression. The difference between *if* and *switch* is that the *switch* statement is used when there are many different expressions to validate, and the *if* statement is more commonly used to validate one expression.

repetition (looping)

repetition – The process of doing some action again, from one to many times

The last control structure is ***repetition***, and it is used when a series of source code is to be repeated. It is often referred to as looping and is commonly used when processing databases or when you want some action to be performed one or many times.

Java implements repetition through the use of the *for*, *while*, and the *do-while* statements.

for statement

When you want to repeat a series of statements a known number of times, you use the *for* statement. The syntax for the statement is:

```
for (variable declaration; expression;
increment/decrement)
{
     statement(s);
}
```

The variable declaration is a variable declared and initialized by the programmer. One of the biggest oversights in working with the *for* loop is to forget to declare the variable used as the counter. All that is needed to accomplish this is to declare a variable with a statement similar to "int iCount".

note **You can also declare the variable within the *for* statement. That variable then becomes visible only within the *for* statement. Once the *for* statement is over, the variable is gone.**

The starting value is the number used to initialize the variable used as the counter and to inform the system of the beginning value used in the loop. The expression is used to check whether or not the statements inside the *for* loop should be executed and act as an ending boundary for processing the loop. The increment/decrement part of the statement is where you either increment or decrement the variable being used as the counter.

```
public class For_Loop {
      public static void main(String[] args) {
             int iCount;
             for (iCount = 1; iCount <= 5; iCount++)
             {
             System.out.println("I am on number " +
             iCount);
             }
      }
}
```

The first *for* loop assigns the value 1 to the variable "iCount" using the "iCount − 1" statement and makes sure that it is less than or equal to the ending value of 5 using the "iCount <= 5" statement. The variable "iCount" is incremented by 1 using the "iCount++" statement so the numbers displayed on the console are 1 through 5.

OUTPUT:

```
I am on number 1
I am on number 2
I am on number 3
I am on number 4
I am on number 5
```

This next *for* loop program repeats the same process as the first loop but instead of using the increment value of 1, the increment statement informs the system to use an increment value of 2 through the use of the "iCount += 2" statement. The numbers displayed on the console are 1, 3, and 5.

```
public class For_Loop2 {
     public static void main(String[] args) {
            int iCount;
            for (iCount = 1; iCount <= 5; iCount+=2)
            {
            System.out.println("I am on number "
            + iCount);
            }
     }
}
```

This next *for* loop program repeats the same process but uses an increment value of −1. The starting value is 5 and the ending value is 1, so the numbers 5 through 1 are displayed on the console.

```
public class For_Loop3 {
     public static void main(String[] args) {
            int iCount;
            for (iCount = 5; iCount > 0; iCount--)
            {
            System.out.println("I am on number "
            + iCount);
            }
     }
}
```

Remember the post- and pre- operations for increment and decrement? They are commonly used when updating the variable used as the counter in the *for* loop. Be careful that you do not mistakenly also update the variable within your loop. It could cause serious consequences as shown in the source code below:

```
int iCount;
for (iCount = 1; iCount <= 5; iCount++)
{
     System.out.println("I am on number " + iCount++);
}
```

OUTPUT:

```
I am on number 1
I am on number 3
I am on number 5
```

Instead of the expected 1 through 5 being listed as the output, the numbers 1, 3, and 5 are displayed. This is because not only is the *for* loop incrementing the variable counter, but the statement within the *for* loop is also incrementing it.

while statement

The *while* statement can be used to process a series of statements for a certain number of times just like the *for* loop. The *while* is considered a precondition loop, meaning that the loop might not execute *at all* as the expression is evaluated before the statements within the loop are executed. The expression part of the statement is a Boolean expression returning a true or false value. If the condition is true then the commands contained between the *do* and *while* statements are executed. The execution process continues until the expression returns false. Here is the syntax of the *while* statement:

```
while (expression)
{
     statements;
}
```

The difference between *while* and *for* is that the *while* statement does not provide a specified area to update the counter. You are responsible for doing so.

```
public class While_Loop {
     public static void main(String[] args) {
            int iCount = 1;
            while (iCount <= 5)
            {
            System.out.println("I am on number " +
            iCount);
            iCount++;
            }
     }
}
```

OUTPUT:

```
I am on number 1
I am on number 2
I am on number 3
I am on number 4
I am on number 5
```

endless loops

One frequent mistake new programmers make when working with loops is forgetting to update the counter. Thus, the loop runs continuously and never stops.

endless loop* – *A segment of repetitious source code that never stops but instead continually repeats

The following source code is an example of an ***endless loop***. Notice that the counter variable iCount is never updated (incremented). Its value always remains 1, which is always less than 5 so the expression that controls the ending of the loop is never satisfied and the loop runs forever.

```
int iCount = 1;
while (iCount <= 5)
{
     System.out.println("I am on number " + iCount);
}
```

OUTPUT:

```
I am on number 1
I am on number 1
I am on number 1
I am on number 1
```

. . . and so on until you kill the program.

11

do/while statement

precondition loop – A loop that checks the expression before any of the source code contained within the loop is executed

The *for* and the *while* loops are considered ***precondition loops,*** meaning that the minimum number of times they execute is zero because the condition is checked before the source code contained in the loop is executed.

The *do-while* statement is another example of repetition and is used mainly when processing a table.

The syntax is:

```
do
{
     statement(s);
} while (expression);
```

postcondition loop – A loop that executes at least one time before the expression is evaluated

The *do-while* is considered a ***postcondition loop***, meaning that the loop executes *at least* one time before the expression is evaluated. The expression part of the statement is a Boolean expression returning a true or false value. If the condition is true, then the commands contained between the *do* and *while* statements are executed. The execution process continues until the expression returns false.

```
public class DoWhile_Loop {
     public static void main(String[] args) {
          int iCount = 1;
          do
          {
          System.out.println("I am on number " +
          iCount);
          } while (iCount++ < 5);
     }
}
```

OUTPUT:

```
I am on number 1
I am on number 2
I am on number 3
I am on number 4
I am on number 5
```

The execution of the loop begins by printing “I am on number 1”. The *do-while* expression is then evaluated to determine whether or not to repeat the loop. Then the variable iCount is incremented. Notice that the expression no longer checks to see if the variable iCount is <= to 5. Instead it checks to see if it is < 5. This is because the *do-while* loop is a postcondition loop and prints “I am on number 6” before determining that the variable iCount is indeed > 5 and exits the loop.

An important item to be aware of is whether or not you use the pre- or post-operator. Look at the same program using the preincrement operator instead of the postincrement:

```
public class DoWhile_Loop2 {
     public static void main(String[] args) {
            int iCount = 1;
            do
            {
            System.out.println("I am on number " +
            iCount);
            } while (++iCount < 5);
     }
}
```

OUTPUT:

```
I am on number 1
I am on number 2
I am on number 3
I am on number 4
```

The loop repeats one less time because the variable was incremented to a value of 5 *before* the expression was checked, thus ending the loop after the fourth output line.

Take a look at our Java program to convert from Celsius to Fahrenheit and from Fahrenheit to Celsius. The program has been modified to prompt the user to enter a temperature in Celsius that the system converts to Fahrenheit. This process continues until the user presses the “e” key to exit.

note Depending on which Java software package you use, the reserved words might appear in a different color, as you see in Converting_Temps2.java here.


```
//Sample Java Program Converting_Temps2

import java.io.*;
public class Converting_Temps2 {
   public static void main(String[] args) {

      InputStreamReader charReader = new
      InputStreamReader(System.in);
      BufferedReader keyboard = new
      BufferedReader(charReader);

      //declare strings to hold the input from the
      //keyboard
      //and double precision floating point variables
      //to hold the temperatures
      String strInput = "";
      double Celsius = 0.0;
      double Fahrenheit = 0.0;

      //program statements should always be included in
      //a "try/catch" block
      try
      {
         //this statement begins a loop
         do {
            //this statement prompts the user to enter a
            //Celsius temperature
            //input from the keyboard comes in as a text
            //string
            System.out.print("Enter the Celsius
            temperature ");
            System.out.print("or type e to exit: ");
            strInput = keyboard.readLine();

            //the if statement tests a condition, then only
            //executes the code in the block if the
            //condition is met
```

```
            if (!(strInput.equals("e")) &&
            !(strInput.equals("E"))) {
              //and must be converted into a floating
              //point number
              //so that it can be used in a calculation
              Celsius = Double.parseDouble(strInput);

              //this statement calculates the Fahrenheit
              //temperature
              Fahrenheit = (9.0/5.0 * Celsius) + 32;

              //This statement will display the converted
              //temperature
              System.out.println("The temperature in
              Fahrenheit is: " + Fahrenheit);
            }

        //this is the end of the do loop
        //the code above will be executed continuously until
        //the user's input is other than a letter e
        } while (!(strInput.equals("e")) &&
        !(strInput.equals("E")));
      }
      //this section catches and displays
      //any errors that occur when the program is running
      catch (IOException e){
        System.out.println("Error " + e.getMessage());
      }
    }
  }
```

Not only does the program check to see if the user enters the "e" key but through the use of the logical ! (not) and the logical && (and) operators, it also checks to see if the input might have been an "E":

```
while (!(strInput.equals("e")) &&
!(strInput.equals("E")));
```

ready, set, go!

Now that you've learned some of the building blocks of Java (variables, operators, and control structures), you're probably wondering what the next steps are to actually start programming. First you have to purchase or download Java.

There are many different vendors of Java, but Sun Microsystems offers a version that is free and also widely used by educators around the world. Sun permits users to download Java and their JDK (Java Developer's Toolkit) for free from their www.sun.com Web site. This provides you with all of the tools you need to compile and run Java programs on your computer.

After you have downloaded, installed, and configured Java to run on your machine, the next step in writing Java programs is to choose an editor. Some Java packages are provided with an Integrated Development Environment (IDE) that consists of a program editor, compiler, debugger, and many more tools. You do not need to have all of those tools to write Java programs, although they do make the development of applications a lot easier and less time consuming.

Java programs can be written in any text editor. You can even use your handy-dandy Windows Notepad to type your Java programs. Make sure that you save your program with the .java file extension and your file is named the same as the public class name in your program.

Once the program has been entered into a text file you can compile it from the command prompt using the *javac* command, like this:

```
javac MyProg1.java
```

This compiles the MyProg1.java program and determines if there are any syntactical errors. If there are errors, reopen your text file, fix the problems, save the changes, and recompile.

Once the compile works, you are ready to try out your program. Java programs are executed through the use of the *java* command:

```
java MyProg1
```

That is all there is to becoming a novice at Java and dangerous enough to take on the world of programming!

object-oriented programming

Now that you have the basic skills needed to begin writing simple Java programs, you can be introduced to the advanced topic of ***object-oriented programming (OOP)***.

object-oriented programming (OOP) – Style of programming that involves representing items, things, and people as objects rather than basing the logic around actions

You deal with objects all the time. Whether you are dealing with a person, car, table, alarm, phone, or any other object, you are experiencing one aspect of object orientation. In object-oriented programming, an object is not simply a noun (person, place, or thing); it also includes the qualities of that object, what it does, and how it responds or interacts with other objects. Objects in OOP can include three distinct features: characteristics, work, and response. As an example, say you have an alarm clock, called the Alarm object. The Alarm object, as with any object in OOP, has the following features (Figure 11-7):

- *Characteristics*—The Alarm object has different characteristics or attributes, such as color, wake time, current time, selected radio station, and so on.
- *Work*—The Alarm object performs some work, such as telling the current time and ringing annoyingly when you'd rather sleep.
- *Response*—The Alarm object responds to certain events. When your wake-up time is reached, the alarm goes off. Or, when you hit the snooze button, the alarm "sleeps" for another five minutes.

Figure 11-7, An object has characteristics, work, and responses

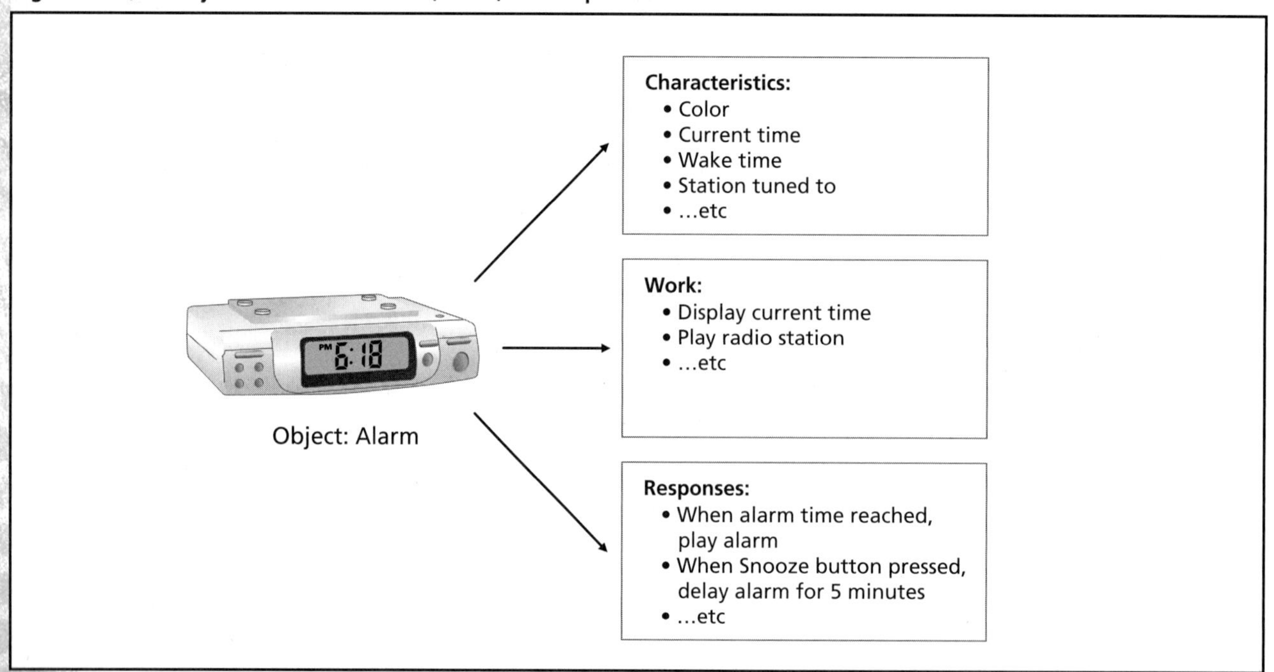

Most of the high-level languages, including Java, support object-oriented programming. A Java application consists of many different objects. Each of these objects incorporates the three characteristics described earlier. For example, the String data type you have already learned about is actually an object, one of many in the Java environment.

learning about objects

The best way to learn all of the objects available in Java is to either search the online help included with many Java software packages or research the Internet for the different Java classes.

OOP can be defined as the ability to represent a part of the application as a self-contained object. The hardest parts about learning OOP are taking the time to create new objects and implement them within your application, and trying to decipher what needs to be an object and what can remain as simple source code.

The main advantages of using an OOP language such as Java are reusability and maintainability. If there were a specific item that is or can be used in many applications it would be silly to write the supporting code over and over again. Instead, you write the source code to represent the item as an object, thus reducing the amount of code you have to write when you want to reuse the object in a different application.

For example, assume you had written all of the necessary source code to represent a person as an object. You included the person source code in a current program and it worked great. Later on, you had to write another program but this time instead of using a generalized person you had to be more specific and represent a student. Because you have already written the source code to work with a person and know that it works, and because the characteristics of a person are very similar to those of a student, you only need to add those items that are more specific to a student such as GPA, grade level, and schedule. Thus, through reusability of objects you can decrease the amount of time you spend generating source code by reusing and modifying the object code that you already have proven to work.

Maintaining the source code is also easier as the use of object-oriented programming requires that the application be broken into smaller more manageable pieces. Consider the example of making a change to a program. If you were to modify how a student logs into a system, you would have to track down every location in the source code where a student could log in and change the program. By representing items as objects you only have to change the source code in one location. The object handles the rest because the code is contained within the object.

how OOP works

To illustrate the principles of object-oriented programming, consider the following example.

Suppose that you work for a toy company and your division is responsible for creating action figures. This week you are charged with creating a Kung-fu action doll. How is the company going to proceed so that they can be profitable? Are they going to give you and every other employee in your division a piece of plastic and tell you to carve out the doll? If so, how much will they charge for the figure and still make enough profit to pay you? What if you make a mistake? It is time to get another piece of plastic. What a waste of time! The company won't stay in business for very long with that approach.

For the company to be profitable, it needs to implement a mold (called a class or template in object-oriented terminology) so that the figure can be mass-produced in the most economic and efficient manner.

making the mold

What do you see when you look at the mold? Is the mold an action figure? No, it is simply the skeleton or form or outline of the finished product. Susie or

Jake are not going to buy the mold to play with and take over to their friends' houses. Instead, they want what comes out of the mold.

The mold describes the type of figure you are going to create. You see two arms, a head, two legs, a certain height, other dimensions, and so on. In other words, the mold defines the attributes or characteristics of the figure that is to be created.

creating the figure

To create the action figure, you must put the plastic into the mold. Once the plastic has been placed in the mold it is formed to the shape of the mold attributes. In other words, putting the plastic in the mold is the creation process of the figure.

Once the plastic has been placed in the mold and a doll is created, you can see that the mold defined the characteristics of the figure. The characteristics or attributes might include height, weight, hair color, eye color, type of figure, name of figure, and any other attribute that describes how the toy looks.

class – A template or a mold used for defining new object types along with their properties and behavior

object – A self-contained entity that consists of both data and procedures

instantiation – The process of creating an object based upon a class. Memory is allocated and assigned to a variable

constructor – A special class function/method used for creating or instantiating an object

property (also called attribute) – Characteristic of an object

method – The work performed by an object; a function that is defined within a class

event – An action or occurrence recognized by a class

event handler – How a class responds to an event

putting the figure to work

In addition to having characteristics, the doll can perform some work or action. For instance, it can stand, the arms and legs can move, the head can turn, and so on. The work of the doll is defined by the type of doll that was created (that is, which type of mold was used). The doll can also respond to specific actions. For instance, assume that the mold used to create the figure was the Kung-Fu mold. When you pull the arm back and release it, the arm shoots forward with a powerful karate chop. In other words, the figure responds to the event of pulling the arm back with a specific action.

Now that you have seen how the process of creating a doll can be compared to creating an object, you can carry the analogy a little further to learn more about OOP terminology (Figure 11-8).

- The mold or template used for creating the doll is called a *class*. It defines the characteristics, work, and available responses for the doll to be created.
- The doll is called an *object*. It is created based upon the mold, or class.
- The creation process is called *instantiation*. Instantiation is simply creating an object and assigning it memory resources. The method used to instantiate an object in a class is called a *constructor*.
- A characteristic of the doll is a called *property* or *attribute*. It defines how the object looks.
- The work performed by an object is called a *method*. It performs a task and is linked specifically to a class.
- The response by an object is called an *event* or *event handler*. Many Java objects have events, which are the responses to some action taken by the end user or the system.

Figure 11-8, Making a plastic doll shows OOP concepts in action

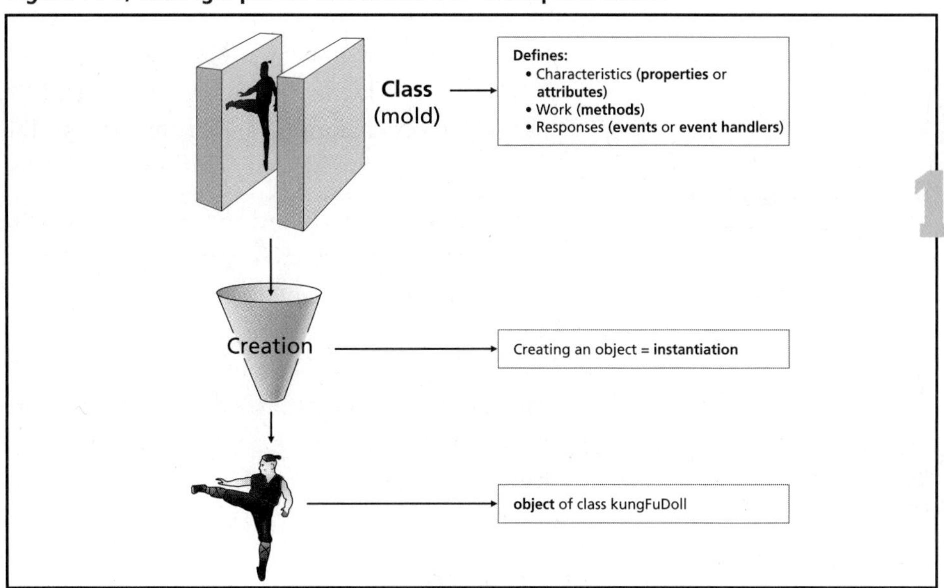

All of these items describe the basic functionality of OOP. The part you must now implement is what items in the program need to be represented by an object and what can be represented by standard source code. The items you want to represent by an object are those that might be required by the Java system and those that you will reuse not only in the current application but many other applications being developed in the future.

Once the object is created using a class, it has access to all of the properties, methods, and events defined for that type. To access information for an object, use the object name, period (.), and the qualifier. For example, to access the String object's equals() method:

```
String sFirstName = "Joe";
String sLastName = "Blow";
if (sFirstName.equals(sLastName))
     System.out.println("The last name equals the first
     name. Strange!");
```

The call to equals() represents calling a method in the String class.

Another example to which you have already been introduced is the parseDouble() method that is part of the Double class.

```
String sInput = "";
     String sInput = "";
     double dFahrenheit = 0.0;
     dFahrenheit = Double.parseDouble(sInput);
```

inheritance

inheritance – The process of providing more class functionality by creating more specific classes based upon generic classes

Take a moment to ponder how you look. Do you look more like your father or your mother? Why? It is because you inherited traits from your parents. Likewise, in programming, "child" objects can inherit properties, methods, or events from "parent" objects. This process is called *inheritance*.

In programming, inheritance is the creation of an object from a parent class. The newly created object receives everything (properties, methods, and events) from the parent class that is not declared as private, plus it can now add any other capabilities it might need that the parent did not offer. As shown in Figure 11-9, inheritance promotes code reusability. Consider the example of a person being represented as an object. The basis of many inherited classes has already been created and tested. Any time you write another program and encounter an item that is similar to the characteristics, work, and responses to that of a person you can inherit from it to provide a "head start" in creating your new class.

Figure 11-9, Inheritance promotes code reusability

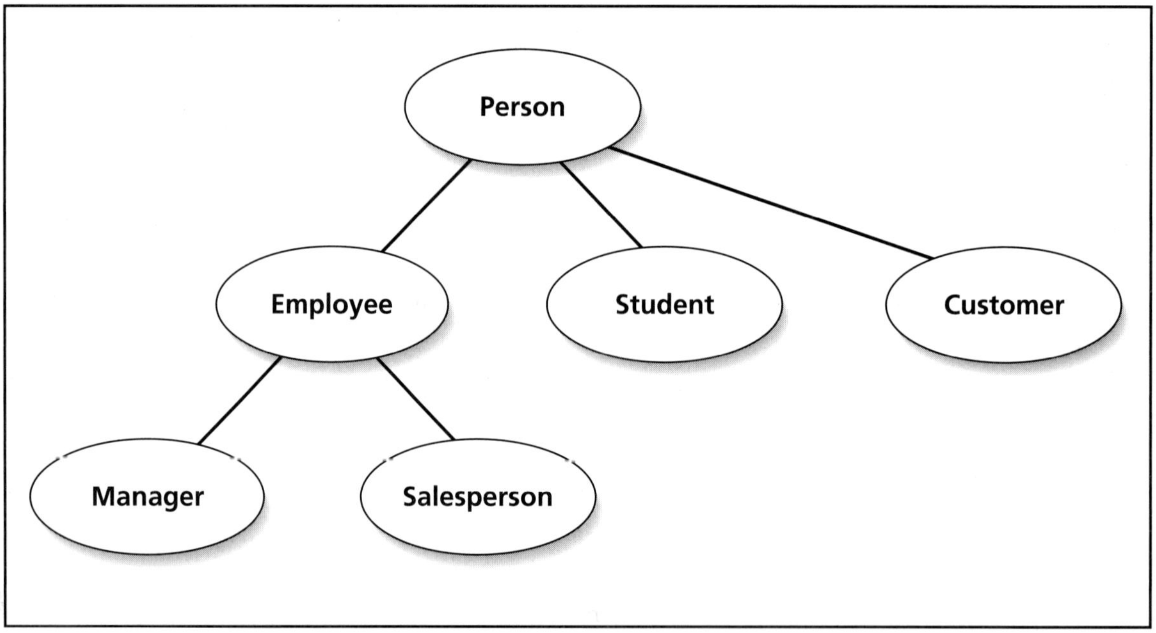

parent class (also called base class) – A generic class from which other classes can be created through the process of inheritance

subclass – The more specific class created through the process of inheritance that has been based upon a parent class

The generic or higher-level class is called the *base* or *parent class*. The new more specific classes that are created through inheritance are called *subclasses* and receive all that the parent or generic class has plus whatever they add to the template.

Some of the inherited classes that can be based upon a person class might include student, employee, manager, salesperson, and customer. The real power of inheritance comes from creating a generic class and then making it more specific to meet your needs. Thus most of the work is already done and you are simply reusing source code with slight modifications.

Calling a method is a chain reaction. Suppose you are asked to mow the lawn. You go out and you mow the lawn. But what if you did not know how to mow the lawn? If the lawn does not get mowed, the person that asked you is going to get real fussy and blow up. What are you going to do? Go to your parent and explain the situation. If your parent knows how to mow the lawn, then the lawn gets mowed. If your parent does not know how to mow the lawn, then they go to their parent (and so on).

This describes the process of calling methods. If a method is called from within a subclass and the subclass does not contain it, then it is passed up the chain to the parent and continues to do so until the method is located and executed or an error is generated.

The nice feature about many OO languages is that you don't care who has been subclassed from who because the documentation makes it appear as though all of the information found within a class was written for that class even though much of the information for a class has been received through inheritance. Do you care that a class has inherited a property instead of a company writing it from scratch? Suppose you just inherited a million dollars and you want to put it in the bank to keep it safe. Is the bank going to say "Wait a minute! Is this inherited money? Get out of here! We don't take inherited money!" In reality, the bank will probably say "Welcome! What can I get you? Would you like a toaster oven to take home?" Inheritance means that it is yours and is treated as such.

One of the biggest questions is "Why do you want to subclass?" The following example demonstrates the answer.

Much like the example of mowing the lawn, you are asked to go clean your room. Being very efficient with your time, you do not want to spend all of it cleaning your room. You would rather have somebody else do the dirty work. Who do you call? Mom. The only problem is that Mom cleans the room just a little bit different than how you are told to clean. When she makes the bed, she pulls the sheet over the pillow and gives it that little tuck under. That was not how the bed was requested to be made. So what do you do? You let Mom clean the room and make the bed and then you come in and pull the sheet back off the pillow.

You subclass an object when it just doesn't do everything you want it to do and you know that you will reuse the new object in other situations.

encapsulation

encapsulation – Process of hiding an object's operations from other objects

Another great advantage of OOP is that you do not need to know how everything works in order to use it. ***Encapsulation*** is often referred to as the black box. In other words, you don't really know how something works and you don't really care as long as it does work. Encapsulation is the process of one object hiding its operations from other objects. This means that if one object interacts with another object and the second object changes functionality, you probably do not have to change the first object because it is encapsulated from all other objects.

Encapsulation helps cut down on the potential for errors to occur. For example, your computer monitor hides its operations from the CPU. If something happens to the monitor, you either fix it or replace it. You do not have to do anything to the CPU.

Another example relates to printing. When you choose the print menu item, do you really think about the packets of data being sent to the printer or do you just want the document to print? Encapsulation hides the details and does the work.

polymorphism

polymorphism – An object's ability to use the same expression to denote different operations

In order to help promote reusability and flexibility, object-oriented programming supports the ability to use the same expression to denote different operations (called ***polymorphism***). For example, consider an application that has objects representing a word-processed document, a report, and an e-mail. Each of these objects has the ability to be printed. If you click on the Print menu item, then the contents contained by the object should be sent to the printer and printed.

Polymorphism states that even though the objects are different, they can each use the print operation. It is the ability to make a call to an operation and the system at runtime determines how the operation is used.

Another example incorporating polymorphism relates to geometric shapes. If you had objects representing squares, triangles, and circles, and wanted to send them to the standard output device (the monitor) and display them, you should be able to call the *Draw* operation for all of them.

There are many different classes, methods, and events you can use while programming in Java. The more Java programming you do, the more of them you'll become familiar with. So, practice, practice, practice!

Java and OOP

Java is tied very closely to the OOP model. Everything in Java revolves around classes and their properties and methods. The sooner you start using OOP in Java, the sooner you begin to know the available classes, reduce the amount of lines of code you are producing by reusing objects you have created or by using someone else's objects, and begin to understand how to implement OOP in your programs.

practice, practice, practice . . .

Learning the many different statements you can use in a programming language, whether assembly language, C++, or Java, is a lot like learning a foreign language—it takes practice before you're fluent. And to maintain fluency, you have to use it. The same concept applies to most skills. Remember those hours of piano lessons when you were a kid? If you're still playing, it's probably because you play and practice regularly.

This same concept applies to learning a programming language. Right now, you are in "piano" lessons learning the language. If you do not spend time at the "keyboard" then you will not learn the language. You have to practice, practice, and then practice some more. The more you practice, the more you will learn, until at some point you realize that you actually know how to do this stuff!

As you are learning, you will also find that there are many resources to help you. There are many free resources on the Internet and also books you can purchase to show you the objects and libraries that are available for you to use. Why is this so important? Because much of the work in writing programs, implementing algorithms, and performing tasks has already been done by someone else. You just need to know where to find the resource and how to use it.

choosing a programming language

So, revisit your earlier dilemma of what "flavor" of programming language to use. Java has been used in the examples, but as you've learned in this chapter, each language has advantages and disadvantages. If the choice of programming language is up to you, choose very carefully which one you want to invest your time and money in. One of the things you need to determine before you dive headfirst into the high-level programming language waters is whether or not there are any "rocks." In other words, be cautious. Look around. Try out some of the demo versions of the language and see if you like what it has to offer. Talk to others who have experience with the language and ask about the pros and cons.

Other things you should consider are:

- Functionality—Does it allow you to do everything you want to do (e.g., database, Internet, etc.)?
- Vendor stability—Is the company that is backing the language financially stable? Will the language be around for the long haul?
- Popularity—How many books do you see at the bookstore regarding the language? The more books there are usually implies popularity and support.
- Job market—How many and what type of jobs are there related to the language you want to use?
- Price—How much does it cost?

- Ease of learning—How quickly can a programmer learn the language before he/she becomes a productive developer?
- Performance—Will the program that is created through the use of the language have suitable response time and processing time?

Never choose a language simply because someone else said it was a good one to use. Choosing a language is like choosing a car (Figure 11-10). You have to test-drive a lot of them before you know which one you really like. Only by comparing the languages to your set of criteria can you best find the language that fits your needs and requirements. But remember, once a language is selected, do not become complacent by thinking that is the only language you ever need to learn. The world of programming is constantly changing and unless you continue to increase your skills and learn new technology your skills will quickly become outdated.

Figure 11-10, Choosing a language is like choosing a car

one last thought

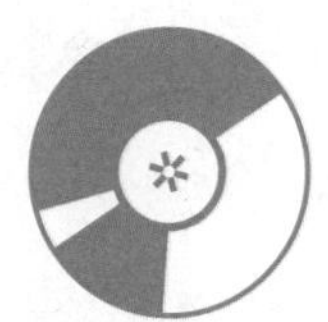

Reinforce your understanding of chapter concepts and terms with the information and activities for Chapter 11 on the student CD.

A program will do whatever you tell it to do. You can write a program that plays your favorite music, destroys the evil space invaders, or calculates how much money you need to pay your bills. In most cases, if the program doesn't work correctly, it is the fault of the person who wrote the program, not the computer.

It all goes back to one word—responsibility! As a programmer, you can create great and wonderful new programs to help society. Then again, the program that you write might have a problem that could have serious ramifications such as inadvertently launching a missile, allowing a breach in national security, or worse yet, knocking out your television reception.

This chapter is just a stepping stone to learning how to program. The ball is now in your court. Now is the time to get started if you want to become a good programmer. Just have patience and practice, practice, and practice!

chapter summary

- A program is only as good as the programmer(s) who wrote it
- Programs are used everywhere and in almost everything you do
- A program can either be interpreted or compiled
- Low-level languages are more closely related to the machine language that a computer understands
- Assembler is a low-level programming language
- High-level languages are more closely related to human language
- Algorithms are created for solving problems through some logical method
- Pseudocode is a way a programmer uses human language to map out how a program is supposed to work
- Creating the algorithm is one of the most important steps in writing a program
- Java is a high-level programming language that was initially designed for the Internet
- Variables are temporary storage locations with a specific type of data and are used within programs for calculations and storing essential information
- Java uses mathematical, relational, and logical operators
- There are four types of control structures used within a program: top down, invocation, selection, and repetition
- Object-oriented programming (OOP) allows programmers to reuse code and make their programs more maintainable
- OOP creates classes, which are like templates or molds from which objects can be created
- Object can have properties, methods, and event handlers
- Java is tied very closely to the OOP model
- In order to become a good programmer you must *practice*, *practice*, and *practice* some more!

key terms

algorithm (*384*)
assembly language (*389*)
assembler (*389*)
class (*448*)
compiler (*384*)
concatenation (*408*)
constructor (*448*)
control structure (*417*)
declaration (*404*)
encapsulation (*451*)
endless loop (*440*)
event (*448*)
event handler (*448*)
expression (*415*)
function (*418*)
high-level language (*389*)
Hungarian notation (*408*)
identifier (*404*)
inheritance (*450*)
insertion point (*422*)
instantiation (*448*)
integrated development environment (IDE) (*395*)
interpreter (*384*)
low-level language (*389*)
machine language (*389*)
method (*448*)
nesting (*433*)
object (*448*)
oriented-oriented programming (OOP) (*445*)
operators (*410*)
parameter (*420*)
parent class (base class) (*450*)
polymorphism (*452*)
postcondition loop (*441*)
precedence (*416*)
precondition loop (*441*)
program (*384*)
property (attribute) (*448*)
pseudocode (*397*)
repetition (*437*)
reserved word (*404*)
scope (*419*)
subclass (*450*)
syntax (*392*)
variable (*403*)
variable initialization (*409*)

test yourself

1. What is an algorithm?
2. Write an algorithm for calculating the balance of your checkbook.
3. Write the pseudocode for a program that can maintain the balance of your checkbook.
4. Write an algorithm for operating a gas pump when filling up a car.
5. Write the pseudocode for a program that maintains the operation of a gas pump.
6. Write an algorithm based on your course syllabus for calculating your final grade.
7. Write the pseudocode for a program based on your course syllabus that calculates your final grade.
8. Describe when to use integer variables in Java. Explain the situation, provide the suggested variable name, and support your recommendation.
9. Describe when to use floating-point variables in Java. Explain the situation, provide the suggested variable name, and support your recommendation.
10. Describe when to use character variables in Java. Explain the situation, provide the suggested variable name, and support your recommendation.
11. Describe when to use string variables in Java. Explain the situation, provide the suggested variable name, and support your recommendation.
12. Write a Java program that prints off truth tables for the "and" and "or" logical operators.
13. Write a Java program that demonstrates the use of the addition, subtraction, division, multiplication, and modulus mathematical operators.
14. Write a Java program that demonstrates how to print five names using the *for*, *while*, and *do-while* statements.
15. Write a Java program that demonstrates how the *if-else-if* statement can be used to determine your final grade in your course. Base the statement on your course syllabus.
16. Repeat Exercise 15 but use a *switch* statement.
17. Discuss when you would use a *do-while* structure versus a *for* structure versus a *while* structure.

18. Discuss inheritance and explain how it works. What are the advantages? What are the disadvantages?

19. Using transportation as a base class, draw a class hierarchy that shows inheritance of at least 3 levels deep (Parent, child, grandchild relationship).

20. Using mammal as a base class, draw a class hierarchy that shows inheritance of at least 3 levels deep (Parent, child, grandchild relationship).

practice questions

1. Which is not an example of a high-level programming language?

    a. Ada
    b. Boolean
    c. C++
    d. Java

2. Java is a high-level programming language used mainly for its readability and maintainability.

    a. True
    b. False

3. Java is case sensitive.

    a. True
    b. False

4. Pseudocode should be written after the program to ensure the program was written correctly.

    a. True
    b. False

5. @JT%name is a valid Java variable identifier.

    a. True
    b. False

6. Which Java data type would you use for the value 14?

    a. Integer
    b. Long
    c. Byte
    d. Char
    e. None of the above

7. Which Java data type would you use for the value 140912?
   a. Integer
   b. Long
   c. Byte
   d. Short
   e. None of the above
8. Which Java data type would you use for the value “e”?
   a. Integer
   b. Long
   c. Byte
   d. Char
   e. None of the above
9. Which Java data type would you use for the value “Joe”?
   a. Integer
   b. Long
   c. Byte
   d. Char
   e. None of the above
10. What is the final result of the expression 5 + 2 * 4 – 2?
    a. 26
    b. 11
    c. 9
    d. 0
    e. Cannot be determined
11. What is the final result of the expression 5 % 4 + 3 – 2?
    a. 2
    b. 6
    c. 1
    d. 0
    e. Cannot be determined
12. The postincrement operator increments the variable and then processes the remainder of the statement.
    a. True
    b. False
13. The preincrement operator increments the variable and then processes the remainder of the statement.
    a. True
    b. False

14. Using the following statements, what value would be displayed?

```
public class test {
  public static void main(String[] args) {
    int iCount;
    iCount = 0;
      System.out.print("iCount has a value of " +
      ++iCount);

    }

}
```

a. 0
b. 1
c. 2
d. unknown

15. Using the following statements, what value would be displayed?

```
public class test {
  public static void main(String[] args) {
    int iCount;
    iCount = 0;
      System.out.print("iCount has a value of " +
      iCount++);

    }
}
```

a. 0
b. 1
c. 2
d. unknown

digging deeper

1. Talk to other students, faculty, and businesses to find out what are the current programming languages being used for C++ development?
2. Talk to other students, faculty, and businesses to find out what are the current programming languages being used for Java development?
3. Talk to other students, faculty, and businesses to find out the advantages and disadvantages of programming in the following languages: C, C++, C#, Java, Pascal, and Visual Basic.
4. How has program development changed in recent years, and where do you predict it is going in the future?
5. Do you feel software engineering for United States companies is increasingly being done in other countries while software design and management remains within the country? Support your opinions.

discussion topics

1. What do you think is the most popular programming language currently being used? Support your argument.
2. On paper, write your own programming language you could use to open a text file, read two numbers stored on separate lines, add them together, print the result, and close the file.
3. What do you think the next great program to change the world will be?
4. What are the most important ways programs have helped you as an individual?
5. What do you expect will be the types of programs you, as a computer scientist, will write?

Internet research

1. What are the number of available jobs and average salaries currently in your state for programmers that use: C++, C#, Java, and Visual Basic?
2. What are the number of available jobs and average salaries currently in your country for programmers that use: C++, C#, Java, and Visual Basic?
3. What are some Web sites that offer free tutorials in Java programming?
4. What are some Web sites that offer free download of Java compilers?
5. Are there any Web sites that offer free downloads of programming languages? If so, also state the programming language.

12

chapter

software engineering

in this chapter you will:

- Learn how software engineering is used to create applications
- Learn some of the different software engineering process models
- Understand what a design document is and how it should be used during software development
- Be introduced to the proper steps in formulating a design document used in creating an application
- Learn how Unified Modeling Language (UML) diagrams can be used as a blueprint in creating an application
- See some of the pitfalls in developing software, and learn how to avoid them
- Gain an understanding of how teams are used in application development

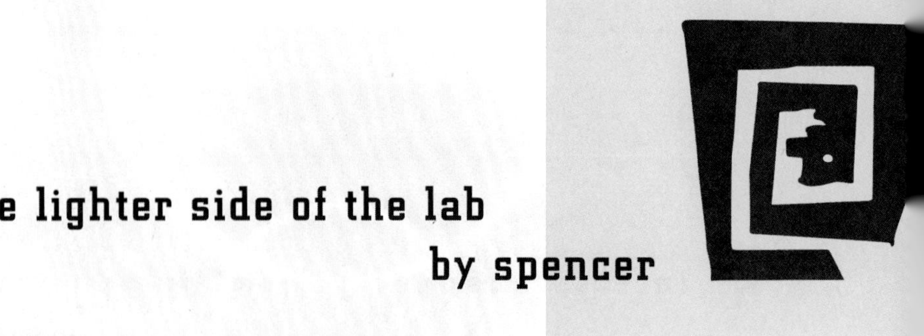

the lighter side of the lab

by spencer

I've got a little problem with procrastination that I've been meaning to take care of. I'm not sure how I've made it through school so far. I can't tell you how many times I've been up all night working on a term project or a research paper that was due the following day.

Unfortunately, I've found that the last minute routine doesn't work in the computer world. Software isn't created overnight (although sometimes it functions like it was). There is an intricate process that goes into creating a program.

First, it's important for your team to get together and argue for hours about which is better: Windows or UNIX. This step serves no purpose, but it is a lot of fun. (HINT to computer programmers: "UNIX vs. Windows debate" <> "Interesting date conversation".)

Next, it's important to come up with a programming strategy. Will the program be completed by teams in pieces and then assembled? Or will the entire programming team work together on the same program? Will there need to be a prototype of the program? Will the Unified Modeling Language be used? Should the programming teams be the same teams for Halo?

After all these decisions are made, it's time to get to work. It's really exciting when the pieces come together and the program starts to work. Although it's sometimes even more exciting when the pieces come together and the program doesn't work. (The Computer Throw and the Monitor Kick could be Olympic events.)

Then, finally, one day the program is complete, or so you think. The program is then sent to a few customers for what is known as a "beta test." No matter how well you think you've programmed, the beta testers will find errors. Eventually those bugs are fixed and the program is shipped to all users. They find many errors that a normal person would never think of.

Support Technician: What seems to be the problem?

Customer: Well, when I enter the entire alphabet backwards into the Date Range box, I get an error.

But the process is a lot of fun, and there's nothing as satisfying as seeing someone using the program that you created with your own two hands (with the exception of finally being able to go to sleep after staying up all night to finish a research paper).

why you need to know about...
software engineering

Every day you are faced with the task of defining a project. Whether it is mowing the lawn, buying groceries, or writing a program, you need to define the scope of the project before you begin the work.

For example, a neighbor hires you to mow his lawn. You show up bright and early, and after three hours of grueling work you finish the job. You ring the doorbell, expecting praise for your good work and a fistful of hard-earned cash. The neighbor opens the door, looks at the lawn with a sour expression and says, "That's not how I wanted it done!" So, off you go, sweating, pushing, and pulling the lawn mower, which feels heavier with each passing moment. Once again, you trudge to the door and ring the doorbell. The neighbor comes to the door and once again you hear the words, "That's not what I wanted!" Finally, you scream, "How *do* you want your lawn mowed?!" The neighbor explains that the proper way to mow the lawn is by pushing the mower diagonally across the yard rather than horizontally. The neighbor releases you from your duty without pay and swears to never hire you to mow the lawn again. Dejected, you leave the lawn mowing business and join a traveling circus.

The moral of this story is, of course, that you must find out exactly what's required *before* you start the job—a principle that you might have already discovered applies to programming. Just because you have problems making your program meet all of the requirements you have been given, you don't have to quit your programming job and join the circus. In fact, if you have been frustrated trying to write your first "perfect" program, you don't even need to change your major from Computer Science to Basket Weaving. All you need to do is properly design the project before you start writing any source code.

It's not enough to know a programming language and be able to write code. Software engineering enables you to design your programs and to communicate with clients and other team members, essential elements of writing applications.

software engineering – Process of producing software applications involving not just the source code of the program but also associated documentation, including UML diagrams, screen prototypes, reports, software requirements, future developmental issues, and data needed to make the programs operate correctly

end user – Someone or something that needs the program to perform a function or meet a need, and who determines the required functionality of the program

what is software engineering?

Designing a project requires you to incorporate software engineering skills in order to meet the requirements of the end user. ***Software engineering*** is the process of producing software applications. It involves not just the source code of the program but also associated documentation, including UML diagrams, screen prototypes, reports, software requirements, future developmental issues, and data needed to make the programs operate correctly.

An ***end user*** is the driving force behind software development. End users are the ones who need the program to perform a function or meet a need and determine the required functionality of the program.

A major part of software engineering is the process of writing or producing software applications. These applications are based upon the needs of the end users. As time goes by, the needs of the end users might change. In fact, the end user's need for the application might even disappear, making the application obsolete. Thus, there is a constant need to communicate with the end user to make the software applicable to their needs.

note

The end user (also called the client or user) can be a person, thing, or a task. It does not always have to be a person. It could be a piece of machinery or even a task that needs to be accomplished.

software development life cycle (SDLC) – Describes the life of the application including all of the stages involved in the development, testing, installation, and maintenance of a program

software development life cycle

During the life of the program, you will continue to maintain, fix, and improve the program. The ***software development life cycle (SDLC)*** includes several elements:

- *Project feasibility*—Determining whether the project is worth doing, and specifying the advantages and disadvantages of this application
- *Software specifications*—Determining specific functions of the software and any constraints or requirements
- *Software design and implementation*—Designing and writing the application to meet the software specifications
- *Software validation*—Testing the software to ensure it meets the software specifications
- *Software evolution*—Modifying or changing the software to meet changing customer needs

There are different models of the software development process that can be used to represent software functionality. Some are:

- *Waterfall*—The fundamental processes involved in creating the program are represented as phases. The output from each phase is used as the input to the next phase.
- *Build and fix (or evolutionary)*—The developer writes a program and continues to modify it until the system is functional.
- *Rapid prototyping*—Tools are available that allow end users to work with **prototypes** of the screens and other interfaces. These prototypes can then be used to build the final product.
- *Incremental*—The application is developed and released in a series of software releases.
- *Spiral*—Spiral starts with an initial pass using the waterfall method. After an evaluation period, the cycle is started again, adding new functionality until the next prototype is released. The process resembles a spiral with the prototype becoming larger and larger until all functionality has been completed and delivered to the end user.

***prototype** – A standard or typical example that gives the end user a good idea of what they will see when their application is completed*

Each model of the software development process varies in the steps that are needed to complete the development tasks. This chapter focuses on the waterfall model (shown in Figure 12-1), which has been around since 1970 and is considered one of the more widely used process models. The waterfall process resembles the process of building a house. You start by excavating the area where the foundation will be placed. You cannot pour the foundation without first completing the excavation process. After the foundation is laid, you can

Figure 12-1, The "waterfall" model of software development

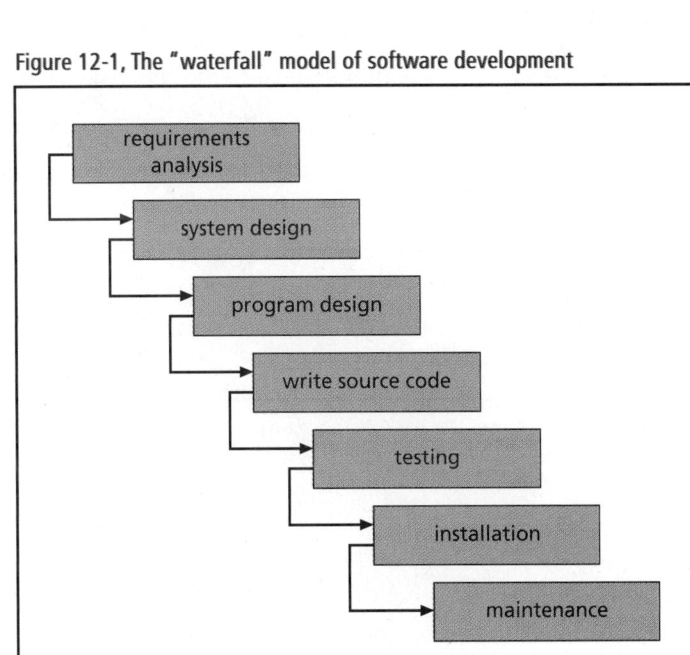

extreme programming (XP)

This is a new (about eight years old) software development process that focuses on customer satisfaction. Emphasis is placed on teamwork and delivering quality software. XP improves software development by enhancing communication, simplicity, feedback, and courage by delivering the product and implementing changes as soon as possible.

agile software development

This is another new software process that focuses on satisfying the customer through early and continuous delivery of software products. Changes are welcomed even in the late stages of the software development.

design document – A document that details all of the design issues for an application

then proceed to the next process of framing the house. The process of completing one step before moving on to the next step continues until the house is finally completed.

The waterfall method follows a similar approach. The first step is to gather all of the requirements for the project. The second step is to design the system and software. After all the requirements have been defined and the project has been designed, it is time to build and implement the application. Once the application is finished, it must be tested and then finally put into operation and maintained to meet the user's needs.

Software need not simply wear out. Instead, it can be modified to meet the changing needs of the end user. Over time the needs that used to be important and for which the program was written might be no longer part of the picture. The requirements and functionality of a program can change and the software can be changed to fit.

Luckily, software engineers are prepared to deal with change because they have a set of "blueprints" to refer to for their software product, called a design document.

creating the design document

A *design document* is a document sometimes compared to the size of a thesis due to the fact that it can be quite large since it details all of the design issues for the application. These design issues include screen layouts, colors, reports, security, paths for files, online help, user documentation, future plans, and more. Every aspect of the application should be documented and maintained within a file or folder. This file or folder is the design document.

One of the fascinating advantages of using a software development environment as your application development tool is the ability to prototype your screens and reports without writing a single line of source code. In other words, you could sit down with the end user and interactively design all of the screens and reports to their specifications, including text, color, and field location. For instance, assume that you have been contacted to write an application to help a person keep track of laboratory tests results. You could sit down with the end user and have him or her help you design the appearance of the input screen by specifying fonts, colors, and locations of the input areas. The end user could also use a word processor to design sample reports that you could use as a prototype for the reports you create in the application. All of this information provides you with a head start in creating the application and making sure that it appears in a manner that is pleasing to the end user.

Another important reason for using a design document is that it acts like a blueprint. If everyone agrees on the design document as being the correct way of doing the work, then there should be no surprises in the final product. If one party says that something was done incorrectly, both parties can return to the design document to resolve the dispute.

The entire process of creating the design document is based upon good communication with the end user in determining the needs and requirements of the application (see Figure 12-2).

Figure 12-2, Process of creating a design document

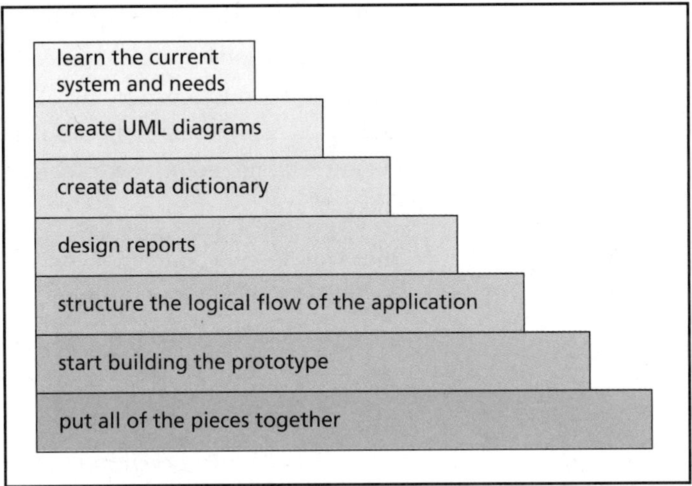

To better understand the process, the following case study is provided to walk you through seven steps involved in creating a design document.

step 1—learn the current system and needs

Assume you are president and programmer for Over Byte, Inc. The owner of the music store Toe-Tappin' Tunes, Mr. B. Bop, comes to you with a proposal for an application to manage their media inventory. Learning the end users or client's current system needs is your initial task.

note RULE: Learn the end user's current system and needs.

First, you have to spend some time with Mr. Bop and find out how he currently handles his inventory. What are his needs? What is his goal of using a computer-based inventory system? In fact, you can even assign him the task of writing or typing a list of reports he would like to be able to generate from the application. Then have him send you a copy of the reports so you can review them before your next meeting.

Your job is to document the meeting's main points and come up with solutions or suggestions to combat the issues of security, colors, printing, and all of the other standard application entities. You don't have to write down every word of the meeting, but do take notes that can be used as a reference later on when you begin creating the design document.

note **RULE: Document the information the client gives you.**

You become a detective trying to determine what the user really wants. If there is a system already in place you can spend time learning how it is used, its good points, and its bad points. You should also talk to the people who will actually be using the product to make sure you will meet their needs with the program you are going to write. In other words, you have to keep digging for information.

Once you have a good handle on what the user really wants, you should write the project objectives or introduction, specifications, and requirements. This part of the design document will act as an overall guide for the major tasks that need to be accomplished (Figure 12-3).

note **RULE: Write objectives or introduction, specifications, and requirements.**

step 2—create UML diagrams

Unified Modeling Language (UML) – Software modeling process that enables system developers to create a blueprint showing the overall functionality of the program being engineered and provides a way for the client and the developer to communicate

After the objectives and requirements have been defined, it is time to start creating diagrams to illustrate what the system is supposed to do. The ***Unified Modeling Language (UML)*** enables system developers to create diagrams to be included in the blueprint showing the overall functionality of the program being engineered and provides a way for the client and the developer to communicate. UML provides a visual modeling approach in specifying the system functionality that needs to be met in order to create a product that meets the project requirements. The visual diagrams are created before any lines of source code are written and help the software developer see what needs to be accomplished.

note **There is a common perception among end users that software is cheap to produce and easy to modify. After you have gained more experience with software engineering, you will find that this perception is false. Software can be very complex and take many hours to produce. Time is translated into money spent by the company or lost by the developer in creating a program.**

Figure 12-3, A design document includes the project introduction, specifications, and requirements

1. **Introduction**

 1.1. **Purpose**

  1.1.1. This document lists all software requirements necessary for the creation and implementation of a Fantasy Basketball Web site. It defines the feasibility study, operational requirements, algorithms, databases, user interfaces, error systems, help systems, cost analysis, and supporting diagrams.

  The intended audience for this document is the end user or client, development team, project manager, and any other stakeholders in the system.

 1.2. **Terms**

- *League Owner:* The creator of the league
- *Commissioner:* The person responsible for overseeing league actions
- *Team Owner:* Any person who owns a team within the specified league
- *Team:* Consists of 12 players each playing in one more positions of guard, forward, and center
- *User:* Any individual that registers to play in a league of Fantasy Basketball

 1.3. **Scope**

  1.3.1 The users of this product are the participants in the Fantasy Basketball game. The user may create their own league or participate in a league already established.

 1.4. **Overview**

  1.4.1. This product will allow individuals to create leagues and organize teams by letting them manage and follow their teams through a basketball season. This product is Web based and will require a server, Internet connection, and a Web browser. Every night, basketball statistics will be downloaded to the server. These statistics will then be updated throughout the league teams to determine a team's final score for a specific game.

2. **Specifications**

 2.1. ...

3. **System Requirements**

 3.1. ...

12

UML

UML helps conceptualize and illustrate software design. It was developed by Grady Booch, James Rumbaugh, and Ivar Jacobson. In the late 1990s, they submitted their UML concept to the Object Management Group (OMG), which has taken over the maintenance of the product. For more information on the Object Management Group refer to *www.omg.org/uml/*.

UML provides many different diagrams that help to visually explain the different parts of a system. Microsoft Visio is one tool that allows you to create UML diagrams, as well as many other types of diagrams that are useful to programmers (Figure 12-4).

Some of the types of UML diagrams and their uses are:

- *Class*—Shows how the different object classes relate to each other
- *Object*—Gives details of an object created from a class
- *Use case*—Describes a system's behavior from a user's standpoint
- *State*—Shows an object's particular state at any given time
- *Sequence*—Shows how one class communicates with another class by sending messages back and forth

Figure 12-4, Creating UML diagrams in Microsoft Visio

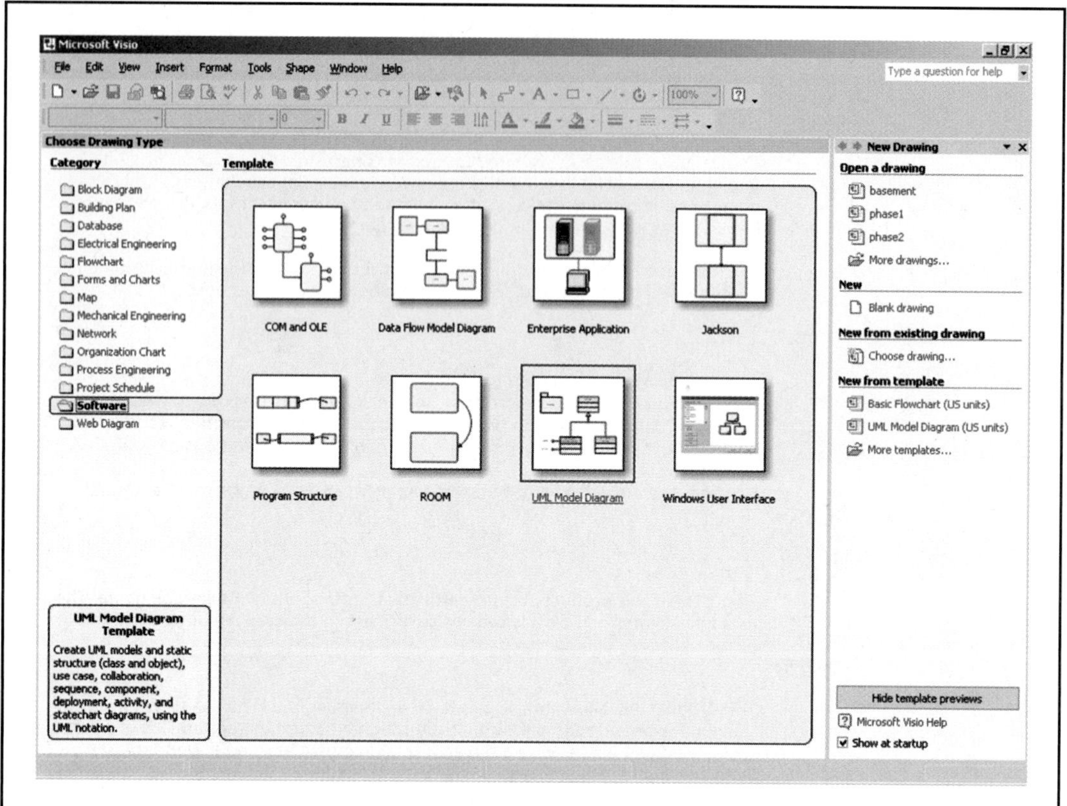

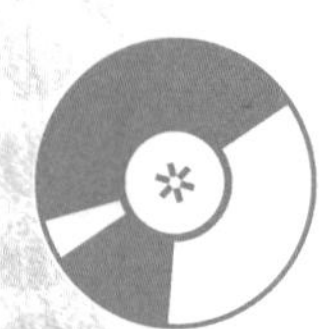

To try your hand at UML, check out the "Working @ UML in Visio" under Chapter 12 tutorials on the student CD.

- *Activity*—Shows activities that occur within a use case or within an object's behavior
- *Collaboration*—Shows how system elements work together to accomplish the system's objectives
- *Component*—Shows how system components relate to each other
- *Deployment*—Shows the physical architecture of a computer-based system

Each of the different types of UML diagrams serves a specific purpose in defining the functionality of the system for each client's viewpoint.

Consider the following scenario. Assume that you are asked to create a software application to help the Toe-Tappin' Tunes music store. The use case diagram (Figure 12-5) shows the overall functionality of the inventory application. It details the main tasks that the application needs to perform and that the system needs to support.

The class diagram shows what object-oriented classes will be involved and need to be included when creating the application (Figure 12-6). It also shows how each of the classes relates to one another. In essence, it can be used as an OOP

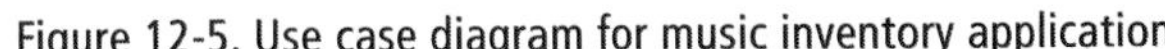

Figure 12-5, Use case diagram for music inventory application

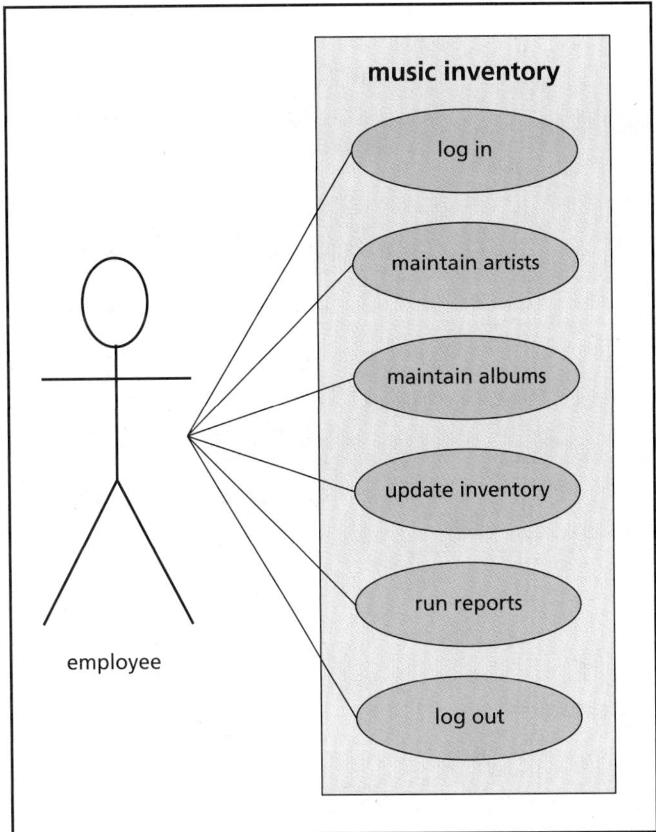

Figure 12-6, Class diagram for music inventory application

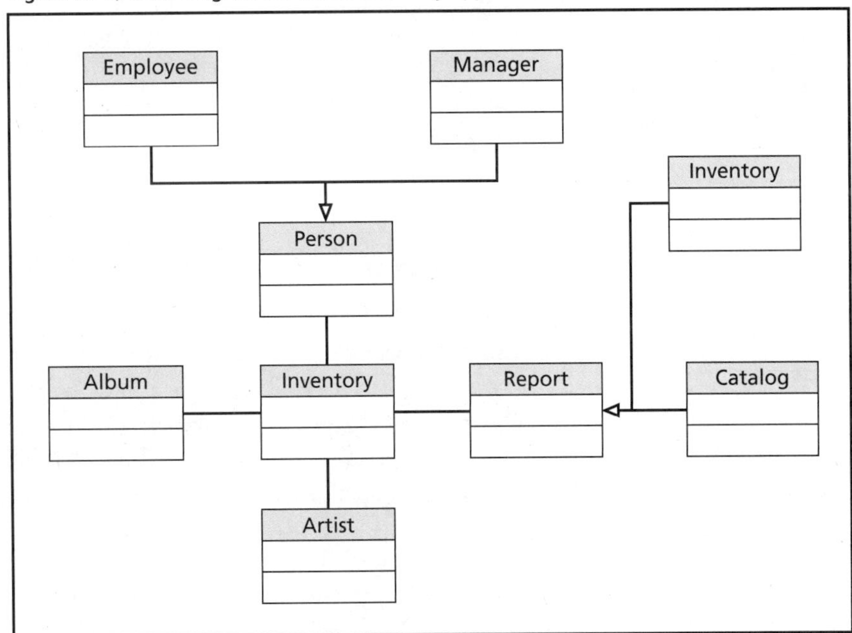

12

blueprint for creating the necessary lines of object-oriented source code built upon the class relationships.

The UML sequence diagram (Figure 12-7) shows what types of messages are passed back and forth between the different classes that were specified in the class diagram.

Figure 12-7, Sequence diagram for music inventory application

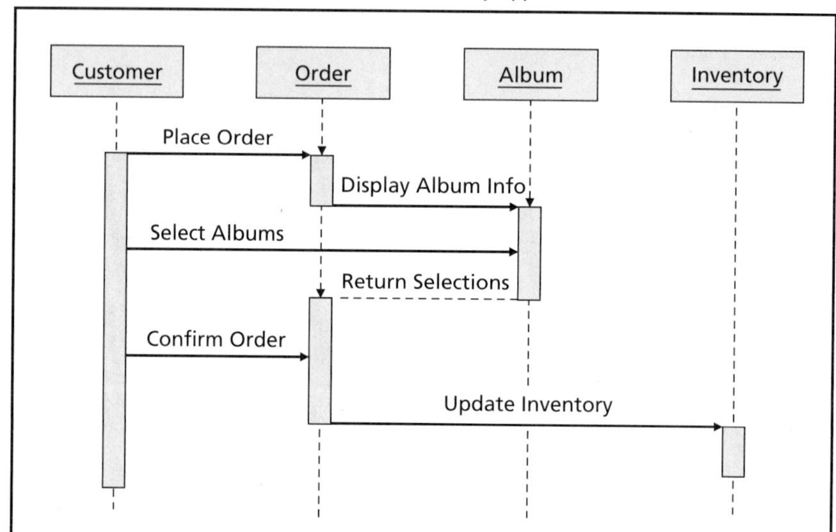

UML tools

There are many tools that can be used in creating UML diagrams, such as Rational Rose and Microsoft Visio. There are also many free UML tools that can be downloaded from the Internet, such as Visual Paradigm and ArgoUML. You can find these free tools and many others by using your favorite Internet search engine.

Each type of UML diagram describes different object-oriented functionality within a system. The developer can use these visual models as a blueprint when writing the actual source code.

UML tools allow you to create a UML diagram in much the same manner that you might paint a picture using a program such as Paint. Each diagram has predefined images that you can drop onto the workspace to represent different functionality within a specific UML diagram.

step 3—create the data dictionary

data dictionary – A document describing the type of data being utilized within the program, showing the table definitions, indexes, and other data relationships

You know the program incorporates a database if the user wants to store information. Unless a database is already in place, it is your job to help define the structure of the database. This might be a secondary role for you. The primary contact in charge of the database could be the database administrator (DBA). If the database is already in place, you should review it for accuracy by comparing it to your meeting notes and the project objectives, specifications, and requirements.

note

RULE: Determine if a database is needed; if so, create a data dictionary.

If the database is not in place and you are responsible for creating the database structure, you can review any reports the end user has provided to devise a list of data tables to use within the application.

The process of defining the database structure is defined more clearly in Chapter 8, "Databases."

note

RULE: Use the information from the end user to summarize the current system and organize a brief plan for the new application.

By reviewing all reports, you will have a good idea of what type of information the user needs to store.

Before you meet again with the end user, review the reports and design the necessary tables to be used within the application. The tables represent the information the end user wants to be stored. This information is what drives the application. For example, what good is an application if it cannot retrieve information so that the user can know the status of the inventory?

note

RULE: Review end-user reports to find possible tables and elements for a data dictionary.

Create a data dictionary of the tables by listing the table name, the order (or indexes) in which the data is sorted, a description of its use, and a comment for each field in the table (Figure 12-8).

The data dictionary becomes a schematic describing the type of data being utilized within the program. Software engineers and end users can both use this document to achieve a clearer understanding of the data available for use in reports, screens, file transfers, and other data operations.

step 4—design reports

It's time to meet with the end user and review your ideas on how you can help the company better maintain the media inventory. Bring along a notebook computer if possible or drag along your desktop loaded with development environment. This might seem like a major task sitting down with the end user at the computer, but in the long run you will reap many benefits by creating a program that specifically meets his or her needs.

Figure 12-8, Creating a data dictionary

Music Inventory Data Dictionary

Database is MIToeTappin written in Oracle 10i

Table: Artist

Indexes: *ByCode* *Artist_CD*
ByName *Artist_NM*

Use: This table contains all of the music artists.

Field	Description
ARTIST_CD	Unique code identifying record
ARTISTS_NM	Artist name

Table: Inventory

Indexes: *ByCode* *Media _CD*
ByType *Media_Type*

Use: This table contains all of the music items found in the store's inventory.

Field	Description
MEDIA _CD	Unique code identifying record
MEDIA_TYPE	Media type (CD, tape, album, etc.)
ON_HAND	Quantity on hand
MRP	Minimum re-order point
COST	Our cost
PRICE	Retail sales price

Start off by reviewing the data dictionary and explaining what data will be stored. Ask the user if there is any other data that needs to be kept. If you haven't accurately planned your data tables before you start the project, you are asking for trouble and planning on a missed deadline.

One of the ways you can include the end user in the design process is through the use of an Integrated Development Environment (IDE). An IDE is made up of different tools, wizards, and designers, making the programmer's job easier during the application development cycle.

note **RULE: Let the user help you design the reports.**

For example, you can use a report wizard or a report generator such as the one shown in Figure 12-9 to generate prototypes of the reports that Mr. Bop at Toe-Tappin' Tunes needs to have in the application.

Figure 12-9, Example of report created with report generator

Music CD Catalog
ToeTappin' Tunes
Sorted by Artist and Song Title

Print Date 1/16/2005

Artist Name	Song Title	CD Title
COUNTING CROWS		
	ANGELS OF THE SILENCES	RECOVERING THE SATELLITES
	MR. JONES	AUGUST AND EVERYTHING AFTER
	RECOVERING THE SATELLITES	RECOVERING THE SATELLITES
	TIME AND TIME AGAIN	AUGUST AND EVERYTHING AFTER
ERIC CLAPTON		
	BLUES BEFORE SUNRISE	ERIC CLAPTON UNPLUGGED
	HEY HEY	ERIC CLAPTON UNPLUGGED
	HOOCHIE COOCHIE MAN	ERIC CLAPTON UNPLUGGED
	LAYLA	ERIC CLAPTON UNPLUGGED
	TEARS IN HEAVEN	ERIC CLAPTON UNPLUGGED
HOWARD JONES		
	CONDITIONING	HUMAN'S LIB
	LOOK MAMA	BEST OF HOWARD JONES
	NEW SONG	BEST OF HOWARD JONES
	PEARL IN THE SHELL	BEST OF HOWARD JONES
	WHAT IS LOVE?	BEST OF HOWARD JONES
MANHATTAN TRANSFER		
	BIRDLAND	THE MANHATTAN TRANSFER ANTHOLOGY
	BOY FROM NEW YORK CITY	THE MANHATTAN TRANSFER ANTHOLOGY
	JAVA JIVE	THE MANHATTAN TRANSFER ANTHOLOGY

When you examine a report, you are presented with a snapshot of data that should exist within your application. Each of the columns in the report might represent a field or column within a data table. Each row of data that is printed on the report represents a record of information found in the data table.

You can sit down with the end user and interactively design the reports, using the reporting tools.

step 5—structuring the logical flow of the application

Now that the data structure is in place and the reports have been roughly designed, it is time to move on to the logical flow of the application.

note RULE: Create a logical flow of the application before you begin writing source code.

flowchart *– A combination of symbols and text that provide a visual description of a process*

The logical flow of the application details the main functionality of the system and the relationship of the different tasks to be completed. This can be done through the use of a ***flowchart***. Although some developers skip this step, it is always a good idea to sketch out or write down how the system should work before you start typing in lines of source code.

Some developers like to use formal flowchart diagrams. Consider the example shown in Figure 12-10, which shows how a student might drive to school.

Figure 12-10, Flowchart example

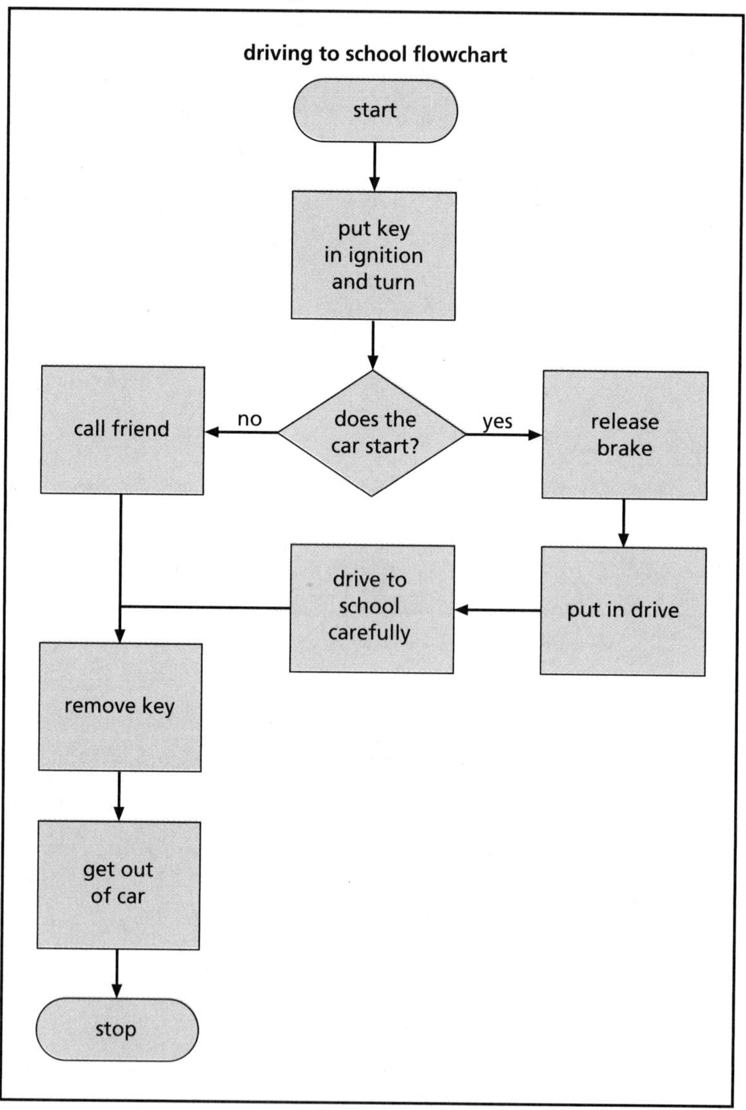

The different symbols in the flowchart represent different functions within a program. Figure 12-11 shows some of the symbols you might encounter in a flowchart.

Figure 12-11, Flowchart symbols

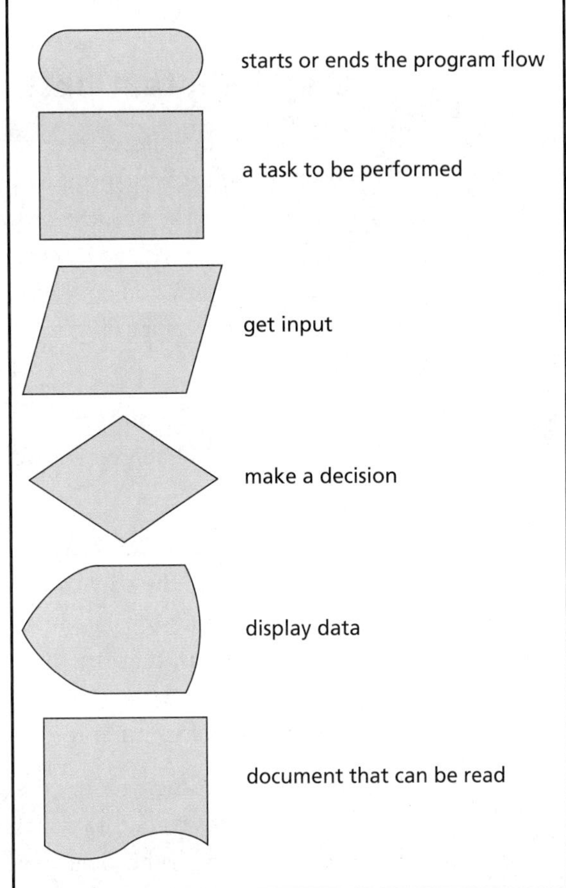

Others simply use pseudocode, as you saw in Chapter 11 on programming. Here is some sample pseudocode for the process of starting your car:

```
Start
Put the key in the car ignition
Turn the key
If the car does not start, call a friend to take you to
school
Else if the car does start
Release the brake
Put the car in drive
Drive to school carefully
End if
Remove key
Stop
```

However you do it, you should create some kind of formal definition of how the system is supposed to work before you start typing in the program. Time spent thinking and designing before actually using the keyboard will save much time later when you have to debug and maintain the program.

step 6—start building the prototype

Because the opening screen is the first thing the end user will see, and because it forms the user's first impression of your program, it is important that this screen reflects the purpose of the client and the main function of the program. The screens can be clever, cute, serious, or whatever the end user would like to make the application appealing. A good way to make sure you create or use screens that are appealing to the end user is to include the end user in the design process.

For example, Mr. Bop's music company focuses on disco music, so his opening screen should be representative of his company and the major task of the program.

When the screens are completed, you should take them to the end user for approval. Once the application startup screen is designed, it is time to move on to the data input screens. In this case, Mr. Bop wants to be able to update the inventory status, track the purchase information, maintain the employee information, and set up some form of program security. You also know that he needs to have a set of routines to manage the data in the table.

Asking the end user more questions opens a world of information you never even thought you had to worry about. For example, by continuing to have an open dialog with the client, you might learn new items that need to be incorporated in your application, such as artists, media produced by each artist, types of media, and so on.

note

RULE: Ask the end user as many questions as possible until you feel that you have a good understanding of the main functionality of the program.

One way to increase your productivity, and also include the end user in the design of the application, is to use some sort of form generator to create prototypes or nonworking samples for each of the screens you and the end user have decided to include in the application. Remember, not one line of code should be written until the user has agreed to the specifications and approves the screen prototypes.

note

RULE: *Do not write any source code until the project specifications are approved!*

A prototype is a standard or typical example that gives the end users a good idea of what they will see when their application is completed. It is *not* the actual product in place, ready to go. Instead, it is considered to be more of an overview of what the screens will look like, how the reports will look, and what the general flow of the application will be.

Let the end users help determine the colors, text, position of fields, anything that enables them to feel that they have a large part in deciding how the application will look and feel when it is complete. By including the end users you are building their sense of ownership of the product.

note **RULE: Let the user help you design the screens.**

The more work the user does, the better the application is when it is completed. In addition, users will like the system more because they feel that they had a major part in developing it.

step 7—putting all of the pieces together

Almost all of the pieces of the application design have been put together and it is time to thank the end users for their time and head back to your office. Take all of the information you have gathered and create the design document. Much of this is simply putting all of the pieces together that you already have, along with dates, time lines, and price estimates.

note **RULE: Be realistic in defining project completion dates.**

Be very careful in giving dates or price estimates to make sure they are realistic and feasible. Remember that end users will hold you to dates or figures that you give, so you have to take the time to be accurate in your estimating process. The end users want that application and they want it now. If the user adds more details to the application, simple logic says that the date of completion should be extended. End users don't always think that way. Although the user might say, "Yeah, yeah, we know that you will need more time to complete the project if you add these other details," they often only remember the date on your earliest estimate.

The design document should contain the following items:

- Header page describing the contents
- Project objective
- Defined terms relating to the project
- Feasibility study
- Project specifications and requirements
- Project cost analysis
- Database dictionary
- Copies of screens (or prototype)
- Copies of reports
- Diagrams (UML and flowchart of all business processes)
- Plans to test the software after it is written
- Plans to gather user feedback regarding the functionality of the system
- Notes from meetings

You can also include information, such as employee bios and company profiles or other material you feel would be appropriate for readers to fully understand the key players involved in the application and how it will be accomplished.

And don't forget this important part of the design document: a place for the end users to sign indicating that they have read the document and that they accept it as the basis for creating the program. By having a signature in the design document you can use it as a contract for work.

Almost always, something changes after the design document is signed. Whether it is a new item that the end user wants to include or an item forgotten by the system designer, the document probably needs to be amended. In this case, you don't need to start over, designing all of the screens and placing copies of the reports, screens, menus, and tables in a document. Simply create an addendum detailing the new items. The end user should be required to sign an agreement to modify the date of the deadline and your fee if necessary, since the scope of the project has changed.

note

RULE: Make the user sign the design document, thus agreeing to the deadline defined by the scope of the project.

If the application is not completed by the deadline because of frequent changes in the scope of the project by the end user, by documenting these changes you have at least protected your reputation (perhaps your job) within your own company.

avoiding the pitfalls

After looking at the process of software engineering, and all the rules involved in creating a design document, you might feel a little hesitant. What if the project fails miserably? What might go wrong, and what can you do to help your projects succeed? The next sections warn of some common problems and pitfalls, and tell you how to avoid them.

user-phobia

What if the end user messes up the whole process? One of the biggest mistakes you can make when designing an application is to be "user-phobic." User-phobia is the fear that if you include the end user in the design process, the application will be a failure.

Some programmers have the attitude that end users are stupid and have no idea of what is needed in creating an application to meet their needs. You need to remember that the end users are actually sitting in the driver's seat. It's their application. If they don't like the colors yellow on blue, then change to whatever colors they want. Just make sure to document everything.

There are some instances when the user's ideas might not be correct. If the end user wants something in the application that simply cannot be done, tell them honestly it cannot be done. Don't get in the habit of saying "Sure. No problem. I can do anything. I am Zeus, master of the keyboard!" Treat the end user as you would any customer. Whether the end users are outside contacts or in-house employees, they are still considered customers and have all the rights and privileges that pertain to that label.

Remember to keep a good line of communication with the end users. Let them know what is happening. A weekly update informing the end users of the progress made on the application is often a good idea. An informed end user is a happy end user.

note **RULE: Keep the lines of communication open with the end user.**

too much work

Another problem that you might run into is the "heap on the work" syndrome. In this scenario, a programmer's manager gives the programmer a deadline to complete a project, but later gives the programmer more work that has a higher priority than the previous work. Of course, the manager specifies that the first deadline cannot change. In this situation, the manager is setting the programmer up for failure on both projects. You, as the programmer, need to be assertive and explain to your manager what will happen to the deadline for the first project if the second project takes priority. By doing so, you save yourself a lot of grief and heartache. Once again, protect yourself by documenting everything.

scope creep

scope creep – Occurs when new changes are continually added to a project thus changing the proposed completion date so that the project is never completed, but is instead in a constant improvement mode

The last big pitfall that can seriously affect whether you meet your deadline is called ***scope creep***. This occurs when the end user keeps adding functionality to the system after you have already agreed upon the project specifications and requirements, thus changing the deadline date. This process of making changes and extending the deadline continues until finally a manager above you steps in and asks, "Will this project ever be completed?"

To avoid scope creep, one common tactic is to use a phased approach. Any changes the user wants that significantly affect the project's deadline can be put into a second phase. The first phase can continue as planned. Once the first phase is finished, tested, and delivered to the end user, you can begin on phase two. As the program is being used, the end user might find problems or other issues that need to be addressed. These can also be placed in phase two, or if needed, pushed into a phase three.

The main point is that you need to deliver something to the end user on schedule! Let the users start working with the product while you continue to make other changes.

the project development team

An application can be developed by one developer or a team of developers. Many software development departments support team development because it allows the individual team members to run the IDE on their workstations while storing the necessary tables on a network.

To help you understand how a successful team is built, the next sections outline the various players that can be included in the team, their roles, and how they interact with other members of the team and with clients.

project manager

project manager – Leader of the software development team who is responsible for choosing the right players for the right positions and making sure the project is on schedule

The ***project manager*** is the leader of the team and is responsible for choosing the right players for the right positions. The project manager is the team builder. The manager is responsible for determining the risks involved with the project, the cost, and the schedule of tasks.

Determining the risks and costs many times comes through experience. Scheduling the various tasks involved in the project and keeping up with team member responsibilities is generally done using project management software

Figure 12-12, A project management tool helps a manager keep track of the status of the project

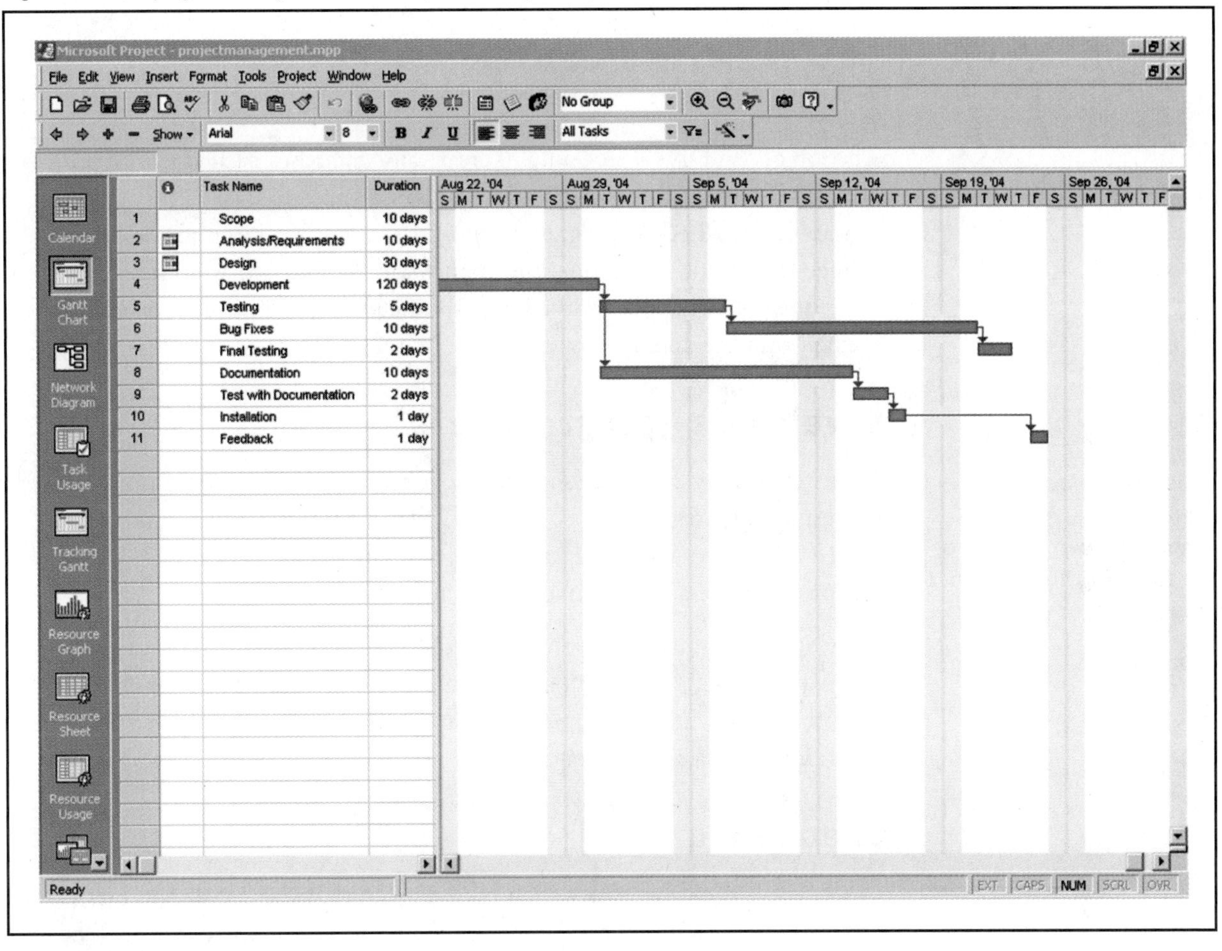

such as Microsoft Project (Figure 12-12). The manager uses a project management tool to track the different tasks that need to be completed, the assignments of the tasks, the status of the tasks, and the costs associated with each.

The project manager is also responsible for pulling together all of the pieces of the project and incorporating them into the design document.

creator of the database

database administrator – Person assigned the role of creating and maintaining the database structure

The individual assigned the role of creating the database is often referred to as the ***database administrator*** or DBA. Creating the database involves taking the information from the design meetings with the end user and creating a data dictionary. The data dictionary serves as a road map for the structures of the data tables. It is created by reviewing the screens and reports the end user would like included in the application and determining which fields are essential to the application.

note

Have only one person in charge of creating and maintaining the databases to reduce confusion and errors.

The job of the DBA is not only to create any databases needed by the project, but also to maintain them and manage changes and updates to the data stored in the files. If all of the programmers on the team were given the ability to change the database structure, the application would once again be heading down the path of application failure. Too many DBAs in the programming kitchen ruin the application.

developers (programmers)

software developer (or programmer) – Person responsible for writing source code to meet the functional requirements of the end user

Teams include one or more ***software developers*** (also called ***programmers***) who are responsible for writing the program. Many times, developers are also involved in creating UML diagrams. The developer takes the design document or blueprint for the application and turns it into a tangible product.

Developers use software development tools and good logical skills to create programs that meet the project requirements and objectives. The lines of source code that they write also implement the UML diagrams such as the class, use case, and sequence UML diagrams.

client (end user)

The client is the driving force behind the project. The client or end user is the one that has a need that can be met by the project development team. The client can be internal (works for the same company as the software developers) or external (does not work for the company that is creating the program).

Clients usually know what they want, but many times do not know how to explain it to the developers. The developers usually know how to meet the needs of the client, but often times do not know how to communicate the process to the client.

note

Clients know what they want. Your job as the software developer is to help them communicate their needs and translate it into a software development project.

tester

Every program has to be tested. An untested program is a program that is doomed to fail. Many corporations have a quality assurance (QA) department responsible for putting out good products. The development team is responsible for testing its program before it is turned over to the quality assurance team. The quality assurance team then puts the program through a series of tests. The results are then communicated back to the software developers who in turn fix the problems, test, and redeliver the product to the quality assurance team for another round of testing.

tester *– Person responsible for making sure the program functions correctly and that it meets all of the specified functional requirements set forth in the design document*

The role of **tester** is one of the most critical roles in application development. Not only should the developers test the application as it is being written, but there should be at least one or two people, including the end user, designated as testers. Too many times a product is written and presented to the end user without being thoroughly tested. This results in wasted time and a lowering of confidence in the application (and its developers). If there are too many bugs in the application, the end user will stop using it and seek a different means of accomplishing the job. This could mean reverting to the previous way of handling day-to-day operations, or finding another developer for the application. Either way, insufficient testing can blemish your reliability and could jeopardize your career.

no bugs?

No application is bug free. You should tell this to the end user when the application is being created, delivered, and tested. Be happy when end users find bugs. Thank them for letting you know, fix the problem fast, and hope that the bug is the last one you encounter!

Here are a few pointers on testing:

- Make sure to run the application through a series of tests that mimic the environment the end user will be using. This environment includes monitors, CPUs, printers, and any other hardware the end user might have or is using.
- Make sure the programmers have developed the application to handle any situation that could arise. Some developers take the stand that the end user would never try to do something a certain way because it just isn't logical. If anyone can break the application, the end user can, so put yourself in his or her place and try to test situations that aren't always logical.
- Keep a log of the errors encountered during testing and after the release of the application. Record the date the error occurred, a description of the error, the procedure that you think created the bug, what was done or needs to be done to fix the problem, and who is responsible for handling the error.

Some day, you might end up hearing or taking part in the following scenario. An end user calls up the developer and in panicked voice says, "I just had a problem occur while I was using the application!" The developer chokes down a question of, "Why me?" and proceeds to calm the end user. The developer asks the end user to explain the process that resulted in the error and asks him or her to describe the error information that appeared on the screen. It is now the end user who chokes down the question of, "Why me?" and informs the developer that the information was not kept. A wave of relief passes over the developer as the popular technical support response of, "Call me if it happens again," is echoed through the telephone receiver. The developer hangs up the phone and says, "Whew! Dodged that bullet!" This situation occurs every day. As a developer you shouldn't be afraid of the errors. Instead, be thankful that the end user has found them and is willing to help you resolve the problem.

customer relations representative

customer relations representative (or support technician) – Person responsible for interfacing with the testers, developers, and end users during the creation and early release of the product and later in an ongoing basis with the end user as long as the product is being used

The *customer relations representative* (or *support technician*) is the interface between the testers, developers, and end users during the creation and early release cycles of the product. After the early release stage, you might want to create a help desk to handle all calls pertaining to the use of the application or errors encountered by using the application.

generator of the application CD

Once the application is completed, tested, and debugged, it is time to create the disks to install on the end user's machine. This is not a full-time job, so the customer relations person might be able to handle this responsibility. The role of the generator of the application disks is to interface with the developers to make sure that all of the necessary files are included on the disks.

note Make sure to scan for viruses before copying the installation program to any distribution media!

Many IDEs include a utility for creating installation disks, which makes the task easier.

installer of the application disks

It's show time! After the installation disks have been created, it is time to install the program on the end user's machine. It is recommended that the customer relations person also take on the role of installer because the customer relations person should already have a good relationship with the end user. Once the installation process is complete, the installer should stay with the end user while the end user test-drives the application. Take the user on a guided tour of the application, showing all the bells and whistles the application has to offer.

note Train the end user well so that he or she can train other end users.

If the end user does not feel comfortable using the application, you might need to schedule additional training sessions. Once one user is trained, that user can train other end users in their own departments.

Reinforce your understanding of chapter concepts and terms with the information and activities for Chapter 12 on the student CD.

one last thought

Good design results in good programs. If you skip some of the steps involved in creating an application or cut corners, you will probably see the results in poor performance, unmet client needs, or a project than runs over budget and over schedule. The project manager's primary responsibilities are to build a team that can work well together, and to keep the project on schedule and within budget. By making sure the project follows all the steps outlined in the design document and is put through a thorough testing cycle, the team can ensure that the program will meet the needs of the client.

chapter summary

- Software engineering involves many different steps that can be followed in order to create an application that meets an end user's needs
- The process of building the application is accomplished by implementing a software development life cycle (SDLC) process
- Each SDLC provides a different way of detailing the steps used in creating a software product
- A design document is created to act as a blueprint for software development. The design document outlines all of the functionality of an application
- There are several steps that can be followed when creating a design document: researching the needs of the end user, communication, logical design of screens, reports, and data structures, and all of the other necessary steps that must take place before any source code is written
- UML or unified modeling language is a tool that enables developers and end users to visually design the functionality of the system
- There are several types of UML diagrams, each serving a particular purpose or describing a part of the system being developed
- Using the reports and the data dictionary can help a developer assess any "holes" that might exist in the design of the system
- Software development is often a team effort; building a team involves knowing the specific roles of each member
- Team members often include a project manager, database administrator, developer/programmers(s), client/end users, a tester, and sometimes customer relations and other roles
- Once the application has been developed, installation disks need to be generated
- After the system is installed on the client's system, spend some time training initial end users, who can in turn train other end users

key terms

customer relations representative (or support technician) (490)

data dictionary (476)

database administrator (487)

design document (470)

end user (468)

flowchart (480)

project manager (486)

prototype (469)

software developer (or programmer) (488)

software development life cycle (SDLC) (468)

software engineering (468)

scope creep (486)

tester (489)

Unified Modeling Language (UML) (472)

test yourself

1. Describe software engineering and how it plays a part in computer science.
2. What is a design document and how does it affect software engineering?
3. Write the pseudocode steps for a program that would process an ATM machine for a savings deposit.
4. Write the pseudo code steps for a program that would process a savings withdrawal from an ATM machine.
5. How can UML help a developer create a program that could meet an end user's needs?
6. How can a data dictionary be used in software development?
7. What is a prototype and how can it be implemented in software engineering?
8. What are some of the mistakes you could make while designing and developing a software program?
9. Describe the Waterfall SDLC process model.
10. List each of the software development team roles and describe the job function.
11. Draw a flowchart for using a microwave to heat up a TV dinner for 2 minutes.
12. Write the pseudo code for using a microwave to heat up a TV dinner for 2 minutes.
13. Draw a flowchart for making a purchase on the Internet.
14. Write the pseudocode for making a purchase on the Internet.
15. Draw a flowchart and write the pseudocode for an application that allows a professor to keep track of 10 student homework assignments, 4 quiz scores, and 2 test scores. The average grade should be calculated for each and then a final grade should be calculated by taking the average of all three.

practice questions

1. End users and clients need to be told what they want and how the program should do their job.

   a. True
   b. False

2. Which is *not* included as a task of software engineering?

   a. Communicating with the clients in meetings
   b. Designing screens
   c. Writing the application
   d. Creating a design document
   e. None of the above

3. A design document is used as:

   a. A way to bill the client more
   b. A blueprint showing the functionality of a system
   c. A replacement for pseudocode when writing a program
   d. Nonc of thc above

4. Which is *not* part of the SDLC?

   a. Project feasibility
   b. Software design
   c. Software implementation
   d. Software proposal to client
   e. All are part of the SDLC

5. Which is *not* a valid software process model?

   a. Waterfall
   b. Degradation
   c. Evolution
   d. Spiral
   e. Incremental

6. UML was designed to:

   a. Assist developers in creating visual models of the system functionality
   b. Assist developers in designing screens and reports
   c. Incorporate object-oriented design topics into application development
   d. Replace the outdated notion of pseudocode

7. The best way to write a good program is to have an initial meeting with the end user to find out what the requirements are for the project, go back to your office and write the program, and then deliver the finished product for installation.

   a. True
   b. False

8. The document responsible for describing the type of data being stored in the database is called the:

    a. Design document
    b. Data dictionary
    c. UML diagram
    d. SDLC
    e. None of the above

9. It is recommended to include the end user during the entire design process. In fact, you can even let them help design the screens and reports.

    a. True
    b. False

10. A ______ is used as a visual model for describing the logical flow of a program.

    a. Flowchart
    b. Class diagram
    c. Use case diagram
    d. Design document
    e. None of the above

11. A ______ is a standard or typical example without all of the built-in functionality of how something might actually work.

    a. Flowchart
    b. Prototype
    c. Design document
    d. Data dictionary
    e. None of the above

12. Which should *not* be included in the design document?

    a. Project objectives and requirements
    b. Cost analysis
    c. Feasibility study
    d. Copies of screens and reports
    e. All should be included

13. Scope creep is good for a project since it is one of the software development life cycles.

    a. True
    b. False

14. If the end users or testers finds a bug in the application, it would be prudent to find out why they insist on breaking the program and get them some training so they will stop making it crash.

    a. True
    b. False

15. The role of the tester is not as critical as other team roles and should be the first role eliminated if the project is behind the scheduled completion date.

    a. True
    b. False

discussion topics

1. Which member of the software development team has the most important role and why?
2. Which software engineering step do you consider to be the most important and why?
3. Do you think UML is a viable way of doing software engineering and will software development departments adopt it? Why or why not?
4. What do you think the biggest challenge is when doing software engineering?
5. The biggest problem with creating a design document is the time spent in meetings trying to determine the client's needs, research, and organization. How can you convince your employer or a client to pay for the time spent in creating a good design document even if it means it will delay the project's completion date?

digging deeper

1. Research and describe the software development life cycle model processes described in this chapter.
2. What are the different software packages available on the market for doing project management? Give a brief description of each product along with the maker and the cost.
3. What are the different software packages available on the market for generating reports? Give a brief description of the products along with the maker and the cost.
4. What are the different software packages available on the market for flowcharting? Give a brief description of the product along with the maker and the cost.
5. Why do you think it is so important to get the end user to sign the design document agreeing that the document meets the requirements for the project? What would you do if the requirements changed after the document had already been signed?

Internet research

1. What are the number of available jobs and average salaries currently in your state or province for software engineers?
2. What are the number of available jobs and average salaries currently in your state for developers that have UML skills?
3. What are the products and their links to free UML drawing packages?
4. What are some Internet links teaching software engineering skills?
5. What are some of the newer software engineering process models currently being discussed in the software development community?

13

chapter

computing security and ethics

in this chapter you will:

- Learn about the origins of computer hacking
- Learn about some of the motivations for hackers and crackers
- Learn about technologies that system intruders use
- Learn about malicious code
- Learn what social engineering is and how it works
- Learn how security experts categorize types of system attacks
- Learn about physical and technical safeguards
- Learn how to select a good password
- Learn about antivirus software
- Learn about encryption
- Learn about preventive system setup, including firewalls and routers
- Learn about laws to protect intellectual property and prosecute cracking
- Learn about ethical behavior in computing
- Learn about privacy in computing and ways to assure it

the lighter side of the lab
by spencer

Have you ever noticed that the only "cool" computer people in the movies are computer hackers? It's not often that you see a scene where dramatic music is playing in the background, while Larry down the hall sits in his cubicle and programs a for-next loop.

Sometimes I wish that I were a computer hacker. Now, I don't want to break into government files or the university database (not even a hacker could make *my* grades look good). I just want to be able to get into my computer the day after I change my password.

We're told that it's important to rotate our passwords frequently in order to make our computers more secure. The only problem with that idea is that my brain seems to contain only "virtual memory" these days. As soon as I "shut down" at night, the password information disappears from my brain.

Trying to guess your password is fun in a way. It's almost like a game. "Okay, I was thinking about my aunt when I created this password. She has a dog named Fluffy. She got Fluffy in the month of May. My password must be 'fluffymay'!" BUZZ! "mayfluffy"? BUZZ! "05fluffy"? BUZZ! "fluffy05"? BUZZ! "$%*&!" BUZZ!!

I've finally resorted to writing my usernames and passwords on yellow sticky notes that I paste all over the front of my computer. So now I'm completely secure . . . as long as someone isn't sitting at my computer. (Professional hackers around the world would have a hard time getting in, but a kindergartener sitting at my desk shouldn't have any problems.)

Yellow sticky notes are an essential tool for any computer person. My computer often resembles a big, yellow piñata. Besides holding all my username and password information, the yellow sticky notes on my computer contain my to-do lists, important phone numbers and dates, reminders to pay bills, and the names of the seven dwarfs (just in case).

One thing I could do to improve computer security would be to clean my desk. I'm currently on the annual cleaning schedule. At this very moment, I face the risk of paper avalanche. I'm personally considering the purchase of one of those cannons they use to prevent avalanches at ski resorts for my office. I'd better check to see if they have one on eBay. Now, what was my password?

why you need to know about...
computing security and ethics

Clifford Stoll, a systems manager at Lawrence Berkeley National Laboratory in California, was tracking a 75-cent accounting error. His search for the source of that error led to a year of investigation, and eventually to a programmer in West Germany who turned out to be part of a spy ring that sold computer secrets to the Soviet Union's KGB in return for money and drugs. Stoll's 1989 book about his experience, *The Cuckoo's Egg*, was a bestseller.

When it comes to computer security and ethics, it's tempting to think in such dramatic images: the clean-cut genius nerd catches the lone wolf, evil scientist hacker. This is not a totally incorrect set of characterizations, as it turns out. But creating computer security and frustrating would-be intruders is a much broader, more complex, and more mundane undertaking than Hollywood's typical portrayal. It involves more than computer detectives and lurking intruders. Good computer security is primarily a matter of prevention—including preventing and recovering from accidental and natural events. And computer security must not exist in a vacuum but must link to good security practices and professional ethical standards for computing. Good computer security, then, is as much about locking doors, storing backups, and following protocol as it is about writing smarter software to catch the bad guys.

Computer security is important because it affects everyone and everyone can affect it. You have probably already been subjected to a virus or worm attack and perhaps played unwittingly into propagating infection to other computers. You have probably already had the unpleasant experience of losing important files (usually right before you have to hand them in to your professor). Being aware of threats and how to prevent or counteract them, as well as being conscious of the possible effects of your actions as a computer scientist, are becoming increasingly important.

the intruder

hacker – *A technically proficient individual who breaks into a computer system; originally connoted good intent, but general usage today is similar to cracker*

cracker – *An unwelcome system intruder with malicious intent*

The term ***hacker*** (or ***cracker***) is often used to refer to an intruder who breaks into a computer system with malicious intent. The term originated in the 1960s, and it originally meant an insider who was able manipulate the system for the good of the system. At that time, programming was a difficult and esoteric art practiced by very few people. The best of the programmers were called hackers as a sign of respect, and a good program that took advantage of the system as best it could was called a "hack." Over time, however, the connotation of "hacker" in the eyes of the general public has become much more negative and synonymous with "cracker," although the computer security industry still differentiates between a hacker (technically proficient individual) and a cracker (unwelcome system intruder).

phreaking – *Subverting the phone system to get free service*

Around the same time, some people began illegally manipulating the AT&T phone system, mimicking certain tones to obtain free long-distance calls. A fellow who called himself Cap'n Crunch discovered that using a whistle that came in a box of cereal by the same name allowed the whistler to subvert the phone system. The practice was called ***phreaking***, and those who did it became known as phreaks.

Some of the phreaks started getting into computers as the microcomputer revolution took hold. In fact, some of these characters went legit and became beneficiaries of the revolution. Cap'n Crunch, whose real name is John Draper, helped write some of the most important applications for Microsoft. Unfortunately, a number of characters also applied their technical proficiency to computers in a negative way. By breaking into mainframes and creating viruses, they subverted the word "hacker" from meaning a technically savvy insider helping to make the system better to a potentially dangerous outsider. The labels "cracker" or just plain "criminal" are also used.

undirected (untargeted) hacker – *A cracker motivated by the challenge of breaking into a system*

directed (targeted) hacker – *Generally, a cracker motivated by greed and/or politics*

These hackers are now the semi-romantic figures from movies, books, and magazines who either wear the "black hat" and threaten the world or the "white hat" and promise to save the world. But, who are they really? Many intruders are fairly innocent browsers or computer users who stumble into a security hole and cause problems. But, intentional intruders are generally divided into two classes: those motivated primarily by the challenge of breaking into a system, called ***undirected*** (or ***untargeted***) ***hackers*** and those motivated by greed or malicious intent, called ***directed*** (or ***targeted***) ***hackers***. In this book "cracker," "malicious hacker," "directed hacker," and "undirected hacker" are used to indicate an unwanted system intruder.

Studies have found the cracker profile to be generally a male between 16 and 35 years old whom many would consider a loner. The person also tends to be intelligent as well as technically savvy. Novice crackers who really only know

script kiddie – An amateur hacker that simply uses the hacking tools that have been developed by others

how to use the tools that already exist earn the moniker ***script kiddie***. Crackers intent on remaining anonymous while they steal or damage (directed hackers) are usually the most proficient.

hacktivism – Cracking into a system as a political act; one political notion is that cracking itself is useful for society

Hacker's Manifesto – A document, written anonymously, that justifies cracking into systems as an ethical exercise

One of the biggest motivators for cracking for the undirected hacker is bragging rights. Often these undirected hackers comb the Internet looking for systems that are vulnerable and have not yet been cracked. Once they've cracked a system they boast about it on Internet Relay Chat (IRC), message boards, or submit to magazines such as *2600: The Hacker Quarterly*. Many crackers close the security hole that they've taken advantage of after they've gained entry so that no other cracker can follow. The justification for this can be to have sole control of the system. Another justification is ***hacktivism***. Many crackers believe they are doing society a favor by discovering these security holes before "real criminals" do. A document on the Internet called the ***Hacker's Manifesto*** justifies cracker activity for this very reason.

Greed tends to motivate directed hackers, who unfortunately tend to be more proficient and do not advertise their exploits. This type of hacker looks for information that can be sold or used to blackmail the organization that holds it. Hackers of this type tend to target corporations that have assets of monetary value.

Malicious hackers—either interested in vandalizing or terrorism—can be both directed and undirected. Undirected hackers tend to write viruses and worms, without knowing where they will end up. They are content with the random violence of the act. These intrusions can damage systems at many levels. Some attacks are fairly benign while others can cause billions of dollars of damage. Directed hackers usually direct their efforts at organizations or individuals where there is some perceived wrong. For example, a directed hacker might vandalize a company's Web site because he was fired or was dissatisfied with the company's product. Directed hackers might also be interested in making political statements. Usually the intent of directed hackers is to damage, not gain quiet access.

Whether directed or undirected, malicious, greedy, or benign, hired by a competing corporation, the Mob, or part of a terrorist organization, hackers are an increasingly expensive and dangerous aspect of computing. In monetary terms, illegal hacking becomes more expensive each year, and there seems no end in sight. So, how do the unwanted visitors do it?

how do they get in?

The sad truth is that, historically, most intrusions could have been avoided with good system configuration, proper programming techniques, and adherence to security policies: neglecting these leads to holes in the system that can quickly be taken advantage of by directed hackers. Even more quick to take advantage of systems are the malicious software programs commonly known as viruses. It takes milliseconds for a virus (or worm) to invade an unprotected system over a network. Finally, crackers take advantage of the innocent human tendency to be helpful. This most non-technical approach—called social engineering—is often one of the most effective tools for intruders.

holes in the system

One major benefit to crackers is the open nature of the Internet. The whole point of the Internet when it was created was that it would allow sharing of information and computer resources. The same could be said of the World Wide Web and networks. Unfortunately, this openness benefited malicious intent. For example, in UNIX, the Network File System (NFS) allows for a user on one machine to mount (or see) a drive on another machine as if it were local (called cross-mounting). In the early days of computers, all a cracker had to do was mount someone else's drive using the appropriate user ID number. Even more dangerous was the fact that the root file system (where passwords and configuration files for the machine reside) was open for reading and writing. Protecting user IDs and system files was something system administrators had to learn quickly. Individual users also became vulnerable to this type of intrusion when they began using remote terminal access or PCAnywhere-type programs to share Windows drives with remote users. A naive user easily could open his entire system to the world without knowing or intending it.

backdoors – Shortcuts into programs created by system designers to facilitate system maintenance but used and abused by crackers

Crackers have taken considerable advantage of ***backdoors*** left by programmers and administrators for their own convenience. The UNIX *rlogin* (remote login) command allows an administrator to log into one system and then remotely log into other machines without having a password. This command benefits system managers in maintaining the machines on their system. Unfortunately, this can also benefit a cracker because a configuration error could easily allow anyone to have the same kind of access. Early versions of the UNIX e-mail program Sendmail had a backdoor in which a three-letter command could gain you access to system level control (called the "root" on Unix systems) where you could delete, modify, and replace protected operating system programs.

Sloppy programming plays a major role in creating holes crackers can exploit. For example, many online shopping sites have kept information about the purchase a customer is making right in the URL string displayed in the address window. If the site doesn't verify the price of the item in the cart at purchase and a cracker modifies the price, then the cracker potentially walks away with some pretty cheap merchandise. Buffer overflows are another vulnerability of many systems. They are fairly easy to fix, even easier to not allow in the first place, but are endemic to computer programs. A ***buffer overflow*** is when a program tries to place more information into a location in memory than that location can handle. For example, if you try to put an 8-byte integer into a 1-byte character variable, that is an overflow. An overflow that overloads

buffer overflow – When a program tries to place more information into a memory location than that location can handle

memory all the way to a section of memory critical to the operation of the machine is what a cracker is aiming for. The most critical memory sections in a computer are in the instruction stack. The goal of a cracker is to stuff an address of a program that they want run onto the stack. Once they do that, they have control of the machine.

viruses, worms, and other nasty things

malicious code – Code designed to breach your system security and threaten your digital information; often called a virus, although technically a virus is only one kind of malicious code

virus – A virus is an uninvited guest program on your computer—with the potential to damage files and the operating system; this term is sometimes used generically to denote a virus, worm, or Trojan horse

Crackers can create ***malicious code*** to do their work for them. This code is designed to breach your system security and threaten your digital information. Malicious code comes in a few major forms: the Trojan horse, the virus, and the worm.

A ***virus*** is a program that, when run, can infect the machine directly or actively searches for programs to infect and embeds itself into those programs. When those programs are run, they activate the virus program which infects the machine. Sometimes the virus is silent or at least silent for a while. Usually, the virus affects the host machine. It can do anything from playing a little tune and then eliminating itself to destroying files on the hard drive. Some other evidence that you have a virus might be:

- Programs do not run properly. Files do not open properly.
- Disk space or memory become far less than they should be.
- Existing files or icons disappear.
- Machine runs very slowly.
- Unknown programs, files, processes appear.

Viruses can also target particular files, such as system files, and become difficult to remove. Technically, viruses, unlike worms, require assistance in moving between machines; users sharing files is a common way they move. The first viruses appear almost quaint now. They appeared in the early 1980s and were spread by individuals swapping floppy disks. Booting from an infected disk was a common means of infection. With the widespread adoption of e-mail, however, viruses can spread like wildfire. Beware of attachments: They can host a virus that runs when the attachment is opened. Figure 13-1 shows a typical virus warning from a system administrator.

worm – A type of bot that can roam a network looking for vulnerable systems and replicate itself onto those systems; the new copies look for still more vulnerable systems

bot – A software program that can roam the Internet autonomously; bots can be quite benign and useful, such as those used by Google and other search engine companies to find links to list on their Web sites

A ***worm*** is a program that actively reproduces itself across a network. This code is a type of ***bot*** (short for robot) because of its ability to work on its own. Worms seek out vulnerable systems, invade them, and continue to seek more systems. It is far more active than a virus, which requires humans to move it between machines. The first catastrophic worm event was the Great Worm or Morris Worm of 1988 written by graduate student Robert T. Morris. It was a "benign" worm—the user intended it to do no damage—yet it brought down over 10 percent of the Internet.

Figure 13-1, A typical virus e-mail warning

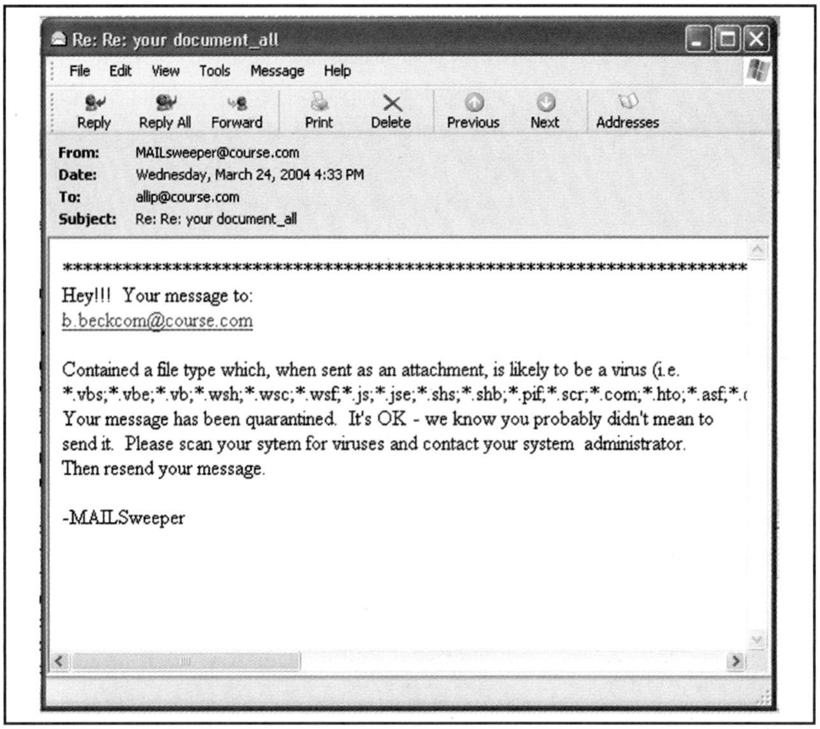

Re: Re: your document_all

File Edit View Tools Message Help

Reply Reply All Forward Print Delete Previous Next Addresses

From: MAILsweeper@course.com
Date: Wednesday, March 24, 2004 4:33 PM
To: allip@course.com
Subject: Re: Re: your document_all

****

Hey!!! Your message to:
b.beckcom@course.com

Contained a file type which, when sent as an attachment, is likely to be a virus (i.e.
.vbs;.vbe;*.vb;*.wsh;*.wsc;*.wsf;*.js;*.jse;*.shs;*.shb;*.pif;*.scr;*.com;*.hto;*.asf;*.(
Your message has been quarantined. It's OK - we know you probably didn't mean to
send it. Please scan your sytem for viruses and contact your system administrator.
Then resend your message.

-MAILSweeper

Trojan horse – A program that poses as an innocent program; some action or the passage of time triggers the program to do its dirty work

A *Trojan horse* program disguises itself as something innocent such as a game or, the worst possible example, an antivirus program. Once on a host system it can lay dormant and then either do obvious damage or clandestine system analysis, potentially compromising the system by finding backdoors, and so on.

the human factor—social engineering

social engineering – Social interaction that preys on human gullibility, sympathy, or fear to take advantage of the target, e.g., to steal money, information, or other valuables—basically, a con

For those crackers intent on breaking into a particular system, the best approach turns out to be not one of exploiting technical holes but one called *social engineering*. A social engineer is a contemporary term for something that has been around for a long time. You might better recognize the labels "con artist," "grifter," or "flimflam man." These individuals use their understanding of human behavior to get important information from trusting "marks."

The ability to lie persuasively is the most effective tool in the social engineer's arsenal. If the social engineer knows an employee's name, the social engineer might pose as that employee, call the human resources department, get just a little more information, and then call computer support looking for a password. Posing as an insider, the social engineer strings together bits of information, gaining more information from various sources. There are many support organizations just doing their jobs that have unwittingly given away passwords to a caller posing as an authorized user. After all, it's the job of technical support to be helpful.

dumpster diving – Picking through people's trash to find things of value; though often innocent, it has been used by thieves to glean information that is potentially damaging

Social engineers can also find information just by hanging out in the right places: the smokers' circle that forms around 10 A.M. outside, or at a favorite coffee shop down the block. If the con artist can't get the kind of information he or she wants over the phone or in person, there's always ***dumpster diving***—essentially sifting through trash, suffering through a few rotten banana peels to find information about companies and individuals. (Of course, with recycling, you don't even have to worry about the banana peels!) Even things as seemingly innocent as the corporate phone book can be used by a social engineer to pick out the right people and just use the right corporate lingo to dupe someone into revealing more than they should. For this reason more and more shredders are used and corporate dumpsters are locked. Individuals might do the same.

Generally, the social engineer tries to maintain a low profile and not show his or her face if possible. Something as simple as browsing the company Web site—which the company wants the casual user to do—is a good way to gather information. Some companies have also combined what should be an internal intranet of information with their public Internet site. In that case, details about employees, corporate events, and other information that is only of value to employees might be available to outsiders. A social engineer might also use traditional cracker techniques to augment the attack. Installing a fake login box on a user's computer that captures the person's name and password is one technique. Another is sending out a spam mail for a chance to win money that requires a username and password. Many people will use the same username and password as they do in other programs.

One notorious social engineer was Kevin Mitnick. At one point in the 1990s he was on the FBI's ten most wanted list. He was subsequently caught, tried, and sent to jail. Since then, in an effort to turn over a new leaf, he has revealed many of his techniques for the benefit of the security community.

types of attacks

As you've seen, crackers use a variety of techniques (both directed and undirected) to gain entry to or compromise a system. Security managers divide these attacks into four primary categories:

- Access
- Modification
- Denial of service
- Repudiation

access attack – An attack on a system that can include snooping, eavesdropping, and interception; it is more basically known as spying or illicitly gaining access to protected information

Access attacks include snooping, eavesdropping, and interception. Snooping can be anything from snooping around a person's desk with the hope of finding something interesting to browsing a person's software files. Eavesdropping is putting a bug in an office, wiretapping, or tapping onto a network to listen

sniffer – A software program that allows the user to listen in on the traffic of a network

to communication across that medium using a ***sniffer***. Interception is a more invasive form of eavesdropping, in which the attacker determines whether the information continues on to its intended receiver. There are many locations where an access attack can occur: backup tapes and CD-ROMs, hard drives, servers, file cabinets, as well as on a network. USB flash drives have become a new source of threat because they are small and easily hidden, hold a great deal of information, and can be easily plugged into all but the older machines. Usually permissions protection can prevent casual snooping. The cracker will try to gain that permission level. This kind of attack is mostly used in espionage.

modification attack – An attack on a system that modifies information illicitly

Modification attacks modify information illicitly. This can occur on the devices on which the information resides or when the information is in transit. In this attack, information is deleted, modified, or newly created. It turns out that electronic information is much easier to modify (especially undetected) than that stored on paper. Electronic information, however, can be easily replicated. As long as the system administrators know what has been modified during an attack, they should be able to restore the information.

denial-of-service attack – An attack which denies legitimate users from using the system or access to information

repudiation attack – An attack on a system that injures the reliability of the information; for example, a repudiation attack might remove evidence that an event (such as a bank transaction) actually did occur

risk – The relationship between vulnerability and threat; total risk also includes the potential affect of existing countermeasures

vulnerability – The sensitivity of the information and the skill level needed by the attacker to threaten that information

Denial-of-service (DoS) attacks deny legitimate users from using resources. The attack can make information, applications, systems, and communications unavailable. This attack is usually pure vandalism. In the physical realm, a cracker could burn the records that users require, or cut the communications cable that users need for communication. Computers can be destroyed or even stolen. Digitally, one way to deny communications is to overwhelm a system or network with information: inundating an address with e-mail messages, for example.

Repudiation attacks seek to create a false impression that an event did not occur when it did, or did occur when it did not. Forging someone's signature on a document is an obvious physical example of repudiation. Electronically, an e-mail, for example, can easily be sent to someone as if from someone else. Or a credit card transaction can be denied. A repudiation attack in the electronic world is much easier than in the physical world because of the potential for eliminating or destroying evidence. Destroying a document with a signature requires that someone with malicious intent gain physical access to the document.

managing security: the threat matrix

In order to manage security in a cost-effective manner, those people involved in system administration and security need to manage risk. Managed risk is the basis of security. ***Risk*** is essentially the relationship between vulnerability and a threat. In risk assessment, ***vulnerability*** is characterized by the sensitivity of the information potentially threatened and the skill level needed by an attacker to

threat – The likely agent of a possible attack, the event that would occur as a result of an attack, and the target of the attack

threaten that information. A **threat** is characterized by three things: *targets* that might be attacked, *agents* or attackers, and *events* or types of actions that are a threat. After identifying risks, measuring total risk also includes evaluating countermeasures.

For example, information on when a bank is open is usually widely available—on the bank's Web site or posted on the door of the bank, for example. It is important for customers to know the hours of operation, and this service to customers outweighs the possible risk of an agent (a bank robber) creating an event (a bank robbery) against the money in the bank (target). The amount of money a robber typically takes in a holdup is very small compared to the assets of the bank, thus lowering the vulnerability. In addition, countermeasures such as cameras, possible witnesses, proximity of police, silent alarms, and so on lower the total risk.

vulnerabilities

Vulnerabilities in a network or computer system might include Internet connections, hard or soft connections to partner organizations, open ports, physical access to the facilities, phone modem access, and more. It is essential to evaluate a system's vulnerabilities.

threat: agents

Who is potentially attacking? You have already learned about crackers and their motivations. In addition to crackers, other possible threat agents include employees, ex-employees, commercial rivals, terrorists, criminals, partners, customers, visitors, natural disasters, and the general public. When you examine these agents, look at their access capability (whether physical or electronic) to the information; their knowledge (for example the agent knows user ID numbers, passwords, names and addresses, file locations, security procedures, and so on); and their possible motivation (such as the challenge of the attack, greed, or some kind of malicious intent).

threat: targets and events

In systems security, targets are broken down into the four main areas:

- Confidentiality
- Integrity
- Availability
- Accountability

confidentiality – Ensuring that only those authorized to access information can do so

encryption – Transforming original data (plaintext) into coded or encrypted data (ciphertext) so that only authorized parties can interpret it

integrity – Assurance that information is what you think it is and that it has not been modified

Confidentiality means that only those authorized to see or modify a certain level of information can see or modify that information. For most organizations, information is classified as public, proprietary (available internally to the company), and restricted (available to only some employees). The government uses Top Secret and has many levels of confidentiality. ***Encryption*** is often used for information that has a high level of confidentiality. Designs for complex weapon systems, employee medical records, your own bank account information—these are targets. An event would be an access attack, viewing the confidential information.

Integrity assures that the information is correct. Mechanisms must exist to assure that information—whether physical files, electronic files, or electronic information—have integrity. Digital signatures on files and encryption for data transmissions are some of the approaches for assuring integrity. A typical target would be a transaction record for a bank account. An example of an event would be removing that record using a repudiation attack, or modifying that record in a modification attack.

availability – Accessibility of information and services on a normal basis

Availability involves making systems on which information sits accessible and useful to those who should use them. Backup electronic and paper copies, the capability for "failover," the reconstruction of information after an intrusion, and disaster recovery plans are techniques that create availability in the face of attack. A denial-of-service attack that denies users access to their e-mail is an example of a successful attack on availability.

accountability – Making sure that a system is as secure as feasible, and that there is a record of activities for reconstructing a break

identification – A technique for knowing who someone is; for example, a Social Security number can be identification (ID)

authentication – A technique for verifying that someone is who they claim to be; a password is one type of authentication

Accountability works with confidentiality, availability, and integrity to assure that those who are authorized (and no others) for access to information have that access. This is where ***identification*** and ***authentication*** (I&A) come in. Accountability is usually not attacked solely. Usually it is a means to attacking one of the other security targets. However, a secret attack on accountability could be used for a future attack against availability, integrity, and confidentiality. For example, a cracker might break into a system and leave a backdoor to return to later. If the cracker eliminates all traces of entering the system, then accountability has been compromised.

measuring total risk

Once vulnerabilities, threats, and existing countermeasures are identified and evaluated, the organization can measure risk and determine what needs adjustment. Unfortunately, risk is sometimes difficult to measure. Money is one way to measure risk. The cost of lost productivity, security consultants, and employee overtime to fix the problem, plus replacing stolen equipment—these things can add up. Less easily calculated is the time the event might take to fix if a key system is down, physical resources that need to be brought to bear, the damage to the organization's reputation, or the opportunity cost of lost business during the crisis. Although risk assessors can look to other cases for a clue to these costs, many of these costs are not calculable until an event actually occurs.

managing security: countermeasures

Start getting paranoid! As should be fairly obvious at this point, there are many avenues for intrusion and system breakdown: from the trash barrel to the corporate firewall to the hard drive on your laptop. The first few parts of this section—clean living, passwords, antivirus software, and encryption—are useful for individuals as well as system administrators. The second half—system setup—concerns the system administrator, but might also benefit the individual user.

clean living (or . . . only the paranoid survive!)

Here are some pointers on keeping computer systems secure:

- *Have a security policy*—None of the advice below will do any good if you or your employees don't follow it. Have a written policy and follow it. As a corporation, have regularly scheduled information and "rah-rah" sessions tying the importance of employees' work with the importance of securing information about them and their work. Some companies even hire consultants to pose as both social engineers and crackers to test the policy.
- *Have physical safeguards*—Do you lock your house when you leave? Well, maybe you don't. Maybe you figure you don't have anything worth stealing or that an open door will convince potential thieves that someone is actually home. You do have something worth stealing even if you think you're the poorest person on the planet: your identity. Records with personal information (bank accounts, social security numbers, tax returns, things related to work, and so on) should be secured or shredded. Don't throw valuable information into the trash. And, secure your trash. Your corporate dumpster should be in a visible, secure location and be locked. Your corporation should have a policy that doesn't allow visitors to roam at will without badge or escort. Computers, even laptops, can be locked to desks. Computers can have removable hard drives that can be locked in a secure location. The premises can be guarded with security guards and cameras. Quitting or terminated employees should be escorted off the premises, passwords terminated, badges removed.
- *Use passwords to protect everything*—Use passwords to protect entry to your computer at startup, entry to your e-mail, entry to your router if you have one, entry to software with personal information, entry to your personal digital assistant (PDA), an entry to your phone. Set your password-protected screen saver to engage after a few minutes of inactivity. See the section below on choosing the right password.

- *Destroy old copies of sensitive material*—Use a shredder for paper and possibly floppy disks and printer ribbons. Incinerate the material for added protection. Overwrite magnetic disks with specialized overwrite software to eliminate any original electronic trace. Another approach is to use a degausser. A degausser can quickly create a magnetic field so powerful that it realigns all the magnetic information on a disk. Some people argue that these techniques are still not enough—that old hard drives should be completely destroyed.
- *Back up everything of value*—This includes copies kept off site or in a bombproof lockbox. Many individuals and corporations have begun to use online backup services that give you the convenience and assurance that someone else does it properly. A typical approach is to have full backups of all systems in at least a couple locations and then to have a number of generations (going back the last three dates modified, for example) of backups for important files. Software developers use programs such as SourceSafe and the UNIX archive program to do this.
- *Protect against system failure*—Use a power surge protector. A surge in electricity from a lightning strike or electrical fluctuations typical in brownouts can damage and even destroy electronic equipment. Some experts recommend replacing surge protectors every couple years. Systems also benefit from an uninterruptible power supply (UPS). This is essentially what your laptop has built in—a battery backup in case the power goes out. A personal UPS will give you enough juice for your computer to work for several hours without electricity. Servers that need to be up can benefit from an industrial power backup—perhaps a diesel generator that keeps running as long as the supply of fuel lasts. Figure 13-2 shows three physical means to secure your system: a surge suppressor, UPS, and lock.

Figure 13-2, Three technologies that help back up your system. From left to right: surge suppressor, UPS, and physical locks

Courtesy of Tripp Lite Courtesy of Belkin Corporation Courtesy of Kensington Technology Group

Acceptable Use Policy (AUP) – Organizational policy that defines who can use company computers and networks, when, and how

callback – Users can connect to a network only by having the network initiate contact to a specified number

virtual private network (VPN) – A private network connection that "tunnels" through a larger, public network and is restricted to authorized users

disaster recovery plan (DRP) – A written plan for responding to natural or other disasters, intended to minimize downtime and damage to systems and data

13

- *Create an Acceptable Use Policy (AUP) for your company*—An ***Acceptable Use Policy (AUP)*** defines who can use the company computers and networks, when, and how. If your employees can or should not use the company resources for personal activities or such use is limited to certain times, then state that. If you allow employees, vendors, or partners to connect to the network from outside, then address that possible vulnerability as well. One requirement you might stipulate is to only allow electronic contact through ***callback*** numbers. This way a user can only connect to a system after it calls them back at an established number. Another approach is to have a ***virtual private network (VPN)***. A VPN is a sophisticated setup in which a "private" connection is established within a larger network, such as the Internet. The private network connection "tunnels" through the larger network, taking advantage of the reach and management facilities of the larger network, but is accessible only to authorized users.
- *Protect against viruses*—Install antivirus software, and configure it to automatically scan any downloaded files and programs, as well as incoming and outgoing e-mail. Even so, be careful with e-mail. You should only open letters, especially attachments, from trusted sources. Mail-filtering programs such as MailFrontier Matador and SpamKiller can be configured to discover fraudulent e-mail messages. Have your antivirus program automatically and regularly check for and download new virus definitions. Don't start a computer with a floppy in the A: drive unless it is a secure disk. Scan any disk before using it—even ones in packaged software can be infected. Have your operating system and second-party applications automatically and regularly check for and download security update patches. Create backups of your important files. If you don't need it, make sure file sharing is turned off in your operating system. Look into antispam, antispyware, and anticookie programs (detailed below in the privacy section). Install intruder detection software that can analyze network traffic and assess vulnerabilities. It also watches for suspicious activity and any unauthorized access.
- *Have a disaster recovery plan (DRP)*—Whether you experience a naturally occurring or human-caused occurrence, a ***disaster recovery plan (DRP)*** is designed to minimize any disruption such a disaster might create. Depending on your situation, a disaster could be anything from the death of the CEO to a major earthquake or fire. DRPs include documentation that, in the event of an emergency, create a chain of command with a checklist of alternative recovery processes depending on the crisis. Disaster recovery support teams should be formed and brainstorm about responding to disasters, examining who and what might be affected and how to react.

Some of the key resources that need to be addressed in a DRP are:

- Data storage and recovery
- Centralized and distributed systems recovery
- End-user recovery

- Network backup
- Internal and external data and voice communications restoration
- Emergency management and decision making
- Customer services restoration

Recovery operations may require off-site storage or operations with or without immediate "go live" capabilities, alternative communication technologies or techniques between recovery team members, and end-user communication parameters. Once a DRP has been completed, it should be tested, performing dry runs through various scenarios. Testing of the DRP should occur on a regular basis.

passwords

Easily guessed passwords are a very serious problem for system security. Common and simple passwords that can be guessed include a carriage return, a person's name, account name, birth date, loved one's birth date or name, or even the word "password" possibly repeated and spelled either frontward or backward. Do you use anything like that? Then you are vulnerable.

Better passwords are ones that are longer and more obscure. Short passwords allow the cracker to simply run through all the possible combinations of letters and numbers. Take an extreme example. Only using capital letters, how many possibilities are there in a single-character password? Twenty-six. Expand that to an eight-character password and there are over 200 million possible combinations (Table 13-1).

A good password should be long (at least eight characters), have no real words in it, and include as many different characters as possible. Maybe something like "io\pw83 mcx?$". Unfortunately, passwords this complicated are often written down and taped up in plain view, which negates the purpose of the password in the first place. One mnemonic that could be used to remember a password is to come up with an easily remembered phrase and use its acronym as a password. Say you take the last sentence of the opening sequence for the original Star Trek: "To boldly go where no man has gone before!" You get "TBGW0MHGB!" (replacing the "n" in "no" with a zero just to confuse things a bit). Not a bad password. Of course, if you have Star Trek posters on your walls, wear Spock ears, and wander around spouting off about "the prime directive" all the time, then a proficient social engineer might still figure it out.

Table 13-1, Password protection using combinations of the letters A through Z

number of characters (A through Z)	possible combinations	human avg. time to discovery (max time/2) tries per second: 1	computer avg. time to discovery (max time/2) tries per second: 1 million
1	26	13 seconds	.000013 seconds
2	$26 \times 26 = 676$	6 minutes	.000338 seconds
4	26 raised to 3 = 17576	2.5 hours	.008788 seconds
8	26 raised to 8 = 208,827,064,576	6640 years	58 hours
10	26 raised to 10 = 1.4×10 raised to 14	4.5 million years	4.5 years

Although individuals can make significant changes to protect themselves and their companies, corporate cultures can include many subtle and dangerous security weaknesses. Proficient directed crackers become aware of corporate cultures and find these weaknesses. For example, back in 1987, as Clifford Stoll tracked the cracker, he became aware that many system administrators thought their VAX minicomputers were secure—and they were certainly capable of being secure. But, the machines had been shipped with an easy access service account—an account named FIELD with the password Service. The cracker had become aware of the account and password—which hadn't been kept a secret—and took advantage of the fact that many system administrators neglected to change the account password after installing the machine.

Many major institutions also confuse what is essentially public identification information (but often perceived as private because it is less readily accessible), such as a social security number or birth date, with a password. What were the questions you were asked to identify yourself the last time you called your credit card company? Name, birth date, last four digits of your social security number possibly? This confuses identification (who the person is) with authentication (proof that the person is who they say they are). Because of the problems with passwords, many secure locations are moving to a combination of three authentication techniques:

· Something you know—like a password
· Something you have—like an ID badge
· Something you are (often called *biometrics*)—like a fingerprint, retinal scan, or DNA sample

biometrics – Biological identification, such as fingerprints, voice dynamics, or retinal scans; considered more secure than password authentication

Figure 13-3 shows the three authentication techniques. Combining these authentication methods over the phone or through the Web, however, can be difficult and expensive.

Figure 13-3, Three potentially combined authentication methods. They are from left to right: what you know, what you have, what you are

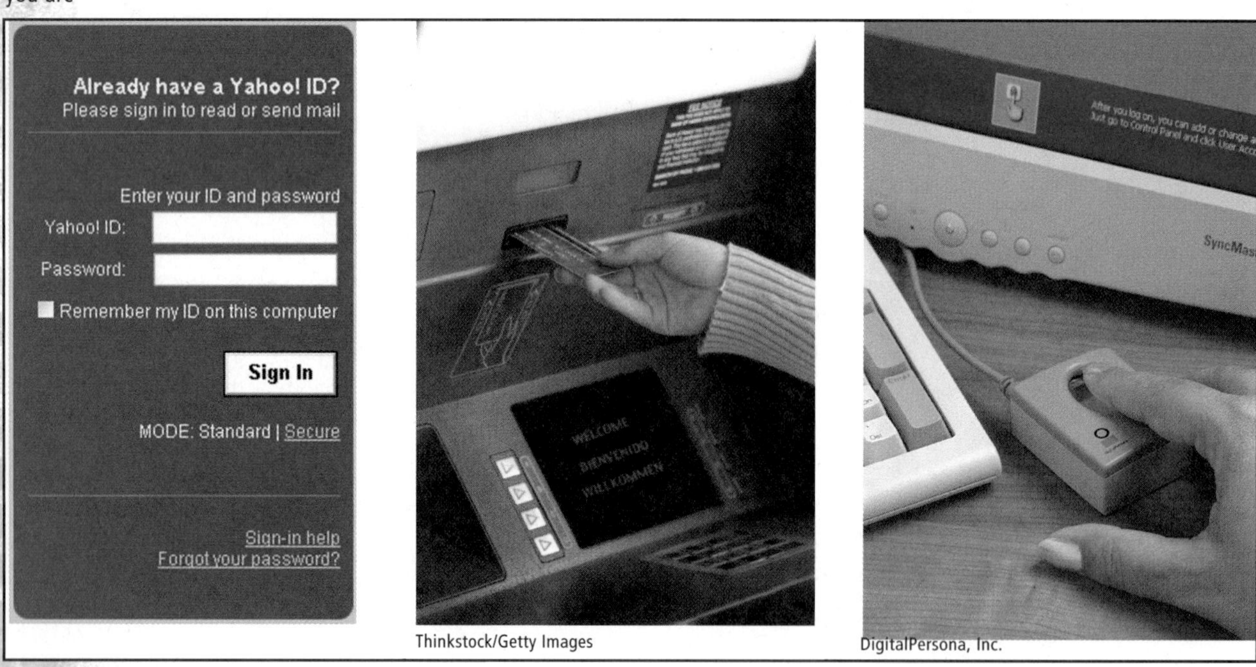

Thinkstock/Getty Images DigitalPersona, Inc.

antivirus software

antivirus software – Program designed to detect and block computer viruses

Installing *antivirus software* is one of the smartest things you can do to protect your machine, software, data, and your sanity—especially on networks on college campuses which are notoriously open and vulnerable to attack. These networks are also where a lot of script kiddies can be found. Popular antivirus software is produced by companies such as eSafe, eTrust, F-Secure, McAfee, Norton, RAV, and AVG.

save your system and your sanity

· Choose a difficult password
· Install antivirus software
· Configure to automatically download antivirus software and operating system updates

virus signature (or virus definition) – *Bits of code that uniquely identify a particular virus*

honeypot – *A trap (program or system) laid by a system administrator to catch and track intruders*

heuristics – *In virus detection, a set of rules that predict how a virus might act; for example, anticipating that the virus will affect certain critical system files*

checksum – *A mathematical means to check the content of a file or value (such as a credit card number) to assure that it has not been tampered with or re-created illicitly*

Antivirus software uses numerous techniques. One technique searches for a match with what's called a ***virus signature*** (or ***virus definition***) of known viruses—bits of code that are unique to that virus software. Usually you can select where to look for the signature match—in the boot sector, all hard drives, certain folders or directories, memory, and so on. This is a very efficient way of searching for and potentially eliminating a virus. The drawback is that the program must have the signature in its database. Antivirus manufacturers are continually watching their ***honeypots*** (programs or systems set up to deliberately lure and then track intruders) and have their ears to the ground, hoping to catch the newest viruses and put out a signature. The idea is that you continually need to update your signature database by downloading the latest signatures before a virus infects your system. Most antivirus programs offer a service that automatically updates virus definitions on a regular basis.

Two other techniques attempt to get around the possible signature match lag by predicting how a virus will behave and then signaling possible anomalies. One of these techniques uses a set of ***heuristics*** (rules) to detect a possible virus. The other uses a ***checksum*** on known clean and likely target files and checks for anomalies between the files. The downsides to both techniques are that they are not as sure as signature matching and both are more likely to give false positives—labeling clean files as infected. One final approach that antivirus software can take is to alert you to activity that might be malicious. Usually, you can select the level of alarm you get: anything from probable virus events such as writing to the boot sector in your hard drive or formatting your hard drive (alarm set to "nonchalant" level) to writing anything at all to your hard drive (alarm set to "really paranoid" level).

Antivirus software has options for scanning and dealing with viruses. For instance, the software can be operating in continuous mode in which it is always scanning the hard drives and system. It can also work in on-demand mode in which the user tells the software to scan. Most antivirus software can repair infected files. Some viruses are particularly nasty, however, and create files that cannot be repaired. They do this by not just attaching to a file but essentially copying over (deleting) the good code. In a case like that, the antivirus software might quarantine the file—labeling it and removing it to a separate location on the hard drive. If the file is important to the operating system this could be a problem, but most antivirus software also allows you to create a recovery disk that has critical OS programs on it. In a worst-case scenario, you might have to reformat your hard drive. That's when a backup of the drive becomes very important.

double safe

Even if you think your system is adequately protected from intrusion, it's essential to back up your system and data files on a regular basis.

Antivirus software continues to add features. If your software supports it, activate the ability to scan macro scripts, incoming and outgoing e-mail messages, files when opened, compressed files, ActiveX controls, Java applets, and potential Trojan horses.

using encryption to secure transmissions and data

The content of the information sent along the Internet could be seen by every computer through which it passes. Your e-mail is like a postcard that anyone can read. Not only that, many different machines owned by many different entities handle your postcard along its way. This means that sensitive e-mail and Web content need to be secured in some way. One way to ensure that your transmissions remain private is to use encryption. Encryption uses a computer code called an ***encryption key*** to scramble the transmission so that only a user or system with the appropriate decoding key can read it. Encryption can be used for securing stored information as well.

encryption key – A string of bits used in an encryption algorithm to encrypt or decrypt data; the longer the key, the more secure the encryption

When you install a Web browser on your machine you usually have a choice of installing a protection level of 40-bit or 128-bit encryption. The number of bits refers to the size of the encryption key. The more bits, the longer the key, the more secure the encryption. If you are going to be doing any credit card transactions or online banking, then you will likely need 128-bit encryption.

note E-mail can be encrypted using programs such as Email Protector and Pretty Good Privacy (PGP); both are shareware programs available online.

Web pages use a secure system such as Secure HTTP (S-HTTP), Secure Electronics Transactions Specification (SET), or Secure Sockets Layer (SSL). Typically, financial institutions use S-HTTP or SET because they are more secure. Their complexity makes them potentially slower, however, and because S-HTTP comes in both 40- and 128-bit flavors, it is also used in some credit card transactions. Credit card transactions do not have the same security needs as online banking because, ultimately, the owner of the credit card is not responsible for fraudulent activity on the card. That is a risk that the credit card companies assume. In addition, unless you specify otherwise, online retailers do not hold your credit card information. That information is passed on directly to credit card-verifying organizations. In many cases, organizations choose to use SSL because it is easy to implement and fast, two things that can increase customer satisfaction and, it is hoped, sales.

S-HTTP and SSL both use what is called a digital certificate. A ***digital certificate*** is issued by a certificate authority to both the user's browser and the vendor's server. The information in the certificate—including user name and certificate number—is encrypted and verified by the certificate authority. VeriSign is one company that manages digital certificates.

digital certificate – The digital equivalent of an ID card; used with encryption and issued by a third-party certificate authority

Encryption has been used to secure information for thousands of years—mostly by spies, the military, and statesmen. With the need for secure financial transactions over the Internet, everyone who makes a purchase over the Web has become a user of cryptography, even if it happens in the background. Encryption uses various simple to sophisticated algorithms to encode (encrypt or encipher) plaintext into ciphertext. Once encrypted, the recipient uses a reverse algorithm to decode (decrypt or decipher) the message back into plaintext. Julius Caesar has been said to be the first to use a fixed-place substitution algorithm (replacing a letter with another a fixed distance away in the alphabet). For example, the letter A might become C which is two letters later (see Table 13-2). The letter B then becomes the letter D and so on.

Table 13-2, Simple substitution encryption algorithm for the alphabet

plaintext	ciphertext
A	C
B	D
C	E
D	F
. . .	. . .
X	Z
Y	A
Z	B

Substitution combined with algorithms for transposition, compaction, and expansion (Table 13-3) can make the original message pretty hard to break—at least by hand.

Table 13-3, The plaintext words "JULIUS CAESAR" converted to ciphertext in turn by substitution, transposition, compaction, and expansion

algorithm	technique	plaintext	ciphertext
Substitution	Replace characters; example: replace with two to the right and make space a #	JULIUS CAESAR	LWNKWU#ECGUCT
Transposition	Switch order of characters; example: put in reverse	LWNKWU#ECGUCT	TCUGCE#UWKNWL
Compaction	Remove characters; example: take every other character and put at end	TCUGCE#UWKNWL	TUC#WNLCGEUKW
Expansion	Insert characters; example: insert "@" after every sixth character	TUC#WNLCGEUKW	TUC#WN@LCGEUK@W

Even with this confused new string of characters—TUC#WN@LCGEUK@Wa cryptanalyst using cryptanalysis (breaking a cipher) will likely decipher it. One weakness in the example given is that the space never changes from the substitution phase. Given enough to work with, a cryptanalyst sees the obvious reuse of the character—or any of the characters for that matter—and begins to deduce their significance.

Encryption and cryptanalysis have become far more sophisticated with the advent of computing and the Internet. Although there are a number of encryption standards, three have become popular in the commercial world. They are known as DES (data encryption standard), RSA (named after the inventors Rivest, Shamir, and Adelman), and AES (advanced encryption standard). These encryption standards are key-based standards. That is, they rely on an agreed upon starting point for encryption and decryption. In the example of substitution above, the key might be something that indicates substitution of two

symmetric encryption – Encryption using a private key to both encrypt and decrypt

asymmetric encryption – Encryption using both a public key and a private key

letters to the right. The key might be secret (also called ***symmetric encryption***) or it might be public (***asymmetric encryption***). Secret keys work pretty well between two individuals but the system begins to break down when more than two people are involved. Even with only two, distributing the keys between people may be difficult because the key must remain secret. For that reason, public keys are often used. Public key systems actually use both a public key and a corresponding private key. Figure 13-4 illustrates asymmetric encryption. As shown in the figure, public/private key encryption can be likened to a process in which the sender sends the information locked in a box that can be opened only with the sender's public key. That box from the sender is in turn locked in a box that can only be opened by the receiver's private key. Only the receiver can open this box with the private key; even the sender can't open this outer box.

Figure 13-4, Using a public and private key (asymmetric encryption)

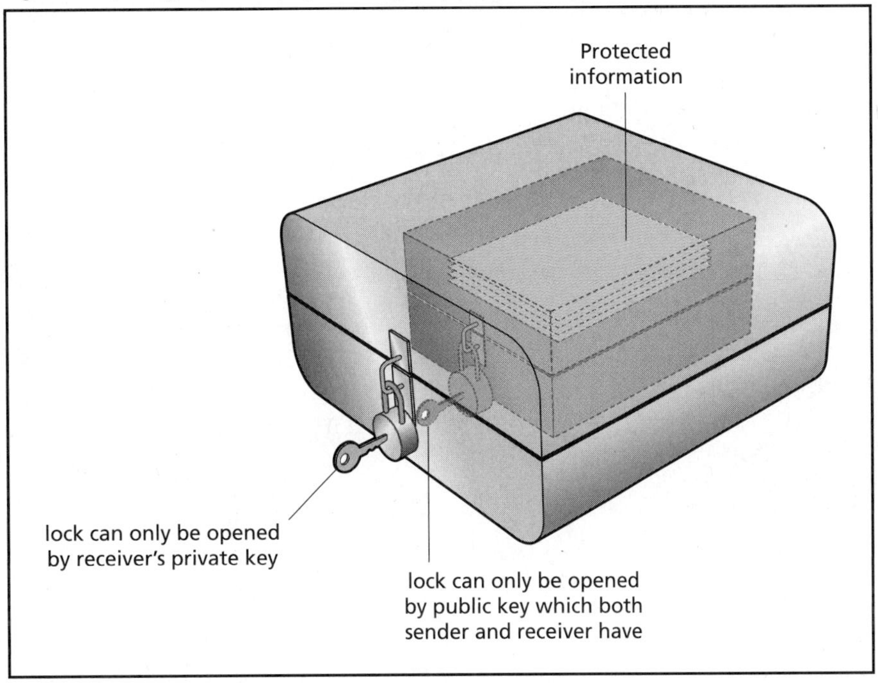

securing systems with firewalls

firewall – Software and/or hardware that sits between an external network and the internal computer system that monitors requests for entry to the internal system and allows entry only to designated or authorized entrants

A ***firewall*** is software or hardware that acts as a protective filter between an internal computer system and an external network such as the Internet. A firewall functions to prevent all traffic into the system except that which is explicitly allowed. At a minimum, it is located between the Internet service provider (ISP) and the rest of the system or between a router (which links to the ISP and is often owned by the ISP) and the rest of the system. Internal firewalls can be set up as well. The outside world should not see the details of the system behind the firewall. Some companies that offer firewall software include BlackICE, McAfee, Symantec, and Sygate. Microsoft began including a firewall (Internet Connection Firewall) in Windows XP. A firewall also can be part of hardware—they are often offered on routers (which you learn more about in the next section).

proxy firewall – A firewall that establishes a new link between each packet of information and its destination; it is slower but more secure than a packet-filtering firewall

packet-filtering firewall – A firewall that inspects each packet and moves it along an established link to its destination; it is usually faster but less secure than a proxy firewall

There are two main types of firewalls. One type is called a *proxy firewall.* It has different software (proxies) that must deal with each type of packet as it comes in (HTTP, FTP, and so on). For each packet that passes inspection, a new link is created between the firewall and the internal network and the packet is sent on its way. Another type is the *packet-filtering firewall* that inspects the packets as they arrive and sends them directly to the required server (again, HTTP, FTP, and so on). No proxies are involved and a new link is not necessary; thus, it is faster. However, it is probably less secure, because the internal IP addresses more easily can be made visible from outside.

The firewall allows you to configure a single entry point to your network. You can configure firewalls to allow traffic based on a number of things: the Internet Protocol (IP) address of either the destination or originator, the identification of the user making a service request, and more. What is called the "rule set" of the firewall should be set to accommodate the needs of high traffic for certain requests (for example, SMTP for a system that has a mail server). You want the firewall to make the fastest reasonable ruling on traffic that you label as high priority without allowing the easy entry of undesirables. A firewall also logs traffic so that an attack can be investigated.

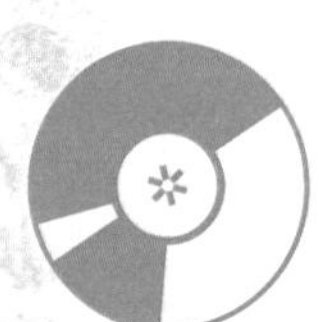

Reinforce your understanding of firewalls, routers, and other system architecture with the information and activities for Chapter 13 on the student CD.

protecting a system with routers

Another way to protect a network is the router. Filtering software in a router can be a front line of defense against certain service requests. The router's job, unlike the firewall's, however, is to move packets as quickly as possible towards their intended destination. With the rise of home networks, however, hybrid router systems have been created especially for the home user that claim to perform both routing and firewall functions adequately.

Placing a system on the Internet, especially one that has numerous services that you want to allow for internal and external users, requires some thought in terms of system architecture. For example, you may want to allow people on the inside to surf the Web, transfer files, access e-mail, or log on to external systems. Each one of these services has a unique port, an opening to the Internet, through which it travels. The point is to close the ports that are not allowed, thus giving fewer points of entry to secure. Table 13-4 shows some typical ports and their associated services.

Table 13-4, Some of the many ports available on a router and what they do

service	port(s)	description
FTP	21, 22	File transfer
HTTP	80	Access the Web
SSH	22	Create a remote session
Telnet	23	Create a remote session
POP-3	110	Access remote e-mail accounts

Keeping your available ports to a minimum goes for those services you want to offer to others on the outside as well. High-risk services include Telnet and FTP (using SSH is more secure for both services), Microsoft NetMeeting (Internet conferencing software that opens a large number of ports at once), and Network File Services (NFS) or NetBios Services (these services allow file sharing).

For more information about Telnet, FTP, and SSH, see Chapter 6, "Networks," and Chapter 7, "The Internet."

In addition to port selection, you can determine where on the network your servers are to be located and what services are offered outside the firewall. For example, the Domain Name System (DNS) is what allows a Web surfer to type in a URL instead of an IP address. Networks often have an internal DNS server to resolve internal names and rely on an external DNS server for external names. You want to keep the internal and external DNS names separate so that an outsider potentially cannot directly access machines behind the wall. This means having a DNS server on the outside of the firewall (either owned by you or your ISP).

Services outside the firewall? Weren't you just advised to keep everything behind the firewall? Well, everything that you want to protect should be behind a firewall. But, there is also the demilitarized zone.

the DMZ

demilitarized zone (DMZ) – A location outside the firewall (or between firewalls) that is more vulnerable to attack from outside

The ***demilitarized zone (DMZ)*** separates those services you want to offer internally from those you want to offer externally. A Web service for your customers is a good example of something you want to offer externally; so is an incoming e-mail server. The database with all the employees' names, addresses, and salaries, however, is not something you want to offer externally. Because the systems in the DMZ are more vulnerable to attack, they need some protection. One source of protection is filters on the router. Another is to only allow each server to serve the service it's intended to serve (say that five times fast). In other words, you don't allow FTP, SMTP, or any other service on your Web server; you have different servers for those services. Another approach is the possibility of yet another firewall on the other side of the demilitarized zone (DMZ).

Figure 13-5 shows a system configuration for a network that includes a firewall, a DMZ, and a router.

Figure 13-5, System configuration of a network that includes a firewall, a DMZ, and a router

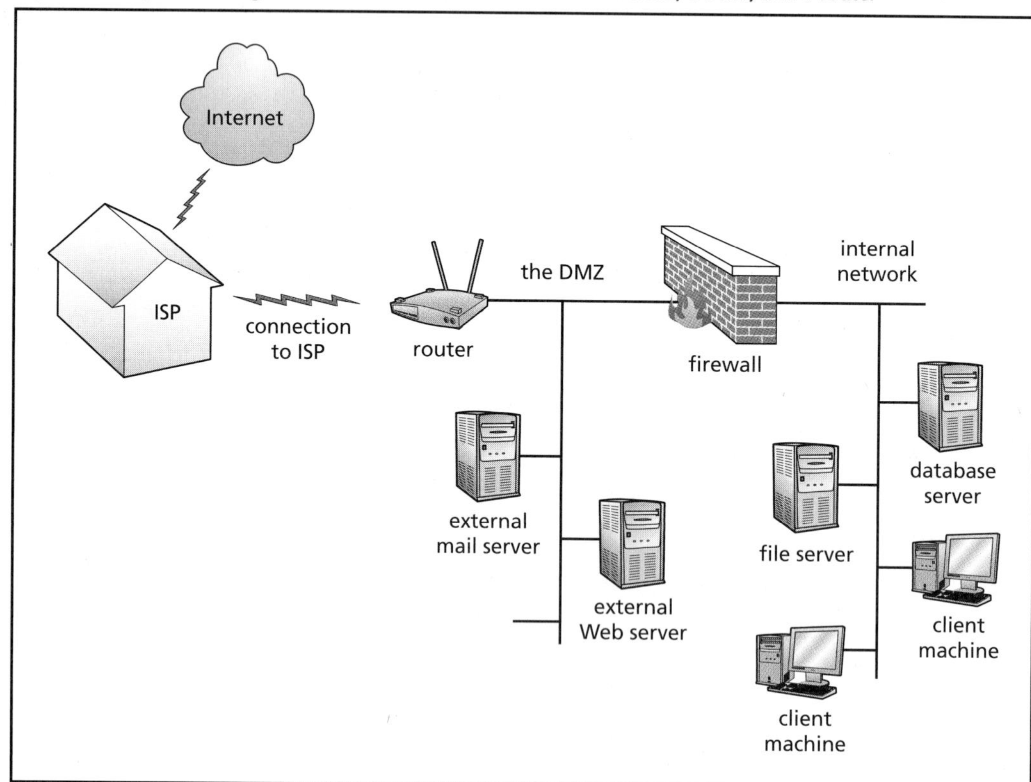

protecting systems with machine addressing

Another critical area for security administration is machine addressing. Because of the limited number of IP addresses in the world (32-bit addresses of the form xxx.xxx.xxx.xxx), organizations from small to large usually have more machines than they have IP addresses. One way this is handled is through dynamically allocating IP addresses (through the Dynamic Host Configuration Protocol (DHCP), for example). Organizations also use private class addressing. Nodes on the internal network have a different address (up to 16 bits) than what is seen on the outside. This conversion of internal to external IP addresses and vice versa is called Network Address Translation (NAT). NAT is usually provided by the firewall.

putting it all together

To ensure that your computer systems are as secure as they can be, the approaches to system security and countermeasures outlined here should be considered as part of a comprehensive security plan, rather than implemented in a piecemeal fashion. An organization doesn't just install a firewall and figure it is immunized. Neither should an individual. Your approach to security is a concerted effort that includes firewalls and antivirus software. It also includes restricting physical access to buildings and hardware utilizing locked doors, identification, and authentication systems. It includes constant reminders of the dangers of letting your guard down and training employees to remain alert to possible threats. It demands a security policy that is continually audited and updated as well as enforced. It demands that systems are continually updated and patched to fix security holes. Files and systems must have appropriate access controls. In many ways, a successful security system can be quite boring (because "nothing ever happens") and you as an administrator might have to deal with people (maybe even yourself) who don't want to bother with all that "bureaucracy" involved in creating and maintaining good security. But, in the end, that's what you want: a boring system where nothing ever really happens.

computer crime

The preceding sections dealt with many approaches to secure the hardware, software, and data on computer systems. If these approaches are not used or fail, and an intrusion occurs, there are some legal safeguards and avenues for prosecuting and punishing computer intruders. The next sections talk about the various types of computer crime and the legislation that applies to it.

defining computer crime

intellectual property – An idea or product based on an idea that has commercial value, such as literary or artistic works, patents, business methods, industrial processes, and trade secrets

copyright – The legal right granted to an author, composer, artist, publisher, playwright, or distributor to exclusive sale, publication, production, or distribution of a literary, artistic, musical, or dramatic work

In the IT world, computer crime most often relates to ***intellectual property*** rather than physical theft (although physical theft can also be a problem, addressed earlier in this chapter). Intellectual property can consist of a trademarked symbol, a patented design or process, a copyrighted program, digital information, or programming and hardware trade secrets. For software and hardware, protections generally fall into three categories:

- Copyright
- Patent
- Trade secrets

Copyright protects the expression of the idea and not the idea itself. In other words, you can copyright Mickey Mouse and how he is drawn, but you can't copyright all drawn mice. Copyright gives the author the exclusive right to make copies of the work. It is very easy to file for a copyright. Actually, if you put a copyright symbol on your work it is essentially marked as copyrighted, although in a legal dispute you have to prove origination. A copyright lasts the life of the human originator plus another 70 years—which is a topic of debate in legal, political, and economic circles. If an unauthorized copy is made of your copyrighted material, you can sue. Your chances of successfully suing increase if an unauthorized copy is made and sold. Copyrights are often used for software. Although there is always the possibility that someone will *reverse engineer* the program, it takes considerable effort to do that kind of programming. The copyright at least protects against someone creating an illegal duplicate. Copyrights (or patents) have not proven very successful for protecting a user interface, however. Lotus Development, for example, tried unsuccessfully to sue Borland Quattro and Microsoft Excel because they felt those companies copied the "look and feel" of the Lotus 1-2-3 spreadsheet in their products.

reverse engineer – To figure out the design of a program or device by "taking it apart" and analyzing individual components; for example, source code can be reverse engineered to determine a design model

patent – A government grant that gives the sole right to make, use, and sell an invention for a specified period of time

A *patent* protects inventions, the workings of a device, or process. In the United States, you file a design at the Patent Office for a fee. The design can be a fairly rough sketch but, again, if the case ever goes to court, the design could be torn apart as insufficient for proving unique origination. Filing for a patent is a fairly expensive and complicated undertaking and requires a specialized lawyer (or someone with a lot of time on their hands). Large corporations, with embedded legal staffs, have become much better at filing for patents. The life of a U.S. patent is 19 years. If the invention is copied you can sue. Software typically is not patented although the U.S. Patent Office no longer discourages software patents (prior to the mid-1980s successful bids for software patents were rare). The problem lies in the typical fast software development and revision cycle compared to the fairly slow patent process. In addition, a patent requires that you show your design which, in the case of software, means showing the source code. Most companies don't want to reveal their source code and so they rely on copyright law and trade secrets to protect their products.

trade secret – A method, formula, device, or piece of information that a company keeps secret and that gives the company competitive advantage

Trade secrets are another form of intellectual property. Trade secrets are methods, formulas, or devices that give their companies competitive advantage, and are kept from the public. One famous long-standing trade secret is the recipe for Coca Cola. There was a considerable length of time when only three people in the organization—and therefore in the world—knew the recipe. There is no time limit on trade secrets. They last as long as they can be kept secret. If trade secrets are stolen, perpetrators can be sued. Privacy laws protect the original owner in some cases.

prosecuting computer crime

The United States has a number of laws designed to protect intellectual property, personal privacy, and computer systems from fraud and abuse. There are many laws that relate to securing intellectual property, for example, with a long history.

The first copyright protection in the United States was created in 1787 and signed into law in 1790. That predates the ratification of the Bill of Rights—before free speech, freedom of the press, and the right to bear arms. The U.S. Patent Office was also created in 1790 to protect the exclusive rights of inventors. Privacy is not written into the Bill of Rights per se, but has been the concern of several acts such as the Fair Credit Reporting Act (1970) and the Video Privacy Protection Act (1988). Table 13-5 lists many of the important U.S. laws of the past 40 years that have been used to prosecute intellectual property theft, computer system intrusion, and invasions of personal privacy.

Table 13-5, Some important U.S. federal laws used to prosecute intellectual property theft, computer system intrusion, and invasion of privacy

law (U.S. code)	date	purpose/notes
Interception Act (18 US Code 2511)	1968	Outlaws wiretapping; a computer network "sniffer" would fall under this statute
Fair Credit Reporting Act (15 US Code 1681)	1970	Allows individuals to review their credit ratings, and disallows companies from releasing credit information
Family Educational Rights and Privacy (20 US Code 1232)	1974	Protects students' records from parties other than the student and parents
Privacy (5 US Code 552)	1974	U.S. statute that stops federal agencies from using "bonus" information—information collected while an agency was investigating—for another purpose
Electronic Funds Transfer (15 US Code 1693)	1978	Prohibits the use, sale, and supply of counterfeit (or obtained without authorization) debit/credit instruments
Computer Fraud and Abuse (18 US Code 1030)	1984	Makes intentional access to a computer without authorization illegal

(continued)

Table 13-5 (*continued*)

law (U.S. code)	date	purpose/notes
Credit Card Fraud (18 US Code 1029)	1984	Makes unauthorized access to 15 or more credit card numbers illegal; that means that accessing a system that has 15 or more numbers on it, even if the individual does not use the cards, is illegal
Access to Electronic Information Act (18 US Code 2701)	1986	Further defines illegal access to electronic communications; also protects access by authorized users and included the owner of the information as an authorized user
Electronic Communications Privacy Act (18 US Code 1367)	1986	Extends privacy protection beyond postal and phone communication to e-mail, cell phones, voice mail, and other electronic communications
Video Privacy Protection Act (18 US Code 2710)	1988	Prohibits retailers from selling or giving away movie rental records
Telephone Consumer Protection Act (15 US Code 5701)	1991	Restricts telemarketing activities to assure privacy
Computer Abuse Amendments	1994	An extension of the 1984 Computer Fraud and Abuse Act that includes transmission of malicious code such as viruses and worms
National Information Infrastructure Protection Act	1996	Further nationalizes the law against stealing information electronically and computer trespassing across state lines; also extends to theft of information related to national defense
Economic Espionage Act (18 US Code 793)	1996	Makes any theft of information or trade secrets across international lines a crime

law (U.S. code)	date	purpose/notes
No Electronic Theft (NET) Act	1997	Further refines copyright law to disallow freely distributing copyrighted material without authorization
Digital Millennium Copyright Act (DMCA)	1998	Makes using anti-antipiracy technology, as well as selling anti-antipiracy technology, a crime
Provide Appropriate Tools Required to Intercept and Obstruct Terrorism (PATRIOT) Act	2001	Gives law enforcement agencies broader rights to monitor the electronic (and other) activities of individuals; in addition, the Computer Fraud and Abuse Act is further refined; causing damage (even unintentionally) to a computer system is punishable

It should be noted that these laws are always open to interpretation in the courts. For example, at this writing, to prosecute computer fraud and abuse, the damage must be shown to exceed $5000. In some cases in the past, it has been proven that entering a system and viewing the information there could not be construed as damage because the plaintiff could not prove the damage exceeded the minimum dollar amount of $5000. With credit card fraud, the attacker has to be shown to be in possession of 15 or more counterfeit or illegally acquired credit card numbers.

As of this writing, all but 16 U.S. states have laws concerning computer crimes but the laws differ widely. Some specify no minimum damage requirements, while others do. Some states, such as Minnesota, specifically target viruses. What constitutes accessing a system—either actual entry or merely an attempt—also differs from state to state.

When you start looking at laws in other countries it gets even messier. First there is the matter of jurisdiction. For the most part, one country has to give another country permission to pursue a case. In most of the Western world, there are established agreements for reciprocity and sharing of information and, that aspect of investigation can go fairly smoothly. In many other cases the United States' Federal Bureau of Investigation (FBI) has had to specifically ask for help from countries that don't have any computer crime laws—even if that country is an ally. For countries openly hostile to the United States, getting that type of assistance is nearly impossible.

Prosecuting a computer crime is also a complex matter. Can you prove there was monetary damage? Can you gather enough evidence? That means that you have to show the traces of the intrusion on your systems. The computers in your organization become part of a criminal investigation, which means that they must be replicated entirely and convincingly, or not used for their normal purposes during the investigation and prosecution. Of course, this all presupposes that you have actually discovered the perpetrator—a very difficult matter in its own right. Unfortunately, while the record is improving, many people have gotten away with a considerable amount of intrusion and even when caught are given no or light sentences.

I fought the law and the law won

So, if computer crimes have been difficult to prosecute, you might as well commit a few, eh? Not so fast!! The Western world has come a long way in prosecuting computer intrusions and other IT related crimes since 1987 when Clifford Stoll had difficulty convincing the FBI to pursue the odd 75-cent usage fees automatically charged for the cracker's time. And, increasing numbers of crackers are being caught and prosecuted. Since 1987, the laws have changed to make prosecution and conviction even more likely. In addition, authorities are far more likely to pursue electronic and computer crime than in the past.

paying the price

In May 2002, a U.S. court sentenced the author of a worm called Melissa, David L. Smith, to 20 months in a federal prison. Two years before, the Melissa worm had done an estimated $80 million in damages and lost business. After 9/11/2001, the U.S. Attorney General's office stated that individuals breaking into computer systems were a threat to the security of the country, and that it would look for harsher penalties and prompter sentencing for electronic break-ins.

For example, corporations are willing to pursue copyright violations much more aggressively. In 2003, the Recording Industry Association of America (RIAA) began to target not just the Web sites, but the end users who had downloaded copyrighted music from such Web sites as Napster and KaZaA. Napster itself had been shut down the year before. At the same time, the music and movie industries have begun to give individuals incentives for staying within legal boundaries. In 2003, Napster was reborn as a Web site for legally downloading songs at a reasonable cost. Apple computer did the same with its iTunes approach. RealNetworks and the Starz Encore Group recently created a similar movie download service.

End users who engage in software piracy are also liable. Individuals can be prosecuted and punished with up to five years in jail and fines of up to $250,000. Corporations can be liable for software piracy as well. For a number of years now, in an effort to avoid prosecution, many organizations have begun to review all machines periodically to check for illegal copies of software. The software industry may also try to thwart potential thieves by making the purchase of a copy of a software title a thing of the past. Currently, when you buy software you don't actually own it. You purchase the right to use a copy with certain conditions, specified in the end-user license (EULA) agreement where you have to click "I accept" to continue, which usually disallows using the software on more than one machine, loaning or renting it out, or otherwise distributing it. A different model exists where you purchase time on a program and connect to it through a network. Microsoft Terminal server software, a program that many organizations are now using, is headed in this direction, in which you link to a server that has, for example, MS Office or Visual Studio running on it. A setup such as this makes stealing software more difficult and protects organizations who want to be sure they are on the right side of the law.

note More information on software piracy can be found online at the Business Software Alliance (BSA) Web site, *www.bsa.org*.

ethics in computing

Although ethics and law are intertwined, they are separate systems for defining right and wrong behavior. Sometimes, they even conflict. Nevertheless, despite differences between them and differences in the way they are viewed by individuals, some strong generalizations can be made about what is ethically and legally acceptable conduct concerning property, general welfare, health, and privacy in the world of information technology. Just because an act you engage in is difficult to prosecute or is even legal does not make it ethical.

ethics – Principles for judging right and wrong, held by an individual or group

Ethics are the moral principles for judging right and wrong behavior held by an individual or group. People often confuse ethics with religious rules because most religions attempt to instill some set of moral principles. However, ethics can be amazingly similar across religions and even for those with no particular religious affiliation. The reason is simple: ethical systems (along with laws) help to create a stable platform from which to live life comfortably with other people and, it is hoped, to benefit all. People generally make fairly rational decisions. The great majority of them can see beyond their own nose enough to know what's rational and right.

Organizations of computer professionals have outlined ethical standards for their members, often predating the laws that now reflect those ethics. The Institute of Electrical and Electronics Engineers (IEEE), the Association for Computing Machinery (ACM), the Data Processing Management Association (DPMA), the Computer Ethics Institute, and other IT organizations created codes of ethics that their members have sworn to uphold. Many companies create codes of ethics as well. Figure 13-6 shows an excerpt from the ACM code of conduct.

Individuals approach ethical reasoning from different perspectives. These approaches can be generalized along two continuums: orientation toward consequences versus orientation toward rules, and orientation toward the individual versus orientation toward the universal. Most people do not fit entirely within one square, or at least not for all situations that they might face. Nevertheless, these approaches can help you understand a situation in terms of ethics no matter what your ethical reasoning.

Figure 13-6, An excerpt from the Association for Computing Machinery (ACM) "Code of Ethics and Professional Conduct"

1.1 Contribute to society and human well-being
1.2 Avoid harm to others
1.3 Be honest and trustworthy
1.4 Be fair and take action not to discriminate
1.5 Honor property rights including copyrights and patents
1.6 Give proper credit for intellectual property
1.7 Respect the privacy of others
1.8 Honor confidentiality

2.1 Strive to achieve the highest quality, effectiveness, and dignity in both process and products of professional work
2.2 Acquire and maintain professional competence
2.3 Know and respect existing laws pertaining to professional work
2.4 Accept and provide appropriate professional review
2.5 Give comprehensive and thorough evaluations of computer systems and their impacts, including analysis of possible risks
2.6 Honor contracts, agreements, and assigned responsibilities
2.7 Improve public understanding of computing and its consequences
2.8 Access computing and communication resources only when authorized to do so

These approaches can be generally described with the following terms:

- Egoism—Ethical principles based on possible consequences to an individual
- Deontology—Ethical principles based on individual duties and rights
- Utilitarianism—Ethical principles based on possible consequences to many or all individuals
- Rule-deontology—Ethical principles based on what an individual considers to be universal rules or duties

Many of the issues facing the information technology industry and those who work in it can be analyzed in terms of the schema shown in Table 13-6, as shown in the next few sections.

software piracy

software piracy – Illegal copying of software; a problem in the United States and Europe, but rampant in the rest of the world

Software piracy is unethical from a number of perspectives. It is illegal and violates one or more rules in all the aforementioned organizations' rules of conduct. That is enough reason to avoid piracy for an honest rule-based person. If you believe that the right to private property is a natural right, then as a

Table 13-6, Individuals base their ethical decisions on different principles

	oriented toward consequences	oriented toward rules
oriented toward the individual	*Egoism* The individual bases his ethics on the possible good and bad consequences to himself. An example: An individual might judge the possibility of getting caught for cheating on a test as high, and therefore not cheat.	*Deontology* The individual bases her ethics on a sense of duty. Consequence is not considered relevant. An example: An individual believes that telling the truth is important no matter what the situation. When she realizes that her team leader has mislead her manager as to the progress of the program she is working on, she tells her boss what her true progress is, even though it puts her own abilities in a worse light.
oriented toward the universal	*Utilitarianism* The individual bases her ethics on the possible good and bad consequences to all individuals, including herself—and to the universe in general. This can include a sense of empathy—i.e., what if I was the victim of X. An example: A programmer might realize that an unintended consequence of the emissions checking program that she is writing will allow some polluting cars to pass. She determines the negative effects will be felt by many people. She thus takes the time to fix the code.	*Rule-deontology* The individual bases his ethics on what he considers universal rights or natural or inherent rules—rules that make people responsible to one another. Consequences are not considered relevant. An example: An individual believes in the right to privacy. His boss asks for the names and addresses of people in his neighborhood as possible customers for their new product. He refuses.

13

rule-deontologist, that should be enough for you. It is detrimental to everyone in a number of ways. As the software is spread illegally, it increases the likelihood of spreading viruses. Because it lowers the revenue of the company that manufactures the software, it increases the cost of software for everyone. In terms of consequence, this would give any good utilitarian pause. It decreases the amount of resources that can be put toward improving the product. It decreases the resources that can be put toward hiring people such as you or improving your salary. Depending on the country, estimates of pirated software run from 60 to 80 percent of all copies. That is a lot of lost revenue for owners of stock in the software company. Even an egoist would find reasons to avoid software piracy—such as the possibility of getting a virus, losing a job, or losing share value on stock holdings.

some famous and humorous virus hoaxes

- Clipper: scrambles all the data on a hard drive, rendering it useless.
- Lecture: deliberately formats the hard drive, destroying all data, and then scolds the user for not catching it.
- SPA: examines programs on the hard disk to determine whether they are properly licensed. If the virus detects illegally copied software, it seizes the computer's modem, automatically dials 911, and asks for help.

viruses and virus hoaxes

What about passing viruses along? It's not just writing them, it's also not doing the small things you can to stop their movement, such as running updated antivirus software, regularly updating your system, and not opening strange e-mail attachments. It's not against the law if you don't put a virus checker on your machine, but it's imprudent and unconscionable not to do so. A number of schools and corporations discipline anyone found passing along a virus—consciously or not. A virus can make your life and anyone else who is affected by the virus miserable. And all the code of ethics of the IT organizations mentioned above cover it in at least one rule. You should do what you can to eliminate viruses and inform others that you communicate with if you get a virus. However, you should *not* pass along ***virus hoaxes***, which only add to the overwhelming amount of information individuals are already receiving via junk e-mail.

virus hoax – E-mail that contains a phony virus warning; started as a prank to upset people or to get them to delete legitimate system files

note Information on virus myths and hoaxes can be found at such sites as *vmyths.com*, *hoaxbusters.ciac.org*, and *internet-101.com.*

weak passwords

It also could be considered unethical to use weak passwords. Weak passwords allow access to the system to online vandals who, in addition to harming your computer, might take advantage of any other system weaknesses and cause further damage.

plagiarism

Many schools have an honor code that includes not only prosecuting the person who cheats, but the one(s) who allow the cheating, including "innocent" bystanders. This means that if you are found to know about the cheating being done by other people, you have also cheated. Cheating usually occurs because students feel under pressure to perform, don't understand that stealing intellectual property is a crime, or don't feel they will be caught. All three situations potentially put the student in an ethical bind but do not make the behavior correct. Cheating usually puts instructors in a bind as well because it forces them to spend time dealing with the issue of cheating rather than instructing.

Cheating might achieve a short term goal of getting through a particular assignment or test. But in the long run, the information represented by that assignment and the skills developed in doing the assignment will not be acquired. Even if the student avoids being caught and bluffs into a job, chances are he or she isn't going to have the skills to do the job properly. That means the former student will possibly be fired. Plagiarism contradicts many ethical standards and rules of conduct, such as Rule 2.1 of the ACM code, which mentions striving to achieve the highest quality of work. And the more plagiarism in which a person is engaged, the more likely the perpetrator will be caught. If you are going to borrow the work of others who freely share, whether it is text or a program, then cite where and who the work came from originally.

cracking

Cracking or hacking into computers is the same as trespassing on someone's land. Would many of the crackers trespassing on computer systems be as bold in the physical world? Unlikely. The physical world contains more deterrents, including the possibility of bodily harm. This is much less the case in the virtual world. Yet, in dollar terms, the damage that someone can cause by trespassing can be even more considerable than in the real world. A cracker could, potentially, wipe out your bank account, run up your credit cards, steal your identity and ruin your credit rating. Or a cracker could wipe out important files and kill your career. Even if a cracker never intended it, he or she ignorantly might do damage. Many writers of worms have been as surprised and impressed as their victims at how effectively the worms have moved across the Internet. Many program and system crackers justify their actions in terms of social Darwinism ("survival of the fittest"). They argue that stupidity should be punished and that society is better off for their actions. Yet, how many privately contact an organization and tell them of a flaw, giving the organization time to fix it?

Mistakes made while programming complex systems are not necessarily a matter of stupidity. Programming is still more art than engineering. There are millions of programs out there running everything from the stock exchange to the charger on your electric toothbrush. The chances that some programmers are better than others are high, but there are many programs that still need writing, many systems that still need administration. The best and brightest can't do everything. If you consider yourself one of the budding best and brightest, and you want to go counterculture, think about joining the open source movement. The evidence from Linux and other open source programs suggests that many great minds working from around the world on a large software program makes for better—or definitely more robust and secure—software.

health issues

Rule 1.2 of the ACM code indicates avoiding harm to others. Rule number 1 for both the IEEE and the Computer Ethics Institute concerns not using a computer to harm others. Computers have been instrumental in many injuries—large and slight—regarding health and the environment. A repetitive strain injury (RSI) such as carpal tunnel syndrome (the nerves are inflamed) and tendonitis (the tendons are inflamed) are frequent injuries for individuals using keyboards and mice. A burning, tingling, or numbness in the hands, arms, or fingers can accompany either. The U.S. Occupational Safety and Health Administration (OSHA) has issued guidelines that address these problems. As a software or hardware designer concerned with user interfaces, you should be aware of the ***ergonomics*** of how your interface will be used as well. In addition, proper disposal of your computer equipment could be considered ethical. Many of the components of computers, monitors, and peripherals are made of toxic materials. For the sake of your water supply, think of disposing of computer equipment properly.

ergonomics – Science of the relationship between people and machines; designing work areas to facilitate both productivity and human ease and comfort

In the end, as stated in the beginning of this section, ethics are principles held by an individual. You can't be forced to write good software that won't harm others, or to eliminate viruses. But, it is hoped that you will. It is also hoped that this section will give you an introduction to the tools required to evaluate complex issues in information technology, intellectual property, rules, laws, and privacy.

privacy

privacy – Freedom from unwanted access to or intrusion into a person's private life or information; the Internet and computerized databases have made invasion of privacy much easier and an increasing cause for concern

Not all cultures have the same set of ethics or laws concerning ***privacy***. In the United States there is much discussion and legislation regarding privacy and there are a number of laws designed to safeguard personal information. However, laws also exist (as do holes in the laws) that allow information about you to be gathered and disseminated by government and corporations without your consent. If you are concerned about your privacy, you may have to proactively defend it. In the workplace, where you are using your employer's equipment on their time, you are likely to have fewer legal protections for your privacy. There are a number of techniques for protecting your private information. You should also be aware of the tools—such as spyware and cookies—that are used to gather information about you and your online activities. Finally, privacy and intellectual property are issues in the area of information accuracy, an area that has been little addressed by legislative action.

With a great deal of information now available online—doctors' records, government records, credit records—that once need to be viewed in person, the importance of information privacy has become paramount. Many people believe that information about them acts as if it was still kept in file cabinets in an office: little movement and little access. This, however, is not the case. Just going to the doctor's office for a checkup passes your information through a number of organizations (credit card, insurance, hospital, lab, and so on). Browsing the Web and buying things online can also leave your Web habits open for viewing. All of this is potentially helpful information for companies trying to sell you something or a government agency interested in determining how suspicious your behavior might be.

In general, starting in the late 1960s, laws related to assuring privacy have become more protective of the privacy of individual residents in the United States. The creation of the "do not call list" in 2003 to thwart telemarketers was the latest effort by Congress to shield Americans from what many consider intrusive marketing behavior and violations of privacy. The one legislative act that runs counter to that trend is the PATRIOT Act (Provide Appropriate Tools Required to Intercept and Obstruct Terrorism) of 2002, which was a response to the destruction of the World Trade Centers in New York City by terrorists on 9/11/2001. It specifies, in part, that law enforcement organizations have the right to monitor individuals' Web and e-mail activity if they are suspected terrorists. At present a debate rages as to the constitutionality of this act, which will likely be challenged in the years to come.

No law currently exists to protect the privacy of employees working for a corporation. Employees' activities can be monitored through e-mail, log records, Web traffic, time spent on various software packages, keystrokes, and other mechanisms. Companies do not need to tell their employees about the types of monitoring and can use the information for performance review, firing, and even legal action. To the company, communicating electronically from within a company, or using a company's equipment, is considered no different than punching a time clock. You are in the company confines, on company property, and the company has a right to know how you are using your (their) time. The use of spyware (discussed below) facilitates this monitoring.

A number of specialized technologies are used to gather information about your Web habits and sell you products and services. Most are fairly harmless, some are used by crackers, and many are considered by many people to be obnoxious.

spam – Unsolicited (and almost always unwanted) e-mail; usually trying to sell something

Spam is the name for an unsolicited (although not always unwanted) e-mail. Most are attempts to sell directly to you. Spammers don't expect a very high return ratio. But, depending on the size of their distribution list, they can be successful with a fraction of one percent of what is called "click through"—or people clicking on the e-mailed advertisement. Most corporations that engage in mass e-mailing do so cautiously. They do not want to alienate their customers. The most successful mass e-mails go where there is a defined relationship to a company's existing customer base. These e-mails tend to make it easy to be removed from the list as well—a sign of goodwill towards the customer that actually reduces the chances that a customer asks to be removed because removal is perceived as something they can do at any time. There is a whole marketing science of mass e-mails that takes the customer response seriously. These types of customer lists have been created mostly through product registration and support logs. In this case you can likely reply to an e-mail with "Unsubscribe" in the subject line and be removed from the list.

The opposite of this approach is the unsolicited e-mail that does not make it clear how it has gotten your e-mail address or how to stop such e-mails from coming. Often they come from a single individual or organization who is using multiple return addresses to fool the antispam programs used by e-mail systems such as Yahoo and Hotmail. Spammers get their addresses from many sources. One technique is to use common sense with addresses. They have programs that search through combinations of common first and last names. Using a slightly odd e-mail name with non-alphabetic characters in it helps to stop this kind of approach. Another approach is to find public declarations of e-mail addresses (on Web pages for example). Yet another approach is to buy or steal lists of names and e-mail addresses. Many people fear that their e-mail address is being sold or given to others by the latest online merchant they visited. Using a special e-mail address, such as a free e-mail account, just for merchant interactions is one way to find out if such is the case. However, many merchants won't sell their lists to the lowest common denominator spammers (who likely couldn't afford them anyway). Those spammers probably used other tools, even spyware, to gather those names. It is best to never reply to spam e-mails.

spyware – Software that can track, collect, and transmit to a third party or Web site certain information about a user's computer habits

Spyware is a catchall phrase for programs that sit on your computer, with or without your knowledge, observing your computer activities. Spyware can collect information about your computer usage: anything from program usage to Web browsing habits. More intrusive spyware can collect e-mail addresses from your address book. Spyware is often passed into your computer through a virus, worm, or Trojan horse. Some legitimate software products also include a spyware program (they might call it adware) and inform you of it in the fine print. Whether spyware will or will not be used in conjunction with a program you install should be specified in the license or registration agreement and you should read it carefully to see whether information about you will be communicated to other vendors or advertisers. Spyware/adware is not necessarily illegal, but it can be, and it is criticized by many as an invasion of privacy, especially if the user is unaware of the program's existence.

cookie – A program that can gather information about a user and store it on the user's machine

Cookies are related to and sometimes used in conjunction with spyware, but considered different because the user is assumed to be aware of their use. ***Cookies*** are files that sit on your hard drive and communicate with Web pages that you visit. Your Web browser searches for a cookie with a unique identification when it is pointed to a Web page. If it doesn't find one, it may download one if the Web page uses them. If one does exist it sends information on to the Web page from the cookie and the Web page might in turn update the cookie. Cookies are used by Web sites for many things, many helpful to the user: keeping track of the items in your shopping cart as you move from page to page on a merchant's site, your Web site preferences, or user names and passwords to alleviate retyping every time you visit the site. Cookies can also be used to track visits to the site and to better target advertisements.

Spyware and cookies can be controlled. Cookies can be tracked, reduced, or eliminated. Your Web browser has settings that allow you to know when a cookie is sent and to block some or all cookies. Occasionally clearing the history files, cookies, and favorites from your browser is also a good move. A number of third-party programs (some are free) can also help manage spyware and cookies. Antispyware programs such as Spy Sweeper, Spyware Eliminator, and AntiSpy work like antivirus checkers; they scan disks for intruders and warn you when spyware exists or is being installed. Cookie manager programs include such names as Cookie Cruncher, Cookie Crusher, CookieCop, and WebWasher. Spam can also be filtered. Antispam programs include Brightmail, MailWasher, and SpamKiller. A final category of privacy tool is an anonymous Web surfer setup such as Anonymizer.com or WebSecure. These programs disallow your Web surfing to be identified with you. To find these kinds of programs, try searching online with your favorite search engine.

Here are a number of other steps that can be taken to secure your privacy—some drastic and some less so:

- Avoid leaving a record of your purchases when possible: Use cash if possible, then cash card, then credit card, then check. Don't join purchasing clubs. Don't give out information to be put on a call or e-mail list. Skip filling out warranty and registration information. You don't need them to get product support. Avoid tempting rebates.
- Guard against telephone and mail intrusion: Have an unlisted phone number. Use caller ID to block unknown numbers. Don't have your telephone number and address printed on your checks.
- Review privacy rules and write to all financial institutions with which you interact: Get off their mailing lists. Inform merchants that you don't want your personal information shared.

Not only access to information, but information accuracy is an issue. Questions arise as to who is ultimately responsible for the accuracy of information that is now so readily available, especially online. You are responsible for assuring that the information held by credit organizations is up to date. Some argue that you should review your credit history once a year from the big three reporting agencies Equifax, Experian, and TransUnion. The same is the case with your medical records.

note You can find more information about your health records at the Medical Information Bureau, *www.mib.com.*

The accuracy of Web pages is another issue. With print media, incorrect or false information is often discovered and corrected in the editorial process. For many of the billions of Web pages that exist, there is no editorial process or "quality control." The possibilities for misleading and even harmful information about almost any subject—including, possibly, information about you—have increased exponentially. And this applies not just to text. Digital pictures can be modified and used to present false or misleading information. On the extreme end, the National Photographers Association has stated that any alteration to an original photograph is dangerous. Legal precedents for determining the accuracy of photographs have yet to be set.

one last thought

This chapter has examined many of the vulnerabilities of computer systems, from technical to social. It has reviewed many of the laws related to system intrusion, intellectual property, and privacy. Most pragmatically, it has explored the ethical imperative of securing computer systems and a number of critical

Reinforce your understanding of chapter concepts and terms with the information and activities for Chapter 13 on the student CD.

ways to make those systems less vulnerable. Operators of computer systems must realize that they are not just individually vulnerable; they are part of an overall vulnerability. For most computer operators, lessening this vulnerability is fairly straightforward: install and constantly update antivirus software, firewalls, and operating system patches. Operators need to guard against communicating information and allowing access that increases vulnerability. And individuals and organizations need to reassess the balance between ease of use, customer service, time, and cost on the one hand, and system security on the other. Maintaining system security is a long-term investment for individual and organizational viability. As a computer user and potential system designer and programmer, you play an essential role in creating and supporting secure systems.

chapter summary

- Computer security is more than the hunt for the intruder, but also includes creating a protective mind-set and abiding by the policies created
- The terms "hacking" and "hacker" did not originally have the negative connotation that they often do today
- Intruders to systems can be classified as directed and undirected hackers, each with different motives but often having a similar effect on the systems they target
- Crackers can find holes in systems put there intentionally or unintentionally by system administrators and programmers
- Viruses, worms, and Trojan horses are programs that crackers use to infiltrate systems
- One of the greatest risks to a company and its computers is through social engineering—human (not technological) manipulation
- There are four types of attacks on computer systems: access, modification, denial of service, and repudiation
- Total risk to an organization is made up of vulnerability, threat, and existing countermeasures
- Intruders target the confidentiality, integrity, availability, or accountability of a system's information
- Countermeasures in managing security include common sense behavior, creating and following security-oriented procedures, using encryption, antivirus software, firewalls, system setup, and architecture
- You need to install antivirus software, perform system updates, physically restrict access to your computers, and have a good backup system
- Users support cracking by using weak passwords—you need to have good passwords
- Authentication and identification are two distinct things
- One way to secure communications over a network is to encrypt the information using one of a number of encryption schemes, such as using private and public keys
- Firewalls and routers can be set up so that certain ports are unavailable and that certain servers—such as the company Web site server—can sit in a DMZ—a more public and less protected part of the network
- It often has been difficult to prosecute computer attackers because of variations in national and international laws, as well as the difficulty of proving a case
- Despite the difficulties in prosecuting computer crimes, there are laws and ethical reasoning that dictate that it is unwise to commit such crimes.

- Law enforcement and the courts are cracking down on computer criminals more than ever
- There are a number of issues in computing that can be viewed from an ethical perspective and seen as wrong: software piracy, virus propagation, plagiarism, breaking into computers, and doing harm to people through computers are some of them
- Privacy is protected by law, but employees have fewer rights to privacy while on the job
- There are many things you can do to protect your privacy; only give out your personal information when you must
- Computer and network security is everyone's responsibility, from basic users to system designers

key terms

Acceptable Use Policy (AUP) (513)
access attack (507)
accountability (510)
antivirus software (516)
asymmetric encryption (521)
authentication (510)
availability (510)
backdoors (504)
biometrics (516)
bot (505)
buffer overflow (504)
callback (513)
checksum (517)
confidentiality (510)
cookie (539)
copyright (525)
cracker (502)
demilitarized zone (DMZ) (523)
denial-of-service (DoS) attack (508)
digital certificate (518)
directed hacker (502)
disaster recovery plan (DRP) (513)
dumpster diving (507)
encryption (510)
encryption key (518)
ergonomics (536)
ethics (531)
firewall (521)
hacker (502)
Hacker's Manifesto (503)
hacktivism (503)
heuristics (517)
honey pot (517)
identification (510)
intellectual property (525)
integrity (510)
malicious code (505)
modification attack (508)
packet-filtering firewall (522)
patent (526)

phreaking (502)

privacy (537)

proxy firewall (522)

repudiation attack (508)

reverse engineer (526)

risk (508)

script kiddie (503)

sniffer (508)

social engineering (506)

software piracy (532)

spam (538)

spyware (539)

symmetric encryption (521)

threat (509)

trade secret (526)

Trojan horse (506)

virtual private network (VPN) (513)

virus (517)

virus hoax (534)

virus signature (or virus definition) (517)

vulnerability (508)

undirected hacker (502)

worm (505)

test yourself

1. Who is Cliff Stoll?
2. What is the term for the individuals that thwarted the AT&T phone system?
3. What did the term "hacker" originally describe?
4. What's the difference between a "directed" and an "undirected" hacker?
5. What other potential intruders do systems managers need to guard against other than crackers?
6. What document justifies hacker activity?
7. How could most computer intrusions be avoided?
8. What login technique on a UNIX system could crackers take advantage of?
9. Explain one sloppy programming problem connected to URLs.
10. Explain a buffer overflow and indicate how a buffer overflow can be used by a cracker.
11. What is the difference between identification and authentication?
12. What is the main difference between a virus and a worm?
13. A system attack that disallows users from accessing their accounts is called what kind of attack?
14. Give an example of a repudiation attack.
15. What four types of targets are there for an information security specialist?

16. Name four ways that you can "get paranoid" and safeguard your system from losing data.
17. What is the term used for the most common and accurate antivirus software search technique?
18. Name three laws that you could use to prosecute a cracker.
19. How expensive should the damage caused by a cracker be in order to be prosecuted by the U.S. Computer Fraud and Abuse Law? Explain.
20. Name four ways you could defend your privacy.

practice exercises

1. Computer security affects:
   - **a.** Programmers and system administrators
   - **b.** Naive users
   - **c.** All users of computers
   - **d.** Everyone
2. John Draper created:
   - **a.** A whistle in Cap'n Crunch cereal
   - **b.** Software for Microsoft
   - **c.** Software for Apple
   - **d.** A secure router
3. The term "hacker" originally had a negative context associated with it.
   - **a.** True
   - **b.** False
4. The term "script kiddie" refers to what?
   - **a.** Con man
   - **b.** Youthful hacker
   - **c.** Unsophisticated cracker
   - **d.** A game for hackers
5. What is the likely motivation of an "undirected hacker"?
   - **a.** Technical challenge
   - **b.** Greed
   - **c.** Anger
   - **d.** Politics, economics, poverty
6. What is the likely motivation of a "directed" hacker?
   - **a.** Technical challenge
   - **b.** Anger, greed, politics
   - **c.** Fear
   - **d.** Improving society

7. The term hacktivists refers to?

    a. Hackers motivated by greed
    b. Hackers motivated by economics
    c. Hackers who use social engineering
    d. Hackers motivated by politics

8. The Hacker's Manifesto does what?

    a. Specifies how to break into systems
    b. Justifies hacking as an end in itself
    c. Justifies prosecuting hackers and crackers for their crimes
    d. Is a Communist document that justifies hacking for its inherent justice

9. What was the backdoor on a basic mail program on early versions of UNIX?

    a. rlogin
    b. login
    c. ls –l
    d. blogin

10. Trojan horse programs are different from viruses because they need to be transported by an e-mail program and viruses do not?

    a. True
    b. False

11. One of the most notorious social engineers of the 1990s was:

    a. Clifford Stoll
    b. John Draper
    c. David L. Smith
    d. Kevin Mitnick

12. In a social engineering attack, the company phone book can be the target.

    a. True
    b. False

13. What kinds of things does a modification attack do?

    a. Denies users access to the system
    b. Changes software and information
    c. Modifies evidence of system entry
    d. Allows access to a computer system

14. One way to ensure you have a backup of information is to use a UPS.

    a. True
    b. False

15. Which of the following doesn't stop virus and worm attacks?

    a. SpamKiller
    b. Opening e-mail attachments
    c. The disaster recovery plan
    d. Updating your virus checker

16. The best passwords are 8 or 10 letters long.

    a. True
    b. False

17. A virus-checking program that uses heuristics uses:

    a. A honeypot
    b. A virus signature
    c. A checksum on files to check their validity
    d. A set of rules to anticipate a virus's behavior

18. Encryption algorithm standards used in computers today are:

    a. Substitution, transcription, compaction, expansion
    b. S-HTTP, SEC, SSL
    c. DES, RSA, AES
    d. Proxy, packet, DMZ

19. SSN is a more secure way of transferring files than Telnet.

    a. True
    b. False

20. What kind of service is best placed in a DMZ?

    a. FTP and SMTP
    b. Internal DNS server
    c. Web server
    d. Database server

21. The legal protection most sought after for software source code is?

    a. A patent
    b. A copyright
    c. A trademark
    d. A trade secret

22. Utilitarianism is a set of ethical principles that focuses on individual consequences of an action.

    a. True
    b. False

23. The set of ethical principles that puts principles in terms of natural rights is:

    a. Rule-deontology
    b. Deontology
    c. Egoism
    d. Utilitarianism

24. According to an argument in the text concerning piracy, an egoist would consider piracy unethical because:

    a. It is illegal
    b. It may affect many systems if a virus is released
    c. It is against the ACM rules of conduct
    d. The company that sells the software could lose share value

25. You should always respond to spam with an e-mail that has "Unsubscribe" in the subject line.
    - a. True
    - b. False

digging deeper

1. Why was a simple whistle able to subvert the phone system in the 1970s?
2. Is a firewall useful in a home computer hooked up to the Internet? When? How?
3. What is likely to happen with IP addresses given that the world is running out of them?
4. A number of system holes were introduced in this chapter that allow crackers to enter a system. Can you find another?
5. How much does the microcomputer revolution owe to cracking and vice versa?

discussion topics

1. What value for society is there in having rogue programmers out there breaking into systems because they say it is valuable for society as a whole? What dangers?
2. The companies that battle viruses and market antivirus software actually share information about new viruses. Do you think this helps the fight against viruses, or is the power of the marketplace not given its proper due?
3. The text notes that it is everyone's responsibility to combat malicious hacking. Do you believe this is true? Why or why not?
4. Who holds the bulk of the blame for the ease with which viruses propagate around the globe: companies or individuals?
5. Examine some of the reasons that people don't bother to protect their systems against intrusions. Look at passwords, software, software updates, architecture, costs, and so on.

Internet research

1. List 10 companies that make antivirus software. Which one is supposedly the best? Why?
2. Find a good online source for the constantly changing vocabulary of the hacker or cracker.
3. Find a Web location that gives awards for antivirus software.
4. Who is Mikko Hypponen?
5. Find the "Hacker's Manifesto." What reasons does the author give for hacking?

14

chapter

emerging technologies

in this chapter you will:

- Understand the performance limitations of Von Neumann architecture
- Learn why computer speed enables new innovation
- Gain an understanding of current and future computing paradigms
- Learn how light and biologic computers can speed processing
- Learn what the Turing Test is and how it applies to computing
- Learn about the changing shape of computers
- Learn how computers are merging with other devices
- Learn about innovations in memory and data storage
- Learn how the Internet will affect future computing
- Gain an understanding of artificial intelligence (AI)
- Learn about developments in AI

the lighter side of the lab
by spencer

Each November, computer and tech geeks from around the world assemble in Las Vegas, Nevada. No, they aren't assembling to carry out the final stages of Bill Gates' plan to take over the world (yet). Rather, they come together for Comdex.

No, Comdex is not Rolo's brother. (Rim shot.) It is an enormous convention where technology companies from around the world showcase their latest and greatest. In past years, as many as 220,000 people (including myself) have attended the weeklong trade show.

I recently logged onto the official Comdex Web site to get a sneak peek at some of the year's coolest technological advancements. One of the first headlines that caught my eye mentioned "Wearable Computers Utilized by Event Coordinators at Comdex." I could barely contain myself as I excitedly clicked on the link.

But instead of seeing wearable computers, I saw the message—"Warning: Bad arguments to implode." I've never known the word "implode" to be used in a positive context (unless it is in the same sentence as "Teletubbies"), so I quickly pressed the Back button. Luckily, nothing imploded. I tried the next link. Same error. Next link. Same error.

I tried clicking on every link in the news section of the Comdex Web site, and each time I was warned of an evil, impending implosion. Luckily, I lived to tell about it. I also learned a valuable lesson: Teletubbies actually have televisions stuck inside their tummies. (Take that, wearable computers!)

Actually, I learned that technology isn't perfect. And why isn't technology perfect? Because if technology were perfect, we would have no reason to upgrade our computers.

COMPUTER SALESMAN: You mean to tell me you've survived the past four weeks on a 1.4 GHz processor?! Are you out of your mind?!

The computers have to be upgraded in order to keep up with the high-speed Internet that is spreading across the globe like wildfire. I can now receive junk mail at speeds never thought possible even a year ago. Pop-ups now pop up so fast that I sometimes mistakenly think I just won solitaire.

Looking back on what's happened to technology in the last 15 years, one can only imagine what the next 15 years have in store for us. Whatever the future brings, we can only hope that King Gates will implode the Teletubbies.

why you need to know about... emerging technologies

Throughout the history of computers, there has been a constant stream of innovation and new technologies. Although many of these have dramatically affected the way people live and have been widely accepted, some have been failures and have faded into obscurity. Much money and time have been invested in the development of new technologies with varying levels of success. This chapter looks at the limitations of current hardware and software and outlines some of the research that is taking place and some new products and services that are on the horizon.

This chapter also will help you recognize current and future needs so that you can make better decisions concerning the purchase and use of emerging technologies. In order to recognize the worth of an innovation to you and to society, you need to be able to assess the impact that the new technology will have and the specific problems it will solve. You will very likely have opportunities to make both hardware and software decisions during your career—certainly so for your own use. You could even become wealthy (assuming that you're not already!) and would want to know what new technologies might be a good investment.

Understanding the current problems or limitations in computing and recognizing valid solutions to them is key to taking advantage of the new technologies.

hardware limitations

As you learned earlier in this book, hardware consists of the CPU, memory, and I/O devices. There is room for improvement in all of these areas.

The main limitations of hardware continue to be related to three factors:

- Speed
- Physical size
- Power requirements

There are tasks that we would like to accomplish with computers that cannot be accomplished because current computers are either too slow, too big, or require too much power. Innovations in hardware will likely revolve around solutions to one or more of these three issues.

limitations of Von Neumann architecture

As you learned in the chapter on computer architecture, virtually all computer CPUs currently in use are built on the Von Neumann architecture. Remember that Von Neumann architecture is defined by the following characteristics:

- Binary instructions are processed sequentially by fetching an instruction from memory, and then executing that instruction.
- Both instructions and data are stored in the main memory system.
- Instruction execution is carried out by a central processing unit (CPU) that contains a control unit (CU), an arithmetic logic unit (ALU), and registers (small storage areas).
- The CPU has the ability to accept input from and provide output to external devices.

Because instructions are processed sequentially in Von Neumann architecture, most computers today are limited by the number of instructions that can be processed each second. If your old personal computer had a clock speed of 2 GHz and your new one has a clock speed of 4 Gig, you would think that the new computer would execute instructions twice as fast. That isn't actually the case, however. Remember that the Von Neumann architecture has to fetch instructions from main memory (RAM) over the system bus, and the bus is limited by physical characteristics to speeds that are less than 200 MHz. Therefore, increasing the CPU clock speed by a given amount seldom results in a proportional overall speed increase in the computer. In addition, input and output devices limit the overall speed even more.

why speed is important

Many tasks currently cannot be accomplished because of the speed limitations of Von Neumann architecture. One example of this is visual recognition. Perhaps you have seen on TV or in person a food-processing assembly line where workers watch produce, such as beans, go by on a conveyer belt. The job of each worker is to let the beans continue down the line to be processed and to remove any nonbean items, such as rocks, spiders, or rodents. Removing nonedible items from the produce assembly line is a very essential job, but most humans would rather not do it. The work is very repetitious and some people actually cannot perform the task because watching the produce move along the conveyor gives them motion sickness. Here is a problem that needs to be solved, and it seems that using computers and robots would be the ideal solution.

Automating the process would first require that a computer system be designed that could visually discriminate reliably between a bean and a nonbean, then another computer robotic system would need to be built that could physically pick out the nonbean items as they move by at high speed. At present, these tasks need more computing power than is currently available.

In addition to visual discrimination, technologies such as speech recognition, character recognition, and many other applications, need more computing power than is currently available. Scientists have long realized that the key to accurate weather prediction may be a computer or network of computers that is fast enough to perform calculations that take into consideration all of the variables involved in global climate and weather.

a new paradigm

paradigm – A theoretical framework, or a way of doing things

A ***paradigm*** is a theoretical framework, or a way of doing things. For over 50 years, computers have been constructed according to the paradigm of the Von Neumann architecture, using switching devices as the basis for the computer digital logic circuits. Computers first used mechanical switches, then vacuum tubes, followed by transistors, and now virtually all computers use complex integrated circuits. These semiconductor circuits have their own speed limitations. Transistors can only switch so fast, and can only be made so small. Transistors are now being built that are barely larger than a molecule in size. It seems that the current semiconductor technology can't get very much faster or smaller.

Von Neumann architecture is discussed in detail in Chapter 3, "Computer Architecture."

To achieve a giant leap in speed will require a paradigm shift in the design of computer hardware. One area where there is much research effort is in new types of computer hardware. One new type of computer uses light instead of electricity to transmit and store data.

light computers

Shifting the paradigm from semiconductor switches and electrical buses to optical switches and fiber optic buses promises a large increase in the speed of computing. Light has advantages over electrons in two important areas. Recall that electrons traveling along a conductor interfere with other conductors through the effects of inductance and capacitance. Light traveling through an optical medium doesn't exhibit these characteristics, so "light" buses would not be limited to the speeds of current electronic buses. Also, light beams can cross without interfering with each other. Electron streams cannot. The main board of your current computer has to go to great lengths to run the bus conductors from the CPU to memory and I/O devices without crossing. Light computers and devices would not have this problem.

honey, I shrunk the computer . . .

Computers get smaller, but hands don't. Miniature keyboards just aren't feasible. As computers become smaller and smaller, new methods of interfacing them will have to be developed.

Electronic semiconductors generate a great deal of heat as electrons move through them. Your computer is designed to dissipate the heat of the CPU and other chips so that they don't melt. Most computers have a fan and large heat sinks to pull the heat away from the CPU. This heat loss is actually an energy loss. Much of the power supplied to semiconductor computers is wasted as heat. Light generates virtually no heat as it travels through optical switches and conductors. Because of this, light computers would require much less power. It might be that a notebook computer using light technology could operate for weeks on a small watch battery! And, because large heat dissipaters would not be required for a light operated CPU, the processor and associated circuitry could be much smaller. Instead of a notebook computer, you might be using that small watch battery to power your new 1000 GHz wrist computer constructed with light technology.

quantum computers

quantum computer – A computer built using the principles of quantum mechanics, which is the study of matter and radiation at an atomic level

The use of this type of light computer could change the future of computing by increasing the speed of computers, while decreasing their size and power requirements. This type of light computer, however, still uses Von Neumann architecture. Another type of computer based on light is the ***quantum computer***. It also operates via light technology, but uses principles of quantum mechanics. In the Von Neumann computer, the fundamental unit of information is a bit. In a quantum computer, the fundamental unit of information is called a quantum bit, or qubit. A bit can represent two values. A qubit can represent four values. Quantum computers are still in the realm of theory, but some scientists predict that quantum computers will come into use in the future with speeds that are many millions of times faster than current computers. Imagine what kinds of games you could play on the new Pentium Q 10,000,000 GHz processor!

biological computers

Research has also been ongoing in the development of a computer based on biological molecules. Prototype biological computers have been created that use enzymes and DNA. These computers can perform operations at the rate of approximately one billion per second, which is comparable to the speed of the Pentium 2.4 GHz CPU. Additionally, biological computers are very small. Billions of simple biological computers could fit in the same space as a current semiconductor CPU. Researchers are trying to design biological computers that can be used inside the body to watch for, and maybe treat, problems.

passing the Turing Test

Turing Test – A test conceived by Alan Turing in 1950 to reveal whether a machine had the equivalent of human intelligence

In 1950, mathematician Alan Turing wrote a paper entitled "Computing Machinery and Intelligence." In this paper, Turing proposed that in time, computers would be programmed with abilities that would rival human intelligence. Part of the paper proposed the idea of an imitation game wherein a human being and a computer would be asked questions by a person. The game would be structured such that the person would not know whether it was the human or the computer that was answering. If the person could not tell the difference from the answers received during the dialog, the computer could then be considered as intelligent as the human. The game that Turing proposed is now usually referred to as the ***Turing Test*** for intelligence. Part of the quest for improving computer speed is to build a computer that can pass the Turing Test.

a Turing tour

Alan Turing has contributed so much to the theory of computing that he is sometimes referred to as the father of computing. Entering his name into an Internet search engine will return tens of thousands of links to articles concerning him and his research.

the computer's changing shape

First-generation electronic computers were very large and had massive power and air-conditioning requirements. The original Eniac computer occupied over 5000 square feet of space. Since then, computers have steadily become smaller. Many of the PDAs (personal digital assistants) in use today have much more computing power than the Eniac, and yet fit in the palm of your hand.

The next evolution in the physical design of a computer involves the shape and location of the computer. For over 20 years, the computer fit on the desktop and was used only when the user was sitting in front of the computer. Now notebook and PDA computers provide portability and computing power that greatly exceeds that of the supercomputers of just a few years ago.

wearable computers

New computers that can be easily worn are now being developed. Research is ongoing into the feasibility of making computers out of clothing (or maybe clothing out of computers). The ability to wear your computer in an unobtrusive fashion would allow you to have your own intelligent assistant with you at all times. Your computer could remember things for you or it could provide you with access to all of the knowledge available on the Internet at any time.

Wearable computers have also been designed to be used as language translators. Imagine having a jacket attached to special eyeglasses that have a camera aimed forward and a special display that can be viewed with the eye. The camera in the glasses would recognize words on a page or sign, translate them to a desired language, and display the translation on the display. The same technology could be used with spoken language. The only thing holding this new technology back is the speed and size of present computers. As computers get faster, this technology will become commonplace. Figure 14-1 shows an example of a wearable computer vest.

Figure 14-1, A wearable computer vest

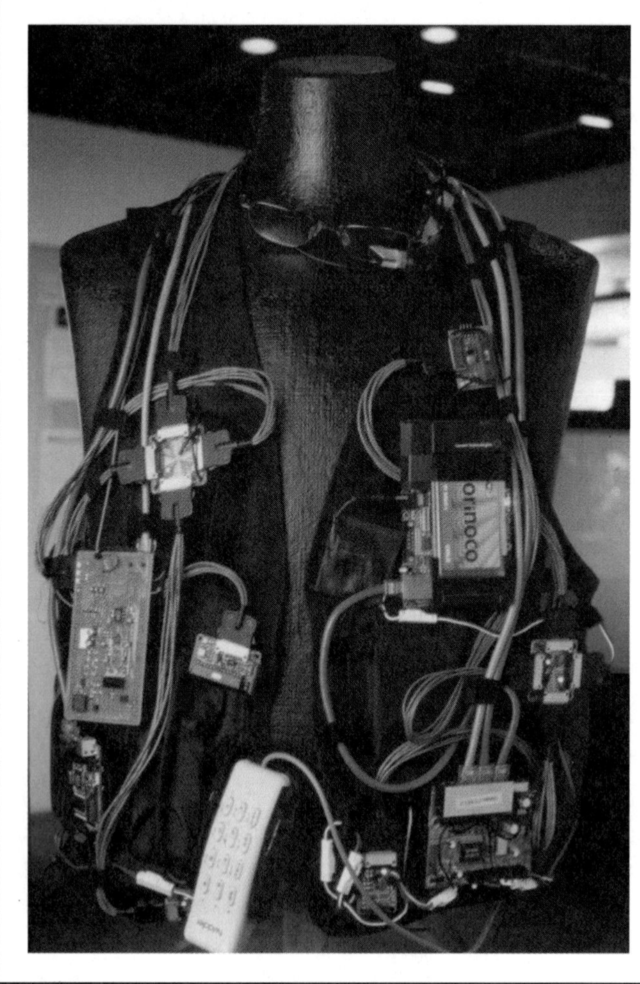

Wearable computers are also being designed to allow people to perform complex tasks without prior training. One example is that of an aircraft mechanic that isn't familiar with a specific maintenance procedure. The mechanic could wear a computer that has a microphone and special "heads up" display glasses. As the mechanic stands in front of the jet engine, a view of the outside of the engine would be displayed on the glasses. The mechanic could then say, "What should I do next?" and the computer would then display a video of the process of opening the cowling of the engine. The mechanic would see in the display exactly the same engine as was being worked on. Using voice commands the mechanic could be walked through the process and know that everything being done was correct. It would be like having your own expert in that procedure standing over your shoulder helping you.

computers in everything

Once computers move off the desktop, where will they end up? Research is being performed on placing computers in nearly everything. Already computers are in nearly every type of electronic equipment, from cell phones to microwave ovens. Computers are in cars and airplanes and even amusement rides. Anything around you that seems to make decisions most likely has a computer in it.

it's everywhere

The concept of each person interacting with many, sometimes invisible computers has been named "ubiquitous computing" by computer scientist Mark Weiser.

merging technologies

As computers begin to be placed into nearly every device, it is only a matter of time until all of these devices begin to merge. Currently, the lines between computer, television, and radio technology have become increasingly fuzzy. You can watch a movie on your computer and you can browse the Internet on your TV. Your phone is now a camera, a music player, and a video game machine. Phones can also now function as PDA devices. Or, are PDA devices functioning as phones? Computers are being incorporated into home appliances. It's entirely possible that you can continue to instant message with your friends while looking in the refrigerator for something to eat. As more and more devices begin to be equipped with computers and the ability to communicate, it is only natural that they should communicate with each other and become a connected part of your home computer network.

The TV is a great example of merging technologies. A television doesn't need a computer to work. But, if you want to be able to record television shows and play them back later, you need some type of device that has enough logic circuitry to watch a clock and turn the recorder on and off at the correct time. VCRs have been used for many years, but in the late 1990s something happened that is changing the concept of watching TV forever. That thing is the advent of the ***digital video recorder (DVR)*** and services like TiVo. The unique thing about the TiVo service is that the first TiVo units were simply Pentium computers running the Linux operating system. The units interfaced with the DirectTV program guide and allowed the user much power and flexibility in deciding which programs to record. Since the TiVo unit was just a normal computer, do-it-yourself instructions for building your own TiVo units sprang up all over the Internet. With a DVR and a service like this, you can have shows you like automatically recorded and then watch them whenever you choose. You can also pause either recorded or live television and continue playback later. In the near future, it may be that all TVs will have a built in DVR and software to interact with the program guide. Or, maybe DVRs will come with TVs. Then again it might be that you will simply be able to plug your desktop computer into your satellite or cable connection and watch and record TV on it. You get the picture. The line between computers and other devices is becoming increasingly blurred.

digital video recorder (DVR) – A specialized computer designed to record and play back video content from cable and satellite sources

TV on your phone?

Effort is ongoing to make streaming video available on cell phones. Nokia and T-Mobile are teaming up to allow subscribers to watch movies on their phones.

Project Oxygen

Project Oxygen – An alliance of educators, students, and researchers formed to create new computing paradigms and products enabling people to interact with computers in a more natural and useful way

In 2000, researchers and students at MIT formed an alliance with the Laboratory for Computer Science (LCS), the Artificial Intelligence Laboratory (AI Lab), and the U.S. government Defense Advanced Research Projects Agency (DARPA) and founded something they called ***Project Oxygen***. This alliance was formed to create a new paradigm of computing that would make computers and communication between computers as natural and all-encompassing as the oxygen that we breathe. The goal of the alliance is to free people from having to interact with the computers around them via special devices such as keyboards, mice, and video screens. The idea was that people should be able to command and interact with the computers that surround them, and do it in a very natural and useful way.

Project researchers have been working to create speech and vision technologies that can enable people to communicate with computers in a natural way. They are also working on new hardware, software, and networking techniques and technologies to help the project achieve its goals.

The concept is that computers will be everywhere and that people will be able to communicate with computers by just talking with them. You will be able to ask for information or ask the computer to do things. Because most of the appliances in homes and businesses will have computers, you could, for example, tell your stove to find you and remind you when the food that you're cooking is done. The main goal of Project Oxygen is to bring computers to the human level and to serve people, rather than having people go to the computers and try to communicate on the computer's level.

innovations in storage

A computer that can't permanently store information is of little use to anyone. Early computers could only store data in electronic memory that was lost as soon as the power was removed. Scientists quickly developed punched cards and paper tape to store programs and data. These methods were slow, and the storage media were very bulky. The advent of magnetic storage greatly accelerated the acceptance of computers. Magnetic tapes and disk drives became the standard method of semipermanent storage for computers well into the personal computer era.

Each type of electronic storage has strengths. Figure 14-2 shows the advantages of various types of currently available memory. Note that flash memory seems to combine the best features of all.

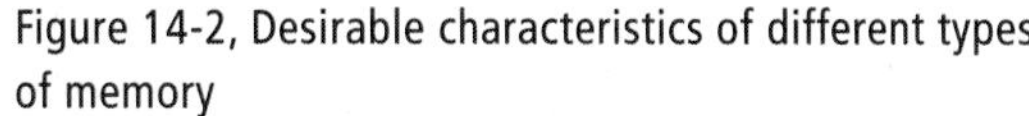

Figure 14-2, Desirable characteristics of different types of memory

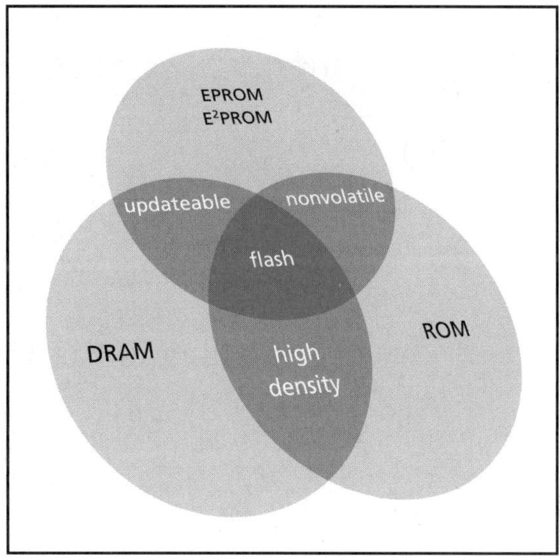

14

optical storage

going, going, gone

The advent of writeable CDs and flash drives has made other removable storage devices such as floppy disks nearly obsolete.

In the early 1980s, optical disks (CDs) began to be used as a storage device for computers. A CD can store approximately 700 MB of storage, compared to the 40 MB of the magnetic drives at that time. Hard drive capacities have steadily increased over the years and have surpassed the CD. Optical storage, however, is more stable than magnetic storage and is unaffected by outside magnetic influences. Optical storage such as the CD also lends itself well to removable storage. The DVD was developed as an improvement to CD technology. DVDs work in a similar way to CDs, but DVDs have higher densities and can store information in multiple layers and on multiple sides of the platter. DVDs can currently store from 4.7 MB to 17 GB depending on the number of layers and sides used.

holographic storage – A method of splitting a laser beam and using a device called a spatial light modulator to store full pages of information in layers on a crystal material

A new type of storage that is currently being researched is ***holographic storage***. Holographic storage is similar to optical disks, in that information is stored and retrieved using light. Holographic memory offers the possibility of storing 1 terabyte (TB) of data in a crystal the size of a sugar cube. A terabyte is a thousand gigabytes. Holographic memory uses a different technique for optically storing information. Instead of a moving platter with a spiral of microscopic bit information, the recording medium of holographic memory is a small crystal cube. Moreover, instead of storing simple ones and zeros in a stream, a laser and spatial light modulator is used to store a full page of information as a single holographic image. These holographic images are stored in many layers of the crystal cube. Although this type of storage is not currently available, scientists predict that it will be in common use in just a few years.

magnetic storage

Hard disk technologies have physical limits that will eventually be reached. Current hard disk technology allows for hard drives with over 500 GB of capacity, but recording densities for the magnetic coating are close to being maxed out. Manufacturers and researchers are trying new technologies that alter the types of magnetic particles or arrange them to achieve even higher densities.

new storage technologies

Both magnetic and optical storage have a problem. That problem is that both use moving parts (spinning disks). Moving parts require higher energy and are prone to mechanical failure. Inertia and other physical laws slow down the transfer of data because of the effort required in moving the parts. The solution to this problem is to develop storage devices that have no moving parts. Another benefit of a storage device with no moving parts is that the cost of manufacturing the device should be considerably less than a conventional hard drive that requires manufacturing to very close tolerances.

Conventional RAM is composed of transistor-capacitor circuits that can each store one bit. These circuits require constant refreshing to maintain the bit. When power is removed from the memory, the digital contents are lost. In response to the need for a device that could function like a hard drive and retain data indefinitely, but have no moving parts, technologies like flash memory have been developed.

flash memory

flash memory – Nonvolatile memory that allows the user to electrically program and erase information

Flash memory functions as erasable, rewriteable ROM memory. While flash memory has been used for some time in electronic devices and as the BIOS memory in computers, using flash memory for removable storage is a relatively new phenomenon, though it is becoming a standard alternative for removable drives. Flash memory comes in various forms. Some common brands are SanDisk CompactFlash, SmartMedia, and Secure Digital (SD). These flash memory modules can be plugged into external connectors on computers, cameras, printers, and many other electronic devices. Computers treat these flash memory modules as just another removable hard drive. You can write and read to them as easily as you could to a floppy disk in the past. These flash drives, however, have much greater storage capacity than the old floppies. Flash memories at this writing come in sizes up to 2 GB. Figure 14-3 shows a flash memory card.

Figure 14-3, A flash memory card

Courtesy of SanDisk Corporation

USB drives

USB drive – Flash memory in a small, durable portable case that can be plugged into a USB port of a computer and used in the same manner as a disk drive

A variation of the flash drive that has become very popular is the *USB drive*, sometimes referred to as a thumb drive. These are small flash drives enclosed in a durable case with a USB connector. The USB drive is attractive to computer users because of its portability. Connecting a flash card to a USB connector and providing drivers for it allows the flash memory to be connected to virtually any computer since most computers now have USB ports. USB drives have become the portable storage of choice among students and others who have a need to carry their files between computers.

These USB drives can be used for carrying your personal documents and files between computers, and new software innovations with Windows and other operating systems will allow you to actually carry your desktop configuration with you. When you plug your USB drive into a computer, the operating system will access a file on the drive and then configure the computer such that it will be an exact duplicate of your home or work computer desktop and environment. This will allow you to have your own computing environment wherever you might be. Figure 14-4 shows a USB drive.

Another new technology that is being used with USB drives to make them more secure is to combine them with fingerprint sensors. The small drive has a fingerprint reader built into the side of it. Unless the drive is plugged into the USB port by the person with the correct fingerprint, the drive is unreadable.

Figure 14-4, A flash memory thumb drive connects to the USB port of a computer and acts as if it were a removable hard drive

Courtesy of Trek 2000 International Ltd

As you learned in Chapter 13, "Computing Security and Ethics," biometric authentication methods such as fingerprint and retinal readers are becoming more widespread.

magnetic RAM

MRAM – Magnetic RAM, memory that uses the polarization of microscopic magnetic layers to store ones and zeros that remain after the power source is removed

Another type of memory that scientists have been working on for a long time is called magnetic RAM (*MRAM*). This type of memory uses the polarization of microscopic magnetic layers separated by an insulating layer to store ones and zeros. Like flash memory, MRAM has the ability to retain the data stored in it after the power source is removed. If used as a computer's main memory, the computer could be turned off and then back on without needing a reboot. MRAM has an added benefit of very low power requirements for reading and writing data. Although the main purpose of MRAM is to replace the DRAM as computer main memory, it could be used for many other purposes as well. Figure 14-5 shows how MRAM works.

Figure 14-5, How IBM's MRAM reads and writes data

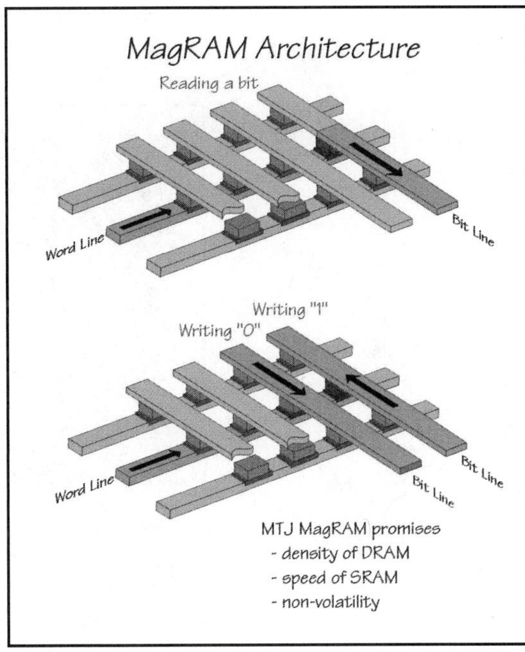

Courtesy of IBM Research

polymer memory – Nonvolatile memory that uses artificial polymers to store ones and zeros; some types of polymer memory can only be written once, while others can be rewritten many thousands of times

nanotechnology – The branch of engineering that deals with things smaller than 100 nanometers and especially the manipulation of individual molecules or atoms

polymer memory

Polymers are chains of complex molecules. Polymers come in natural forms such as DNA, and artificial forms such as plastics. Scientists have been working on ways to use polymers to store data. A few different types of ***polymer memory*** have emerged. One type uses ***nanotechnology*** to burn microscopic pits in a thin polymer coating inside the memory chip. The pits, or lack of them, are then interpreted as ones and zeros when read back. The other type of polymer memory uses electrical currents to burn through microscopic segments in the polymer. The first type can be burned, restored, and rewritten hundreds of thousands of times and could work in the same manner as flash memory. The second type can only be written once, but read back as often as desired. This type will probably replace audio CDs in the near future. These polymer memory chips are very small. In fact, over 1000 CDs worth of music could be placed on polymer memory the size of your little fingernail (if you keep your nails trimmed short!). Figure 14-6 shows how one form of polymer memory works.

nanotubes

One of the greatest technological areas of promise is nanotechnology. There are many research areas in nanotechnology, but perhaps the most important to computing is the development of nanotubes, which can function as transistors, but are much smaller, faster, and require less power to operate.

Figure 14-6, An artist's rendering of the Millipede nanomechanical storage device illustrates how an individual tip creates an indentation in a polymer surface (bottom) and how a large number of such tips operate in parallel (top)

Courtesy of IBM Research

the end of the mechanical storage device

The development, introduction, and acceptance of these new types of storage will make mechanical storage devices such as the magnetic hard drive, CD, and DVD obsolete in the future. These new devices have power requirements that are much lower than the mechanical drives, and they are also much smaller than the mechanical drives in use today. The use of these new technologies will enable computers and computer equipment to become much smaller. The lower power requirements will enable computers of the future to run on small batteries for a much longer time than is currently possible. Imagine a small notebook computer that runs for months on a single charge!

miniature storage and security

As removable storage devices become ever smaller with ever greater capacity, government and corporate entities are having to deal with the possibility that employees might use the devices to remove sensitive information from the premises. Many organizations are enacting bans on devices such as USB drives and other flash memory in the workplace to avoid this problem.

the Internet and future computing

So far, the Internet has been used mostly for e-mail, online chatting, and browsing Web pages. In the future, the Internet will become an extension of your computer bus. It will be just as easy, and just as fast, to store your files on a storage device thousands of miles away as it will be to store them on your local storage device. As Internet speed capabilities increase, and as more and more people and businesses are connected to this high-speed network, the merging of computers, radio, television, and even appliances will be able to become complete. All devices connected to the Internet, which will be virtually everything, will be able to communicate with one another and to share and transfer data from one device to another.

audio and video

Already, many forms of audio and video communication are taking place via the Internet. You have probably viewed Webcams over the Internet and perhaps talked with friends or family over the Internet. Certainly you have used the Internet to listen to music and to watch various forms of video entertainment. In the future, television and movies will be delivered to your home via the Internet. Movie theaters will also receive the movies via the Internet. Much of this is taking place already, but as time goes on, transmission of audio and video via the Internet will most likely become the standard.

wireless technology

Wireless networking technology is in its infancy. Scientists envision a future in which you will have connectivity to the Internet everywhere in the world. You will be able to have your notebook computer, PDA, or wearable computer clothing with you all the time and have it connected to the Internet. As is the goal in Project Oxygen, your computer can become your connection to the rest of the world and you will be able to interface to it and find and share information at any time and at any place.

jobs without end?

Cell phones, PDAs, and 24-hour jobs—as people become more and more connected, it is becoming increasingly difficult to get away from the office.

artificial intelligence

As you learned earlier in the chapter, the Turing Test was proposed as a method to determine if a computer can think and reason like a human. Since the invention of the computer, computer scientists have been striving to create a computer that can reason and think. The concept of a computer with these human characteristics is referred to as artificial intelligence (***AI***), but there are actually many different levels of AI that scientists are working with. Some of these different levels are:

AI – Artificial intelligence, the science and engineering of making intelligent machines, especially intelligent computer programs

- Fuzzy logic
- Neural networks
- Speech recognition
- Visual pattern recognition
- Machine learning (expert systems)
- Natural language processing
- Robotics

All of these have to do with trying to make a computer that is more humanlike. There are many things that humans do that might be more suited to computers. Many dangerous or undesirable tasks could be delegated to robots. For a robot to accomplish these tasks, however, requires a high level of human emulation. The robot would need the ability to make decisions. Conventional computer programs have the ability to act the same way every time that they are executed. AI requires a computer program that can adjust to the situation and actually "think." So far, computer scientists have had a difficult time making that possible.

In earlier chapters, you learned that computers use Boolean logic in their circuits to solve problems. You have dealt with logic such as *if-then-else* when programming. This either/or situation programming doesn't lend itself to AI. A computer needs to have "fuzzy" logic in order to complete AI-type problems.

fuzzy logic

One of the problems involved in programming a computer using Boolean logic is that the programmer has to provide for every circumstance. How often have you typed something into the computer and caused it to crash? The computer crashes because the programmer who wrote the program you are running (remember that the operating system is a program too) didn't account for what you did. Had the programmer planned for what you entered, everything would have gone smoothly. With ***fuzzy logic***, the program would have some other alternatives in dealing with your keystrokes.

fuzzy logic – A superset of conventional (Boolean) logic that has been extended to handle the concept of partial truth—truth values between "completely true" and "completely false"

fuzzy pioneer

The concept of fuzzy logic was conceived by Lotfi Zadeh, a professor at the University of California at Berkeley as part of his work with set theory.

Imagine that you are developing a robot that can walk from one end of the room to the other. You have programmed the robot to take one step at a time until it hits the wall. It should work well unless something happens for which you have not programmed. What if there is an obstacle in the robot's path? A human would examine the situation and then go around or climb over the obstacle without having been told how to do it. As a human, you are frequently faced with situations for which you didn't plan. When this happens, you probably just consider all of the possibilities and then take the course that seems to have the least amount of problems attached to it. That is the core of fuzzy logic. It involves deciding on an alternate approach or action when the primary isn't available.

neural networks

The Von Neumann architecture used in most computers today is based on the input, process, and output that humans perform naturally. Early design of computers was an attempt to build a machine that acted in a way similar to the human brain. Research since that time has discovered that the brain works very differently than was first thought. The brain consists of billions of neurons. These neurons are interconnected in three dimensions. It is thought that each neuron in the brain may have as many as 10,000 connections to adjacent neurons. The structure of this network of neurons allows for a massive degree of parallel processing. Remember that the Von Neumann architecture only allows for serial processing. Scientists have speculated that in order to create a computer with as much processing and calculating power as the human brain, an artificial neural network would need to be created. Neural networks are a different paradigm for computing than Von Neumann architecture. ***Neural networks*** are based on the parallel architecture of human and animal brains. Artificial neural networks consist of parallel interconnection of simple processing units. Figure 14-7 shows a simple neural network diagram.

neural networks – A parallel interconnection of simple processing units based on the architecture of human and animal brains; an alternate computing paradigm to Von Neumann architecture

Because neural networks have the ability to process many pieces of data at the same time, they are well suited to such applications as visual and speech recognition applications. Any problem that can be solved more quickly by working on it in parallel can benefit from using a neural network instead of a computer with Von Neumann architecture.

Research has been going on for many years in the area of neural networks. Applications, such as visual and audio discrimination, are greatly benefiting from being implemented as neural networks rather than conventional Von Neumann architecture. Yet, while some applications such as these can benefit from capabilities of artificial neural networks, it seems that scientists are still a long way off from imitating the capabilities of the biological neural networks of human (and animal) brains.

Figure 14-7, Neural networks can take many inputs, send the inputs through a network of simple processors, and then combine the results to form multiple outputs

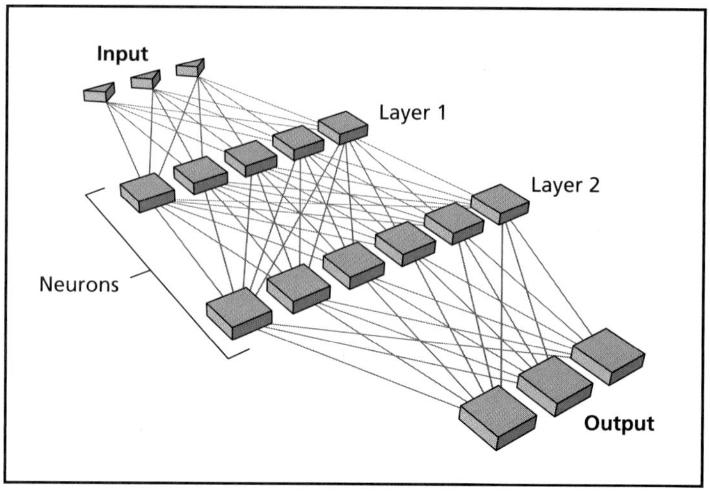

speech recognition

As you communicate with others, through either speech or reading, there are many things going on in your brain that allow you to understand what you perceive. Think how difficult it would be to program a computer to understand all of the different accents, dialects, and speech problems you encounter in your daily routine. Your brain constantly applies fuzzy logic to the things you hear and read to try to make sense of it. Consider the following paragraph:

> *Yuor biarn is albe to mkae snece of wodrs eevn if tehy are slpeeld wnrnog. It semes taht the mnid msolty jsut lokos at the fsirt and lsat ltertes and the orvarel cnotetx of the snetnece.*

You can probably figure out what the sentence means even though none of the longer words are spelled correctly. All of the letters in each word are correct, but they have been arranged out of sequence.

For a human to be able to communicate more easily with computers, the computers must be able to understand the nuances of human speech. Much work has gone into the development of speech recognition systems that can allow for these nuances. With the advent of the faster CPUs, speech recognition has become much more accurate. It is currently being used in many areas. You have probably had opportunity to talk to computers while performing online banking, online surveys, or picking up your voicemail. In the next generation of computers, it is probable that speech recognition will finally become usable.

visual pattern recognition

> **look out!**
>
> Pattern recognition is one of the core technologies developed by companies such as Mobileye. Their system is used for obstacle detection and classification in traffic situations such as the Adaptive Cruise Control System that recognizes obstacles in front of a vehicle.

Earlier in the chapter, you learned that having a computer recognize visual patterns was something that computer scientists are trying hard to achieve. The main problem is that Von Neumann architecture computers aren't fast enough to perform all of the calculations and comparisons necessary to allow for real-time visual discrimination. As computers get faster, scientists and researchers get closer to solving the problem. Much research has also been done in the area of using neural networks to achieve workable visual pattern recognition.

If scientists are to create a machine that can perform human tasks, it is essential that the machine have the ability to recognize shapes, colors, and motion and to discern what an object is. It's even more important that the machine be able to recognize the shapes in time to be able to act on them. Visual pattern recognition is a vital aspect of artificial intelligence.

machine learning (expert systems)

You are able to apply fuzzy logic in situations because your brain supports fuzzy logic. Fuzzy logic is effective because you also have the ability to learn, especially from your mistakes. Each time you encounter a situation you haven't prepared (been programmed) for, you apply the principles of fuzzy logic and choose a course of action. Sometimes it seems you didn't choose the best action. That fact gets added to your knowledge base and is factored into the decision the next time something similar occurs.

In order for a computer to emulate human behavior and reasoning, it needs to have the ability to learn. When the personal computer was first sold in stores, many of these stores had a display computer running the "What am I?" program. This program is an early example of how computers can "learn." The program starts out by saying,

"Think of an animal and I will guess what you're thinking of."

The first person playing the game would think of an animal, and the computer would immediately give up, because it hadn't learned about any animals yet.

The computer would then ask the person, "What animal were you thinking of?" and the person would type the name of the animal.

The computer would then ask, "What yes or no question could I have asked to determine that you were thinking of that animal?" The person then would type in an appropriate question.

If the next person to play the game picked a different animal, the process would be a little different.

The computer would start with the same question, "Think of an animal and I will guess what you are thinking of." Then the computer would ask the question typed in by the first person and ask for a yes or no answer. If the person answered yes, the computer would guess the first person's animal. If the person answered no, the computer would ask for a question that would differentiate between the first and second animal.

After a number of people had played the game, the computer could nearly always guess the animal correctly.

This game is an example of creating a learning computer. Computers that learn like this can come to resemble an expert in a topic. Because of this, computers that have this kind of program are referred to as *expert systems*.

expert system – A computer program that simulates the judgment and behavior of a human or an organization that has expert knowledge and experience in a particular field

There are many applications for expert systems. Telephone support and hotlines, such as a poison control center, can make use of this technology. For the first while, a person who is an expert on the subject can answer the phone and record the questions asked and answers given. Much like the game, the expert can formulate what questions to ask to get to the correct answer. After a period of this learning activity, a person with no knowledge of the subject could begin to answer the phones. Questions to ask would be displayed on the computer along with possible answers. If the person calling responds with a different answer than is given, the call is transferred to the expert, the new answer is recorded in the correct place, and the next question and possible responses are entered into the system. Expert systems like this continue to learn as time goes on and eventually can very nearly approximate the questions and answers that an expert would give. At that point, it is possible for many people to respond in the same manner as the expert. Systems like this are in use in many technical and medical support operations.

use an expert

Expert systems are currently used in many different fields such as tax preparation, equipment repair, financial planning, production control, training, and many others.

natural language processing

Programming a computer requires that you learn how to speak to the computer in a programming language such as C++ or Java. These languages also require that the programmer give a command for every little detail that the computer should do. Humans communicate in a very different way. Your mother might ask you, "Could you run to the store and pick up some milk?" You naturally understand the meaning of the request is that you should:

1. Get into the car.
2. Drive the car to a particular store.
3. Find the milk.
4. Put the kind you normally buy into the cart.

5. Take the milk to the checkout and purchase it.
6. Drive home.
7. Come back into the house.

Actually, many more small steps were left out of that set of instructions. If you were to try to write a program in a conventional programming language such that a robot could accomplish the task, you would need to specify every single detail of the process, even to the point of specifying exactly how to move the robot legs to get from the house to the car.

To achieve a level of artificial intelligence, a computer needs to be able to process the human language naturally and to infer many actions based on receiving a simple command. Although there are some good efforts being made in this area, we are still far away from having ***natural language processing*** that approximates human capabilities.

natural language processing – Computer applications that can recognize and interact with natural language text

robotics – The development, study, and use of robots; in most cases robotics also involves work with artificial intelligence

robotics

Robotics is perhaps the final branch of artificial intelligence. When all of the other aspects of AI have been achieved to some degree, it will be possible for robots to begin carrying out humanlike activity. Robots are not just the stereotypical human-shaped machines from the science fiction movies. Special-purpose robots are used today to assemble cars, perform medical operations, and defuse bombs. You can even buy a robotic lawn mower or vacuum cleaner. The science of robotics is primarily concerned with the mechanics and electronics that are used to carry out the results of the other areas of artificial intelligence. In the bean conveyer example earlier in the chapter, it should be obvious that even if visual pattern recognition is achieved, it would be useless without the robots to pick out the nonbean items. New humanlike robots are constantly being developed (Figure 14-8). In addition to the challenge of creating a robot that can think like a human, scientists also struggle to make a robot that can mimic human movements.

who is that man?

What will happen when robots are indistinguishable from humans? Many movies have addressed this topic, but it could become a reality in your lifetime.

Figure 14-8, Jogging robot developed by Sony

Courtesy of Sony Electronics

one last thought

One thing is certain, and that is that computers and computer scientists will play an increasingly important role in our future. Computers are becoming part of every aspect of life and there's no reason to think that the use of computers and computer technology is going to stop. It is amazing to think that just a few decades ago, computers didn't even exist, and now it's hard to imagine life without them.

Technology is currently changing so rapidly that even a chapter like this one can quickly become outdated. The speed, physical size, and power requirements of computers will continue to evolve to better suit the needs of current and future computers users and applications.

The key to a successful career in computer science is your ability to stay current with technology. Computer years are much like dog years (one dog year is said to be equal to about seven person years). One computer year is like ten years in most other fields. The information that you have learned in the study of this text will prepare you to continue to learn about new and emerging technologies. There are discoveries on the horizon that are impossible to conceive of now.

Reinforce your understanding of the chapter concepts and terms with the information and activities for Chapter 14 on the student CD.

Years ago there were no computers. Then mainframe computers started to be used by governments and large corporations. Then small businesses began to automate. The personal computer and the software that accompanied it brought computers into the home. The Internet brought them all together. Sometime in the future, the computing paradigm will shift once again. What will be the next big breakthrough in computing? How will it affect your life? As these new technologies emerge and are put into use, problems may arise concerning their ethical use. This is especially true in the areas of visual recognition, artificial intelligence, and miniature high-capacity storage. As a computer scientist, you need to take what you know now and ethically apply it to the future to move to the next level of computing.

chapter summary

- Understanding past technologies helps you evaluate new innovations
- Current hardware devices have limitations of speed, size, and power requirements
- Speed limitations are inherent in Von Neumann architecture
- The limitations on computer speed have made some applications impossible or impractical at this time
- Computing paradigms, or ways of computing, change on an ongoing basis
- Light computers may provide tremendous computer speed increases
- Mathematician Alan Turing proposed a test to determine the intelligence of a computer
- Computers will not be constrained to a desktop in the future
- Computers will become part of nearly all devices and appliances
- Computers and other technologies are merging
- Research is ongoing to allow people to interact more naturally with computers
- Storage devices with moving parts will be replaced with optical and magnetic innovations
- Polymer memory may become the standard in future storage products
- The Internet will be a prominent part of the future of computing
- Scientists have been working to give computers artificial intelligence capability
- Branches of AI include fuzzy logic, neural networks, speech recognition, visual pattern recognition, machine learning, natural language processing, and robotics

key terms

AI (568)
digital video recorder (DVR) (559)
expert system (572)
flash memory (562)
fuzzy logic (568)
holographic storage (561)
MRAM (564)
nanotechnology (565)
natural language processing (573)
neural networks (569)
paradigm (555)
polymer memory (565)
Project Oxygen (560)
quantum computer (556)
robotics (573)
Turing Test (557)
USB drive (563)

test yourself

1. What are the three main limitations of current computer hardware?
2. What has been the main computing paradigm for the last 50 years?
3. What is the effect of inductance and capacitance on light computing?
4. Much of the power supplied to semiconductor computers is wasted as ________________.
5. Do quantum computers use Von Neumann architecture?
6. Who conceived the idea of the Turing Test?
7. What is the problem with moving parts in a storage device?
8. Which of the new memory types cannot be rewritten?
9. Fuzzy logic is a superset of what type of logic?
10. Which type of computer architecture is thought to best mimic the brain?

practice questions

1. Which of the following is not one of the main hardware limitations?

   a. Power requirements
   b. ALU size
   c. Physical size
   d. Speed

2. In Von Neumann architecture, instructions are processed:

   a. In parallel
   b. Serially
   c. Both serially and in parallel
   d. None of the above

3. Light is subject to capacitance and inductance the same as electron flow.

   a. True
   b. False

4. The fundamental unit of information in a quantum computer is a:

   a. Bit
   b. Byte
   c. Quit
   d. Qubit

5. A test conceived to reveal whether a machine has the equivalent of human intelligence is the:

   a. IQ test
   b. AI equivalence paradigm
   c. Timing test
   d. Turing Test

6. DVDs can store up to 17 GB.

   a. True
   b. False

7. Which of the following is not a technology that uses light?

   a. Holographic storage
   b. CD storage
   c. DVD storage
   d. Polymer storage

8. Thumb drives use what type of memory?

   a. CD
   b. DVD
   c. Flash
   d. Holographic

9. Magnetic RAM is volatile.

   a. True
   b. False

10. Which of the following is not a branch of artificial intelligence?

   a. Light computing
   b. Fuzzy logic
   c. Natural language processing
   d. Machine learning

digging deeper

1. What is the current size of the smallest transistor? Theoretically, how small could one be made?
2. In what other ways has Alan Turing contributed to the field of computer science?
3. What ethical issues are involved in the creation and use of robots in society?
4. What new forms of memory have been created and adopted since the publishing of this text?
5. What is the technology that allows computers to be created in the form of things such as clothing?

discussion topics

1. What computer applications are impossible now because computers aren't fast enough?
2. What technological hurdles must be overcome for the light computer to be feasible?
3. How would your life be different if you could wear your computer?
4. How much storage would it require to store all of your audio CDs as MP3 files?
5. What are some applications that would be well suited to artificial intelligence?

Internet research

1. What are the physical factors limiting electronic bus speed?
2. How does flash memory store ones and zeros?
3. What is the current state of quantum computer research?
4. What is a Turing Machine?
5. What other branches of artificial intelligence have been defined?

appendix

answers to test yourself exercises

chapter 1

1. Measuring resources, land, dimensions for construction, navigation, understanding the cycle of the year, etc.
2. Probably the Chinese abacus. While clay tablets and other counting mechanisms predate this, it was likely the first object with moving parts for doing calculation.
3. Both used stored information from a card (or roll of paper in the piano's case) with holes in it.
4. He borrowed the idea of stored information on cards with holes.
5. Ada Lovelace is considered the mother of programmers for her work with Babbage's Analytic engine.
6. The idea of the program loop.
7. Using vacuum tubes
8. The Mark I in the United States, the Colossus in Britain, and the Z1 in Germany
9. Machine code is difficult for humans to read. Assembly language code makes it easier to program the machine code.
10. Big Blue refers to IBM and its successful blue-suited sales force.
11. The transistor and magnetic core random access memory
12. Hard drives or any kind of magnetic disk storage device
13. The first UNIX was written in 'B'. They had to invent the 'C' programming language to create the UNIX we know today.
14. It was written on a minicomputer; a Digital Equipment Corporation PDP-7
15. Calculators
16. The Microsoft BASIC programming language
17. Steve Wozniak and Steve Jobs; Visicalc, the first spreadsheet program
18. It launched the Apple Macintosh. Microsoft later came out with Windows.
19. It was originally conceived for the telephone system but never adopted.
20. We can go all the way back to the 1940s for the origins of hypertext from a paper by Vannevar Bush.

chapter 2

1. Word Processor, Text Editor
2. Microsoft Word – Windows documents

   WordPerfect – Windows and UNIX/Linux documents

Windows Notepad and Windows WordPad – text document

Star Office – UNIX/Linux

VI – UNIX/Linux

NOTE: There could be many more.

3. Microsoft PowerPoint

   Corel Presentations

   Star Office – UNIX / Linux

   NOTE: There could be many more.

4. BMP – Background images for desktops

   GIFs – Mainly used for buttons, banners, simple images, and animated images on the Internet

   JPG – Most efficient storage method that is great for photos and widely used on the Internet

   TIF – Widely used in professional photographic settings

5. Lossless removes only the redundant area of an image while Lossy removes redundant areas and areas that are not perceptible by the human eye.

6. Scaling can be used to change a graphic's display size without changing the underlying size of the graphic. It is commonly used when a graphic in its original format does not fit an output location's size.

7. Rotation moves an image by rotating it around a 360-degree layout. It is used when the image in its original size does not conform to the layout of the page (landscape or portrait) or if the user simply desires the image to be presented in a different angle.

8. Cropping allows you to cut portions that are not needed from an image. It is used when the user would like to focus on a particular part of the image and remove the non-essential areas.

9. There are many graphic packages available. This list by no means should be used as a restrictive answer limiting the student to only these five choices.

   1. Paintshop Pro
   2. Adobe Photoshop
   3. Microsoft Paint
   4. Macromedia Fireworks
   5. Star Office Draw

10. Flowcharting involves building diagrams that visually explain the logical steps in creating a program. Through the use of flowcharting a designer or developer can provide an easy-to-understand picture of how something is supposed to work.

11. There are many flowcharting packages available. This list by no means should be used as a restrictive answer limiting the student to only these three choices.

    1. Microsoft Visio
    2. SmartDraw
    3. Microsoft Excel

12. There are many e-mail packages available. This list by no means should be used as a restrictive answer limiting the student to only these six choices.

    1. Microsoft Outlook
    2. Microsoft Outlook Express
    3. Netscape Navigator
    4. Pine
    5. ELM
    6. Novell GroupWise

13.

RLE (Run Length Encoding)	Lossless
LZW (Lempel-Zif-Welch)	Lossless
Zip Encoding	Lossless
Huffman	Lossless

14. There are many compression packages available. This list by no means should be used as a restrictive answer limiting the student to only these three choices.

    1. Winzip
    2. Compress
    3. gzip

15. There are many ftp packages available. This list by no means should be used as a restrictive answer limiting the student to only these three choices.

    1. WS_FTP Pro
    2. WS_FTP LE
    3. UNIX ftp command

16. Program editor

    Graphics editor

    Compiler

    Debugger

    Components or objects

    Compiler and linker

    Project manager

    Help system

17. There are many spreadsheet packages available. This list by no means should be used as a restrictive answer limiting the student to only these two choices.

    1. Microsoft Excel
    2. Star Office Calc

18. There are many Web development packages available. This list by no means should be used as a restrictive answer limiting the student to only these three choices.

    1. Macromedia Dreamweaver
    2. Microsoft FrontPage
    3. Adobe GoLive

19. The project manager is responsible for building the development team, keeping the lines of communication open between the client and the team, keeping track of the project schedule, helping organize and motivate developers, and making sure that the product meets the requirements.

20. There are many project management packages available. This list by no means should be used as a restrictive answer limiting the student to only this choice.

    Microsoft Project

chapter 3

1. A motherboard provides a physical location for the CPU and supporting circuitry. It also allows for attaching additional devices via expansion slots and ports.
2. Central Processing Unit
3. Adding, decoding, shifting, and storing
4. A decoder is used to select memory addresses and I/O devices.
5. Collector, base, and emitter
6. AND, OR, NOT
7. Truth table
8. Decoder
9. Zero (0)
10. NOT
11. The plus symbol (+)
12. The flip-flop
13. SRAM
14. Binary instructions are processed sequentially by fetching an instruction from memory, then executing that instruction.

    Both instructions and data are stored in the main memory system.

Instruction execution is carried out by a central processing unit (CPU) that contains a control unit (CU), an arithmetic logic unit (ALU) and registers (small storage areas).

The CPU has the ability to accept input from and provide output to external devices.

15. A bus is a set of wires and protocols designed to facilitate communication between computer devices.
16. Address, Data, and Control
17. Cache memory is used to speed processing in a computer.
18. Polling is the process of the CPU interrogating each I/O device to see if it needs servicing.
19. Interrupt handling
20. Resolution is normally measured in terms of the number of pixels or dots in a horizontal and/or vertical direction.

chapter 4

1. That the number is a base 10 number.
2. That the number 2 will be raised to the 10th power.
3. 256
4. 16
5. 16
6. 256
7. 170
8. 101011001
9. 7243
10. A10
11. BEAD
12. 1100010000111010
13. 11000
14. 10001010
15. 256
16. 786,432
17. 41
18. 16,777,216
19. BMP
20. 1

chapter 5

1. Operating system
2. Device drivers
3. Kernel
4. The ability of a computer operating system to effectively support more than one process running at a time
5. The coordinated processing of a program by more than one processor at the same time
6. Provide a user interface, Manage processes, Manage resources, Provide security
7. Command line and graphical user interface
8. A small program running on a computer that may be part of a larger program
9. Time slicing
10. To allow processes and hardware I/O devices to interrupt the processor's normal executing in order to handle specific tasks
11. Tree structure
12. By using the "man" command
13. The process of formatting arranges the disk surface into addressable areas and sets up the basic directory tree structure on the disk. It may also install the operating system on the disk.
14. Unix, Linux
15. MD or MKDIR
16. The "ls" command
17. A special character used to allow pattern matching in filenames
18. The F2 key
19. To allow the operating system and hardware to work together to automatically detect and configure I/O devices
20. Yes

chapter 6

1. Guided and unguided
2. Bandwidth, Signal to noise ratio, Bit error rate, and Attenuation
3. Coaxial and twisted
4. 100 MHz
5. What are examples of networking protocols?

6. Seven
7. Wide Area Network
8. Bus, Star, and Token Ring
9. Bus
10. Network interface card
11. Gateway
12. A switch can create a point-to-point connection between an input port and an output port.
13. Firewall
14. 300 to 3300 Hz
15. 256 Kbps to 1.5 Mbps
16. The speed a transmission medium is able to handle, measured in bits per second
17. A WLAN is a LAN that uses wireless transmission instead of guided media.
18. AM places information on a carrier by modulating the amplitude. FM places information by modulating the frequency of the carrier.
19. 24
20. FDM

chapter 7

1. LANs and WANs
2. No single person or entity owns the Internet. It is owned in part by all who have networks or devices attached to it.
3. Internet Service Provider
4. National Backbone Provider. NBPs provide high speed communication lines to ISPs.
5. Sending e-mail
6. TCP
7. TCP
8. TCP
9. 32
10. Class C
11. Network broadcasts to every computer on the network.
12. ARIN (American Registry for Internet Numbers)
13. It automates the assignment of IP addresses in an organization's network.

14. A device or software in a computer that determines the next network point to which a packet should be forwarded toward its destination
15. The use of the Time To Live field in the IP header
16. To provide reliable file transfer between devices
17. DNS (Domain Name Server)
18. ipconfig
19. HTML (Hypertext Markup Language)
20. Bots (or spiders)

chapter 8

1. Data that has been organized and logically related into a file or set of files to allow access and usage

   There could be a wide variety of answers for the examples of the database currently being used. Some might be:

   Registration

   Student Transcripts

   Grocery store checkout

   Grading

   Library

   Health Insurance
2. Record #
3. select * from teams order by wins desc;

   The table name could vary since it is not provided in the documentation. Case does not matter.

   Students might be tempted to leave off the desc column. You will need to decide if you feel that is right or wrong. As an end user looking at the results, they will most probably want to see the team with the most wins at the top.
4. select * from teams order by wins desc, team;

   Students will be tempted to put the desc after team, but make sure you point out that it only applies to that column and NOT the wins column. The student might also list out each field rather than using the wildcard '*'.
5. insert into teams values (6, 'Bears', 3, 9);

   OR

   insert into teams (record_num, team, wins, losses) values (6, 'Bears', 3, 9);

6. insert into teams values (7, 'Lions', 9, 3);

   OR

   insert into teams (record_num, team, wins, losses) values (7, 'Lions', 9, 3);

   The record number could be different depending on whether or not problem #5 was executed.

7. select * from teams;

   OR

   select record_num, team, wins, losses from teams

8. Normalization is the process of database design that structures tables to eliminate duplication and inconsistencies in the data structure.

   The first problem is that if a database is not properly normalized, it cannot represent certain real-world information items.

   The second problem occurs when the database contains redundancies (repetitions) in the data. This simply wastes time and storage space.

   The third problem occurs when important information has been excluded during the design of the data structures.

9. first normal form (1NF) – Eliminates repeating fields or groups of fields from the table and confirms that every column has only one value by creating a new record in the table

   second normal form (2NF) – First normal form has already been applied to the table and every column that is not part of the key is fully dependent upon the primary key

   third normal form (3NF) – Eliminates columns that are not dependent only on the primary key

10. step 1—investigate and define
    The first step in the database design process is to investigate and research the information you will model. Define the purpose of the database and how it will be used.

    step 2—make a master column list
    Create a list of all the fields for which you need to store information along with their properties.

    step 3—create the tables
    Logically group the fields into tables.

    step 4—work on relationships
    Define the relationships showing how one entity works with or relates to another.

    step 5—analyze the design
    Analyze the work completed by searching for design errors and refining the tables as needed.

    step 6—reevaluate
    Reevaluate database performance and ensure that it meets all of your reporting and form needs.

11. This could vary. Please see accompanying CD for example.

12. This could vary. Please see accompanying CD for example.

13. This could vary. Please see accompanying CD for example.

14. The Not Null statement could vary.

```
CREATE TABLE ErrorDesc
(Error_Code char(4) NOT NULL,
Error_Code_Desc char(40) NOT NULL
);
CREATE TABLE Errors
(Error_Log_Date DateTime NOT NULL,
Error_Log_Time DateTime NOT NULL,
User_Code char(8) NOT NULL,
Error_Code char(4) NOT NULL,
Error_Log_Desc char(80),
Error_Status_Code char(1),
Error_Priority_Code number
);
CREATE TABLE Users
(User_Code char(8) NOT NULL,
User_First char(15) NOT NULL,
User_Last char(25) NOT NULL,
User_Password char(10) NOT NULL
);
```

15. The answer provided is an example of what a student might provide for the Users table. Please be aware that the values will most definitely be different.

    insert into users values('mrooney', 'mickey', 'rooney', 'dance');

    insert into users values('bboop', 'betty', 'boop', 'cartoon');

    insert into users values('bbunny', 'bugs', 'bunny', 'rabbit);

16. select User_Code, User_First, User_Last from Users order by User_Last, User_First;

17. select Error_Log_Date, Error_Log_Time, Errors.Error_Code, Error_Status_Code, Error_Priority_Code, Error_Code_Desc, Error_Log_Desc from Errors, ErrorDesc order by Error_Log_Date, Error_Log_Time;

    If you are using MS Access and you specified the Error_Code column you might have seen an error message displayed stating that the specified field "Error_Code" could refer to more than one table listed in the FROM clause. If you have more than one field with the same name being used in two different tables then it is proper to precede the field name with the table name followed by a period and then the field name (i.e., Errors.Error_Code)

18. select Error_Log_Date, Error_Log_Time, Errors.Error_Code, Error_Status_Code, Error_Priority_Code, Error_Log_Desc, Errors.User_Code, User_Last, User_First from Errors, Users order by Error_Log_Date, Error_Log_Time;

    If you are using MS Access and you specified the Error_Code and User_Code columns you might have seen an error message displayed stating that the specified field "Error_Code" and "User_Code" could refer to more than one table listed in the FROM clause. If you have more than one field with the same name being used in two different tables, then it is proper to precede the field name with the table name followed by a period and then the field name (i.e., Errors.Error_Code and Errors.User_Code).

19.

```
CREATE TABLE ErrorStatus
(Error_Status_Code char(1) not null,
Error_Status_Desc char(50) not null
);
```

20.

```
CREATE TABLE PriorityDesc
(Error_Priority_Code number not null,
Error_Priority_Desc char(50) not null
);
```

chapter 9

1. Any time you need to store information that should or can be accessed in sequential order.
2. int [ ][ ] aiGrades = new int[5][2];
3. Values may vary.

```
aiGrades[0][0] = 1234;
aiGrades[0][1] = 100;

aiGrades[1][0] = 4321;
aiGrades[1][1] = 90;

aiGrades[2][0] = 2212;
aiGrades[2][1] = 85;

aiGrades[3][0] = 8374;
aiGrades[3][1] = 75;

aiGrades[4][0] = 7758;
aiGrades[4][1] = 92;
```

4. A stack allows you to push (add) items on to the list and pop (remove) them from the list. The new item goes to the top of the list. The items are removed from the top of the list. This means that the last item added would be the first item removed.

5. A queue allows you to push (add) items on to the list and pop (remove) them from the list. The new item goes to the bottom of the list. The items are removed from the top of the list.

6. A binary tree represents a hierarchal format of data. Nodes have values associated with them. A node may or may not have leaf nodes or child nodes. The child's lower value is always placed to the left of the parent node, while the child's greater value is placed to the right of the parent node. As you proceed through the search tree you should compare to see if the value you are searching for is found in the current node. If not you check to see if your value is greater than the current node value. If so, you move to the node on the right. Otherwise, you move to the node on the left and begin the comparison process again.

7. (See two diagrams)

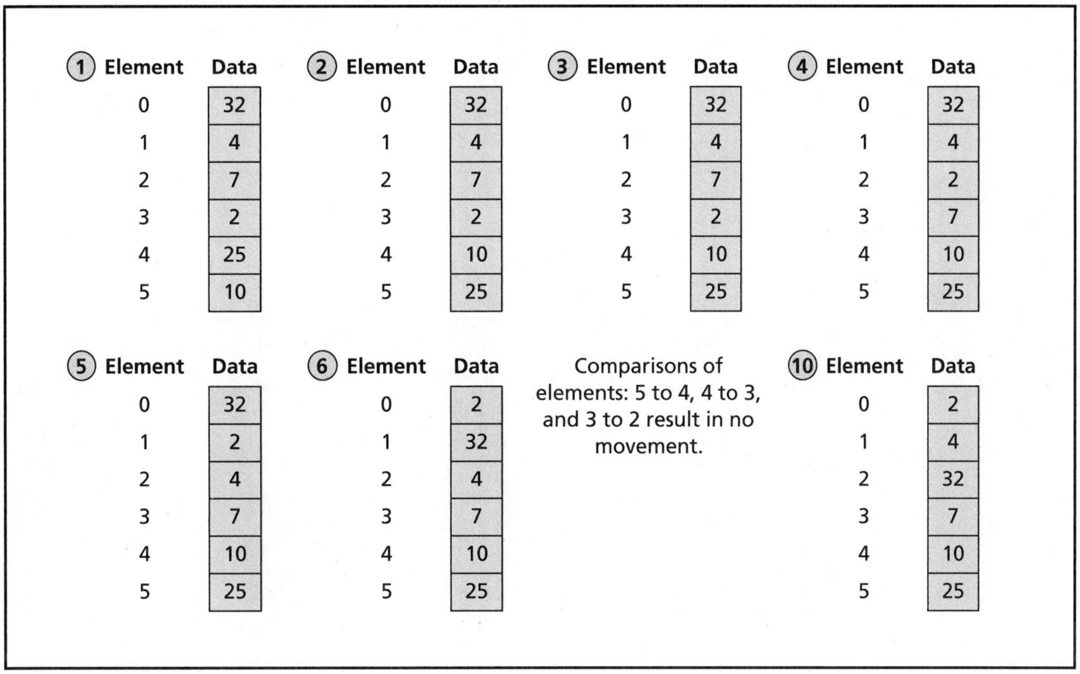

(1) Element	Data	(2) Element	Data	(3) Element	Data	(4) Element	Data
0	32	0	32	0	32	0	32
1	4	1	4	1	4	1	4
2	7	2	7	2	7	2	2
3	2	3	2	3	2	3	7
4	25	4	10	4	10	4	10
5	10	5	25	5	25	5	25

(5) Element	Data	(6) Element	Data	(10) Element	Data
0	32	0	2	0	2
1	2	1	32	1	4
2	4	2	4	2	32
3	7	3	7	3	7
4	10	4	10	4	10
5	25	5	25	5	25

Comparisons of elements: 5 to 4, 4 to 3, and 3 to 2 result in no movement.

(11)

Element	Data
0	2
1	4
2	32
3	7
4	10
5	25

Comparisons of elements: 5 to 4, and 4 to 3 result in no change.

(14)

Element	Data
0	2
1	4
2	7
3	32
4	10
5	25

Comparison of element 5 to 4 results in no change.

(16)

Element	Data
0	2
1	4
2	7
3	10
4	32
5	25

(17)

Element	Data
0	2
1	4
2	7
3	10
4	25
5	32

8. (See diagram)

(1)

Element	Data
0	2
1	4
2	7
3	32
4	25
5	10

(2)

Element	No Change Data
0	2
1	4
2	7
3	32
4	25
5	10

(3)

Element	No Change Data
0	2
1	4
2	7
3	32
4	25
5	10

(4)

Element	Data
0	2
1	4
2	7
3	10
4	25
5	32

No more changes.

9. (See two diagrams)

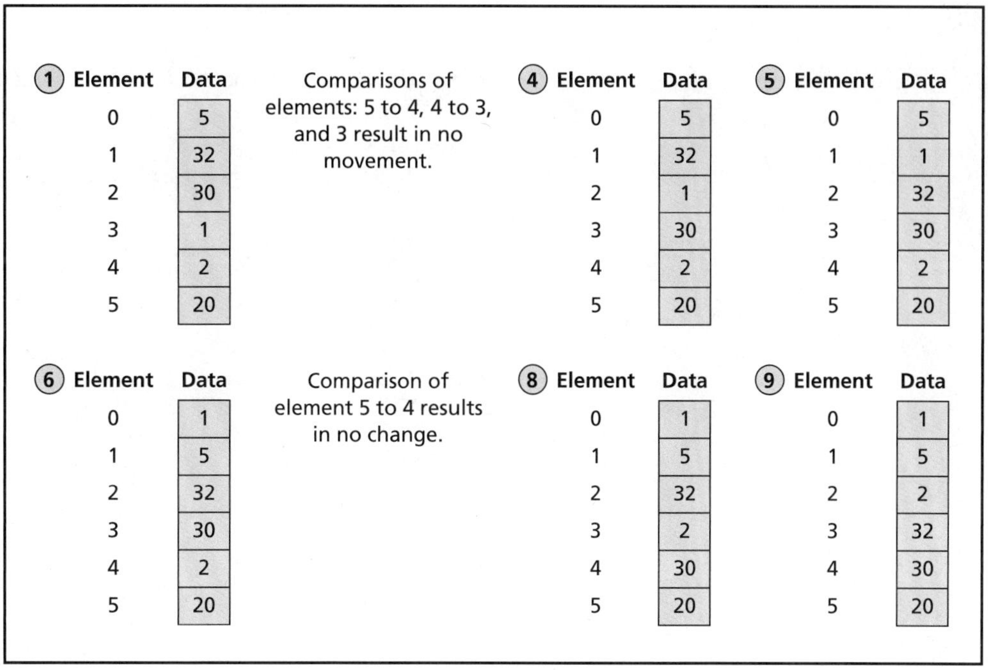

①

Element	Data
0	5
1	32
2	30
3	1
4	2
5	20

Comparisons of elements: 5 to 4, 4 to 3, and 3 result in no movement.

④

Element	Data
0	5
1	32
2	1
3	30
4	2
5	20

⑤

Element	Data
0	5
1	1
2	32
3	30
4	2
5	20

⑥

Element	Data
0	1
1	5
2	32
3	30
4	2
5	20

Comparison of element 5 to 4 results in no change.

⑧

Element	Data
0	1
1	5
2	32
3	2
4	30
5	20

⑨

Element	Data
0	1
1	5
2	2
3	32
4	30
5	20

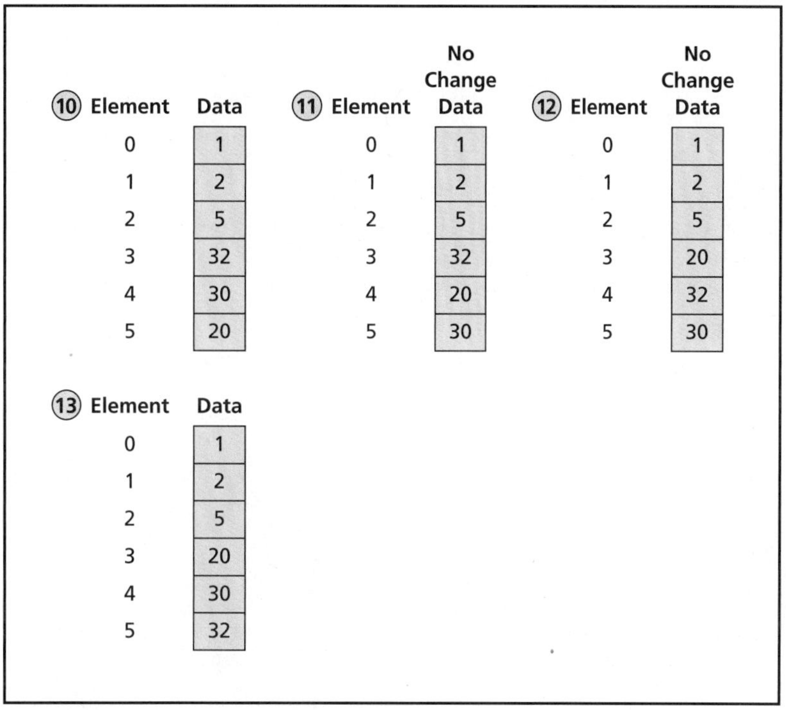

⑩

Element	Data
0	1
1	2
2	5
3	32
4	30
5	20

⑪

Element	No Change Data
0	1
1	2
2	5
3	32
4	20
5	30

⑫

Element	No Change Data
0	1
1	2
2	5
3	20
4	32
5	30

⑬

Element	Data
0	1
1	2
2	5
3	20
4	30
5	32

10. (See diagram)

①

Element	Data
0	5
1	32
2	30
3	1
4	2
5	20

②

Element	Data
0	1
1	32
2	30
3	5
4	2
5	20

③

Element	Data
0	1
1	2
2	30
3	5
4	32
5	20

④

Element	Data
0	1
1	2
2	5
3	30
4	32
5	20

⑤

Element	Data
0	1
1	2
2	5
3	20
4	32
5	30

⑥

Element	Data
0	1
1	2
2	5
3	20
4	30
5	32

11. (See diagram)

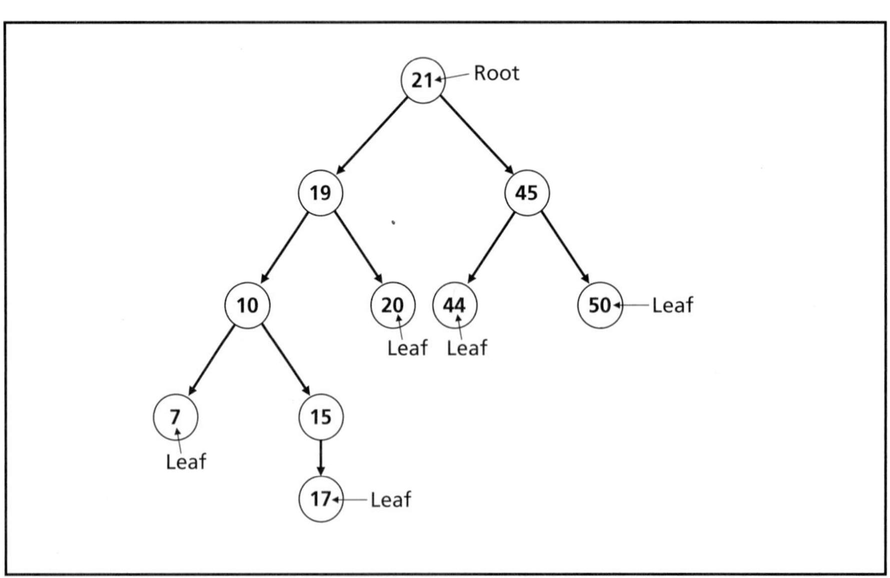

12. Four (21, 19, 10, 15, 17)
13. Three
14. Seven comparisons
    1. 7 = 21? No
    2. 7 > 21? No. Go left.
    3. 7 = 19? No.
    4. 7 > 19? No. Go left.
    5. 7 = 10? No.
    6. 7 > 10? No. Go left.
    7. 7 = 7? Yes.
15. Nine comparisons
    1. 17 = 21? No
    2. 17 > 21? No. Go left.
    3. 17 = 19? No.
    4. 17 > 19? No. Go left.
    5. 17 = 10? No.
    6. 17 > 10? Yes. Go right.
    7. 17 = 15? No.
    8. 17 > 15? Yes. Go right.
    9. 17 = 17? Yes.

chapter 10

1. A file system is responsible for creating, manipulating, renaming, copying, and removing files to and from a stored device.
2. The file management system organizes the hard drive into several different areas. FAT uses a table to keep track of which files are using which clusters. It also keeps track of which clusters are good and bad. FAT is implemented as a linked list. The clusters of a file are linked together until the last cluster of a file is stored. It has a special code indicating that it is the last cluster being used by the file.
3. As more and more files are stored on the hard drive, clusters become less contiguous. The system will try to recover open disk space. As time goes by, spaces might not be contiguous and the file could have clusters stored all over the disk drive.
4. Disk defragmentation reorganizes the clusters on a hard drive so that the files are contiguous. Having contiguous clusters for a stored file increases performance since the read head does not have to move as much. Thus, the speed of the system is increased when working with files.
5. FAT uses a file allocation table which means that large files do not have to be stored contiguously. They can be placed wherever they fit on the drive. NTFS uses a master file table that stores information about the files and directories. The MFT acts as a database table that keeps track of file/directory information. FAT is used on small drives less than 10 GB whereas NTFS is geared toward larger hard drives.

6. Using FAT might promote fragmentation on the hard drive causing the system performance to degrade. System performance also degrades just by the amount of files that are being stored on the system. FAT lacks many security features found in NTFS. It can also have integrity problems with clusters.
7. NTFS is implemented through the use of a master file table (MFT). The MFT resembles a database table that holds information regarding each file and volume. As new files or directories are created, new entries are added to the MFT. NTFS is a journaling system that keeps track of all of the transactions performed when working with files and directories. That way, if there is a problem, the system can "roll back" to a secure state.
8. NTFS is fast and reliable. The system can also recover from problems without significant loss of data. NTFS also supports greater security by way of providing security on users or groups of users based upon files or directories. NTFS also supports file compression and file encryption. The main disadvantage of NTFS is that it is only feasible to use on larger hard drives.
9. The MFT is similar to a database table that stores data entries for each file and directory on a volume. It contains various attributes about different files and resembles a table of contents for the files and folders in the volume. When a file or directory is created, a new record is also created in the MFT.
10. The advantages of file compression is that it will allow you to save disk space and is transparent to the user that the compressing and uncompressing is handled by the system. The disadvantage of file compression is that it can slow down the file management since the system has to compress and uncompress the files.
11. All files are stored as binary information but a text file consists of ASCII or unicode characters and the binary file contains ones and zeroes. Text files are kept in the human language form and are more readable. Binary files are not readable by humans but are more compact and faster to access since the system already understands binary.
12. Sequential file access starts at the beginning of a file and processes it line by line until it reaches the end. The stored data can be thought of as one long row of information. Random file access allows you to access a particular record in a file without having to process through all of the information stored before it.
13. The writing process used in sequential file access is very fast since all information is appended to the end of the file. Retrieving or reading the information can be very slow since you have to start at the beginning of the file and process through all of the data until you find the specified information. Inserting, deleting, and modify existing records would require you to rewrite the contents of the file to a new file. Random file access is very useful for accessing records quickly since you do not have to process all of the file information. You can also update records without having to rewrite the file contents. Thus, you can see that speed is an advantage of random file access. The disadvantage is that it can waste disk space if the data does not fill the entire record area or if a record does not have any data associated with it.

14. Hashing creates and uses a hash key value that acts like an identifier for data. The process of hashing involves creating an algorithm that calculates a hash value that would be suitable for identifying records while at the same time avoid as many collisions or duplicates as possible. The goal is to make data searches, updates, deletions, and modifications more efficient.

15. There are many different algorithms that could be used to solve this question. If you follow the example in the book, then the algorithm would be based upon determining the maximum number of records you might have. The records should have a key value of 0 to the highest number minus 1. You would need to identify how many students you might have in the system. This number will vary. For our example, we will follow the book and say that there are approximately 2000 students. Divide 9999999 by 2000 to come up with approximately 5000 as the key. If the first student number were 1002394, you would divide that number by 5000 to create the key of 200 for that record.There is no right or wrong algorithm that could be used as a solution for this question. Instead, this question is intended to make the student think creatively and design an algorithm to answer it.

chapter 11

1. A logically ordered set of statements used to solve a problem.

2. If the amount is to be deposited, then take the current balance and add the amount to it. If the amount is to be withdrawn, then take the amount and subtract it from the current balance.

3. Ask for the current balance of checking account

   Ask if deposit or withdrawal (check written)

   Ask for amount

   Ask for date

   If Deposit

       Current balance = Current balance + amount

   Else if Withdrawal (check written)

       Current balance = Current balance – amount

   Store information

4. When the gas pump lever is lifted up and the gas grade is selected, reset the dollar amount, the amount of gas pumped, and display the price per gallon. When the pump handle lever is lifted, begin pumping gas and updating the dollar amount and gas pumped display areas. Continue pumping gas until the sensor clicks off the gas pump handle or until the user releases the handle. Turn off pump when gas lever is pushed down.

5. System is idle

   Continue checking to see if gas lever is lifted

   While gas lever is lifted

   If gas grade selected = Unleaded

   Begin pumping unleaded gas

   Else if gas grade selected = Premium

   Begin pumping premium gas

   Update gas pump display area

   End while

   Put system back in idle state

6. This will vary depending on the course. It should represent a high level description of accepting assignments, tests, quizzes, projects, and a final exam score. It should then show the formula for calculating the grade and assigning a letter grade for the resulting percentage.

7. This will vary depending on the course. This should be a step-by-step description of a professor entering grades into a system to calculate the scores for a class based upon a syllabus.

8. Integer variables are used in Java when the value associated with the variable is a whole number. Some examples might be for storing inventory counts, miles driven, points scored in a sporting event, etc. A suggested variable name could be iCount, iMilesDriven, iPoints, etc. Placing the letter "i" in front of the variable name increases readability within the source code since a person debugging the program could make the assumption that any variables starting with the letter "i" must contain an integer value. The different integer types are: byte, short, int, and long.

   An example of declaring the variable would be:

   int iMilesDriven;

9. Float variables are used in Java when the value associated with the variable is not a whole number and might contain precision data (decimal values). Some examples might be storing a student's class percentage, the cost of an item, averages, etc. A suggested variable name could be fPercent, fCost, fAverage, etc. Placing the letter "f" in front of the variable name increases readability within the source code since a person debugging the program could make the assumption that any variables starting with the letter "f" must contain a float value. The different float types are: float and double.

   An example of declaring the variable would be:

   float fCost;

10. Character variables are used in Java when the value associated with the variable is exactly one character. Some examples might be storing a student's middle initial, a letter grade that does not include minuses and

plusses, gender, etc. A suggested variable name could be cMiddleInit, cGrade, cGender, etc. Placing the letter "c" in front of the variable name increases readability within the source code since a person debugging the program could make the assumption that any variables starting with the letter "c" must contain a character value.

An example of declaring the variable would be:

char cGender;

11. String variables are used in Java when the value associated with the variable is a combination of one or more characters. Some examples might be storing a student's first name, a letter grade that does include minuses and plusses, a street address, etc. A suggested variable name could be sFirstName, sGrade, sAddress1, etc. Placing the letter "s" in front of the variable name increases readability within the source code since a person debugging the program could make the assumption that any variables starting with the letter "s" must contain a string value.

An example of declaring the variable would be:

string sFirstName;

12.

```
public class chap11_12 {
        public static void main(String[] args) {
         boolean bFirst = true;
         boolean bSecond = true;
         if((bFirst) && (bSecond))
              System.out.print("T");
         else if((bFirst) && (! bSecond))
              System.out.print("F");
         else if((! bFirst) && (bSecond))
              System.out.print("F");
         else if((! bFirst) && (! bSecond))
              System.out.print("F");
     }
}
```

Try changing the values for the variables bFirst and bSecond and see the results.

For example:

```
public class chap11_12 {
        public static void main(String[] args) {
         boolean bFirst = false;
         boolean bSecond = true;
         if((bFirst) && (bSecond))
              System.out.print("T");
```

```
            else if((bFirst) && (! bSecond))
                System.out.print("F");
            else if((! bFirst) && (bSecond))
                System.out.print("F");
            else if((! bFirst) && (! bSecond))
                System.out.print("F");
        }
    }
```

13.

```
public class Arithmetic {
        public static void main(String[] args) {
         int iFirstNum = 15;
         int iSecondNum = 10;
         int iResult;
         System.out.print("Addition: ");
         iResult = iFirstNum + iSecondNum;
         System.out.print("15 + 10 = ");
         System.out.println(iResult);
         System.out.print("Subtraction: ");
         iResult = iFirstNum - iSecondNum;
         System.out.print("15 - 10 = ");
         System.out.println(iResult);
         System.out.print("Multiplication: ");
         iResult = iFirstNum * iSecondNum;
         System.out.print("15 * 10 = ");
         System.out.println(iResult);
         System.out.print("Division: ");
         iResult = iFirstNum/iSecondNum;
         System.out.print("15/10 = ");
         System.out.println(iResult);

         System.out.print("Modulus: ");
         iResult = iFirstNum%iSecondNum;
         System.out.print("15%10 = ");
         System.out.println(iResult);
        }
}
```

14.

```
public class Looping {
public static void main(String[] args) {
      int iCount = 1;

      for (iCount = 1; iCount <= 5; iCount++)
      {
         System.out.println("For Loop -
         Dr. Doolittle # " + iCount);
      }

      iCount = 1;

      while (iCount <= 5)
      {
         System.out.println("While Loop -
         Dr. Doolittle # " + iCount);
          iCount++;
      }

      iCount = 1;

      do
      {
         System.out.println("Do While Loop -
         Dr. Doolittle # " + iCount);
      } while (iCount++<5);
   }
}
```

15. The answers could vary.

```
public class Grade_If {
public static void main(String[] args) {
      int iGrade = 72;

     if (iGrade >= 90)
         System.out.println("You get an A");
     else if ((iGrade >= 80) && (iGrade < 90))
         System.out.println("You get a B");
     else if ((iGrade >= 70) && (iGrade < 80))
         System.out.println("You get a C");
     else if ((iGrade >= 60) && (iGrade < 70))
         System.out.println("You get a D");
     else
         System.out.println("See you next
         semester!");
  }
}
```

16.

```
public class Grade_Switch {
public static void main(String[] args) {
      int iGrade = 82;

      switch (iGrade)
      {
        case 100 :
        case 99 :
        case 98 :
        case 97 :
        case 96 :
        case 95 :
        case 94 :
        case 93 :
        case 92 :
        case 91 :
        case 90 :
           System.out.println("You get an A");
           break;
        case 89 :
        case 88 :
        case 87 :
        case 86 :
        case 85 :
        case 84 :
        case 83 :
        case 82 :
        case 81 :
        case 80 :
           System.out.println("You get a B");
           break;
        case 79 :
        case 78 :
        case 77 :
        case 76 :
        case 75 :
        case 74 :
        case 73 :
        case 72 :
        case 71 :
        case 70 :
           System.out.println("You get a C");
           break;
```

```
            case 69 :
            case 68 :
            case 67 :
            case 66 :
            case 65 :
            case 64 :
            case 63 :
            case 62 :
            case 61 :
            case 60 :
               System.out.println("You get a D");
               break;
            default :
               System.out.println("See you next
               semester!");
            }
      }
   }
```

17. A do-while is used when you want to execute the loop at least 1 time and have the condition checking at the end of the loop. The for loop executes for a known number of times while the do-while executes as long as the condition is true. The while loop checks the condition before the statements within the loop are executed and might not even execute the statements at all if the condition evaluates to a false.

18. Inheritance is when you create one class based upon another class. The newly created class is called a subclass or child class. It receives everything the parent had plus whatever else it has. An advantage of inheritance is reusability of classes so that the programmer does not have to recreate or rewrite source code. A disadvantage is that if you continue to inherit many levels deep it can become quite confusing to keep the class hierarchy in order.

19. (See diagram)

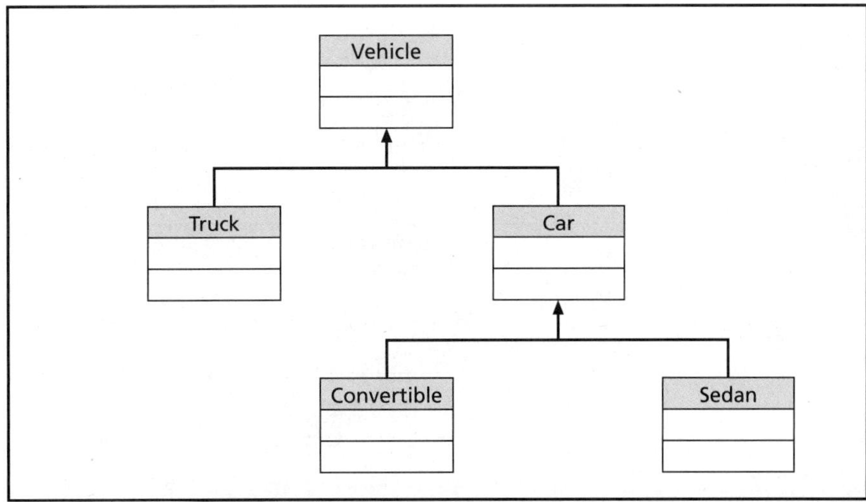

20. (See diagram)

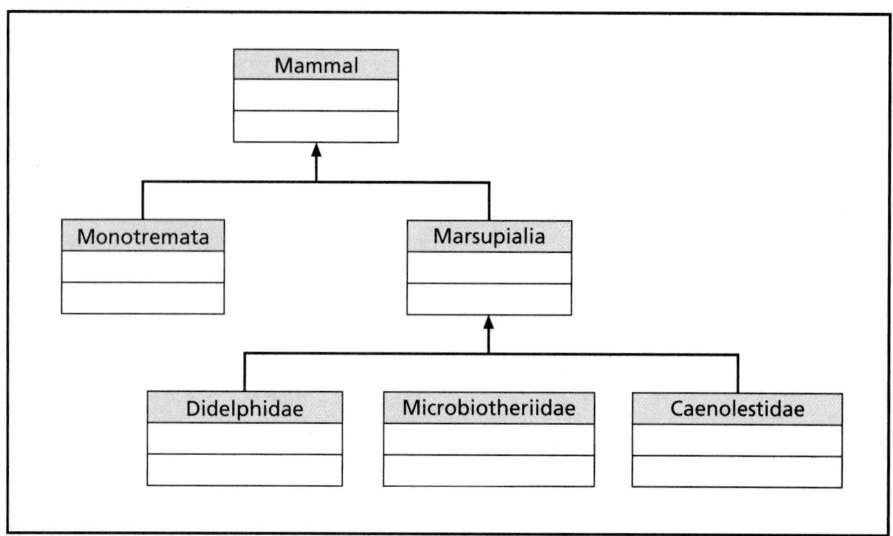

chapter 12

1. Software engineering is the process of producing software applications involving not just the source code of the program but also associated documentation including UML diagrams, screen prototypes, reports, software requirements, future developmental issues, and data needed to make the programs operate correctly. It is the heart of computer science and is related to all aspects that a computer scientist might encounter including hardware components, networking, database, Web development, software applications, etc.

2. A design document is a document that details all of the design issues for an application. Without a properly defined design document, a project is doomed for failure. Aspects such as scope creep can delay the completion of the project. The application being created might not even be close to what the end user initially perceived. A design document will encompass the functionality, appearance, and distribution of the application.

3. Prompt for card

When card is entered, read card

Ask for PIN

Confirm that PIN matches card

If there is a match, continue on with transaction. Otherwise, display an error message.

Ask for dollar amount to add to savings

Add dollar amount to savings and update account

Ask if they would like to do another transaction

If so, continue by going back to step 6. Otherwise, display a thank you message and quit.

Eject card

4. Prompt for card

   When card is entered, read card

   Ask for PIN

   Confirm that PIN matches card

   If there is a match, continue on with transaction. Otherwise, display an error message.

   Ask for dollar amount to add to remove from account

   Subtract dollar amount from account and update the account

   Ask if they would like to do another transaction

   If so, continue by going back to step 6. Otherwise, display a thank you message and quit.

   Eject card

5. UML is a software modeling process that enables the system developers to create a blueprint showing the overall functionality of the program being engineered and provides a way for the client and the developer to communicate. Better communication will hopefully result in a better project.

6. A data dictionary is a document describing the type of data being utilized within the program showing the table definitions, indexes, and other data relationships. This document is used by developers in making sure that the application meets the initial defined look of the data. The document can also be used by developers or end users during the report creation process. The document acts as a master guide for making sure all data is consistent.

7. A prototype is a standard or typical example that gives the end user a good idea of what they will see when their application is completed. A software engineer can design all of the screens and reports before any lines of source code are actually written. This allows the end user to see what the product will look like and give approval for the proposed application. The result should be a product agreed upon by both the user and the developer, thus promoting good communication throughout the entire process.

8. Not including the end user in the design process

   Writing your application without getting user approval for the prototype

   Not testing the application

   Using poor coding procedures

   Not creating a design document

   Thinking that the end user doesn't know what they want so you instead tell them what they are going to get

   There are many more items that the student could add to this list.

9. The waterfall SDLC process model represents each of the fundamental processes involved in creating the program as phases. The output from each phase is used as the input to the next phase. The first step is to gather all of the requirements for the project. The second step is to design the system and software. After all of the requirements have been defined and the project has been designed it is time to build and implement the application. Once the application is finished it must be tested and then finally put into operation and maintained to meet the user's needs. If a problem in the design is encountered, then you must return to the first step and continue repeating the process until the final product has met all of the user's functional requirements.

10. Project Manager – Leader of the team and is responsible for choosing the right players for the right positions and keeping the project on schedule.

    Database Administrator (DBA) – Person assigned the role of creating and maintaining the structure of the database.

    Software Developer (or programmer) – Person responsible for writing source code to meet the functional requirements of the end user.

    Client – Person that has a need that can be met through the process of software engineering. The client is the one that knows what they really want and why.

    Tester – Person responsible for making sure the program functions correctly and that it meets all of the specified functional requirements set forth in the design document.

    Customer Relations Representative (or support technician) – Person responsible for interfacing with the testers, developers, and end users during the creation and early release of the product and on an ongoing basis with the end user as long as the product is being used.

11. (see diagram)

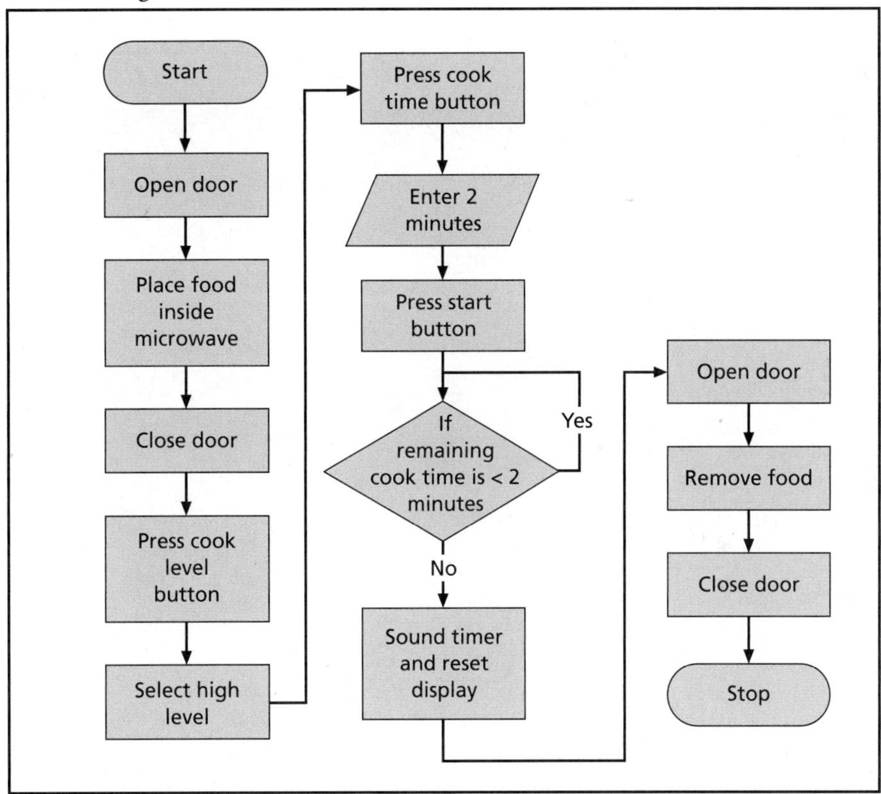

Answer could vary

12. Open microwave door
Place food inside microwave
Close microwave door
Press the cook level button
Select High
Press the cook time button
Enter 2 minutes
Press the start button
When timer goes off, open door
Remove food
Close door

Answer could vary

13. (See diagram)

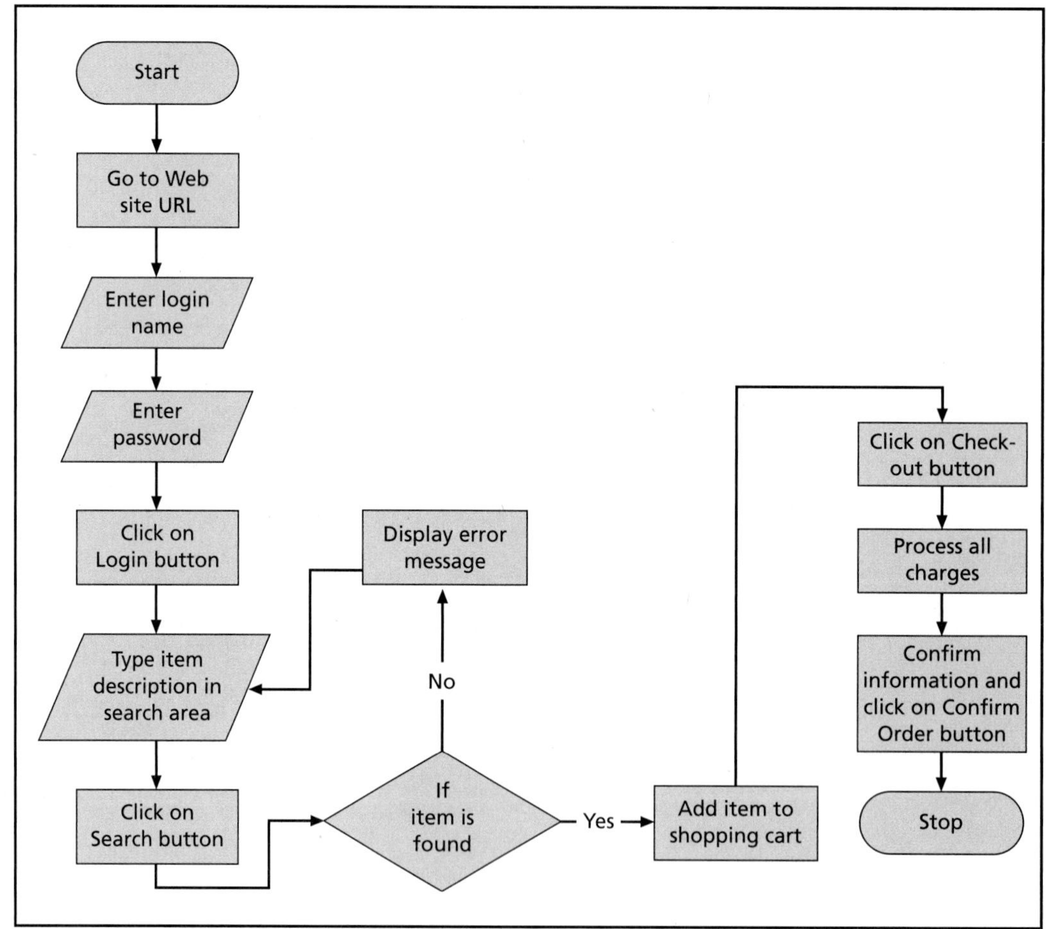

Answer could vary

14. Go to Web site URL
Enter login name
Enter password
Click on Login button
Type in item description in search area
Click on Search button
If found, enter quantity and click on Add item to shopping cart
If not found, display error message and return to screen
Click on Checkout button
Confirm information and click on Confirm button
Click on Logout button

Answer could vary

15. (See diagram)

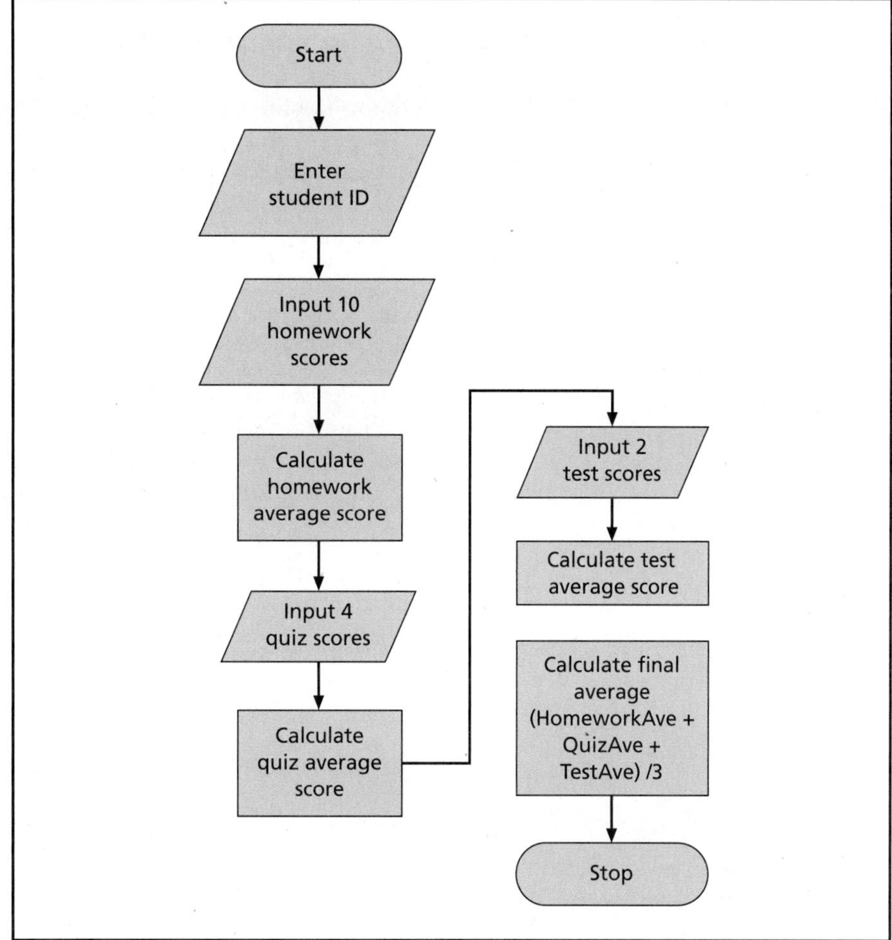

Enter student ID
Input 10 homework scores
Calculate the homework average score
Input 4 quiz scores
Calculate the quiz average score
Input 2 test scores
Calculate test average score
Calculate final average (HomeworkAve + QuizAve + TestAve)/3

Answer could vary

chapter 13

1. Clifford Stoll is most famous for writing the 1989 book *The Cuckoo's Egg: Tracking a Spy through the Maze of Computer Espionage* where he describes his year-long effort to track the cracker who intruded on his and many other government and private systems.

2. They have been called "Phreaks" or "Phone Phreaks". They engaged in "Phreaking" or finding ways to use AT&T phones or phone lines for free.
3. The term originated in the 1960s to describe a programmer with a very high skill level. The name took on a negative connotation in the 1980s with the widespread viruses and costly intrusions of computer systems. The term "cracker" can be used to describe an unwelcome outsider as compared to a welcome insider. But, the common use of hacker may have made the distinction irrelevant to the general public. It is a good distinction to know, however, since many system security professionals make the distinction.
4. A directed or targeted hacker directs his attack at particular machines for purposes of theft or damage. An undirected or untargeted hacker is motivated by the desire to break into any system or systems.
5. One intruder is the worm or virus that doesn't target any particular machine but makes use of security holes in operating systems and applications to wreck havoc. Another is the general user who, if not disallowed entry to parts of the system, might, even innocently, damage the system.
6. The "Hacker's Manifesto". This document is easily found on the Web. Among other things, it justifies breaking into systems just because they can be broken into.
7. Good system configuration. Rules and communicating those rules. Updating system and virus definitions regularly. Having the user base be aware of the dangers of seemingly innocent communication.
8. The rlogin command allowed an administrator to log into one system and then remotely log onto other machines without needing a password.
9. Many online shopping sites kept information about the purchase a customer makes in the URL string. A clever thief could change the price in the URL if the server side of the program didn't verify the item and price.
10. A buffer overflow is when a program tries to place more information into a location than that location can handle and it overflows into other areas. A cracker aims to overflow a buffer to get to memory that is critical to the operation of the machine and insert their own code into that area.
11. Identification is the mechanism by which an operation determines what something is. Authentication is the proof that the person is who they say they are. Your name is your identification. Your fingerprint might be proof that you are who you say you are.
12. A worm can actively search for vulnerable systems and replicate itself across systems. A virus must depend on some other mechanism (such as a human moving a file) to infect other systems.
13. A denial-of-service attack denies legitimate users from using resources.
14. A repudiation attack seeks to create a false impression that an event that didn't occur did or an event that actually did occur did not. Attacking a system so that a credit card transaction that occurred appears as if it did not is an example.

15. Confidentiality, Integrity, Availability, Accountability

16. Some ways to safeguard your data:

Have a security policy and communicate it and follow it.

Have physical safeguards against intrusion: locks, secure trash, ID badges, security guards.

Password protect everything and make the passwords difficult to discover.

Make backup copies of everything and physically secure those backups.

Protect against system failures.

Use up-to-date antivirus programs and anti-spyware and anti-cookie programs to protect privacy.

In case the worst happens, have a disaster recovery plan.

Use encryption.

Use firewalls.

Use secure system setups and programs with frequent security updates.

17. The technique that uses a virus signature (virus definition)

18. The 1968 law outlawing wire tapping would cover a network "sniffer"

The 1984 law on computer fraud and abuse would cover unauthorized use of a computer.

The 1986 law on electronic communications privacy would cover unwanted viewing of email contents

There are many laws that could be used depending on what occurred.

Intellectual property violations, consumer protection, threats to national defense, avoiding taxation, and fraud might be used.

19. $5000. This seems like a lot but an argument can be made for not just computer time but lost processing time and its effect on business operations.

20. Avoid a record of your purchases when possible.

Have an unlisted phone number.

Write explicitly to all companies you do business with to get off mailing lists.

Install anti-spyware software.

chapter 14

1. Speed, physical size, and power requirements
2. Von Neumann architecture
3. It has no effect.
4. Heat
5. Yes
6. Alan Turing
7. They require higher energy and are prone to mechanical failure.
8. Polymer memory
9. Boolean logic
10. Neural network

B

appendix

ASCII (American Standard Code for Information Interchange) table

The following table shows the ASCII character set.

ASCII

	0	1	2	3	4	5	6	7	8	9
0	nul	soh	stx	etx	eot	enq	ack	bel	bs	ht
1	lf	vt	ff	cr	so	si	dle	dc1	dc2	dc3
2	dc4	nak	syn	etb	can	em	sub	esc	fs	gs
3	rs	us	b	!	"	#	$	%	&	'
4	(	)	*	+	,	-	.	/	0	1
5	2	3	4	5	6	7	8	9	:	;
6	<	=	>	?	@	A	B	C	D	E
7	F	G	H	I	J	K	L	M	N	O
8	P	Q	R	S	T	U	V	W	X	Y
9	Z	[	\	]	^	_	`	a	b	c
10	d	e	f	g	h	i	j	k	l	m
11	n	o	p	q	r	s	t	u	v	w
12	x	y	Z	{	|	}	~	del		

C

appendix

Java reserved words

reserved word	description
abstract	Declares that a class or method is abstract
assert	Declares a boolean variable or return type
boolean	Declares a boolean variable or return type
break	Prematurely exits a loop
byte	Declares a byte variable or return type
case	Declares a case statement within a switch statement
catch	Handles an exception
char	Declares a character variable or return type
class	Signals the beginning of a class definition
continue	Prematurely returns to the beginning of a loop
default	Default action within a switch statement
do	Begins a do-while loop
double	Declares a double variable or return type
else	Signals the code to execute when an if statement is not true
extends	Specifies that a class is a subclass of another class
final	Declares that a class may not be subclassed or that a field or method may not be overridden
finally	Declares a block of code that is guaranteed to be executed
float	Declares a floating point variable or return type
for	Begins a for loop
if	Declares a block of code to be executed if a condition is true
implements	Declares that the class implements a given interface
import	Permits access to a class or group of classes within a package
instanceof	Tests whether a class is an instance of another class
int	Declares an integer variable or return type
interface	Signals the beginning of an interface definition
long	Declares a long integer variable or return type
native	Declares that a method is implemented in native code
new	Declares and allocates memory for a new object

reserved word	description
package	Defines the package in which the source code file belongs
private	Declares a method or member variable to be private
protected	Declares a class, method, or member variable to be protected
public	Declares a class, method, or member variable to be private
return	Returns a value from a method
short	Declares a short integer variable or return type
static	Declares that a field or a method belongs to a class rather than an object
super	References the parent of an object
switch	Tests a true condition in the possible cases
synchronized	Indicates that a section of code is not thread-safe
this	References the current object
throw	Raises an exception
throws	Declares the exceptions thrown by a method
transient	Declares that the field should not be serialized
try	Attempts an operation that might throw or raise an exception
void	Declares that a method does not return a value
volatile	Warns the compiler that a variable changes asynchronously
while	Begins a while loop

glossary

10Base2 An Ethernet networking cable made up of a thin coaxial cable capable of transmitting at rates up to 10 Mbps

10Base5 An Ethernet networking cable made up of a thick coaxial cable capable of transmitting at rates up to 10 Mbps

10BaseT A twisted pair Ethernet networking cable capable of transmitting at rates up to 10 Mbps

100BaseT A fast Ethernet networking cable made up of four twisted pairs of wire and capable of transmitting at 100 Mbps

802.11 A family of specifications for WLANs developed by IEEE; there are currently four specifications in the family: 802.11, 802.11a, 802.11b, and 802.11g

Acceptable Use Policy (AUP) Organizational policy that defines who can use company computers and networks, when, and how

access attack An attack on a system that can include snooping, eavesdropping, and interception; it is more basically known as spying or illicitly gaining access to protected information

accountability Making sure that a system is as secure as feasible, and that records of activity are kept so that breaks can be identified and traced back to the attacker

adder The circuit in the CPU responsible for adding binary numbers

AI Artificial Intelligence, the science and engineering of making intelligent machines, especially intelligent computer programs

algorithm A logically ordered set of statements used to solve a problem

AM (amplitude modulation) A technique of placing data onto an alternating carrier wave by varying the amplitude of the signal; this technique is often used in modems

American National Standards Institute (ANSI) An organization that works with industry groups in the formulation and publication of standards

American Standard Code for Information Interchange (ASCII) A standard for storing text characters in computers; the ASCII standard allows for 128 possible characters to be represented by seven bits

AND Boolean operator that returns a true value only if both operands are true

antivirus software Program designed to detect and block computer viruses

ARIN (American Registry of Internet Numbers) The organization in the United States that manages IP address numbers for the country and assigned territories

arithmetic logic unit (ALU) The portion of the CPU responsible for mathematical operations, specifically addition

array A set of contiguous memory cells used for storing the same type of data

ASP (Active Server Page) A page that combines features of HTML and JavaScript or VBScript programming code used on a Web server to dynamically create Web pages

assembler Reads the assembly language code and converts it into machine language

assembly language A language that resides in between the lowest-level language and a higher-level language; it assigns letter codes to each machine language instruction

asymmetric encryption Encryption using both a public key and a private key

attenuation A reduction in the strength of an electrical signal as it travels along a medium

authentication A technique for verifying that someone is who they claim to be; a password is one type of authentication

availability Accessibility of information and services on a normal basis

backdoors Shortcuts into programs created by system designers to facilitate system maintenance but used and abused by crackers

bandwidth A measurement of how much information can be carried in a given time period over a wired or wireless communications medium, usually measured in bits per second (bps)

binary Numbering system with two digits, 0 and 1; the basis for modern computer systems. Also known as base 2

binary search tree (BST) A binary tree where the left child's data is less than the parent node and the right child's data is greater than the value of the parent node

biometrics Biological identification, such as fingerprints, voice dynamics, or retinal scans; considered more secure than password authentication

BIOS (basic input/output system) A ROM (or programmable ROM) chip on the motherboard of a computer; the BIOS provides the initial startup (boot) program for the computer as well as the basic interrupt routines for I/O processing

bit The abbreviation for a binary digit; a bit is either a one or a zero, and is the smallest unit of representation in a common computer system

bit error rate The percentage of bits that have errors relative to the total number of bits received in a transmission; a measure of the quality of a communication line

Bluetooth A specification for short-range radio links between mobile computers, mobile phones, digital cameras, and other portable devices

BMP (bitmap) A Windows graphic format that is compact and used for images needing up to 16.7 million colors

Boolean basic identities A set of laws that apply to Boolean expressions and define ways in which expressions may be simplified; they are similar to algebraic laws

Boolean operator A word used in Boolean algebra expressions to logically test two values; the main Boolean operators are AND, OR, and NOT

booting The process of starting up a computer system

bot A small software program, also called a spider or a crawler, that can roam the Internet autonomously to gather their content for search engine indexes; bots can be quite benign and useful, such as those used by Google and other search engine companies to find links to list on their Web sites

bridge A special type of network switch that can be configured to allow only specific network traffic through, based on destination address

browser Software that allows you to view Web pages

bubble sort Compares each item in the list with the item next to it. If the first item is greater than the second, then it swaps them. The algorithm repeats this process until it makes a pass all the way through the list without swapping any items

buffer overflow When a program tries to place more information into a memory location than that location can handle

bus A collection of conductors, connectors, and protocols that facilitate communication between the CPU, memory, and I/O devices

bus protocol The set of rules governing the timing and transfer of data on a computer bus

byte A group of eight bits that are considered as one unit and is used as the basic unit of measurement in a computer system; memory is measured in the number of bytes the computer has

cable modem A type of digital modem that connects to a local cable TV line to provide a continuous connection to the Internet

cache memory High-speed memory used to hold frequently accessed instructions and data in a computer to avoid having to retrieve them from the slower-speed system DRAM

callback Users can connect to a network only by having the network initiate contact to a specified number

cardinality Shows the numeric occurrences between entities in an entity relationship (ER) model

Cat 5 A popular Ethernet twisted pair communication cable capable of carrying data at rates up to 100 Mbps

CCITT (Comite Consultatif International de Telegraphique et Telephonique or **International Telegraph and Telephone Consultative Committee)** A standards group that was involved in the development of the ISO/OSI networking model

CD-ROM A 120-mm disc used to store data, music, and video in a computer system using laser technology; CD-ROM discs are capable of holding up to 850 MB of information

CGI (Common Gateway Interface) An older Web server technology that provides for dynamic Web page creation

checksum A mathematical means to check the content of a file or value (such as a credit card number) to assure that it has not been tampered with or re-created illicitly

class A template or a mold used for defining new object types along with their properties and behavior

cluster Contains a group of the smallest units that can be accessed on a disk (sectors)

coaxial Communication cable that consists of a center wire surrounded by insulation and then a grounded foil shield that is wrapped in steel or copper braid

collision In hashing, when the hashing algorithm generates the same relative key for more than one original key value

column Represents a field within a row or record (e.g., First Name)

column, field, or **attribute** A specific piece of information in a table row

command prompt Words and symbols displayed on the monitor that indicate to the user of a command-line operating system that it is waiting for user input

command-line interface A method of communicating with the operating system by typing commands and receiving responses in plain text

compiler A program that reads all of the statements from a program and converts them into a computer language

composite key A key that is made up of more than one column

concatenation The process of combining or joining strings into one value

confidentiality Ensuring that only those authorized to access information can do so

constructor A special class function/method used for creating or instantiating an object

control structure An instruction that dictates the order in which the statements in a program are executed

control unit (CU) The part of the CPU that controls the flow of data and instructions in and out of the CPU

cookie A program that can gather information about a user and store it on the user's machine

copyright The legal right granted to an author, composer, artist, publisher, playwright, or distributor to exclusive sale, publication, production, or distribution of a literary, artistic, musical, or dramatic work

cracker An unwelcome system intruder with malicious intent

cropping Modifying an image by cutting or trimming parts from the image

CRT (cathode ray tube) The technology used in the conventional computer display monitor; CRTs use electron beams to light up phosphor displays on the screen

customer relations representative (support technician) Person responsible for interfacing with the testers, developers, and end users during the creation and early release of the product and later in an ongoing basis with the enduser as long as the product is being used

data compression A method that uses a compression format to reduce the size of a file

data dictionary A document describing the type of data being utilized within the program, showing the table definitions, indexes, and other data relationships

data structure A way of organizing data in memory, such as arrays, lists, stacks, queues, and trees, or on storage media, such as file structures

database A collection of data logically organized into a table, a file or set of files to allow access and usage.

database administrator Person assigned the role of creating and maintaining the database structure

database management system (DBMS) A tool used to extract, organize, and maintain data stored in a database

datagram A packet of information used in a connectionless network service that is routed to its destination using an address included in the datagram's header

deadlock A rare situation where I/O devices and/or processes are waiting on each other for the use of resources; this situation would continue indefinitely without intervention by the operating system

declaration A statement that associates an identifier with a variable (or an action, or some other element of the programming language that can be given a name)

decoder A digital circuit used in computers to select memory addresses and I/O devices

decompression Restoring a compressed file to its original format

demilitarized zone (DMZ) A location outside the firewall (or between firewalls) that is more vulnerable to attack from outside

denial-of-service attack An attack which denies legitimate users from using the system or access to information

depth or level The distance from the node to the root node. The root's depth or level is 0

dequeue To remove an item from a queue

design document A document that details all of the design issues for an application

desktop publisher Software used to create documents that use pages laid out in brochure, magazine, newspaper, or book format

determinant A determinant in a database is any column or columns you can use to determine the value assigned to another column (or columns) in the same row

DHCP (Dynamic Host Configuration Protocol) A communications protocol that automates that assignment of IP addresses in an organization's network

DHTML (Dynamic HTML) An extension to HTML tags and options that allow for Web pages that are responsive to user interaction

digital certificate The digital equivalent of an ID card; used with encryption and issued by a third-party certificate authority

digital video recorder (DVR) A specialized computer designed to record and play back video content from cable and satellite sources

directed (targeted) hacker Generally, a cracker motivated by greed and/or politics

directory An organizational unit within a storage medium that stores files, folders, and subdirectories; same as folder; folder terminology is often used in Windows, while directory/subdirectory is more often used in DOS and UNIX

disaster recovery plan (DRP) A written plan for responding to natural or other disasters, intended to minimize downtime and damage to systems and data

disk fragmentation Occurs when files have clusters scattered in different locations on the storage medium rather than in contiguous locations

DNS (Domain Name System) A method of translating Internet domain names into IP addresses (DNS servers are servers that are used in the process)

domain Set of possible values for a column

domain name A name used to locate the IP address of an organization or other entity on the Internet, such as *www.course.com*

DOS disk operating system; a single-user, singletasking, command-line operating system that was the Microsoft predecessor to Windows

DRAM Dynamic RAM, a generic term for a type of RAM that requires constant refreshing to maintain its information; various types of DRAM are used for the system main memory

driver A special program designed to provide an interface to a specific I/O device

DSL (digital subscriber line) A method of sending and receiving data over regular phone lines using a combination of FDM and TDM

dumpster diving Picking through people's trash to find things of value; though often innocent, it has been used by thieves to glean information that is potentially damaging

DVD A technology that uses laser and layering technology to store data, music, and video on 120- mm discs; DVD discs are capable of holding up to 9 GB of information

element A memory cell in an array

encapsulation Process of hiding an object's operations from other objects

Encrypting File System (EFS) Encryption technology that converts the data within a file using an encryption algorithm and key value to nonreadable information; in order to make the information understandable again you must decrypt it using another key value

encryption Transforming original data (plaintext) into coded or encrypted data (ciphertext) so that only authorized parties can interpret it

encryption key A string of bits used in an encryption algorithm to encrypt or decrypt data; the longer the key, the more secure the encryption

end user Someone or something that needs the program to perform a function or meet a need, and who determines the required functionality of the program

endless loop A segment of repetitious source code that never stops but instead continually repeats

enqueue To insert an item into a queue

entity relationship (ER) model A data model that visually represents how all of the tables interact and relate to each other within the database

ergonomics Science of the relationship between people and machines; designing work areas to facilitate both productivity and human ease and comfort

ethics Principles for judging right and wrong, held by an individual or group

event An action or occurrence recognized by a class

event handler How a class responds to an event

expert system A computer program that simulates the judgment and behavior of a human or an organization that has expert knowledge and experience in a particular field

exponent In scientific notation, the exponent is the power of the base that is multiplied by the mantissa to give the actual number

expression A programming statement that returns a value when executed

Extended ASCII A method for storing characters using an 8-bit code; extended ASCII is an extension of 128 characters beyond the original 7-bit ASCII code that was developed by the American National Standards Institute

FAT (file allocation table) File management system used to locate files on a storage medium

FDM A technique for combining many signals on a single circuit by dividing the available transmission bandwidth by frequency into narrower bands, each used for a separate communication channel

fiber optic Guided network cable consisting of bundles of thin glass strands surrounded by a protective plastic sheath

file compression Process of reducing file size and thus taking up less disk space

file system Responsible for creating, manipulating, renaming, copying, and removing files to and from a storage device

firewall Software and/or hardware that sits between an external network and the internal computer system that monitors requests for entry to the internal system and allows entry only to designated or authorized entrants; a firewall protects a network by filtering out potentially harmful incoming and outgoing traffic

first in, first out (FIFO) The last item placed on the stack is the last item removed from the stack, and the first item removed from the stack is the first item placed onto the stack

first normal form (1NF) Eliminating repeating fields or groups of fields from the table and confirming that every column has only one value by creating a new record in the table

flash drive A small, thumbsize memory device that functions as if it were a disk drive; flash drives normally plug into the USB port of a personal computer

flash memory Nonvolatile memory that allows the user to electrically program and erase information

flip-flop or latch A digital circuit that has the ability to retain the binary value to which it was set after the input is removed; static RAM is constructed using flip-flop circuits

floating point or scientific notation A method of representing numbers that have fractional values in a consistent manner; the numbers are represented as a mantissa and an exponent, such as 3.144543E+8

flowchart A combination of geometric symbols and text that provide a visual and logical description of a program or process

FM (frequency modulation) A technique of placing data onto an alternating carrier wave by varying the frequency of the signal; this technique is often used in modems

folder Structure on a formatted disk that enables storage and organization of files; also known as directory or subdirectory

foreign key (FK) A column in one table that is a primary key in another table

format Organizing the disk surface in such a manner as to be able to have folders and files written to it

format conversion Converting an image from one file format to another

freeware Software that is offered to the user at no cost

FTP (File Transfer Protocol) A protocol designed to exchange text and binary files via the Internet

function A block of source code that performs a task and can return a value

functional dependency When a column's single value is dependent upon another column's value

fuzzy logic A superset of conventional (Boolean) logic that has been extended to handle the concept of partial truth—truth values between "completely true" and "completely false"

gate A transistor-based circuit in the computer that implements Boolean logic by creating a single output value for a given set of input values

gateway A network component, similar to a bridge, that allows networks of different types to be connected

GIF (Graphics Interchange Format) A graphic format that supports up to 256 colors and is mainly used for buttons, banners, and both simple and animated images

graphical user interface (GUI) A method of interacting with the operating system wherein information is displayed in a graphical format and the user can select items using a pointer object such as a mouse

guided media Physical transmission media such as wire or cable

hacker A technically proficient individual who breaks into a computer system; originally connoted good intent, but general usage today is similar to cracker

Hacker's Manifesto A document, written anonymously, that justifies cracking into systems as an ethical exercise

hacktivism Cracking into a system as a political act; one political notion is that cracking itself is useful for society

hash key Unique value used in hashing algorithms and identifying records

hashing A common method used for accessing data either in a file or a database table through the use of a unique value called the hash key

hashing algorithm A routine of logic used for determining how hash values are created

head pointer A pointer that points to the beginning of the first element in a data structure

height The longest path length in the tree

heuristics In virus detection, a set of rules that predict how a virus might act; for example, anticipating that the virus will affect certain critical system files

hexadecimal (hex) Numbering system with 16 digits, 0–9 and A–F. Often used as shorthand for binary (1 hex digit 5 4 binary digits). Also known as base 16

high-level language Programming language that is more human-friendly or more natural for humans to read

holographic storage A method of splitting a laser beam and using a device called a spatial light modulator to store full pages of information in layers on a crystal material

honeypot A trap (program or system) laid by a system administrator to catch and track intruders

HTML (Hypertext Markup Language) A set of markup symbols or codes inserted in a file that specify how the material is displayed on a Web browser page

HTTP (Hypertext Transfer Protocol) A protocol designed for transferring files (primarily content files) on the World Wide Web

hub A network device that functions as a multiport repeater; signals received on any port are immediately retransmitted to all other ports of the hub

Hungarian notation Variable naming method that gives each variable an identifier at the beginning of the variable name describing the data type of the variable

hyperlink A link that allows the user to select a connection from one word, picture, or information object to another

IANA (Internet Assigned Numbers Authority) The organization under contract with the U.S. government to oversee the allocation of IP addresses to ISPs

IDE (integrated development environment) A workspace providing tools to support application development using a programming language

identification A technique for knowing who someone is; for example, a Social Security number can be identification (ID)

identifier Name of a variable

IEEE (Institute of Electrical and Electronics Engineers) An organization involved in the formulation of networking and electronics standards

IEEE-754 A standard for the binary representation of floating-point numbers; it is the 754th standard proposed by the IEEE

IMAP (Internet Message Access Protocol) A standard protocol for accessing e-mail from a mail server

impedance The opposition that a transmission medium has toward the flow of alternating electrical currents

index A special type of file that occupies its own space and specifies that one or more columns in a table determines how the information stored in the table is organized

index (subscript) How an array accesses each element stored in its data structure

inductance The magnetic field around a conductor that opposes changes in current flow

inheritance The process of providing more class functionality by creating more specific classes based upon generic classes

insertion point Where the cursor is ready to display data

instantiation The process of creating an object based upon a class. Memory is allocated and assigned to a variable

Institute of Electrical and Electronics Engineers (IEEE) An organization involved in the formulation of networking and electronics standards

integrated development environment (IDE) An interface provided with software development languages that incorporates all of the necessary tools needed to write, compile, and distribute programs; these tools often include an editor, compiler, graphic designer, and more

integrity Assurance that information is what you think it is and that it has not been modified

intellectual property An idea or product based on an idea that has commercial value, such as literary or artistic works, patents, business methods, industrial processes, and trade secrets

interpreter A program included with an executable application that acts as the translator between the program and the computer by converting program statements one by one into a language the computer understands

interrupt handling A method of allowing processes and hardware I/O devices to interrupt the processor's normal processing of instructions in order to handle specific tasks

IP (Internet Protocol) The protocol that provides for the addressing and routing of Internet packets from one computer to another

IP address A unique, 32-bit number assigned to network devices that use the Internet Protocol

IPCONFIG A Windows command-line utility that can be used to display the network settings currently assigned and given by a network

IPv4 Version 4 of the Internet Protocol, the most widely used version of IP

IPv6 Version 6 of the Internet Protocol has greater capability than IPv4, including the provision for a much greater number of IP addresses

ISO (International Organization for Standardization) An organization that coordinates worldwide standards development

ISO/OSI reference model A data communications model consisting of seven application layers

ISP (Internet service provider) A company that provides access to the Internet and other related services such as Web site building and virtual hosting

JavaScript An interpreted programming or script language from Netscape; somewhat similar in capability to Microsoft VBScript

JPG or JPEG (Joint Photographic Experts Group) A commonly used Internet graphic format that is the most efficient of all graphic formats and supports up to 16.7 million colors

JSP (Java Server Pages) Comparable to Microsoft's Active Server Page (ASP) technology, except that it runs only programs written in Java

kernel The core of an operating system that controls processor, disk, memory, and other central functions

key In a database table, one or more columns used to determine the sort order of the data

LAN (local area network) A network of computers within a single building or in close proximity

last in, first out (LIFO) The last item placed on the stack is the first item removed from the stack

LCD (liquid crystal display) A type of electronic device used as a computer display monitor; LCD displays have been popular in notebook computers and PDA devices, and have now also become used widely as desktop monitors

leaf node A node that does not have any children nodes

left child The child node to the left of the parent node

level The distance from the node to the root node. The root's depth or level is 0

linked list A data structure that uses noncontiguous memory locations to store data; each element in the linked list points to the next element in line and does not have to be contiguous to the previous element

Linux A multitasking, multiuser, open-source operating system patterned after the popular UNIX operating system

lossless compression A compression format used to remove redundant areas of an image without losing any image data; when the image is decompressed it returns to its original state

lossy compression A compression format that eliminates redundant data and information that is not perceptible to the human eye; the image loses some of its quality when it is decompressed

lower bound The lowest position in an array

low-level language Programming language that resembles more what a computer can understand rather than a human

machine language The lowest-level language, which is directly understood by a computer

main board or **motherboard** The physical circuit board in a computer that contains the CPU and other basic circuitry and components

malicious code Code designed to breach your system security and threaten your digital information; often called a virus, although technically a virus is only one kind of malicious code

mantissa In scientific notation, the mantissa contains the actual digits of the number and is placed before the exponent

many-to-many (M:M) relationship Many instances of one entity or table (parent table) are associated with many instances of another entity (child table)

master file table (MFT) Table used in NTFS to store data about every file and directory on the volume

metadata In XML and in database systems, information about the characteristics of the data contained in the data file; sometimes referred to as "data about data"

method The work performed by an object; a function that is defined within a class

modem A device that converts binary signals into audio signals for transmission over standard voice-grade telephone lines and also converts the audio signals back into binary

modification attack An attack on a system that modifies information illicitly

MP3 (MPEG-1 Audio Layer-3) A standard technology and format for compressing a sound sequence into a small file as compared to an uncompressed sound file such as a WAV file

MRAM Magnetic RAM, memory that uses the polarization of microscopic magnetic layers to store ones and zeros that remain after the power source is removed

multidimensional array An array consisting of two or more single-dimensional arrays

multiprocessing The coordinated processing by more than one processor at the same time

multitasking The ability of a computer operating system to effectively support more than one process running at a time

NAND A logical AND followed by a logical NOT that returns a false value only if both operands are true

nanotechnology The branch of engineering that deals with things smaller than 100 nanometers and especially the manipulation of individual molecules or atoms

NAT (Network Address Translation) The translation of an inside IP address to an outside IP address; NAT is often used to allow multiple computers to share one Internet connection

natural language processing Computer applications that can recognize and interact with natural language text

NBP (national backbone provider) A provider of high-speed network communication lines for use by ISPs

nesting Putting one control structure inside of another

network operating system An operating system designed to provide strong network services

neural networks A parallel interconnection of simple processing units based on the architecture of human and animal brains; an alternate computing paradigm to Von Neumann architecture

nibble A term sometimes used to refer to four bits

NIC (network interface card) A circuit board that connects a network medium to the system bus of a computer device and converts the binary information of a computer into a format suitable for the transmission medium in use; each NIC has a unique, 48-bit address

node or vertex Each position in the tree

NOR Logical OR followed by a logical NOT that returns a true value only if both operands are false

normalization A process of database design that structures tables to eliminate duplication and inconsistencies in the data structure

NOT Boolean operator that returns a false value if the operand is true and a true value if the operand is false

NTFS (New Technology File System) File management system implemented with Windows NT and incorporated into Windows 2000, XP, and 2003; used to locate files on a storage medium

null value The absence of a value meaning that there is no value stored; null is not the same as blank or zero

object A self-contained entity that consists of both data and procedures

object-oriented programming (OOP) Style of programming that involves representing items, things, and people as objects rather than basing the logic around actions

offset Used to specify the distance between memory locations

one-to-many (1:M) relationship One instance of an entity (parent table) is associated with zero to many instances of another table (child table)

one-to-one (1:1) relationship One instance of one entity (parent table) is associated with only one instance of another entity (child table)

open source Computer programs, including operating systems, that have been developed as a public collaboration and made freely available for use or modification

operating system (OS) The program on a computer system responsible for managing the user interface, system resources, and processes

operators Symbols used to manipulate the data

OR Boolean operator that returns a true value if either operand is true

overflow area Area in a file that is used in case a collision occurs during the hashing algorithm

packet-filtering firewall A firewall that inspects each packet and moves it along an established link to its destination; it is usually faster but less secure than a proxy firewall

paradigm A theoretical framework, or a way of doing things

parameter A received value assigned to a variable that is used by a block of source code

parent class (base class) A generic class from which other classes can be created through the process of inheritance

partition An area of a hard disk that has been reserved to hold files of a particular operating system type

patent A government grant that gives the sole right to make, use, and sell an invention for a specified period of time

PCI (Peripheral Component Interconnect) A system bus to connect a microprocessor with memory and I/O devices; PCI is widely used in personal computers

PDU (protocol data unit) A data communications packet that contains protocol information in addition to a data payload

peeking Looking at the top item in the stack without removing it from the stack

Perl A script programming language similar in syntax to the C language, often used to develop CGI dynamic Web pages

PHP In Web programming, a script language and interpreter that is freely available and used primarily on Linux Web servers

phreaking Subverting the phone system to get free service

pixel (picture element) The basic unit of programmable color on a computer display or in a computer image; the physical size of a pixel is dependent on the resolution of the display device

platform The operating system running on a computer

PM (phase modulation) A technique of placing data unto an alternating carrier wave by varying the phase of the signal; PM is the most often used modulation type in modems

PnP (Plug and Play) A technology that allows the operating system and hardware to work together to automatically detect and configure I/O devices

pointer A memory variable that points to a memory location

polling A technique wherein the CPU periodically interrogates I/O devices to see if they require attention; polling requires many more CPU resources than interrupt handling

polymer memory Nonvolatile memory that uses artificial polymers to store ones and zeros; some types of polymer memory can only be written once, while others can be rewritten many thousands of times

polymorphism An object's ability to use the same expression to denote different operations

pop Remove an item from the stack

POP (point of presence) An access point to the Internet

POP3 (Post Office Protocol version 3) The most recent version of a standard protocol for receiving e-mail from a mail server

port In the context of I/O devices, a port is the physical connection on the computer to allow an I/O device to be plugged in

port number An addressing mechanism used in TCP/IP as a way for a client program to specify a particular server program on a computer in a network and to facilitate Network Address Translation

positional value The numerical value that each position in a number has; the value of a position is calculated by raising the base of the number to the power of the position

POST Power-on self test; a procedure performed by the computer boot routine

postcondition loop A loop that executes at least one time before the expression is evaluated

precedence The order in which something is executed; those symbols that have a higher precedence are executed before those with a lower precedence

precondition loop A loop that checks the expression before any of the source code contained within the loop is executed

presentation tool Software that presents information in the form of a slide show

primary key (PK) A column or combination of columns that uniquely identifies a row within a table

privacy Freedom from unwanted access to or intrusion into a person's private life or information; the Internet and computerized databases have made invasion of privacy much easier and an increasing cause for concern

procedure A group of one or more computer statements that perform a task

process A small program running on a computer that may be part of a larger program

program A collection of statements or steps that solve a problem and need to be converted into a language that the computer understands to perform one or more tasks

project management software Software used to keep track of project progress, schedule, and expenses

project manager Leader of the software development team who is responsible for choosing the right players for the right positions and making sure the project is on schedule

Project Oxygen An alliance of educators, students, and researchers formed to create new computing paradigms and products enabling people to interact with computers in a more natural and useful way

property (attribute) Characteristic of an object

protocol A set of rules designed to facilitate communication; protocols are heavily used in networking

prototype A standard or typical example that gives the end user a good idea of what they will see when their application is completed

proxy firewall A firewall that establishes a new link between each packet of information and its destination; it is slower but more secure than a packetfiltering firewall

pseudocode A readable description of an algorithm written in human language

push Place an item on the stack

Python An interpreted, object-oriented programming language similar to Perl that has gained popularity in recent years

quantum computer A computer built using the principles of quantum mechanics, which is the study of matter and radiation at an atomic level

queue A list in which the next item to be removed is the item that has been in the list the longest

radix point The point that divides the fractional portion from the whole portion of a number; in the decimal numbering system, it is referred to as a decimal point

RAID (redundant array of independent disks) A collection of connected hard drives that are arranged for increased access speed or high reliability

RAM (random access memory) A generic term for volatile memory in a computer; RAM is fast and can be randomly accessed, but requires power to retain its information

random access Reading or writing data directly anywhere on disk

recursion In programming, when one line or function calls itself

refresh rate The number of times per second an image is renewed on the screen of a display monitor; a higher refresh rate results in less flickering on the display

register A small, very high-speed amount of memory located on the CPU; registers are used to store the data and instructions used by the CPU

relationship How one entity or table works with another

repeater A network device that is used to amplify signals on long cables between nodes

repetition The process of doing some action again, from one to many times

repudiation attack An attack on a system that injures the reliability of the information; for example, a repudiation attack might remove evidence that an event (such as a bank transaction) actually did occur

reserved word A key word that has a specific instructional meaning; the name cannot be redefined as it is already being used by the programming language as an instruction

resolution A measurement of the granularity of a computer monitor or printer; it is usually given as either a pair of numbers indicating the number of dots in a horizontal and vertical direction or as the number of dots per inch

resources Devices connected to the CPU of a computer such as main memory, hard disk, and CD-ROM drive; all running processes have to share these devices

reverse engineer To figure out the design of a program or device by "taking it apart" and analyzing individual components; for example, source code can be reverse engineered to determine a design model

RGB (red, green, blue) A type of computer monitor that displays color as a function of these three colors

RGB encoding A method of defining the color and brightness of a pixel in terms of the intensity of each of the colors: red, green, and blue

right child The child node to the right of the parent node

risk The relationship between vulnerability and threat; total risk also includes the potential affect of existing countermeasures

robotics The development, study, and use of robots; in most cases robotics also involves work with artificial intelligence

ROM (read-only memory) A type of memory that retains its information without power; some types of ROM can be reprogrammed

root The node that begins the tree

root level The main or base folder/directory level on a drive

rotating Modifying an image by moving the image from its current layout to a different position based upon a 360-degree circle

router A device or software in a computer that determines the next network point to which a packet should be forwarded toward its destination

row, record, or **tuple** Represents logically related information stored in a table, often described as a collection of columns

scaling Changing the display size of an image with or without changing the underlying size of the graphic

scope Where something can be seen and what other source code can see and use it

scope creep Occurs when new changes are continually added to a project thus changing the proposed completion date so that the project is never completed, but is instead in a constant improvement mode

script kiddie An amateur hacker who simply uses the hacking tools that have been developed by others

SCSI (Small Computer System Interface) A high-speed bus designed to allow personal computers to communicate with peripheral hardware such as disk drives, tape drives, CD-ROM drives, printers, and scanners

search engine A program, usually accessed on the Web, that gathers and reports information available on the Internet

second normal form (2NF) First normal form has already been applied to the table and every column that is not part of the key is fully dependent upon the primary key

selection sort Selects the smallest unsorted item remaining in the list, and then swaps it with the item in the next position to be filled

semiconductor A medium that is neither a good insulator nor a good conductor of electricity, used to construct transistors

sequential access Reading and writing in order from the beginning

SGML (Standard Generalized Markup Language) A standard for how to specify a document markup language or tag set

shareware Software distributed on a trial basis with the understanding that the user might want to pay for it later

shifter Circuit that converts a fixed number of inputs to outputs that have bits shifted to the left or right, often used with adders to implement multiplication and division

signal to noise ratio A measure of the quality of a communications channel

single-tasking An operating system that only allows one process (task) to be running at a time

SMTP (Simple Mail Transfer Protocol) A TCP/IP related, high-level protocol used in sending e-mail

sniffer A software program that allows the user to listen in on the traffic of a network

social engineering Social interaction that preys on human gullibility, sympathy, or fear to take advantage of the target, e.g., to steal money, information, or other valuables—basically, a con

software developer (programmer) Person responsible for writing source code to meet the functional requirements of the end user

software development life cycle (SDLC) Describes the life of the application including all of the stages involved in the development, testing, installation, and maintenance of a program

software engineering Process of producing software applications involving not just the source code of the program but also associated documentation, including UML diagrams, screen prototypes, reports, software requirements, future developmental issues, and data needed to make the programs operate correctly

software piracy Illegal copying of software; a problem in the United States and Europe, but rampant in the rest of the world

spam Unsolicited (and almost always unwanted) e-mail; usually trying to sell something

spider Also called bot or crawler, a program that visits Web sites and reads their pages and other information in order to create entries for a search engine index

spreadsheet A document that consists of rows and columns that facilitates organizing information and making calculations

spyware Software that can track, collect, and transmit to a third party or Web site certain information about a user's computer habits

SRAM (synchronous random access memory) Static RAM, a type of high-speed memory constructed using the flip-flop circuit

stack A list in which the next item to be removed is the item most recently stored

stack pointer A pointer that keeps track of where to either remove or add an item to the list in a data structure

Structured Query Language (SQL) A special language used to maintain the structure of a database and also modify, query, or extract information

subclass The more specific class created through the process of inheritance that has been based upon a parent class

subnet A portion of a network that shares part of an address with other portions of the network and is distinguished by a subnet number

switch A network repeater with multiple inputs and outputs; each input can be switched to any of the outputs creating a point-to-point circuit

symmetric encryption Encryption using a private key to both encrypt and decrypt

syntax Refers to the spelling and grammar used within a programming language's statements

system bus The main bus that is used by the CPU to transfer data and instructions to and from memory and I/O devices

system clock A crystal oscillator circuit on a computer motherboard that provides timing and synchronization for the operation of the CPU and other circuitry

T1 line A digital transmission link with a capacity of 1.544 Mbps; T1 uses two pairs of normal twisted wires, the same as found in most residences

table or **entity** Data arranged in rows and columns much like a spreadsheet

tail pointer Keeps track of the end or rear position of the data structure

TCP (Transmission Control Protocol) An OSI transport level, connection-oriented protocol designed to exchange messages between network devices

TCP/IP (Transmission Control Protocol/Internet Protocol) The suite of communications protocols used to connect hosts on the Internet

TDM A technique for combining many signals on a single circuit by allocating each of the signals a fixed amount of time, but allowing each of the signals the full bandwidth during the allotted time

tester Person responsible for making sure the program functions correctly and that it meets all of the specified functional requirements set forth in the design document

text editor A program that contains basic functions for creating and editing text documents

third normal form (3NF) Eliminates columns that are not dependent only on the primary key

threat Consists of three elements: the agent of the possible attack, the resulting event of an attack, and the target of the attack

TIF or TIFF (Tag Image File Format) A graphic format that is widely used in professional photographic settings; the image is very realistic, but the files are very large

time slicing A method of allocating fixed time units to processes running on a computer such that it appears to the user that all of the processes are running simultaneously

time to live (TTL) A field in the IP header that enables routers to discard packets that have been traversing the network for too long

trade secret A method, formula, device, or piece of information that a company keeps secret and that gives the company competitive advantage

transitive dependency When one column is dependent upon another column that is not part of the primary key

transmission medium A material with the capability to conduct electrical and/or electromagnetic signals

tree A data structure that represents a hierarchical structure similar to that of organizational or genealogy charts

Trojan horse A program that poses as an innocent program; some action or the passage of time triggers the program to do its dirty work

truth table A table representing the inputs and outputs of a logic circuit; truth tables can represent basic logic digital circuits as well as complex ones

Turing Test A test conceived by Alan Turing in 1950 to reveal whether a machine had the equivalent of human intelligence

twisted pair A pair (sometimes pairs) of insulated wires twisted together and used as a transmission medium in networking

two's complement A method of representing negative numbers in a computer system; a binary number is converted to two's complement format by flipping, or reversing the state of each bit and then adding 1 to the entire word

undirected (untargeted) hacker A cracker motivated by the challenge of breaking into a system

unguided media Transmission media that you can't see, such as air or space, which carry radio or light signals

Unicode The Unicode Worldwide Character Standard is a 16-bit standard for storing text or script information, and it defines 34,168 unique characters and control codes

Unified Modeling Language (UML) Software modeling process that enables system developers to create a blueprint showing the overall functionality of the program being engineered and provides a way for the client and the developer to communicate

UNIX A multitasking, multiuser command-line operating system that is known for its stability and reliability

upper bound The highest position in an array

URL (Uniform Resource Locator) The Englishlike address of a file accessible on the Internet

USB (universal serial bus) A high-speed interface between a computer and I/O devices; multiple USB devices can be plugged into a computer without having to power off the computer

USB drive Flash memory in a small, durable portable case that can be plugged into a USB port of a computer and used in the same manner as a disk drive

variable Name used to identify a certain location and value in the computer memory

variable initialization or initializing Providing an initial value when the variable is first declared

VBScript An interpreted script language from Microsoft that is a subset of the Visual Basic programming language often used by Web browsers and ASP servers

Very Large-Scale Integration (VLSI) The current point of evolution in the development of the integrated circuit; VLSI chips typically have more than 100,000 transistors

virtual private network (VPN) A private network connection that "tunnels" through a larger, public network and is restricted to authorized users

virus An uninvited guest program on your computer—with the potential to damage files and the operating system; this term is sometimes used generically to denote a virus, worm, or Trojan horse

virus hoax E-mail that contains a phony virus warning; started as a prank to upset people or to get them to delete legitimate system files

virus signature (virus definition) Bits of code that uniquely identify a particular virus

vulnerability The sensitivity of the information and the skill level needed by the attacker to threaten that information

WAN (wide area network) A network in which the computer devices are physically distant from each other, typically spanning cities, states, or even continents

WAV An audio file format that has become a standard for everything from PC system and game sounds to CD-quality audio

Web server A program running on a computer that responds to HTTP requests for Web pages and returns the pages to the requesting client

Web service Programming and data on a Web server that is designed to make that data available to other Web programs

whole (integer) numbers A number (positive, zero, or negative) that has no fractional portion; also referred to as an integer number

wildcard A symbol that stands for one or more characters, used in selecting files or directories

Windows A popular Microsoft GUI operating system for Intel-based processors

WLAN (wireless LAN) A local network that uses wireless transmission instead of wires; the IEEE 802.11 protocol family is often used in WLANs

word A group of bits in a computer system; the number of bits in a word is machine dependent, although common word sizes are 16, 32, and 64 bits; a typical computer system manipulates bits in word increments

word processor Text editing and formatting software used to create a wide variety of documents

worm A type of bot that can roam a network looking for vulnerable systems and replicate itself onto those systems; the new copies look for still more vulnerable systems

WYSIWYG What You see Is What You Get. In word processing or Web design, the ability to output text and images onscreen exactly as they will appear in print or in a browser window

XML (Extensible Markup Language) A markup language designed to create common information formats and share both the format and the data on the World Wide Web

XOR (exclusive OR) Logical operator that returns a true value if one, but not both, of its operands is true

index

special characters